An Introductory German Course
Fourth Edition

WIE GEHT'S?

An Introductory German Course

Dieter Sevin
Vanderbilt University

Ingrid Sevin

Katrin T. Bean

Holt Rinehart and Winston, Inc.

Fort Worth
Philadelphia
London
Chicago
Montreal
Sydney
San Francisco
Toronto
Tokyo

Publisher   *Ted Buchholz*
Senior Acquisitions Editor   *Jim Harmon*
Developmental Editor   *Barbara Caiti Baxter*
Production Manager   *Annette Dudley Wiggins*
Cover and Text Design   *World Composition, Inc., Rosemary L. Moak*
Text Illustrations   *World Composition, Inc., Ginny Baier*
Photo Research   *Judy Mason*
Editorial, Design, and Production   *World Composition, Inc.*
Photographic credits appear on page xii

Library of Congress Cataloging-in-Publication Data

Sevin, Dieter.
    Wie Geht's? : an introductory German course / Dieter Sevin, Ingrid
Sevin, Katrin T. Bean.—4th ed., instructor's annotated ed.
        p.   cm.
    Includes index.
    ISBN 0-03-049494-X
    1. German language—Grammar—1950–   2. German language—Textbooks
for foreign speakers—English.   I. Sevin, Ingrid.   II. Bean, Katrin
T.   III. Title.
PF3112.S4   1991b
438.2′421—dc20   90-24140
                                                           CIP

ISBN-0-03-049494-X

Request for permission to make copies of any part of the work should be mailed to: Copyrights and Permissions Department, Holt, Rinehart and Winston, Inc., Orlando, Florida 32887.

Address for editorial correspondence: Holt, Rinehart and Winston, Inc., 301 Commerce Street, Suite 3700, Fort Worth, TX 76102.

Address for orders: Holt, Rinehart and Winston, Inc., 6277 Sea Harbor Drive, Orlando, FL 32887, 1-800-782-4479 or 1-800-433-0001 (in Florida)

Printed in the United States of America.

    3 4   0 6 9   9 8 7 6 5 4 3 2

Holt, Rinehart and Winston, Inc.
The Dryden Press
Saunders College Publishing

I. Changes in the New Edition

The enthusiastic response to the first three editions of *Wie geht's?* confirmed the soundness of the basic concept of our introductory text. In this fourth edition we have made revisions, many of them suggested by colleagues, in most of the course materials without abandoning our original purpose: to create an introductory German text that is flexible, practical, and appealing in format and presentation, focusing on the essential elements of effective communication. The result is a text that lends itself readily to various teaching styles and student backgrounds.

The four skills (listening comprehension, speaking, reading, and writing) are practiced as the student is introduced to various cultural aspects of the German-speaking countries. The double meaning of the title *Wie geht's?* reflects the double goal of the book, which is to show the language at work and how the language works. We believe that explaining how the language works is not an end in itself but only a means of achieving communicative competence in natural, modern German.

- Learning objectives (*Lernziele*) introduce each chapter.

- Study hints (*Lerntips*) address the students in the pre-units and the first three chapters.

- All aspects of the book have been evaluated and revised where improvement seemed desirable. Several of the introductory dialogues have been replaced. Many of the grammar exercises have been contextualized.

- The reading texts have been updated. Those in Chapters 5, 10, 12, 14, and 15 have been considerably revised; those in Chapters 1 and 9 have been replaced.

- The tremendous political changes in Germany have been incorporated in the text. The maps reflect the new realities.

- Cultural notes in English have been revised and expanded.

- Pre-reading activities have been included in the annotations of the instructor's edition.

- An entirely new section (*Sprechsituationen*), focusing on functional-notional expressions, has been added to provide extra conversational practice.

- The text has been enhanced with color photographs and new illustrations.

- The lab manual / workbook has been updated. In response to suggestions from users, the answer key for the lab manual / workbook has been placed in the tapescript.

- A supplementary video program (*Zielpunkt Deutsch*) highlights language and situations students would actually encounter abroad.

- Text-specific software has been added to the package to encourage students to practice grammatical structures.

▪ A computerized testing program allows instructors to customize the tests to meet their individual needs.

II. Planning the Course

Wie geht's? is designed for a one-year college-level course. In planning the schedule, take into consideration the number of class hours available per week and student background and motivation. In most situations, there will be enough time not only to complete the book and use the lab and workbook materials, but also to enrich the course with slides, films and / or a supplementary first-year reader. On the other hand, those who have only three hours of instruction time per week, or who feel that some grammar topics are better left for the second year, may prefer to spread the work over three semesters.

It is important not to regard a schedule as unchangeable, but to remain flexible and respond to the special needs of a class. Overly strict adherence to a schedule can be detrimental to the success of the course. Below are scheduling suggestions for the semester and quarter system. Normally, 1½ days per *Schritt* and 1½ weeks per *Kapitel* should be appropriate.

1. The Semester System

(Note: *S* = Schritt; 1, 2, 3 usw. = Kapitel; *R* = Rückblick)

Week	1st Semester	Week	2nd Semester
1 2	S1 − S6, R	1 2 3	8 + 9
3 4 5	1 + 2	4 5 6	10 + 11
6 7	3, R, Test	7	R, Test
8 9 10	4 + 5	8 9 10	12 + 13
11 12 13	6 + 7	11 12 13	14 + 15
14	R, Test	14	R, Test

2. The Quarter System

Week	1st Qtr.	Week	2nd Qtr.	Week	3rd Qtr.
1 2	S1 – S6, R	1 2	6	1 2	11, R
3 4 5	1 + 2	3 4	7, R	3 4	12
6 7	3, R, Test	5 6	Test, 8	5 6	13, Test
8 9 10	4 + 5, Test	7 8	9	7 8	14
		9 10	10, Test	9 10	15, R, Test

If you plan well in advance your Learning Resources Center can make slides and transparencies of charts, maps, menus, ads, TV or radio programs, pictures from books and magazines, etc. for you. Sources of supplementary materials are, among others: the German Consulate in your area, the German Information Center, the AATG, Inter Nationes, and the International Film Bureau.

III. Aims and Methods

A. General Objectives

Wie geht's? focuses on the essential elements of effective communication. By the end of the course, the students have acquired a degree of competence in the four language skills and gained insights into life in the German-speaking countries. We hope that they will come to like German-language study and continue it. What can be expected at the end of the first year, and how do the textbook, tape program, and lab manual / workbook combine to achieve these goals?

1. Aural Comprehension   The students should be able to understand German that is spoken at moderate conversational speed and that deals with everyday topics. Sound discrimination is presented systematically in the book, the lab program, and the pronunciation section of the workbook. The lab program contains a variety of listening comprehension exercises. Most important, however, the text itself presents numerous opportunities for enhancing the students' listening skills.

2. Speaking   The students should be able to engage in simple conversations with speakers of German in everyday situations. The text encourages them to express themselves in German. They get a good start in the pre-units, where the focus is on speaking. Throughout the book, topics tend toward practical and everyday matters. Each pre-unit and chapter provides ample opportunity for oral practice in meaningful contexts

3. Reading   The students should be able to read nontechnical German of moderate difficulty on various aspects of German culture. Reading skills are developed through the study of dialogues, reading texts, and exercises in the workbook.

4. Writing The students should be able to write simple sentences correctly on the topics presented in the text. Written exercises extend and reinforce oral exercises (*Zusammenfassung*). The book and the workbook provide suggestions for writing dialogues and compositions on the chapter theme.

5. Cultural Insights The students should acquire basic knowledge about the countries where German is spoken and become aware of essential differences and similarities between these countries and the United States or Canada. The reading texts and numerous cultural notes in English deal with life in German-speaking countries. Most texts are followed by special questions that focus on differences between these countries and the United States or Canada. The workbook section of each chapter also includes cultural materials, as does the video program.

B. Some Dos and Don'ts of Language Teaching

- Make maximum use of German.
- Don't constantly lapse back into English.

- Speak distinctly and accurately.
- Don't speak too slowly, since the students need to get used to German spoken at a normal conversational speed.

- Use words and constructions that are within the students' comprehension.
- Don't use German that is beyond their current level.

- Organize each class meeting into a variety of activities.
- Don't stretch any activity beyond the students' attention span.

- Make it clear when one activity ends and another begins.
- Don't confuse students by suddenly asking them to do something else without clear instructions.

- Maintain a fairly lively pace, especially in choral responses.
- Don't let one student hold up the class too long. Special discussions that don't benefit the entire class should be saved until after class.

- Be flexible, imaginative, and attentive. Take advantage of special situations and student interests.
- Don't give the impression that it is impossible to deviate from your plan and that there is no time for anything else.

- Be well prepared.
- Don't be caught without things to do.

- Be honest.
- Don't make mistakes by improvising. Sometimes students will have to wait a whole day for an answer; that's better than telling them something wrong.

- Encourage all students to participate actively.

- Praise good performances and originality. Positive feedback makes all the difference!

- Ignore minor mistakes if the answer is original. Repeat a correct version of the answer to the rest of the class.

- Be tactful in correcting mistakes; some students are very sensitive. Gently remind them that they are all in the same boat, that only "practice makes perfect" (*Es ist noch kein Meister vom Himmel gefallen*). They are all there to learn and to help one another learn.

- Address questions to the entire class before asking individual students. This will get everyone thinking.

- Stop an exercise when all students understand and know the material.

- Be clear and strict with assignments. Spot-check once in a while.

- Encourage the students to attend the language lab regularly. Use lab and workbook materials on tests.

- Be enthusiastic, pleasant, and helpful. Usually the students will try to live up to your expectations.

- Don't monopolize class time yourself.

- Don't take special efforts for granted.

- Don't discuss every little mistake. That only inhibits the students.

- Don't embarrass a student in front of the class.

- Don't put students on the spot, unless they habitually don't pay attention.

- Don't bore students.

- Don't accept sloppy work.

- Don't underestimate the usefulness of the lab. It is an important means for acquiring a degree of fluency in the language.

- Don't be too critical and pedantic. Don't forget that humor and a personal touch are very effective.

C. Sources of Information on Foreign Language Teaching

Much useful information on foreign language teaching can be found in journals such as *Die Unterrichtspraxis, Foreign Language Annals,* and *The Modern Language Journal* and in books by such experts as E. Allen and R. Vallette, K. Chastain, A. Omaggio, and W. Rivers, to name just a few. These books contain, in addition to the theory and practice of foreign language teaching, substantial bibliographies.

IV. General Methodological Suggestions

A. *Schritte (Pre-units)*

1. Objectives   After completing the *Schritte*, the students will have learned approximately 200 words and phrases (not counting numerals) on such topics as the classroom, greetings, colors, clothes, weather, days, months, seasons, and telling time. They will be able to respond to German classroom directions and to answer questions about themselves. They will know about genders, plural forms, and some verb endings, and will be able to produce simple statements, yes / no questions, information questions, and imperatives.

Of the four skills, listening and speaking are given primary importance in the *Schritte*. For this reason, pronunciation practice and vocabulary learning are stressed, while discussion of grammar is all but avoided. The *Rückblick* following the last pre-unit summarizes what students should know after completing all the *Schritte*. (Students who prefer to understand the principles behind what they are doing can be told to use the *Rückblick* for guidance.) At the end of the pre-units, the students should have a feeling of accomplishment and should approach the main chapters with confidence.

2. Pacing   The pacing of the *Schritte* will depend on the number of class hours available per week and on student motivation, aptitude, and background. On the average, a day and a half per pre-unit (or 8 to 10 hours for the six pre-units) should be appropriate. Pacing should be adjusted to student response.

- Day 1: Introduction to the course: Dialogue of *Schritt* 1

- Day 2: *Schritt* 1; Dialogue of *Schritt* 2

- Day 3: *Schritt* 2; Dialogue of *Schritt* 3

- Day 4: *Schritt* 3

- Day 5: Review; Dialogue of *Schritt* 4

- Day 6: *Schritt* 4; Dialogue of *Schritt* 5

- Day 7: *Schritt* 5; Dialogue of *Schritt* 6

- Day 8: *Schritt* 6; *Sprechsituationen*

- Day 9: *Rückblick*; Quiz

If the course is 3 hours per week, spend about 7 hours with the pre-units, covering about one pre-unit per class period.

3. Methodology   For the *Schritte*, direct methods are appropriate. After an introductory explanation of aims and methods, it should be possible to conduct classes almost entirely in German. The instructor must be energetic, lively, and willing to act out sentences and phrases. Each class period must be carefully planned to allow for a maximum of practice, a variety of activities, and a smooth flow from one activity to another. No activity should last longer than eight to ten minutes, and the pace should be brisk. While new materials are constantly added, it is essential to review regularly the material already learned in the previous pre-units. Planning includes collecting realia or pictures to teach new vocabulary without resorting to English.

Much of the work can be done in chorus, but this should alternate with choral responses by sections of the class and with individual responses. Occasionally the class should also be divided into groups of two students working together on

Wiederholungsübungen and the like. The listening skills can be developed by having the students act out instructions and by dictation. To train their short-term memory, the students should learn to write down brief sentences (two to five words) of familiar material after only *one* hearing.

4. General Suggestions for the Individual Parts of Each *Schritt*

a. *Gespräche* Read the first dialogue slowly and clearly and try to demonstrate the meaning implied in what you say. Let students follow the text in the book. Then have the students repeat after you in chorus, in small groups, and individually. Now they should not look at their books, but concentrate on sound, stress, and intonation. If a sentence is too long, use a "backward buildup." Here is such a buildup for *Für morgen lesen Sie bitte das Gespräche noch einmal!*

> *noch einmal / / das Gespräche noch einmal / / lesen Sie bitte das Gespräch noch einmal / / Für morgen lesen Sie bitte das Gespräch noch einmal! / /*

The students should not be expected to memorize entire dialogues, but should be able to read them correctly and fluently, answer questions about them, and write them as part of a dictation. It may be a good idea to introduce the dialogue of the next pre-unit during the last part of the class, so that the students can practice it at home in preparation for work on the other materials presented in that unit.

b. *Wortschatz* The vocabulary listed in this section is considered active and must be mastered by the students, including the gender and plural forms of nouns and spelling. It may be useful to read each word in the list and have the students repeat it in chorus, or to pick out those words which may prove difficult. Point out that vocabulary listed as headings must also be learned. However, words under *Passives Vokabular* do not have to be mastered actively, i.e., students only need to understand them, not use them. Avoid including them in quizzes, other than for comprehension.

c. *Aussprache* Each *Schritt* focuses on a particular set of sounds, which are also contained in the tape program. In addition, the workbook offers a Summary of Pronunciation with brief explanations of sound production and exercises available on a separate tape in the tape program. This summary can be used for additional practice in the classroom or for individual practice by the students. Draw the students' attention to this resource.

Before a pronunciation drill, it would be helpful to explain similarities and differences between the production of sounds in American English and German and to describe and demonstrate the production of the German sounds. The students must *hear* the differences before being asked to make new sounds. Some of the more difficult sounds should be reviewed regularly. To practice listening and to test how well the students hear, have them write down words you say which contain sounds recently learned. Point out how spelling reflects sound.

d. *Mündliche Übungen* Phrases from the dialogues and the vocabulary of each pre-unit are drilled in the *Mustersätze*. It is important here to have realia or pictures of the new vocabulary, as, for example, pens and pencils, pieces of construction paper for colors, a clock, etc., or to use drawings on the board or posters. Also use personal belongings and other objects in the classroom, such as clothes worn by you and your students.

First read the entire pattern, i.e., the cue and model sentence (*Heinz Fiedler: Ich heiße Heinz Fiedler*), then repeat *Heinz Fiedler* and let the entire class respond. Continue with the next cue. Keep the pace of these drills brisk while listening carefully for pronunciation problems. Demonstrate difficult words again and have them repeated in chorus.

All previously learned material recurs in the *Wiederholung* exercises. This section can be used as a warm-up to start the next class period. Quiz questions can be selected from it.

e. *Aufgabe* This section is to be assigned orally and / or in writing. The students should be able to answer questions and do other tasks readily on the day for which they are assigned.

f. *Im Sprachlabor und zu Hause (Laboratory Manual / Workbook)* There is a brief 15-minute tape program for each pre-unit. The workbook section consists of a short list of English vocabulary and phrases to be written in German as practice in spelling and writing.

B. *Kapitel (Chapters)*

1. Objectives While the pre-units focus on listening and speaking, the main chapters add explanations and drill in structure as well as practice of all four skills. Both practice and understanding of structure are essential for adults learning a foreign language.

2. Pacing and Lesson Plans As with the pre-units, the pacing of the chapter will depend on various factors: hours per week, quarter or semester system, the students' background, etc. For an average class meeting five times a week on the semester system, here is how a schedule for the teaching of Chapter 1 might look:

	Class	Assignment
Day 1	• Review of *Rückblick* • Quiz on pre-units • Introduce *Gespräche*, Ch. 1	• Prepare to read fluently and understand meaning of *Gespräche* • Start *Wortschatz I: Familie* • Read *Struktur I*; learn endings
Day 2	• Warm-up: personal questions • Review *Gespräche*: in chorus, groups of 2, "perform" • *Zum Thema A* • *Strukturübungen A–C*	• *Wortschatz I: Länder und Sprachen* • Fill in *Strukturübung D*, write out E • Study *Struktur II*
Day 3	• Warm up: *Zum Thema B* • Ask content questions on *Gespräche* • *Zum Thema C* • *Strukturübungen F–H* • Check vocabulary	• Complete *Wortschatz I: Weiteres* • Prepare *Zum Thema D* • Study *Struktur III*

Continued

	Class	Assignment
Day 4	• Warm-up: *Zum Thema D* • *Strukturübungen I, J* • Start *Einblicke: Wortschatz 2, Was ist das?*, pre-reading activity	• Read *Struktur IV* • Write out *Strukturübung L* • Learn *Wortschatz 2*
Day 5	• Warm-up: *Etwas Geographie* (base questions on *Zum Text C*) • *Aussprache* • *Strukturübung K* • Collect *Strukturübung L* • Text of *Einblicke*	• Review *Einblicke* • Prepare *Zum Text A* • Read *Sprechsituationen*
Day 6	• Warm-up: questions on text • *Zum Text A, B* (C, if not done before text) • Return *Strukturübung L*, discuss • *Sprechsituationen*	• Workbook • *Übungsblatt* (lab) • Prepare for quiz
Day 7	• Collect *Übungsblatt* • Quiz • Introduce *Gespräche*, Ch. 2	• Read fluently and understand meaning of *Gespräche*, Ch. 2 • Learn *Wortschatz I: Lebensmittel* • Read *Struktur I*

Again, pacing should be adjusted to the students' response. Don't be driven by the idea you must finish the book. At times you should proceed more slowly so as to ensure quality and then catch up later—perhaps by deleting less important items. For the scheduling of the entire course, see pp. IAE 2–IAE 3.

To make good use of the available time, prepare for class a variety of focused activities. Constant recycling of material is necessary. With that in mind, we have included some suggestions for additional warm-ups, permitting the instructor to start each class in German while systematically reviewing familiar vocabulary and structure. After a chapter is completed, listening and speaking skills can be sharpened by talking about the chapter pictures, thus indirectly reviewing vocabulary, cultural information, and structure through visual cues. Slides or films would be a stimulating addition. Songs, too, are a pleasant way to review and enhance language learning. If there is no time for songs in class, you might want to add some to the lab program.

3. General Suggestions for the Individual Parts of each *Kapitel*

a. *Gespräche* Each chapter starts out with one or two dialogues. These are not meant to demonstrate new structures but to be models for everyday speech. They set the scene for the topic of the chapter. All subsequent activities focus on this theme. It might be helpful to have the students read the English equivalent of the dialogues at home, in order to facilitate comprehension and free more time for oral practice in class. While the dialogues as a whole need not be memorized, the students should become so familiar with them that individual sentences are virtually committed to memory.

Dramatization is effective in activating useful words and phrases. These dialogues should be read and / or acted out with natural intonation and gestures. The following steps provide a number of activities for several practice sessions:

- Practice the dialogue until the students can repeat it reasonably well.

- Have the students practice the dialogue in groups of two or three, until they sound fairly fluent. Walk around and listen; correct and answer questions while the students practice.

- Have the students "perform," i.e., read or act out the dialogue before the entire class.

- Practice variations on the basic dialogue by means of the *Mustersätze* and the dialogue exercise in *Zum Thema*.

- Ask the students content questions on the dialogue or personal questions.

- Give the students selected English cues and ask for the German equivalents.

- Give the students a few key words and have them say the entire sentence.

- Give the students one line and have them provide the next line or an appropriate response.

- Ask the students to write a similar dialogue. After you have corrected their sketches, it might be fun to let some students act theirs out.

Needless to say, the amount of practice with a dialogue depends on the time available.

b. *Wortschatz* This vocabulary section is organized by topic, with the nouns listed alphabetically by gender. Have the students mark all words with an unpredictable word stress before they begin to learn the vocabulary. Include here words with unstressed prefixes until the students have developed some familiarity with German word-formation patterns.

Divide the list into manageable groups and have the students start to learn it as soon as you introduce the dialogue of a new chapter. With many vocabulary items, the students can be helped considerably if realia or visuals (slides, transparencies) are provided, either to introduce the items or to check the students' mastery of the terms. Frequent brief quizzes, emphasizing genders and plurals of new nouns, are useful throughout the year. Constant reuse of active vocabulary is important.

Help students reduce the amount of memory work by pointing out those nouns whose gender is readily predictable (see Appendix p. 423).

c. *Zum Thema* The goal of this section is oral practice. Depending on the time available, you may have to be selective. Choose those exercises which best suit the background and interests of the class. Don't try to do all the exercises in one day; spread them over several days as you progress through the chapter. If your students find it difficult early in the chapter to answer some of the *Fragen* (which involve the new vocabulary, but not the new grammar), reserve those particular items for a later warm-up or a summary and review exercise.

d. *Struktur und Übungen* Either introduce the grammar in class and then have the students read the explanations or have them read the explanations first and explain only what remains unclear; which system you adopt depends on your teaching style, your students, and how much time is available. Keep in mind, however, that understanding the rule cannot replace practice and that practice time should far outweigh time spent on explaining (and on speaking English). All irrelevant questions and those going beyond the scope of the chapter presentation or the general interest of the students should be answered after class. Avoid writing on the board with your back to the class for extended periods of time. If an overhead projector is available, transparencies can save a great deal of time.

It is not desirable to spend entire class periods practicing structural patterns, so plan in such a way that there is some regular grammar practice, but also some reading, free speaking, etc., each day. Remember that additional graded drills are available in the tape program which are most effective when used simultaneously with the work in class. Instructions for the drills and exercises are given in German, but they are supplemented in English when they appear for the first time or when extra explanations seem necessary. Using German instructions in class helps to keep the class hearing and speaking German. It is more effective to have at least some exercises done in groups of two or three rather than by the entire class, since it gives each student more opportunity to practice.

Many sections contain brief English-to-German exercises. They often bring out contrasts between English and German and are meant for quick oral practice. The exercises in the *Zusammenfassung*, on the other hand, are intended as written practice. It might benefit the whole class to have the German answers for the translation exercise in the *Zusammenfassung* written on the board before discussing them; assign several students to this task ahead of time. If time for correcting this exercise is not available, provide the students with an answer key for self-correction.

c. *Einblicke* While some books start out the chapter with a reading passage to exemplify structure, we have chosen to put a reading selection at the end of the chapter. After ample practice with the new chapter vocabulary and grammar, we follow it up with a reading text on the chapter topic. As a result, the students review familiar vocabulary and structure in an extended context.

Each reading selection is introduced by a short set of cognates and compounds (*Was ist das?*) which the students can recognize but do not have to master actively. Since German spelling baffles some students and since the stress in many of these words is unpredictable for speakers of English, it is useful to read through the list, have the students repeat each item in chorus, have them mark the stress, and encourage them to ask the meaning if they are not entirely sure of it. By first going over *Was ist das?* orally in class, you will make the reading text easier and help the students develop recognition skills, which should enlarge their passive vocabulary considerably.

All vocabulary that is to become active through the reading text is listed under *Wortschatz* 2. This group of about fifteen words consists of useful vocabulary that could not easily be integrated into the topical sections of *Wortschatz* 1. Try to use these words actively in the classroom and make sure that students learn them, as they will appear in subsequent chapters.

For those who wish to prepare students further for the contents of the reading text, we have suggested pre-reading activities in the margin.

Since most students do not know how to read a long passage in a foreign language, take time to give them instructions. You might suggest the following approach:

- First read through the assignment for general content without worrying about unfamiliar words and phrases.

- Reread carefully and always finish a paragraph, or at least a sentence, before looking up an unfamiliar word or phrase. Look up as little as possible. Underline and pronounce the words in question, but do not scribble the English translation into the text; this will only distract you from the German.

- Read the text a third time after having guessed or looked up all the underlined words. See how many of them you remember. Try to learn them now, at least passively, so as to avoid looking them up again and again. If a word or phrase still remains unclear, circle it and ask your instructor instead of spending more time on it.

The treatment of the text itself should change in the course of the year, as the students' knowledge of German increases. In the beginning, the reading text is another means of developing good pronunciation, intonation, and fluency in reading. Therefore one of the major objectives of an assignment may involve having them prepare to read the assigned part fluently and correctly. Demonstrate and practice this in class. In the beginning of the first semester, it is advisable to introduce the text in class. Read a few sentences, have the students repeat them in chorus, drill them on difficult words, and ask detailed questions to make sure the students have understood the text. Information questions (*wo, wer, wie, was . . .?*) are more productive than yes / no questions, unless you want to check comprehension only. Assign the text in several small segments, telling the students precisely what you expect at the next meeting. Then listen to them read (it may pay off to grade a few students each time on their performance!) and ask questions. After that, prepare the next segment of the text.

As the students progress, you might have them read parts of the passage instead of reading them yourself. One entertaining way is called "*Fehlerlesen*": have one student start to read and be stopped only when a mistake is made (which you and / or the class corrects); then the next one automatically continues until another error is made, etc. This goes fairly fast and keeps the students attentive and in a state of suspense. Instead of reading through the whole passage, the students can be asked to quiz one another about the text, to define a word in German, or to give a definition and let the others guess the word. You can pick out—or, better yet, have the students find—further examples of the grammar of the chapter. Students could be asked to develop as many questions as they can on one paragraph, or the reading text could be divided among them for this purpose. Finally, you can summarize the content by means of the general questions and provide a personal touch by asking personalized questions. In the second semester the students should be able to read the text on their own. It is important to use the reading text also to develop listening comprehension. Brief dictations of familiar sentences are useful to train the students' short-term memory. Encourage the students to make use of the tapes of the reading texts to enhance their listening skills.

The exercises following the reading text are intended to test the students' comprehension of the text, to encourage them to review the main grammar topics in another context, and to expand on the topic.

f. *Sprechsituationen* The pre-units and all chapters are followed by a section which presents notional-functional expressions and provides extra conversational practice in small groups and should motivate students to converse in German. Make sure they understand what to do and stick to the time limit of five to ten minutes. Move around the room and answer questions during this time. Please note that not all of the expressions are active. Situation cards, available from the publisher, provide additional ideas for conversational exchanges. The cards include a booklet with indices for appropriate situations.

C. *Rückblicke (Reviews)*

Wie geht's? has five review sections: after the pre-units and after Chapters 3, 7, 11, and 15. These are periodic summaries of what has been introduced in the chapters. They are intended for reference and as preparation for quizzes, tests, and finals. The first part sums up points of structure; the second part practices familiar structures and vocabulary. While the students can easily read through the first part themselves, it would be helpful to do the second part—the *Wortschatz* and *Strukturwiederholung*—orally in class. The workbook contains written review exercises. If there is no time in class to go over them, make the answer keys (in the tape-script) available to the students for self-study.

D. *Aussprache (Pronunciation)*

All the pre-units and chapters include a section on pronunciation that corresponds to the lab program (*Im Sprachlabor*). Also, you and / or the students are encouraged to use the pronunciation section of the workbook. (Note the reference to that section with each *Aussprache*.) Encourage students to work with the tapes if they have difficulties.

One of the goals of the first semester is to teach the students to develop good auditory discrimination and an acceptable pronunciation—one that can be understood by a native speaker of German. While the heaviest emphasis on pronunciation naturally occurs in the beginning of the year, good habits must be constantly monitored and reinforced.

Most students are very interested in practicing pronunciation early in the year and will do so if enough tapes can be made available in the lab. Encourage the students not only to listen and repeat, but if at all possible to record themselves and compare their own pronunciation with that on the master track. To provide an incentive for practicing pronunciation, have each student read words, sentences, or a paragraph from a supplied text on tape and then record the same material toward the end of the semester.

In the beginning of the year, everything you do in class should develop pronunciation; dialogues, vocabulary practice, questions and answers, as well as the practice of individual sounds. Chorus repetition is very useful, since it allows practice without the individual student's feeling "on the spot." However, keep a sharp ear out for problems and repeat difficult words until the group has mastered them. Be generous with praise for honest efforts and good results and assure frustrated students that it will soon become quite easy. Early in the year, the students should also read dialogues and reading texts aloud in class, and difficult words should be practiced by the whole group. Don't draw attention to incorrect pronunciation every time; rather, repeat the German correctly.

Be aware of two sources of difficulties for your students: (1) their speech organs must be trained to produce certain sounds that do not exist in English; (2) they must learn to respond with different sounds to quite a few letters to which they respond automatically with English sounds. The explanations in the pronunciation section are short and nontechnical. For more information, see William G. Moulton's comparative study, *The Sounds of English and German* (Chicago: University of Chicago Press, 1962). Correct pronunciation and stress of individual words is found in the *Duden Aussprachewörterbuch* (Mannheim: Bibliographisches Institut, most recent edition).

V. Testing
A. General Guidelines

Tests should be considered not only evaluation instruments but also teaching devices. They evaluate both the students' mastery and the instructor's effectiveness, and they motivate students to learn. Frequent brief quizzes can encourage students to learn in continuous small steps. Tests covering several chapters help them review and summarize what they have been introduced to and remind them of the cumulative nature of language learning.

Quizzes given during the work on a chapter can be very brief (5–8 minutes), those given at the end of a chapter a little longer (15–20 minutes). Regular quizzes, two to three 1-hour tests, and a 2-hour final provide enough of an objective basis for evaluation, but the semester grade should also reflect preparation and classroom performance. Since students often let tests determine what they stress in their studies, it is desirable to test them orally, too, at least once each term. Here are some general guidelines for testing:

- Test only what you have taught.

- Tell the students clearly beforehand what the test will cover and what it will be like.

- Give clear directions.

- Keep tests short enough so that all but extremely slow students can complete the test comfortably.

- Make tests reasonably easy to grade.

- Check carefully for errors and typos; you expect accuracy from your students, too.

- Return the corrected tests as soon as possible.

- Go over the tests in class item by item.

- Have the bad test papers corrected and returned to you.

- Discuss study habits with unsuccessful students and make suggestions for improvement.

Testing should cover the sound system, grammar, vocabulary, listening comprehension, speaking, reading, writing, and cultural knowledge.

1. The Sound System   Students should be tested for:

- Sound discrimination: Can they tell whether they hear a German or an English word? Can they tell two similar German words apart?

- Sound production: Can they say words so that a native speaker will readily understand them? Do they put the stress on the correct syllable?

- Fluency: Can they read and speak more or less fluently, with correct interpretation of orthographic symbols and appropriate intonation?

Sound discrimination can be included in a regular quiz or test; sound production must be tested individually and orally.

- On a list of minimal pairs, have students mark the words they hear.

- Have each student read you a passage after he / she has had time to become familiar with it. Mark ahead of time the sounds or words you want to check and rate each one as acceptable or unacceptable. Also evaluate the general quality of the reading. One could test each student early in the semester to make specific suggestions for improvement and then reevaluate the pronunciation late in the semester for a grade.

2. Grammar   Mastery of grammar points can be tested in a variety of ways:

- Fill-ins: This is an effective way to test adjective endings, verb forms, relative pronouns, time expressions, conjunctions, prepositions, forms of articles, etc. A word of caution: sometimes it is not necessary to make specific indications as to how the blank is to be filled in (e.g., with adjective endings), but often a German or English cue is essential. Students cannot anticipate what you are testing and may not answer as you wish. If you use English cues, it is best to put them below the blank to be filled in:

  Dein Pullover liegt _____ Sofa. Inge ist _____ ich.
  behind the   older than

- Restated sentences: Sentences can be restated as questions or commands; in another tense, mood, or voice; with a substitute for one of the sentence elements (a different subject, a pronoun, etc.); negatively; or with something added (a modal, an adjective, etc.).

- Connected sentences: Sentences can be connected with conjunctions or with relative pronouns.

- Questions and answers: Questions can be answered positively or negatively. They can be phrased in a certain tense or mood to elicit a particular grammatical item.

- Synthetic sentences: Synthetic or dehydrated sentences test more than one item at a time. They give students an opportunity to show to what extent they have mastered several grammar points.

- English-into-German sentences: Sentences in English to be expressed in German place the greatest demands on the students, in that the students have to provide vocabulary and idioms in addition to the structure. This type of test item should be used to test contrastive use in English and German. Such sentences should test only one or two specific things at a time and not be overloaded. Use two brief sentences rather than one long one.

3. Vocabulary   Mastery of vocabulary is, of course, tested in everything the students hear, say, read, or write, but it is so important that it should be tested specifically as well. If you include the vocabulary-building section from the Workbook in your regular work, also use items from that section in quizzes and tests.

- German equivalents: In the case of nouns, also ask for gender and plural.

- Items to identify in a picture

- Fill-ins: The students can be asked to choose one of several words given or supply a word suggested by an English cue.

- Synonyms or antonyms

- Definitions: Students can be asked to define a word in German or to use a word in a sentence.

- Matching: German words can be matched with their English definitions.

- Derivations: Ask the students to derive certain words from familiar ones (a noun from an adjective, a verb from a noun, etc.); to make compound nouns; to give the English definition of a derived word.

- Paraphrasing: Ask the students to restate a sentence using different vocabulary.

4. Listening Comprehension   A check of listening comprehension should be included in every quiz and test. The lab manual contains a listening exercise and a dictation for every *Schritt* and *Kapitel*. Use them as patterns for listening tests.

- Dictations: Since spelling is a minor problem in German, dictations should focus on developing the students' short-term memory. Sentences should involve a familiar topic and contain only familiar vocabulary. They should gradually get longer.

- True / False statements: The students hear statements about a familiar topic (a recent reading, dialogue, or film) or a picture they see while listening.

- Comprehension passages: The students hear a passage or a dialogue, followed by true / false statements, questions with multiple-choice answers, or English questions. True / false statements and questions should usually be read only once, entire passages or anecdotes twice. The reading pace should be somewhat slower than normal speaking, but never so slow that students lose track of what is being said.

- A map: The students mark a path on a map according to the instructor's directions.

- Questions: Ask the students questions in German.

- Retelling: Have the students summarize an anecdote or passage they have heard.

5. Speaking   The students' ability to respond to questions can be tested on all written quizzes and tests, but their ability to speak can be evaluated only in an oral test. They can occasionally be graded in class on their responses, but a brief test (8–10 minutes) in the instructor's office or in the language lab is far more informative, though time-consuming. An oral test can evaluate pronunciation, intonation, fluency, appropriate choice of vocabulary, and correctness. It might consist of the following:

- Questions and answers: Questions are an obvious way to test speaking. Look through the book and write out personal questions from all the chapters studied; then choose from that list a few questions for each student. Evaluate them for pronunciation, correctness of structure and vocabulary, fluency and spontaneity, and appropriateness. Rate them on a scale of 1–5 in each of these areas.

- Take a role in a dialogue

- Rejoinders: Have them react to questions and statements, as in *Was paßt?*

- Talk about personal experiences

- Talk about a picture or a reading: Provide the necessary picture or refer to information from a reading passage. Ask them for personal opinions or let them talk about content. Rate the response as above.

6. Reading   While reading is usually not tested in short quizzes, it could easily be included in a test or final. Here are a few suggestions:

- True / false statements

- Choosing correct rejoinders

- Fill-ins: Complete a passage by filling in blanks.

- Comprehension passages: Read a passage and mark sentences based on it as true or false; choose the correct answer(s) from a set of statements about it; answer content questions on it; complete sentences or formulate questions on it; summarize it.

7. Writing   Although we claim to teach four skills, tests often rely very heavily on the writing skill, as in dictations, fill-ins, synthetic sentences; English-into-German sentences; questions and answers; sentence completions; etc. Here are a few techniques to test specifically the writing skill:

- Writing a role in a dialogue

- Writing a complete dialogue (letter, story, essay, etc.)

- Writing questions on a story

- Summarizing a story
- Rewriting a passage

8. Cultural Knowledge The cultural information contained in the *Gespräche*, *Einblicke*, and cultural notes (*Übrigens*) should be included in tests and quizzes. Here are some specific ways to do it:

- True / False statements
- Questions with or without multiple-choice answers
- Sentence completions
- Writing a paragraph or essay

The computerized testing program available from the publisher simplifies test construction considerably.

B. Grading

Evaluating tests and grading can be accomplished through various procedures. Besides the commonly used approach of putting all points on a curve, the following system seems objective, workable, and fair to the students.

In your gradebook, keep track of how many points each quiz and test was worth, and the number of points a student earned. (In addition, you may want to keep a percentage figure which gives you a clear picture of the student's achievement.) At the end of the term you will have a column that adds up the total number of points a student could have earned in the course. In addition to tests and quizzes, that column may include an oral test grade, and grades for preparation and participation, if you choose. Add up all the points each student earned and compare it with the total number possible. Then translate this percentage grade into the grading system at your institution.

How does one determine the number of points a test or quiz is worth? Here are some suggestions:

- Dictation: half as many points as there are words. Take off ½ point per error.
- Multiple-choice: 1 point per item.
- True/False statements: 1 point per sentence.
- Restated sentences: Mark the points where the students have to make changes or adjustments and count 1 point for each (including word order).
- Fill-ins: 1 point for each item, e.g., . . . *neben dem* . . . (2 points).
- Completions: Undirected sentence completions can be graded on a basis of 2 or 3 points each.
- Synthetic sentences: Allow 1 point for each adjustment the students have to make, e.g., *du / sich anziehen / Mantel! Zieh dir den Mantel an!* (4 points).
- Questions and answers: Grade consistently for appropriateness and correctness on a basis of 3–5 points each.

- <u>English-into-German sentences:</u> Calculate all substantial input, which usually means all words. However, as the students become more proficient, don't count such pronouns as *ich* or words like *und; She writes home only when she needs money.* (7 points)

- <u>Dialogue completion:</u> This is more difficult to predict; allow perhaps 2 or 3 points per line.

- <u>Composition:</u> Assign a number of points corresponding to the amount of time allotted to this section (20–50 points, depending on the length of the test) and take off according to your overall estimate of the quality of the essay. This is the least objective part of any test, since you want to give credit not only for correctness but also for style and content.

To calculate a quiz or a test grade, divide the number of points earned by 1% of the number of total points possible.

$$120 \text{ points possible}$$
$$\underline{-\ 12} \text{ errors}$$
$$108 \text{ points earned}$$

$$1.2 \overline{)108} = 90\%$$

Check the validity of your test by figuring the average grade. Keep in mind that grades will naturally be quite high in the beginning of the first semester, but that this will normalize quickly. The advantage of this system is that you don't have to struggle to get all tests or quizzes to reach a magic figure of 50 or 100 points.

VI. Ancillaries

A. Tape Program and Laboratory Manual / Workbook

The tape program and its corresponding laboratory manual / workbook provide additional opportunity for students to practice listening, speaking, and writing skills. A complete transcript is available from the publisher. It includes the texts of the stories read and the answer keys for the *Übungsblätter* AND for the exercises in the workbook.

Each chapter in the workbook combines materials for use in the language laboratory (*Im Sprachlabor*) and written exercises for review and practice at home (*Zu Hause*). The lab program contains: (1) the chapter dialogues; (2) supplementary grammar exercises which follow the presentation of structural points in the chapter; (3) a pronunciation review concentrating on special sounds and sound discrimination; (4) an aural comprehension passage; (5) a dictation based on the general content of the reading text; and (6) the reading text of the chapter. A special *Übungsblatt* is provided for each chapter to check the students' mastery of the material. <u>Remind students to have the *Übungsblatt* ready as they begin the lab session, since constant reference is made to it.</u> The lab program is divided into two parts—two 20–30 minute sessions that we suggest as a mandatory assignment for each chapter. By collecting the *Übungsblätter* you can monitor the students' effort and progress.

The exercises in the workbook focus on vocabulary, structure, and cultural enrichment. They develop skills in word recognition and word formation, review chapter grammar in context, and add cultural information through visual material and short reading texts. You may want to assign and collect the exercises regularly, or at least spot-check periodically whether students actually use the workbook by collecting a few pages of it. Include items from it on quizzes and tests. If there is no class time available to go over the exercises, you can provide the answer key from the tapescript for self-correction.

B. Video

Video is a superlative medium for letting students experience the richness of the German-speaking world. The two-hour video cassettes (*Zielpunkt Deutsch*), designed to supplement any first-year German text, can add excitement to your classroom. The video program is proficiency-based and highlights language and situations students would actually encounter abroad. Each of the 16 units includes three theme-related modules: *Szene*, *Minidrama*, and *Aus dem Alltag*. The *Szenen* contain short dialogues stressing survival situations, such as ordering a meal in a restaurant. The *Minidramen* feature longer conversations or interviews. The *Aus dem Alltag* sections show authentic footage, such as news and weather reports. The viewer's manual that accompanies the video program contains written and oral activities for students. The complete script with suggestions to the instructor is also available.

Correlation of video episodes with text chapters

(Note: 4.1 = episode 4, scene 1; 4.M = episode 4, minidrama; SP = suitable for Sprechsituationen)

Wie geht's?	*Zielpunkt Deutsch*
S1	1.1
S2	
S3	
S4	
S5	
S6	SP:1.1
K1	
K2	4.1 9.1 SP:9.2
K3	4.2 SP:4.M
K4	9.M
K5	5.1 5.2 5.M 12.1 12.2
K6	2.1 2.M
K7	13.1 13.2 13.M
K8	6.1 6.2 6.M 12.M 14.1
K9	3.1 10.1 10.2 10.M 14.M
K10	16.M 17.1 17.2 17.M
K11	SP:10.1 SP:10.2 SP:10.M

K12	7.1	7.2	7.M	16.1	12.2	
K13	1.2	1.M	2.2	8.1	8.2	8.M	16.M
K14	5.M					
K15	3.1	14.2	15.1	15.2	15.M	

C. Computerized Testing Program

The computerized testing program, which accompanies the fourth edition of *Wie geht's?*, provides two tests for each chapter. The program comes in a bound book with perforated pages so that the tests may be easily reproduced. It is also available on computer disk so that instructors may customize the tests to meet their individual needs. Answer keys for all tests are found at the end of the program.

Each test includes sections evaluating mastery of chapter vocabulary and grammatical structures as well as listening, reading comprehension, and writing skills. The Situation Cards for Oral Evaluation (see p. 22) may be used to test speaking skills.

D. Text-Specific Software

A set of tutorial disks accompany the fourth edition of *Wie geht's?*. They encourage the students to practice grammatical structures introduced in each chapter in a medium most of them will find enjoyable. The program features error analysis.

Depending upon the computer facilities at your institution, make the software available to students as freely as possible. The software can be used by students as a general drill or for review of specific problem structures.

E. Overhead Transparencies

Two sets of 34 and 35 full-color overhead transparency acetates contain a variety of materials: visual representations of vocabulary items arranged thematically (e.g., food, sports, travel), scenes for description, and cultural materials. These transparencies can be used for vocabulary review, communicative situations, oral and written testing, and grammar practice.

Correlation of overhead transparencies with text chapters

Wie geht's?	*Neue Freunde*	*Wir, die Jugend*
S1	1, 2	
S2		
S3	29	
S4	3, 6, 15, 29	
S5	9	
S6	7, 9	
K1	15, 17	
K2	19, 21, 29	
K3	10, 20, 23	4, 5, 13, 25, 26
K4	15, 22, 23, 24, 28, 30	
K5	5, 13, 18	7, 23
K6	7, 16, 10	7, 8, 9, 23

K7	12, 26	22, 24
K8	12, 13, 14, 21	10, 21, 22
K9	8, 9, 10, 22, 25	4, 6, 17, 20, 25
K10	10, 24, 25, 26, 27	18, 20, 22, 24
K11	17	1, 3, 10, 13, 14
K12		1, 11, 12, 15, 17, 19, 21, 27, 29
K13		11, 12, 14, 15, 16, 27, 28
K14	17	2, 15, 16, 28, 29
K15		

F. Situation Cards for Oral Evaluation

A set of 144 situation cards may be used to evaluate students' oral proficiency. Each card contains a situation to which the student is to react orally in German. They are written in English so that students are not given key German vocabulary and structures. The booklet accompanying the cards contains useful suggestions for evaluating speaking skills. The cards can also be used as additional material for the *Sprechsituationen*.

Correlation of situation cards with text chapters

Wie geht's?	*Situation cards*
Schritte	1, 2
K1	12
K2	
K3	42, 43, 52, 53, 56
K4	22, 23, 24, 29, 30, 58, 59, 61, 64
K5	44, 46, 55
K6	14, 40, 45, 135, 136
K7	139, 140
K8	15, 26, 27, 28, 48, 125, 126, 141
K9	13, 31, 33, 34, 50, 51, 53, 65, 66, 69, 70, 71, 97, 101, 107, 108, 112, 115, 119, 124, 127, 128
K10	5, 6, 21, 36, 57, 98, 105, 106, 109, 110, 117, 129
K11	9, 10, 16, 17, 18, 19, 20, 67, 68, 73, 74, 75, 76, 80, 90, 91, 99, 104, 111
K12	8, 37, 38, 39, 41, 47, 49, 60, 63, 77, 78, 79, 89, 92, 93, 113, 114, 116, 122, 123
K13	3, 4, 7, 11, 25, 32, 72, 81, 83, 85, 86, 87, 88, 100, 102, 103, 118, 120, 121, 130, 131, 133, 134, 143, 144
K14	35, 62, 82, 84, 94, 95, 96, 137, 138
K15	132, 142

VII. ACTIVE VOCABULARY LIST

This section will help you prepare tests and supplementary practice. Nouns are grouped by *gender* and *alphabetically within that group*. Words preceded by G are introduced in the grammar section. The symbol (—) is used to mark the beginning of *Wortschatz 2*.

CII.	NOUNS		VERBS	ADJECTIVES	OTHER
S1	Herr Fräulein Frau		ich bin ich heiße Sie heißen	gut / schlecht müde wunderbar	auch Auf Wiedersehen! danke / bitte Es geht mir . . . Freut mich. Guten Abend / Morgen! Guten Tag! ja / nein Mein Name ist . . . nicht und wie? Wie geht's? Wie geht es Ihnen? Wie heißen Sie?
S2	Bleistift Kuli Stuhl Tisch Bild Buch Fenster Heft Papier Zimmer	Farbe Kreide Tafel Tür Wand	antworten fragen hören lernen lesen sein wiederholen	blau braun gelb grau grün orange rosa rot schwarz weiß richtig / falsch	auf deutsch / englisch Das ist (nicht). für morgen hier / da noch einmal Was ist das? Welche Farbe hat . . .? Wo ist . . .?
S3	Mantel Pullover Rock Schuh Gegenteil Hemd Kleid	Bluse Hose Jacke Kleidung	gehen sagen schreiben sprechen verstehen	dick / dünn groß / klein kurz / lang langsam / schnell neu / alt sauber / schmutzig	aber Gehen Sie an die Tafel! Ich weiß nicht. oder Passen Sie auf! Sprechen Sie laut! Wie bitte? zu
S4	Zahl		brauchen kosten nehmen öffnen zählen		auf Seite Das kostet . . . Was kostet / kosten . . .? eins, zwei . . . eine Mark / ein Pfennig heute / morgen nur von . . . bis . . . wie viele?
S5	Frühling . . . Januar . . . Monat Montag . . . Tag	Jahr Wetter Woche	finden	furchtbar heiß / kalt prima schön warm / kühl	Die Sonne scheint. Die Woche hat . . . Es ist . . . Es regnet. Es schneit. Ich finde es . . . nicht wahr? sehr Wann sind Sie geboren? Ich bin im Mai geboren. wieder wirklich

CH.	NOUNS		VERBS	ADJECTIVES	OTHER
S6	Minute		beginnen	fertig	Danke schön!
	Sekunde		essen		Bitte schön!
	Stunde		haben		Wie spät ist es?
	Uhr		Tennis spielen		Wieviel Uhr ist es?
	Vorlesung				Es ist ein Uhr.
	Zeit				Es ist eins.
					jetzt
					morgens / mittags
					nachmittags / abends
					um (halb) . . .
					um Viertel vor / nach . . .
					Ich habe keine Zeit.
1	Berg	Eltern	kommen	—	Ich bin aus . . .
	Bruder	Familie	liegen		im Norden . . .
	Deutsche . . .	Frage	wohnen	wichtig	nördlich von . . .
	Fluß	Frau			mein(e) / dein(e) / Ihr(e)
	Großvater	Großeltern			woher?
	Junge	Großmutter			G: du, er, sie, ihr; wer? was?
	Mann	Hauptstadt			kein(e)
	Onkel	Landkarte			—
	Satz	Leute			ungefähr
	See	Mutter			so . . . wie . . .
	Sohn	Prüfung			
	Vater	Schwester			
		Sprache			
	Deutsch . . .	Stadt			
	Deutschland. . .	Tante			
	Kind	Tochter			
	Land	—			
	Mädchen				
		Mensch			
		Nachbar			
		Teil			
2	Apfel	Bäckerei	kaufen	frisch	doch
	Fisch	Banane	machen	—	etwas
	Kaffee	Bohne	verkaufen	billig / teuer	gern
	Käse	Buchhandlung	G: haben	offen / zu	Ich esse / trinke gern . . .
	Kuchen	Butter	sein		Ich möchte . . .
	Markt	Cola	es gibt		natürlich
	Saft	Erbse			ein Pfund . . .
	Salat	Erdbeere			ein Stück . . .
	Supermarkt	Gurke			was für ein?
	Tee	Karotte			G: wen? was?
	Wein	Lebensmittel			durch, für, gegen,
		Limonade			ohne, um;
	Bier	Marmelade			aber, denn, oder,
	Brot	Milch			und
	Brötchen	Orange			—
	Ei	Tomate			alles
	Fleisch	Wurst			ein Glas . . .
	Gemüse	Zitrone			eine Tasse . . .
	Geschäft	G: Student . . .			ein paar
	Kaufhaus	—			Ich gehe . . . einkaufen.
	Obst	Durst / Hunger			Ich habe Hunger / Durst.
	Pfund	Glas			montags . . .

CH.	NOUNS		VERBS	ADJECTIVES	OTHER
	Plätzchen	Apotheke			oft
	Stück	Blume			warum?
	Wasser	Drogerie			
		Studentin			
		Tasse			
3	Kellner	Gabel	bestellen		Fräulein!
	Löffel	Kartoffel	(be)zahlen		Herr Ober!
	Nachtisch	Kellnerin	bringen		Das schmeckt gut.
	Ober	Mensa	empfehlen		Guten Appetit!
	Pfeffer	Nudel	G: danken		Danke gleichfalls!
	Pudding	Rechnung	fahren		etwas (zu)
	Reis	Serviette	geben		nichts (zu)
	Teller	Speisekarte	gefallen		noch ein(e)
	Zucker	Suppe	gehören		viel(e)
		—	helfen		wieviel? / wie viele?
	Café	Freund	laufen		zu Hause / nach Hause
	Eis	Freundin	sehen		zum Frühstück . . .
	Essen	Flasche	tragen		G: wem? aus, außer, bei,
	Frühstück	Hand	werden		mit, nach, seit, von, zu
	Mittagessen		—		
	Abendessen		schlafen		eine Flasche
	Messer				besonders
	Restaurant				dann
	Salz				gewöhnlich
					man
					manchmal
					nicht nur . . . sondern auch
					überall
					vielleicht
4	Feiertag	Ferien	bekommen	sicher	erste . . .
	Geburtstag	Party	dauern	—	Der wievielte ist . . .?
	Sekt	Überraschung	denken	laut	Heute ist der . . .
			feiern	lustig	Ich habe am . . . Geburtstag.
	Datum	—	gratulieren	verrückt	vom . . . bis zum . . .
	Fest	Lied	schenken		am Wochenende
	Geschenk	Kerze	singen		gerade
			tanzen		gestern / morgen
			tun		vorgestern / übermorgen
			überraschen		noch
			—		vor einer Woche
			arbeiten		wie lange?
			bleiben		Bis später!
			fallen		Tschüß!
			Spaß machen		zum Geburtstag
			studieren		zu Ostern
					zu Weihnachten
					zu Silvester
					G: bevor, daß, ob, obwohl,
					weil, wenn
					—
					dort
					eigentlich
					ein bißchen

CH.	NOUNS		VERBS	ADJECTIVES	OTHER
					immer
					(noch) nie
5	Bahnhof	Bank	besichtigen	nah / weit	da drüben
	Bus	Bibliothek	halten	—	Entschuldigen Sie!
	Dom	Brücke	zeigen	bekannt	Es tut mir leid.
	Park	Dame	zu Fuß gehen	gemütlich	Fahren Sie mit . . .!
	Platz	Haltestelle	G: dürfen	interessant	gegenüber von
	Stadtplan	Kirche	können	lieb-	(immer) geradeaus
	Tourist	Post	mögen	toll	in der Nähe von
	Weg	Schule	müssen		links / rechts
		Straße	sollen		schade
	Auto	Straßenbahn	wollen		sondern
	Hotel	Touristin	—		Vielen Dank!
	Kino	U-Bahn	bummeln		G: mir, mich . . .;
	Museum	Uni(versität)			sondern vs. aber
	Rathaus				—
	Schloß				Das macht nichts.
	Taxi				einmal
	Theater				genug
					leider
					schon
					stundenlang
6	Balkon	Ecke	baden	hell / dunkel	im Parterre
	Baum	Garage	duschen	praktisch	im ersten Stock
	Fernseher	Kommode	kochen	(un)bequem	im Monat
	Flur	Küche	mieten	—	oben / unten
	Garten	Lampe	vermieten	ausgezeichnet	sogar
	Kühlschrank	Möbel	G: hängen		ziemlich
	Schrank	Toilette	legen		G: an, auf, hinter, in,
	Schreibtisch	Wohnung	liegen		neben, über, unter,
	Sessel	—	sitzen		vor, zwischen
	Teppich	Wald	stehen		wo? wohin?
	Vorhang	Fahrrad	stellen		—
			kennen		am Abend
	Arbeitszimmer		wissen		am Tag
	Bad		—		auf dem Land
	Bett		bauen		aufs Land
	Eßzimmer		leben		außerdem
	Haus		lieben		mitten in
	Radio		sparen		noch nicht
	Regal				trotzdem
	Schlafzimmer				
	Sofa				
	Studentenheim				
	Telefon				
	Wohnzimmer				
7	Ausgang	Bank	lassen	frei	Wann machen Sie auf / zu?
	Ausweis	Kasse	(um)wechseln	geöffnet	Wie steht . . .?
	Dollar	Nacht	unterschreiben	geschlossen	G: dieser, jeder, mancher
	Eingang	Nummer	G: anrufen	möglich	solcher, so ein, welcher,
	Gast	Tasche	aufmachen	ruhig	alle; mein, dein . . .;
	Koffer	Uhrzeit	aufpassen	—	aber, denn, doch, ja
	Paß	—	aufschreiben	einfach	—

CH.	NOUNS		VERBS	ADJECTIVES	OTHER
	Reisescheck	Gasthof	aufstehen		fast
	Schalter	Jugendherberge	ausgehen		meistens
	Scheck	Pension	einkaufen		
	Schlüssel	Reise	einlösen		
			mitbringen		
	Doppelzimmer		mitgehen		
	Einzelzimmer		mitkommen		
	Geld		mitnehmen		
	Bargeld		umwechseln		
	Kleingeld		vorbeigehen		
	Gepäck		zuhören		
	Hotel		zumachen		
			zurückkommen		
			—		
			ankommen		
			bedeuten		
			Glück / Pech haben		
			kennenlernen		
			packen		
			reisen		
			reservieren		
			übernachten		
8	Absender	Abfahrt	abfahren		in einer (Drei)viertelstunde
	Aufenthalt	Adresse	abfliegen		in einer halben Stunde
	Bahnsteig	Ankunft	aussteigen		G: wessen?
	Brief	Bahn	einsteigen		(an)statt, trotz,
	Briefkasten	Briefmarke	umsteigen		während, wegen;
	Fahrplan	Fahrkarte	ausfüllen		früh, morgen,
	Flug	Fahrt	besuchen		vormittag, mittag,
	Flughafen	Post	fahren mit		nachmittag, abend,
	Wagen	(Post)karte	fliegen		nacht; jeden Tag,
	Zug	Rückfahrkarte	landen		eines Tages
	—	—	schicken		
	Flugzeug	Dorf	telefonieren		sofort
	Gleis	Gegend	—		1291 . . .
	Paket	Geschichte	Geld ausgeben		im Jahre
			erzählen		
			hinauffahren		
			weiterfahren		
9	Arm	Freizeit	fernsehen	gesund / krank	Ich habe . . .schmerzen.
	Bauch	Gitarre	photographieren	phantastisch	Ich habe (keine) Lust . . .
	Finger	Hand	sammeln	—	Mit tut . . . weh.
	Fuß	Idee	schwimmen	ander-	Was gibt's Neues?
	Fußball	Karte	schwimmen gehen	ganz	nichts Besonderes
	Hals	Kassette	Schach spielen		Was ist los?
	Kopf	Nase	Ski laufen gehen		G: zu (+ inf.), um . . . zu
	Körper	(Schall)platte	spazierengehen		—
	Mund	—	wandern		anders
	Zahn	Sport	wünschen		etwas anderes
		Leben	—		(genauso) wie
	Auge	Musik	G: s. anhören		
	Bein		s. ansehen		
	Gesicht		s. anziehen		
	Haar		s. ausziehen		

CH.	NOUNS		VERBS	ADJECTIVES	OTHER
	Hobby		s. beeilen		
	Klavier		s. duschen		
	Knie		s. erkälten		
	Ohr		s. fragen		
	Spiel		s. fühlen		
			s. (hin)legen		
			s. kämmen		
			s. . . . putzen		
			s. rasieren		
			s. (hin)setzen		
			s. waschen		
			—		
			ausgehen		
			s. ausruhen		
			s. fit halten		
			s. langweilen		
			vorziehen		
10	Anfang	Oper	anfangen	dumm	am Anfang / Ende
	Autor	Pause	anmachen	komisch	Was gibt's im Fernsehen?
	Chor	Unterhaltung	ausmachen	langweilig	G: damit, womit;
	Film	Vorstellung	klatschen	letzt-	einige, mehrere,
	Komponist	Werbung	lachen	spannend	viele, wenige
	Krimi	Zeitschrift	weinen	traurig	—
	Plattenspieler	Zeitung	G: denken an	—	vor allem
	Roman	—	erzählen von		weder . . . noch
	Schauspieler		halten von	amerikanisch	
		Bürger	schreiben an	leicht / schwer	
		Zuschauer	sprechen von	monatlich . . .	
	Ende	Fernsehen	warten auf	öffentlich / privat	
	Konzert	Nachricht	s. ärgern über	verschieden	
	Orchester	Sendung	s. freuen auf		
	Programm		s. interessieren		
	Stück		für		
11	Partner		einladen	attraktiv	auf diese Weise
	Wunsch		heiraten	charmant	beid-
			recht haben	faul / fleißig	bestimmt
	Ehe		setzen	geschieden	Du hast (un)recht.
	Eigenschaft		suchen	häßlich / hübsch	jemand
	Hochzeit		träumen (von)	intelligent	G: als, wenn, wann;
	Liebe		vergessen	jung	nachdem
	Scheidung		s. verlieben (in)	ledig	—
	—		verlieren	nett	bald
	König		s. verloben (mit)	reich / arm	endlich
			versuchen	schick	niemand
			s. wünschen	schlank	plötzlich
			—	temperamentvoll	
			aufhören	(un)freundlich	
			geschehen	(un)gebildet	
			hereinkommen	(un)glücklich	
			kaputtgehen	(un)musikalisch	
			s. lustig machen	(un)sportlich	
			über	(un)sympathisch	
			rennen	(un)talentiert	
			ziehen	(un)verheiratet	

CH.	NOUNS		VERBS	ADJECTIVES	OTHER
				unternehmungslustig	
				verliebt (in)	
				verlobt (mit)	
				verständnisvoll	
				—	
				böse	
				stolz	
12	Arbeiter	Arbeit	s. gewöhnen an	anstrengend	Ich will . . . werden.
	Arzt	Ausbildung	glauben an	eigen-	Was willst du werden?
	Beamte	Firma	verdienen	gleich	—
	Beruf	Geschäftsfrau	—	hoch	darum
	Geschäftsmann	Hausfrau	gewinnen	selbständig	früher
	Haushalt	Krankenschwester	hoffen	sicher	so daß
	Ingenieur	Sekretärin	teilen	G: besser . . .	
	Journalist	Stelle	s. vorstellen	—	
	Lehrer	Zukunft		breit	
	Plan	G: Deutsche . . .		verantwortungsvoll	
	Polizist	—			
	Rechtsanwalt	Erde			
	Verkäufer	Gefahr			
	Wissenschaftler	Luft			
	Zahnarzt	Umwelt			
		Welt			
	Büro				
	Einkommen				
	Geschäft				
13	Hörsaal	Arbeit	belegen	—	wieso?
	Kurs	Note	bestehen	ausländisch	—
	Professor	Prüfung	s. entscheiden		an deiner Stelle
	Zimmerkollege	Vorlesung	holen		erst
		Wissenschaft	lehren		gar nicht
	Fach	Zimmerkollegin	eine Prüfung		jedenfalls
	Hauptfach	—	schreiben		sowieso
	Nebenfach	Problem	—		
	Labor		teilnehmen (an)		
	Semester				
	Seminar				
	Stipendium				
	Studium				
14	Frieden	—	aussehen (wie)	einmalig	damals
	Krieg	Gedanke	bieten	historisch	eben
	Turm	Heimat	erinnern (an)	kulturell	mitten durch
		Insel	s. erinnern (an)	witzig	rings um
	Gebäude	Jugend	nennen	wunderschön	G: der, den, dem,
	Volk	Macht	stören	—	dessen . . .
		Mitte	teilen	berühmt	—
	Grenze	—			kaum
	Mauer		austauschen		nun
	Umgebung		erkennen		
			scheinen		
			verlassen		
15	Staat		abreißen	gemeinsam	Wo ein Wille ist, ist
			erklären	vereint	auch ein Weg

CH.	NOUNS	VERBS	ADJECTIVES	OTHER
	Denkmal	erlauben	—	—
	—	finanzieren	geteilt	schließlich
	Bevölkerung	garantieren	typisch	
	Hilfe	gebrauchen	wirtschaftlich	
	Landschaft	parken		
	(Wieder)ver-	planen		
	einigung	reden		
	Wirtschaft	renovieren		
		restaurieren		
		retten		
		(s.) verändern		
		verbieten		
		(wieder)aufbauen		
		zerstören		
		G: habe, sei . . .		
		—		
		s. (auseinander)-		
		entwickeln		
		s. einsetzen für		
		eine Frage stellen		

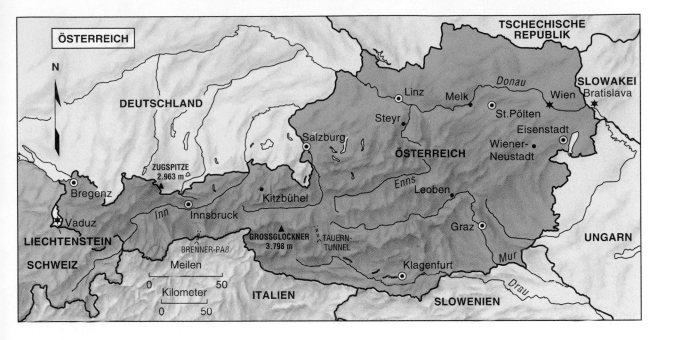

ÖSTERREICH

N

DEUTSCHLAND

TSCHECHISCHE REPUBLIK

SLOWAKEI

Linz
Melk
Donau
Wien
Bratislava

Steyr
St.Pölten

Salzburg
ÖSTERREICH
Eisenstadt
Wiener-Neustadt

ZUGSPITZE
2.963 m

Enns
Leoben

Bregenz

Kitzbühel

Innsbruck
Inn

Graz

Vaduz

GROSSGLOCKNER
3.798 m
TAUERN-TUNNEL

UNGARN

LIECHTENSTEIN

BRENNER-PAß

SCHWEIZ

Meilen

Mur

Klagenfurt

0   50

Kilometer

0   50

ITALIEN

Drau

SLOWENIEN

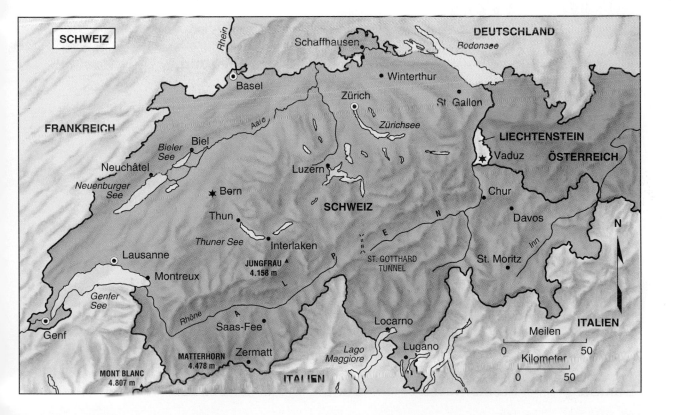

SCHWEIZ

DEUTSCHLAND

Rhein

Schaffhausen

Bodensee

Winterthur

Basel

Zürich

St. Gallen

FRANKREICH

Aare

Zürichsee

LIECHTENSTEIN

Bieler See
Biel

Vaduz

ÖSTERREICH

Neuchâtel

Luzern

SCHWEIZ

Chur

Neuenburger See

Bern

Davos

Thun

Inn

N

Thuner See
Interlaken

E

St. Moritz

Lausanne

JUNGFRAU
4.158 m

P

ST. GOTTHARD
TUNNEL

Montreux

L

N

Genfer See

Rhône

A

Locarno

ITALIEN

Meilen

Genf

Saas-Fee

Lugano

0   50

MATTERHORN
4.478 m
Zermatt

Lago Maggiore

Kilometer

0   50

MONT BLANC
4.807 m

ITALIEN

iii

Flensburg

Kassel

Bern

München

Ludwigshafen

Leipzig

Schwerin

Weimar

Wien

Darmstadt

Bonn

Speyer

Koblenz

Würzburg

Rostock

Gotha

Lübeck

Mannheim

Solingen

Suhl

Bamberg

Bremerhaven

Berlin

Offenbach

Liechtenstein

Fourth Edition

WIE GEHT'S?

An Introductory German Course

Dieter Sevin
Vanderbilt University

Ingrid Sevin
Katrin T. Bean

Harcourt Brace Jovanovich College Publishers

Fort Worth   Philadelphia   San Diego
New York   Orlando   Austin   San Antonio
Toronto   Montreal   London   Sydney   Tokyo

Publisher   *Ted Buchholz*
Senior Acquisitions Editor   *Jim Harmon*
Developmental Editor   *Barbara Caiti Baxter*
Production Manager   *Annette Dudley Wiggins*
Cover and Text Design   *World Composition, Inc., Rosemary L. Moak*
Text Illustrations   *World Composition, Inc., Ginny Baier*
Photo Research   *Judy Mason*
Editorial, Design, and Production   *World Composition, Inc.*

Photographic credits appear on page xii.

Library of Congress Cataloging-in-Publication Data

Sevin, Dieter.
    Wie Geht's? : an introductory German course / Dieter Sevin, Ingrid
 Sevin, Katrin T. Bean.—4th ed.
        p.   cm.
    Includes index.
    ISBN 0-03-049493-1
        1. German language—Grammar—1950–   2. German language—Textbooks
 for foreign speakers—English.   I. Sevin, Ingrid.   II. Bean, Katrin
 T.   III. Title.
 PF3112.S4   1991
 438.2′421—dc20   90-24141
                                                                             CIP

ISBN-0-03-049493-1

Request for permission to make copies of any part of the work should be mailed to: Copyrights and Permissions Department, Harcourt Brace Jovanovich, Inc., Orlando, Florida 32887.

Address for editorial correspondence: Harcourt Brace Jovanovich, Inc., 301 Commerce Street, Suite 3700, Fort Worth, TX 76102.

Address for orders: Harcourt Brace Jovanovich, Inc., 6277 Sea Harbor Drive, Orlando, FL 32887, 1-800-782-4479 or 1-800-433-0001 (in Florida)

Printed in the United States of America.

    3 4   0 6 9   9 8 7 6 5 4

Harcourt Brace Jovanovich, Inc.
The Dryden Press
Saunders College Publishing

CONTENTS

PREFACE

The double meaning of *Wie geht's?* reflects the double goal of the text: to show the German language at work and to show how the language works. The main text is divided into six pre-units (*Schritte*), fifteen chapters (*Kapitel*), five review sections (*Rückblicke*), and an appendix.

The purpose of the pre-units is to acquaint you with the German language and the language learning process by focusing on listening and speaking. When you have completed the last pre-unit, you should be able to greet others, describe your classroom and your clothes, use numbers, discuss the weather, and tell time, all in German.

Each chapter begins with one or two dialogues (*Gespräche*) which introduce the chapter topic and are models for conversations. English translations help you understand the content. Cultural notes (*Übrigens*) following the dialogues and later in the chapter explain differences between life in the United States or Canada and countries where German is spoken.

Most of the new vocabulary is listed in *Wortschatz 1;* it is arranged thematically, and nouns are listed in alphabetical order according to gender. The vocabulary list is followed by exercises (*Zum Thema*) which foster communication and help you learn the new words.

Each chapter introduces two or three major points of grammar. A variety of exercises (*Übungen*) provides practice of the principles presented.

A reading passage (*Einblicke*) features one or more cultural aspects related to the chapter topic. It offers additional examples of the new grammar and a review of the chapter vocabulary. A list of cognates and other easily recognized words precedes the text (*Was ist das?*); other words which are not part of the active vocabulary are given in the margin. Those few additional words that must be mastered actively are listed in *Wortschatz 2*; they will recur in later chapters. The reading text is followed by exercises (*Zum Text*) which check comprehension and provide additional grammar, writing, and speaking practice. They are preceded and followed by additional cultural notes in English.

The *Sprechsituationen* (Speaking Situations) at the end of the pre-units and each chapter list and practice expressions that are useful in social situations, such as extending, accepting, or declining invitations.

After the pre-units and chapters 3, 7, 11, and 15, you will find reviews (*Rückblicke*) of structures and vocabulary. The appendix includes information on predicting the gender of some nouns, a grammar summary in chart form, tables of all basic verb forms, lists of irregular verbs, a German-English and an English-German vocabulary, and a grammar index.

The tape program and the lab manual/workbook provide additional practice in listening, speaking, and writing. On the tapes you will find the dialogues and reading texts, supplementary grammar exercises, listening-comprehension exercises, and pronunciation practice. The lab manual section of the workbook (*Im Sprachlabor*) contains instructions and examples for all the grammar and pronunciation exercises, and a worksheet which will let you check your progress. The following section (*Zu Hause*) focuses on vocabulary building, structure, and cultural enrichment. The workbook also includes a complete pronunciation guide with brief explanations of correct sound production and corresponding exercises that are available on a separate tape.

The computer disks let you practice and review most of the exercises in the book on your own; error analysis will guide you to correct answers.

We hope that you will find this course enjoyable. You will be surprised at the rapid progress you will make in just one year. Many students have been able to study abroad after only two years of studying German!

ACKNOWLEDGMENTS

We would like to thank the following colleagues who reviewed the manuscript during its various stages of development:

Eckhard Bernstein, College of the Holy Cross; Joseph L. Brockington, Kalamazoo College; M. Jane Autenrieth Chapman, Moorpark College; David R. Connor, Minot State University; Maria Constanz, Community College of Allegheny County; William L. Cunningham, University of Louisville; Reinhard Czeratzki, Walla Walla College; Harold P. Fry, Kent State University; George A. Everett Jr., University of Mississippi; Rolf J. Goebel, The University of Alabama In Huntsville; Ingeborg M. Goessl, University of Missouri-St. Louis; Marie E. James, Grossmont College; Dwight A. Klett, Rutgers The State University of New Jersey; Kriemhilde I. R. Livingston, The University of Akron; Kay Mittnik, Texas Tech University; W. Lee Nahrgang, University of North Texas; Peggy W. Nickson, University of South Carolina At Spartanburg; Richard Packham, City College of San Francisco; Dieter Saalmann, Wichita State University; Erika Scavillo, Converse College; Elfriede W. Smith, Drew University; Robert Stanley, University of Tennessee At Chattanooga; Carol Starrels, Bucks County Community College; Cordelia Stroinigg, University of Cincinnati; Ronald C. Warner, Ball State University; Garrett Welch, West Texas State University.

We wish to extend special thanks to Joe Rea Phillips of the Blair School of Music at Vanderbilt University for his musical interludes in the tape program. Finally, we are grateful to the following of Holt, Rinehart and Winston: Jim Harmon, Senior Acquisitions Editor; Barbara Caiti Baxter, Developmental Editor; Annette Dudley Wiggins, Production Manager; Shirley Kizer, Editorial Assistant; and Patricia Meyer, Production Manager of World Composition Services.

We also wish to thank the holder of copyright of „Immer schön fressen und nicht so viel nachdenken!" from *Frankfurter Rundschau*, reprinted by permission of Stefan Schüch.

Photo Credits

1, Margot Granitsas/Photo Researchers, Inc. 2, Ulrike Welsch. 6, Owen Franken/Stock Boston. 11, Fredrik D. Bodin/Stock Boston. 16, Inter Nationes. 22, Peter Menzel. 27, Inter Nationes. 39, Peter Menzel/Stock Boston. 48, Inter Nationes. 54, Dagmar Fabricius/Stock Boston. 55, Eric Carle/Stock Boston. 57, Inter Nationes. 59, Alan Carey/The Image Works. 61, Inter Nationes. 63, Inter Nationes. 69, Inter Nationes. 74, Cary Wolinsky/Stock Boston. 78 *(top)*, Inter Nationes. 78 *(bottom)*, DIA-Verlag. 81, Peter Menzel. 84, Beryl Goldberg. 86, Martha Bates/Stock Boston. 96, Goethe Institut München. 97, Margot Granitsas/The
(Continued on page 466)

Schritte *Pre-units*

Hallo! Wie geht's?

■ LERNZIELE *Learning Objectives*

The pre-units will help you take your first steps in German. You will learn to . . .

- introduce yourself and say hello and good-bye.
- describe your classroom.
- use articles of clothing and adjectives to describe them.
- use numbers.
- describe the calendar and the weather.
- tell time.

Sprechsituationen *Communication*

- Greetings and good-byes
- Expressing Incomprehension

1

1 Guten Tag!

For suggestions on how to deal with various points of the "Schritte," see "Instructor's Preface."

Begin by saying in German who you are (**Ich heiße . . .**), then write your name on the board. Repeat **Ich heiße . . .** and ask a student **Wie heißen Sie?** Repeat until students understand and can respond.

Draw two faces or stick figures on the board, label one **Herr Sanders** and one **Frl. Lehmann.** Point to each figure while introducing the first dialogue and have students repeat after you. Then walk around the room and greet several students, using the patterns they've just heard.

Remind students to read the following dialogues aloud until they can do so fluently. They are not expected to memorize entire dialogues but should be prepared to answer questions about them.

Wie geht's?

HERR SANDERS	Guten Tag!
FRÄULEIN LEHMANN	Guten Tag!
HERR SANDERS	Ich heiße Sanders, Willi Sanders. Und Sie, wie heißen Sie?
FRÄULEIN LEHMANN	Mein Name ist Erika Lehmann.
HERR SANDERS	Freut mich.
HERR MEIER	Guten Morgen, Frau Fiedler! Wie geht es Ihnen?
FRAU FIEDLER	Danke, gut. Und Ihnen?
HERR MEIER	Danke, es geht mir auch gut.
HEIDI	Guten Abend, Ute. Wie geht's?
UTE	Ach, ich bin müde.
HEIDI	Ich auch. Auf Wiedersehen!
UTE	Tschüß!

How Are You? MR. SANDERS: *Hello.* MISS LEHMANN: *Hello.* MR. SANDERS: *My name is Sanders, Willi Sanders. And what's your name?* MISS LEHMANN: *My name is Erika Lehmann.* MR. SANDERS: *I'm glad to meet you.*

MR. MEIER: *Good morning, Mrs. Fiedler. How are you?* MRS. FIEDLER: *Fine, thank you. And how are you?* MR. MEIER: *I'm fine too, thank you.*

HEIDI: *Good evening, Ute. How are you?* UTE: *Oh, I'm tired.* HEIDI: *Me too. Good-bye!* UTE: *Bye!*

WORTSCHATZ *Vocabulary*

You are responsible for knowing all the vocabulary in this section, including the headings. Be sure to learn the gender and plural forms of nouns. Words and phrases listed under "Passives Vokabular" are intended for comprehension only; you will not be asked to produce them actively.

- In German, all nouns are capitalized.

- The pronoun **ich** (*I*) is NOT capitalized unless it stands at the beginning of a sentence.

der	Herr, die Herren *(pl.)*	*Mr.; gentleman*
das	Fräulein, die Fräulein *(pl.)*[1]	*Miss, Ms.; young lady*
die	Frau, die Frauen *(pl.)*	*Mrs., Ms.; woman; wife*

Guten Morgen! / Guten Abend!	*Good morning. / Good evening.*
Guten Tag!	*Hello.*
Wie heißen Sie?	*What's your name? (formal)*
Mein Name ist . . .	*My name is . . .*

heißen	*to be called*
ich heiß**e**	*my name is . . .*
Sie heiß**en**	*your name is . . . (formal)*

Freut mich.	*I'm glad to meet you.*
Wie geht es Ihnen?	*How are you? (formal)*
Wie geht's?	*How are you? (informal)*
wie?	*how?*
Es geht mir gut.[2]	*I'm fine.*
gut / schlecht	*good, fine / bad(ly)*
wunderbar	*wonderful(ly), great*
Ich bin müde.[2]	*I'm tired.*
ja / nein	*yes / no*
danke / bitte	*thank you / please*
auch	*also, too*
nicht	*not*
und	*and*
Auf Wiedersehen!	*Good-bye.*

Ich bin müde!

---

1 More and more often the title **Fräulein** is being replaced by **Frau** for adult women, regardless of a woman's age or marital status.

2 Es geht mir gut (schlecht, wunderbar). BUT Ich bin müde.

PASSIVES VOKABULAR ach *oh*   ich auch *me too*   **Tschüß!** *Good-bye! Bye! (colloquial).*

See III 1–21 in the pronunciation section of the Workbook. Have students familiarize themselves with it.

AUSSPRACHE *Pronunciation*

a, e, er, i, o, u

The words listed below are either familiar words, cognates (words related to English), or proper names (**Erika, Amerika**). A simplified phonetic spelling for each sound is given in brackets. The colon (:) following a vowel means that the vowel is long. Pay particular attention to word stress as you hear it from your instructor or the tape. For a while, you may want to mark words for stress.

For pronunciation practice, have students do the pronunciation exercises on the tapes. The exercises are printed in the Workbook.

Hören Sie gut zu und wiederholen Sie! *(Listen carefully and repeat.)*

[a:] **A**dam, **A**bend, Kl**a**ra, D**a**vid, T**a**g, Ban**a**ne, N**a**me, j**a**
[a]   **A**nna, **A**lbert, H**a**ns, w**a**s, d**a**s, d**a**nke, H**a**nd
[e:] **E**rika, L**e**hmann, **E**duard, P**e**ter, Am**e**rika, g**e**ht, T**ee**, S**ee**
[e]   **E**llen, H**e**rmann, **e**s, schl**e**cht
[ə]   *(unstressed* **e***)* Ut**e**, dank**e**, heiß**e**, gut**e**n, Morg**e**n, Ihn**e**n
[ʌ]   *(final* **-er***)* Diet**er**, Fiedl**er**, Rain**er**, Mei**er**, Wern**er**, Schneid**er**
[i:] **Ih**nen, Mar**i**a, Sab**i**ne, m**i**r, W**ie**dersehen, w**ie**, S**ie**
[i]   **I**ngrid, L**i**nda, **i**ch, b**i**n, b**i**tte, n**i**cht, W**i**lli, Schr**i**tt
[o:] **R**ob**e**rt, M**o**nika, R**o**se, H**o**se, B**oo**t, s**o**, w**o**, Z**oo**
[o]   **O**lga, **O**skar, **O**liver, **o**ft, M**o**rgen, S**o**mmer, k**o**sten
[u:] **U**te, **U**we, G**u**drun, H**u**go, g**u**t, N**u**del, Sch**u**h
[u]   **U**rsula, G**u**stav, **u**nd, w**u**nderbar, Ges**u**ndheit, H**u**nger, B**u**tter

■ As you may have noticed, double vowels (**Tee**), vowels followed by **h** (**geht**), and the combination **ie** (**wie**) are long. Vowels followed by double consonants (two identical consonants as in **Willi**) are short.

MÜNDLICHE ÜBUNGEN *Oral Exercises*

A: You can also use the models as patterns for role-playing activities.

A. Mustersätze *(Patterns and cues)*
These patterns give you a chance to practice phrases from the dialogues and the vocabulary of each "Schritt." Listen carefully and repeat the sentences until you can say them fluently.
  1. Willi Sanders: **Ich heiße** Willi Sanders.
     Hugo Schmidt, Helmut Rose, Gudrun Kleese, Anna Peters
  2. Erika Lehmann: **Heißen Sie** Erika Lehmann?
     Monika Schulz, Brigitte Fischer, Wolfgang Friedrich, Hermann Ohler
  3. Hugo Schmidt: **Ja, ich heiße** Hugo Schmidt.
     Helmut Rose, Hans Holbein, Brigitte Fischer, Gudrun Kleese
  4. Oskar Meier: **Nein, ich heiße nicht** Oskar Meier.
     Gustav Mahler, Clara Schumann, Wolfgang Amadeus Mozart
  5. Frau Fiedler: **Wie geht es Ihnen,** Frau Fiedler?
     Fräulein Lehmann, Herr Sanders, Frau Bauer, Herr Meier
  6. gut: **Es geht mir** gut.
     auch gut, nicht gut, schlecht, nicht schlecht, wunderbar

A.6: Act out the meaning of these adjectives.

B. Das Alphabet

1. **Lesen Sie laut!** *(Read aloud.)*

a b c d e f g h i j k l m n o p
ah beh tseh deh eh eff geh hah ih jot kah ell emm enn oh peh

q r s t u v w x y z
kuh err ess teh uh fau weh iks üppsilon tsett

ä ö ü ß
äh (a-umlaut) öh (o-umlaut) üh (u-umlaut) ess-tsett

For capital letters say **Großes A (B, C . . .)**. For further explanation of the ß-sound, see III A.6 in the pronunciation section of the Workbook.

2. **Buchstabieren Sie auf deutsch!** *(Spell in German.)*
ja, gut, müde, danke, schlecht, heißen, Fräulein, Name, wunderbar

LERNTIP

What's it like to learn a language?

Learning another language is more like learning a musical instrument or a sport than studying philosophy or history. Just as you can't learn to play the piano or swim by reading about it, you can't learn a foreign language by thinking or reading about it. You must practice. Listen to your instructor, to tapes, to the answers of your fellow students. Speak German every chance you get. Whenever possible, read the language aloud and write it.

Remember also that you are still improving your English, so don't expect perfection in another language. You made mistakes while learning English; when learning a foreign language, mistakes are also inevitable. But with daily practice, your fluency in German will make great progress.

AUFGABE *Assignment*

Prepare all assignments so that you can answer fluently in class.

A. Buchstabieren Sie Ihren Namen auf deutsch! *(Spell your name in German.)*

B. Was sagen Sie? *(What do you say?)* Read the cue lines and prepare appropriate responses.

x Guten Tag!
Y _____ .
x Ich heiße _____. Und Sie, wie heißen Sie?
Y Ich heiße _____.
x Freut mich.
Y Wie geht es Ihnen?
x _____. Und Ihnen?
Y _____.
x Auf Wiedersehen!

SCHRITT 2

Das Zimmer und die Farben

Warm-ups: 1. Guten Tag! Ich heiße .... Wie heißen Sie? Heißen Sie ...? Ja / nein ... 2. Wie geht's? Geht es Ihnen gut? Ja / nein ... 3. Ich sage „Guten Tag." Was sagen Sie?

Act out the dialogue as you introduce it so that students understand most of it without reference to the English. Bring a yellow pencil and a blue notebook.

Was ist das?

DEUTSCHPROFESSOR	Hören Sie jetzt gut zu, und antworten Sie auf deutsch! Was ist das?
JIM MILLER	Das ist der Bleistift.
DEUTSCHPROFESSOR	Welche Farbe hat der Bleistift?
SUSAN SMITH	Gelb.
DEUTSCHPROFESSOR	Bilden Sie einen Satz, bitte!
SUSAN SMITH	Der Bleistift ist gelb.
DEUTSCHPROFESSOR	Ist das Heft auch gelb?
DAVID JENKINS	Nein, das Heft ist nicht gelb. Das Heft ist blau.
DEUTSCHPROFESSOR	Richtig! Für morgen lesen Sie bitte das Gespräch noch einmal, und lernen Sie die Wörter! Das ist alles für heute.

What's That? GERMAN PROFESSOR: *Now listen carefully and answer in German. What is that?* JIM MILLER: *That's the pencil.* GERMAN PROFESSOR: *What color is the pencil?* SUSAN SMITH: *Yellow.* GERMAN PROFESSOR: *Make a sentence, please.* SUSAN SMITH: *The pencil is yellow.* GERMAN PROFESSOR: *Is the notebook yellow too?* DAVID JENKINS: *No, the notebook isn't yellow. The notebook is blue.* GERMAN PROFESSOR: *Correct. For tomorrow please read the dialogue again and learn the words. That's all for today.*

6

WORTSCHATZ

- In English the DEFINITE ARTICLE has just one form: *the*. The German singular definite article has three forms: **der, das, die.** Some nouns take **der** and are called MASCULINE; some take **das** and are called NEUTER; and some take **die** and are called FEMININE. This is a grammatical distinction and has little to do with biological sex, although it is true that most nouns referring to females are feminine and most referring to males are masculine.

der Herr, **die** Frau, BUT **das** Fräulein

Inanimate objects such as table, blackboard, and book can be of any gender.

der Tisch, **das** Buch, **die** Tafel

Because the gender of many nouns is unpredictable, the article must always be learned with the noun.

- In German the plural of nouns is formed in various ways that are often unpredictable. You must therefore learn the plural together with the article and the noun. Plurals are given in an abbreviated form in vocabulary lists. These are the most common plural forms and their abbreviations.

Abbreviation	Listing	Plural Form
-	das Fenster, -	die Fenster
⸚	der Mantel, ⸚	die Mäntel
-e	der Tisch, -e	die Tische
⸚e	der Stuhl, ⸚e	die Stühle
-er	das Bild, -er	die Bilder
⸚er	das Buch, ⸚er	die Bücher
-en	die Frau, -en	die Frauen
-n	die Farbe, -n	die Farben
-s	der Kuli, -s	die Kulis

- The plural article for all nouns is **die.** In this book, when the noun is not followed by one of the plural endings, either it does not have a plural or the plural is rarely used.

DIE FARBE, -N *color*

blau

rot

orange

gelb

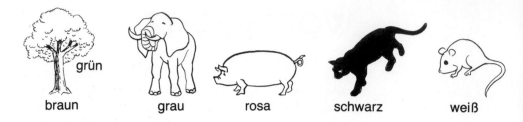

grün

braun   grau   rosa   schwarz   weiß

The vocabulary section is organized by topic, with the nouns listed alphabetically by gender.

DAS ZIMMER, - *room*

der	Bleistift, -e	*pencil*		das	Heft, -e	*notebook*
	Kuli, -s	*pen*			Papier, -e	*paper*
	Stuhl, ⸚e	*chair*		die	Kreide	*chalk*
	Tisch, -e	*table*			Tafel, -n	*blackboard*
das	Bild, -er	*picture*			Tür, -en	*door*
	Buch, ⸚er	*book*			Wand, ⸚e	*wall*
	Fenster, -	*window*				

WEITERES *Additional words and phrases*

auf deutsch / auf englisch	*in German / in English*
für morgen	*for tomorrow*
hier / da	*here / there*
noch einmal	*again, once more*
richtig / falsch	*correct, right / wrong, false*
Was ist das?	*What is that?*
Das ist (nicht) . . .	*That is (not) . . .*
Welche Farbe hat . . .?	*What color is . . .?*
Wo ist . . .?	*Where is . . .?*
antworten	*to answer*
fragen	*to ask*
hören	*to hear*
lernen	*to learn*
lesen	*to read*
wiederholen	*to repeat*
sein	*to be*
ich bin	*I am*
es ist	*it is*
sie sind	*they are*
Sie sind	*you (formal) are*

PASSIVES VOKABULAR der Artikel, - (von) der Plural (von) das Beispiel, -e *example* das Gespräch, -e *dialogue* das Wort, ⸚er *word* **alle zusammen** *all together* **Bilden Sie einen Satz!** *Make a sentence.* **Das ist alles für heute.** *That's all for today.* **Hören Sie gut zu!** *Listen carefully.* **jetzt** *now* **zum Beispiel = z.B.** *for example = e.g.*

AUSSPRACHE

ä, ö, ü, eu, äu, au, ei, ie

Hören Sie gut zu und wiederholen Sie!

[e:]	**E**rika, K**ä**the, g**e**ht, l**e**sen, Gespr**ä**ch, B**ä**r
[e]	**E**llen **Ke**ller, B**ä**cker, W**ä**nde, H**ä**nde, h**ä**ngen
[ö:]	**Ö**l, h**ö**ren, L**ö**wenbräu, G**oe**the, **Ö**sterreich
[ö]	**Ö**tker, P**ö**ppel, **ö**ffnen, W**ö**rter
[ü:]	**Ü**bung, T**ü**r, St**ü**hle, B**ü**cher, f**ü**r, m**ü**de, gr**ü**n, t**y**pisch
[ü]	J**ü**rgen M**ü**ller, G**ü**nter H**ü**tter, m**ü**ssen, k**ü**ssen, Tsch**ü**ß
[oi]	d**eu**tsch, fr**eu**t, **Eu**ropa, Fr**äu**lein, Löwenbr**äu**
[au]	Fr**au** P**au**la B**au**er, Klaus Br**au**n, **au**f, **au**ch, bl**au**grau
[ai]	R**ai**ner, H**ei**nz, H**ei**di, Kr**ei**de, w**ei**ß, h**ei**ßen, n**ei**n

- Pay special attention to the pronunciation of **ei** and **ie** (as in *Eisenhower's niece*):

[ai]	**ei**ns, h**ei**ßen, H**ei**di, H**ei**nz, M**ei**er
[i:]	S**ie**, w**ie**, W**ie**dersehen, D**ie**ter F**ie**dler
[ai / i:]	H**ei**nz F**ie**dler, B**ei**sp**ie**l, H**ei**di Th**ie**lemann

MÜNDLICHE ÜBUNGEN

A. Mustersätze
1. der Tisch: **Das ist** der Tisch.
   das Zimmer, die Tür, das Fenster, die Tafel, die Wand, das Bild, der Stuhl, das Papier, der Kuli, der Bleistift, die Kreide
2. das Papier: **Wo ist** das Papier? **Da ist** das Papier.
   der Kuli, die Kreide, die Tür, der Bleistift, das Buch, der Tisch, die Tafel, das Fenster, das Bild
3. das Buch: **Ist das** das Buch? **Ja, das ist** das Buch.
   der Bleistift, das Fenster, die Tür, der Kuli, die Kreide
4. die Tafel: **Ist das** die Tafel? **Nein, das ist nicht** die Tafel.
   der Tisch, das Papier, der Bleistift, der Kuli, der Stuhl
5. schwarz: **Das ist** schwarz.
   rot, gelb, grün, braun, orange, grau, rosa, blau, weiß
6. der Bleistift: **Welche Farbe hat** der Bleistift?
   der Kuli, das Papier, das Buch, die Tafel, die Kreide
7. lesen: Lesen **Sie bitte!**
   antworten, hören, fragen, lernen, wiederholen

B. Fragen und Antworten (*Questions and answers*)
1. Ist das Papier weiß? **Ja, das Papier ist weiß.**
   Ist das Buch gelb? die Tafel grün? die Kreide weiß? der Kuli rot?
2. Ist die Kreide grün? **Nein, die Kreide ist nicht grün.**
   Ist die Tafel rot? der Bleistift weiß? das Buch rosa? das Papier braun?

See also II.23–41 in the pronunciation section of the Workbook.

[e:] For most speakers, **Erika** and **Käthe** have the same long vowel. For [ö:] and [ü:] you may need the additional examples in the Workbook. The easiest way to learn to say [ö:] and [ü:] is to start from the tongue position for [e:] and [i:] and then round the lips. [ü:] and [ö:] need to be reviewed regularly, as students find it hard to hear and make these sounds.

A: Bring with you a pencil, a ball-point pen, some paper, a picture, and items with the colors mentioned.

B: Modify sentences to fit your particular surroundings.

3. Die Kreide ist weiß.   Ist das richtig? **Ja, das ist richtig.**
   Die Tafel ist schwarz. Ist das richtig? **Nein, das ist nicht richtig.**

   Das Papier ist weiß. Die Tür ist orange. Der Kuli ist blau. Das Buch ist rosa. Der Tisch ist braun.

C. Wiederholung *(Review)*
   1. **Was sagen sie?** *(What are they saying?)*

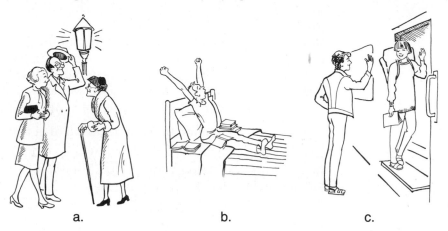

   a.   b.   c.

   2. **Buchstabieren Sie auf deutsch!**
      Elefant, Maus, Tiger, Löwe, Katze, Hund, Giraffe, Orang-Utan, Ratte

LERNTIP

How to get organized

Take a few minutes to get acquainted with your textbook. Read the table of contents, find the index, the vocabulary lists, and the appendix. Find out how each chapter is organized. Familiarize yourself with the Workbook, too. See how the lab work and the supplementary exercises are arranged. Find out whether the language lab is set up to duplicate tapes, and what other support is available to you.

Divide your assignments into small units. It's almost impossible to cram in a foreign language; so don't fall behind. Study and review daily.

AUFGABE

Fragen und Antworten
1. Was ist der Artikel? **Tür → die Tür**
   Zimmer, Bleistift, Bild, Kreide, Kuli, Stuhl, Tafel, Buch, Tisch, Fenster, Farbe, Papier, Wand, Heft, Wort, Herr, Frau, Fräulein
2. Was ist der Plural? **Kuli → die Kulis**
   Tür, Bild, Bleistift, Buch, Heft, Tisch, Fenster, Tafel, Stuhl, Wort, Farbe
3. Welche Farben hat das Deutschbuch?

3 *Kleidungsartikel*

Im Kleidungsgeschäft

VERKÄUFERIN	Na, wie ist die Hose?
HERR SEIDL	Zu groß und zu lang.
VERKÄUFERIN	Und die Krawatte?
FRAU SEIDL	Zu teuer.
HERR SEIDL	Aber die Farbe ist wunderbar. Schade!
HERR SEIDL	Mensch, wo ist meine Jacke?
FRAU SEIDL	Ich weiß nicht.
VERKÄUFERIN	Welche Farbe hat die Jacke?
HERR SEIDL	Blau.
VERKÄUFERIN	Ist das die Jacke?
FRAU SEIDL	Ja, danke!

In the Clothing Store SALESCLERK: *Well, how are the pants?* MR. SEIDL: *Too big and too long.* SALESCLERK: *And the tie?* MRS. SEIDL: *Too expensive.* MR. SEIDL: *But the color is beautiful. Too bad!*

MR. SEIDL: *Hey, where's my jacket?* MRS. SEIDL: *I don't know.* SALESCLERK: *What color is the jacket?* MR. SEIDL: *Blue.* SALESCLERK: *Is that the jacket?* MRS. SEIDL: *Yes, thank you.*

11

WORTSCHATZ

Optional vocabulary:
der Sportschuh,-e; der
Tennisschuh,-e *sneaker*;
die Socke,-n; die Jeans
(pl.); die Sandalen *(pl.)*;
das T-Shirt,-s; das
Sweatshirt,-s.

DIE KLEIDUNG *clothing*

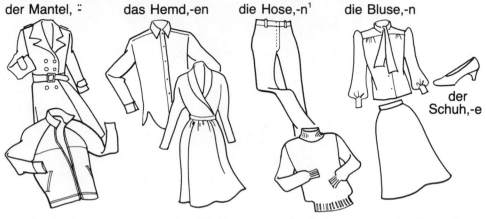

der Mantel, ⸚   das Hemd,-en   die Hose,-n¹   die Bluse,-n

der Schuh,-e

die Jacke,-n   das Kleid,-er   der Pullover,-   der Rock, ⸚e

DAS GEGENTEIL, -E *opposite*

dick / dünn	*thick, fat / thin, skinny*
groß / klein	*big, large / small, little*
lang / kurz	*long / short*
langsam / schnell	*slow(ly) / fast, quick(ly)*
neu / alt	*new / old*
sauber / schmutzig	*clean, neat / dirty*

WEITERES

aber	*but, however*
oder	*or*
zu	*too (+ adjective or adverb)*
gehen	*to go*
sagen	*to say, tell*
schreiben	*to write*
sprechen	*to speak*
verstehen	*to understand*
Gehen Sie an die Tafel!	*Go to the board.*
Ich weiß nicht.	*I don't know.*
Passen Sie auf!	*Pay attention.*
Sprechen Sie laut!	*Speak up.*
Wie bitte?	*What did you say, please?*

1 Note that **die Hose** is singular in German.

PASSIVES VOKABULAR **das Geschäft, -e** *store*   **die Krawatte, -n** *tie*
die Verkäuferin, -nen *salesclerk, f.*   **Mensch!** *Man! Boy! Hey!*   **Schade!** *Too bad!*

AUSSPRACHE

l, s, st, sp, sch, x

Hören Sie gut zu und wiederholen Sie!

[l]   lernen, lesen, langsam, alle, Pullover, Kuli, klein, blau, alt, Stuhl, Tafel,
      Mantel, Beispiel, schnell
[z]   so, sagen, sauber, sie, sind, lesen, Bluse, Hose
[s]   Professor, passen, heißen, was, groß, weiß
[st] ist, kosten, Fenster
[št] Stephan, Stuhl, Stein, Bleistift, verstehen
[šp] sprechen, Sport, Beispiel, Gespräch, Aussprache
[š]   schlecht, schnell, schmutzig, schwarz, schreiben, falsch, deutsch
[ks] Axel, Max, Felix, Beatrix

MÜNDLICHE ÜBUNGEN

A. Mustersätze
1. der Schuh: **Das ist** der Schuh.
   die Jacke, das Hemd, der Mantel, das Kleid, die Bluse, der Pullover,
   der Rock, die Hose
2. alt / neu: **Das Gegenteil von** alt **ist** neu.
   groß / klein; lang / kurz; dick / dünn; langsam / schnell; sauber /
   schmutzig; richtig / falsch; ja / nein; hier / da
3. der Mantel / alt: **Ist** der Mantel alt? **Nein,** der Mantel **ist nicht** alt.
   die Jacke / dick; das Kleid / lang; der Pullover / dünn; das Hemd /
   sauber
4. Jacken / klein: **Sind die** Jacken **zu** klein? **Ja,** die Jacken **sind zu** klein.
   Hosen / lang; Röcke / kurz; Blusen / dünn; Pullover / dick; Kleider /
   groß; Schuhe / schmutzig
5. schreiben: Schreiben **Sie bitte schnell!**
   lesen, sprechen, gehen, wiederholen, antworten
6. verstehen: Verstehen **Sie das? Ja, ich** verstehe **das.**
   sagen, hören, wiederholen, lernen, lesen

B. Fragen und Antworten
1. Ist der Rock rot? **Ja, der Rock ist rot.**
   Ist die Bluse rosa? die Jacke braun? der Kuli neu? das Papier dünn?
   der Bleistift kurz?
2. Ist der Rock blau? **Nein, der Rock ist nicht blau.**
   Ist das Buch dick? das Wort kurz? das Fenster klein? der Pullover neu?
   Sind die Schuhe weiß? die Fenster groß? die Bücher neu?

See also III. 1, 6, 9, 11–12 in the pronunciation section of the Workbook.

A.1: Make use of gestures and point to the various objects. Vary the cues and add to them, especially when books are closed. Make use of actual objects carried or worn by your students.

A.2: If possible, bring pictures or realia to demonstrate contrasting words from the "Wortschatz."

B: Adapt to your situation. After students have mastered ja / **nein** answers, mix questions.

C. Wiederholung

1. **Fragen**

   a. Geht es Ihnen schlecht? Sind Sie müde?

   b. Was ist rot? braun? blau? weiß? gelb? orange? rosa? schwarz? grau?

   c. Ist der Tisch orange? die Tafel grün? das Buch rot? . . .

2. **Wie fragen Sie?** What questions would elicit the following answers?

   BEISPIEL: Ja, ich bin müde.   **Sind Sie müde?**

   a. Danke, gut.

   b. Nein, ich heiße nicht Heinz Fiedler.

   c. Das Buch ist blau.

   d. Da ist die Tür.

   e. Das ist das Bild.

   f. Mein Name ist Schneider.

   g. Ja, das ist richtig.

   h. Ja, ich antworte auf deutsch.

C.3: Expect and encourage a variety of responses to make this section more personal.

3. **Was sagen Sie?** Point to a familiar object in the room and ask your neighbor questions, using the left-hand column as a guideline.

   x Ist das die Tafel?

   y Nein, das ist nicht die Tafel. Das ist die Wand.

   x Wo ist die Tafel?

   y Da ist die Tafel.

   x Welche Farbe hat die Tafel?

   y Die Tafel ist grün.

   x Was ist auch grün?

   y Das Buch ist auch grün.

   x Ist das _____?

   y Nein, das ist nicht _____. Das ist _____.

   x Wo ist _____?

   y _____.

   x Welche Farbe hat _____?

   y _____ ist _____.

   x Was ist auch _____?

   y _____ ist auch _____.

4. **Buchstabieren Sie auf deutsch!**

   Thomas Mann, Arthur Schnitzler, Christa Wolf, Ilse Aichinger, Friedrich Nietzsche, Heinrich Böll, Günter Grass

LERNTIP

Cognates

Because German and English are both members of the Germanic branch of the Indo-European language family, they share a lot of vocabulary. Some of these related words, called cognates, are identical in spelling (e.g., **der Name, der Winter***); others are very similar (e.g.,* **das Buch, der Schuh, der Sommer***). As the two languages developed, certain cognates acquired different meanings, such as* **die Hose** *(pair of pants) versus "hose" (stockings).*

AUFGABE

A. Fragen

1. Was ist der Artikel von Kleidung? Mantel? Pullover? Bluse? Hemd? Rock? Hose? Kleid? Jacke? Schuh?

2. Was ist der Plural von Schuh? Jacke? Rock? Kleid? Hose? Hemd? Bluse? Pullover? Mantel?

3. Sprechen Sie langsam oder schnell? Hören Sie gut oder schlecht? Sind Sie groß oder klein?

4. Was ist das Gegenteil von lang? dick? sauber? da? richtig? alt? schlecht? schnell? schmutzig? nein? danke?

5. Welche Farbe hat das Buch? das Papier? die Hose? der Rock? die Bluse? . . .

B. Beschreiben Sie bitte! Describe some of your clothing or one or two items you have with you.

BEISPIEL: Die Hose ist blau. Die Schuhe sind . . .

4

Zahlen und Preise

Was kostet das?

VERKÄUFER	Guten Tag, Frau Ziegler! Was brauchen Sie heute?
FRAU ZIEGLER	Ich brauche ein paar Bleistifte, zwei Kulis und Papier. Was kosten die Bleistifte?
VERKÄUFER	Fünfundneunzig Pfennig (0,95 DM).
FRAU ZIEGLER	Und der Kuli?
VERKÄUFER	Zwei Mark fünfundsiebzig (2,75 DM[1]).
FRAU ZIEGLER	Und was kostet das Papier da?
VERKÄUFER	Nur sechs Mark zwanzig (6,20 DM).
FRAU ZIEGLER	Gut. Ich nehme sechs Bleistifte, zwei Kulis und das Papier.
VERKÄUFER	Ist das alles?
FRAU ZIEGLER	Ja, danke.
VERKÄUFER	Siebzehn Mark vierzig (17,40 DM), bitte!

[1] Note the difference between English and German: *$2.75* but **2,75 DM**; *$1,600.00* but **1 600,00 DM** (or **1.600,00 DM**).

How Much Is It? SALESCLERK: *Hello, Mrs. Ziegler. What do you need today?* MRS. ZIEGLER: *I need some pencils, two pens and paper. How much are the pencils?* SALESCLERK: *Ninety-five pfennig.* MRS. ZIEGLER: *And the pen?* SALESCLERK: *Two marks seventy-five.* MRS. ZIEGLER: *And how much is the paper over there?* SALESCLERK: *Only six marks twenty.* MRS. ZIEGLER: *Fine. I'll take six pencils, two pens and the paper.* SALESCLERK: *Is that all?* MRS. ZIEGLER: *Yes, thank you.* SALESCLERK: *Seventeen marks forty, please.*

WORTSCHATZ

To help you remember, note these similarities between English and German:
-teen = **zehn** (*fourteen* / **vierzehn**); *-ty* = **zig** (*forty* / **vierzig**).

- 21–29, 31–39, and so on to 91–99 follow the pattern of "four-and-twenty
  (**vierundzwanzig**) blackbirds baked in a pie."

- Any number up to 1 million is written in one word, no matter how long it is:
  234 567 (**zweihundertvierunddreißigtausendfünfhundertsiebenundsechzig**).

DIE ZAHL, -EN *number*

1 eins	11 elf	21 einundzwanzig	0 null
2 zwei	12 zwölf	22 zweiundzwanzig	10 zehn
3 drei	13 dreizehn	30 dreißig	100 hundert
4 vier	14 vierzehn	40 vierzig	200 zweihundert
5 fünf	15 fünfzehn	50 fünfzig	1 000 tausend
6 sechs	16 sechzehn	60 sechzig	10 000 zehntausend
7 sieben	17 siebzehn	70 siebzig	100 000 hunderttausend
8 acht	18 achtzehn	80 achtzig	1 000 000 eine Million
9 neun	19 neunzehn	90 neunzig	
10 zehn	20 zwanzig	100 hundert	

WEITERES

ein Pfennig (zehn Pfennig)	*one pfennig (ten pfennigs)*
eine Mark (zwei Mark)[1]	*one mark (two marks)*
auf Seite 2	*on / to page 2*
heute / morgen	*today / tomorrow*
nur	*only*
von ... bis ...	*from ... to ...*
Was kostet / kosten ...?	*How much is / are ...?*
Das kostet ...	*That comes to ...*
wie viele?	*how many?*
brauchen	*to need*
kosten	*to cost, come to (a certain amount)*
nehmen	*to take*
öffnen	*to open*
zählen	*to count*
ich zähle	*I count*
wir ⎫	*we count*
sie ⎬ zählen	*they count*
Sie ⎭	*you (formal) count*

1 eins BUT **eine Mark!**

PASSIVES VOKABULAR der Preis, -e der Verkäufer, - *salesclerk, m.*
ein paar *a couple of* **plus / minus** **und so weiter = usw.** *and so on = etc.*

AUSSPRACHE

z, w, v, f, pf, qu

Hören Sie gut zu und wiederholen Sie!

[ts]   Fri**tz**, **Z**immer, **Z**ahl, **z**u, **z**usammen, **z**ählen, **z**wei, **z**ehn, **z**wölf, **z**wanzig, **z**weiund**z**wanzig, **z**weihundert**z**weiund**z**wanzig, je**tz**t

[z / ts]   sech**s**, **s**ech**z**ehn, **s**ech**z**ig, **s**ech**s**und**s**ech**z**ig, **s**ech**s**hundert**s**ech**s**und**s**ech-**z**ig, **s**ieben, **s**ieb**z**ig, **s**ieben**und**siebzig, **s**ieben**hunderts**iebenund**s**iebzig, Sa**tz**

[v]   **W**illi, **W**olfgang, **W**and, **W**ort, **w**ie, **w**as, **w**o, **w**elche, **w**eiß, **w**iederholen, **V**olvo, **V**ase

[f]   **v**ier, **v**ierzehn, **v**ierzig, **v**ierund**v**ierzig, **v**ierhundert**v**ierund**v**ierzig, **v**iele, **v**erstehen, **V**olkswagen

[f]   **f**ünf, **f**ünfzehn, **f**ünfzig, **f**ünfund**f**ünfzig, **f**ünfhundert**f**ünfund**f**ünfzig, **f**ür, **F**enster, öf**f**nen, Ta**f**el, au**f**, el**f**, zwöl**f**

[pf]   **Pf**ennig, **Pf**effer, **Pf**efferminz, Dummko**pf**, **pf**ui

[kv]   **Qu**alität, **Qu**antität, **Qu**artal, **Qu**artett, **Qu**intett, Ä**qu**ivalent

MÜNDLICHE ÜBUNGEN

A. Hören Sie gut zu und wiederholen Sie!
1. Wir zählen von eins bis zehn: eins, zwei, drei, vier, fünf, sechs, sieben, acht, neun, zehn.
2. Wir zählen von zehn bis zwanzig: zehn, elf, zwölf, dreizehn, vierzehn, fünfzehn, sechzehn, siebzehn, achtzehn, neunzehn, zwanzig.
3. Wir zählen von zwanzig bis dreißig: zwanzig, einundzwanzig, zweiundzwanzig, dreiundzwanzig, vierundzwanzig, fünfundzwanzig, sechsundzwanzig, siebenundzwanzig, achtundzwanzig, neunundzwanzig, dreißig.
4. Wir zählen von zehn bis hundert: zehn, zwanzig, dreißig, vierzig, fünfzig, sechzig, siebzig, achtzig, neunzig, hundert.
5. Wir zählen von hundert bis tausend: hundert, zweihundert, dreihundert, vierhundert, fünfhundert, sechshundert, siebenhundert, achthundert, neunhundert, tausend.

B. Lesen Sie laut auf deutsch!
1. **Seitenzahlen**
   Seite 1, 5, 7, 8, 9, 11, 12, 17, 19, 22, 25, 31, 42, 57, 66, 89, 92, 101
2. **Plus und minus**

   BEISPIEL: $4 + 4 = 8$ **Vier plus vier ist acht.**
   $8 - 4 = 4$ **Acht minus vier ist vier.**

See also III. 1, 4–5, 7–8, 19, 21 in the pronunciation section of the Workbook.

Initial z [ts] is difficult. Point out to students that they have no trouble with [ts] in *rats* or *pizza* and that initial z is the same sound.

You could introduce part A on the first day by repeating several times in chorus the numbers from 1 to 12, 13 to 20, 21 to 30, 31 to 100, and do part B the next day. Keep reviewing numbers. To sharpen listening skills, say a few every day and let students write them as numerals.

When counting, Germans use the thumb (not the index finger) to indicate number 1. Have students count students, women, men, fingers, feet, windows, chairs, etc.

$$3 + 2 = 5 \qquad 8 + 1 = 9 \qquad 8 - 2 = 6$$
$$7 + 3 = 10 \qquad 10 - 2 = 8 \qquad 7 - 6 = 1$$
$$1 + 1 = 2 \qquad 9 - 4 = 5 \qquad 5 - 5 = 0$$

Show some German, Austrian, or Swiss money and explain its value in relation to the dollar.

3. Preise

BEISPIEL: 0,10 DM   **zehn Pfennig**
           1,20 DM   **eine Mark zwanzig**

0,25 DM   0,31 DM   0,44 DM   0,67 DM   0,72 DM   0,88 DM
2,50 DM   4,75 DM   8,90 DM   5,60 DM   10,40 DM   3,25 DM

4. Inventar. With an employee, played by a partner, you are making the inventory of the items you have in stock in your store.

BEISPIEL: Jacke / 32   **Wie viele Jacken? Zweiunddreißig Jacken.**

a. Pullover / 42
b. Rock / 14
c. Hemd / 66
d. Kleid / 19
e. Hose / 21

f. Jacke / 37
g. Mantel / 12
h. Krawatte / 89
i. Schuh / 58

C. Mustersätze

1. das Papier: **Was kostet** das Papier?
   die Kreide, die Hose, der Mantel, die Jacke, der Pullover
2. Bleistifte: **Was kosten** die Bleistifte?
   Kulis, Bücher, Schuhe, Hemden, Bilder
3. brauchen: **Was** brauchen **Sie?**
   sagen, hören, schreiben, lesen, zählen, nehmen
4. brauchen: Brauchen **Sie das? Nein, ich** brauche **das nicht.**
   hören, sagen, verstehen, zählen, wiederholen, öffnen
5. brauchen: **Wir** brauchen **das.**
   lesen, nehmen, zählen, verstehen, wiederholen, öffnen

D. Wiederholung

1. **Gegenteile.** Tell which adjectives best describe each pair.

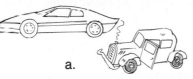
a.

b.

c.   d.

e.

2. **Fragen und Antworten.** Ask a classmate the following questions.
   a. Wie geht's?
   b. Heißen Sie Meier?
   c. Wie heißen Sie? Wie heiße ich?
   d. Was ist das? *(Point to items in the classroom.)*
   e. Ist das Buch dick oder dünn? der Bleistift lang oder kurz? das Zimmer groß oder klein? die Tafel schwarz oder grün?
   f. Welche Farbe hat das Buch? der Kuli? die Bluse? die Hose? die Jacke?

3. **Antworten Sie mit ja!** *(Answer with yes.)*

   BEISPIEL: Wiederholen Sie das?   **Ja, ich wiederhole das.**

   a. Sprechen Sie langsam?
   b. Verstehen Sie die Frage?
   c. Nehmen Sie die Kreide?
   d. Öffnen Sie das Fenster?
   e. Lesen Sie das noch einmal?
   f. Gehen Sie an die Tafel?
   g. Lernen Sie das für morgen?

4. **Antworten Sie mit nein!** *(Answer with no.)*

   BEISPIEL: Sind die Schuhe neu?   **Nein, die Schuhe sind nicht neu.**
   Nein, die Schuhe sind alt.

   a. Sind die Fenster klein?
   b. Sind die Bücher alt?
   c. Sind die Jacken sauber?
   d. Sind die Bleistifte dick?
   e. Sind die Mäntel lang?

5. **Geben Sie Befehle!** *(State as requests.)*

   BEISPIEL: antworten   **Antworten Sie bitte!**

   fragen, wiederholen, gehen, lesen, schreiben, lernen

6. **Buchstabieren Sie auf deutsch!** Blume *(flower)*, Rose, Tulpe, Narzisse, Gladiole, Nelke *(carnation)*, Sonnenblume, Dahlie, Iris

AUFGABE

A. **Wieviel ist das?** *(How much is that?)*

$$15 + 9 = ? \qquad 20 - 1 = ? \qquad 72 + 8 = ?$$
$$28 + 4 = ? \qquad 12 + 48 = ? \qquad 114 - 16 = ?$$
$$22 - 8 = ? \qquad 60 - 5 = ? \qquad 1\,000 - 25 = ?$$

B. **Wie geht's weiter?** *(What comes next?)*

$$100 - 10 = 90 \qquad 90 - 10 = 80 \qquad 80 - 10 = ?$$
$$70 - 7 = 63 \qquad 63 - 7 = 56 \qquad 56 - 7 = ?$$

C. Was kostet das zusammen?

1. Sechs Bleistifte kosten 2,40 DM, der Kuli kostet 1,60 DM, das Buch 24,55 DM und das Papier 3,—DM. Das kostet zusammen _____.
2. Die Jacke kostet 75,—DM, die Bluse 48,—DM, und die Schuhe kosten 84,—DM. Das kostet zusammen _____.
3. Das Buch kostet 5,50 DM. Was kosten drei Bücher?
4. Das Hemd kostet 28,50 DM und die Hose 125,—DM. Das kostet zusammen _____.

D: Let students adapt this exercise to their own situation.

D. Was sagen Sie?

VERKÄUFER Guten Tag, Herr (Frau, Fräulein) _____! Wie geht es Ihnen?

x _____.

VERKÄUFER Was brauchen Sie heute?

x _____ ein paar _____ und ein paar _____. Was kosten / kostet _____?

VERKÄUFER _____ DM.

x Und was kostet _____?

VERKÄUFER _____ DM.

x Ich nehme zwei (drei . . .) _____

VERKÄUFER Ist das alles?

x _____

VERKÄUFER _____ DM, bitte!

LERNTIP

Learning vocabulary

To remember vocabulary, you must use it. Name things as you see them in the course of your day. Practice new words aloud—the use of your auditory and motor memory will quadruple your learning efficiency. Be sure to learn the gender and plural with each noun. For some, the gender and plural are predictable, so study p. 423 in the Appendix.

5 Das Jahr und das Wetter

Warm-ups: 1. **Schreiben Sie, was Sie hören!** Have students write down numerals, prices, or telephone numbers that they hear you say. 2. **Wieviel ist . . .?** Give simple arithmetic problems.

Das Wetter im April

NORBERT	Es ist schön heute, nicht wahr?
JULIA	Ja, wirklich. Die Sonne scheint wieder!
RUDI	Aber der Wind ist kühl.
JULIA	Ach, das macht nichts.
NORBERT	Ich finde es prima.
DOROTHEA	Das Wetter ist furchtbar, nicht wahr?
MATTHIAS	Das finde ich auch. Es regnet und regnet!
SONJA	Und es ist wieder kalt.
MATTHIAS	Ja, typisch April.

The Weather in April NORBERT: *It's nice today, isn't it?* JULIA: *Yes indeed. The sun is shining again.* RUDI: *But the wind is cool.* JULIA: *Oh, that doesn't matter.* NORBERT: *I think it's great.*

DOROTHEA: *The weather is awful, isn't it?* MATTHIAS: *I think so, too. It's raining and raining.* SONJA: *And it's cold again.* MATTHIAS: *Yes, typical of April.*

WORTSCHATZ

DAS JAHR, -E *year*

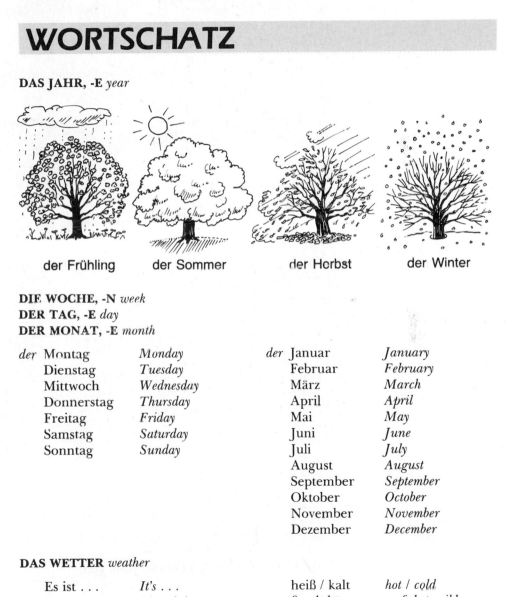

| der Frühling | der Sommer | der Herbst | der Winter |

DIE WOCHE, -N *week*
DER TAG, -E *day*
DER MONAT, -E *month*

der	Montag	*Monday*	der	Januar	*January*
	Dienstag	*Tuesday*		Februar	*February*
	Mittwoch	*Wednesday*		März	*March*
	Donnerstag	*Thursday*		April	*April*
	Freitag	*Friday*		Mai	*May*
	Samstag	*Saturday*		Juni	*June*
	Sonntag	*Sunday*		Juli	*July*
				August	*August*
				September	*September*
				Oktober	*October*
				November	*November*
				Dezember	*December*

DAS WETTER *weather*

Es ist . . .	*It's . . .*	heiß / kalt	*hot / cold*
Es regnet.	*It's raining.*	furchtbar	*awful, terrible*
Es schneit.	*It's snowing.*	prima	*great, wonderful*
Die Sonne scheint.	*The sun is shining.*	schön	*nice, beautiful, fine*
		warm / kühl	*warm / cool*

Optional Vocabulary: **schwül** *humid;* **sonnig** *sunny;* **windig** *windy;* **neblig** *foggy;* **stürmisch** *stormy;* **es donnert** *it's thundering;* **es blitzt** *there's lightning;* **es gießt** *it's pouring.*

WEITERES

Die Woche hat . . .	*The week has . . .*
nicht wahr?	*isn't it?*
sehr	*very*
wieder	*again*
wirklich	*really, indeed*
Wann sind Sie geboren?	*When were you born?*
Ich bin im Mai[1] geboren.	*I was born in May.*
finden	*to find*
Ich finde es . . .	*I think it's . . .*

1 Im is used with the names of the months and seasons: **im Mai, im Winter.**

PASSIVES VOKABULAR der Wind   die Jahreszeit, -en *season*   **Das macht nichts.** *It doesn't matter.*   **typisch**

AUSSPRACHE
r; p, t, k; final b, d, g; j, h

Hören Sie gut zu und wiederholen Sie!

See also III. 2, 3, 10, 17 in the pronunciation section of the Workbook.

[r]   **r**ichtig, **r**egnet, **r**ot, **r**osa, **R**ock, b**r**aun, g**r**ün, d**r**ei, f**r**agen, **Fr**au, **Fr**eitag, P**r**eis, hö**r**en, gebo**r**en, o**r**ange

The **r** requires substantial practice. For additional examples, use German names: **Renate, Rita, Rainer, Rudolf, Karin, Barbara, Marion, Marika, Andreas, Friedrich, Gerhard, Hermann.**

[ʌ]   wi**r**, vie**r**, ode**r**, abe**r**, nu**r**, seh**r**, fü**r**, wiede**r**, Fenste**r**, Papie**r**, Wette**r**, Somme**r**, Winte**r**, Oktobe**r**, Dezembe**r**
BUT [ʌ / r] Tü**r** / Tü**r**en; Jah**r** / Jah**r**e; Uh**r** / Uh**r**en

[p]   **P**eter **P**öppel, **P**apier, **P**ullover, **P**lural, **p**lus, ka**p**utt
AND [p] Herb**st**, Jako**b**, gel**b**, hal**b**
BUT [p / b] gel**b** / gel**b**e; hal**b** / hal**b**e

Point out that **th** in German is [t]: **Ruth.** Final **b, d,** and **g** must be practiced repeatedly.

[t]   **Th**eo, **T**ür, **T**isch, Doro**th**ea, Mat**th**ias, bi**tt**e
AND [t] un**d**, tausen**d**, Bil**d**, Klei**d**, Hem**d**, Wan**d**
BUT [t / d] Bil**d** / Bil**d**er; Klei**d** / Klei**d**er; Hem**d** / Hem**d**en; Wan**d** / Wän**d**e

[k]   **k**lein, **k**ühl, **k**urz, **K**uli, **K**leidung, dan**k**e, dic**k**
AND [k] sa**gt**, fra**gt**, Ta**g**
BUT [k / g] sa**gt** / sa**g**en; fra**gt** / fra**g**en; Ta**g** / Ta**g**e

[j]   **J**akob, **J**osef, **J**ulia, **j**a, **J**anuar, **J**uni, **J**uli

[h]   **H**err, **H**erbst, **H**emd, **H**ose, **h**ören, **h**eiß, **h**at, **h**undert

[:]   **z**ählen, ne**h**men, ge**h**en, verste**h**en, **I**hnen, Stu**h**l, Schu**h**

MÜNDLICHE ÜBUNGEN

A: Read and practice in chorus several times.

A. Hören Sie gut zu und wiederholen Sie!

1. Das Jahr hat vier Jahreszeiten. Die Jahreszeiten heißen Frühling, Sommer, Herbst und Winter.
2. Das Jahr hat zwölf Monate. Die Monate heißen Januar, Februar, März, April, Mai, Juni, Juli, August, September, Oktober, November und Dezember.
3. Die Woche hat sieben Tage. Die Tage heißen Montag, Dienstag, Mittwoch, Donnerstag, Freitag, Samstag und Sonntag.

B: Act out the meaning of these adjectives.

B. Mustersätze

1. schön: **Es ist heute** schön.
   wunderbar, furchtbar, kalt, heiß, warm, kühl
2. sehr kalt: **Es ist** sehr kalt.
   sehr heiß, sehr schön, schön warm, furchtbar heiß, furchtbar kalt
3. prima: **Ich finde es** prima.
   schön, gut, wunderbar, schlecht, furchtbar
4. Juli: **Ich bin im** Juli **geboren.**
   Januar, März, Mai, Juni, August, Sommer, Winter
5. 19: **Ich bin** neunzehn.
   20, 21, 26, 27, 31

C. Wiederholung

1. **Antworten Sie mit ja!**

   BEISPIEL: Verstehen Sie das? **Ja, wir verstehen das.**

   a. Zählen Sie schnell?
   b. Fragen Sie auf deutsch?
   c. Hören Sie gut zu?
   d. Lernen Sie die Wörter?
   e. Lesen Sie auf Seite dreißig?
   f. Passen Sie auf?
   g. Sprechen Sie laut?

C.2: **Wie geht's weiter?** is a type of exercise that can be used frequently; the more varied the responses, the better.

2. **Wie geht's weiter?**

   BEISPIEL: Wo ist _____? **Wo ist das Fräulein?**

   a. Ich heiße _____.
   b. Ich bin _____.
   c. Es geht mir _____.
   d. Das Gegenteil von _____.
   e. Der Artikel von _____.
   f. Der Pullover _____.
   g. Das kostet _____.

C.3: For additional practice on numbers have students work in pairs: one student says a number in German, the partner writes it down. They check and alternate.

3. **Zahlen, Preise, Telefonnummern und Temperaturen**
   a. **Wieviel ist das?**

$3 + 6 = ?$	$65 + 15 = ?$	$50 - 20 = ?$
$9 + 9 = ?$	$75 + 25 = ?$	$33 - 11 = ?$
$23 + 10 = ?$	$100 - 60 = ?$	$16 - 6 = ?$
$40 + 50 = ?$	$80 - 15 = ?$	$12 - 11 = ?$

C.3b: Have students count even / odd numbers from 1–20, 30–40, etc.

   b. **Lesen Sie laut auf deutsch!**
   101 / 315 / 169 / 555 / 1 110 / 20 000 / 88 888 / 267 315 / 987 654
   100,10 DM / 212,25 DM / 667,75 DM / 1 920,— DM / 9 999,99 DM

TEMPERATUREN

GRAD		
Fahrenheit		Celsius
100		38
98,6		37 ◄
96		36
95		35
94		34
90		32
86		30
84		29
82		28
79		26
77		25
72		22
70		21
68		20
64		18
59		15
53		12
50		10
46		8
41		5
37		3
32		0 ◄
28		− 2
23		− 5
14		−10
5		−15
− 4		−20
−13		−25

Körpertemperatur

Gefrierpunkt

c. **Was ist Ihre Telefonnummer?** Ask another student.

BEISPIEL: Was ist Ihre Telefonnummer?
Meine Telefonnummer ist 646-0195
(sechs vier sechs, null eins neun fünf).

D. **Temperaturen**

European thermometers use the Celsius scale. On that scale water freezes at **0°C** and boils at **100°C.** Normal body temperature is about **37°C,** and fever starts at about **37.6°C.** To convert Fahrenheit into Celsius, subtract 32, multiply by 5, divide by 9. To convert Celsius into Fahrenheit, multiply by 9, divide by 5, add 32.

1. **Wieviel Grad Celsius sind das?** *(How many degrees Celsius?)* Use the thermometer as a reference.

BEISPIEL: $32°F = 0°C$
Zweiunddreißig Grad Fahrenheit sind null Grad Celsius.

100°F, 96°F, 84°F, 68°F, 41°F, 23°F, −4°F, −13°F

2. **Wie ist das Wetter?** *(What's the weather like?)*

BEISPIEL: 12°C (zwölf Grad Celsius) **Es ist kühl.**

21°C, 0°C, 30°C, 38°C, −10°C, −25°C

AUFGABE

Fragen

1. Welcher Tag ist heute? morgen?
2. Wie viele Tage hat die Woche? Wie heißen die Tage?
3. Wie viele Tage hat der September? der Oktober? der Februar?
4. Wie viele Monate hat das Jahr? Wie heißen die Monate?
5. Wie viele Wochen hat das Jahr?
6. Wie viele Jahreszeiten hat das Jahr? Wie heißen die Jahreszeiten?
7. Wie heißen die Wintermonate? die Sommermonate? die Herbstmonate?
8. Wie ist das Wetter heute? Scheint die Sonne, oder regnet es?
9. Wie ist das Wetter hier im Winter? im Sommer? im Frühling? im Herbst?
10. Was ist der Artikel von Montag? September? Donnerstag? Herbst? Juni? Monat? Jahr? Woche?

6 *Die Uhrzeit*

Wie spät ist es?

RITA	Axel, wie spät ist es?
AXEL	Es ist zehn vor acht.
RITA	Mensch, in zehn Minuten habe ich Philosophie. Danke schön!
AXEL	Bitte schön!

HERR HUBER	Hallo, Frau Lange! Wieviel Uhr ist es?
FRAU LANGE	Es ist halb zwölf.
HERR HUBER	Gehen Sie jetzt essen?
FRAU LANGE	Ja, die Vorlesung beginnt erst um Viertel nach eins.

HERR RICHTER	Wann sind Sie heute fertig?
HERR HEROLD	Um zwei. Warum?
HERR RICHTER	Spielen wir heute Tennis?
HERR HEROLD	Ja, prima! Es ist jetzt halb eins. Um Viertel vor drei dann?
HERR RICHTER	Gut! Bis später!

How Late Is It? RITA: *Axel, what time is it?* AXEL: *It's ten to eight.* RITA: *Boy, in ten minutes I have philosophy. Thanks a lot.* AXEL: *You're welcome.*

MR. HUBER: *Hi, Ms. Lange. What time is it?* MS. LANGE: *It's eleven thirty.* MR. HUBER: *Are you going to lunch now?* MS. LANGE: *Yes, the lecture doesn't start till a quarter past one.*

MR. RICHTER: *When are you finished today?* MR. HEROLD: *At two. Why?* MR. RICHTER: *Shall we play tennis today?* MR. HEROLD: *Yes, great. It's twelve-thirty now. At a quarter to three, then?* MR. RICHTER: *Fine. See you later.*

WORTSCHATZ

▪ German has a formal (see Chapter 7) and informal way of telling time. The informal system is used in everyday speech and varies somewhat from region to region. The system below is a compromise, but certain to be understood everywhere.

WIE SPÄT IST ES? *How late is it?*
WIEVIEL UHR IST ES? *What time is it?*

die				
	Minute, -n	*minute*	morgens	*in the morning*
	Sekunde, -n	*second*	mittags	*at noon*
	Stunde, -n[1]	*hour*	nachmittags	*in the afternoon*
	Uhr, -en	*watch, clock*	abends	*in the evening*
	Zeit -en	*time*		

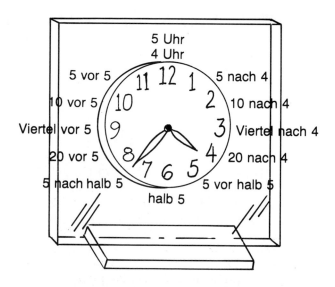

---

1 Stunde refers to duration or a particular class. (Die Deutsch**stunde** ist von acht bis Viertel vor neun.) **Uhr** refers to clock time.

WEITERES

die Vorlesung, -en	*lecture, class (university)*
Es ist ein Uhr (zwei Uhr).[2]	*It's one o'clock (two o'clock).*
Es ist eins (zwei).	*It's one (two).*
(um) eins[2]	*(at) one o'clock*
(um) Viertel nach eins	*(at) a quarter past one*
(um) halb zwei, 1.30[3]	*(at) half past one, 1:30*
(um) Viertel vor zwei, 1.45	*(at) a quarter to two, 1:45*
fertig	*finished, done*
jetzt	*now*
Danke schön!	*Thank you very much. Thanks a lot.*
Bitte schön!	*You're welcome.*
beginnen	*to begin*
essen	*to eat*
Tennis spielen	*to play tennis*
haben	*to have*
ich habe	*I have*
es hat	*it has*
wir	*we have*
sie ⎬ haben	*they have*
Sie	*you (formal) have*
Ich habe eine Frage.	*I have a question.*
Ich habe keine Zeit.	*I don't have any time.*

2 um ein Uhr BUT **um eins**
3 Note the difference in punctuation between English (*1:30*) and German (**1,30**)

PASSIVES VOKABULAR **die Uhrzeit, -en** *time of day* **Bis später!** *See you later.* **dann** *then* **erst** *only, not before* **Hallo!** *Hi! Hello!* **warum?** *why?*

AUSSPRACHE

ch, ig, ck, ng, gn, kn, ps

See also III. 13–15, 20, 22–23 in the pronunciation section of the Workbook.

Hören Sie gut zu und wiederholen Sie!

[x] a**ch**, a**ch**t, a**ch**thundert**ach**tunda**ch**tzig, Joa**ch**im, ma**ch**t, au**ch**, brau**ch**en, Wo**ch**e, Mittwo**ch**, Bu**ch**

[ç] i**ch**, mi**ch**, ni**ch**t, wirkli**ch**, Ri**ch**ard, Mi**ch**ael, wel**ch**e, schle**ch**t, spre**ch**en, Gesprä**ch**e, Bü**ch**er

[iç] richt**ig**, fert**ig**, sech**zig**, fünf**zig**, vier**zig**, drei**ßig**, zwan**zig**, Pfenn**ig**

[ks] se**chs**, se**chs**undse**chz**ig, se**chs**hundertse**chs**undse**chz**ig, Da**chs**hund

[k] **Ch**ristian, **Ch**ristine, **Ch**rista, **Ch**aos

[k] Ja**ck**e, Ro**ck**, di**ck**, Pickni**ck**

[ŋ] I**ng**e La**ng**e, Wolfga**ng** E**ng**el, e**ng**lisch, si**ng**en, Fi**ng**er, Hu**ng**er

[gn] **Gn**om, re**gn**et, resi**gn**ieren, Si**gn**al

[kn]   **Kn**irps, **Kn**ie, **Kn**oten
[ps]   **Ps**ychologie, **Ps**ychiater, **Ps**ychoanalyse, **Ps**eudonym

MÜNDLICHE ÜBUNGEN

It would be helpful to have a model clock or to draw a clock face on the board to show **eins, Viertel nach eins, halb zwei, Viertel vor zwei,** etc.

A. Wie spät ist es? Wieviel Uhr ist es?
   1. 1.00: **Es ist** ein **Uhr.**
      3.00, 5.00, 7.00, 9.00, 11.00
   2. 1.05: **Es ist** fünf **nach** eins.
      3.05, 5.05, 7.05, 9.10, 11.10, 1.10, 4.20, 6.20, 8.20
   3. 1.15: **Es ist Viertel nach** eins.
      2.15, 4.15, 6.15, 8.15, 10.15.
   4. 1.30: **Es ist halb** zwei.
      2.30, 4.30, 6.30, 8.30, 10.30
   5. 1.40: **Es ist** zwanzig **vor** zwei.
      3.40, 5.40, 7.40, 9.50, 11.50, 1.50, 12.55, 2.55, 4.55
   6. 1.45: **Es ist Viertel vor** zwei.
      3.45, 5.45, 7.45, 9.45, 11.45, 12.45

B. Wann ist die Vorlesung? *(When is the lecture?)*
   1. 9.00: **Die Vorlesung ist um** neun.
      3.00, 11.00, 1.00, 9.15, 12.15, 9.45, 12.45, 1.30, 3.30
   2. 0.05: **Die Vorlesung beginnt in** fünf **Minuten.**
      2, 10, 12, 15, 20
   3. morgens: **Die Vorlesung ist** morgens.
      nachmittags, abends, um acht, um Viertel nach acht, um halb neun, um Viertel vor neun.

C. Mustersätze
   1. essen: Essen **Sie jetzt? Ja, ich** esse **jetzt.**
      geben, fragen, schreiben, lernen, antworten, beginnen
   2. heute: **Ich spiele** heute **Tennis.**
      jetzt, morgens, nachmittags, abends, wieder
   3. Sie: **Wann** sind Sie **heute fertig?**
      wir, Horst, ich, Rolf und Maria
   4. ich: Ich habe **keine Zeit.**
      wir, Maria, Maria und Rita

D. Wiederholung
   1. **Wie ist das Wetter?**

a.   b.   c.   d.

joggen

reiten

schwimmen

Golf spielen

Tennis spielen

Ski laufen

angeln

segeln

campen

2. **Was sagen Sie?** Talk about the weather with a classmate.

   x Wie ist das Wetter heute?

   Y _____.

   x Wie finden Sie das Wetter?

   Y _____.

   x Typisch _____, nicht wahr?

   Y _____.

3. **Wie fragen Sie?** Formulate the questions for these answers.

   BEISPIEL: Das ist die Tafel. **Was ist das?**

   a. Da sind die Schuhe.

   b. Der Bleistift ist gelb.

   c. Das Papier kostet 1,50 DM.

   d. Ich brauche Zeit.

   e. Heute ist es furchtbar heiß.

   f. Ich finde das nicht schön.

   g. Fünf plus sechzehn ist einundzwanzig.

   h. Der Januar hat einunddreißig Tage.

   i. Heute ist Dienstag.

4. **Und Sie?** Answer, then ask someone else.

   a. Wie alt sind Sie? (**Ich bin _____. Und Sie?**)

   b. Wann sind Sie geboren? (**Ich bin im _____ geboren. Und Sie?**)

5. **Was tun Sie wann?** *(What do you do when?)* Match months or seasons with the activities based on the drawings.

   BEISPIEL: Was tun Sie im Sommer?

           Im Sommer spiele ich Tennis.

AUFGABE

Fragen

1. Wie viele Stunden hat der Tag? Wie viele Minuten hat die Stunde?
2. Wie viele Sekunden hat die Minute?
3. Wie spät ist es? (8.45, 9.30, 10.15, 11.30, 1.05, 2.20, 2.45, 6.59)
4. ~~Was studieren Sie?~~ *(What courses are you taking?)*
     Welche Vorlesungen hast du?
   Biologie, Chemie, Deutsch, Englisch, Französisch *(French)*, Geographie, Geologie, Geschichte *(history)*, Informatik *(computer science)*, Kunst *(art)*, Latein, Mathematik, Musik, Philosophie, Physik, Politik, Psychologie, Soziologie, Spanisch, Sport
5. Welche Vorlesungen haben Sie heute? Wann? (**Ich habe Deutsch um _____ und Englisch um _____.**) Und morgen?
6. Wie heißt der Deutschprofessor (Englischprofessor. . .)?
7. Wann sind Sie heute fertig? (**Ich bin heute um _____ fertig.**)
8. Wann essen Sie morgens? mittags? abends?

SPRECHSITUATIONEN

Most of the vocabulary in these sections is already familiar. Some expressions are optional.

These sections focus on practical language functions. In German as in English, there are many ways to say the same thing, but what you choose depends on the circumstances. Your instructor will indicate which expressions you will need to learn.

Greetings and Good-byes

1. In formal situations or when meeting strangers, you can use these expressions:

    Guten Tag!
    Guten Morgen! *(until about 10:00 a.m.)*
    Guten Abend! *(from about 5:00 to 10:00 p.m.)*
    Wie geht es Ihnen?
    Auf Wiedersehen!

    Speakers of German usually shake hands whenever they meet, not only when they meet for the first time. **Wie geht es Ihnen?** is an inquiry, and an answer is expected.

2. Here is a list of greetings for informal situations or when meeting friends:

Tag! Wie geht's?	Wiedersehen! Tschüß!
Morgen! Abend!	Bis später! *(See you later!)*
Gute Nacht! *(Good night!)*	Bis bald! *(See you soon!)*

    Other informal ways of saying "Hi" are **Grüß dich! Servus!** (in Bavaria and Austria), and **Gruezi!** (in Switzerland). **Gute Nacht!** is normally used to wish someone who lives in the same house a good night's sleep.

3. Here are some responses to **Wie geht es Ihnen?** or **Wie geht's?**

    Gut, danke. Und Ihnen? . . .
    Sehr gut, danke.
    Prima! *(informal)*
    Es geht mir gut / nicht gut / nicht besonders gut *(not particularly well)*.
    Es geht mir schlecht / nicht schlecht.

4. To introduce yourself, you should say:

    Mein Name ist . . .
    Ich heiße . . .

5. When meeting someone for the first time, the following expressions are used:

(Es) freut mich!	*(I'm) glad to meet you.*
(Es) freut mich auch.	*Likewise. Glad to meet you, too.*
Sehr angenehm!	*My pleasure. (formal)*
Ganz meinerseits.	*The pleasure is all mine. (formal)*

Expressing Incomprehension

Especially when speaking a foreign language, you need to be able to say that you don't understand or that you'd like to have something repeated.

Entschuldigen Sie!	*Excuse me.*
Ich habe eine Frage.	*I have a question.*
Ich verstehe das nicht.	*I don't understand that.*
Wie bitte?	*I beg your pardon?*
Sagen Sie das noch einmal, bitte!	*Say that again, please.*
Wiederholen Sie (das), bitte!	*Please repeat that.*
Was bedeutet . . .?	*What does . . . mean?*
Sprechen Sie nicht so schnell, bitte!	*Please don't speak so fast.*
Sprechen Sie langsamer, bitte!	*Please speak more slowly.*

A. Was paßt? What are they saying?

B: This exercise could easily be done in small groups.

B. Was sagen Sie? What would you say in response to these statements?
1. Mein Name ist Taeger, Dr. Kai Taeger.
2. Guten Morgen! Wie geht es Ihnen?
3. Auf Wiedersehen!
4. Sprechen Sie nicht so schnell, bitte!
5. Dort drüben ist die Straßenbahnhaltestelle.
6. Tag! Wie geht's?

C. Was sagen Sie? What would you say in reponse to these situations?
1. You got called on in class and didn't hear the question.
2. You were unable to follow your instructor's explanation.
3. You have to ask your instructor to repeat something.
4. You want to say good-bye to the host after an evening party.
5. You are staying with the family of a friend in Austria. What do you say as you go to bed?
6. You have asked a native of Berlin for directions and she is speaking much too fast.
7. In a conversation the word "Geschwindigkeitsbegrenzung" keeps coming up. You want to ask for clarification.

D. Kurzgespräche. In small groups create short conversations along the following lines.
1. You run into a friend between classes. Say hi and ask how things are going. Your friend tells you that he / she is doing great. You say that is wonderful; you're glad. Your friend then asks how you are. You say you're very tired. You part, saying *See you later.*
2. You meet someone for the first time. Say hello and introduce yourself. Ask for his / her name. When he / she answers, say *Glad to meet you.*

RÜCKBLICK Review: SCHRITTE

The "Rückblick" explains the grammatical structures encountered so far. It should not lead to long, involved discussions; but if students read it at home, it should clarify much of what they have learned. For additional suggestions, see IAE p. 14.

By now you know quite a few German words and a number of idiomatic expressions. You have learned how to pronounce German and to say a few things about yourself. You also have learned a good deal about the structure of the German language.

I. Nouns

1. German has three genders: MASCULINE, NEUTER, and FEMININE. Nouns are distinguished by **der, das,** and **die** in the singular. In the plural there are no gender distinctions; the article is **die** for all plural nouns:

der Herr, **der** Bleistift		Herren, Bleistifte
das Fräulein, **das** Bild	**die**	Fräulein, Bilder
die Frau, **die** Tafel		Frauen, Tafeln

2. There are several ways to form the plural of nouns. You have learned how to interpret the most common plural abbreviations found in dictionaries and vocabulary lists:

das Fenster, -		Fenster
der Mantel, ̈		Mäntel
der Tag, **-e**		Tage
der Stuhl, ̈**e**		Stühle
das Kleid, **-er**	die	Kleider
das Buch, ̈**er**		Bücher
die Uhr, **-en**		Uhren
die Sekunde, **-n**		Sekunden
der Kuli, **-s**		Kulis

3. When you learn a noun, you must also learn its gender and plural forms.

4. All nouns are capitalized.

   Ich brauche **B**leistifte, **K**ulis und **P**apier.

II. Pronouns

You have used the following pronouns:

ich	*I*	Ich heiße Sanders.
es	*it*	Es regnet.
wir	*we*	Wir zählen von eins bis zehn.
sie	*they*	Sind sie neu?
Sie	*you (formal)*	Wann sind Sie heute fertig?

- The pronoun **ich** is not capitalized unless it stands at the beginning of a sentence.

Ja, **ich** finde das Wetter schön.

- The pronoun **Sie** (*you*), which is always capitalized, is used in all formal relationships, and always when others are addressed with such titles as **Herr, Frau,** and **Fräulein.** It is used to address one or more persons.

Fräulein Thielemann, verstehen Sie das?
Fräulein Thielemann und Herr Fiedler, verstehen Sie das?

III. Verbs

1. You have noticed that German verbs have different endings—that is, they are INFLECTED, or CONJUGATED. You have used the following verb endings:

We've also had two examples of the 3rd person sg.: **es kostet, es regnet.**

ich	-e	Ich brauch**e** Papier.
wir	-en	Wir brauch**en** Papier.
sie, Sie	-en	Sie brauch**en** Papier.

2. **Sein** *to be* and **haben** *to have* are two important verbs. They are frequently used as AUXILIARY, or helping verbs. As in English, their forms are not regular.

ich	bin	Ich bin groß.
es	ist	Es ist groß.
sie, Sie	sind	Sie sind groß.

ich	habe	Ich habe Zeit.
es	hat	Es hat Zeit.
sie, Sie	haben	Sie haben Zeit.

IV. Sentence Structure

You have encountered three basic sentence types: STATEMENTS, QUESTIONS, and IMPERATIVES. In all of them, verb position plays a significant role.

1. Statements

One of the most important observations you will make is that the verb is always the second element in a statement. (As you see from the examples, a SENTENCE ELEMENT can consist of more than one word.)

Sie **schreiben** schön.
Mein Name **ist** Dieter Schneider.
Gerda und Dorothea **sind** fertig.
Der Rock und die Bluse **kosten** 150,—DM.

2. Questions

You have practiced two types of questions: INFORMATION QUESTIONS and QUESTIONS THAT ELICIT YES / NO ANSWERS.

a. Information questions begin with a question word or phrase and ask for specific information: *what, where, how.* In information questions, too, the verb is the second element. You have learned the following question words and phrases. Note that all question words begin with **w**!

Wann **haben** Sie Deutsch?
Was **kostet** das?
Wo **ist** der Stuhl?
Wie **geht** es Ihnen?
Welche Farbe **hat** das Buch?
Wieviel Uhr **ist** es?
Wie viele Tage **hat** die Woche?

b. Yes / no questions, on the other hand, begin with the verb.

Haben Sie Zeit?
Regnet es morgen?
Spielen wir heute Tennis?
Ist das richtig?

3. Imperatives

Imperatives (commands, requests, suggestions) also begin with the verb.

Antworten Sie bitte!
Nehmen Sie die Kreide!
Öffnen Sie das Buch!
Sagen Sie das noch einmal!
Zählen Sie von zwanzig bis dreißig!

WIEDERHOLUNG

A. Was sagen sie?

This vocabulary review could easily be expanded into an hour's review of what has been learned. After that, students should be ready for a quiz on the material covered so far.

Optional practice: Was ist . . .? 1. der Artikel von Tisch, Mantel, Hemd, Pfennig, Mark, Tag, Woche, Jahr. 2. der Plural von Tür, Schuh, Buch, Kuli, Mantel, Pullover, Minute, Bild, Wand. 3. das Gegenteil von bitte, dick, falsch, gut, heiß, heute, hier, klein, kühl, lang, nein, neu, sauber, schön

Optional practice:
Zählen Sie von 1 bis 10,
11 bis 20, 61 bis 70, 121
bis 130!

B. Zahlen und Zeiten

1. **Wie geht's weiter?** Add to or subtract from the previous sum. Continue from one person to another.

BEISPIEL: $7 + 5 = 12 + 9 = 21 - ? = ? \ldots$

2. **Was kostet das?** A student writes prices on the board for others to read aloud.

B.3: Point out that the telephone number can also be read as **vierundsechzig vierundneunzig.**

3. **Was ist die Telefonnummer?** Ask each other for the telephone number of persons listed below.

BEISPIEL: Welche Telefonnummer hat Helene Hartmann?
Helene Hartmann hat Nummer 64 94.

Fischer Ulrich Berliner-1 71 29	**Harms Ralf** (Du) 18 93	**Jung Detlef** 73 35	**Kreissparkasse Alfeld Leine**
Fittje Herta Heinsen 4B 67 44	Alte Mühlen-8	Heinrich-Sohnrey-Weg 13	Geschäftsstellen
Flentje Isabella Alte-12 74 99	**Harstick Alfred** Landw. (Du) 5 98	—**Walter** 73 24	Duhnser-1 64 01
Flor Andrea Heinser-4 65 74	Deinsen	Heinrich-Sohnrey-Weg 11	Deilmissen 71 00
Forstverwaltung	—**Werner** Landw. (Du) 5 08	**Junge Kurt** Alte-1 65 00	Deinsen (Du) 5 28
o Staatl. Revierförsterei (Du) 5 92	Deinsen 14	—**Rolf** Betriebswirt Am Knick 78 76 45	**Krempig Dieter** Dunser-13 63 64
Deinsen	**Hartig Jürgen** KfzRep. Dorf-36 72 71	—**Wilhelm** RohrMstr. 61 36	**Kreth Erich** Am Knick 33 71 17
Freimut Ella Breslauer-1 71 45	**Hartmann Helene** 64 94	Am Knick 78	—**Harald** Kampweg 6 76 85
Freund Achim Im Külfeld 6 62 40	Schachtweg 30	**Kahle Wolfgang** (Du) 12 86	—**Hugo** Königsberger-7 72 87
—**Friedrich** Haupt-49 61 39	**Haushaltswaren- und** 66 63	Lange-22	**Kreutz Kurt** Drogerie Haupt-1 66 08
—**Helga** Fußpflege Am Knick 32 65 97	**Geschenkartikel-Vertriebs**	**Kaiser Rolf** Bantelner-12 65 69	**Kreybohm Erich** (Du) 14 03
—**Klaus** Haupt-49 68 80	**GmbH** Haupt-17A	—**Siegfried** SparkassenOInsp. 66 82	Landw. Deinsen 23
Frie August Wassertor-18 76 54	**Hausmann Christian** 61 35	Breslauer-19	**Krieter Franz** (Du) 65 85
Friebe Martha Alte-10 74 17	Kampweg 5	—**Willi** Bantelner-29 68 91	Aschenkamp 3
—**Paul** Deilmissen Dorf-29 73 55	—**Heinz** Schachtweg 12 74 59	**Kalkof Carsten** Mühlen-3 68 35	**Krömer Alfred** 72 41
Friedrich Leo Berliner-19 72 60	**Hebisch Ernst** Haupt-5 62 09	—**Otto** Mühlen-3 73 59	Wilhelm-Raabe-4
—**Norbert** Wassertor-10 75 13	—**Heinrich** jun. Dunser-14 66 70	**Kanngießer Wolfgang** 63 40	**Krüger Horst** Neue-3 65 22
Friese Horst Heinser-2 70 84	—**Heinrich** sen. Dunser-16 68 27	Dunser-46	—**Selma** Dunser-56 73 19
Fritsche Herbert 62 24	—**Karl** Deilmissen Dorf-22 69 44	**Kasper Bernhard** 72 11	**Krumfuß Anna** Haupt-30 75 92
Unter den Tannen 9	—**Karl** Deilmissen Dorf-20A 71 52	Schachtweg 85	**Kube Klemens** (Du) 17 62
Frömming H. 72 06	**Hecht Friedrich W.** 62 84	**Kassebeer Horst** 65 66	Schlesierweg 102
Am Bahndamm 21	Bantelner-6	Im Külfeld 2	**Kuchenbach Waldtraut** 73 37
Frohns Gustav Landw. 68 13	**Hehr W.** Gronauer-14 70 31	**Kassing Uwe** 69 88	Wassertor-9
Deilmisser-6	**Hein Alfred** Ing. Gastst. 66 50	Unter den Tannen 10	**Kuckuck Friedhelm** 66 57
Fromm Josef Berg-10 69 43	Haupt-41	**Katt Günter** Berg-30 61 76	Kampweg 6
	—**Günter** Neue-1 60 89	**Kaufmann Friedel** 62 55	—**Karl-Heinz** ElektroMstr. 74 88

C. Buchstabieren Sie bitte! Mozart, Wagner, Händel, Schubert, Brahms, Bach

D. Wann ist die Deutschstunde? At the registration desk of your school, you are giving information about the schedule of next semester's classes. Use the suggested cues from both groups.

BEISPIEL: 9.00: **Die Deutschstunde ist um neun.**

Politik, Musik, Spanisch, Deutsch, Geologie, Kunst, Soziologie, Informatik, Psychologie, Geschichte, Sport, Physik, Philosophie, Biologie, Chemie

3.30, 4.00, 11.15, 10.45, 12.50, 8.30, 2.00, 5.45, 10.30

E. Wie ist das Wetter im April? Describe the weather in your state to an exchange student from Switzerland who has just arrived in this country.

BEISPIEL: Wie ist das Wetter im Januar?
Es ist sehr kalt.

1 Familie, Länder, Sprachen

Herr und Frau Fuchs
mit *(with)* Tochter
Helga und Sohn
Bernd

▌ LERNZIELE

Gespräche and **Wortschatz.** In this chapter, you will talk about yourself, your family, and the countries of Europe.

Struktur. You will become familiar with . . .

▪ the present tense of regular verbs.

▪ the nominative case.

▪ some elements of sentence structure.

▪ compound nouns.

Einblicke. Languages in Europe

Sprechsituationen

▪ Making small talk

▪ Asking for personal information

◆◆◆◆◆ GESPRÄCHE

Im Goethe Institut[1]

Warm-ups: 1. **Wie ist das Wetter heute? Wie geht es Ihnen?** 2. **Was ist das?** Point to various things in the classroom and have students identify them. 3. **Wie ist . . .?** Have them describe various things: color, size, etc. 4. **Buchstabieren Sie . . .!** Have them spell various German words.

Remind students to read the following dialogues aloud until they can do so fluently. They are not expected to memorize entire dialogues but should be prepared to answer questions about them.

SHARON   Roberto, woher kommst du[2]?
ROBERTO   Ich bin aus Rom. Und du?
SHARON   Ich komme aus Sacramento, aber jetzt wohnt meine Familie in Seattle.
ROBERTO   Wie groß ist deine Familie?
SHARON   Wir sind fünf—mein Vater, meine Mutter, mein Bruder, meine Schwester und ich.
ROBERTO   Ich habe nur eine Schwester. Sie wohnt in Montreal, in Kanada.
SHARON   Wirklich? Mein Onkel wohnt auch da.

Später

ROBERTO   Sharon, wann ist die Prüfung?
SHARON   In zehn Minuten. Du, wie heißen ein paar Flüsse in Deutschland?
ROBERTO   Im Norden ist die Elbe, im Osten die Oder, im Süden . . .
SHARON   Die Donau?
ROBERTO   Und im Westen der Rhein. Wo liegt Düsseldorf[3]?
SHARON   Düsseldorf? Hm. Wo ist eine Landkarte?
ROBERTO   O hier. Im Westen von Deutschland, nördlich von Bonn, am Rhein.
SHARON   Ach ja, richtig! Na, viel Glück!

Übrigens

1. The Goethe Institute supports the study of the German language and culture through study centers for students and teachers of German throughout the world.

2. There is now no equivalent form of address in English for **du,** but its cognate *thou* is still in poetic and religious use. Although it has become customary for university students to address each other with the **du**-form, all adults must be addressed with **Sie** unless they are relatives or close friends (see also p. 45).

3. **Düsseldorf** (pop. 590,000) is the capital of North Rhine-Westphalia and the administrative center for the state's heavy industry. An affluent city, it is also a university town, an art and fashion center, and the site of numerous conventions and trade fairs.

1. Woher kommt Roberto? 2. Woher kommt Sharon? 3. Wo wohnt Sharons Familie? 4. Wann ist die Prüfung? 5. Was sind die Elbe, die Oder, die Donau und der Rhein? 6. Wo ist die Elbe? die Oder? die Donau? der Rhein? 7. Wo liegt Düsseldorf?

At the Goethe Institute SHARON: *Roberto, where are you from?* ROBERTO: *I'm from Rome. And you?* SHARON: *I come from Sacramento, but now my family lives in Seattle.* ROBERTO: *How big is your family?* SHARON: *There are five of us—my father, my mother, my brother, my sister, and I.* ROBERTO: *I only have one sister. She lives in Montreal, Canada.* SHARON: *Really? My uncle lives there, too.*

Later ROBERTO: *Sharon, when is the exam?* SHARON: *In ten minutes. What are the names of some rivers in Germany?* ROBERTO: *In the north is the Elbe, in the east the Oder, in the south . . .* SHARON: *The Danube?* ROBERTO: *And in the west the Rhine. Where is Düsseldorf?* SHARON: *Düsseldorf? Hm. Where is a map?* ROBERTO: *Oh, here. In the west of Germany, north of Bonn, on the Rhine.* SHARON: *O yes, right! Well, good luck!*

WORTSCHATZ 1

DIE FAMILIE, -N *family*

Urge students to look at the Appendix. Point out those nouns whose genders are predictable.

Optional vocabulary: **die Geschwister** *pl., siblings;* **Stiefvater / Stiefmutter** *step. . .;* **Schwiegervater / Schwiegermutter** *father / mother-in-law;* **Schwager, - / Schwägerin, -nen** *brother / sister in law;* **Urgroßvater / Urgroßmutter** *great-grandfather / mother;* **Vetter, -n / Cousin, -s / Kusine, -n; Neffe, -n / Nichte, -n** *nephew / niece;* **Enkelkind, -er** *grandchild*

der	Bruder, ⸚	brother	die	Frau, -en	woman; wife
	Junge, -n	boy		(Groß)mutter, ⸚	(grand)mother
	Onkel, -	uncle		Schwester, -n	sister
	Mann, ⸚er	man, husband		Tante, -n	aunt
	Sohn, ⸚e	son		Tochter, ⸚	daughter
	(Groß)vater, ⸚	(grand)father		(Groß)eltern (pl.)	(grand)parents
das	Kind, -er	child			
	Mädchen, -	girl			

DAS LAND, ⸚ER *country, state*
DIE SPRACHE, -N *language*

der	Berg, -e	mountain		Deutsch[1]	German
	Fluß, Flüsse	river		Englisch	English
	See, -n	lake		Französisch	French
die	Landkarte, -n	map		Italienisch	Italian
	Stadt, ⸚e	city		Spanisch	Spanish
	Hauptstadt, ⸚e (von)	capital (of)			
	Leute (pl.)	people			

die	Schweiz	*Switzerland*	der Schweizer, - / die Schweizerin, -nen[2]
(das)	Deutschland[3]	*Germany*	der Deutsche, -n / die Deutsche, -n
	Österreich	*Austria*	der Österreicher, - / die Österreicherin, -nen

Point out that it is **die Schweiz.** Other examples would be **die DDR, die Bundesrepublik, die Sowjetunion (UdSSR), die Tschechoslowakei, die Türkei.** Some countries are plural nouns like **die USA, die Niederlande.**

1 Antworten Sie **auf deutsch** (*in German*)! BUT Ich spreche **Deutsch** (*the German language*).

2 Many feminine nouns can be derived from masculine nouns by adding **in** (der Schweizer / **die Schweizerin**). Their plurals end in **-nen (die Schweizerinnen).** BUT der Deutsche, -n / **die Deutsche, -n** (see p. 338).

3 All countries and cities are neuter unless indicated otherwise **(die Schweiz).**

(das) Frankreich	*France*	der Franzose, -n / die Französin, -nen
Spanien	*Spain*	der Spanier, - / die Spanierin, -nen
Italien	*Italy*	der Italiener, - / die Italienerin, -nen
England	*England*	der Engländer, - / die Engländerin, -nen
Amerika	*America*	der Amerikaner, - / die Amerikanerin, -nen
Kanada	*Canada*	der Kanadier, - / die Kanadierin, -nen

WEITERES

der	Satz, ⸚e	*sentence*
die	Frage, -n	*question*
	Prüfung, -en	*test, exam*
	kommen	*to come*
	liegen	*to lie (be located)*
	wohnen	*to live, reside*
	woher?	*from where?*
	Ich bin aus . . .	*I'm from . . . (a native of)*
	im Norden / Süden / Osten / Westen[4]	*in the north / south / east / west*
	nördlich / südlich / östlich / westlich von . . .	*north / south / east / west of. . .*
	mein(e)[5]	*my*
	dein(e) / Ihr(e)[5]	*your (informal / formal)*

4 im is used with months, seasons, and points of the compass (**im** Mai, **im** Winter, **im** Norden). **in** is used with names of cities, countries, and continents (**in** Berlin, **in** Deutschland, **in** Europa).

5 mein, dein, and **Ihr** have no ending when used before masculine and neuter nouns. Before feminine and plural nouns, **meine, deine,** and **Ihre** are used (see p. 49): dein Bruder, mein Vater, Ihr Kind; deine Schwester, meine Mutter, Ihre Eltern.

PASSIVES VOKABULAR: na . . . *well . . .*   Viel Glück! *Good luck!*

ZUM THEMA

A. Mustersätze
1. Ihre Familie: **Woher kommt** Ihre Familie?
   Ihr Vater, Ihre Mutter, Ihr Onkel, Ihre Tante
2. Rom: **Ich bin aus** Rom.
   Frankfurt, Österreich, Amerika, Berlin
3. Hamburg / Norden: Hamburg **liegt im** Norden.
   Berlin / Osten; München / Süden; Bonn / Westen; Wien / Osten

4. die Schweiz / westlich; Die Schweiz **liegt** westlich **von Österreich.**
   die Tschechoslowakei / nördlich; Italien / südlich; Deutschland / nördlich

5. Österreich / Deutsch: **In Österreich sprechen die Leute** Deutsch.
   Frankreich / Französisch; England / Englisch; Italien / Italienisch; Spanien / Spanisch.

NOTE: Unlike English, German does not use an indefinite article before nationalities.

B. **Was sind sie?** Say from what city and country each person comes.

1. BEISPIEL: Uwe und Monika sind aus Frankfurt.
   Uwe ist Frankfurter, und Monika ist Frankfurterin.

   a. Robert und Evi sind aus Berlin.
   b. Klaus und Inge sind aus Hamburg.
   c. Rolf und Katrin sind aus Wien.
   d. Ulrich and Johanna sind aus Zürich.

2. BEISPIEL: Juan ist Spanier. Und Juanita?
   Juanita ist Spanierin.

   a. Antonio ist Italiener. Und Luisa?
   b. Hugo ist Österreicher. Und Lieselotte?
   c. Walter ist Schweizer. Und Helga?
   d. Pierre ist Franzose. Und Monique?

C. **Was paßt?** For each question or statement on the left, select one or more appropriate responses from the right-hand column, or give your own.

_____ 1. Woher kommst du?
_____ 2. Wie groß ist deine Familie?
_____ 3. Meine Schwester wohnt in Seattle.
_____ 4. Wann ist die Prüfung?
_____ 5. Wo liegt Düsseldorf?

a. Sehr klein. Ich habe keine Brüder und Schwestern.
b. Am Rhein.
c. Mein Onkel wohnt auch da.
d. Aus Seattle, und du?
e. Um Viertel nach zehn.
f. Im Westen von Deutschland.
g. In zwanzig Minuten.
h. Nördlich von Bonn.
i. Ich bin aus Rom.
j. Wir sind sechs.
k. Wirklich?
l. Ich weiß nicht.

D: After completing the exercise, have students work in smaller groups. Each member draws his / her family tree and describes his / her background: **Meine Mutter ist die Tochter von . . . Sie heißt . . . und ist . . . Jahre alt. Sie wohnt . . . usw.**

D. Stammbaum. Look at Wolfgang's family tree and explain who each person is.

BEISPIEL: **Wolfgang ist der Sohn von Gerhard und Gertrud.**
Wolfgang ist der Bruder von Ingrid.

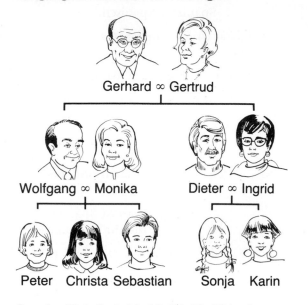

All pronunciation exercises are recorded on tape (see *Lab Manual*).

E. Aussprache. See also II. 1, 3–4, 11–13, 17, 19–20 in the pronunciation section of the Workbook.

1. [i:] **Ih**nen, l**ie**gen, w**ie**der, **Wi**en, B**e**rlin
2. [i] **i**ch b**i**n, b**i**tte, K**i**nd, r**i**chtig
3. [a:] Fr**a**ge, Spr**a**che, Amerik**a**ner, Sp**a**nier, **Va**ter
4. [a] St**a**dt, L**a**ndkarte, K**a**nada, S**a**tz, T**a**nte
5. [u:] g**u**t, Br**u**der, K**u**li, Min**u**te, d**u**
6. [u] **u**nd, St**u**nde, J**u**nge, M**u**tter, Fl**u**ß
7. Wortpaare

E.7: To sharpen listening skills, use variations (e.g., **still / Stil, Stil / still, still / still, Stil / Stil**), and let students tell you through signals (left hand / right hand) which one within each pair they hear.

a. still / Stil	c. Kamm / komm	e. Rum / Ruhm
b. Stadt / Staat	d. Schiff / schief	f. Ratte / rate

Lerntip

Studying grammar

Don't let the idea of grammar scare you. It's a shortcut to learning, providing you with the patterns native speakers follow when they use the language. The fact that German and English are closely related will be both a help and a hindrance: note well the instances when German functions differently from English. As a bonus, your study of German will make you more aware of the fine points of English grammar.

STRUKTUR

I. The Present Tense

1. You are already familiar with some of the PERSONAL PRONOUNS; there are four others: **du, er, sie,** and **ihr.**

	singular	plural	singular / plural
1st person	ich	wir	
2nd person	**du**	**ihr**	Sie
3rd person	**er** / **es** / **sie**	sie	

I   *we*
you (familiar)   *you (familiar)*   *you (formal)*
he, it, she   *they*

- **du** and **ihr** are intimate forms of address used with family members, close friends, children up to the age of fourteen, and animals.

- **Sie,** which is always capitalized when it means *you,* is used in formal relationships and when others are addressed with titles such as **Herr, Frau,** and **Fräulein.** It is used to address one or more persons. **Sie** (*you*) and **sie** (not capitalized) can be distinguished in conversation only through context.

  BEISPIEL: Herr Schmidt, wo wohnen **Sie?** Und Ihre Eltern, wo wohnen **sie?**
  Mr. Schmidt, where do you live? And your parents, where do they live?

- The pronouns **sie** (*she, it*) and **sie** (*they*) can be distinguished through the personal endings of the verb.

  BEISPIEL: **Sie** komm**t** im Mai, und **sie** komm**en** im Juni.
  She comes in May, and they come in June.

2. The INFINITIVE is the form of the verb that has no subject and takes no personal ending (e.g. *to learn*). Almost every German infinitive ends in **-en: lernen, antworten.** The stem of the verb is the part that precedes the infinitive ending **-en.** Thus the stem of **lernen** is **lern-,** and that of **antworten** is **antwort-.**

   •English verbs have at most one personal ending in the present tense, *-s:* I (*you, we, they*) *learn,* BUT *he* (*it, she*) *learns.* In German, endings are added to the verb stem for all persons.

   > stem + personal ending = present tense verb form

   German verb endings vary, depending on whether the subject is in the FIRST, SECOND or THIRD PERSON, and in the SINGULAR or PLURAL. The verb must agree with the subject. You have already learned the endings used for some persons.

To give students experience in using **du** and **Sie,** have them address you with **Sie** and one another with **du.** Address them with **Sie.**

Here is the complete list:

	singular	plural	formal (sg. / pl.)
1st person	ich lerne	wir lernen	
2nd person	du lernst	ihr lernt	Sie lernen
3rd person	er / es / sie lernt	sie lernen	

NOTE: The verb forms for formal *you* (**Sie**) and plural *they* (**sie**) are identical. The same holds true for **er / es / sie.** For that reason we won't repeat **Sie** and **es / sie** in future chapters.

> Caution: Students cannot be expected yet to use these verbs to write their own sentences, since most require objects.

These verbs, which you already know from the "Schritte," follow the model of **lernen.** Be sure to review them.

beginnen	*to begin*	sagen	*to say, tell*
brauchen	*to need*	schreiben	*to write*
fragen	*to ask*	spielen	*to play*
gehen	*to go*	verstehen	*to understand*
hören	*to hear*	wiederholen	*to repeat, review*
kommen	*to come*	wohnen	*to live, reside*
liegen	*to be (located)*	zählen	*to count*

> Here's the rule for "certain consonant combinations": If the stem ends in **-d, -t,** or a combination of any consonant (other than **l** or **r**), plus **n** or **m,** then the ending adds an **-e,** like **atmen / atmet, regnen / regnet.** We think it's too complex for this level.

3. When a verb stem ends in **-d** or **-t** (**antwort-**), or in certain consonant combinations (**öffn-, regn-**), an **-e** is inserted between the stem and the **-st** and **-t** endings to make these endings clearly audible.

	singular	plural	formal (sg. / pl.)
1st person	ich antworte	wir antworten	
2nd person	du antwortest	ihr antwortet	Sie antworten
3rd person	er / es / sie antwortet	sie antworten	

These familiar verbs follow the model of **antworten:**

finden	*to find*
kosten	*to cost*
öffnen	*to open*

4. The **du**-form of verbs with a stem ending in any **s**-sound (**-s, -ss, -ß, -tz, -z**) adds only a **-t** instead of **-st: ich heiße, du heißt.** Thus, the **du**-form is identical with the **er**-form of these verbs: **du heißt, er heißt.**

5. German has only one verb form to express what can be said in English in several ways.

Ich **wohne** in Köln.
> *I live in Cologne.*
> *I'm living in Cologne.*
> *I do live in Cologne.*

Wohnst du in Köln?
> *Are you living in Cologne?*
> *Do you live in Cologne?*

6. In both languages the present tense is frequently used to express future time, particularly when a time expression clearly indicates the future.

In dreißig Minuten **gehe** ich in die Stadt.	*I'm going downtown in thirty minutes.*
Er **kommt** im Sommer.	*He's coming in the summer.*

ÜBUNGEN

For a quick introductory practice, have students add subjects to any of the familiar verbs under I.2 and I.3, e.g. **brauchen: er, wir, du, ich.**

A. Du, ihr oder Sie? How would you address these people? Explain why.
1. your father   2. members of your family   3. your German professor   4. a store clerk   5. two police officers   6. your roommate   7. friends of your three-year-old niece   8. your classmates   9. a group of strangers who are older than you

B. Ersetzen Sie das Subjekt! Replace the subject by using the words in parentheses.

BEISPIEL: Ich sage das noch einmal. (wir, Maria)
   Wir sagen das noch einmal.
   Maria sagt das noch einmal.

1. Wir antworten auf deutsch. (Roberto, du, ich, die Mutter)
2. Ich wiederhole die Frage. (er, wir, ihr, Sie)
3. Ihr lernt die Wörter. (ich, du, die Kinder, wir)
4. Du öffnest das Buch auf Seite 3. (der Franzose, ich, ihr, sie / *sg.*)
5. Heidi Bauer geht an die Tafel. (ihr, sie / *pl.*, ich, du)
6. Brauchst du Papier und Bleistifte? (wir, ich, Sie, ihr)
7. Wie finden Sie das? (ihr, du, Ihre Familie, die Leute)

C. Kombinieren Sie! Create sentences by combining items from each column.

BEISPIEL: Er kommt aus Kanada.

1	2	3
ich	beginnen	auf deutsch
du	hören	auf englisch
er	kommen	aus . . .
es	kosten	(das) nicht
sie	regnen	heute
das	schreiben	in . . .
die Deutschvorlesung	spielen	jetzt
das Mädchen	wohnen	morgen
wir	zählen	(nicht) gut
ihr		Tennis
Sie		um . . .
sie		vier Mark
		von zehn bis zwanzig

D. After students complete the dialogue, have them use it as a model for a role-playing activity.

D. Was fehlt? *(What's missing?)* Fill in the missing verb forms.

JENS Inge und Heidi, woher _____ ihr? (kommen)

HEIDI Ich _____ aus Heidelberg. (kommen)

INGE Und ich _____ aus Berlin. (sein)

JENS Wirklich? Meine Großmutter _____ auch aus Berlin. (kommen) Aber sie _____ jetzt in Hamburg. (wohnen) Wie _____ ihr es hier? (finden)

HEIDI Wir _____ es hier prima. (finden)

INGE Ich _____ die Berge wunderbar. (finden)

JENS Ich auch!

Im Hamburger Hafen *(harbor)*

E. Auf deutsch, bitte!

1. We're learning German.
2. I'm counting slowly.
3. Where do you *(pl. fam.)* come from?
4. They come from Canada.
5. I'm from America.
6. Do you *(sg. fam.)* answer in English?
7. No, I'll speak German.
8. She's opening the book.
9. I do need the book.
10. What does she say?
11. Do you *(sg. fam.)* understand that **(das)?**
12. Is she repeating that?

II. The Nominative Case

The nominative case is the case of the subject and of the predicate noun. (The latter is discussed in Section III. 2, p. 51.)

In the English sentence *The boy asks the father,* the SUBJECT of the sentence is *the boy*; he does the asking. We know that the boy is the subject of the sentence because in English the subject precedes the verb. This is not always true in German, where one frequently knows the function of a word or phrase from its form rather than from its position. In the sentence **Der Junge fragt den Vater,** the phrase **der Junge** tells us we are dealing with the subject, whereas **den Vater** tells us we are dealing with a direct object (more about this in Chapter 2). In dictionaries and vocabulary lists, nouns are given in the nominative. The nominative answers the questions *who?* for persons or *what?* for objects and ideas.

Der Junge fragt den Vater.	*The boy asks the father.*
Der See ist schön.	*The lake is beautiful.*

1. The nominative forms of the INTERROGATIVE PRONOUNS are **wer** (*who*) and **was** (*what*).

	persons	things and ideas
nom.	wer?	was?

Wer fragt den Vater? **Der Junge.**	*Who is asking the father? The boy.*
Was ist schön? **Der See.**	*What is beautiful? The lake.*

2. The nominative forms of the DEFINITE ARTICLE **der** (*the*) and the INDEFINITE ARTICLE **ein** (*a, an*) are already familiar. Note that the indefinite article does not distinguish between masculine and neuter nouns because it has no ending. It also has no plural: *I have a pencil,* BUT *I have pencils.*

This table will be augmented gradually and used to teach cases. You might make a poster-size reproduction or a transparency of it for future use.

	singular			plural	
	masc.	**neut.**	**fem.**		
nom.	der	das	die	die	*the*
	ein	ein	eine		*a, an*
	kein	kein	keine	keine	*no, not a*

The possessive adjectives **mein** (*my*), **dein** (*your*), and **Ihr** (*your*) follow the pattern of **ein** and **kein.**

Die Frau, der Junge und das Mädchen sind aus Österreich.
Mein Onkel und meine Tante wohnen auch da. Wo wohnen deine Eltern?

3. Nouns can be replaced by PERSONAL PRONOUNS. In English we replace persons with *he, she,* or *they,* and objects and ideas with *it* or *they.* In German the pronoun used depends on the gender of the noun. You already know the nominative forms of the third-person pronouns. Note how similar they are to the forms of the articles: **der → er; das → es; die → sie.**

According to Duden das Mädchen, das Fräulein, das Kind = es BUT: Fräulein Meyer = sie. In everyday speech you also hear sie for das Mädchen, das Fräulein.

der Vater = **er** (*he*)		der Stuhl = **er** (*it*)	
das Kind = **es** (*it*)		das Buch = **es** (*it*)	
die Mutter = **sie** (*she*)		die Tafel = **sie** (*it*)	
die Eltern = **sie** (*they*)		die Kulis = **sie** (*they*)	

Da ist **der Stuhl. Er** ist neu.	*There is the chair. It's new.*
Das Buch liegt hier. **Es** ist dick.	*The book is here. It's thick.*

Das Kind heißt Elke. **Es** ist fünf.	*The child's name is Elke. She's five.*
Wo ist **die Tafel?** Da ist **sie.**	*Where is the board? There it is.*
Die Kulis kosten 2,00 DM. **Sie** sind blau.	*The pens cost 2 marks. They're blue.*
Da sind **die Eltern. Sie** sind aus Zürich.	*There are the parents. They're from Zurich.*

Note that German uses three pronouns (**er, es, sie**) for objects where English uses only one *(it)*.

ÜBUNGEN

F. Ersetzen Sie die Wörter mit Pronomen! Replace the nouns with pronouns.

BEISPIEL: Fritz   **er**
             die Landkarte   **sie**

der Vater, der Berg, das Land, die Großmutter, der Junge, die Stadt, der Bleistift, der Pullover, Österreich, der Österreicher, die Schweiz, die Schweizerin, Deutschland, das Kind

G. Have students work in small groups.

G. Die Geographiestunde

1. **Was ist das?** As the instructor of a geography course, describe some features of Europe to your class. Use the appropriate form of **ein.**

   BEISPIEL: Frankfurt / Stadt   **Frankfurt ist eine Stadt.**

   Österreich / Land; die Donau / Fluß; Italienisch / Sprache; Berlin / Stadt; der Main / Fluß; das Matterhorn / Berg; Französisch / Sprache; Kanada / Land; der Bodensee / See; Bremen / Stadt

2. **Ist das richtig?** Now test your students to see what they do and don't know about Europe. Use the appropriate form of **kein.**

   BEISPIEL: die Donau / Land?
              Ist die Donau ein Land?—Nein, die Donau ist kein Land. Die Donau ist ein Fluß.

   Frankfurt / Fluß; Frankreich / Sprache; Heidelberg / Berg; der Rhein / Stadt; die Schweiz / See; Spanien / Sprache; Bonn / Land

3. **Ethnisches Mosaik.** Working in pairs, find out the ethnic background of one of your classmates. Use the appropriate form of **mein** and **dein.**

   BEISPIEL: Woher kommt dein Vater?   **Mein Vater kommt aus Salzburg.**

   Woher kommt dein Vater oder dein Stiefvater *(stepfather)*? deine Mutter oder deine Stiefmutter *(stepmother)*? dein Großvater? deine Großmutter? dein Urgroßvater *(great-grandfather)*? deine Urgroßmutter?

H. Ersetzen Sie das Subjekt!

1. **Antworten Sie mit ja!** A curious neighbor asks you questions about the new family in the neighborhood. In your answer, use pronouns.

   BEISPIEL: Die Eltern kommen aus Italien, nicht wahr?
              Ja, sie kommen aus Italien.

a. Der Sohn antwortet auf italienisch, nicht wahr?   **b.** Die Tochter versteht Deutsch, nicht wahr?   **c.** Das Kind ist fünf Jahre alt, nicht wahr?   **d.** Die Großmutter heißt Maria, nicht wahr?   **e.** Der Großvater wohnt auch da, nicht wahr?   **f.** Die Familie kommt aus Rom, nicht wahr?

2. **Antworten Sie, bitte!** One student asks, another answers, using pronouns.

   BEISPIEL: Wann beginnt Ihr Tag?   **Er beginnt morgens um sechs.**

   a. Wann beginnt die Deutschvorlesung?   **b.** Ist das Vorlesungszimmer groß?   **c.** Wie heißt das Deutschbuch?   **d.** Ist dein Kuli schwarz?   **e.** Welche Farbe hat dein Heft?   **f.** Welche Farbe hat deine Jacke?   **g.** Wo ist das Fenster?   **h.** Wie ist das Fenster?   **i.** Wie viele Monate hat das Jahr?   **j.** Wie viele Wochen hat der Monat?   **k.** Wie viele Tage hat die Woche?   **l.** Wie viele Stunden hat der Tag?   **m.** Wie viele Minuten hat die Stunde?

III. Sentence Structure

1. In English the subject usually precedes the verb, and more than one element may do so.

   They *speak Italian.*
   There **they** *speak Italian.*

   In German, however, only one sentence element may precede the verb, and this element is not necessarily the subject. If another element precedes the verb, the subject then follows the verb.

   Sie sprechen Italienisch
   Da sprechen **sie** Italienisch.

   REMEMBER: In statements and information questions the verb is always the second sentence element.

The verbs **sein** and **heißen** work like an equal sign: **Er ist Schweizer (Er = Schweizer). Er heißt Stefan Wolf (Er = Stefan Wolf).** This is the best time to practice this concept and the absence of **ein** before nationalities. As soon as students learn the accusative (Chapter 2), they'll want to use it in analogy with *It's me.* Practice sentences like *He's an Austrian, I'm an American,* etc,

2. The verbs **sein** *(to be)* and **heißen** *(to be called)* are LINKING VERBS. They normally link two words referring to the same person or thing, both of which are in the nominative: the first is the subject, the other a PREDICATE NOUN.

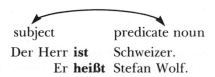

subject   predicate noun
Der Herr **ist**   Schweizer.
     Er **heißt** Stefan Wolf.

The verb **sein** can be complemented not only by a predicate noun, but also by a PREDICATE ADJECTIVE. Both are considered part of the verb phrase (i e, the complete verb). This is an example of a typical and important feature of German sentence structure: when the verb consists of more than one part, the inflected part (V1), i.e. the part of the verb that takes a personal ending, is the second element in the sentence. The uninflected part (V2) stands at the very end of the sentence.

Stefan Wolf **ist** auch **Schweizer.**

$$\text{Er } \underline{\text{ist}} \text{ heute } \underline{\text{sehr müde.}}$$
$$\text{V1} \qquad\qquad \text{V2}$$

REMEMBER: In German no indefinite article is used before nationalities. **Er ist Österreicher** (*an Austrian*).

ÜBUNGEN

I. **Sagen Sie es anders!** *(Say it differently.)* Begin the sentence with the word or phrase in boldface.

BEISPIEL: Mein Bruder kommt **morgen.**   **Morgen kommt mein Bruder.**

1. Es geht **mir** gut.
2. Ich bin nicht **müde.**
3. Der Bleistift ist **da.**
4. Wir lesen **für morgen** das Gespräch.
5. Die Schuhe sind auch **sehr schmutzig.**
6. Das kostet **zusammen** 12,60 DM.
7. Es ist **heute** 27°C.
8. Es ist **schön** heute!
9. Die Sonne scheint **jetzt** wieder.
10. Es regnet oft **im April.**
11. Es schneit aber **im Winter** nicht.
12. Sie finden die Wörter **auf Seite 50.**
13. Ich habe **morgen** keine Zeit.
14. Rita hat **in zehn Minuten** Philosophie.
15. Wir spielen **um halb drei** Tennis.
16. Die Leute sprechen **hier** nur Deutsch.

J. **Was sind sie?** Professor Händel of the Goethe Institute is determining the nationality of his summer-class students. Follow the model.

BEISPIEL: Pierre kommt aus Frankreich.   **Er ist Franzose.**

1. Roberto kommt aus Italien.
2. Sam kommt aus Amerika.
3. Carla kommt aus Spanien.
4. James kommt aus England.
5. Helen kommt aus Kanada.
6. Maria und Caroline kommen aus Amerika.
7. Marie und Simone kommen aus Frankreich.
8. Evita und Pia kommen aus Spanien.

IV. Compound Nouns

German typically uses many compound nouns that consist of two or more nouns, a verb and a noun, or an adjective and a noun. The last component determines the gender and the plural form.

das Land + die Karte = die Landkarte, -n
der Arm + das Band + die Uhr = die Armbanduhr, -en

schreiben + der Tisch = der Schreibtisch, -e
klein + die Stadt = die Kleinstadt, ¨e

ÜBUNG

K. Was bedeuten die Wörter? Was sind die Artikel? Determine the meaning and gender of the following words.

BEISPIEL: Kleinkind   *little child, toddler;* **das**

Wochentag, Abendkleid, Morgenmantel, Altstadt, Großstadtkind, Neujahr, Lesebuch, Sprechübung, Bergsee, Familienvater, Sommerbluse, Zimmertür, Jungenname, Frühlingswetter, Wanduhr, Deutschstunde, Uhrzeit

ZUSAMMENFASSUNG

These sentences include the material introduced in this chapter and in the "Schritte." Watch carefully for differences between English and German patterns.

L. Sprachstudenten. Auf deutsch, bitte!
   1. Tomorrow my parents will come.   **2.** My father is (a) French(man), and my mother is (an) Austrian.   **3.** In France they (the people) speak French, and in Austria they speak German.   **4.** France is west of Germany, and Austria is south of Germany.   **5.** I do understand French and German, but I answer in English.   **6.** Where are you (*fam.*) from?   **7.** I'm from Texas.   **8.** There's Thomas. Thomas is (an) American.   **9.** He's learning Spanish.   **10.** I think it's beautiful here.   **11.** But I am very tired.

LERNTIP

Reading German texts

First read for general content without worrying about unfamiliar words and phrases. Then reread carefully and always finish a paragraph, or at least a sentence, before looking up an unfamiliar word or phrase. Look up as little as possible. Underline and pronounce the words in question, but do not scribble the English translation into the text. It will only distract you from the German.

   Read the text a third time after having guessed or looked up all the underlined words. See how many of them you remember. Try to learn them now, at least passively, so as to avoid looking them up again and again. If a word or phrase still remains unclear, circle it and ask your instructor instead of spending more time on it.

Students can form many other compound nouns. This exercise can be done throughout the course, e.g. **Wintermantel (Sommer-, Regen-); Deutschkurs (Französisch-, Englisch-); Kinderbuch (-bild, -pullover).** There are additional vocabulary-building exercises in the Workbook.

L: 1. Morgen kommen meine Eltern. 2. Mein Vater ist Franzose, und meine Mutter ist Österreicherin. 3. In Frankreich sprechen sie Französisch, und in Österreich sprechen sie Deutsch. 4. Frankreich ist (liegt) westlich von Deutschland, und Österreich ist (liegt) südlich von Deutschland. 5. Ich verstehe Französisch und Deutsch, aber ich antworte auf englisch. 6. Woher kommst du? 7. Ich bin aus Texas. 8. Da ist Thomas. Thomas ist Amerikaner. 9. Er lernt Spanisch. 10. Ich finde es hier schön (schön hier). 11. Aber ich bin sehr müde.

EINBLICKE ◆◆◆◆◆◆◆◆◆◆◆

Frankfurt am Main ist groß und modern.

During the 1990s, plans for the total economic integration of Western Europe are being implemented. This will create a single, frontier-free market of over 330 million consumers, which will become one of the richest economies in the world and of great attraction for other European countries. This European Community, or EC **(Europäische Gemeinschaft = EG)**, is an economic association of Western European nations dedicated to the unrestricted movement of goods, capital, services, and people among member countries. Created in 1957 by the Treaty of Rome, the six original Community members (Belgium, France, Italy, the Netherlands, Luxemburg, and West Germany) have been joined by Denmark, Great Britain, Greece, Ireland, Portugal, and Spain.

In 1949, as a result of World War II, two German states were created: the Federal Republic of Germany, FRG **(die Bundesrepublik Deutschland = BRD),** and the German Democratic Republic, GDR **(die Deutsche Demokratische Republik = DDR)**. Although only the FRG belonged to the European Community, the GDR had indirect access to the EC, because West Germany insisted on not imposing any tariffs in trading with East Germany. With the opening of the Berlin Wall, starting on November 9, 1989, the process towards German reunification and East Germany's integration into the EC was set into motion. On July 2, 1990, the deutschmark (DM) became the official currency of the GDR and all border controls between the two German states were eliminated. On September 12, 1990, the major Western powers as well as the Soviet Union agreed to a united and sovereign Germany. Official reunification took place on October 3, 1990.

WORTSCHATZ 2

Exercise C, p. 57, can
be used as a pre-read-
ing activity.

These reading texts expand on the chapter topic. All vocabulary that is to become active is listed under **Wortschatz 2.** Learn these words well; they will recur in future exercises. Each reading selection is introduced by **Was ist das?**, a short set of cognates and compounds that you should be able to recognize but do not have to master actively.

der Mensch, -en	*human being, person (pl. people)*
Teil, -e	*part*
Nachbar, -n / die Nachbarin, -nen	*neighbor*
ungefähr	*about, approximately*
so . . . wie . . .	*as . . . as . . .*
wichtig	*important*

Make sure that students
can pronounce these
words correctly and that
they fully understand
their meaning. You can
also use this vocabulary
to lay the groundwork
for students' under-
standing of the reading
text.

Bankier is pronounced
[baŋkje':]

WAS IST DAS? der Ausländer, Bankier, Europäer, Großteil, Tourismus; (das) Europa, Sprachenlernen, Westeuropa; die Muttersprache, Politik; die USA (pl.); Dänisch, Finnisch, Griechisch, Holländisch, Norwegisch, Polnisch, Portugiesisch, Schwedisch, Tschechisch; studieren; europäisch, interessant

Viele Länder, viele Sprachen

of course

by far not

Europa hat viele Länder und viele Sprachen. In Deutschland hören Sie natürlich° Deutsch. Aber die Nachbarn im Norden sprechen Dänisch, Schwedisch, Norwegisch und Finnisch. Die Nachbarn im Osten sprechen Polnisch und Tschechisch, und im Westen sprechen sie Holländisch und Französisch. Im Süden von Europa sprechen die Menschen Italienisch, Spanisch, Portugiesisch und Griechisch. Und das sind noch lange nicht° alle Sprachen!

5

as
of the / work
in / this way

trade

more than / in the / most
of the / EC
abroad
tells
already

at home
as never before

Deutsch ist sehr wichtig. Ungefähr 90 Millionen Europäer sprechen Deutsch als° Muttersprache: die Deutschen, die Österreicher, die Liechtensteiner und ein Großteil der° Schweizer. Viele Ausländer arbeiten° oder studieren in Deutschland, Österreich und in der° Schweiz und lernen so° auch Deutsch. Sehr viele Menschen in Europa sprechen zwei oder drei Sprachen. Sie finden das interessant und auch wichtig für Tourismus, Handel° und Politik. 10

In Westeuropa wohnen ungefähr 350 Millionen Menschen; das sind mehr Menschen als° in den° USA und in Kanada zusammen. Die meisten° Länder sind ein Teil der° Europäischen Gemeinschaft (EG)°. Viele Europäer wohnen und arbeiten im Ausland°. Ein Beispiel ist Familie Bruegel. Pieter Bruegel erzählt°: „Ich bin aus Brüssel, und meine Frau Nicole ist Französin. Wir sind Bankiers. Wir wohnen schon° zwei Jahre in Frankfurt¹. Wir finden 20 es hier sehr schön. Wir haben zwei Kinder, Maude und Dominique. Sie sprechen zu Hause° Französisch, aber in der Schule sprechen sie Deutsch. Das freut mich. Das Sprachenlernen ist heute so wichtig wie nie zuvor°." 15

1 Superscript numbers in the reading texts refer to additional cultural information in the "Übrigens" section at the end of most chapters.

ZUM TEXT

A. Richtig oder falsch?

___ 1. In Europa hören Sie viele Sprachen.
___ 2. Alle Europäer sprechen Schwedisch.
___ 3. Ungefähr 900 000 Europäer sprechen Deutsch.
___ 4. Die Liechtensteiner sprechen Deutsch als Muttersprache.
___ 5. In Westeuropa wohnen so viele Menschen wie in Kanada und in den USA zusammen.
___ 6. Alle Länder in Europa sind ein Teil der EG.
___ 7. In Deutschland wohnen keine Ausländer.
___ 8. Herr und Frau Bruegel sind Bankiers.
___ 9. Herr Bruegel ist Franzose.
___ 10. Familie Bruegel wohnt schon fünf Jahre in Frankfurt.
___ 11. Sie finden es da sehr schön.
___ 12. Die Eltern und die Kinder sprechen zu Hause Deutsch.

Optional practice:
1. **z.B. (das) Europa >
es.** Deutschland, Teil Berlin, Menschen, Norden, Deutsch, Sprache, Nachbar, Europäerin.
2. **Was bedeuten die Wörter und was sind die Artikel?** Menschenzahl, Nachbarland, Zimmernachbar, Satzteil, Stadtteil, Teilzeit, Stadtmensch. 3. **z.B. Herr und Frau Watzlik sind aus Warschau. > Er ist Warschauer / Pole; sie ist Warschauerin / Polin.** Okko und Antje sind aus Amsterdam. Pierre und Nadine sind aus Paris. Bjorn und Christina sind aus Oslo. usw.

B. Interview. Imagine yourself to be Mr. / Mrs. Bruegel. Respond to the reporter's questions.
1. Guten Tag! Woher kommen Sie? **2.** Warum sind Sie hier in Frankfurt? **3.** Wie heißt Ihre Frau / Ihr Mann? **4.** Haben Sie Kinder? **5.** Sind die Kinder auch hier? **6.** Was sprechen Sie zu Hause, Deutsch oder Französisch? **7.** Sprechen die Kinder noch andere Sprachen? **8.** Wie finden Sie es hier in Frankfurt?

C. Etwas Geographie. Look at the maps of Europe and of Germany. Then, together with a classmate, work out the answers to the questions below.

1. **Sehen Sie auf die Landkarte von Europa!**
    a. Wie viele Nachbarn hat Deutschland? Wie heißen sie?
    b. Wo liegt Dänemark? Belgien? Spanien? Frankreich? Italien? die Tschechoslowakei? Schweden?
    c. Wie heißt die Hauptstadt von Deutschland? Dänemark? Belgien? Frankreich? Spanien? Italien? Jugoslawien? Finnland? Norwegen? Schweden? England? Polen?
    d. Welche Sprache sprechen die Leute wo?

2. **Sehen Sie auf die Landkarte von Deutschland!**
    a. Welche Flüsse, Seen und Berge gibt es in Deutschland?
    b. Wo liegt die Nordsee? die Ostsee? die Insel *(island)* Rügen? die Insel Helgoland? Wo liegen die Nord- / Ostfriesischen Inseln?
    c. Wo liegt . . .? *Ask each other about the location of various towns in Germany.*

For maps of Europe and Germany, see front of the book. To foster listening skills, have students look only at the maps.

C.1c: Discuss with students the current situation with regard to Berlin and Bonn.

C.2b: Point out the difference between **der See** and **die See** (**die See** is not active vocabulary).

Wasserburg am Bodensee

Übrigens

1. **Frankfurt am Main** (pop. 660,000), nicknamed "Mainhattan" or "Bankfurt," is the transportation hub and the most important financial center in Germany. Some 320 banks have headquarters or branch offices there. The city's stock exchange is the most important in Germany, and its airport handles more freight than any other in Europe.

SPRECHSITUATIONEN

Making Small Talk

When you meet someone for the first time, it is useful to be able to make small talk. The weather is a typical point of departure.

Es ist wirklich schön heute, nicht wahr?	*It's really beautiful today, isn't it?*
Furchtbares Wetter heute, nicht wahr?	*It's awful today, isn't it?*
Heute ist es aber heiß!	*Is it ever hot today!*
Jetzt regnet es schon wieder!	*It's raining again!*

Asking for Personal Information

You have already learned many words which make it possible for you to ask questions, e.g., **was? wo? woher? wer? wann? wie? wieviel? wie viele?** Here is a list of expressions you can use to elicit personal information.

Ich bin aus . . . . Woher sind Sie / bist du?
Ach, Sie sind / du bist (auch) aus . . .!
Sind Sie / bist du auch Student(in) . . .?
Was studieren Sie / studierst du?
Wo wohnen Sie / wohnst du?
Wo wohnt Ihre / deine Familie?
Wie finden Sie / findest du es hier / da?
Wie alt sind Sie / bist du?
Haben Sie / hast du Geschwister *(siblings)?*

The confirmation tag **nicht wahr?**—abbreviated to **nicht** in informal speech—is used to get someone to agree with the speaker.

BEISPIEL: Sie lernen auch Deutsch, nicht wahr?—Ja, natürlich.
Sie sind auch Amerikanerin, nicht?—Ja!

Optional practice: Have students work in small groups. Tell them to select a dialogue from the "Gespräche" or a paragraph from the reading text, and to come up with as many questions about the content as possible.

A. Das Opfer

Select one classmate and ask him / her questions very rapidly; the "victim" **(das Opfer)** will answer as many as possible. Then pick the next "victim" from those who are slow to ask questions. Here are a few to start with: **Was ist das? Wo ist . . .? Welche Farbe hat . . .? Wie ist . . .? Wieviel ist . . .?** etc.

B. Kurzgespräche

1. As you wait for a class to start, you begin a conversation with the student next to you by commenting on the weather. You then ask what the other student is studying and learn that he / she is also learning German. Respond appropriately.
2. Ask another student some personal questions, i.e., where he / she is from, how he / she likes it here, where the family lives, how big the family is, what the names of the family members are, and what language they speak at home **(zu Hause).** Then report to the class.

2

Lebensmittel und Geschäfte

Ich hab' in Biskin gebadet!

Eine Bäckerei. Hier gibt es Brot und Kuchen.

▌ LERNZIELE

Gespräche and **Wortschatz.** In this chapter you will talk about food and shopping.

Struktur. You will learn about . . .

▪ the present tense of **sein** and **haben.**

▪ the accusative case.

▪ sentence structure (verb complements, negation, and coordinating conjunctions).

Einblicke. Stores and opening hours

Sprechsituationen

▪ Making a purchase

◆◆◆◆◆ # GESPRÄCHE

Im Lebensmittelgeschäft[1]

VERKÄUFER	Guten Tag! Was darf's sein?
HERR SCHÄFER	Ich brauche etwas Obst. Haben Sie keine Bananen?
VERKÄUFER	Doch, hier!
HERR SCHÄFER	Was kosten sie?
VERKÄUFER	1,80 DM das Pfund.
HERR SCHÄFER	Und die Orangen?
VERKÄUFER	60 Pfennig das Stück.
HERR SCHÄFER	Gut, dann nehme ich zwei Pfund Bananen und sechs Orangen.
VERKÄUFER	Sonst noch etwas?
HERR SCHÄFER	Ja, zwei Kilo[2] Äpfel.
VERKÄUFER	14,20 DM bitte! Danke schön! Auf Wiedersehen!

In der Bäckerei

VERKÄUFERIN	Guten Morgen! Was darf's sein?
FRAU MEYER	Ich möchte sechs Brötchen. Ist der Apfelstrudel frisch?
VERKÄUFERIN	Natürlich.
FRAU MEYER	Gut, dann nehme ich vier Stück.
VERKÄUFERIN	Es gibt heute auch Schwarzbrot[3] im Sonderangebot.
FRAU MEYER	Nein, danke. Aber was für Plätzchen haben Sie?
VERKÄUFERIN	Butterplätzchen, Schokoladenplätzchen . . .
FRAU MEYER	Ach, ich nehme 300 Gramm[2] Schokoladenplätzchen.
VERKÄUFERIN	Sonst noch etwas?
FRAU MEYER	Nein, danke. Das ist alles.
VERKÄUFERIN	13,50 DM bitte!

 *Übrigens*

1. In Germany, Switzerland, and Austria small specialty shops are still very common. Particularly in small towns, shoppers buy their groceries almost daily, going from the butcher shop to the bakery, then to the grocery store and the fish market. They usually bring their own shopping bags (**Einkaufstaschen**) or buy plastic bags at the check-out counter, and pay cash rather than using checks or credit cards.

2. In Europe the metric system is used to measure distances and weights. A shopper may ask for various amounts: **100 Gramm Leberwurst, ein Pfund**

Kaffee, or **ein Kilo (2 Pfund) Äpfel.**

German:	
1g = 1 Gramm	
125 g = 1 Viertelpfund	
250 g = 1 halbes Pfund	
500 g = 1 Pfund	
1000 g = 1 Kilo(gramm)	

U.S.: 1 oz. = 28.3 g
        1 lb. = 454 g

In the metric system a pound is about 10 percent heavier than an American pound (500 g rather than 450 g). To convert approximately U.S. pounds to metric pounds: deduct 10 percent (120 lbs. − 12 = 108 lbs.); metric pounds to U.S. pounds: add 10 percent (108 lbs. + 11 = 119 lbs).

As a quick and easy measurement guide, some cookbooks round off these figures: 1 oz. = 30 g; 1 lb. = 500 g; 2 lbs. = 1 kg; 4 cups = 1 liter.

3. When Germans think of **Brot,** they probably think first of a firm, heavy loaf of rye bread, and not of the soft white bread so common in America. White loaves and rolls are prized for their crisp crust. There are over two hundred varieties of bread available in Central Europe. For Germans, bread is the most important food—on the average, they eat four slices of bread and one roll a day.

Der Supermarkt hat Sonderangebote.

Fragen: 1. Was braucht Herr Schäfer? 2. Was kosten die Bananen? die Orangen? 3. Wie viele Bananen und wie viele Orangen kauft er? 4. Was kauft er noch? 5. Was kostet alles zusammen? 6. Wie viele Brötchen möchte Frau Meyer? 7. Was ist frisch? 8. Wieviel Apfelstrudel kauft sie? 9. Was für Plätzchen kauft sie? 10. Was gibt es im Sonderangebot?

At the Grocery Store CLERK: *Good morning. May I help you?* MR. SCHÄFER: *I'd like some fruit. Don't you have any bananas?* CLERK: *Certainly. Here they are.* MR. SCHÄFER: *How much are they?* CLERK: *1 mark 80 a pound.* MR. SCHÄFER: *And the oranges?* CLERK: *60 pfennig each.* MR. SCHÄFER: *Fine, then I'll take two pounds of bananas and six oranges.* CLERK: *Anything else?* MR. SCHÄFER: *Yes, 2 kilos of apples.* CLERK: *14 marks 20, please. Thank you very much. Good-bye.*

In the Bakery CLERK: *Good morning. May I help you?* MRS. MEYER: *I'd like six rolls. Is the apple strudel fresh?* CLERK: *Of course.* MRS. MEYER: *Fine. Then I'll take four pieces.* CLERK: *Today there's also a special on rye bread.* MRS. MEYER: *No, thank you. But what kind of cookies do you have?* CLERK: *Butter cookies, chocolate cookies* . MRS. MEYER: *Oh, I'll take 300 grams of chocolate cookies.* CLERK: *Anything else?* MRS. MEYER: *No, thank you. That's all.* CLERK: *13 marks 50, please.*

WORTSCHATZ 1

DIE LEBENSMITTEL *(pl.) groceries*

der	Apfel, ⸚	apple	die	Banane, -n	banana
	Fisch, -e	fish		Bohne, -n	bean
	Kaffee	coffee		Butter	butter
	Käse	cheese		Cola	coke
	Kuchen, -	cake		Erbse, -n	pea
	Saft, ⸚e	juice		Erdbeere, -n	strawberry
	Salat, -e	lettuce, salad		Gurke, -n	cucumber
	Tee	tea		Karotte, -n	carrot
	Wein, -e	wine		Limonade, -n	soft drink,
das	Bier	beer			lemonade
	Brot, -e	bread		Marmelade, -n	jam
	Brötchen, -	roll		Milch	milk
	Ei, -er	egg		Orange, -n	orange
	Fleisch	meat		Tomate, -n	tomato
	Gemüse, -	vegetable(s)		Wurst, ⸚e	sausage
	Obst	fruit		Zitrone, -n	lemon
	Plätzchen, -	cookie			
	Wasser	water			

WEITERES

der	(Super)markt, ⸚e	(super)market
das	(Lebensmittel)geschäft, -e	(grocery) store
	Kaufhaus, ⸚er	department store
	Pfund[1]	pound
	Stück, -e[1]	piece
die	Bäckerei, -en	bakery
	Buchhandlung, -en	bookstore

doch	yes, sure, certainly, of course
es gibt[2]	there is, there are
etwas . . .	a little, some . . . (used with sg. collective nouns)
frisch	fresh
gern	gladly
Ich esse (trinke) gern . . .	I like to eat (drink) . . .
Ich möchte . . .[3]	I would like (to have) . . .
kaufen / verkaufen	to buy / sell
machen	to make, do
natürlich	of course
was für (ein)?[4]	what kind of (a)?

1 One says **ein Pfund Fleisch, zwei Pfund Fleisch; ein Stück Kuchen, zwei Stück Kuchen.** Remember also **eine Mark, zwei Mark.**

2 See Struktur II. 1 d.

3 möcht- is a special verb form that will be explained later: **ich möchte, du möchtest, er möchte, wir möchten, ihr möchtet, sie möchten.**

4 Treat this phrase as you would treat **ein** by itself: Das ist **ein** Kuchen. Was für **ein** Kuchen? Das ist **eine** Wurst. Was für **eine** Wurst? There's no **ein** in the plural: Das sind Plätzchen. Was für Plätzchen? Don't use **für** in answers to a **was für ein** question: Was für Obst essen Sie gern? Ich esse gern Bananen.

PASSIVES VOKABULAR der Apfelstrudel   Sonst noch etwas?
Anything else?   **das Kilo / vier Kilo   Was darf's sein?** *May I help you?*   **im Sonderangebot** *on sale, special*

Eine Metzgerei (*butcher shop*). Hier gibt es Fleisch und Wurst.

ZUM THEMA

A. Mustersätze

1. Bananen: **Ich esse gern** Bananen.
   Äpfel, Erdbeeren, Orangen, Gurken, Plätzchen
2. Fisch: **Die Kinder essen nicht gern** Fisch.
   Salat, Tomaten, Karotten, Gemüse, Eier
3. Cola: **Wir trinken gern** Cola.
   Limonade, Kaffee, Tee, Bier, Wein
4. Obst: **Ich brauche etwas** Obst.
   Brot, Fleisch, Marmelade, Käse, Wurst
5. Bananen: **Haben Sie keine** Bananen?
   Erdbeeren, Bohnen, Erbsen, Zitronen, Brötchen

B. Was paßt nicht?

1. die Butter, der Käse, die Wurst, die Bohne
2. das Brötchen, die Zitrone, das Plätzchen, der Kuchen
3. die Tomate, die Erdbeere, die Gurke, der Salat
4. das Gemüse, der Apfel, die Orange, die Banane
5. das Obst, das Gemüse, der Salat, der Tee
6. der Wein, das Bier, die Zitrone, die Milch
7. das Geschäft, die Lebensmittel, die Bäckerei, das Kaufhaus

C. Was bedeuten die Wörter, und was sind die Artikel?

Bohnensalat, Buttermilch, Delikatessengeschäft, Erdbeermarmelade, Fischbrötchen, Kaffeemilch, Milchkaffee, Obstsalat, Orangenlimonade, Schreib-
warengeschäft, Teewasser, Wurstbrot, Zitronensaft.

D. Was paßt?

_____	1. Der Fisch ist nicht frisch.	a. Wirklich?
_____	2. Möchten Sie etwas Obst?	b. Wie bitte.
_____	3. Die Bäckerei verkauft Wurst, nicht wahr?	c. Ich nicht.
		d. Ja, gern.
_____	4. Wir kaufen auch Kuchen.	e. Ja, bitte.
_____	5. Ich trinke morgens gern Cola.	f. Natürlich nicht.
		g. Prima!
		h. Wir auch.
		i. Richtig.
		j. Nein, danke.
		k. Doch.

E. Und Sie? Interview a classmate to find out what foods he / she likes and what his / her eating habits are.
1. Was für Obst essen Sie (nicht) gern?   **2.** Was für Gemüse essen Sie (nicht) gern?   **3.** Was für Kuchen, Plätzchen, Salat essen Sie gern?   **4.** Was trinken Sie (nicht) gern?   **5.** Was essen Sie morgens, mittags, abends?

F. Aussprache. See also II. 2, 5, 14–16, 18, and 21 in the pronunciation section of the Workbook.
1. [e:]   g**eh**en, K**ä**se, M**ä**dchen, Apoth**e**ke, Am**e**rika, n**eh**men, **Tee, See**
2. [e]   **e**s, **e**twas, spr**e**chen, M**e**nsch, Gesch**ä**ft, **e**ssen, H**e**md
3. [o:]   **oh**ne, **o**der, **O**bst, w**oh**nen, Br**o**t, B**oh**ne, M**o**ntag, s**o**
4. [o]   **O**sten, k**o**mmen, N**o**rden, Kar**o**tte, d**o**ch, S**o**nne
5. Wortpaare

a. _gate_ / geht	c. zähle / Zelle	e. Ofen / offen
b. den / denn	d. _shown_ / schon	f. Bonn / Bann

STRUKTUR

I. The Present Tense of sein _(to be)_ and haben _(to have)_

	sein		haben	
1st person	ich bin	wir sind	ich habe	wir haben
2nd person	du bist	ihr seid	du hast	ihr habt
3rd person	er ist	sie sind	er hat	sie haben

ÜBUNGEN

A. Ersetzen Sie das Subjekt!

BEISPIEL: Haben Sie Zeit? (du, ihr) **Hast du Zeit? / Habt ihr Zeit?**

1. Ich bin fertig. (er, wir, sie / *sg.*)
2. Sind Sie müde? (du, ihr, sie / *pl.*)
3. Sie hat die Landkarte. (ich, er, wir)
4. Haben Sie Papier? (sie / *sg.*, ihr, du)
5. Wir sind Amerikaner. (er, sie / *pl.*, ich)
6. Er hat eine Frage. (ich, wir, Sie)
7. Seid ihr aus Wien? (Sie, du sie / *sg.*)
8. Er hat Orangensaft (sie / *pl.*, ich, ihr)

II. The Accusative Case

The accusative case has two major functions: it is the case of the direct object and it follows certain prepositions.

1. In the English sentence *The boy asks the father*, the DIRECT OBJECT of the sentence is *the father*. He is being asked; he is the target of the verb's action. One determines what the direct object is by asking *who* or *what* is directly affected by the verb's action. In other words, the person you see, hear, or ask, or the thing you have, buy, or eat is the direct object.

Der Junge fragt **den Vater.**	*The boy asks the father.*
Ich kaufe **den Kuchen.**	*I buy the cake.*

   a. The accusative forms of the INTERROGATIVE PRONOUN are **wen** (*whom*) and **was** (*what*). You now know two cases for this pronoun.

	persons	things and ideas
nom.	wer?	was?
acc.	**wen?**	**was?**

Wen fragt der Junge? **Den Vater.**	*Whom does the boy ask? The father.*
Was kaufe ich? **Den Kuchen.**	*What do I buy? The cake.*

   b. Only the ARTICLES for masculine nouns have special forms for the accusative. In the other genders the nominative and accusative are identical in form.

	singular			plural
	masc.	neut.	fem.	
nom.	der	das	die	die
	ein	ein	eine	—
	kein	kein	keine	keine
acc.	**den**	**das**	**die**	**die**
	einen	**ein**	**eine**	—
	keinen	**kein**	**keine**	**keine**

PETER Der Käse, das Obst, die Wurst und die Brötchen sind frisch.
PETRA Dann kaufe ich den Käse, das Obst, die Wurst und die Brötchen.
PETER Aber wir brauchen keinen Käse, kein Obst, keine Wurst und keine Brötchen.

This pattern is true of all possessive adjectives, but these are the only ones introduced so far.

The POSSESSIVE ADJECTIVES **mein, dein,** and **Ihr** follow the pattern of **ein** and **kein:**

Brauchen Sie mein**en** Bleistift? Nein danke, ich brauche Ihr**en** Bleistift nicht.

c. German has a few masculine nouns that have an **-n** or **-en** ending in all cases (singular and plural) except in the nominative singular. They are called N-NOUNS. Note how they are listed in vocabularies and dictionaries: the first ending refers to the singular for cases other than the nominative, the second one to the plural. You are already familiar with most of the n-nouns below.

der **Herr, -n, -en**   *gentleman*
　　Junge, -n, -n   *boy*
　　Mensch, -en, -en   *human being, person*
　　Nachbar, -n, -n   *neighbor*
　　Student, -en, -en   *student*

	singular	plural
nom.	der Student	die Studenten
acc.	**den Studenten**	die Studenten

Many students need to develop a sense of the accusative case. It may help to go through the list of these verbs. Point out that these verbs take or even require objects in English, too. If you say I need or I would like, someone is bound to ask What? What you need, buy, sell, take, etc., is the direct object of the verb.

Der Herr heißt Müller. Fragen Sie Herr**n** Müller!
Da kommt ein Student. Fragen Sie den Student**en**!

d. Verbs that can take accusative objects are called TRANSITIVE. (Some verbs are INTRANSITIVE, i.e., they can't take a direct object: **gehen** *to go.*) Here are some familiar transitive verbs.

brauchen	*to need*	machen	*to make, do*
es gibt	*there is, there are*	möcht-	*would like*
essen	*to eat*	nehmen	*to take*
finden	*to find*	öffnen	*to open*

fragen	*to ask*	sagen	*to say*
haben	*to have*	schreiben	*to write*
hören	*to hear*	sprechen	*to speak, talk*
kaufen	*to buy*	trinken	*to drink*
lernen	*to learn*	verkaufen	*to sell*
lesen	*to read*	verstehen	*to understand*

Sie kauft den Rock und die Bluse.
Schreiben Sie den Satz!
Ich esse einen Apfel und eine Banane.
Wir haben einen Supermarkt und ein Kaufhaus.
Das Geschäft verkauft keinen Fisch und kein Fleisch.

▪ The idiom **es gibt** is always followed by the accusative case in the singular or in the plural.

Es gibt hier einen Markt.   *There's a market here.*
Es gibt auch Lebensmittel-   *There are also grocery stores.*
geschäfte.

The pronoun **es** is the subject of the sentence. What "there is," is in the accusative. **es gibt** implies a general, unspecified existence, unlike **Hier / da ist,** which points to a specific item.

Gibt es hier einen Markt?   *Is there a market here (in town)?*
Ja, **es gibt** einen Markt.   *Yes, there's a market.*

Wo ist ein Markt?   *Where is a market?*
Da ist ein Markt.   *There's a market. (There it is.)*

2. ACCUSATIVE PREPOSITIONS are always followed by the accusative case.

durch	*through*	Britta kommt **durch die Tür.**
für	*for*	Das Obst ist **für die Kinder.**
gegen	*against*	Was hast du **gegen den Kaffee?**
ohne	*without*	Wir essen das Brötchen **ohne den Käse.**
um	*around*	Die Kinder laufen **um den Tisch.**
	at	Wir kommen **um 12 Uhr.**

▪ Some prepositions may be contracted with the definite article. These forms are especially common in everyday speech.

durch + das = **durchs**
für + das = **fürs**
um + das = **ums**

NOTE: A sentence can contain two accusatives, one the direct object and the other the object of a preposition.

Sie kauft den Fisch für den Fischsalat.

ÜBUNGEN

B. Wiederholen Sie die Sätze noch einmal mit ein und kein!

BEISPIEL: Er kauft den Bleistift, das Buch und die Landkarte.
Er kauft einen Bleistift, ein Buch und eine Landkarte.
Er kauft keinen Bleistift, kein Buch und keine Landkarte.

1. Sie möchte den Rock, das Kleid und die Bluse.
2. Du brauchst das Hemd, die Hose und den Pullover.
3. Ich esse das Brötchen, die Orange und den Apfel.

C. Einkaufen. Small talk while you are shopping with some friends.

BEISPIEL: Wir kaufen den Saft. (Salat) **Wir kaufen den Salat.**

1. Möchtest du das Fleisch? (Gemüse, Obst, Schwarzbrot)
2. Die Wurst essen wir nicht. (Marmelade, Tomate, Gurke)
3. Meine Schwester trinkt keinen Saft. (Limonade, Cola, Wasser)
4. Hast du den Tee? (Saft, Milch, Käse)
5. Gibt es hier eine Buchhandlung? (Markt, Delikatessengeschäft, Kaufhäuser)
6. Fragen Sie den Herrn! (Junge, Mensch, Student, Studenten / *pl.*)
7. Den Verkäufer verstehe ich nicht! (Verkäuferin, Nachbar, Fräulein)

D. Umzug. *(Moving.)* You are giving instructions to the movers who are bringing your belongings into your new apartment. Use the cues.

BEISPIEL: durch / Zimmer
Durch das Zimmer, bitte!

1. gegen / Wand	4. durch / Tür	7. gegen / Fenster *(sg.)*
2. um / Tisch	5. ohne / Tisch	8. um / Ecke *(f., corner)*
3. ohne / Bücher	6. für / Kinderzimmer *(pl.)*	

E. Sagen Sie es noch einmal! Replace the noun following the preposition with another noun.

BEISPIEL: Ich möchte etwas für meinen Vater. (Mutter, Kind)
Ich möchte etwas für meine Mutter.
Ich möchte etwas für mein Kind.

1. Wir gehen durch die Geschäfte. (Supermarkt, Kaufhaus, Bäckerei)
2. Er kommt ohne das Bier. (Wein, Cola, Kaffee, Käsebrot, Salat)
3. Was haben Sie gegen den Herrn? (Frau, Mädchen, Junge, Nachbarin)
4. Wiederholen Sie das für Ihren Großvater! (Bruder, Schwester, Nachbar, Eltern)

F. Kombinieren Sie! You are a salesperson in a clothing store. Ask your customers what kind of items they need. Also indicate how you would address your customers if they were: (a) a friend, (b) a stranger, (c) two of your relatives.

BEISPIEL: **Was für einen Pullover möchten Sie?**

If students have difficulties with C and D because they can't remember the genders of the nouns used, point out how crucial it is to learn the article with the noun. Ask them to state the article of each noun before giving the accusative form.

1	2	3	4
was für (ein)	Rock	brauchen	du
	Hemd	möchten	ihr
	Jacke		Sie
	Schuhe		
	usw.		

Optional practice:
Write the title of a recipe on the board: (Salat). Begin with the question **Was kaufen Sie für den Salat?** One student answers **Ich kaufe Tomaten für den Salat.** He / she then asks a classmate **Was kaufen Sie / kaufst du noch?** etc. Students keep on adding to the list.

Do the same with articles of clothing and seasons: **Was brauchen Sie / brauchst du für den Winter?** Ich brauche einen Pullover. **Was brauchen Sie noch?** Ich brauche einen Pullover, einen Mantel, etc.

Heute ist Markt. Die Frau verkauft Obst.

G. Was kaufen Sie? Answer each question with four to six items, drawing on all the vocabulary you have had so far. Use articles whenever possible.

BEISPIEL: Sie sind im Supermarkt. Was kaufen Sie?
Ich kaufe einen Kuchen, eine Cola, ein Pfund Butter, ein Stück Käse, etwas Obst . . .

1. Sie sind in der Bäckerei. Was kaufen Sie?
2. Sie sind im Lebensmittelgeschäft. Was kaufen Sie?
3. Sie sind im Kaufhaus. Was kaufen Sie?
4. Sie sind in der Buchhandlung. Was kaufen Sie?

H. Wie bitte? Your grandfather, who is hard of hearing, always asks you to repeat whatever you say.

BEISPIEL: Meine Freunde spielen Tennis.
Wer spielt Tennis?
Was spielen deine Freunde?

1. Vater hört den Nachbarn.
2. Matthias fragt Tante Martha.
3. Die Mutter kauft Obst.
4. Die Kinder möchten einen Apfel.
5. Helga und Britta verstehen die Engländer nicht.
6. Wir lernen Deutsch.

I. Im Kaufhaus. Sagen Sie es auf deutsch!

x Hello! May I help you?

y Hello! I need a sweater for my son.

x The sweater here is from England. Would you like a sweater in blue **(in Blau)?**

y No. Don't you have any sweater in red?

x Of course we do—here.

y Fine. I think the color is very beautiful. **(finden)**

x Do you also need a shirt or (a pair of) slacks *(sg.)*?

y No, he doesn't need any shirt or (any) slacks. (He needs no shirt and no slacks.)

III. Sentence Structure

1. Objects and Verbs as Verb Complements (V2)

As you know from Chapter 1, predicate nouns and predicate adjectives are VERB COMPLEMENTS (V2). Sometimes objects or another verb also become part of the verb phrase, i.e., verb complements, and in that combination they complete the meaning of the main verb (V1).

Sie **sprechen Deutsch.**
Sie **sprechen** gut **Deutsch.**
Sie <u>**sprechen**</u> wirklich gut <u>**Deutsch.**</u>
   V1   V2

Wir **spielen Tennis.**
Wir **spielen** gern **Tennis.**
Wir <u>**spielen**</u> morgens gern <u>**Tennis.**</u>
   V1   V2

Er **geht essen.**
Er **geht** hier **essen.**
Er <u>**geht**</u> mittags hier <u>**essen**</u>.
  V1   V2

2. Negation

a. **kein** must be used to negate a sentence containing either a predicate noun or an object that is preceded by the indefinite article **ein (ein** Apfelkuchen) or not preceded by any article (Zitronen).

> **kein** + noun = *no, not a(n), not any*

Ist das **ein** Apfelkuchen?
Nein, das ist **kein** Apfelkuchen.
Ist er Kanadier?
Nein, er ist **kein** Kanadier.

Is that an apple cake?
No, that's no (not an) apple cake.
Is he a Canadian?
No, he isn't a Canadian.

Kaufen Sie **einen** Mantel?   *Are you buying a coat?*
Nein, ich kaufe **keinen** Mantel.   *No, I'm not buying a coat.*

Haben Sie Zitronen?   *Do you have (any) lemons?*
Nein, wir haben **keine** Zitro-   *No, we have no (don't have any) lemons.*
nen.

b. **nicht** is used under all other circumstances. Its position is determined as follows:

- **nicht** (usually) comes after the subject and verb, after all objects, and after time expressions. Therefore, it stands at the end of many sentences.

Der Junge fragt **nicht.**
Der Junge fragt den Vater **nicht.**
Der Junge fragt den Vater heute **nicht.**

- **nicht** (usually) comes before adverbs of manner (*how?*) or place (*where?*), before adverbial phrases with prepositions, and before verb complements (V2).

Ich kaufe das **nicht** gern.   *I don't like to buy that.*
Ich kaufe das **nicht** hier.   *I don't buy that here.*
Ich kaufe das **nicht** für Ute.   *I don't buy that for Ute.*
Das Buch ist **nicht** neu.   *The book isn't new.*
Das ist **nicht** mein Buch.   *That's not my book.*
Sie sprechen **nicht** Deutsch.   *They don't speak German.*
Wir spielen **nicht** Tennis.   *We don't play tennis.*
Ich gehe heute **nicht** essen.   *I'm not going out to eat today.*

Discuss sample senten-
ces in detail. Remind
students to check the
sentences they write
against the sentence-
structure formula.

S	VI	O	time expression	↑ other adverbs or adverbial phrases	V2.
				nicht	

c. **kein** vs. **nicht**

COMPARE: Ich kaufe **ein** Brot.   Ich kaufe **kein** Brot.
           Ich kaufe Brot.   Ich kaufe **kein** Brot.
           Ich kaufe das Brot.   Ich kaufe das Brot **nicht.**

d. **ja, nein, doch**

COMPARE: Hast du das Buch?   **Ja!**   *Yes.*
                                       Nein!   *No.*
           Hast du das Buch **nicht?** **Doch!**   *Of course I do.*

doch is an affirmative response to a negative question.

Wohnt Erika Schwarz **nicht** in Salzburg?—**Doch!**
Haben Sie keine Wintermäntel?—**Doch,** hier sind sie.

3. Joining Sentences

Two independent clauses can be joined into one sentence by means of COORDI-

NATING CONJUNCTIONS. Each of the two clauses keeps the original word order.

aber	*but*
denn	*because, for*
oder	*or*
und	*and*

Ich kaufe Erdbeeren, **und** er kauft Äpfel.
Ich kaufe Erdbeeren, **denn** sie sind frisch.
Wir essen Fisch, **aber** sie essen Fleisch.
Nehmen Sie Käsekuchen, **oder** möchten Sie Apfelstrudel?

You could point out that a COMMA separates two independent clauses, each with its own subject.

ÜBUNGEN

J. Die Nachbarin. Every time you visit your elderly neighbor, she insists that you eat or drink something. Use the negative **kein.**

BEISPIEL: Möchten Sie eine Banane?   **Möchten Sie keine Banane?**

1. Nehmen Sie Erdbeeren? **2.** Essen Sie Gurkensalat? **3.** Trinken Sie Limonade? **4.** Essen Sie Käsekuchen? **5.** Möchten Sie ein Stück Brot? **6.** Möchten Sie eine Cola? **7.** Nehmen Sie ein Wurstbrötchen? **8.** Essen Sie Tomaten? **9.** Trinken Sie ein Glas Milch? **10.** Möchten Sie einen Apfel?

K: Extra practice: 1. Was essen / trinken Sie nicht gern? 2. Welche Farbe finden Sie nicht schön? 3. Wie ist das Wetter heute nicht?

K. Das ist nicht richtig! Shortly after you have joined your new class, some misconceptions have arisen. Tell your classmates what is not true about you. Use **nicht.**

BEISPIEL: Mein Name ist Fiedler.   **Mein Name ist nicht Fiedler.**

1. Ich komme aus Italien. **2.** Meine Familie wohnt in Österreich. **3.** Zu Hause sprechen wir Finnisch. **4.** Meine Familie kommt morgen. **5.** Ich finde es hier schön. **6.** Es geht mir gut. **7.** Ich bin 25 Jahre alt.

L. Nein! To get your attention, your little brother negates everything you say. Use either **nicht** or **kein.**
1. Heute ist es heiß. **2.** Ich trinke jetzt Wasser. **3.** Das Geschäft verkauft Limonade und Eistee *(ice tea)*. **4.** Die Cola ist teuer. **5.** Ich möchte ein Käsebrötchen. **6.** Ich esse das Käsebrötchen! **7.** Wir gehen in die Buchhandlung. **8.** Vater braucht eine Landkarte und einen Stadtplan *(city map)*. **9.** Er braucht die Landkarte! **10.** Das Buch ist gut, nicht wahr? **11.** Ich finde es hier kalt. **12.** Wir haben Zeit.

M. Ja, nein oder doch! You are the instructor of your German class. Ask your students the following questions to check how much they know about German-speaking countries.

BEISPIEL: Ist der Rhein im Westen von Deutschland? **Ja!**
Ist der Rhein im Osten von Deutschland? **Nein!**
Ist der Rhein nicht im Westen von Deutschland? **Doch!**

1. Sprechen die Österreicher nicht Deutsch?
2. Hat Deutschland viele Nachbarn?
3. Ist Bonn die Hauptstadt von Deutschland?
4. Ist Wien nicht die Hauptstadt von Österreich?
5. Hamburg liegt in Norddeutschland, nicht wahr?
6. Gibt es in Deutschland keine Supermärkte?
7. Sind 500 Gramm ein Pfund?
8. Ein Viertelpfund ist nicht 125 Gramm?
9. Ein Kilogramm ist ein halbes Pfund, nicht wahr?

N. Eine Postkarte. After your first week in Munich, write a brief postcard home. Join the two sentences with the conjunctions indicated.

Liebe *(dear)* Mutter, lieber Vater!
1. Ich schreibe nicht viel. Ich habe keine Zeit. *(because)*
2. Ich finde es hier sehr schön. Ich lerne auch sehr viel. *(and)*
3. Meine Zimmerkolleginnen / Zimmerkollegen *(roommates)* kommen aus Kanada. Sie sind 21 Jahre alt. *(and)*
4. Sie sprechen Französisch. Sie verstehen kein Englisch. *(but)*
5. Sonntag spielen wir Minigolf. Wir gehen in die Stadt. *(or)*

ZUSAMMENFASSUNG

O. Im Lebensmittelgeschäft. Auf deutsch, bitte!
1. What would you like? **2.** What kind of vegetables do you have today? **3.** I'll take two pounds of beans. **4.** The eggs are fresh, aren't they?—Of course. **5.** We don't need (any) eggs. **6.** But we need some fish and lettuce. **7.** I'm not eating any fish. **8.** Do you have any carrot juice **(Karottensaft)**? **9.** Don't you like (to drink) carrot juice?—No, I don't. **10.** Do you have any coke? I like to drink coke. **11.** She's buying a coke and some orange juice. **12.** That's it?—No, I'd also like two pieces of strawberry cake.

O: 1. Was möchten Sie? 2. Was für Gemüse haben Sie heute? 3. Ich nehme zwei Pfund Bohnen. 4. Die Eier sind frisch, nicht wahr? —Natürlich! 5. Wir brauchen keine Eier. 6. Aber wir brauchen etwas Fisch und Salat. 7. Ich esse keinen Fisch. 8. Haben Sie Karottensaft? 9. Trinkst du nicht gern Karottensaft? —Nein. 10. Haben Sie Cola? Ich trinke gern Cola. 11. Sie kauft eine Cola und etwas Orangensaft. 12. Ist das alles? —Nein, ich möchte auch zwei Stück Erdbeerkuchen.

LERNTIP

Developing listening comprehension

Being able to understand spoken German is probably your most important skill. Without it, you can't learn to speak. Use class time well, listen carefully to the instructor and your classmates. Use the tape program in the lab. Listen to the reading text with the book closed. Take advantage of opportunities to hear German in the German Club or German House, if there is one on your campus. Watch plays or movies; listen to tapes and records. Even if you can't understand much of it in the beginning, you will be able to pick out key words, and learn to "tune in" to German.

EINBLICKE ◆◆◆◆◆◆◆◆◆◆◆◆

Fußgängerzone in München. Hier gibt es keine Autos.

   Most European cities have developed traffic-free areas called **Fußgängerzonen,** usually in the center of town. Since no motor vehicles or streetcars are allowed, these areas are free of traffic noise and exhaust fumes. In warm weather people sit on benches or have refreshments in sidewalk cafés. Although merchants initially feared a decrease in business from closing streets to traffic, there has been an increase instead. Establishing these areas provided an incentive for property owners to refurbish older buildings, which typically combine apartments in the upper stories and retail businesses on the first and second floors.

WORTSCHATZ 2

Exercise E.1, p. 77, can be used as a pre-reading exercise with some adjustments.

der	Durst / Hunger	*thirst / hunger*
das	Glas, ¨er[1]	*glass*
die	Apotheke, -n[2]	*pharmacy*
	Blume, -n	*flower*
	Drogerie, -n[2]	*drugstore*
	Studentin, -nen	*student (f.)*
	Tasse, -n[1]	*cup*
	alles	*everything*
	billig / teuer	*inexpensive, cheap / expensive*
	ein paar[3]	*a few, some (used with plural nouns)*
	montags (dienstags usw.)	*on Mondays (Tuesdays, etc.)*
	offen / zu	*open / closed*
	oft	*often*

warum?	*why?*
Ich gehe . . . einkaufen.	*I go shopping . . .*
Ich habe Hunger / Durst.	*I'm hungry / thirsty.*

1 Möchten Sie **ein Glas Milch** *(a glass of milk)* oder **eine Tasse Kaffee** *(a cup of coffee)*?

2 The **Drogerie** sells over-the-counter drugs, cosmetics, and toiletries. An **Apotheke** sells prescription and non-prescription drugs.

3 ein paar Tomaten, **ein paar** Äpfel *(pl.)* BUT **etwas** Kaffee, **etwas** Butter *(sg. collective noun)*

WAS IST DAS? das Auto, Café, Sauerkraut, Spezialgeschäft; die Boutique, Medizin; romantisch, studieren

Sonntags sind die Geschäfte zu

Carolyn ist Studentin. Sie studiert ein Jahr in Regensburg. In der Studentenheim-küche° findet sie zwei Regensburger Studenten, Ursula und Peter.

CAROLYN	Guten Morgen! Mein Name ist Carolyn.	
URSULA	Freut mich. Das ist Peter, und ich heiße Ursula.	5
PETER	Guten Morgen, Carolyn! Woher kommst du?	
CAROLYN	Ich komme aus Colorado.	
PETER	Du, wir essen gerade° Frühstück°. Möchtest du eine Tasse Kaffee?	
CAROLYN	Ja, gern. Ich habe wirklich Hunger.	
URSULA	Hier hast du ein Stück Brot, etwas Butter und Marmelade.	10
CAROLYN	Danke schön!	
PETER	Etwas Milch für den Kaffee?	
CAROLYN	Ja, bitte.	
PETER	Auch ein Ei?	
CAROLYN	Nein, danke.—Mm, das Brot ist gut!—Wo gibt es hier Geschäfte?	15
URSULA	Um die Ecke° gibt es ein Lebensmittelgeschäft, eine Metzgerei° und eine Drogerie.	
CAROLYN	Prima! Ich brauche auch etwas Medizin.	
URSULA	Da findest du auch eine Apotheke.	
CAROLYN	Ist das Lebensmittelgeschäft sehr teuer?	20
PETER	Billig ist es nicht. Wir gehen oft in die Stadt, denn da findest du alles. Da gibt es Spezialgeschäfte, Supermärkte und auch Kaufhäuser.	
URSULA	Regensburg ist wirklich sehr schön. Es ist alt und romantisch, und um den Dom° gibt es viele Boutiquen.	
PETER	Ich finde die Fußgängerzone° prima, denn da gibt es keine Autos, nur Fußgänger. Da beobachte° ich gern die Leute.	25
URSULA	Du meinst° die Mädchen.	
PETER	Na und°!	
URSULA	Da gehen wir auch oft in ein Café² und essen ein Stück Kuchen.	

Margin glosses:

dorm kitchen

just now / breakfast

corner / butcher shop

cathedral
pedestrian area
watch
mean
So what!

to the	PETER	Oder wir gehen an die Donau zur° „Wurstküche", essen ein paar 30 Würstchen und trinken ein Glas Bier.
farmers	URSULA	Samstags ist Markt. Da verkaufen die Bauern° Obst, Gemüse, Eier und Blumen³. Alles ist sehr frisch.
	CAROLYN	Und wann sind die Geschäfte offen?
	URSULA	Die Kaufhäuser sind von morgens um neun bis abends um halb 35 sieben offen, donnerstags sogar bis abends um halb neun. Aber hier
out here		draußen° ist mittags von halb eins bis zwei alles zu.
	CAROLYN	Gut, dann gehe ich heute nachmittag einkaufen.
that won't work	PETER	Das geht nicht°.
	CAROLYN	Warum nicht? 40
	PETER	Heute ist Samstag. Samstags sind die Geschäfte nur bis zwei offen, und sonntags ist alles zu.
	CAROLYN	Aber nicht die Kaufhäuser, oder?
once a month	URSULA	Doch! Nur einmal im Monat° sind sie samstags bis vier offen.
	CAROLYN	Wirklich? Dann gehe ich jetzt schnell einkaufen. Danke fürs Früh- 45 stück!
	PETER	Bitte schön!

Donnerstag bis 20.30 Uhr geöffnet

ZUM TEXT

A. Was paßt wo? Find the correct places for the listed words.

Apotheke, einkaufen, Hunger, Kaffee, Kuchen, Kaufhäuser, Lebensmittelgeschäft, samstags, Studenten, Studentin

1. Carolyn ist _____ . **2.** Peter und Ursula sind auch _____ . **3.** Carolyn hat wirklich _____ . **4.** Um die Ecke gibt es ein _____ und eine _____ . **5.** Die Leute im Café essen _____ und trinken _____ . **6.** Donnerstags sind die _____ bis abends um halb neun offen. **7.** _____ sind die Geschäfte nur bis um zwei offen. **8.** Carolyn geht schnell noch *(still)* _____ .

B. Verstehen Sie? Answer according to the reading. Use **ja, nein** or **doch.**
1. Essen Peter und Ursula zum Frühstück Wurst und Käse?
2. Gibt es um die Ecke eine Apotheke?
3. Regensburg ist nicht sehr alt, nicht wahr?
4. Ist samstags Markt?
5. Verkaufen die Bauern da Kuchen und Kaffee?
6. Sind die Geschäfte samstags nicht offen?

C. Verneinen Sie die Sätze! *(Negate the sentences.)*
1. Sie möchte ein Ei.
2. Sie möchte Milch für den Kaffee.

3. Die Kaufhäuser sind samstags zu.
4. Verkauft die Drogerie Medizin?
5. Das Lebensmittelgeschäft ist billig.
6. Gibt es da Autos?
7. Die Blumen sind frisch.
8. Mittags sind die Geschäfte offen.

D. Carolyns Einkaufsliste. Consult Carolyn's shopping list where she has checked what she needs. Then complete the sentences below.

1. **Was hat sie, und was braucht sie nicht?**
   a. Carolyn hat noch etwas ＿＿＿＿ , ein paar ＿＿＿＿ und ein Stück ＿＿＿＿ .
   b. Sie braucht kein(e / en) ＿＿＿＿ .
2. **Was hat sie nicht, und was kauft sie?**
   a. Carolyn hat kein(e / en) ＿＿＿＿ .
   b. Sie kauft ein paar ＿＿＿＿ , ein Pfund ＿＿＿＿ und etwas ＿＿＿＿ .

E. Interviews
1. **Einkaufen hier.** Ask a partner about the stores in his / her native town and his / her shopping habits.
   a. Welche Geschäfte sind billig? teuer?
   b. Gibt es hier eine Fußgängerzone? Wo? Was für Kaufhäuser gibt es da?
   c. Gibt es einen Markt? Was kaufen die Leute da?
   d. Wann sind die Geschäfte offen? Sind sonntags auch alle Geschäfte zu?
   e. Gehst du gern einkaufen? Was kaufst du oft? Kaufst du oft Blumen?

Was darf's sein?
Brauchen Sie ein
paar Blumen?

2. **Einkaufen in Regensburg.** On your first day in Regensburg, you find out about shopping from a fellow student who answers your questions.

You want to know . . .
a. where stores are.   **b.** when they are open.   **c.** if the grocery store is expensive.   **d.** where the drugstore is.   **e.** if the department store is closed on Sundays.   **f.** if there is a pedestrian area.   **g.** if the city is very beautiful.   **h.** if there is a (farmers') market and when.

◆◆◆◆◆◆◆◆◆◆◆◆◆◆◆◆◆◆◆◆◆◆◆◆◆◆◆◆◆◆◆◆

Regensburg an der Donau. Die Brücke (*bridge*) ist 800 Jahre alt.

1. **Regensburg** (pop. 124,500) dates back to Roman times. This city is one of the few in Germany that was not seriously damaged during World War II, so a varied architecture spanning the centuries has survived. A tour through the old section of town reveals Romanesque, Gothic, and baroque buildings, many of which are being restored.

2. **Cafés** and **Konditoreien** are favorite places for conversation or for breaks in shopping excursions. Coffee, tea, and hot chocolate are served, along with a great variety of delicious cakes and pastries.

3. Germans are very fond of having fresh flowers in their homes. It is customary for coffee or dinner guests to bring their hosts a small gift, usually flowers.

SPRECHSITUATIONEN

Making a Purchase

Here are some useful phrases for shopping.

1. In response to offers of assistance, such as . . .

Was darf's sein?
Ja, bitte?

you may say:

Ich brauche . . .   Haben Sie . . . ?
Ich möchte . . .   Gibt es . . .?
Ich hätte gern . . . *(I'd like to*   Was kosten / kostet . . .?
have . . .)   Ich nehme . . .
Ich suche . . . *(I'm looking for . . .)*

2. After you have made a selection, you may hear the following and respond accordingly:

Sonst noch etwas?   Ja, ich brauche (auch) noch . . .
                                           Nein, danke! (Das ist alles.)

Ist das alles?   Ja, danke! (Das ist alles.)
                                           Nein, ich brauche (auch) noch . . .

After adding up the bill, the salesclerk might say:

Das macht (zusammen) . . .

When you get your change back, you may hear:

Und . . . Mark zurück *(back).*

A. Wir kaufen ein Buch. Organize the sentences below in proper sequence.
___ Ist das alles?
___ 35,— DM.
___ Ich suche ein Bilderbuch von Österreich für meinen Großvater.
___ Auf Wiedersehen!
___ Ach, es ist wirklich sehr schön!
___ Das macht dann 35 Mark.
___ Guten Tag! Was darf's sein?
___ Was kostet es?
___ Hier, wie finden Sie dieses *(this)* Buch?
___ Gut, ich nehme es.
___ Vielen Dank! Auf Wiedersehen!
___ Ja, danke.

B: In groups of two, have students complete this dialogue about shopping. They tell the salesclerk what they need, ask about prices, make their choice, and respond to the salesclerk's final question. They then reverse roles. Other stores can also be used: **Bäckerei, Buchhandlung, Kaufhaus.**

C.3: Before doing the exercise, have students write on the board the ingredients for the fruit salad: **Äpfel, Erdbeeren, Bananen, Kirschen, Zitronen- und Orangensaft, Zucker, usw.**

B. Im Lebensmittelgeschäft

x Guten Tag! was darf's sein?

y Ich brauche _____ und _____ . Was kosten / kostet _____ ?

x _____ .

y Und was kosten / kostet _____ ?

x _____ .

y Gut, dann nehme ich _____ und _____ .

x Sonst noch etwas?

y _____ .

x _____ DM, bitte!

C. Kurzgespräche

1. You want to buy a sweater in a department store. Describe to the salesclerk what you are looking for. After viewing and commenting on several items the clerk has shown you, you decide to buy one, pay for it, and leave.

2. You stop at a refreshment stand in a railways station. You're asked what you'd like. You purchase some food for your seven-hour trip. You're asked if that is all and then told what the total comes to. You pay with two fives and are told you are getting back DM _____ .

3. At the beginning of the semester you want to organize a welcome party for your new roommate. At the grocery store buy cookies, the ingredients for a fruit salad, soft drinks, etc. Always ask the clerk for the price of each item to make sure that anything you are buying is within reach of your limited budget. Try to include phrases like *half a pound, a quarter of a pound,* and *a dozen* (**ein halbes Pfund, ein Viertelpfund, ein Duzend).**

KAPITEL

3

Im Restaurant

Studenten im Café

▌LERNZIELE

Gespräche and **Wortschatz.** This chapter deals with meals and restaurants.

Struktur. You will use . . .

- verbs with vowel changes.

- the dative case.

Einblicke. Eating habits in German-speaking countries

Sprechsituationen

- Choosing and ordering a meal

- Expressing likes and dislikes

81

◆◆◆◆◆ GESPRÄCHE

Warm-ups: 1. **Was essen / trinken Sie (nicht) gern?** 2. **Was für Getränke und Lebensmittel gibt es** mit F, B, K, S, E, W? (z.B. F: Fisch). 3. **Was ist das Gegenteil von** kaufen, offen, frisch, im Süden, Westen? 4. **Was ist der Artikel von** Blume, Glas, Tasse, Markt, Geschäft, Bäckerei, Kaufhaus, Zeit, Familie, Tag, Woche, Jahr, Kleidung, Farbe? 5. **Was für Länder gibt es** in Europa? Wie heißen die Hauptstädte? Was für Sprachen sprechen welche Leute? 6. **Wie alt sind Sie?** Haben Sie Schwestern oder Brüder? Wie viele? Wie heißen sie? (Ask about other family members.)

For menu, see **Sprechsituationen,** p. 103.

Im Restaurant[1]

AXEL   Herr Ober, die Speisekarte bitte!
OBER   Hier bitte!
AXEL   Was empfehlen Sie heute?
OBER   Die Menüs sind sehr gut.
AXEL   Gabi, was nimmst du?
GABI   Ich weiß nicht. Was nimmst du?
AXEL   Ich nehme Menü eins: Schnitzel und Kartoffelsalat.
GABI   Und ich nehme Menü zwei: Rindsrouladen mit Kartoffelklößen.
OBER   Möchten Sie etwas trinken?
GABI   Ein Glas Apfelsaft, und du?
AXEL   Mineralwasser. *(Der Ober kommt mit dem Essen.)* Guten Appetit![2]
GABI   Danke, gleichfalls. Du, das schmeckt gut.
AXEL   Das Schnitzel auch.

Später

GABI   Herr Ober, wir möchten zahlen!
OBER   Ja, bitte. Alles zusammen?
GABI   Ja. Geben Sie mir die Rechnung, bitte!
AXEL   Nein, nein, nein!
GABI   Doch, Axel! Heute bezahle ich.
OBER   Also, einmal Menü eins, einmal Menü zwei, ein Apfelsaft, ein Mineralwasser, zwei Tassen Kaffee. Sonst noch etwas?
AXEL   Ja, ein Brötchen.[3]
OBER   Das macht 45,30 DM, bitte.
GABI   46,—Mark, bitte.[4]
OBER   Und vier Mark zurück. Vielen Dank!

◆◆◆◆◆◆◆◆◆◆◆◆◆◆◆◆◆◆◆◆◆◆◆◆◆◆◆◆◆◆◆

1. Many Europeans still eat the main meal at noon. It often consists of soup, meat or fish, vegetables, and a dessert. Salads are not eaten before the meal but with the main course. Europeans do not usually drink water with the meal but rather (if anything) mineral water, beer, or wine. Coffee is never served with a meal, but afterward.

2. It shows good manners to wish others a pleasant meal (**Guten Appetit!** or **Mahlzeit!**) before they begin to eat. The appropriate response is **Danke gleichfalls.**

3. There is a separate charge for any bread or roll that is not part of a particular dish.

4. A service charge (**Bedienung**) of 10 to 15 percent and 14 percent for value-added tax (**Mehrwertsteuer**) is included in the bill, but it's customary to add a small amount to round up the total. The tip (**Trinkgeld**) is given directly, not left on the table.

Fragen: 1. Wer bringt die Speisekarte? 2. Was empfiehlt der Ober? 3. Was bestellen Gabi und Axel? 4. Was trinken sie? 5. Was bringt der Ober am Ende? 6. Wer bezahlt? 7. Was essen Gabi und Axel zum Nachtisch? 8. Was kostet alles zusammen? 9. Gabi gibt (*gives*) dem Ober 50 Mark. Wieviel Geld bekommt sie zurück? 10. Wieviel Trinkgeld (*tip*) gibt Gabi dem Ober?

In the Restaurant AXEL: *Waiter, the menu, please.* WAITER: *Here you are.* AXEL: *What do you recommend today?* WAITER: *The complete dinners are very good.* AXEL: *Gabi, what are you having?* GABI: *I don't know. What are you going to have?* AXEL: *I'll take dinner number one: veal cutlet and potato salad.* GABI: *And I'll take dinner number two: stuffed beef rolls with potato dumplings.* WAITER: *Would you like to drink something?* GABI: *A glass of apple juice. And you, Axel?* AXEL: *Mineral water.* (Soon the waiter comes with the food.) *Enjoy your food!* GABI: *Thanks, the same to you. That tastes good.* AXEL: *The veal cutlet, too.*

Later GABI: *Waiter, we'd like to pay.* WAITER: *Yes. All together?* GABI: *Yes. Please give me the bill.* AXEL: *No, no, no.* GABI: *Yes, Axel. Today I'm paying.* WAITER: *Well, one menu 1, one menu 2, one apple juice, one mineral water, two cups of coffee. Anything else?* AXEL: *Yes, one roll.* WAITER: *That comes to DM 45.30 DM, please.* GABI: *[Make it] 46 marks, please.* WAITER: *And four marks back. Thank you very much.*

WORTSCHATZ 1

DAS RESTAURANT, -S *restaurant*
DAS CAFÉ, -S *café*
DIE MENSA *student cafeteria*

der			die		
der	Kellner, -	*waiter*	die	Gabel, -n	*fork*
	Ober,-			Kellnerin, -nen	*waitress*
	Löffel, -	*spoon*		Rechnung, -en	*check / bill*
	Teller, -	*plate*		Serviette, -n	*napkin*
das	Messer, -	*knife*		Speisekarte, -n	*menu*

DAS ESSEN *food, meal*

der			das		
der	Nachtisch	*dessert*	das	Eis[1]	*ice cream*
	Pfeffer	*pepper*		Salz	*salt*
	Pudding	*pudding*	die	Kartoffel, -n	*potato*
	Reis	*rice*		Nudel, -n	*noodle*
	Zucker	*sugar*		Suppe, -n	*soup*

WEITERES

Explain to students that **Herr Ober! / Fräulein!** is used to address a waiter or a waitress, while **der Kellner / die Kellnerin** and **der Ober / das Fräulein** are job descriptions.

	Herr Ober!	*Waiter!*
	Fräulein!	*Waitress!*
das	Frühstück	*breakfast*
	Mittagessen	*lunch*
	Abendessen	*supper*

zum Frühstück (Mittagessen usw.)	*for breakfast (lunch, etc.)*
Guten Appetit!	*Enjoy your meal!*
Danke gleichfalls!	*Thanks, the same to you!*
Das schmeckt (gut)!	*That tastes (good)!*
etwas (zu) / nichts (zu)	*something (to) / nothing (to)*
noch ein(e)	*another*
viel(e)[2]	*much, many*
wieviel? / wie viele?[2]	*how much? / how many?*
zu Hause / nach Hause[3]	*at home / (toward) home*
bestellen	*to order*
(be)zahlen	*to pay*
bringen	*to bring*
empfehlen	*to recommend*

1 Eis means both *ice* and *ice cream*. If you ask for **Eis** in a restaurant, you will get ice cream. Ice water is not served in German-speaking countries.

2 viel Obst *(sg., collective noun)*, **Wieviel** Obst? BUT **viele** Äpfel *(pl.)*, **Wie viele** Äpfel?

3 Ich bin **zu Hause.** BUT Ich gehe **nach Hause.** (See Struktur II.3.)

PASSIVES VOKABULAR **der Kartoffelsalat**   **der Kloß, ⸚e** *dumpling*
das Menü, -s *dinner, daily special*   **das Mineralwasser**   **das Schnitzel** *veal cutlet*
die Rindsroulade, -n *stuffed beef roll.*

Delikatessengeschäft
Dallmayr in
München

ZUM THEMA

A. Mustersätze

1. die Speisekarte: **Herr Ober,** die Speisekarte **bitte!**
   ein Glas Mineralwasser, eine Tasse Kaffee, ein Stück Kuchen, ein Eis,
   die Rechnung
2. eine Tasse: **Fräulein, ich brauche** eine Tasse.
   einen Teller, einen Löffel, ein Messer, eine Gabel
3. ein Glas Mineralwasser: **Ich möchte noch** ein Glas Mineralwasser.
   eine Tasse Kaffee, eine Tasse Tee, ein Glas Limonade, einen Teller
   Suppe
4. gut: **Das Schnitzel schmeckt** gut.
   auch gut, wunderbar, nicht schlecht, furchtbar
5. ein Eis: **Zum Nachtisch nehme ich** ein Eis.
   Schokoladenpudding, etwas Käse, ein Stück Apfelkuchen, ein paar
   Erdbeeren

B. Was paßt nicht?

1. der Teller, das Messer, die Speisekarte, die Gabel
2. das Frühstück, der Nachtisch, das Mittagessen, das Abendessen
3. das Salz, der Zucker, der Pfeffer, die Serviette
4. die Rechnung, die Kartoffeln, die Nudeln, der Reis
5. das Café, der Appetit, das Restaurant, die Mensa
6. bestellen, empfehlen, sein, bezahlen

C. Was paßt?

____	1. Die Suppe ist eiskalt.	a. Danke schön!
____	2. Der Kartoffelsalat schmeckt prima.	b. Wirklich?
____	3. Möchten Sie etwas zum Nachtisch?	c. Freut mich.
____	4. Guten Appetit!	d. Das finde ich auch.
____	5. Möchtest du nichts trinken?	e. Ja, bitte.

a. Danke schön!
b. Wirklich?
c. Freut mich.
d. Das finde ich auch.
e. Ja, bitte.
f. Ja, wirklich.
g. Doch!
h. Nein, danke.
i. Ja, sie schmeckt furchtbar.
j. Ja, gern.
k. Natürlich.
l. Danke, gleichfalls.

D: 1. ein Stück Papier, Käse, Kuchen, Brot, Fleisch, Wurst 2. ein Glas Saft, Wein, Bier, Wasser, Cola, Milch, Limonade 3. eine Tasse Kaffee, Milch, Tee 4. ein paar Wörter, Bilder, Bücher, Sätze, Fragen, Stühle, Kinder, Minuten, Äpfel, Brötchen, Eier, Bohnen, Blumen, Kartoffeln. 5. etwas Butter, Gemüse, Obst, Wurst, Salz, Zucker, Reis, Pfeffer, Marmelade, Milch, Wasser, Eis, Kaffee, Suppe, Pudding, Fleisch... 6. ein Pfund Kartoffeln, Reis, Zucker... 7. viel Kuchen, Brot, Wurst, Käse... 8. viele Äpfel, Tomaten, Eier, Plätzchen.

D. Was noch? (*What else?*) See how many items you can find for each word or phrase.

BEISPIEL: ein Stück . . .   **Ich möchte ein Stück Brot.**

1. ein Stück . . .
2. ein Glas . . .
3. eine Tasse . . .
4. ein paar . . .
5. etwas . . .
6. ein Pfund . . .
7. viel . . .
8. viele . . .

E. Persönliche Fragen. At the exit of your cafeteria a marketing specialist, who is studying what college students eat and drink, asks you to answer some questions. Work in pairs.

1. Was essen Sie zum Frühstück?
2. Trinken Sie morgens Kaffee, Tee, Milch oder Kakao? Trinken Sie Ihren Kaffee schwarz oder mit *(with)* Milch? mit oder ohne Zucker?
3. Was essen Sie gern zum Nachtisch? Essen Sie oft Nachtisch? Wann?
4. Trinken Sie Wein oder Bier? Wenn *(if)* ja, wann? Wenn nicht, was trinken Sie auf *(at)* Parties?

Leute mit wenig *(little)* Zeit gehen gern zur Imbißstube.

F. Aussprache. See also II. 22–28 in the pronunciation section of the Workbook.

1. [ü:] über, Tür, für, Frühling, Prüfung, Gemüse, südlich, grün, natürlich, müde
2. [ü] Flüsse, Würste, Stück, Müller, München, fünf, fünfundfünfzig, dünn
3. Wortpaare
    a. vier / für
    b. missen / müssen
    c. Stuhle / Stühle
    d. Mutter / Mütter
    e. fühle / fülle
    f. Goethe / Güte

STRUKTUR

1. Verbs with Vowel Changes

Some very common verbs have a STEM-VOWEL CHANGE in the SECOND and THIRD PERSON SINGULAR. These changes will be clearly noted in all vocabulary lists.

	e > i	e > ie	a > ä	au > äu
	sprechen *to speak*	**sehen** *to see*	**fahren** *to drive*	**laufen** *to walk, run*
ich	spreche	sehe	fahre	laufe
du	**sprichst**	**siehst**	**fährst**	**läufst**
er	**spricht**	**sieht**	**fährt**	**läuft**
wir	sprechen	sehen	fahren	laufen
ihr	sprecht	seht	fahrt	lauft
sie	sprechen	sehen	fahren	laufen

A few verbs in this group have additional changes:

	nehmen *to take*	**werden** *to become, get*	**essen** *to eat*	**lesen** *to read*
ich	nehme	werde	esse	lese
du	**nimmst**	**wirst**	**ißt**	**liest**
er	**nimmt**	**wird**	**ißt**	**liest**

Note that the second and third person singular forms of **essen** and **lesen** are identical (**du liest, er liest**). As you know from Chapter 1, the **du**-form of verbs with a stem ending in any s-sound (**-s, -ß, -tz, -z**) adds only a **t**-ending instead of an **-st**: lesen, du lies**t**.

You need to know the following common verbs with stem vowel changes. Only those in boldface are new; the others are being reviewed.

essen	**ißt**	*to eat*
empfehlen	**empfiehlt**	*to recommend*
fahren	**fährt**	*to drive*
geben	**gibt**	*to give*
gefallen	**gefällt**	*to please*
helfen	**hilft**	*to help*
laufen	**läuft**	*to run; walk*
lesen	**liest**	*to read*
nehmen	**nimmt**	*to take; have (food)*
sehen	**sieht**	*to see*
sprechen	**spricht**	*to speak*
tragen	**trägt**	*to carry; wear*
werden	**wird**	*to become, get*

ÜBUNGEN

A. Ersetzen Sie das Subjekt!

BEISPIEL: Der Ober trägt die Teller. (ich, ihr)   **Ich trage die Teller.**
Ihr tragt die Teller.

1. Fahren Sie zum Kaufhaus? (wir, er, ihr, du)
2. Wir nehmen Nudelsuppe. (er, ich, sie / *pl.*, du)
3. Ich werde müde. (das Kind, wir, sie / *sg.*, sie / *pl.*)
4. Sie empfehlen das Schnitzel. (der Ober, ich, du, das Fräulein)
5. Sehen Sie die Apotheke nicht? (du, ihr, er, die Leute)
6. Ich esse Käsekuchen. (wir, sie / *pl.*, er, du)
7. Sprechen Sie Deutsch? (er, du, sie / *pl.*)
8. Hilfst du heute nicht? (ihr, Sie, sie / *sg.*)
9. Lesen Sie gern Bücher? (du, ihr, er, sie / *pl.*)

B. Was tun sie? Answer logically, telling what others do. Make use of pronouns and irregular verbs.

BEISPIEL: Ich esse schnell. Und Ihr Großvater?   **Er ißt sehr langsam.**

1. Ich spreche Englisch. Und Ihre Großmutter?
2. Ich helfe gern. Und Ihr Nachbar?
3. Ich nehme Apfelstrudel. Und Gabi?
4. Ich empfehle den Schweinebraten. Und der Ober?
5. Ich laufe langsam. Und Ihr Bruder oder Ihre Schwester?
6. Ich lese gern. Und Ihre Mutter?
7. Ich fahre im Sommer nach Deutschland. Und Ihre Familie?
8. Ich sehe alles. Und Ihre Nachbarin?
9. Ich trage gern blau. Und Ihr Bruder oder Ihre Schwester?
10. Ich gebe gern Hausaufgaben. Und Ihr Englischprofessor?
11. Ich esse Käsekuchen. Und Axel?
12. Ich helfe heute nicht. Und Erika?

II. The Dative Case

The dative case has three major functions: it is the case of the INDIRECT OBJECT, it follows certain verbs, and it follows certain prepositions.

1. In English the INDIRECT OBJECT is indicated in two ways:

   ▪ with a preposition: *The boy gives the plate **to the father.***

   ▪ through word order: *The boy gives **the father** the plate.*

   In German this function is expressed through case form and word order. One finds the indirect object by asking for whom or in reference to whom (or occasionally what) the action of the verb is taking place.

Der Junge gibt **dem Vater** den Teller.   *The boy gives the father the plate.*

Point out that students
have already used the
dative forms of **ich**
(**mir**) and **Sie** (**Ihnen**).

a. The dative form of the INTERROGATIVE PRONOUN is **wem** *(to whom)*.

	persons	things and ideas
nom.	wer?	was?
acc.	wen?	was?
dat.	**wem?**	—

Wem gibt der Junge den
Teller? **Dem Vater.**

*To whom does the boy give the plate? To
the father.*

b. The dative forms of the DEFINITE and INDEFINITE ARTICLE are as follows:

	singular			plural
	masc.	neut.	fem.	
nom.	der ein kein	das ein kein	die eine keine	die — keine
acc.	den einen keinen			
dat.	dem einem keinem	dem einem keinem	der einer keiner	den — keinen

Der Ober empfiehlt dem Vater, der Mutter und den Kindern das Schnitzel. Er bringt dem Kind einen Löffel, aber er gibt einem Kind kein Messer und keine Gabel.

- The POSSESSIVE ADJECTIVES **mein, dein,** and **Ihr** follow the pattern of **ein** and **kein**:

  Was empfiehlt er Ihr**em** Vater und Ihr**er** Mutter?
  Er empfiehlt mein**em** Vater und mein**er** Mutter den Fisch.

The dative pl. **n**-ending
needs a lot of practice.
Give students familiar
nouns; have them give
you the dative pl. form
in short sentences.

- In the dative plural all nouns add an **-n** ending, unless the plural form already ends in **-n** or **-s**.

  die Väter / den Väter**n**   BUT die Eltern / den Eltern
  die Kinder / den Kinder**n**   die Mädchen / den Mädche**n**
  die Äpfel / den Äpfel**n**   die Kulis / den Kulis

- N-nouns also have an **-n** or **-en** ending in the dative singular, as they do in the accusative singular: Das Eis schmeckt dem Student**en**.

Such verbs include **bringen, empfehlen, geben, kaufen, öffnen, sagen, schreiben, verkaufen.** Point out that the verbs listed here can have two objects in English, too. Give English sample sentences and have students identify the dative and the accusative object.

c. Many verbs can have both accusative and dative objects. Note that the direct object is usually a thing and the indirect object a person.

Der Ober bringt dem Kind den Kuchen.	*The waiter brings the child the cake.*
Er empfiehlt der Studentin den Fisch.	*He recommends the fish to the student.*

Note the difference in meaning:

Der Onkel trägt der Tante die Lebensmittel. BUT Der Onkel trägt die Tante.

d. In sentences with two objects, the direct object, if it is a noun, generally follows the indirect object.

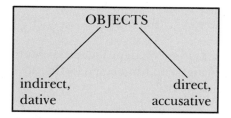

OBJECTS

indirect, dative   direct, accusative

Die Kellnerin bringt dem Herrn den Tee.

2. Dative Verbs
Some verbs take only dative objects, such as:

Warn students that **antworten** is used with a dative if the answer is given to a *person*. They should not try to use "letter" or "questions" as the dative object.

antworten	*to answer*	**gehören**	*to belong to*
danken	*to thank*	helfen	*to help*
gefallen	*to please*		

Der Bruder antwortet der Schwester.	*The brother answers (gives an answer to) the sister.*
Alex dankt dem Kellner.	*Alex thanks (gives thanks to) the waiter.*
Die Mensa gefällt den Studenten.	*The students like the cafeteria (the cafeteria pleases the students).*
Der Mantel gehört dem Mädchen.	*The coat belongs to the girl.*
Ich helfe dem Nachbarn.	*I'm helping (giving help to) the neighbor.*

3. Dative Prepositions

These prepositions are always followed by the dative case:

Point out that **nach Hause** does not follow the rule that "**nach** is used for cities, countries, continents."

aus	*out of* *from (a place of origin)*	Sie kommt aus dem Geschäft. Er kommt aus Berlin.
außer	*besides*	Außer dem Café ist alles zu.
bei	*at (for)* *near* *at the home of*	Sie arbeitet bei VW. Die Drogerie ist bei der Buchhandlung. Er wohnt bei Familie Angerer.
mit	*with* *together with*	Ich schreibe mit einem Kuli. Alex kommt mit Gabi.
nach	*after (time)* *to (cities, countries,* *continents)* *to (used idiomatically)*	Kommst du nach dem Mittagessen? Fahrt ihr auch nach Österreich? Gehen Sie nach Hause!
seit	*since* *for (time)*	Sie wohnen seit Mai in Bonn. Sie wohnen seit drei Tagen da.[1]
von	*of* *from* *by*	Das Gegenteil von billig ist teuer. Wir fahren von Berlin nach Hamburg. Das Bild ist von Albrecht Dürer.
zu	*to (in the direction of)* *at (used idiomatically)* *for (purpose)*	Sie fährt zum Supermarkt. Sie sind zu Hause. Was gibt es zum Nachtisch?

[1] **seit** translates as *for* in English when it expresses duration of time (three minutes, one year) that began in the past and still continues in the present: *They have been living there for three days.*

- In everyday speech, some of these prepositions may be contracted with the definite article.

bei + dem = **beim**   zu + dem = **zum**
von + den = **vom**   zu + der = **zur**

- Pay particular attention to the contrasting use of these pairs of prepositions:

Sie fährt **zum** (*to the*) Supermarkt.   Fahrt ihr **nach** (*to*) Deutschland?
Wir fahren **von** (*from*) Salzburg nach   Er kommt **aus** (*from*) Salzburg.
München.
Gehen Sie **nach** Hause (*home*)!   Sie sind nicht **zu** Hause (*at home*).

ÜBUNGEN

C. Sagen Sie die Sätze im Plural! Restate in the plural the phrases in boldface.

BEISPIEL: Wir sprechen mit **dem Kanadier.**
               Wir sprechen mit den Kanadiern.

1. Er lernt seit **einem Jahr** Deutsch. (drei)
2. Das Restaurant gehört **dem Schweizer.**
3. Sie kommen aus **dem Geschäft.**
4. Der Bleistift liegt bei **dem Buch.**
5. Nach **einem Monat** bezahlt er die Rechnung. (zwei)
6. Ich gehe nur mit **dem Kind.**
7. Die Stadt gefällt **dem Amerikaner.**
8. Sie gibt **dem Engländer** eine Landkarte.
9. Die Löffel liegen bei **dem Teller.**
10. Die Kellnerin kommt mit **der Serviette.**

D. Ersetzen Sie das Dativobjekt!

BEISPIEL: Der Kellner bringt dem Kind ein Eis. (Großvater)
            Der Kellner bringt dem Großvater ein Eis.

1. Die Kellnerin empfiehlt dem Vater die Rouladen. (Bruder, Spanier, Schweizer)
2. Der Junge gibt der Mutter ein Bild. (Schwester, Studentin, Frau)
3. Der Ober bringt den Eltern das Essen. (Leute, Amerikaner / *pl.*, Studenten / *pl.*)
4. Die Drogerie gehört meiner Großmutter. (Großvater, Eltern, Familie)
5. Axel dankt dem Bruder. (Schwester, Vater, Leute)
6. Meine Großmutter hilft meinem Vater. (Mutter, Schwestern, Brüder)

E. Sagen Sie es noch einmal! Replace the nouns following the prepositions with the words suggested.

BEISPIEL: Eva geht zum Lebensmittelgeschäft. (Apotheke)
   Eva geht zur Apotheke.

1. Paula kommt aus dem Kaufhaus. (Drogerie, Café, Mensa)
2. Seit Sonntag ist er wieder hier. (zwei Tage, eine Stunde, ein Monat)
3. Wir gehen mit dem Großvater. (Frau, Fräulein, Großeltern)
4. Ich wohne bei meinen Eltern. (Bruder, Schwester, Familie)
5. Er möchte etwas Salat zu den Rouladen. (Schnitzel, Suppe, Würstchen / *pl.*, Fleisch)
6. Das Café ist bei der Apotheke. (Kaufhaus, Lebensmittelgeschäft, Drogerie)
7. Nach dem Mittagessen spielen sie Tennis. (Frühstück, Kaffee, Deutschstunde)
8. Außer meinem Bruder sind alle hier. (Vater, Mutter, Nachbar, Studentin)

F. Wer, wem oder was? At your son's graduation party you are talking to a friend. Because of the loud music, he / she can't hear what you are saying.

BEISPIEL: Oskar gibt dem Bruder die Bücher.
   Wer gibt dem Bruder die Bücher?—Oskar!
   Wem gibt Oskar die Bücher?—Dem Bruder!
   Was gibt Oskar dem Bruder?—Die Bücher?

1. Der Nachbar verkauft Onkel Willi den Volkswagen.
2. Onkel Willi gibt dem Jungen den Volkswagen.
3. Großmutter empfiehlt Irene ein paar Tage Ferien (*vacation*).
4. Die Kinder zahlen der Mutter die Hotelrechnung.

G. Was gehört wem? You and some friends are unpacking your family's boxes after a move. Tell what belongs to whom.

BEISPIEL: Wem gehört die Krawatte?   **Sie gehört meinem Bruder.**

das Familienbild	gehört	mein Bruder
die Kochbücher (*cook . . .*)	gehören	meine Schwester
das Taschenmesser (*pocket . . .*)		meine Mutter
die Teller und Tassen		mein Vater
das Sporthemd		mein Großvater
die Hausschuhe		meine Großmutter
die Tennishose		
die Winterpullover		
die Golduhr		
die Ringe (*pl., rings*)		
die Landkarten		
das Bilderbuch		
die Jacken		
die Gläser		
der Mantel		
das Deutschbuch		

H. Was gefällt wem?

1. Ersetzen Sie das Dativobjekt!
   a. Das Restaurant gefällt dem Onkel. (Tante, Großmutter, Kinder, Student, Studentin, Studenten)
   b. Aber die Preise gefallen der Familie nicht. (Frau, Leute, Nachbar, Herren)
2. Auf deutsch, bitte!
   a. Ms. Bayer likes the country.   **b.** My father likes the city.   **c.** My mother likes the South.   **d.** My sister likes the lakes.   **e.** My brothers like the mountains.   **f.** My grandparents like the student.   **g.** The student likes my grandparents.   **h.** I like German (**mir**).

I: Preferably with books open.

I. Was kaufen wir wem?

The Christmas season is approaching, and you and your roommate are coming up with ideas for presents. Working with a classmate, form sentences using one word from each list. Follow the model.

BEISPIEL: Mutter / das Kochbuch, ¨er
Meiner Mutter gefallen Kochbücher.
Prima! Ich kaufe meiner Mutter ein Kochbuch.

1. Bruder, Schwester, Mutter, Vater, Großeltern, Onkel, Tante, Freund *(friend)*, Freundin
2.

die Blumenvase, -n	die Kassette, -n	der Pullover, -
die Bluse, -n	die Kette, -n *(necklace)*	der Ring, -e
das Buch, ¨er	die Krawatte, -n *(tie)*	die Tasche, -n *(handbag)*
der Kalender, -	das Portemonnaie, -s *(wallet)*	das Taschenmesser, - *(pocket . . .)*

J. nach Hause oder zu Hause?

1. Heute essen wir _____ .
2. Ich habe die Bilder _____ .
3. Jürgen kommt oft spät _____ .
4. Ich lese das Buch _____ .
5. Bringst du die Großeltern _____ ?
6. Geht ihr um sechs _____ ?
7. Er ist jetzt nicht _____ .

ZUSAMMENFASSUNG

K: Discuss synthetic exercises. Tell students that they'll have to add articles to the key words given in order to make complete sentences (books open). This exercise can also be done in writing.

K. Bilden Sie Sätze!

BEISPIEL: das / sein / für / Onkel   **Das ist für den Onkel.**

1. Ober / kommen / mit / Speisekarte
2. Mutter / kaufen / Kind / Apfelsaft
3. Fräulein / empfehlen / Studentin / Apfelkuchen
4. er / sehen / Großvater / nicht
5. kommen / du / von / Mensa?
6. Familie / fahren / nicht / nach Berlin

L. Guten Appetit! Was fehlt?

1. Zu_____ Essen braucht man ein_____ Messer und ein_____ Gabel. **2.** Suppe ißt man mit ein_____ Eßlöffel (tablespoon), und für d_____ Kaffee braucht man ein_____ Kaffeelöffel. **3.** Wir haben kein_____ Messer, kein_____ Gabel und kein_____ Löffel (sg.). **4.** Gibt es hier kein_____ Salz und kein_____ Pfeffer? **5.** Doch, d_____ Salz steht bei d_____ Pfeffer. **6.** Jetzt habe ich alles außer ein_____ Speisekarte. **7.** Der Ober empfiehlt d_____ Studentin d_____ Schweinebraten (m.) **8.** Nach d_____ Essen bringt er ein_____ Eis und ein_____ Kaffee. **9.** D_____ Restaurant gefällt d_____ Studenten (pl.). **10.** Aber sie haben etwas gegen d_____ Preise. **11.** Wir sprechen von d_____ Professor und von d_____ Prüfung. **12.** Ich bestelle noch ein_____ Cola. **13.** Hier trinke ich d_____ Cola aus ein_____ Glas, aber zu Hause aus ein_____ Flasche (f., bottle). **14.** Da kommt der Ober mit d_____ Rechnung. **15.** Ohne d_____ Rechnung geht's nicht. **16.** Danke für d_____ Mittagessen!

M. In der Mensa. Auf deutsch, bitte!

1. We're going through the cafeteria with the students. **2.** They're from Hamburg. They're Hamburgers. **3.** Paul lives with (at the home of) a family, and Helga lives at home. **4.** Helga, what are you having? **5.** I'll take the roast (**der Braten**), peas and carrots, and a glass of juice. **6.** Would you (formal) like a piece of cake for dessert? **7.** No, I'm not eating any cake because it's fattening (**dick machen**). **8.** I have no knife, no fork, and no spoon. **9.** Paul brings the student (f.) a knife, a fork, a spoon, and (some) ice cream. **10.** Whose ice cream is that? (To whom does the ice cream belong?) **11.** Would you (fam.) like some ice cream with a cookie? **12.** She thanks the student. **13.** Who's paying for (the) lunch?

M: 1. Wir gehen mit den Studenten durch die Mensa. 2. Sie sind aus Hamburg. Sie sind Hamburger. 3. Paul wohnt bei einer Familie, und Helga wohnt zu Hause. 4. Helga, was nimmst du? 5. Ich nehme den Braten, Erbsen und Karotten und ein Glas Saft. 6. Möchten Sie ein Stück Kuchen zum Nachtisch? 7. Nein, ich esse keinen Kuchen, denn das macht dick. 8. Ich habe kein Messer, keine Gabel und keinen Löffel. 9. Paul bringt der Studentin ein Messer, eine Gabel, einen Löffel und etwas Eis. 10. Wem gehört das Eis? 11. Möchtest du etwas Eis mit einem Plätzchen? 12. Sie dankt dem Studenten. 13. Wer bezahlt das Mittagessen?

LERNTIP

Reviewing for Tests

If you have taken full advantage of all class sessions, kept up with your work and reviewed regularly, you should not have to spend much time preparing for tests. Concentrate on the areas that give you the most trouble. Use the "Rückblicke" for efficient reviewing. Go over the vocabulary lists of the chapters that will be covered by the test; make sure you know genders and plurals of nouns. Mark any words you seem to have trouble remembering; review them again. Begin your review early enough so that you can clear up any questions with your instructor.

EINBLICKE ◆◆◆◆◆◆◆◆◆◆

Heidelberger Studentenrestaurant. Nicht nur Studenten essen hier.

"Food and drink are the glue that holds body and soul together," claims an old Viennese saying. The sentiment is popular in all of the German-speaking countries.

German cooking has many regional specialties. In addition to excellent hams and sausages, there are numerous fish dishes, such as Helgoland lobster, Hamburg eel soup, or Black Forest trout. Some of the regional meat dishes include **Sauerbraten, Kasseler Rippchen** (*smoked loin of pork*), or Bavarian **Leberkäse** (*meat loaf made from minced pork*). In the South dumplings and pasta dishes (e.g., **Spätzle**) are popular. Germany also boasts a large variety of pastries, such as **Schwarzwälder Kirschtorte** or **Frankfurter Kranz** (*a rich cake ring decorated with whipped cream and nuts*).

Most famous among Austrian dishes are **Schnitzel, Gulasch,** and a variety of salted and smoked meats, as well as dumplings. But desserts like **Strudel, Palatschinken** (*dessert crêpes*), or **Sachertorte** delight visitors even more. Swiss cooking has also developed many specialties of its own, such as **Geschnetzeltes** (*minced veal in a cream sauce*), **Berner Platte** (*dish with a variety of hams and sausages*), or **Röschti** (*fried potatoes with bacon cubes*). The most famous Swiss dish is probably the cheese fondue (**Käsefondue**), a reminder that Switzerland produces a great variety of excellent cheeses (e.g., **Schweizer Käse, Gruyère, Emmentaler, Appenzeller**).

WORTSCHATZ 2

der	Freund, -e	*(boy)friend*
die	Freundin, -nen	*(girl)friend*
	Flasche, -n; eine Flasche . . .	*bottle; a bottle of. . .*
	Hand, ¨e	*hand*

besonders	*especially*
dann	*then*
gewöhnlich	*usual(ly)*
man	*one (they, people)*
manchmal	*sometimes*
nicht nur . . . sondern auch	*not only . . . but also*
überall	*everywhere*
vielleicht	*perhaps*
schlafen (schläft)	*to sleep*

WAS IST DAS? der Kaffeeklatsch, Kakao; das Büro, Joghurt, Omelett; die Bratwurst, Großstadt, Hand, Schule, Spezialität, Kartoffelchips *(pl.)*; interessant, lokal, relativ, voll

Man ist, was man ißt

Die Deutschen, Österreicher und Schweizer beginnen den Tag gewöhnlich mit einem guten Frühstück. Zum Frühstück gibt es Brot oder Brötchen, Butter, Marmelade, vielleicht auch ein Ei, etwas Wurst oder Käse und manchmal auch etwas Joghurt. Dazu° trinkt man Kaffee, Milch, Tee oder Kakao.

Mittags ißt man warm. Um die Zeit sind die Schulen aus[1], und die Kinder   5
kommen zum Mittagessen nach Hause. Manche° Geschäfte und Büros machen mittags zu. Viele Leute essen mittags zu Hause. Andere° gehen nicht

company cafeteria

chicken
fresh eel in herb sauce
pig's knuckles / dumplings

no matter
special / when / try / once
right
left
sit / at the / this way

little / snack bar
shish kebab / usually
better than
most
comfortably
chat

nach Hause, sondern in die Kantine° oder in ein Restaurant.

Im Restaurant gibt es gewöhnlich ein Tagesmenü. Das ist oft besonders gut und billig. Außer Bratwurst, Omelett oder Hühnchen° findet man natürlich auch lokale Spezialitäten, wie zum Beispiel Berliner Aal grün° oder in Bayern Schweinshax'n° mit Knödeln°. Zum Mittagessen trinkt man gern Saft, Mineralwasser, Bier oder Wein, aber kein Wasser und auch keinen Kaffee. Den (Kaffee) trinkt man manchmal nach dem Essen! Egal° wo, überall findet man etwas Besonderes°. Wenn° Sie in Europa sind, probieren° Sie mal° so eine Spezialität! Nehmen Sie auch das Messer in die rechte° Hand und die Gabel in die linke° Hand, und dann Guten Appetit! Noch etwas: Manchmal sitzen° auch andere Leute bei Ihnen am° Tisch². So° gibt es hier und da interessante Gespräche. Fürs Mittagessen braucht man gewöhnlich Zeit. Leute mit wenig° Zeit gehen gern zu einer Imbißstube°. Da gibt es Bratwurst, Fischbrötchen oder Schaschlik°. In Großstädten finden Sie meistens° auch McDonald's. Schnell essen ist manchmal besser als° nichts, aber ein Mittagessen ist das für die meisten° Leute nicht.

Nachmittags sieht man viele Menschen in Cafés³. Sie sitzen gemütlich° bei einer Tasse Kaffee und reden°. Kaffeeklatsch gibt es aber nicht nur im Café, sondern auch zu Hause. Besonders sonntags kommt man oft mit Freunden zusammen zu einer Tasse Kaffee und einem Stück Kuchen.

10

15

20

25

Eine Tasse Kaffee und ein Stück Kuchen schmecken wunderbar.

stomach

pickles

pretzel sticks

Abends ißt man gewöhnlich kalt und nicht so viel wie mittags. Man sagt: Mit einem vollen Bauch° schläft man schlecht. Was man abends ißt, macht dick. So gibt es nur etwas Brot mit Käse, Wurst oder Fisch, ein paar Tomaten oder saure Gurken°. Dazu gibt es vielleicht eine Tasse Tee oder ein Bier. Abends öffnet man auch gern eine Flasche Wein⁴ für Freunde. Dazu gibt es Salzstangen° oder Kartoffelchips.

30

Den meisten Deutschen, Österreichern und Schweizern ist wichtig, was
sie essen. Wie bei uns° essen sie relativ viel Obst, Salat und Gemüse. Auch   35
haben sie etwas gegen Farbstoffe° und Konservierungsmittel°. Sie wissen°:
,,Man ist, was man ißt."

as we do here

artificial colors / preserva-
tives / know

Students may need
some help with the vo-
cabulary on the poster.

Richtig oder falsch?
1. Zum Frühstück ißt
man oft Brötchen mit
Butter und Marmelade.
(R) 2. Mittags essen
viele zu Hause. (R)
3. Viele Restaurants ha-
ben gewöhnlich Tages-
menüs. (R) 4. Beim
Essen nimmt man die
Gabel in die rechte
Hand und das Messer
in die linke Hand. (F)
5. Nachmittags sieht
man viele Leute in
Cafés. (R) 6. Sonntags
kommt man gern mit
Geschäftsleuten zum
Kaffeeklatsch zusam-
men. (F) 7. Abends ißt
man gewöhnlich kalt.
(R) 8. Abends öffnet
man auch gern eine
Flasche Wein für
Freunde. (R) 9. Aber
oft gibt es abends nur
Brot und Wasser. (F)
10. Die Deutschen es-
sen zu viel Obstsalat.
(F) 11. Sie haben et-
was gegen Konservie-
rungsmittel. (R)
12. Aber Farbstoffe
finden sie o.k. (F)

ZUM TEXT

A. Welche Antwort paßt? Indicate the correct answer according to the text.
1. Zum Frühstück gibt es . . . .
   a. Sauerbraten
   b. Kuchen und Plätzchen
   c. viel Obst und Gemüse
   d. Brot, Butter und Marmelade
2. Mittags essen die Schulkinder . . . .
   a. in der Schule
   b. zu Hause
   c. im Restaurant
   d. etwas Besonderes
3. Zum Mittagessen trinkt man gern . . . .
   a. Kaffee, Milch oder Tee
   b. Eiswasser
   c. Mineralwasser, Bier oder Wein
   d. Cola
4. Zum Abendessen ißt man gewöhnlich . . . .
   a. Kaffee und Kuchen
   b. Brot, Wurst, Käse und Fisch
   c. Suppe, Fleisch und Gemüse
   d. Salzstangen und Kartoffelchips
5. Die Deutschen, Österreicher und Schweizer essen . . . Obst und
   Gemüse.
   a. wenig
   b. kein
   c. nur
   d. viel

B. Guten Appetit! Was fehlt?

1. Ich beginne den Tag gewöhnlich mit ein____ guten Frühstück: mit ein____ Brötchen, ein____ Ei und ein____ Tasse Tee.   **2.** Gehst du mittags ____ Hause?   **3.** Ja, ____ Hause ist es nicht so teuer.   **4.** Bei d____ Preisen (pl.) esse ich gern ____ Hause.   **5.** Warum gehst du nicht zu____ Mensa?   **6.** D____ Essen schmeckt nicht.   **7.** Manchmal gehe ich zu ein____ Imbißstube (f.).   **8.** Dann esse ich nichts außer ein____ Bratwurst, und die Cola trinke ich schnell aus d____ Flasche.   **9.** Oft habe ich kein____ Hunger.   **10.** Dann esse ich nur ein____ Apfel oder ein____ Banane.   **11.** Möchtest du etwas Brot mit ein____ Stück Käse?   **12.** Es ist von d____ Reformhaus (n., health-food store) und hat kein____ Konservierungsmittel (pl.)!

C. Vergleichen Sie! With a classmate make two lists that compare German and North American food and drink preferences.

	in den deutschsprachigen Ländern	in Nordamerika
zum Frühstück		
ißt man		
trinkt man		
zum Mittagessen		
ißt man		
trinkt man		
zum Abendessen		
ißt man		
trinkt man		

D. Schreiben Sie! Write eight to ten sentences, describing your eating habits, i.e., when you eat, what you eat and drink at various meals, and what you like and dislike.

E. Käsefondue für vier bis sechs Personen

500 g° geriebener° Gruyère- und Emmentalerkäse
etwas Knoblauch°
1/2 1° leichter° Weißwein

2 Teelöffel Kartoffelmehl°
2 Teelöffel Kirsch°
etwas Salz, Pfeffer und Muskat°
Weißbrotwürfel°

Den Fonduetopf° innen° mit Knoblauch ausreiben°. Den Wein hineingeben° und langsam erwärmen°. Den Käse dazugeben° und unter Rühren° schmelzen lassen° und zum Kochen° bringen (ungefähr 5 Minuten). Das Kartoffelmehl mit dem Kirsch kombiniert daruntermischen°. Das Fondue ist jetzt cremig° dick. Mit Salz, Pfeffer und Muskat würzen°. Das Fondue zusammen mit den Brotwürfeln servieren. Beim Essen Würfel mit der Gabel in das Fondue tauchen°. Guten Appetit!

Optional vocabulary: der Honig, Hamburger, -, Krapfen, -, donut; Schinken ham; Senf mustard; Speck bacon; Pfannkuchen, -, Toast, -s; das Müsli, Rührei, -er scrambled egg; Spiegelei, -er fried egg; ein gekochtes Ei boiled egg, ein belegtes Brötchen open-faced sandwich; (pl.) die Cornflakes, Haferflocken oatmeal; Waffeln

E: You can also say die Fondue.

4 cups / grated / potato starch
cherry brandy
garlic / nutmeg
2 cups / light / . . . bite-size pieces
. . .pot / inside / rub / pour in
heat / add / stirring
let melt / boil
blend in
creamy / season

dip into

Schweizer Fondue
schmeckt besonders
gut.

Übrigens

1. In Germany and Austria schools generally let out between 12 noon and 1:30 pm; children usually eat their main meal at home after school. The afternoons are for homework and play. In Switzerland children attend school from 8 to 12 and from 2 to 4, but Wednesday and Saturday afternoons are free.

2. Unlike in America, German restaurants normally don't have hostesses to greet and seat you. Instead you look for a free table yourself. If the restaurant is crowded and no other table is available, people share a table with others. Courtesy, however, requires that you first ask permission of those already seated before joining them (**Entschuldigen Sie, ist hier noch frei?**).

3. In Austria, many people have a favorite café **(das Kaffeehaus),** where they can relax over such items as **Kaffee mit Schlag** *(coffee with whipped cream)* or a piece of **Linzertorte.** The tradition of the coffee house goes back to the early 1900s, when it was the preferred meeting place not only of the literati, reformers, artists, and philosophers, but also of middle-class society.

4. German wines are produced mainly in western and southwestern Germany. The Rhine and Moselle **(Mosel)** rivers have given their names to two great wines famous throughout the world. The Swiss, too, love wine, which is for them what beer is to a Bavarian. Out of 23 cantons 18 grow wine. In Austria there are excellent vineyards along the Danube around Vienna. Wines are classified as **Tafelwein** *(table or ordinary wine)*, **Qualitätswein** *(quality wine)*, and **Qualitätswein mit Prädikat** *(superior wine)*. A wine's classification and vintage year reflect its quality.

SPRECHSITUATIONEN

Choosing and Ordering a Meal

To order a meal, you can use the following expressions:

Herr Ober / Fräulein, die (Speise)karte, bitte!
Ich möchte bestellen.
Was empfehlen Sie?
Was ist heute besonders gut?

Ich nehme . . .
Ich möchte . . .
Ich hätte gern . . . *(I'd like to have . . .)*
Bringen Sie mir bitte . . . !

To request the bill, you should say:

Herr Ober / Fräulein, ich möchte (be)zahlen!
Zahlen, bitte!
Die Rechnung, bitte!

Expressing Likes and Dislikes

1. Likes

   Ich esse / trinke gern . . .
   Ich finde . . . gut.
   . . . schmeckt wunderbar.
   . . . ist prima.
   . . . gefällt mir.
   Wie gefällt Ihnen / dir . . .

2. Dislikes

   Ich esse / trinke nicht gern . . .
   Ich finde . . . nicht gut.
   . . . schmeckt nicht gut (furchtbar).
   . . . ist zu heiß / kalt, teuer, usw.
   . . . gefällt mir nicht.

NOTE: **gefallen** is usually not used to talk about food, but rather when you want to say that a city, a picture, an item of clothing, or a person is pleasing to you. **schmecken** is used with food and beverages.

A. Im Ratskeller

Ratskeller

Tagesmenü:	I Nudelsuppe, Schnitzel und Kartoffelsalat, Eis	DM 15,20
	II Gemüsesuppe, Rindsrouladen mit Kartoffelklößen, Eis	18,25

Tagesspezialitäten:

Bratwurst und Sauerkraut	9,50
Omelett mit Schinken°, Salat	11,00
Kalbsleber°, Erbsen und Karotten, Pommes frites	13,50
Sauerbraten°, Kartoffelbrei°, Salat	15,40
Schweinebraten°, Kartoffelbrei, Salat	16,75
Hühnchen° mit Weinsoße°, Reis, Salat	18,70
Gemischte Fischplatte, Kartoffeln, Salat	20,00

Suppen:

Tomatensuppe, Erbsensuppe, Bohnensuppe, Kartoffelsuppe	3,50

Salate:

Grüner Salat, Tomatensalat, Gurkensalat°, Bohnensalat	3,50

Getränke°:

Apfelsaft	2,75	Bier (0,2 l)[1]	2,40
Limonade	2,75	Wein (0,2 l)	3,20
Tee	3,00	Mineralwasser	1,80
Kaffee	3,50		

Zum Nachtisch:

Schokoladenpudding	2,40	Käsekuchen	3,55
Vanilleeis	2,50	Apfelstrudel	3,80
Frische Erdbeeren	3,25	Erdbeerkuchen	3,90
Schlagsahne	-,70	Kirschtorte°	4,10

(margin glosses)
ham
calves' liver
marinated pot roast / mashed . . .
pork . . .
chicken / . . .sauce

cucumber . . .

beverages

cherry cake

Optional practice:
1. Was hat Menü eins? Menü zwei? Was haben die Menüs zum Nachtisch? 2. Was für Suppen gibt es? was für Salate? was für Getränke? 3. Was kostet eine Tasse Kaffee? ein Glas Apfelsaft? ein Teller Suppe? ein Salat? 4. Was finden Sie besonders gut / nicht gut auf der Speisekarte?

1. **Wir möchten bestellen!** In groups of two to five students, take turns ordering from the menu.
2. **Zahlen, bitte!** Ask for the check. Tell the server what you had, e.g. **einmal Bratwurst . . .,** and let him / her figure out what you owe. Round up your bill to include an appropriate tip.

1 A liter is a little more than a quart. 0,2 l therefore is approximately three-fourths of a cup.

B. Wie gefällt dir das? In pairs, ask each other about three likes and three dislikes, using various expressions, e.g., **gern** + verb, **gefallen, schmecken, finden.** You might ask about people, places, restaurants, food and beverages, and so on.

BEISPIEL: Wie gefällt es dir hier? Was schmeckt dir besonders gut? Was für Obst ißt du gern? Wie findest du Fisch? usw.

C. Kurzgespräche

1. You are in a Bavarian restaurant. The server asks what you would like, and you ask what he / she recommends. He / she says that today the pork roast is very good. You order potato soup, pork roast, and cucumber salad. The server asks what you'd like to drink. You order a mineral water.

2. You have just met another student in the cafeteria for the first time and ask how he / she likes it here. Very much, he / she says. The other student asks you if the soup tastes good. You say it is not bad, but too hot. You ask how your fellow student likes the chicken. You are told it doesn't taste particularly good and it is cold. You say the food is usually cold.

300
Jahre Wiener
Kaffeehaus

RÜCKBLICK

I. Verbs

This section gives a periodic summary of what has been introduced in the preceding chapters. It is intended for reference and as a preparation for quizzes, tests, and finals. The first part sums up points of structure, and the second part practices familiar structures and vocabulary. For additional practice, there are also review exercises in the Workbook. Remind students of the verb charts in the Appendix.

1. Forms: PRESENT TENSE

   a. Most verbs inflect like **danken:**

singular	plural
ich dank**e**	wir dank**en**
du dank**st**	ihr dank**t**
er dank**t**	sie dank**en**

   b. Verbs whose stem ends in **-d, -t,** or certain consonant combinations inflect like **antworten,** e.g., finden, kosten, öffnen, regnen.

singular	plural
ich antworte	wir antworten
du antwort**est**	ihr antwort**et**
er antwort**et**	sie antworten

   c. Some verbs have vowel changes in the second and third person singular, e.g., gefallen, tragen; essen, geben, helfen, nehmen, werden; empfehlen, lesen.

	a > ä **fahren**	au > äu **laufen**	e > i **sprechen**	e > ie **sehen**
ich	fahre	laufe	spreche	sehe
du	**fährst**	**läufst**	**sprichst**	**siehst**
er	**fährt**	**läuft**	**spricht**	**sieht**

   d. Some verbs are irregular in form:

	haben	**sein**	**werden**	**essen**	**nehmen**
ich	habe	**bin**	werde	esse	nehme
du	**hast**	**bist**	**wirst**	ißt	**nimmst**
er	**hat**	**ist**	**wird**	ißt	**nimmt**
wir	haben	**sind**	werden	essen	nehmen
ihr	**habt**	**seid**	werdet	**eßt**	nehmt
sie	haben	**sind**	werden	essen	nehmen

2. Usage

   a. German has only one verb to express what English says with several forms:

   Er antwortet meinem Vater.
   { *He answers my father.*
   { *He's answering my father.*
   { *He does answer my father.*

   b. The present tense occasionally expresses future time.

   Im Mai fährt sie nach Bonn.   *She's going to Bonn in May.*
   She'll go to Bonn in May.

II. Nouns and Pronouns

1. You have learned three of the four German cases.

   a. The NOMINATIVE is the case of the subject:

   Da kommt **der Ober. Er** bringt das Essen.

   It is also used for PREDICATE NOUNS following the linking verbs **heißen, sein,** and **werden.**

   Der Herr **heißt** Oskar Meyer.
   Er **ist**   Wiener.
   Er **wird**   Vater.

   b. The ACCUSATIVE is the case of the direct object:

   Wir fragen **den Freund.** Wir fragen **ihn.**

   It follows these prepositions: durch, für, gegen, ohne, um

   c. The DATIVE is the case of the indirect object:

   Rotkäppchen *(Little Red Riding Hood)* bringt **der Großmutter** den Wein. Es bringt **ihr** den Wein.

   It follows these prepositions: aus, außer, bei, mit, nach, seit, von, zu

   It also follows these verbs: antworten, danken, gefallen, gehören, helfen.

   Nouns in the dative plural have an **-n** ending unless the plural ends in **-s:**

   die Freunde / den Freunde**n**   BUT   die Kulis / den Kulis

   d. N-NOUNS. Some masculine nouns have an **-n** or **-en** ending in all cases (singular and plural) except in the nominative singular.

der Herr, **-n**, -en   der Nachbar, **-n**, -n
der Junge, **-n,** -n   der Student, **-en**, -en
der Mensch, **-en,** -en

Der Junge fragt den Nachbar**n**. Der Nachbar antwortet dem Jung**en**.

2. These are the case forms of the DEFINITE and INDEFINITE ARTICLES.

		singular		plural
	masc.	**neut.**	**fem.**	
nom.	der ein kein	das ein	die eine	die —
acc.	den einen keinen	kein	keine	keine
dat.	dem einem keinem	dem einem keinem	der einer keiner	den — keinen

Mein, dein, and **Ihr** follow the pattern of **ein** and **kein.**

3. These are the case forms of the INTERROGATIVE PRONOUN.

	persons	things and ideas
nom.	wer?	was?
acc.	wen?	was?
dat.	wem?	—

III. Sentence Structure

1. Verb position

   a. In a German statement the verb must be the second grammatical ELEMENT. The element before the verb is not necessarily the subject.

   Ich **sehe** meinen Vater morgen.
   Morgen **sehe** ich meinen Vater.
   Meinen Vater **sehe** ich morgen.

   b. A verb phrase consists of an INFLECTED VERB and a COMPLEMENT that completes its meaning. Such complements include predicate nouns, predicate adjectives, some accusatives, and other verbs. When the verb consists of more than one part, the inflected part (V1) is the second element in a statement, and the other part (V2) stands at the very end of the sentence.

Das	**ist**		**meine Schwester.**
Du	**bist**		**prima.**
Er	**spielt**	sehr gut	**Tennis.**
Jetzt	**gehen**	wir schnell	**essen.**
	V1		V2

2. Negation

a.

> nicht + (ein)___ = kein___

Möchten Sie **ein** Eis?	Nein, ich möchte **kein** Eis.
Möchten Sie Erdbeeren?	Nein, ich möchte **keine** Erdbeeren.

b.

> S V1 0 time expression ↑ other adverbs or adverbial phrases V2.
>   **nicht**

Wir spielen heute **nicht** mit den Kindern Tennis.

3. Clauses

Coordinate clauses are introduced by COORDINATING CONJUNCTIONS.

> aber, denn, oder, und

Coordinating conjunctions do not affect the original word order of the two sentences.

Ich bezahle den Kaffee, **und** du bezahlst das Eis.

WORTSCHATZWIEDERHOLUNG

Most of these exercises can and should be done with books closed. As an alternative, students can work with each other in groups of two, with the instructor answering questions and monitoring progress.

A. Welches Wort kommt Ihnen in den Sinn? *(What word comes to mind?)*

BEISPIEL: Winter   **kalt**

Sprache, Fluß, Gemüse, Glas, Bäckerei, Frühstück, Suppe, Rechnung, trinken, Restaurant, Geschäft, schlafen, Sommer, Tasse, Schokoladenkuchen, Mensa, Messer, Nachtisch

B. Geben Sie das Gegenteil!
kaufen, fragen, kommen, nördlich, im Westen, offen, alles, bitte

C. Geben Sie den Artikel!
Buttermilch, Bananeneis, Buttermesser, Frühstückstisch, Gurkensalat, Kaffeetasse, Kartoffelsalat, Obstkuchen, Lebensmittelrechnung, Marmeladenbrot, Salatkartoffel, Suppenteller, Teelöffel, Weinglas, Zitronenpudding

D. Was fehlt?
1. Vater, Mutter und Kinder sind zusammen eine _____ .
2. In Deutschland ißt man Brot mit Wurst, Käse oder Fisch zum _____ .
3. Für Suppe, Pudding oder Eis braucht man einen _____ .
4. Orangen, Bananen, Erdbeeren und Äpfel sind _____ .
5. Karotten, Erbsen und Bohnen sind _____ .
6. Der Vater von meiner Mutter ist mein _____ , aber der Bruder von meiner Mutter ist mein _____ .
7. Zum Schreiben braucht man einen _____ oder einen _____ und ein Stück _____ .
8. Im Winter braucht man einen _____ oder eine _____ .
9. Hier essen die Studenten: _____ .
10. Hier essen die Leute Kuchen, und sie trinken Kaffee oder Tee: _____ .
11. Hier kauft man Röcke und Blusen, Jacken und Hosen, auch Schuhe: _____ .

STRUKTURWIEDERHOLUNG

E: Read the base sentences to the class, have students repeat it in chorus. Then give them English cues for varying the base sentence; let individual students answer. This is intended as a quick oral review, not a translation exercise; certainly not one to be written out.

E. Verben. Variieren Sie die Sätze! Vary the German base sentence as suggested.
1. **Ich trinke Saft.**
   We drink juice. Do you drink juice? (3 ×) She doesn't drink juice.
2. **Sie antwortet den Leuten.**
   I'm answering the people. They answer the people. Does she answer the people? Answer the people. Don't answer the people. Why aren't you answering the people? (3 ×)
3. **Er fährt nach Berlin.**
   They're driving to Berlin. Why is she driving to Berlin? I'm not going to drive to Berlin. Are you driving to Berlin? (3 ×) Drive to Berlin. Don't drive to Berlin.
4. **Wir essen Fisch.**
   Who's eating fish? Are you eating fish? (3 ×) They don't eat fish. Eat fish.
5. **Sie werden müde.**
   I'm getting tired. She's not getting tired. Don't get tired. Who's getting tired? We're getting tired, too.
6. **Er hat Hunger.**
   I'm hungry. Are you hungry? (3 ×) Who's hungry? They're hungry. They're not hungry. We're hungry.
7. **Sie ist sehr groß.**
   You're very tall. (3 ×) They're not very tall. I'm very tall. Isn't he tall?

F: It may be necessary to have books open for some or all of this exercise.

F. Nominativ, Akkusativ und Dativ. Variieren Sie die Sätze!
1. **Herr Díaz ist Spanier.**
   Mr. Schmidt is (an) Austrian. No, he's from Switzerland. Is Miss Bayer an Austrian? She's not an Austrian either. (She's also not an Austrian.)

They say Miss Klein is an American. Joe is an American, too.

2. **Hier gibt es einen Supermarkt.**
   There's a river here. (a restaurant, no cafeteria, no lake) There are mountains here. (bakeries, lakes, no stores, no cafés)

3. **Das Geschäft gehört den Großeltern.**
   Who does the store belong to? (To whom does the store belong?) What belongs to the grandfather? She says it doesn't belong to the brother. It doesn't belong to the aunt.

4. **Der Herr bringt dem Fräulein Blumen.**
   What is he bringing to the young lady? Who's he bringing flowers to? (To whom is he bringing flowers?) Who's bringing the flowers? Why is he bringing flowers? Isn't he bringing flowers to the young lady? They're bringing the children some cookies. Is she bringing the friends a bottle of wine? He's bringing the neighbors apples. I'm bringing the sisters some books.

G: For variety, have students make their own sentences with these prepositions.

G. Präposition. Kombinieren Sie die Präpositionen mit den Wörtern!

BEISPIEL: durch / Land   **durch das (durchs) Land**

DURCH	Stadt, Zimmer / *pl.*, Kaufhaus, Supermarkt
FÜR	Kuchen, Vater, Junge, Eltern, Familie
GEGEN	Leute, Restaurant, Kinder, Ober, Mensch
OHNE	Essen, Speisekarte, Pudding, Herr, Freunde
UM	Geschäft, Markt, Mensa, Tisch

AUS	Flasche, Gläser, Supermarkt, Bäckerei, Café
AUßER	Bruder, Eltern, Schwester, Leute, Student
BEI	Supermarkt, Familie Schmidt, Apotheke, Nachbar
MIT	Herr, Freundin, Leute, Messer, Gabel
NACH	Frühstück, Mittagessen, Vorlesung, Kaffee
SEIT	Abendessen, Frühling, Zeit
VON	Ober, Fräulein, Kinder, Mutter, Studentin
ZU	Restaurant, Mensa, Markt, Apotheke

H. Verneinen Sie die Sätze mit kein oder nicht!

1. Heute gibt es Schokoladen-pudding.
2. Der Junge hilft dem Vater.
3. Sehen Sie den Ober?
4. Ich habe ein Messer.
5. Wir brauchen heute Milch.
6. Geht ihr nach Hause?
7. Haben Sie Rindsrouladen?
8. Er trinkt Kaffee.
9. Sie ißt gern Eis.
10. Joachim ist mein Freund.
11. Hast du Durst?
12. Heute ist es sehr kalt.

KAPITEL

4 *Feste und Daten*

Festzug in Bad Ems

▌LERNZIELE

Gespräche and **Wortschatz.** This chapter deals with holidays and dates.

Struktur. You will learn to use . . .

▪ the present perfect with **haben.**

▪ the present perfect with **sein.**

Einblicke. Holidays in Germany

Sprechsituationen

▪ Offering congratulations and best wishes

▪ Expressing surprise

▪ Expressing gratitude

◆◆◆◆◆ GESPRÄCHE

Am Telefon

Warm-ups: 1. Frau X ist im Supermarkt, in der Bäckerei, auf dem Markt. **Was kauft sie?** 2. Zum Mittagessen sind Sie im Restaurant. **Was möchten Sie?** 3. **Was ist der Artikel von** Suppenlöffel, Nudelsuppe, Obstsalat, Saftflasche, Käsebrot, Wurstbrötchen? 4. **Wie geht's weiter? ein Stück . . . etwas** (viel, ein Glas, eine Flasche, ein Pfund) 5. **nach Hause oder zu Hause?** Meine Familie ist _____ . Jetzt geht sie _____ . Wir tragen die Lebensmittel _____ . Sie sprechen _____ Deutsch.

CHRISTA   Hallo, Michael!
MICHAEL   Hallo, Christa! Was gibt's?
CHRISTA   Was machst du am Wochenende?
MICHAEL   Nichts Besonderes. Warum?
CHRISTA   Klaus hat übermorgen Geburtstag, und wir geben eine Party.
MICHAEL   Bist du sicher? Klaus hat doch vor einem Monat Geburtstag gehabt!
CHRISTA   Quatsch! Klaus hat am dritten Mai (3.5.) Geburtstag. Und Samstag ist der dritte.
MICHAEL   Na gut! Wann und wo ist die Party?
CHRISTA   Samstag um sieben bei mir. Aber nichts sagen! Es ist eine Überraschung.
MICHAEL   Ach so! Also, bis dann!
CHRISTA   Tschüß! Mach's gut!

Richtig oder falsch? 1. Michael hat Geburtstag. (F) 2. Klaus hat vor einem Monat Geburtstag gehabt. (F) 3. Am 3. Mai gibt es eine Party. (R) 4. Die Party ist bei Christa. (R) 5. Gerda, Kurt und Sabine kommen auch. (R) 6. Zum Geburtstag sagt man „Grüß dich!" (F) 7. Klaus gratuliert zum Geburtstag. (F) 8. Der Mensch ist eine Überraschung. (F) 9. Alle gratulieren. (R)

Klaus klingelt bei Christa.

CHRISTA   Tag, Klaus! Herzlichen Glückwunsch zum Geburtstag!
KLAUS   Grüß dich! Danke!
MICHAEL   Alles Gute zum Geburtstag!
KLAUS   Tag, Michael . . . Gerda, Kurt, Sabine! Was macht ihr denn hier?
ALLE   Wir gratulieren dir zum Geburtstag!
KLAUS   Danke! Was für eine Überraschung!

On the Telephone CHRISTA: *Hi, Michael!* MICHAEL: *Hi, Christa! What's up?* CHRISTA: *What are you doing on the weekend?* MICHAEL *Nothing special. Why?* CHRISTA: *Klaus has a birthday the day after tomorrow, and we're giving a party.* MICHAEL: *Are you sure? Klaus had his birthday a month ago.* CHRISTA: *Nonsense. Klaus's birthday is on the third of May (5/3). And Saturday is the third.* MICHAEL: *All right. When and where is the party?* CHRISTA: *Saturday at seven at my place. But don't say anything. It's a surprise.* MICHAEL: *Oh, I see. All right, see you then.* CHRISTA *Good-bye. Take care!*

Klaus Rings Christa's Doorbell CHRISTA: *Hello, Klaus! Happy birthday!* KLAUS: *Hi! Thanks!* MICHAEL: *All the best on your birthday!* KLAUS: *Hi, Michael . . . Gerda, Kurt, Sabine. What are you doing here?* ALL: *Congratulations on your birthday!* KLAUS: *Thanks! What a surprise!*

WORTSCHATZ 1

Point out the difference between **Feiertag** and **Ferien**. **Feiertag** refers to a special day, a holiday, and can be in either the singular or the plural, whereas **Ferien** refers to school or university vacation time. A vacation from work is **der Urlaub**.

Optional vocabulary: der Abschluß *here: graduation;* das Jubiläum, -en *anniversary*

DAS FEST, -E *celebration, festival*

der	Feiertag, -e	*holiday*	die	Ferien (*pl.*)	*vacation*
	Geburtstag, -e	*birthday*		Party, Parties	*party*
	Sekt	*champagne*		Überraschung, -en	*surprise*
das	Geschenk, -e	*present*			

bekommen	*to get, receive*	schenken	*to give (a present)*
dauern	*to last (duration)*		
denken	*to think*	singen	*to sing*
feiern	*to celebrate, party*	tanzen	*to dance*
gratulieren (+ *dat.*)	*to congratulate*	tun[1]	*to do; to put*
		überraschen	*to surprise*

DAS DATUM, DIE DATEN (*calendar*) date

Der wievielte ist heute?	*What's the date today?*
Heute ist der erste Mai (1.5.).[2]	*Today is the first of May (5/1).*
Ich habe am ersten Mai (1.5.) Geburtstag.[2]	*My birthday is on the first of May (5/1).*
Die Ferien sind vom 9. Juli (9.7.) bis zum 18. August (18.8.).	*The vacation is from July 9 (7/9) until August 18 (8/18).*

1. **erste**[3]	3. **dritte**	5. fünfte	7. **siebte**
2. zweite	4. vierte	6. sechste	8. **achte**

1 The present tense forms of **tun** are: **ich tue, du tust, er tut, wir tun, ihr tut, sie tun.**

2 In writing dates, Americans give the month and then the day: *5/1 (May 1), 1/5 (January 5).* In German one usually gives the day first and then the month. The ordinal number is followed by a period: **1.5. (1. Mai), 5.1. (5. Januar).** So 1.5. reads **der erste Mai,** and 5.1. reads **der fünfte Januar.** Note the **-en** after **am, vom,** and **zum: am ersten Mai, vom neunten Juli bis zum achtzehnten August.**

3 From 1 to 19, the ordinal numbers have a **-te(n)** ending. Starting with 20, they end in **-ste(n).** Note the irregularities within the numbers.

9. neunte	15. fünfzehnte	21. einundzwanzigste
10. zehnte	16. **sechzehnte**	22. zweiundzwanzigste
11. elfte	17. **siebzehnte**	30. dreißigste
12. zwölfte	18. achtzehnte	
13. dreizehnte	19. neunzehnte	
14. vierzehnte	20. zwanzigste	

WEITERES

am Wochenende	*on the weekend*
gerade	*just, right now*
noch	*still; else*
sicher	*sure, certain*
vor einer Woche[4]	*a week ago*
vorgestern	*the day before yesterday*
gestern / morgen	*yesterday / tomorrow*
übermorgen	*the day after tomorrow*
Wie lange?	*How long?*
Bis später!	*See you later. So long.*
Tschüß!	*Good-bye. So long.*
zum Geburtstag	*on the / for the birthday*
(zu) Ostern	*(at / for) Easter*
(zu) Weihnachten	*(at / for) Christmas*
(zu) Silvester	*(on / for) New Year's Eve*

Bis can be combined with other time expressions, e.g., **Bis dann (morgen, Montag)!**

4 vor meaning *ago* is PREpositional rather than POSTpositional as it is in English: **vor einem Monat** *(a month ago)*, **vor zwei Tagen** *(two days ago)*.

PASSIVES VOKABULAR **Ach so!** *Oh, I see.* **Alles Gute!** *All the best!* **Grüß dich!** *Hi! Hello!* **Herzlichen Glückwunsch zum Geburtstag!** *Happy birthday!* **klingeln** *to ring* **Mach's gut!** *Take care.* **na gut** *all right* **Quatsch!** *Nonsense!* **Was gibt's?** *What's up?* **nichts Besonderes** *nothing special*

Silvester — Party
Es spielen für Sie die
FRANKY BOYS
Beginn: 19.30 Uhr / Ende?
Tischreservierungen erbeten unter Tel. 34600

ZUM THEMA

Write several dates on the board (**31.12., 1.4., 7.6.**, etc.). Have the students repeat the dates after you. Then point to the dates at random; let individual students read them. Now go to exercise A.

Chain reaction. Start with any date, then follow through: 1. **z.B. Heute ist der 2.7., morgen ist der 3.7., und übermorgen ist der 4.7.**

A. Sagen Sie das Datum!

1. **Der wievielte ist heute?** Someone asks you for today's date. Answer according to the cues.

BEISPIEL: Unabhängigkeitstag *(Independence Day)*
Heute ist der vierte Juli.

a. Neujahr **b.** Martin Luther Kings Geburtstag **c.** Washingtons Geburtstag **d.** Valentinstag **e.** Totensonntag *(Memorial Day)* **f.** der erste Sommertag **g.** Tag der Arbeit *(Labor Day)* **h.** Columbustag **i.** Ihr Geburtstag **j.** der erste Weihnachtstag **k.** Silvester

2. z.B. Die Party ist am Tag nach dem Geburtstag. Der Geburtstag ist am 1.5. Wann ist die Party?

2. Geburtstage. The personnel director of your company is making a list of the birthdays of all employees. Read aloud.

BEISPIEL: Katrin (3.5.)   **Katrin hat am dritten Mai Geburtstag.**

Petra (1.11.), Barbara (2.12.), Gerhard (3.1.), Claudia (4.2.), Uli (5.3.), Rita (15.4.), Rainer (25.5.), Stefan (20.6.), Hilde (21.7.), Werner (31.8.)

B. Die Oper. You work at the box office of the opera house in Bonn. Give patrons information about dates and times of the upcoming performances. Read aloud.

BEISPIEL: Aida (3.9.) **Aida ist am dritten September.**

Spartakus (24.9.), Madame Butterfly (14.10.), Der Nußknacker (19.11.), Die wundersame Schusterfrau *(The Shoemaker's Wife*, 10.12.), Macbeth (11.2.), Der Barbier von Sevilla (8.3.), Der Ring des Nibelungen (29.4.), Die Fledermaus (11.5.), Kammerballett (17.6.), Liederabende (23.10., 20.11., 18.12., 22.10., 2.3., 28.4., 21.5.)

C: Note die Waage, die Jungfrau. All other signs of the zodiac are masculine.

C. Wann hast du Geburtstag, und was bist du? Ask each other your birthday, and find out what sign of the zodiac you are.

BEISPIEL: Wann hast du Geburtstag, und was bist du?
 Ich habe am 2. Februar Geburtstag. Ich bin Wassermann.

Schütze
23.11.-21.12.

Steinbock
22.12-20.

Skorpion
24.10.-22.11

Wassermann
21.1.-19.2.

Waage
24.9.-23.10.

Fisch(e)
20.2.-20.3.

Jungfrau
24.8.--23.9.

Widder
21.3.-20.4.

Löwe
23.7.-23.8.

Stier
21.4.-20.5.

Krebs
22.6.-22.7.

Zwilling(e)
21.5.-21.6.

Die Tierkreiszeichen
(signs of the zodiac)

Optional vocabulary:
der Schlips, -e *tie;*
Gürtel, - *belt;* Schlaf-
anzug, ̈e *pajamas;* das
Nachthemd, -en *night-
gown;* Parfüm, -e *perfume;*
T-shirt, -s; die Rose, -n,
Platte, -n *record.*

Other holidays: 1.1. Neujahr, 6.1. Heilige Drei
Könige, 1.5. Tag der Ar-
beit *(Labor Day),* Karfrei-
tag *(Good Friday),* Fron-
leichnam *(Corpus Christi
Day),* Himmelfahrt *(As-
cension Day),* Pfingsten
(Pentecost), 1.8. Bundes-
feiertag in der Schweiz,
2.10. Erntedankfest
(Thanksgiving), 3.10. Na-
tionalfeiertag in
Deutschland, 26.10. Na-
tionalfeiertag in Öster-
reich, 31.10. Reforma-
tionstag, 11.11.
Allerheiligen *(All Saints
Day),* 20.11. Totensonn-
tag *(Memorial Day),* 6.12.
Nikolaustag

D. Fragen. Ask a classmate the following questions.
1. Wie alt bist du?
2. Was für Geschenke bekommst du gewöhnlich zum Geburtstag? Was möchtest du gern?
3. Was für Geschenke schenkst du zum Muttertag? zum Vatertag?
4. Welcher Feiertag gefällt dir besonders gut? Welcher Feiertag ist bald *(soon)*?

E. Ferienkalender für deutsche Schulen. The German vacation schedule is staggered in order to relieve overcrowding on the freeways during holidays and vacations. Every **Land** *(state)* except Bavaria changes its vacation schedule from year to year so that no state will always have a very late or very early summer vacation.

	OSTERN	PFINGSTEN	SOMMER	HERBST	WEIHNACHTEN
Baden-Württemberg	17.4.–21.4.	28.5.– 8.6.	17.7.– 1.9.	29.10.– 3.11.	24.12.– 5.1.
Bayern	9.4.–21.4.	5.6.–16.6.	27.7.–10.9.	–	21.12.– 7.1.
Berlin	7.4.–21.4.	2.6.– 5.6.	12.7.–25.8.	27.10.– 3.11.	22.12.– 5.1.
Hessen	2.4.–20.4.	5.6.	9.7.–18.8.	8.10.–20.10.	24.12.–12.1.
Niedersachsen	24.3.–17.4.	2.6.– 5.6.	12.7.–22.8.	24.10.– 3.11.	22.12.– 5.1.
Schleswig-Holstein	9.4.–21.4.	–	6.7.–18.8.	15.10.–27.10.	24.12.– 7.1.

1. Wie viele Länder gibt es in Deutschland? Wie heißen sie?
2. Was für Ferien gibt es? Wie lange sind sie ungefähr?
3. Wo gibt es keine Herbstferien? keine Pfingstferien?
4. Von wann bis wann sind die Osterferien in Bayern? die Pfingstferien in Baden-Württemberg? die Sommerferien in Berlin und in Schleswig-Holstein? die Herbstferien in Niedersachsen? die Weihnachtsferien in Hessen? usw.
5. Was für Ferien gibt es hier? Wann sind sie? Wie lange dauern sie?
6. Wann beginnen die nächsten (next) Ferien? Wann enden sie? Was tun Sie dann?

F. Aussprache. See also III.13–15 in the pronunciation section of the Workbook.

1. [ç]   **ich, dich, nicht, nichts, sicher, furchtbar, vielleicht, manchmal, möchten, sprechen, Rechnung, Mädchen, Milch, durch, gewöhnlich, richtig, wichtig, sechzig**

2. [x]   **ach, acht, machen, nach, Weihnachten, Sprache, auch, brauchen, Woche, noch, doch, Buch, Kuchen**

3. [ks]   **sechs, sechste**

4. [k]   **dick, Zucker, Bäcker, Rock, Jacke, Frühstück, Glückwunsch, schmecken**

5. Wortpaare
   a. mich / misch
   b. Kirche / Kirsche
   c. nickt / nicht
   d. lochen / locken
   e. Nacht / nackt
   f. möchte / mochte

STRUKTUR

I. The Present Perfect with haben

1. The PRESENT PERFECT corresponds closely in form to the English present perfect. In both languages it consists of an inflected auxiliary verb and an unchanging past participle.

*You **have learned** that well.*	Du **hast** das gut **gelernt.**
*She **has brought** the books.*	Sie **hat** die Bücher **gebracht.**
*We **haven't spoken** any English.*	Wir **haben** kein Englisch **gesprochen.**

2. In the USE of this tense, however, there is a considerable difference between German and English. In everyday conversation English makes much use of the simple past, whereas German uses the present perfect.

Du **hast** das gut **gelernt.**	*You **learned** that well.*
Sie **hat** die Bücher **gebracht.**	*She **brought** the books.*
Wir **haben** kein Englisch **gesprochen.**	*We **didn't speak** any English.*

The German present perfect corresponds to four past-tense forms in English.

Wir haben das gelernt.
$$\begin{cases} \textit{We have learned that.} \\ \textit{We learned that.} \\ \textit{We did learn that.} \\ \textit{We were learning that.} \end{cases}$$

3. Most German verbs FORM the present perfect by using the present tense of **haben** (V1) with the past participle (V2).

ich **habe** . . . gelernt		wir **haben** . . . gelernt	
du **hast** . . . gelernt		ihr **habt** . . . gelernt	
er **hat** . . . gelernt		sie **haben** . . . gelernt	

4. German has two groups of verbs that form their past participles in different ways: T-VERBS (also called "weak verbs") with the participle ending in **-t (ge-lernt),** and n-verbs (also called "strong verbs") with the participle ending in **-en (gesprochen).** Any verb not specifically identified as an irregular t-verb or as an n-verb can be assumed to be a regular t-verb.

a. The majority of German verbs are regular t-verbs. They form their past participles with the prefix **ge-** and the ending **-t.** They correspond to such English verbs as *learn, learned,* and *ask, asked.*

ge + stem + t   lernen →   ge lern t

Verbs that follow this pattern include: brauchen, danken, dauern, feiern, fragen, hören, kaufen, machen, sagen, schenken, spielen, tanzen, wohnen, zählen.

- Verbs with stems ending in **-d, -t,** or certain consonant combinations make the final **-t** audible by inserting an **-e.**

ge + stem + et   kosten →   ge kost et

Other verbs that follow this pattern include: antworten, öffnen, regnen.

- A few t-verbs are irregular (MIXED VERBS), i.e., they usually change their stem. They can be compared to such English verbs as *bring, brought,* and *think, thought.*

ge + stem (change) + t   bringen →   ge brach t

Here are the participles of familiar irregular t-verbs:

bringen	**gebracht**	haben	**gehabt**
denken	**gedacht**		

b. A smaller but extremely important group of verbs, the N-VERBS, form their past participles with the prefix **ge-** and the ending **-en**. They correspond to such English verbs as *write, written,* and *speak, spoken*. The n-verbs frequently have a stem change in the past participle; their forms are not predictable. (Many of them also have a stem change in the second and third person singular of the present tense: **sprechen, du sprichst, er spricht.** Note: those that do have this change are always n-verbs.)

ge + stem (change) + en	geben →	ge geb en	
	finden →	ge fund en	

You need to learn the past participles of these n-verbs:

essen	**gegessen**	schlafen	**geschlafen**
finden	**gefunden**	schreiben	**geschrieben**
geben	**gegeben**	sehen	**gesehen**
heißen	**geheißen**	singen	**gesungen**
helfen	**geholfen**	sprechen	**gesprochen**
lesen	**gelesen**	tragen	**getragen**
liegen	**gelegen**	trinken	**getrunken**
nehmen	**genommen**	tun	**getan**
scheinen	**geschienen**		

5. Two groups of verbs have no **ge**-prefix.

   a. Inseparable-prefix verbs
   In English as in German, many verbs have been formed by the use of inseparable prefixes, e.g. *to belong, to impress, to proceed*. In both languages the stress is on the verb, not on the prefix. The German inseparable prefixes are **be-, emp-, ent-, er-, ge-, ver-,** and **zer-**.

bestellen → be stell t
verstehen → ver stand en

Familiar t-verbs that also follow this pattern include: bezahlen, gehören, verkaufen, überraschen, wiederholen (although **über-** and **wieder-** are not always inseparable prefixes).

You will need to learn the past participles of these familiar n-verbs:

beginnen	**begonnen**	gefallen	**gefallen**
bekommen	**bekommen**	verstehen	**verstanden**
empfehlen	**empfohlen**		

   b. Verbs ending in **-ieren** (all of which are t-verbs): gratulieren, gratuliert; studieren, studiert.

ÜBUNGEN

A. Geben Sie das Partizip (*participle*)!

BEISPIEL: fragen   **gefragt**

1. dauern, feiern, danken, wohnen, tanzen, antworten, kosten, öffnen, regnen, verkaufen, bezahlen, gratulieren, denken, bringen, studieren
2. essen, finden, tun, helfen, lesen, heißen, trinken, schlafen, scheinen, singen, bekommen, empfehlen, beginnen, gefallen, verstehen

B. Ersezten Sie das Subjekt!

BEISPIEL: Ich habe eine Flasche Sekt gekauft. (er, sie / *pl.*)
Er hat eine Flasche Sekt gekauft.
Sie haben eine Flasche Sekt gekauft.

1. Du hast nichts gesagt. (ihr, man, ich)
2. Ich habe auf englisch geantwortet. (wir, du, er)
3. Er hat Klaus Geschenke gebracht. (ihr, sie / *pl.*, ich)
4. Sie haben nur Deutsch gesprochen. (du, ihr, Robert und Silvia)

C: This exercise requires that students be familiar with all past participles. It may have to be done with open books.

C. Was habt ihr gemacht? Tell your roommate what happened at Klaus' party.

BEISPIEL: Ich habe Klaus ein Buch gegeben. (schenken)
Ich habe Klaus ein Buch geschenkt.

1. Wir haben viel gefeiert. (tanzen, spielen, essen, tun, servieren)
2. Christa und Joachim haben Kuchen gekauft. (bestellen, nehmen)
3. Susanne hat Klaus gratuliert. (danken, helfen, überraschen, empfehlen)
4. Klaus hat viel gegessen. (trinken, singen, bekommen)
5. Wie gewöhnlich hat Peter nur gelesen. (schlafen, lernen, sprechen)
6. Sabine hat Helmut nicht gesehen. (fragen, antworten, schreiben)

D: This is just a quick oral English to German drill to bring out differences between the two languages.

D. Auf deutsch, bitte!

1. She was still sleeping.
2. They helped, too.
3. Have you (*3x*) just eaten?
4. Did you (*formal*) find it?
5. I didn't understand that.
6. Have you (*sg. fam.*) read that?
7. I repeated the question.
8. Who took it?
9. They bought winter coats.
10. My aunt recommended the store.
11. Did you (*sg. pl.*) sell the books?
12. I was paying the bills.

II. Present Perfect with sein

Whereas most German verbs use **haben** as the auxiliary in the perfect tenses, a few common verbs use **sein**. You will probably find it easiest to memorize **sein** together with the past participles of those verbs requiring it. But you can also determine which verbs take **sein** by remembering that they must fulfill two conditions:

▪ They are INTRANSITIVE, i.e., they do not take an accusative (direct) object, like **gehen, kommen, laufen** and **fahren.**

- They express a CHANGE OF PLACE OR CONDITION. **sein** and **bleiben** (see Wortschatz 2) are exceptions to this rule.

Wir **sind** nach Hause **gegangen.**	*We went home.*
Er **ist** müde **geworden.**	*He got tired.*

CAUTION

A change in prefix may cause a change in auxiliary because the meaning of the verb changes.

Ich **bin** nach Hause **gekommen.**	*I came home.*
Ich **habe** ein Geschenk **bekommen.**	*I received a present.*

The present perfect of the following verbs is formed with the present tense of **sein** (V1) and the past participle (V2).

ich **bin** . . . gekommen	wir **sind** . . . gekommen
du **bist** . . . gekommen	ihr **seid** . . . gekommen
er **ist** . . . gekommen	sie **sind** . . . gekommen

The following verbs form the present perfect with **sein.** They are all n-verbs.

sein	**ist gewesen**	kommen	**ist gekommen**
gehen	**ist gegangen**	laufen	**ist gelaufen**
fahren	**ist gefahren**	werden	**ist geworden**

Occasionally **fahren** takes an object. In that case the auxiliary **haben** is used:

Sie **sind** nach Hause **gefahren.**	*They drove home.*
Sie **haben** mein Auto nach Hause **gefahren.**	*They drove my car home.*

ÜBUNGEN

E. Sein oder haben? Geben Sie das Partizip!

BEISPIEL: empfehlen   **hat empfohlen**   gehen   **ist gegangen**

essen, bringen, werden, sein, gefallen, liegen, sprechen, laufen, helfen

F. Ersetzen Sie das Subjekt!

BEISPIEL: Sie ist gerade gegangen. (sie / *pl.*)   **Sie sind gerade gegangen.**

1. Wir sind spät nach Hause gekommen. (er, ich, Sie, du)
2. Sie sind müde gewesen. (ihr, sie / *sg.*, du, ich)
3. Sie sind zum Supermarkt gefahren. (er, wir, ihr)

G. Auf deutsch, bitte!
1. Have you (*pl. fam.*) eaten?—No, we haven't had time 'til now.
2. Did you like the restaurant, Uncle Georg?—Yes, the food tasted good.

3. Where have you been, Andrea?—I drove to the supermarket.
4. Did you buy the book, Mom?—No, the bookstore was closed.
5. What did you get for your birthday, Kirsten?—My parents gave me a watch.
6. When did you (*pl. fam.*) get home?—I don't know. It got very late.

H. Sommerferien. Michael is explaining what he did during his last summer vacation. Use the present perfect. In each case decide whether to use the auxiliary **haben** or **sein.**

BEISPIEL: Im August habe ich Ferien.   **Im August habe ich Ferien gehabt.**

1. In den Ferien fahre ich nach Zell.
2. Ich nehme zwei Wochen frei.
3. Ich wohne bei Familie Huber.
4. Das Haus liegt direkt am See.
5. Zell gefällt mir gut.
6. Nachmittags laufe ich in die Stadt.
7. Manchmal gehen wir auch ins Café.
8. Das Café gehört Familie Huber.
9. Mittwochs hilft Renate da.
10. Renate bringt mir (*me*) oft Kuchen.
11. Ich bekomme alles frei.
12. Sie empfiehlt die Sahnetorte.
13. Die schmeckt wirklich gut.
14. Den Apfelstrudel finde ich besonders gut.
15. Renate ist in den Sommerferien bei uns.
16. Wir werden gute Freunde.
17. Leider regnet es viel.
18. Wir lesen viel und hören Musik.

I. Interview. Find out the following information from your classmate and then tell the class what he / she said.
1. wann er / sie gestern ins Bett (*to bed*) gegangen ist
2. ob er / sie viel für die Deutschstunde gelernt hat
3. wie er / sie geschlafen hat und wie lange
4. was er / sie heute zum Frühstück gegessen und getrunken hat
5. wie er / sie zur Uni(versität) gekommen ist, ob er / sie gelaufen oder gefahren ist
6. wie viele Vorlesungen er / sie heute schon gehabt hat und welche

III. Subordinate Clauses

You already know how to join sentences with a coordinating conjunction. Clauses can also be joined with SUBORDINATING CONJUNCTIONS. Subordinating conjunctions introduce a subordinate or dependent clause, i.e., a statement with a subject and a verb that cannot stand alone as a complete sentence.

because it's his birthday
that they have left already

While coordinating conjunctions don't affect word order, subordinating conjunctions do. German subordinate clauses are always set off by a COMMA, and the inflected verb (V1) stands at the very end.

1. Six common subordinating conjunctions are:

bevor	*before*
daß	*that*
ob	*if, whether*
obwohl	*although*
weil	*because*
wenn	*if, when(ever)*

kaffee HAG
Weil er schmeckt

> **CAUTION**

When it is possible to replace *if* with *whether*, use **ob**; otherwise use **wenn.**

BEISPIEL: Ich kaufe ein Geschenk.
Ich frage Helga, **bevor** ich ein Geschenk kaufe.
I'll ask Helga before I buy a present.

Klaus hat Geburtstag.
Sie sagt, **daß** Klaus Geburtstag hat.
She says that Klaus has a birthday.

Ist sie sicher?
Ich frage, **ob** sie sicher ist.
I ask if she is sure.

Sie hat nicht viel Zeit.
Sie kommt zur Party, **obwohl** sie nicht viel Zeit hat.
She's coming to the party although she doesn't have much time.

Er trinkt gern Sekt.
Wir bringen eine Flasche Sekt, **weil** er gern Sekt trinkt.
We bring a bottle of champagne because he loves to drink champagne.

Ich habe Zeit.
Ich komme auch, **wenn** ich Zeit habe.
I'll come, too, if I have time.

2. Information questions (**wer? was? wann?**) can become subordinate clauses by using the question word as a conjunction and putting the verb last.

Wie schmeckt der Salat?   Sie fragt, **wie** der Salat **schmeckt.**
She asks how the salad tastes.

Wo sind die Brötchen?   Sie fragt, **wo** die Brötchen **sind.**
She asks where the rolls are,

Note the similarity with English·

Where are *the rolls?*   *She asks where the rolls* **are.**

3. Yes / no questions require **ob** as a conjunction.

Schmeckt der Salat gut?   Sie fragt, **ob** der Salat gut **schmeckt.**
She asks whether the salad tastes good.

Sind die Würstchen heiß?   Sie fragt, **ob** die Würstchen heiß **sind.**
She asks if the franks are hot.

4. Subordinate Clauses as the First Sentence Element

If the subordinate clause precedes the main clause, the inflected verb of the main clause—the second sentence element—comes right after the comma.

Ich **komme,** wenn ich Zeit habe.
Wenn ich Zeit habe, **komme** ich.

5. The Present Perfect in Subordinate Clauses

In subordinate clauses in the present perfect, the inflected verb **haben** or **sein** (V1) stands at the end of the sentence.

Er hat ein Radio bekommen.
Er sagt, **daß** er ein Radio bekommen **hat.**

Er ist überrascht gewesen.
Er sagt, **daß** er überrascht gewesen **ist.**

When listening or reading, pay special attention to the end of the sentence, which often contains crucial sentence elements. As Mark Twain said in *A Connecticut Yankee in King Arthur's Court,* "Whenever the literary German dives into a sentence, that is the last we are going to see of him till he emerges on the other side of his Atlantic with his verb in his mouth."

ÜBUNGEN

J. Verbinden Sie die Sätze!

BEISPIEL: Eva geht zur Bäckerei. Sie braucht noch etwas Brot. *(because)*
    Eva geht zur Bäckerei, weil sie noch etwas Brot braucht.

1. Der Herr fragt die Studentin. Kommt sie aus Amerika? *(whether)*
2. Die Stadt gefällt den Amerikanern. Sie ist alt und romantisch. *(because)*
3. Eine Tasse Kaffee tut gut. Man ist müde. *(if)*
4. Zählen Sie alles! Sie bezahlen die Rechnung. *(before)*
5. Wir spielen nicht Tennis. Das Wetter ist schlecht. *(if)*
6. Sie hat geschrieben. Sie ist in Österreich gewesen. *(that)*
7. Ich habe Hunger. Ich habe gerade ein Eis gegessen. *(although)*

K. Sagen Sie die Sätze noch einmal!
1. **Er sagt, daß ...** A friend of yours has just come back from Europe. Tell the class what he has observed. Follow the model.

BEISPIEL: Die Luxemburger sprechen auch Deutsch.
    Er sagt, daß die Luxemburger auch Deutsch sprechen.

a. Im Winter regnet es viel. **b.** Das Essen schmeckt sehr gut. **c.** In Europa leben sehr viele Menschen. **d.** Die Kleidung ist dort sehr teuer. **e.** In Italien hat die Sonne oft geschienen. **f.** Griechenland ist besonders schön gewesen. **g.** Es hat den Studenten dort gut gefallen. **h.** Sie sind im August nach Hause gekommen.

2. **Sie fragt, . . .** Your mother wants to know about Carla's graduation party. Follow the model.

BEISPIEL: Wer ist Carla? **Sie fragt, wer Carla ist.**

a. Wo wohnt Carla? **b.** Was für Leute sind das? **c.** Was macht der Vater? **d.** Wie viele Leute sind da gewesen? **e.** Wie lange hat die Party gedauert? **f.** Was habt ihr gegessen und getrunken? **g.** Mit wem hast du getanzt? **h.** Wie bist du nach Hause gekommen?

3. **Er fragt, ob . . .** Your parents are celebrating their 30th anniversary and your sister is in charge of the party. Now she asks if you and your brothers have completed the tasks she assigned a week ago.

BEISPIEL: Hast du Servietten gekauft?
Sie fragt, ob du Servietten gekauft hast.

a. Seid ihr gestern einkaufen gegangen? **b.** Hat Alfred Sekt gekauft? **c.** Haben wir jetzt alle Geschenke? **d.** Habt ihr den Kuchen beim Bäcker *(baker)* bestellt? **e.** Hat Peter mit den Nachbarn gesprochen? **f.** Habt ihr auch Onkel Werner gefragt? **g.** Hast du deinen Tisch gebracht? **h.** Haben wir genug Gläser und Salatteller? **i.** Hat Alfred die Kamera gefunden?

L. **Beginnen Sie mit dem Nebensatz** *(subordinate clause)*!

BEISPIEL: Ich trinke Wasser, wenn ich Durst habe.
Wenn ich Durst habe, trinke ich Wasser.

1. Ich habe ein Stück Käse gegessen, weil ich Hunger gehabt habe.
2. Ich verstehe nicht, warum die Lebensmittel Farbstoffe brauchen.
3. Ihr habt eine Party gegeben, weil ich 21 geworden bin.
4. Ich finde (es) prima, daß ihr nichts gesagt habt.
5. Ich bin nicht müde, obwohl wir bis morgens um sechs gefeiert haben.

ZUSAMMENFASSUNG

M. **Was haben Sie gestern gemacht?** Schreiben Sie acht Sätze im Perfekt!

BEISPIEL: Ich habe bis 10 Uhr geschlafen. Dann . . .

N. **Die Abschlußparty** *(graduation party)*
1. **Wir planen eine Party.** With one or several partners, work out a plan for your cousin's graduation party. Be prepared to outline your ideas.

Sagen Sie, . . .!

a. wann und wo die Party ist **b.** wie lange sie dauert **c.** wer kommt **d.** was Sie trinken und essen **e.** was Sie noch brauchen

2. **Wie ist die Party gewesen?** Describe what happened at the party.

O: 1. Vorgestern habe
ich eine Geburtstags-
party gegeben. 2. Sind
Volker und Bettina
gekommen? 3. Ja, sie
sind auch gekommen.
4. Alle haben Geschen-
ke gebracht. 5. Mein
Vater hat eine Flasche
Sekt geöffnet. 6. Wie
lange habt ihr gefei-
ert? 7. Bis um drei.
Wir haben getanzt, gut
gegessen und viel Cola
getrunken. 8. Die
Nachbarn haben gesagt,
daß die Musik zu laut
gewesen ist. 9. Hast
du das gehört?
10. Gestern ist ein
Nachbar / eine Nach-
barin gekommen und
hat mit meinen Eltern
gesprochen. 11. Die
Party hat mir gefallen.

O. Die Geburtstagsparty. Auf deutsch, bitte!

1. The day before yesterday I gave a birthday party.   **2.** Did Volker and Bettina come?   **3.** Yes, they came, too. **4.** All **(alle)** brought presents.   **5.** My father opened a bottle of champagne.   **6.** How long did you (*pl. fam.*) celebrate?   **7.** Until three o'clock. We danced, ate well, and drank a lot of Coke.   **8.** The neighbors said that the music was too loud **(laut)**.   **9.** Did you (*sg. fam.*) hear that?   **10.** Yesterday one neighbor came and spoke with my parents.   **11.** I liked the party.

LERNTIP

Studying Verbs

The main difference between verbs in English and in German are the personal endings. The best way to master them is through frequent practice, such as pattern drills. It may also help to write out some charts on cards (see Appendix pp. 424–26) which you can review easily. When it comes to learning the principal parts of n-verbs, memorization and frequent review are necessary. Use the lists of principal parts in the Appendix, checking off verbs as they are presented in the text.

EINBLICKE ◆◆◆◆◆◆◆◆◆◆

Karnevalumzug
(. . . *parade*) in Bonn

Germany is a thoroughly modern industrial society, no less so than the United States or Canada. But it also has a long history and many traditions with roots in various historical periods and events. Some of these are carried on, no doubt, not only out of reverence for tradition, but also to foster tourism which accounts for a considerable part of the healthy trade balance.

The **Oktoberfest** in Munich, the world's biggest beer festival, is attended by several million visitors each year. It started with a royal wedding more than 150 years ago. Similar events on a much smaller scale take place elsewhere, with carrousels and game booths for children and young adults. In late summer and early fall, wine festivals (**Winzerfeste**) are celebrated in wine-growing regions, especially along the Rhine, Main, and Moselle rivers. Wine production, too, is economically significant.

Some towns attract visitors by recreating historical events in their carefully preserved surroundings: The **Meistertrunk** in Rothenburg ob der Tauber recalls an event from the Thirty Years' War (1618–1648); Landshut involves many of its citizens in the reenactment of the 1475 wedding of the son of Duke Ludwig to a Polish princess (**Fürstenhochzeit**); and the *Play of the Pied Piper* in Hameln commemorates the Children's Crusade of 1284 when 130 children of the city mysteriously vanished.

Carnival time, which starts in January and ends with Ash Wednesday, has its roots in the pre-Christian era. Its purpose was to exorcise the demons of winter. Celebrated in the South as **Fasching** and along the Rhine as **Karneval**, it ends just before Lent with parades and merry-making in the streets. Such picturesque events have parallels in other cultures and are but one aspect of life in Germany.

WORTSCHATZ 2

das	Lied, -er	*song*
die	Kerze, -n	*candle*

»Ich tue, was mir Spaß macht«

dort	*(over) there*
eigentlich	*actual(ly)*
ein bißchen	*some, a little bit*
immer	*always*
laut	*loud, noisy*
lustig	*funny, amusing*
(noch) nie	*never, never before*
verrückt	*crazy*
arbeiten	*to work*
bleiben, ist geblieben	*to remain, stay*
fallen (fällt), ist gefallen	*to fall*
Spaß machen[1]	*to be fun*
studieren[2]	*to study a particular field, be a student at a university*

Pre-reading exercise:
1. Welche religiösen Feste feiern wir hier?
2. Gibt es hier historische Feste? Wann gibt es hier Karussels, Buden *(booths)*, Spaß für alle?   3. Was machen die Leute hier gern am 4. Juli?

[1] Das **macht Spaß**. *(It's fun.)* Tanzen **macht Spaß**. *(Dancing is fun.)*
[2] Ich **studiere** *(I am a student)* in Heidelberg. Ich **studiere** Philosophy. BUT Ich **lerne** *(I'm learning / studying)* Vokabeln.

WAS IST DAS? der Prinz, Studentenball; das Kostüm, Musikinstrument, Weihnachtsessen, Weihnachtslied; die Adventszeit, Brezel, Kontaktlinse, Konversationsstunde, Prinzessin, Weihnachtsdekoration, Weihnachtszeit; Ende Juli; ins Bett fallen; authentisch, enorm, erst, exakt, historisch, Hunderte von, wunderschön

Deutsche Feste

reports

(Carolyn berichtet° für die Konversationsstunde.)

only

vintage festival

stiff
them

. . . tent

was / parade in traditional costumes / (festival) grounds

Wie ihr gehört habt, habe ich gerade ein Jahr in Deutschland studiert. Ich bin erst° vor einem Monat wieder nach Hause gekommen, weil ich dort mit der Uni erst Ende Juli fertig geworden bin. Es ist wunderschön gewesen. 5
Ich habe viel gesehen und viel gelernt. Heute habe ich ein paar Bilder gebracht.

Im September bin ich mit Freunden beim Winzerfest° in Bacharach am Rhein gewesen. Da haben wir etwas Wein getrunken, gesungen und getanzt. 10
Ich habe immer gedacht, daß die Deutschen etwas steif° sind. Aber nicht, wenn sie feiern! So lustig und verrückt habe ich sie° noch nie gesehen. Zwei Wochen später sind wir zum Oktoberfest nach München gefahren. Im Bierzelt° haben wir Brezeln gegessen und natürlich auch Bier getrunken. Die Musik ist mir ein bißchen zu laut gewesen. Was mir aber besonders 15
gefallen hat, war° der Trachtenzug° zur Wies'n°.

Beim Münchner
Oktoberfest

instead

like

gypsy

dead-tired

these

booths / toys

*gingerbread / mulled wine /
. . . angel*

. . . wreath / . . . tree

Halloween gibt es in Deutschland nicht, aber dafür° gibt es im Februar
den Fasching. Das ist so etwas wie° Mardi Gras in New Orleans, mit Umzügen
und Kostümen. Ich bin als Zigeunerin° zu einem Studentenball gegangen.
Wir haben lange gefeiert, und morgens bin ich dann todmüde° ins Bett   20
gefallen.

Außer diesen° Festen gibt es natürlich noch viele Feiertage. Die Weihnachtszeit hat mir besonders gut gefallen. Beim Christkindlmarkt in Nürn-
berg¹ gibt es Hunderte von Buden° mit Weihnachtsdekorationen, Spielzeug°,
Lebkuchen° und auch Buden mit Glühwein°. Den Weihnachtsengel° habe   25
ich dort gekauft. Schön, nicht wahr? In der Adventszeit hat man nur einen
Adventskranz°. Den Weihnachtsbaum° sehen die Kinder erst am 24. Dezember, am Heiligabend. Aber dann bleibt er bis zum 6. Januar im Zimmer.

Christkindlmarkt in
Nürnberg

their / real / dangerous
festive

Zu Weihnachten bin ich bei Familie Fuchs gewesen. Die Kerzen auf ihrem° Baum sind echt° gewesen. Ich habe das etwas gefährlich° gefunden, aber es ist sehr festlich°. Bevor das Christkind² die Geschenke gebracht hat, haben wir Weihnachtslieder gesungen. Am 25. und 26. Dezember sind alle Geschäfte zu. Die zwei Feiertage sind nur für Familie und Freunde. Das finde ich eigentlich gut. Zum Weihnachtsessen hat es übrigens Gans° mit Rotkraut° und Knödeln° gegeben. Die Weihnachtsplätzchen und der Stollen² haben mir besonders gut geschmeckt.

goose
red cabbage / dumplings

at midnight
church bells / rang

Silvester habe ich mit Freunden gefeiert. Um Mitternacht° haben alle Kirchenglocken° geläutet°, und wir haben mit Sekt und „Prost Neujahr!" das neue Jahr begonnen.

30

35

Landshuter Fürsten-
hochzeit

forget / medieval
knights
tournaments
glasses
Middle Ages / was lucky
every

more than

Das Bild hier ist von der Fürstenhochzeit in Landshut. Da bin ich im Juni gewesen. Das vergesse° ich nie. Viele Landshuter haben mittelalterliche° Kleidung getragen, und alles ist sehr authentisch gewesen: die Ritter°, Prinzen und Prinzessinnen, die Musikinstrumente und Turniere°. Man ist historisch so exakt, daß Leute mit Brillen° Kontaktlinsen tragen, weil es im Mittelalter° noch keine Brillen gegeben hat. Übrigens habe ich Glück gehabt°, weil man das Fest nur alle° drei Jahre feiert.

40

45

Ich habe immer gedacht, daß die Deutschen viel arbeiten. Das tun sie, aber sie haben auch enorm viele Feiertage³, viel mehr als° wir. Und Feiern in Deutschland macht Spaß.

ZUM TEXT

A. Was hat Carolyn gesagt? Match the sentence fragments from the two groups.

_____ 1. Wie ihr gehört habt,
_____ 2. Ich bin erst vor einem Monat wieder nach Hause gekommen,
_____ 3. Ich habe immer gedacht,
_____ 4. Im Bierzelt haben wir
_____ 5. Der Weihnachtsbaum bleibt
_____ 6. Bevor das Christkind die Geschenke gebracht hat,
_____ 7. Was mir besonders gut gefallen hat,
_____ 8. Man ist historisch so exakt,

a. haben wir Weihnachtslieder gesungen.
b. war der Trachtenzug.
c. Brezeln gegessen.
d. bis zum 6. Januar im Zimmer.
e. weil ich dort mit der Uni erst Ende Juli fertig geworden bin.
f. daß Leute mit Brillen Kontaktlinsen tragen.
g. habe ich gerade ein Jahr in Deutschland studiert.
h. daß die Deutschen etwas steif sind.

B. Feiern in Deutschland. Complete these sentences with the appropriate verb in the present perfect.

bringen, fahren, feiern, gefallen, gehen, kaufen, kommen, sein, studieren

1. Carolyn _____ _____ vor einem Monat nach Hause _____.
2. Sie _____ ein Jahr in Deutschland _____. 3. Es _____ wunderbar _____. 4. Sie _____ ein paar Bilder in die Deutschstunde _____. 5. Im September _____ sie mit Freunden zum Winzerfest nach Bacharach _____. 6. Im Fasching _____ sie als Zigeunerin zu einem Studentenball _____. 7. Die Weihnachtszeit _____ Carolyn besonders gut _____. 8. In Nürnberg _____ sie einen Weihnachtsengel _____. 9. Sie _____ Weihnachten bei der Familie Fuchs _____.

C. Interview. Fragen Sie einen Nachbarn / eine Nachbarin, . . . !
1. wie und wo er / sie das (Ernte)dankfest feiert
2. wie er / sie gewöhnlich Weihnachten (oder Hannukah) feiert
3. wie und wo er / sie das letzte Silvester gefeiert hat
4. ob er / sie zum 4. Juli auch Kracher (_firecrackers_) gehabt oder ein Feuerwerk gesehen hat

D. Schriftliche Übung. Jot down some key words about two of the holidays Carolyn mentions, then write three to five sentences about each.

BEISPIEL: Winzerfest
Bacharach am Rhein, September, Wein, singen

Carolyn ist zum Winzerfest nach Bacharach gefahren. Bacharach liegt am Rhein. Das Winzerfest ist im September. Die Leute haben Wein getrunken, gesungen und getanzt. Es ist sehr lustig gewesen.

Frohe Weihnachten und viel Glück im neuen Jahr

E. Plätzchen für die Feiertage: Spritzgebäck

1. Lesen Sie das Rezept!

¾ cup	175 g° Butter oder Margarine
½ cup	100 g° Zucker
	1 Teelöffel Vanille
	1 Eigelb
2 cups / flour	300 g° Mehl°
	1 / 4 Teelöffel Salz

350°F / preheat / cream until fluffy
add / sift
mix / dough / cookie press / put
different / greased / cookie
sheet / press

Erst Ofen auf 175–190 Grad° wärmen°. Butter schaumig rühren°, Zucker, Vanille und Eigelb dazu geben°. Mehl und Salz sieben° und in die Masse geben, gut mischen°. Den Teig° in eine Teigspritze° füllen° und verschiedene° Formen auf ein gefettetes° Backblech° spritzen°. Acht bis zehn Minuten backen, oder bis die Plätzchen braun werden.

Guten Appetit!

2. Wie haben Sie die Plätzchen gemacht? Tell your classmates how you made these cookies. Except for **backen / gebacken,** all new verbs in this recipe are t-verbs.

BEISPIEL: Erst habe ich den Ofen auf 175 Grad gewärmt. Dann habe ich . . .

1. Nuremberg's outdoor **Christkindlmarkt** is the largest German Christmas market. Over two million people visit it during the four weeks before Christmas. Booths offer Christmas decorations, candy, toys, etc. The smell of hot punch, burnt almonds, and roasted chestnuts is in the air, and there are performances by choirs and instrumentalists. Nuremberg is also the source of the fancy gingerbread called **Nürnberger Lebkuchen.**

2. In Germany, Christmas includes a late afternoon or midnight church service on Christmas Eve **(Heiligabend).** Presents, usually not wrapped but displayed on tables, are exchanged on Christmas Eve. In southern Germany the **Christbaum** and gifts are brought by the **Christkind;** in northern Germany the **Weihnachtsbaum** is brought by the **Weihnachtsmann.** No Christmas is complete without the traditional **Weihnachtsplätzchen** and especially **Stollen,** a fragrant buttery yeast bread filled with almonds, currants, raisins, and candied citrus peel.

3. Germans observe their "Labor Day" **(Tag der Arbeit)** on the first day of May. Good Friday, Easter Monday, Ascension Day, and the Monday after Pentecost **(Pfingsten)** are legal holidays. Other religious holidays are observed only in predominantly Catholic states. No holiday on a fixed date is ever moved to a Friday or Monday.

SPRECHSITUATIONEN

Offering Congratulations and Best Wishes

What do you say to wish someone well on a birthday or a similar occasion, or a special holiday? Here are some useful expressions.

Ich gratuliere dir / Ihnen zum Geburtstag.
Alles Gute zum Geburtstag!
Herzlichen Glückwunsch zum Geburtstag!
Herzliche Glückwünsche! *(Best wishes.)*

Ich wünsche dir / Ihnen . . . *(I wish you . . .)*
Fröhliche Weihnachten!
Frohe Ostern!
Ein gutes neues Jahr!
Ein schönes Wochenende!
Alles Gute!
Viel Glück (und Gesundheit)! *(Good luck and good health!)*
Gute Besserung! *(Get well soon.)*

365 Tage Gesundheit und Glück
♥ 52 Wochen Lebensfreude und Liebe
12 Monate reichlich Geld und Erfolg

Expressing Surprise

Here are a few ways to express surprise.

Zum Geburtstag herzliche Glückwünsche

Was für eine Überraschung!
Das ist aber eine Überraschung!
Das ist ja unglaublich! *(That's unbelievable.)*
Wirklich?
Wie nett! *(How nice!)*
Mensch! *(Boy!)*

Expressing Gratitude

There are many ways to express your gratitude:

Danke (sehr)! / Danke schön!
Vielen Dank! / Herzlichen Dank!
Ich bin dir / Ihnen sehr dankbar.   *I'm very grateful to you.*
Das ist sehr nett von dir / Ihnen.   *That's very nice of you.*

Appropriate responses include:

Bitte (schön)! / Bitte, bitte! / Bitte   *You're welcome*
  sehr!
Gern geschehen!   *Glad to . . .*
Nichts zu danken!   *No need to thank me.*

133

A. Was sagen Sie? Use the appropriate expression for each of the following situations.

1. Ein Freund oder eine Freundin hat heute Geburtstag.
2. Sie haben Geburtstag. Ein Freund oder eine Freundin aus der Oberschule *(high school)* telephoniert und gratuliert Ihnen.
3. Sie schreiben Ihrer Großmutter zu Weihnachten.
4. Sie haben einen Aufsatz *(paper)* geschrieben. Sie haben nicht viel Zeit gebraucht und doch ein "A" bekommen.
5. Sie haben mit einer Freundin in einem Restaurant gegessen. Die Freundin zahlt fürs Essen.
6. Sie sind im Supermarkt gewesen und haben viel gekauft. Die Tür zu Ihrem Studentenheim ist zu. Ein Student öffnet Ihnen die Tür.
7. Ihre Eltern haben Ihnen etwas Schönes zu Weihnachten geschenkt.
8. Sie haben eine Million Dollar gewonnen.
9. Sie danken Ihrem Zimmernachbarn, weil er Ihnen geholfen hat. Was antwortet der Nachbar?
10. Ein Freund fragt, ob Sie zu einer Party kommen möchten.
11. Ihre beste Freundin sagt, daß sie im Herbst ein Jahr nach Deutschland geht.
12. Sie studieren in Deutschland. Ein deutscher Student fragt, ob Sie Weihnachten bei seiner *(his)* Familie feiern möchten.
13. Sie haben Weihnachten bei Familie Schmidt gefeiert. Sie fahren wieder nach Hause. Was sagen Sie zu Herrn und Frau Schmidt?
14. Ihr Onkel hat Ihnen 100 Dollar geschenkt.

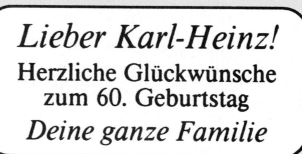

Lieber Karl-Heinz!
Herzliche Glückwünsche zum 60. Geburtstag
Deine ganze Familie

B. Kurzgespräche

1. You meet a fellow student on campus. After engaging in small talk, you tell him / her that a mutual friend has a birthday on Friday. Since you are giving a party, ask the other student to come, and give him / her the necessary information as to where and when the party will take place. After he / she thanks you for the invitation, you both say goodbye.
2. Your parents call you up and ask whether you have plans for the weekend. They are driving through the town where you are studying and would like to see you **(dich).** You are surprised and pleased. It is your mother's birthday, and you wish her a happy birthday. Tell her you have bought a present and that she'll get it when they come. You conclude the conversation.

In der Stadt

▮ LERNZIELE

Gespräche and **Wortschatz.** This chapter deals with life in the city.

Struktur. You will learn about . . .

- personal pronouns.
- modal auxiliary verbs.
- **sondern** vs. **aber.**

Einblicke. The Danube and a visit to Vienna

Sprechsituationen

- Getting someone's attention
- Asking for directions
- Understanding directions

◆◆◆◆◆ GESPRÄCHE

Entschuldigen Sie! Wo ist . . . ?

Warm-ups: 1. **Der wievielte ist das?** Ist das Ihr Geburtstag? z.B. Das ist der 1. Mai. Ich habe am 3. August Geburtstag. (Write various dates on the board; have students answer.) 2. **Geben Sie das Partizip!** (arbeiten, bekommen, beobachten, bleiben, denken, gefallen, fahren, fallen, finden, gehen, gratulieren, helfen, laufen, lesen, singen, tragen, tun, überraschen)

Fragen: 1. Wo ist das Hotel Sacher? 2. Wie kommt man von der Staatsoper zum Stephansdom? 4. Wen fragt der Tourist im zweiten Gespräch? 5. Ist der Herr Wiener? 6. Wie kommt der Tourist zum Burgtheater? 7. Wo ist die Haltestelle? 8. Was ist gegenüber vom Burgtheater?

TOURIST	Entschuldigen Sie! Können Sie mir sagen, wo das Hotel Sacher[1] ist?
WIENER	Erste Straße links hinter der Staatsoper[2].
TOURIST	Und wie komme ich von da zum Stephansdom[3]?
WIENER	Geradeaus, die Kärntnerstraße entlang.
TOURIST	Wie weit ist es zum Dom?
WIENER	Nicht weit. Sie können zu Fuß gehen!
TOURIST	Danke schön!
WIENER	Bitte schön!

Da drüben!

TOURIST	Entschuldigen Sie bitte! Wo ist das Burgtheater[4]?
HERR	Es tut mir leid. Ich bin nicht aus Wien.
TOURIST	Entschuldigen Sie! Ist das das Burgtheater?
DAME	Nein, das ist nicht das Burgtheater, sondern die Staatsoper. Fahren Sie mit der Straßenbahn zum Rathaus! Gegenüber vom Rathaus ist das Burgtheater.
TOURIST	Und wo hält die Straßenbahn?
DAME	Da drüben links!
TOURIST	Vielen Dank!
DAME	Bitte schön!

Übrigens

◆◆◆◆◆◆◆◆◆◆◆◆◆◆◆◆◆◆◆◆◆◆◆◆◆◆◆◆◆◆◆◆

1. **Hotel Sacher** is probably the best-known hotel in Vienna. One of the reasons for its popularity is its famous café, for which a rich, delicious cake **(Sachertorte)** has been named.

2. Vienna's Opera **(Staatsoper)**, inaugurated in 1869, was built in the style of the early French Renaissance and is one of the foremost European opera houses.

3. St. Stephen's **(Stephansdom)** is a masterpiece of Gothic architecture dating from the twelfth century. Its roof of colored tile and its 450-foot-high spire make it the landmark of Vienna.

4. Vienna's **Burgtheater** was declared Austria's national theater in 1776 by Emperor Joseph II. The Burgtheater has always been devoted to classical drama and has developed a stylized mode of diction, giving it an aura of conservatism. Most of the ensemble, numbering more than a hundred, have lifetime contracts.

Wiener Burgtheater

Excuse Me! Where Is . . .? TOURIST: *Excuse me! Can you tell me where the Sacher Hotel is?* VIENNESE: *First street to the left behind the opera.* TOURIST: *And how do I get from there to St. Stephen's Cathedral?* VIENNESE: *Straight ahead along Kärtnerstraße.* TOURIST: *How far is it to the cathedral?* VIENNESE: *Not far. You can walk there.* TOURIST: *Thank you very much.* VIENNESE: *You're welcome.*

Over There TOURIST: *Excuse me. Where is the Burgtheater?* GENTLEMAN: *I'm sorry. I'm not from Vienna.* TOURIST: *Excuse me. Is that the Burgtheater?* LADY: *No, that's not the Burgtheater but the opera house. Take the streetcar to city hall. The Burgtheater is across from city hall.* TOURIST: *And where does the streetcar stop?* LADY: *Over there to the left.* TOURIST: *Thank you very much.* LADY: *You're welcome.*

WORTSCHATZ 1

DER STADTPLAN, ‟E *city map*

der	Bahnhof, ‟e	*train station*	*die*	Bank, -en	*bank*
	Bus, -se	*bus*		Bibliothek, -en	*library*
	Dom, -e	*cathedral*		Brücke, -n	*bridge*
	Park, -s	*park*		Haltestelle, -n	*(bus etc.) stop*
	Platz, ‟e	*place; square*		Kirche, -n	*church*
	Weg, -e	*way; trail*		Post	*post office*
das	Auto, -s	*car*		Schule, -n	*school*
	Hotel, -s	*hotel*		Straße, -n	*street*
	Kino, -s	*movie theater*		Straßenbahn, -en	*streetcar*
	Museum, Museen	*museum*		U-Bahn	*subway*
				Universität, -en	*university*
	Rathaus, ‟er	*city hall*		Uni, -s	
	Schloß, ‟sser	*palace*			
	Taxi, -s	*taxi*			
	Theater, -	*theater*			

WEITERES

der	Tourist, -en, -en	*tourist*
die	Dame, -en	*lady*
	Touristin, -nen	*tourist*

da drüben	*over there*
Entschuldigen Sie!	*Excuse me!*
Es tut mir leid.	*I'm sorry.*
Fahren Sie mit dem Bus!	*Go by bus.*
gegenüber von (+ *dat.*)	*across from*
(immer) geradeaus	*(always) straight ahead*
in der Nähe von (+ *dat.*)	*near (in the vicinity of)*
links / rechts	*on the left / on the right*
nah / weit	*near / far*
schade	*too bad*
sondern	*but (on the contrary)*
Vielen Dank!	*Thank you very much.*
besichtigen	*to visit (palace, etc.)*
halten (hält), gehalten[1]	*to stop; to hold*
zeigen	*to show*
zu Fuß gehen, ist zu Fuß gegangen	*to walk*

Point out that **fahren** expresses *to go* when a vehicle is involved.

The difference between **sondern** and **aber** will be discussed in Struktur III, on p. 146.

1 When **halten** is intransitive (i.e., without an accusative object), it means *to come to a stop:* Der Bus **hält** hier. When it is transitive, it means *to hold:* **Halten** Sie mir bitte das Buch!

PASSIVES VOKABULAR die **Oper, -n** *opera house*   **entlang** *along* **hinter** *behind*

Der Stadtplan zeigt (*shows*) den Weg.

ZUM THEMA

A. Mustersätze

1. das Theater / die Oper: **Das ist nicht** das Theater, **sondern** die Oper.
   das Rathaus / die Universität; das Museum / die Bibliothek; die Bank / die Post; die Bushaltestelle / die Straßenbahnhaltestelle

2. zur Universität: **Können Sie mir sagen, wie ich** zur Universität **komme?**
   zum Rathaus, zur Bibliothek, zum Museum, zur Schulstraße

3. erste / links: **Die** erste **Straße** links.
   zweite / rechts; dritte / links; vierte / rechts

4. Straßenbahn: **Fahren Sie mit** der Straßenbahn!
   Bus, Auto, U-Bahn, Taxi

5. da drüben: **Die Straßenbahn hält** da drüben.
   da drüben rechts, beim Bahnhof, in der Nähe vom Park, gegenüber vom Theater

B. Was bedeuten die Wörter, und was sind die Artikel?

Domplatz, Fußgängerweg, Schloßhotel, Postbus, Touristenstadt, Kirchenfest, Schulferien, Studentenkino, Bahnhofsdrogerie, Universitätsparkplatz, Parkuhr

C. Was paßt nicht?

1. der Bus, das Taxi, die Straßenbahn, das Kino
2. das Theater, der Weg, das Museum, die Bibliothek
3. die U-Bahn, die Bank, die Post, das Rathaus
4. die Straße, die Brücke, der Stadtplan, der Platz
5. da drüben, gegenüber von, in der Nähe von, schade
6. fahren, zu Fuß gehen, halten, laufen

Optional vocabulary: der Parkplatz, ⸚e; das Büro, -s, Gebäude, - *building*, Labor, -s, Stadion, -dien, Studentenheim, -e; die Turnhalle, -n *gym*

D. Wo ist . . . ? Ask for various places in your town or on campus.

x Entschuldigen Sie! Ist das _____ ?

y Nein, das ist nicht _____ , sondern _____ .

x Wo ist _____ ?

y _____ ist in der Nähe von _____ .

x Und wie komme ich von hier zu _____ ?

y _____ .

x Wie weit ist es zu _____ ?

y _____ .

x Vielen Dank!

y _____ !

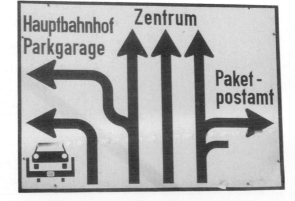

E. Aussprache. See also II.29–36 in the pronunciation section of the Workbook.

1. [ö:] Österreich, Brötchen, Bahnhöfe, Klöße, Goethe, schön, gewöhnlich, französisch, hören
2. [ö] öffnen, östlich, können, Löffel, zwölf, nördlich, möchten, Wörter, Röcke
3. Wortpaare
   a. kennen / können   c. große / Größe   e. Sühne / Söhne
   b. Sehne / Söhne   d. schon / schön   f. Höhle / Hölle

STRUKTUR

I. Personal Pronouns

Encourage students to use pronouns whenever possible. Have them practice the forms of the personal pronouns regularly over several days in simple sentences, e.g., **Das ist für euch** *(for us, for them, for me, etc.).*

1. In English the PERSONAL PRONOUNS are *I, me, you, he, him, she, her, it, we, us, they,* and *them.* Some of these pronouns are used as subjects, others as direct or indirect objects, or objects of prepositions.

SUBJECT:	*He is coming.*
DIRECT OBJECT:	*I see him.*
INDIRECT OBJECT:	*I give him the book.*
OBJECT OF A PREPOSITION:	*We'll go without him.*

The German personal pronouns are likewise used as subjects, direct or indirect objects, or objects of prepositions. Like the definite and indefinite articles, personal pronouns have special forms in the various cases. You already know the nominative case of these pronouns. Here now are the nominative, accusative, and dative cases together.

	singular					plural			sg. / pl.
nom.	ich	du	er	es	sie	wir	ihr	sie	Sie
acc.	**mich**	**dich**	**ihn**	**es**	**sie**	**uns**	**euch**	**sie**	**Sie**
dat.	**mir**	**dir**	**ihm**	**ihm**	**ihr**	**uns**	**euch**	**ihnen**	**Ihnen**

SUBJECT:	**Er** kommt.
DIRECT OBJECT:	Ich sehe **ihn.**
INDIRECT OBJECT:	Ich gebe **ihm** das Buch.
OBJECT OF A PREPOSITION:	Wir gehen **ohne ihn.**

▪ Note the similarities between the definite article of the noun and the pronoun that replaces it.

	masc.	neut.	fem.	pl.
nom.	**der** Mann = **er**	**das** Kind = **es**	**die** Frau = **sie**	**die** Leute = **sie**
acc.	**den** Mann = **ihn**	**das** Kind = **es**	**die** Frau = **sie**	**die** Leute = **sie**
dat.	**dem** Mann = **ihm**	**dem** Kind = **ihm**	**der** Frau = **ihr**	**den** Leuten = **ihnen**

2. As in English, the dative object usually precedes the accusative object, unless the accusative object is a pronoun. If that is the case, the accusative object pronoun comes first.

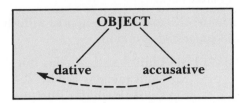

Ich gebe **dem Studenten**	den Kuli.	*I'm giving the student the pen.*
Ich gebe **ihm**	den Kuli.	*I'm giving him the pen.*
Ich gebe ihn	**dem Studenten.**	*I'm giving it to the student.*
Ich gebe ihn	**ihm.**	*I'm giving it to him.*

ÜBUNGEN

A. Ersetzen Sie die Hauptwörter durch Pronomen! Replace each noun with a pronoun in the appropriate case.

BEISPIEL: den Bruder   **ihn**

1. der Vater, dem Mann, den Großvater, dem Freund, den Ober
2. die Freundin, der Großmutter, der Dame, die Frau, der Familie
3. die Eltern, den Herren, den Frauen, die Freundinnen, den Schweizern
4. für die Mutter, mit den Freunden, gegen die Studenten, außer dem Großvater, ohne den Ober, von den Eltern, zu dem Fräulein, bei der Großmutter

B. Kombinieren Sie mit den Präpositionen! Was sind die Akkusativ- und Dativformen?

BEISPIEL: ich (ohne, mit)   **ohne mich, mit mir**

1. er (für, mit)
2. wir (durch, von)
3. Sie (gegen, zu)
4. du (ohne, bei)
5. ihr (für, außer)
6. sie / *sg.* (um, nach)
7. sie / *pl.* (für, aus)
8. es (ohne, außer)

Optional practice: Have students put these phrases into complete sentences, e.g., **Tun Sie das ohne mich!**

C. Antworten Sie! Ersetzen Sie die Hauptwörter durch Hauptwörter und Pronomen!

BEISPIEL: Wo ist das Hotel?   Es ist da drüben. (Bank)
Und die Bank?   Sie ist da drüben.

1. Wo ist die Post? Da ist sie. (Dom, Rathaus, Apotheke)
2. Ist das Museum weit von hier? Nein, es ist nicht weit von hier. (Kirche, Geschäft, Platz)
3. Zeigen Sie der Dame den Weg? Ja, ich zeige ihr den Weg. (Mann, Leute, Touristin)
4. Helfen Sie dem Herrn? Ja, ich helfe ihm. (Kind, Damen, Touristin)

C: Let students add other nouns of their choice, such as **Fluß, Brücke, Museum.**

5. Haben Sie die Straßenbahn genommen? Ja, ich habe sie genommen. (Bus, U-Bahn, Taxi)
6. Wie hat dir die Stadt gefallen? Sie hat mir gut gefallen. (Hotel, Universität, Park)

D: Write the nominative forms of all personal pronouns on the board, then point to the one the students are to use.

D. Was fehlt? Complete the sentences with the appropriate German case forms of the suggested pronouns.

BEISPIEL: Sie kauft _____ das Buch. (*me, you / formal*)
   Sie kauft mir das Buch.
   Sie kauft Ihnen das Buch.

1. Siehst du _____ ? (*them, him, her, me, us*)
2. Geben Sie es _____ ! (*him, me, her, us, them*)
3. Sie braucht _____ . (*you / sg., you / pl., you / formal, me, him, them, us*)
4. Wie geht es _____ ? (*he, they, you / formal, she, you / sg., you / pl.*)
5. Das Fräulein hat _____ das Eis gebracht. (*you / sg., you / pl., us, him, her, me, you / formal*)
6. Hat die Party _____ überrascht? (*you / formal, me, you / sg., us, her, him, you / pl.*)

E. Auf deutsch, bitte!
1. Did you (*sg. fam.*) thank him?
2. We congratulated her.
3. I surprised them.
4. We'll show you (*pl. fam.*) the palace.
5. Did they answer you (*pl. fam.*)?
6. I was writing (to) you (*sg. fam.*).
7. Are you (*sg. fam.*) going to give him the present?

F: Instead of giving students English text cues, you could give them names and have them respond with pronouns. 1. **Es tut mir leid.** (Mark, Barbara, Holger und Birgit) 2. **Es tut ihm nicht leid.** (Karin, Rolf, meinem Mann und mir, meinem Vater und meiner Mutter) 3. **Wien gefällt mir.** (Andreas und mir, meinen Freunden und deinen Freunden, meinem Onkel, meiner Tante, Herrn und Frau Meyer)

F. Variieren Sie die Sätze!
1. **Es tut mir leid**
   a. He's sorry. **b.** She's sorry. **c.** They're sorry. **d.** Are you (*3×*) sorry? **e.** We aren't sorry. **f.** Why are you (*sg. fam.*) sorry? **g.** I was sorry. **h.** We weren't sorry. **i.** Who was sorry?
2. **Wien gefällt mir.**
   a. They like Vienna. **b.** Do you (*3×*) like Vienna? **c.** He doesn't like Vienna. **d.** We like Vienna. **e.** I liked Vienna. **f.** How did you (*sg. fam.*) like Vienna? **g.** Who didn't like Vienna? **h.** She didn't like Vienna.

G: Books open.

G. Wem gibt sie was? Carolyn has just cleaned out her closet and is going to give away all the souvenirs from her European trip. Explain to whom she is going to give them.

BEISPIEL: ihrer Schwester / die Bilder
   Sie gibt ihrer Schwester die Bilder.
   Sie gibt sie ihrer Schwester.
   Sie gibt sie ihr.

1. ihrem Vater / den Stadtplan **2.** ihren Großeltern / die Landkarte **3.** ihrer Mutter / den Zuckerlöffel **4.** ihrer Schwester / das Kleingeld (*small change*) **5.** Eva / die Kassette von Udo Lindenberg **6.** Markus und Charlotte / die Posters **7.** dir / das T-Shirt

II. Modal Auxiliary Verbs

1. Both English and German have a small group of MODAL AUXILIARY VERBS that modify the meaning of an ordinary verb. Modal verbs express such ideas as the permission, ability, necessity, obligation, or desire to do something.

dürfen	*to be allowed to, may*
können	*to be able to, can*
müssen	*to have to, must*

sollen	*to be supposed to*
wollen	*to want to*
mögen	*to like*

- The German modals are irregular in the singular of the present tense:

	dürfen	**können**	**müssen**	**sollen**	**wollen**	**mögen**	
ich	**darf**	**kann**	**muß**	**soll**	**will**	**mag**	**möchte**
du	**darfst**	**kannst**	**mußt**	**sollst**	**willst**	**magst**	**möchtest**
er	**darf**	**kann**	**muß**	**soll**	**will**	**mag**	**möchte**
wir	**dürfen**	**können**	**müssen**	sollen	wollen	mögen	möchten
ihr	**dürft**	**könnt**	**müßt**	sollt	wollt	mögt	möchtet
sie	**dürfen**	**können**	müssen	sollen	wollen	mögen	möchten

- The **möchte**-forms of **mögen** occur more frequently than the **mag**-forms. **mögen** is usually used in a negative sentence.

Ich **möchte** eine Tasse Tee. *I would like (to have) a cup of tea.*
Ich **mag** Kaffee nicht. *I don't like coffee.*

2. Modals are another example of the two-part verb phrase. In statements and information questions, the modal is the inflected second element of the sentence (V1). The modified verb (V2) appears at the very end of the sentence in its infinitive form.

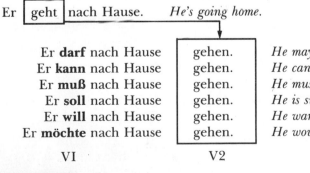

Er | geht | nach Hause.   *He's going home.*

Er **darf** nach Hause	gehen.	*He may (is allowed to) go home.*
Er **kann** nach Hause	gehen.	*He can (is able to) go home.*
Er **muß** nach Hause	gehen.	*He must (has to) go home.*
Er **soll** nach Hause	gehen.	*He is supposed to go home.*
Er **will** nach Hause	gehen.	*He wants to go home.*
Er **möchte** nach Hause	gehen.	*He would like to go home.*

VI   V2

CAUTION

The English set of modals is frequently supplemented by such forms as *is allowed to, is able to, has to, is supposed to.* The German modals, however, do not use such supplements. They follow the pattern of *may, can,* and *must:* **Ich muß gehen.** *(I must go.)*

Ihr sollt gehen always expresses *you're supposed to go* (outer compulsion), not *you should go* (inner compulsion). *Should* must be avoided at this point, since it is a subjunctive form. Students may grasp this if you refer to the Bible: *Thou shalt not kill* (a command), not *you shouldn't kill* (an appeal to one's conscience).

Because modals use two different forms in the present perfect, we have avoided sentences with modals in that tense. The simple past of the modals will be discussed in Chapter 11.

In a dependent clause, two-part verb structures appear in the sequence V2 V1.

3. Modals can be used without an infinitive, provided the modified verb is clearly understood. This happens particularly with verbs of motion.

   Mußt du jetzt nach Hause?—Ja, ich **muß.**
   Willst du zum Supermarkt?—Ja, ich **will,** aber ich **kann** nicht.

4. Watch these important differences in meaning:

   a. **gern** vs. **möchten**

      Ich **esse gern** Kuchen. BUT Ich **möchte** ein Stück Kuchen **(haben).**

      The first sentence says that I am generally fond of cake (*I like to eat cake*). The second sentence implies a desire for a piece of cake at this particular moment (*I'd like a piece of cake*).

   b. **wollen** vs. **möchten**

      Notice the difference in tone and politeness between these two sentences:

      Ich **will** Kuchen. BUT Ich **möchte** Kuchen.
      The first might be said by a spoiled child (*I want cake*), the second by a polite adult (*I would like cake*).

5. Modals in Subordinate Clauses

   a. Remember that the inflected verb stands at the very end of clauses introduced by subordinate conjunctions such as **bevor, daß, ob, obwohl, wenn,** and **weil.**

      Sie sagt, **daß** du nach Hause gehen **kannst.**
      Du kannst nach Hause gehen, **wenn** du **möchtest.**

   b. If the sentence starts with the subordinate clause, then the inflected verb of the main sentence (the modal) follows right after the comma.

      Du **kannst** nach Hause gehen, wenn du möchtest.
      Wenn du möchtest, **kannst** du nach Hause gehen.

Parksünder ist wer parkt, wo man nicht parken darf.

ÜBUNGEN

H. Ersetzen Sie das Subjekt!

BEISPIEL: Wir sollen zum Markt fahren. (ich)   **Ich soll zum Markt fahren.**

1. Wir wollen zu Hause bleiben. (er, sie / *pl.*, du, ich)
2. Sie müssen noch die Rechnung bezahlen. (ich, ihr, du, Vater)
3. Du darfst zum Bahnhof kommen. (er, ihr, die Kinder, ich)
4. Möchtet ihr ein Eis haben? (sie, du, er, das Fräulein)
5. Können Sie mir sagen, wo das ist? (du, ihr, er, die Damen)

I. Am Sonntag. Say what these people will do on Sunday.

BEISPIEL: Carolyn spricht nur Deutsch. (wollen)
   Carolyn will nur Deutsch sprechen.

1. Volker und Silvia spielen Tennis. (wollen)
2. Paul fährt mit ein paar Freunden in die Berge. (möchten)
3. Friederike bezahlt Rechnungen. (müssen)
4. Helmut hilft Vater zu Hause. (sollen)
5. Herr und Frau Ahrendt besichtigen Schloß Schönbrunn. (können)
6. Die Kinder gehen in den Prater (*a Viennese entertainment park*). (dürfen)

J. Besuch (*Visitors*)
1. **Stadtbesichtigung.** (*Sightseeing in town.*) Mitzi and Sepp are visiting their friends Heike and Dirk in Quedlinburg. Dirk tells Mitzi and Sepp what Heike wants to know.

   Beginnen Sie mit **Heike fragt, ob . . . !**

   a. Könnt ihr den Weg in die Stadt allein finden?
   b. Wollt ihr einen Stadtplan haben?
   c. Möchtet ihr zu Fuß gehen?
   d. Soll ich euch mit dem Auto zum Stadtzentrum bringen?
   e. Müßt ihr noch zur Bank?

2. **Fragen.** Mitzi has several questions. Tell us what she asks.

   Beginnen Sie mit **Mitzi fragt, . . . !**

   a. Wo kann man hier in der Nähe Blumen kaufen?
   b. Was für ein Geschenk sollen wir für den Vater kaufen?
   c. Wie lange dürfen wir hier bleiben?
   d. Wann müssen wir abends wieder hier sein?
   e. Wer will mit in die Stadt?

K. Auf deutsch, bitte!
1. He wants to see the cathedral.
2. They have to go to the post office.
3. I can't read that.
4. You (*pl. fam.*) are supposed to speak German.
5. You (*sg. fam.*) may order a piece of cake.
6. She's supposed to study (**lernen**).
7. We have to find the way.

8. Can't you (*3×*) help me?
9. We'd like to drive to Vienna.
10. Are we allowed to see the palace?

Have students complete
the dialogue with a
classmate or in small
groups. Have them
compare answers to see
how meaning is affected
by the modal chosen.

L. Welches Modalverb paßt?

UWE   Till, _____ du mit mir gehen? Ich _____ einen Stadtplan
kaufen.

TILL   Wo _____ wir einen Stadtplan bekommen?

UWE   Die Buchhandlung _____ Stadtpläne haben.

TILL   Gut. Ich _____ zwei Bücher für meinen Bruder kaufen. Ich
gehe mit dir.

UWE   _____ wir zu Fuß gehen, oder _____ wir mit dem Fahrrad
(*bicycle*) fahren?

TILL   Ich _____ mit dem Fahrrad fahren. Dann _____ wir noch
zur Bank, bevor sie zu ist. Die Bücher sind bestimmt nicht billig. _____ du nicht auch zur Bank?

UWE   Ja, richtig. Ich _____ diese Rechnung bezahlen.

III. sondern vs. aber

German has two coordinating conjunctions corresponding to the English *but*.

aber	*but, however*
sondern	*but on the contrary, but rather*

▪ **sondern** must be used when the first clause is negated AND the meaning *but on
the contrary* is implied (frequently with opposites).

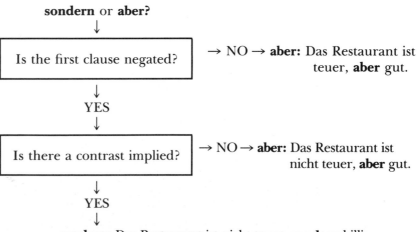

▪ **nicht nur . . . sondern auch . . .**

Das Restaurant ist **nicht nur** gut, **sondern auch** billig.
The restaurant is not only good, but also inexpensive.

ÜBUNGEN

M. sondern oder aber? Insert the appropriate conjunction.

1. Wien ist sehr schön, _____ Salzburg gefällt mir besser *(better)*.
2. Die Straßenbahn hält nicht hier, _____ gegenüber von der Post.
3. Gehen Sie beim Theater nicht rechts, _____ geradeaus!
4. Die Kirche ist nicht alt, _____ neu.
5. Das Rathaus ist nicht besonders schön, _____ sehr alt.
6. Das ist kein Museum, _____ eine Bibliothek.
7. Die Mensa ist billig, _____ nicht gut.

ZUSAMMENFASSUNG

N. Können Sie mir sagen, . . . ? Ask for directions.

BEISPIEL: können / Sie / sagen / mir / / wo / sein / Universität?
Können Sie mir sagen, wo die Universität ist?

1. können / du / sagen / ihm / / wie / heißen / Straße?
2. können / er / sagen / uns / / wie / weit / es / sein / zu / Bahnhof?
3. können / sie *(pl.)* / sagen / euch / / ob / es / geben / hier / Straßenbahn oder Bus?
4. können / Sie / sagen / ihr / / wo / Bus / hält?
5. können / ihr / sagen / mir / / wie / lange / Geschäfte / sein / offen?

O. Wo ist eine Bank? Auf deutsch, bitte!

1. Excuse me *(formal)*, can you tell me where there's a bank?   **2.** I'm sorry, but I'm not from Vienna.   **3.** Whom can I ask?   **4.** Who can help me?   **5.** May I help you?   **6.** I'd like to find a bank.   **7.** Near the cathedral (there) is a bank.   **8.** Can you tell me whether that's far from here?   **9.** You can walk (there), but the banks close (are closed) in twenty minutes.   **10.** Take the subway or a taxi!

Im Wiener Süd-
bahnhof

EINBLICKE ◆◆◆◆◆◆◆◆◆◆◆

Der Stephansdom ist das Wahrzeichen (*landmark*) von Wien.

Vienna **(Wien)** is the capital of Austria and with 1.6 million inhabitants also its largest city. The center of Vienna (the **Innenstadt**) dates from medieval times. The city reached its zenith of power and wealth as the capital of the Austro-Hungarian Empire during the reign of Emperor Franz Joseph (1848–1916), when it developed into one of Europe's most important cultural centers.

Composers such as Haydn, Mozart, Beethoven, Schubert, Brahms, Johann and Richard Strauß, Mahler and Schönberg, who all lived and worked there for at least part of their lives, have left a lasting imprint on the city's cultural life.

The 400-year rule of the House of Habsburg came to an end in 1918, when Emperor Charles I abdicated and Austria was declared a republic. **(Republik Österreich).** In 1938 Austria was incorporated into Hitler's Third Reich by the Anschluss but regained its sovereignty in 1955. Since then the country has pledged to remain neutral, which refers largely to a commitment to armed neutrality. Austria is an active participant in the United Nations, a host for many international conferences, and a gateway for refugees from all over the world.

WORTSCHATZ 2

bekannt	*well-known*
Das macht nichts.	*That doesn't matter.*
einmal	*once, (at) one time*

gemütlich	*pleasant, cozy*
genug	*enough*
interessant	*interesting*
leider	*unfortunately*
lieb[1]	*dear*
schon	*already*
stundenlang	*for hours*
toll	*great, super*
bummeln, ist gebummelt	*to stroll*

1 liebe Eltern, lieber Michael, liebe Elisabeth

Exercise E, p. 153, can be used as a pre-reading activity.

WAS IST DAS? der Sport, Stop, Walzer; das Gästehaus, Schiff; die Großstadt, Innenstadt, Studentengruppe, Winterresidenz; kunsthistorisch, romantisch, zentral

greetings

Grüße° aus Österreich

Liebe Eltern!

Jetzt muß ich Euch† aber wirklich wieder einmal schreiben! Ich habe so viel gesehen, daß ich gar nicht weiß, wo ich beginnen soll. Vor einer Woche *was* war° unsere Studentengruppe noch in Passau[1]. Von dort sind wir mit dem   5 *traveled down* Schiff die Donau hinuntergefahren°. Wir haben einen Stop in Linz[2] gemacht und haben die Stadt, das Schloß und den Dom besichtigt. Dann sind wir mit

Kloster Melk an der Donau

† When writing a letter, it is proper to capitalize pronouns (**Ihr, Euch**) and possessive adjectives (**Euer**) that refer to the addressee.

vineyards / castles
monastery

dem Schiff weiter bis nach Wien gefahren. Die Weinberge°, Burgen° und besonders Kloster° Melk[3] haben mir sehr gut gefallen. Das Wetter ist auch prima gewesen.

Jetzt sind wir schon ein paar Tage in Wien. Ich finde es toll hier! Unser Gästehaus liegt sehr zentral, und wir können alles zu Fuß oder mit der

reach
in the

U-Bahn erreichen°. So viel bin ich noch nie gelaufen! Am Freitag sind wir stundenlang durch die Innenstadt gebummelt. Die Geschäfte in der° Kärntnerstraße sind sehr teuer, aber man muß ja nichts kaufen. Wir haben natür-

elevator
went to the top of the tower /
* all of*
Magic Flute

lich auch den Stephansdom besichtigt und sind mit dem Aufzug° im Turm hinaufgefahren°. Von dort kann man ganz° Wien sehen. Abends haben wir Mozarts *Zauberflöte*° in der Staatsoper gehört.

10

15

of the / emperors
riding academy / white horses
riding

restaurant / was

ferris wheel

Am Samstag haben wir die Hofburg besichtigt. Das ist einmal die Winterresidenz der° Habsburger Kaiser° gewesen. Dort ist auch die Spanische Reitschule°, und man kann die Lipizzaner° beim Training sehen. Das haben wir auch getan. Wirklich prima! Da ist das Reiten° kein Sport, sondern Kunst. Am Abend sind wir mit der Straßenbahn nach Grinzing[4] gefahren und haben dort Marks Geburtstag mit Musik und Wein gefeiert. Die Weinstube° war° sehr gemütlich.

Heute besichtigen wir das Museum für Völkerkunde, und später wollen ein paar von uns noch zum Prater[5]. Das Riesenrad° dort soll toll sein. Das muß man doch gesehen haben!

20

25

MUSEUM FÜR VÖLKERKUNDE

A-1014 WIEN, NEUE HOFBURG

TELEFON (0222) 93 45 41

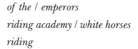

monuments

traffic

simply

we get going again

Richtig oder falsch?
1. Michaels Reise hat in Salzburg begonnen. (F)
2. Sie sind mit dem Schiff bis nach Wien gefahren. (R) 3. Sie haben viele Weinberge und Burgen gesehen. (R) 4. Michael wohnt in der Hofburg. (F)
5. Die Kärntnerstraße ist eine Fußgängerzone, und man kann dort schön bummeln gehen (R) 6. Besonders interessant hat Michael die Spanische Reitschule gefunden. (R) 7. Im Stephansdom haben sie Mozarts *Zauberflöte* gehört. (F) 8. In Grinzing haben sie Marks Geburtstag gefeiert. (R) 9. Der Prater soll ein Museum sein. (F)
10. Michael will nicht nach Budapest. (F)
11. Er bleibt noch ein paar Tage in Wien. (F)
12. Sie wollen noch bis nach Innsbruck. (R)

Passau an der Donau

A: 1. Passau 2. die Donau 3. Wien
4. Melk 5. Linz
6. die Kärntnerstraße
7. der Turm vom Stephansdom 8. die Hofburg 9. die Spanische Reitschule 10. die Staatsoper 11. der Prater 12. Grinzing

Wien ist wirklich interessant. Überall findet man Denkmäler° oder Straßen mit bekannten Namen wie Mozart, Beethoven, Johann Strauß, usw. 30 Aber Ihr dürft nicht denken, daß man hier nur Walzer hört und alles romantisch ist. Wien ist auch eine Großstadt mit vielen Menschen und viel Verkehr°. Aber es gefällt mir hier so gut, daß ich gern noch ein paar Tage bleiben möchte. Das geht leider nicht, weil wir noch nach Salzburg[6] und Innsbruck[7] wollen. Eine Woche ist einfach° nicht lang genug für so eine 35 Reise. Nach Budapest können wir leider auch nicht. Nun, das macht nichts. Das kann ich dann im Frühling machen.

So, jetzt muß ich schnell frühstücken, und dann geht's wieder los°! Tschüß und viele liebe Grüße!

Euer Michael

PS: Ich schreibe auf deutsch, weil ich Euch zeigen möchte, daß ich auch etwas 40 gelernt habe. Mein Freund Wolfgang hat mir natürlich etwas geholfen, aber es geht schon viel besser.

ZUM TEXT

A. Wer, was oder wo ist das? Match the descriptions with the places or people in the list below.

die Donau, Grinzing, die Hofburg, die Kärntnerstraße, Linz, Melk, Passau, der Prater, die Spanische Reitschule, die Staatsoper, der Turm vom Stephansdom, Wien

1. Hier hat die Flußfahrt nach Wien begonnen.
2. Auf diesem *(on this)* Fluß kann man mit dem Schiff bis nach Wien fahren.

Ich soll
Sie schön
grüßen...

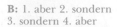

3. Das ist die Hauptstadt von Österreich.
4. Hier gibt es ein Barockkloster. Es ist sehr bekannt.
5. Da haben die Studenten einen Stop gemacht und die Stadt besichtigt.
6. Hier kann man schön bummeln, aber die Geschäfte sind sehr teuer.
7. Von hier kann man ganz Wien sehen.
8. Das ist einmal die Winterresidenz der (of the) Habsburger Kaiser gewesen.
9. Hier kann man die Lipizzaner trainieren sehen.
10. Hier kann man Mozarts *Zauberflöte* hören.
11. Hier gibt es ein Riesenrad.
12. Dort kann man gemütlich essen und Wein trinken.

B: 1. aber 2. sondern
3. sondern 4. aber

B. sondern oder aber? Insert the appropriate conjunction.
1. Das Gästehaus ist nicht sehr elegant, _____ es liegt zentral.
2. Wir sind nicht viel mit dem Bus gefahren, _____ gelaufen.
3. Bei der Spanischen Reitschule ist das Reiten kein Sport, _____ Kunst.
4. Die Geschäfte in der Kärntnerstraße sind teuer, _____ sie gefallen mir.

C. Fahrt (trip) nach Österreich. Mr. Schubach tells about his travel plans. Use modal verbs.

BEISPIEL: Ihr fahrt mit uns mit dem Schiff bis nach Wien. (müssen)
Ihr müßt mit uns mit dem Schiff bis nach Wien fahren.

1. Unsere Fahrt beginnt in Passau. (sollen)
2. In Linz machen wir einen Stop. (wollen)
3. Meine Frau besichtigt Kloster Melk. (möchten)
4. Vom Schiff sieht man viele Weinberge und Burgen. (können)
5. Wir bleiben fünf Tage in Wien. (wollen)
6. Dort gibt es viel zu sehen. (sollen)
7. Man hat natürlich gute Schuhe dabei (along). (müssen)
8. Ich laufe aber nicht so viel. (dürfen)
9. Meine Frau bummelt gemütlich durch die Kärntnerstraße. (möchten)
10. Ich sehe viele Museen. (wollen)

Optional practice: Er-
setzen Sie die Haupt-
wörter durch Prono-
men: z.B. Er zeigt der
Dame den Weg: Er
zeigt ihr den Weg. Er
zeigt ihn ihr. (Er zeigt
den Eltern den Stadt-
plan. Wir zeigen dem
Touristen das Rathaus.
Ich zeige der Studentin
die Museen. Ich zeige
dem Kind den Park.)

Have students work in
pairs or use the ques-
tions as guidelines for a
written assignment.

D. Interview. Fragen Sie einen Nachbarn / eine Nachbarin, . . . !
1. ob er / sie schon einmal in Wien gewesen ist
2. wenn ja, was ihm / ihr in Wien besonders gut gefallen hat **(Was hat dir . . . ?)** wenn nein, was er / sie sehen möchte, wenn er / sie einmal nach Wien fährt
3. ob er / sie in einer Großstadt oder Kleinstadt wohnt
4. ob die Stadt eine Altstadt hat, und ob sie schön ist
5. ob es dort auch eine Straßenbahn, eine U-Bahn oder Busse gibt
6. was ihm / ihr dort besonders gefällt, und was nicht
7. ob er / sie schon einmal in einem Schloß gewesen ist; wenn ja, wo; wenn nein, welches Schloß er / sie einmal sehen möchte
8. was für Denkmäler und Straßen mit bekannten Namen es hier gibt

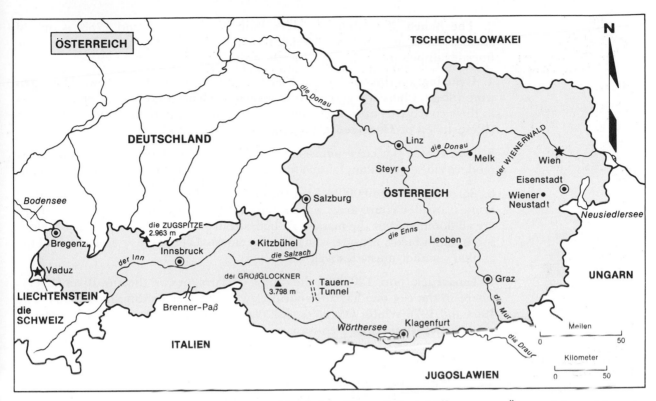

E. Etwas Geographie. Sehen Sie auf die Landkarte von Österreich und beantworten Sie die Fragen!

1. Wie viele Nachbarländer hat Österreich? Wie heißen sie, und wo liegen sie?
2. Wie heißt die Hauptstadt von Österreich? Wie heißen ein paar Städte in Österreich?
3. Welcher Fluß fließt (*flows*) durch Wien? Salzburg? Innsbruck? Linz? Graz?
4. Welcher See liegt nicht nur in Österreich, sondern auch in Deutschland und in der Schweiz? Welcher See liegt zum Teil in Österreich und zum Teil in Ungarn? An welchem See liegt Klagenfurt?
5. Wo liegt der Brenner-Paß? der Großglockner? der Tauern-Tunnel?

Übrigens

◆◆◆◆◆◆◆◆◆◆◆◆◆◆◆◆◆◆◆◆◆◆◆◆◆◆◆◆◆

1. **Passau** (pop. 51,000), not far from the Austrian and Czechoslovakian borders, is known as the "town of the three rivers" since it lies at the confluence of the Danube, Inn, and Ilz rivers. It is the starting point for regular steamer service down the Danube to Vienna and the Black Sea.

2. **Linz** (pop. 208,000) is the capital of Upper Austria and, after Vienna and Graz, Austria's third largest city. Located on the Danube river, it is a large port and commercial center.

3. The Benedictine Abbey of **Melk,** built between 1702 and 1783, is one of Austria's most splendid monasteries. Its twin-towered church ranks as one of the finest examples of the baroque north of the Alps.

4. **Grinzing,** on the outskirts of Vienna, is probably the best-known **Heurigen** wine village, where the young, fresh wine **(der Heurige)** is sold by wine-growers in their courtyards or houses, some of which they have turned into restaurants **(Weinstuben** or **Heurigenschänken).**

5. The **Prater** is a large amusement park with a giant ferris wheel and many modern rides, a stadium, fairgrounds, race tracks, bridle paths, pools, and ponds.

6. **Salzburg** (pop. 140,000) is a very beautiful city. Its narrow streets, tall medieval houses, arcaded courtyards, and the palaces and cathedral of the prince-bishops are all dominated by the massive Hohensalzburg Castle. Salzburg's most famous son is undoubtedly Mozart, who is commemorated at the music academy and the annual summer music festival.

7. **Innsbruck** (pop. 120,000), the capital of Tirol, lies on the Inn River. Everywhere in the city one has a beautiful view of the surrounding mountains. The 1964 and 1976 Winter Olympics took place there, and its sports facilities attract tourists and winter-sports enthusiasts from all over the world.

Überall in Innsbruck
sieht man die Berge.

SPRECHSITUATIONEN

It is very important to be able to ask for and understand directions when traveling or living abroad. But first you must get someone's attention.

Getting Someone's Attention

Entschuldigen Sie, bitte!
Verzeihen Sie! *(Pardon.)*

Asking for Directions

Bitte, wo ist . . . ?
Können Sie mir (bitte) sagen, wo . . . ist?
Ich möchte zum / zur . . .
Ich kann . . . nicht finden.
Wie kommt man (von hier) zum / zur . . . ?
Ist hier in der Nähe . . . ?
Wo gibt es hier . . . ?
Wie weit ist es . . . ?

ST.-STEPHANS-DOM

TURM

Eintrittskarte für Studenten
INKLUSIVE 8% MEHRWERTSTEUER

S 8.—   №   43524

Understanding Directions

Gehen Sie / Fahren Sie . . . !
(immer) geradeaus
die erste Straße links / rechts
die Hauptstraße entlang

bis Sie zum / zur . . . kommen
bis Sie . . . sehen

Fahren Sie mit dem Auto / der Straßenbahn!
Nehmen Sie den Bus / die U-Bahn / ein Taxi!
Sie können zu Fuß gehen.
Kommen Sie! Ich kann Ihnen . . . zeigen.
Fragen Sie dort noch einmal!

A. Fragen zum Stadtplan auf Seite 156

1. **Wo ist . . . ?** Ask for directions to several buildings on the map. For each one use as many different ways of asking as you can.

2. **Wie komme ich dorthin** *(there)*? In groups of two, practice asking and giving directions from one place to another.

   BEISPIEL: vom Bahnhof zum Dom
   Entschuldigen Sie, bitte! Können Sie mir sagen, wie ich von hier zum Dom komme?—Gern. Gehen Sie rechts zur Moritzbrücke! Gehen Sie über die Brücke, dann links die Parkstraße entlang! Gehen Sie die zweite Straße rechts! Dort ist dann der Dom.

You could start by giving directions and have students follow you, e.g., **Ich komme aus dem Hotel Regina und gehe rechts; ich komme zur ersten Straße und gehe wieder rechts, dann geradeaus über die Brücke. Was ist links? (der Bahnhof)** Check comprehension! Then let students work in groups of two.

a. vom Dom zum Kaufhaus
b. vom Kaufhaus zur Schule
c. von der Schule zum Hotel

d. vom Hotel zum Museum
e. vom Museum zur Universität
f. von der Universität zum Rathaus

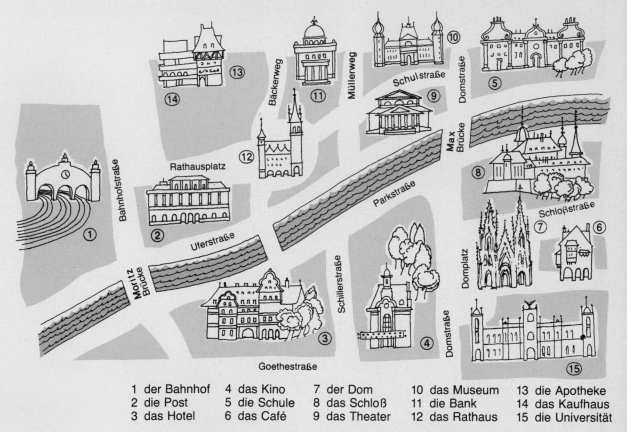

1 der Bahnhof	4 das Kino	7 der Dom	10 das Museum	13 die Apotheke
2 die Post	5 die Schule	8 das Schloß	11 die Bank	14 das Kaufhaus
3 das Hotel	6 das Café	9 das Theater	12 das Rathaus	15 die Universität

B. Kurzgespräche

For optional vocabulary,
see p. 139.

1. You are new in town or on campus, and you're looking for a particular building. Ask someone, starting with *Pardon me, is that . . .?* The stranger tells you that that's not what you're looking for but rather something else. So you ask for directions, and inquire if the building is close by or far away. After your *Thank you very much*, the stranger replies with *You're welcome.*

2. You and a friend are in a Viennese coffee house. Your friend suggests visiting the *Museum für Völkerkunde.* You ask someone at the table next to you where the museum is located. You find out that it is not too far away, but that it is unfortunately closed today. You reply that that's too bad and thank the person for his / her information. As an alternative, your friend says you can stroll along the *Kärntnerstraße* and in the evening **(heute abend)** go to Grinzing. You like the idea very much, but wonder how to get to Grinzing. Your friend informs you that you can take the street car, which stops near the hotel.

6 *Das Haus und die Möbel*

Hamburg, Woh-
nungen am Nikolai-
kanal

▊ LERNZIELE

Gespräche and **Wortschatz.** This chapter talks about housing.

Struktur. You will learn about . . .

- two-way prepositions.
- the imperative.
- **wissen** vs. **kennen.**

Einblicke. Living in the city

Sprechsituationen

- Describing locations
- Offering apologies
- Expressing forgiveness

◆◆◆◆◆ GESPRÄCHE

Warm-ups: 1. **Was ist der Artikel von . . . ?** (Refer to clothing and food.) 2. **Was ist der Plural von** Bus, Brücke, Kino, Museum, . . . ? 3. **Können Sie mir sagen,** wie spät es ist? der wievielte heute ist? was für ein Tag heute ist? auf welcher Seite vom Buch wir sind?

Wohnung zu vermieten

INGE	Hallo, Sie haben eine Zwei-Zimmer-Wohnung zu vermieten, nicht wahr?
VERMIETER	Ja, in der Nähe vom Dom.
INGE	Wie alt ist die Wohnung?
VERMIETER	Ziemlich alt, aber sie ist renoviert[1] und schön groß und hell. Sie hat sogar einen Balkon.
INGE	In welchem Stock liegt sie?
VERMIETER	Im dritten Stock[2].
INGE	Ist sie möbliert oder unmöbliert?
VERMIETER	Unmöbliert[3].
INGE	Und was kostet die Wohnung?
VERMIETER	800 Mark.
INGE	O, das ist ein bißchen zu teuer. Vielen Dank! Auf Wiederhören!
VERMIETER	Auf Wiederhören!

In der Wohngemeinschaft[4]

Richtig oder falsch? 1. In der Nähe vom Dom gibt es eine Wohnung zu vermieten. (R) 2. Die Wohnung hat vier Zimmer. (F) 3. Die Wohnung soll etwas dunkel sein. (F) 4. Sie liegt im Parterre. (F) 5. Horst wohnt in einer Wohngemeinschaft. (R) 6. Von da ist es nur ein Katzensprung zum Dom. (F) 7. Für das Haus bezahlen sie 200 DM pro Nase. (R) 8. Horst möchte, daß Inge auch dort wohnt. (R) 9. Aber das gefällt Inge nicht. (F) 10. Sie hat eine Katze. (F)

INGE	Euer Haus gefällt mir!
HORST	Wir haben noch Platz für dich! Komm, ich zeige es dir! . . . Hier links ist unsere Küche. Sie ist klein, aber praktisch.
INGE	Wer kocht?
HORST	Wir alle: Jens, Gisela, Renate und ich.
INGE	Und das ist das Wohnzimmer?
HORST	Ja. Es ist ein bißchen dunkel, aber das geht.
INGE	Eure Sessel gefallen mir.
HORST	Sie sind alt, aber echt bequem. Oben sind dann vier Schlafzimmer und das Bad.
INGE	Nur ein Bad?
HORST	Ja, leider! Aber hier unten ist noch eine Toilette.
INGE	Was bezahlt ihr im Monat?
HORST	200 DM pro Nase.
INGE	Nicht schlecht! Und wie kommst du zur Uni?
HORST	Zu Fuß natürlich! Es ist ja nur ein Katzensprung!
INGE	Das klingt gut!

Übrigens

1. Although in the fifties and sixties many new apartments were built in the Federal Republic to alleviate the postwar housing shortage, more recently people have rediscovered the beauty of older buildings, many of which are being reno-

vated and modernized with the help of subsidies and tax incentives. In the former GDR the renovation of old housing units lagged behind, except in highly visible sections of cities such as Weimar and Wittenberg.

2. For German-speakers the first floor (ground floor) is **das Parterre** or **das Erdgeschoß.** Only the floors above the ground floor are numbered. When we say *on the second floor,* they say **im ersten Stock.** Homes and apartments usually have a foyer, or hallway **(Flur),** with doors opening into the various rooms. Because these hallways are generally not heated, doors to the heated rooms in homes (as well as in offices) are usually kept closed. Many Germans feel uncomfortably exposed when doors are open, whereas Americans prefer open doors.

3. Furnished apartments are relatively rare. Unfurnished is usually to be taken literally: no light fixtures, built-in cabinets, closets, kitchen cupboards, appliances—just bare walls. The tenant is responsible for the regular maintenance of the apartment, especially interior painting and decorating and, in some places, for cleaning the stairs between the floors.

4. **Wohngemeinschaften,** where several students share an apartment or a house, are quite common because rooms in dormitories are still scarce and waiting lists are long.

Apartment for Rent INGE: *Hello, you have a two-room apartment for rent, don't you?* LANDLORD: *Yes, near the cathedral.* INGE: *How old is the apartment?* LANDLORD: *Quite old, but it's renovated and quite big and bright. It even has a balcony.* INGE: *What floor is it on?* LANDLORD: *On the fourth floor.* INGE: *Is it furnished or unfurnished?* LANDLORD: *Unfurnished.* INGE: *And how much is the rent?* LANDLORD: *800 marks.* INGE: *Oh, that's a little too expensive. Thank you very much. Good-bye!* LANDLORD: *Good-bye!*

With a Group Sharing a House INGE: *I like your house.* HORST: *We still have room for you. Come, I'll show it to you . . . Here to the left is our kitchen. It is small but practical.* INGE: *Who cooks?* HORST: *We all (do): Jens, Gisela, Renate and I.* INGE: *And that's the living room?* HORST: *Yes. It's a bit dark, but that's all right.* INGE: *I like your chairs.* HORST: *They're old but really comfortable. Upstairs are four bedrooms and the bathroom.* INGE: *Only one bathroom?* HORST: *Yes, unfortunately. But down here is another toilet.* INGE: *How much do you pay per month?* HORST: *200 marks per person.* INGE: *Not bad. And how do you get to the university?* HORST: *I walk, of course. It's only a stone's throw from here.* INGE: *That sounds good.*

WORTSCHATZ 1

DAS HAUS, -ER *house*
　　STUDENTENHEIM, -E *dorm*
DIE WOHNUNG, -EN *apartment*

der Balkon, -s	*balcony*	*die* Ecke, -n	*corner*
Baum, -e	*tree*	Garage, -n	*garage*
Flur	*hallway, foyer*	Küche, -n	*kitchen*
Garten, -	*garden, yard*	Toilette, -n	*toilet*

das	Bad, -̈er	*bathroom*
	Arbeitszimmer, -	*study*
	Eßzimmer, -	*dining room*
	Schlafzimmer, -	*bedroom*
	Wohnzimmer, -	*living room*

DIE MÖBEL (*pl.*) *furniture*

der	Farbfernseher, -	*color-TV set*	das	Bett, -en	*bed*
	Kühlschrank, -̈e	*refrigerator*		Radio, -s	*radio*
	Schrank, -̈e	*closet, cupboard*		Regal, -e	*shelf, bookcase*
	Schreibtisch, -e	*desk*		Sofa, -s	*sofa*
	Sessel, -	*armchair*		Telefon, -e	*telephone*
	Teppich, -e	*carpet*	die	Kommode, -n	*dresser*
	Vorhang, -̈e	*curtain*		Lampe, -n	*lamp*

For optional vocabulary, see p. 161.

WEITERES

hell / dunkel	*bright / dark*
im Parterre	*on the first floor (ground level)*
im ersten Stock	*on the second floor*
im Monat	*per month*
oben / unten	*upstairs / downstairs*
praktisch	*practical(ly)*
sogar	*even*
(un)bequem	*(un)comfortable; (in)convenient*
ziemlich	*quite, rather*
baden	*to take a bath; swim*
duschen	*to take a shower*
kochen	*to cook*
mieten / vermieten	*to rent / rent out*

PASSIVES VOKABULAR **die Wohngemeinschaft, -en** *group sharing a place* **Auf Wiederhören!** *Good-bye / on phone* **Das klingt gut.** *That sounds good.* **ein Katzensprung zu** *a stone's throw from, lit. a cat's jump away* **Das geht.** *That's all right.* **pro Nase** *per person, lit. per nose* **renoviert** *renovated* **unmöbliert** *unfurnished*

ZUM THEMA

A. Mustersätze
1. das Haus: Das Haus **gefällt mir.**
   das Wohnzimmer, die Küche, das Bad, der Garten
2. der Sessel: **Wie gefällt dir** der Sessel?
   das Sofa, der Teppich, das Regal, das Radio
3. die Möbel: Die Möbel **gefallen mir.**
   Sessel, Stühle, Vorhänge, Schränke

4. sehr praktisch: **Die Wohnung ist** sehr praktisch.
schön hell, ziemlich dunkel, zu klein, sehr gemütlich, wirklich bequem
5. unten: **Die Wohnung ist** unten.
oben, im Parterre, im ersten Stock, im zweiten Stock, im dritten Stock

B. Beschreiben Sie das Haus! Tell what furniture is in what room. You may need the optional vocabulary below.

PASSIVES VOKABULAR: *bathtub* **die Badewanne**   *closet* **der Kleiderschrank, -̈e** *dining room cabinet* **das Büffet**   *dishwasher* **die Spülmaschine** *dryer* **der Trockner**   *fireplace* **der Kamin**   *freezer* **der Gefrierschrank**   *kitchen cabinet* **der Küchenschrank, -̈e**   *microwave oven* **der Mikrowellenherd**   *mirror* **der Spiegel, -** *nightstand* **der Nachttisch, -e**   *oven* **der Ofen**   *pool* **der Pool**   *range* **der Herd**   *roof* **das Dach**   *shower* **die Dusche**   *sink* **das Waschbecken**   *stairway* **die Treppe**   *stereo set* **die Stereoanlage**   *terrace* **die Terrasse, -n**   *VCR* **die Videoanlage**   *washing machine* **die Waschmaschine**

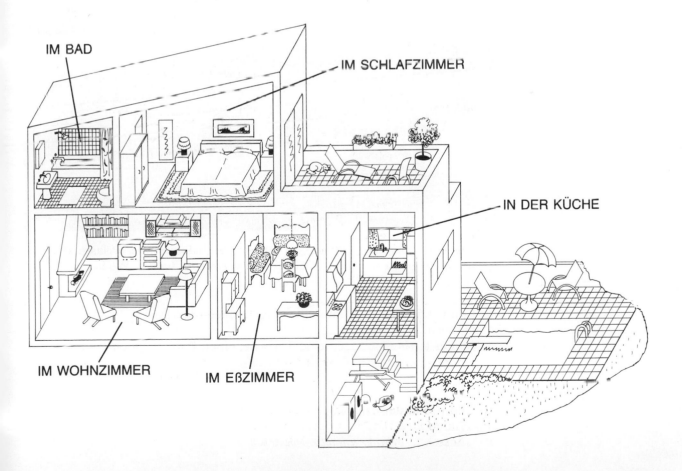

IM BAD

IM SCHLAFZIMMER

IN DER KÜCHE

IM WOHNZIMMER

IM EßZIMMER

C. Was bedeutet das, und was ist der Plural?

Balkontür, Bücherregal, Duschvorhang, Elternschlafzimmer, Eßzimmer, Farbfernseher, Garagentür, Gartenmöbel, Kinderzimmer, Küchenfenster, Kleiderschrank, Kochecke, Nachttisch, Schreibtischlampe, Sitzecke, Waschecke, Wohnzimmerteppich

D. Interview. Fragen Sie einen Nachbarn / eine Nachbarin, . . . !
1. ob er / sie eine Wohnung hat, oder zu Hause oder im Studentenheim wohnt
2. wie lange er / sie schon da wohnt
3. ob er / sie eine Küche hat; wenn ja, was es in der Küche gibt
4. was für Möbel er / sie im Zimmer hat
5. was man vom Zimmerfenster sehen kann

Hildesheim mit Blick auf die Michaelis-kirche

E. Eine Wohnung zu vermieten. Complete the dialogue with a classmate.
x Ich habe gelesen, daß Sie ein Haus zu vermieten haben. Wo ist das Haus?
Y _____ .
x Können Sie mir das Haus etwas beschreiben *(describe)*?
Y Ja, gern. Es hat _____ .
x Gibt es auch _____ (eine Terrasse, einen Balkon, einen Pool . . .)?
Y _____ .
x Wie weit ist es zu _____ ?
Y _____ .
x Und was kostet das Haus?
Y _____ .
x _____ . *(Make a final comment.)*

F. Aussprache. See also II.37–39 in the pronunciation section of the Workbook.

1. [ai] **Ei**, H**ei**zung, w**ei**t, w**ei**l, l**ei**der, **ei**gentlich, **ei**nmal, z**ei**gen, f**ei**ern, bl**ei**ben
2. [au] **au**f, **au**ch, br**au**n, bl**au**grau, K**au**fhaus, B**au**m, br**au**chen, l**au**fen, d**au**ern
3. [oi] **eu**ch, n**eu**, h**eu**te, t**eu**er, d**eu**tsch, L**eu**te, Fr**eu**nde, H**äu**ser, B**äu**me, Fr**äu**lein
4. Wortpaare
   - a. *by* / bei
   - b. *Troy* / treu
   - c. *mouse* / Maus
   - d. Haus / Häuser
   - e. aus / Eis
   - f. euer / Eier

STRUKTUR

I. Two-Way Prepositions

You have learned some prepositions that are always followed by the dative and some that are always followed by the accusative. You will now learn a set of prepositions that sometimes take the dative and sometimes the accusative.

1. The basic meanings of the nine TWO-WAY PREPOSITIONS are:

an	*to, at (the side of), on (vertical surface)*
auf	*on (top of, horizontal surface)*
hinter	*behind*
in	*in, into, inside of*
neben	*beside, next to*
über	*over, above*
unter	*under, below*
vor	*before, in front of; ago*
zwischen	*between*

Most of these prepositions may be contracted with articles. The most common contractions are:

an das = **ans**	in das = **ins**
an dem = **am**	in dem = **im**
auf das = **aufs**	

In colloquial speech you will also hear: hinter**s**, hinter**m**, über**s**, über**m**, unter**s**, unter**m**, vor**s**, vor**m**.

To practice the meaning of the prepositions, give the students sentences in English and have them state the appropriate German preposition: *My car is in front of the house.* (**vor**) *I left my books on top of the car.* (**auf**) *I saw them when I went to the window.* (**an**)

CAUTION

The preposition **vor** precedes a noun (**vor dem Haus**). The conjunction **bevor** introduces a clause (**. . ., bevor du das Haus mietest**).

2. **Wo? Wohin?**

a. German has two words to ask *where:* **wo?** *(in what place?)* and **wohin?** *(to what place?).* **Wo** asks about location, where something is, or an activity within a place. **Wohin** asks about destination or a change of place.

LOCATION: **Wo** ist Horst?   *Where's Horst? (in what place)*
DESTINATION: **Wohin** geht Horst? *Where's Horst going? (to what place)*

b. The difference between location and destination also plays a role in determining the case following two-way prepositions. If the question is **wo?,** the dative is used. If the question is **wohin?,** the accusative is used.

Wo ist Horst? **In der Bibliothek.**   *Where's Horst? In the library.*

Wohin geht Horst? **In die Bibliothek.**   *Where's Horst going? To the library.*

| **wo?** | location | → DATIVE |
| **wohin?** | destination | → ACCUSATIVE |

3. The difference lies entirely in the verb!

- Some verbs denoting location or activity within a place (→ DATIVE) are:

arbeiten, baden, bleiben, essen, finden, kaufen, kochen, lesen, schlafen, schreiben, sein, spielen, studieren, tanzen, trinken, wohnen

And also:
hängen	**gehangen**	*to hang (be hanging)*
liegen	**gelegen**	*to lie (be lying flat)*
sitzen	**gesessen**	*to sit (be sitting)*
stehen	**gestanden**	*to stand (be standing)*

NOTE: **hängen, liegen, sitzen,** and **stehen** are new n-verbs. They are all intransitive, i.e., they don't have direct objects: Der Mantel hängt im Schrank.

- Typical verbs implying change of place (→ ACCUSATIVE) are:

bringen, fahren, gehen, kommen, laufen, tragen

And also:
hängen	**gehängt**	*to hang (up)*
legen	**gelegt**	*to put (flat), lay*
stellen	**gestellt**	*to put (upright)*

NOTE: **hängen, legen,** and **stellen** are new t-verbs. They are all transitive, i.e., they have direct objects: Ich hänge den Mantel in den Schrank.

WOHIN? Der Junge hängt den Teppich **über das** Balkongeländer *(. . . railing).*
WO?   Der Teppich hängt **über dem** Balkongeländer.
WOHIN? Die Mutter stellt die Leiter *(ladder)* **an die** Wand.
WO?   Die Leiter steht **an der** Wand.
WOHIN? Das Kind legt den Teddy **auf die** Bank *(bench).*
WO?   Der Teddy liegt **auf der** Bank.

WOHIN?

WO?

In addition to the drawings, you could act things out: 1. Ich gehe an die Tafel / Ich stehe . . . 2. Ich lege das Buch auf den Tisch / Es liegt . . . 3. Ich stelle den Stuhl hinter den Tisch / Er steht . . . 4. Ich werfe das Papier in den Papierkorb / Es liegt . . . 5. Ich hänge das Bild an die Wand / Es hängt . . . 6. Ich lege das Heft unter das Buch / Es liegt. . . 7. Die Kreide fällt vom Tisch / Sie liegt vor . . . 8. Ich gehe zwischen den Tisch und die Tafel / Ich stehe . . .

WOHIN?	Das Auto fährt **neben das** Haus.
WO?	Das Auto steht **neben dem** Haus.
WOHIN?	Das Kind läuft **hinter die** Mutter.
WO?	Das Kind steht **hinter der** Mutter.
WOHIN?	Der Hund läuft **vor das** Auto.
WO?	Der Hund steht **vor dem** Auto.
WOHIN?	Der Großvater nimmt die Pfeife (*pipe*) **in den** Mund (*mouth*).
WO?	Der Großvater hat die Pfeife **in dem** Mund.
WOHIN?	Das Huhn (*chicken*) läuft **unter die** Bank **zwischen die** Bankbeine (*. . . legs*).
WO?	Das Huhn sitzt **unter der** Bank **zwischen den** Bankbeinen.

Note particularly these sets of verbs:

to put (upright)	Sie stellt die Leiter an die Wand.
to be standing	Die Leiter steht an der Wand.
to put (flat), lay	Das Kind legt den Teddy auf die Bank.
to be lying (flat)	Der Teddy liegt auf der Bank.

Note also these uses of **an, auf** and **in**; you are already familiar with most of them:

Die Stadt liegt **am** Rhein / **an der Donau.**	*The city is on the Rhine / on the Danube.*
Sie spielen **auf der** Straße.	*They're playing in the street.*
Sie leben **in** Deutschland / **in der** Schweiz.	*They live in Germany / in Switzerland.*
Sie leben **im** Süden / **in** Stuttgart.	*They live in the South / in Stuttgart.*
Sie wohnen **in der** Schillerstraße.	*They live on Schiller Street.*
Sie wohnen **im** Parterre / **im** ersten Stock.	*They live on the first / second floor.*

- With feminine names of countries, like **die Schweiz** or **die Tschechoslowakei**, **in** is used rather than **nach** to express *to*.

Wir fahren **in die** Schweiz.	*We're going to Switzerland.*
Wir fahren **nach** Österreich.	*We're going to Austria.*

- If you plan to see a film or play, or to attend a church service, **in** must be used. **zu** implies going *in the direction of, up to,* BUT NOT *into a place.*

Wir gehen **ins** Kino / **in die** Kirche.	*We're going to the movies / to church.*

ÜBUNGEN

A: Remind students that most nouns end in **-n** in the dative plural.

A. Sagen Sie es noch einmal! Replace the nouns following the prepositions with the words suggested.

BEISPIEL: Der Bleistift liegt unter dem Papier. (Jacke)
     Der Bleistift liegt unter der Jacke.

1. Die Post ist neben der Bank. (Bahnhof, Kino, Apotheke)
2. Ursula kommt in die Wohnung. (Küche, Eßzimmer, Garten)
3. Die Mäntel liegen auf dem Bett. (Sofa, Kommode, Stühle)
4. Mein Schlafzimmer ist über der Küche. (Wohnzimmer, Garage, Bad)
5. Willi legt den Pullover auf die Kommode. (Bett, Schreibtisch, Sessel)

Optional practice: Fragen an die Studenten:
1. Wo schläft man?
2. Wo kocht man?
3. Wohin tut man die Lebensmittel? 4. Wo essen Sie gewöhnlich?
4. Wo ist Ihr Fernseher? 5. Wo machen Sie Ihre Hausaufgaben *(assignments)*? 6. Wo sitzen Sie gewöhnlich mit Ihren Freunden?

B. Wieder zu Hause. After you and your family come home from a camping trip, your mother has many questions. Form questions with **wo** and **wohin!**

BEISPIEL: Vater ist in der Garage.   **Wo ist Vater?**
     Jochen geht in den Garten.   **Wohin geht Jochen?**

1. Der Rucksack *(backpack)* liegt im Flur.
2. Günther legt die Schlafsäcke *(sleeping bags)* aufs Bett.
3. Gabi hängt die Badehosen über den Stuhl.
4. Die Handtücher *(towels)* sind auf dem Balkon.
5. Die Schuhe liegen in der Ecke.

6. Gabi und Günther haben die Lebensmittel in die Küche gebracht.
7. Günther hat die Milch in den Kühlschrank gestellt.
8. Gabi hat den Schuh unterm Baum gefunden.

C. Ein paar Fragen, bevor Sie gehen! Before you leave on vacation, answer the questions of your house sitter.

BEISPIEL: Wo ist das Telefon? (an / Wand)   **An der Wand!**

chap. 7

1. Wo darf ich schlafen? (auf / Sofa; in / (unser) Zimmer; in / Arbeits-zimmer)
2. Wohin soll ich meine Kleider hängen? (in / Schrank; an / Wand; über / Stuhl)
3. Wo gibt es ein Lebensmittelgeschäft? (an / Ecke; neben / Bank; zwischen / Apotheke und Café)
4. Wo können die Kinder spielen? (hinter / Haus; unter / Baum; auf / Spielplatz)
5. Wohin gehen sie gern? (in / Park; an / Fluß; in / Kino)
6. Wohin soll ich den Hund (*dog*) tun? (vor / Tür; in / Garten; auf / Balkon)

D. Wir bekommen Besuch. Tell what you still have to do by filling in the blanks. **1.** Die Gläser sind in _____ Küche. **2.** Ich muß die Gläser in _____ Wohnzimmer bringen und sie auf _____ Tisch stellen. **3.** Der Wein ist noch in _____ Kühlschrank. **4.** Wir müssen die Teller neben _____ Gläser stellen. **5.** Ich muß in _____ Küche gehen und die Wurst und den Käse auf _____ Teller legen. **6.** Haben wir Blumen in _____ Garten? **7.** Wir stellen die Blumen auf _____ Tischchen (*sg.*) vor _____ Sofa. **8.** Sind die Kerzen in _____ Schrank? **9.** Nein, sie sind in _____ Kommode auf _____ Flur.

Das Massivhaus
Zukunft und Behaglichkeit unter einem Dach

Hauskonzepte ab 195 000,- DM.
Festpreis ohne Grundstück.

E. Im Wohnzimmer

Additional questions:
Wo kauft man Blumen?
(Bücher, Medizin, Klei-
dung, Brot, Fleisch . . .)
**Wohin geht man, wenn
man Geld braucht?**
(einen Film sehen will,
duschen möchte . . .)
Wo liegt . . .? (Ask
about various geo-
graphic locations, using
**in / in der / im, an der /
am . . .**)

1. **Wohin sollen wir das stellen?** Tell where the movers are supposed to put things.

BEISPIEL: Kommode / an / Wand   **Stellen Sie die Kommode an die Wand!**

a. Regal / auf / Kommode
b. Radio / in / Regal
c. Fernseher / neben / Radio
d. kleine Regal / unter / Fenster
e. Blumen / an / Fenster
f. Glasschrank / zwischen / Kommode
g. Bücher / auf / Kommode
h. Tisch / vor / Sessel
i. Bild / in / Regal

2. **Was ist wo?** As you check the picture on the following page, make ten statements telling where things are standing, lying, or hanging.

BEISPIEL: Das Glas steht auf dem Fernseher.

3. **Mein Zimmer.** Describe your room in eight to ten sentences. Use a two-way preposition in each sentence.

II. The Imperative

You are already familiar with the FORMAL IMPERATIVE, which addresses one individual or several people. You know that the verb is followed by the pronoun **Sie**:

Herr Schmidt, **lesen Sie** das bitte!
Frau Müller und Fräulein Schulz, **kommen Sie** später wieder!

1. The FAMILIAR IMPERATIVE has two forms: one for the plural and one for the singular.

   a. The plural corresponds to the **ihr**-form of the verb WITHOUT the pronoun **ihr.**

ihr schreibt	ihr tut	ihr antwortet	ihr nehmt	ihr lest	ihr eßt
Schreibt!	**Tut!**	**Antwortet!**	**Nehmt!**	**Lest!**	**Eßt!**

   b. The singular usually corresponds to the **du**-form of the verb WITHOUT the pronoun **du** and WITHOUT the -st ending:

du schreibst	du tust	du antwortest	du nimmst	du liest	du ißt
Schreib!	**Tu!**	**Antworte!**	**Nimm!**	**Lies!**	**Iß!**

   NOTE: **lesen** and **essen** retain the **s** of the verb stem. **Lies! Iß!**

   ▪ There is an OPTIONAL **-e** ending in the **du**-form. However, the more informal the situation, the less likely its use.

   Schreib(e) mir! **Sag(e)** das noch einmal!

   ▪ Verbs ending in **-d, -t, -ig,** or in certain other consonant combinations USUALLY have an **-e** ending in the **du**-form.

   Finde das! **Antworte** ihm! **Entschuldige** bitte! **Öffne** die Tür!

The complete rule is: If the stem ends in **-m** or **-n** preceded by a consonant other than **-l-** and **-r-**, the imperative of the **du**-form ends in **-e.**

▪ Verbs with vowel changes from **e** > **i(e)** in the present singular NEVER have an **-e** ending in the **du-**form.

Sprich Deutsch! **Sieh** mal!

▪ Verbs with vowel changes from **a** > **ā** in the present singular DO NOT MAKE THIS CHANGE in the imperative.

Fahr langsam! **Lauf** nicht so schnell!

2. English imperatives beginning with *Let's* . . . are expressed in German as follows:

Sprechen wir Deutsch!	*Let's speak German.*
Gehen wir nach Hause!	*Let's go home.*

3. Here is a summary chart of the imperative.

Schreiben Sie!	Schreibt!	Schreib(e)!	Schreiben wir . . .!
Antworten Sie!	Antwortet!	Antworte!	Antworten wir . . .!
Fahren Sie!	Fahrt!	**Fahr(e)!**	Fahren wir . . .!
Nehmen Sie!	Nehmt!	**Nimm!**	Nehmen wir . . .!
Lesen Sie!	Lest!	**Lies!**	Lesen wir . . .!
Essen Sie!	Eßt!	**Iß!**	Essen wir . . .!

Frau Schmidt, **schreiben Sie** mir!
Kinder, **schreibt** mir!
Helga, **schreib(e)** mir!
Schreiben wir Lisa!

NOTE: The German imperative is always followed by an EXCLAMATION MARK!

An *infinitive* can also be used as an imperative, especially on signs: **Langsam fahren! Nicht mit dem Fahrer sprechen!**

ÜBUNGEN

Additional practice: bitte kommen, jetzt beginnen, Golf spielen, schön feiern, zusammen singen, auch tanzen, nicht so schnell laufen, im See baden, schwimmen gehen, das wieder finden, auf deutsch antworten, nicht so viel arbeiten, die Wohnung mieten, ihm danken, den Dom besichtigen, die Suppe empfehlen, mal sehen, nicht so viel rauch

F. Geben Sie den Imperativ! First form the plural familiar and then the singular familiar.

BEISPIEL: Bleiben Sie bitte!   **Bleibt bitte! Bleib bitte!**

1. Fragen Sie ihn!
2. Entschuldigen Sie bitte!
3. Bitte helfen Sie uns!
4. Zeigen Sie uns den Weg!
5. Geben Sie mir die Landkarte!
6. Fahren Sie immer geradeaus!
7. Wiederholen Sie das bitte!
8. Halten Sie da drüben!
9. Hören Sie mal!

10. Schlafen Sie nicht!
11. Essen Sie einen Apfel!
12. Trinken Sie eine Cola!

G. Geben Sie Befehle (commands)! Form formal and familiar commands, using the phrases below.

BEISPIEL: an die Tafel gehen   **Gehen Sie an die Tafel!**
Geht an die Tafel!
Geh an die Tafel!

1. die Kreide nehmen   **2.** ein Wort auf deutsch schreiben.   **3.** von 1 bis 10 zählen   **4.** wieder an den Platz gehen   **5.** das Deutschbuch öffnen **6.** auf Seite 150 lesen   **7.** mit dem Nachbarn auf deutsch sprechen   **8.** mir einen Kuli geben   **9.** nach Hause gehen   **10.** das nicht tun

H. Was tun? Decide with your friend what to do with the rest of the day.

BEISPIEL: zu Hause bleiben   **Bleiben wir zu Hause!**

1. in die Stadt gehen   **2.** mit der Straßenbahn fahren   **3.** durch die Geschäfte bummeln   **4.** eine Pizza essen   **5.** das Schloß besichtigen   **6.** ins Kino gehen

I. Geben Sie Befehle an (to) . . .! Address three commands to each.
1. einen Touristen oder einen Angestellten (employee at work)
2. einen Freund oder eine Freundin
3. zwei kleine Kinder

BEISPIEL: **Fahren Sie mit dem Bus!**
Hilf mir!
Fallt nicht!

Schreib mal wieder...

Absender

_____

_____

Ein Brief muß nicht immer lang sein.

III. wissen vs. kennen

In German two verbs correspond to the English to know:

kennen, gekannt	to know (to be acquainted with a person or thing)
wissen, gewußt	to know a fact (the fact is often expressed in a subordinate clause)

Whereas **kennen** is regular in the present tense, the forms of **wissen** are very similar to the forms of the modals.

**Volkswagen –
da weiß man, was man hat.**

ich	weiß
du	weißt
er	weiß
wir	wissen
ihr	wißt
sie	wissen

Ich **kenne** das Buch.   BUT Ich **weiß, daß** es gut ist.
Ich **kenne** den Lehrer.   BUT Ich **weiß, daß** er aus Wien ist.

ÜBUNGEN

Optional practice: Have students indicate whether to use **kennen** or **wissen** in the following sentences. 1. Do you know Dr. Schumann? 2. No, I don't know him. 3. But I know that he teaches here. 4. What else do you know about him? 5. Do you know where to find him? 6. No, I don't know. 7. I don't know the university that well.

J. kennen oder wissen? Fill in the appropriate forms.

ANGELIKA Entschuldigen Sie! ____W____ Sie, wo die Wipplinger Straße ist?

DAME Nein. Ich ____K____ Wien gut, aber das ____W____ ich leider nicht.

MICHAEL Danke! Du, Angelika, ____W____ du, wie spät es ist?

ANGELIKA Nein, aber ich ____W____, daß ich Hunger habe.

MICHAEL Hallo, Holger und Sabine! Grüßt euch! Sagt mal, ____K____ ihr Angelika?

SABINE Ja, natürlich.

MICHAEL Wir haben Hunger. ____W____ ihr, wo es hier ein Restaurant gibt?

HOLGER Ja, da drüben ist das Bastei Beisl. Wir ____K____ es nicht, aber wir ____W____, daß es gut sein soll.

MICHAEL ____W____ ihr was? Gehen wir essen!

ZUSAMMENFASSUNG

K. Bilden Sie Sätze! Add suitable subjects and verbs.

BEISPIEL: über dem Tisch **Die Lampe hängt über dem Tisch.**

1. in den Schrank
2. unter dem Bett
3. über dem Sofa
4. hinter der Staatsoper
5. in die Bank
6. vor das Haus
7. neben dem Telefon
8. zwischen der Schulstraße und dem Domplatz
9. auf den Schreibtisch
10. unter dem Baum
11. ins Regal
12. ans Fenster

L: 1. Hallo, Hans! Wo bist du gewesen? 2. Ich komme vom Studentenheim. 3. Wohin gehst du?—In die (zur) Bibliothek. 4. Ich möchte auch in einem Studentenheim wohnen. 5. Wo wohnst du jetzt? 6. In einer Wohnung. Leider ist sie über einer Disko und neben einem Restaurant. 7. Ich höre, daß die Zimmer im Studentenheim schön sind. 8. Mein Zimmer gefällt mir, aber die Möbel gefallen mir nicht. 9. In welchem Stock wohnst du?—Im zweiten Stock. 10. Weißt du, wieviel es kostet?—270 DM im Monat. 11. Da ist Reinhart. 12. Wer ist das? Woher soll ich ihn kennen? 13. Ich habe nicht gewußt, daß du ihn nicht kennst. 14. Sagen wir „Hallo" („Guten Tag")!

L. An der Uni. Auf deutsch, bitte!
1. Hello, Hans! Where have you been? **2.** I'm coming from the dorm. **3.** Where are you going?—To the library. **4.** I'd like to live in a dorm, too. **5.** Where do you live now? **6.** In an apartment. Unfortunately it's over a disco (**die Disko**) and next to a restaurant. **7.** I hear that the rooms in the dorm are nice. **8.** I like my room, but I don't like the furniture. **9.** Which floor do you live on?—On the third floor. **10.** Do you know how much it costs?—270 marks a month. **11.** There's Reinhart. **12.** Who's that? Where am I supposed to know him from? **13.** I didn't know that you don't know him. **14.** Let's say hello.

EINBLICKE ◆◆◆◆◆◆◆◆◆◆◆

Moderne Wohnsilos

During the sixties modern high-rise communities were built around many old German cities in the FRG, often contrasting sharply with the traditional architecture. Today, such high-rise apartment clusters (**Wohnsilos**) have become unpopular and are no longer built. New housing developments are designed to fit into the landscape and conform to local building styles. Also, strict zoning laws have been passed to prevent loss of open space and agricultural land. In the former GDR, where most building was done by the government, the development of modern satellite cities continued, as in the Berlin suburb **Marzahn.** Yet in smaller towns the old appearance has been preserved, since little building was done before the seventies. Thus, the visitor to the East can get more of a feel of the old Germany than in most towns of western Germany.

WORTSCHATZ 2

der	Wald, ⁻er	*forest, woods*
das	Fahrrad, ⁻er	*bicycle*
	am Abend	*in the evening*
	am Tag	*during the day*
	aufs Land	*in (to) the country(side)*
	auf dem Land	*in the country*
	ausgezeichnet	*excellent*

außerdem	*besides (adverb)*
mitten in	*in the middle of*
noch nicht	*not yet*
trotzdem	*nevertheless, in spite of that*
bauen	*to build*
leben	*to live*
lieben	*to love*
sparen	*to save (money)*

Point out the difference between **leben** (*to live*) and **wohnen** (*to reside*): Dürer hat in Nürnberg gelebt. Er lebt nicht mehr. Er hat in dem Haus da drüben gewohnt.

Exercise E, p. 177, can be used as a pre-reading activity.

WAS IST DAS? der Clown, Dialekt, Fahrradweg, Münchner, Musiker, Spielplatz, Stadtpark, Wanderweg; das Bauland, Feld, Leben, Konsulat, Zentrum; die Arbeit, Energie, Innenstadt, Wirklichkeit; frei, idyllisch, jung, relativ; Ball spielen, eine Pause machen, formulieren, picknicken

Schaffen°, sparen, Häuschen° bauen

work hard / little house

Dieser Spruch° aus Schwaben (im Dialekt[1] heißt es „Schaffe, spare, Häusle baue") ist nicht nur typisch für die Schwaben, sondern für die meisten° Deutschen, Österreicher und Schweizer.

this saying

most

In den drei Ländern leben viele Menschen, aber es gibt wenig° Land. Die meisten wohnen in Wohnungen und träumen von° einem Haus mit Garten. Für viele bleibt das aber nur ein Traum°, denn in den Städten ist Bauland sehr teuer. Es gibt auch nicht genug Bauland, weil man nicht überall bauen darf.   5

little

dream of

dream

Oft muß man an den Stadtrand° oder aufs Land ziehen°, wo es mehr Platz gibt und wo Land noch nicht so teuer ist. Aber nicht alle möchten so weit draußen° wohnen und stundenlang hin und her pendeln°. Das kostet Energie, Zeit und Geld°. Abends kommt man auch nicht leicht° ins Kino oder ins Theater. Das Leben zwischen Wäldern und Feldern ist oft idyllisch, aber nicht immer sehr bequem.   10

edge of . . . / move

out(side) / commute back and forth

money / easily

Fahrradweg mitten in Karlsruhe

necessarily
sidewalks
public transportation
on time
commuter train / with them
all across

display . . .
entertainment
. . . artists
going on

In der Stadt kann man eigentlich sehr gut leben. Die Wohnungen sind   15
oft groß und schön. Man braucht nicht unbedingt° ein Auto, weil alles in
der Nähe liegt. Überall gibt es Bürgersteige° und Fahrradwege, und die
öffentlichen Verkehrsmittel° sind ausgezeichnet. Die Busse kommen relativ
oft und pünktlich°. In Großstädten gibt es auch Straßenbahnen, eine U-Bahn
und eine S-Bahn°. Damit° können Sie nicht nur aus der Stadt oder quer   20
durch° die Stadt, sondern auch mitten ins Zentrum, in die Fußgängerzonen
fahren, wo die Leute am Tag einkaufen und am Abend gern bummeln
gehen. Man sieht ein bißchen in die Schaufenster° und geht vielleicht in ein
Restaurant.   Oft   bekommt   man   auch   freie   Unterhaltung°   durch
Straßenkünstler°, Musiker und Clowns. In der Innenstadt ist eigentlich im-   25
mer etwas los°.

Bushaltestelle in
Hamburg

any time
out into nature
dependent / ocean

almost
whole / appear
bigger than

Wenn man in der Stadt wohnt, kann man aber auch jederzeit° leicht ins
Grüne° fahren. Viele tun das gern und oft. Wenn man nicht jeden Tag vom
Auto abhängig° ist, fährt man am Wochenende gern einmal an die See°,
aufs Land oder in die Berge. Überall in Wäldern und Feldern findet man   30
Wanderwege³ und oft auch Fahrradwege. Fast° alle Wege sind öffentlich. So
ist das ganze° Land dem Menschen offen, und die Länder scheinen° größer
als° sie sind. Unterwegs findet man oft auch ein Café, wo man gemütlich
Pause machen kann.

Man muß aber nicht unbedingt aufs Land fahren, wenn man ins Grüne   35
will. Fast alle Städte, ob groß oder klein, haben Stadtparks. Die Münchner z.B.
lieben ihren Englischen Garten (in der Nähe vom amerikanischen Konsulat).

benches
rowboats

Dort gibt es nicht nur Wanderwege, sondern auch Spielplätze und Bänke°,
Platz zum Picknicken und zum Ball spielen und Seen mit Ruderbooten°.

Traumhaus in Garmisch-Partenkirchen

even if

condominium

hard

Die meisten leben eigentlich gern in der Stadt, selbst wenn° sie dort 40
nur eine Eigentumswohnung° haben können oder vielleicht eine Wohnung
mieten. In der Stadt gibt es viel zu sehen und zu tun. Alles ist ziemlich nah,
nicht nur der Arbeitsplatz, die Geschäfte und die Schulen, sondern auch die
Theater, Kinos, Museen und Parks. Natürlich träumen viele trotzdem von
einem Haus mit Garten, einem Häuschen im Grünen. Sie wissen, daß sie 45
schwer° arbeiten und sparen müssen, wenn der Traum Wirklichkeit werden
soll. Und das tun auch viele.

ZUM TEXT

A. Richtig oder falsch? Wenn falsch, sagen Sie warum!
___ 1. In Deutschland, in Österreich und in der Schweiz gibt es nicht viel Bauland, besonders nicht in den Städten.
___ 2. Die meisten Leute dort wohnen in einem Haus mit Garten.
___ 3. Auf dem Land ist Bauland nicht so teuer wie in der Stadt.
___ 4. Das Leben zwischen Wäldern und Feldern ist sehr bequem.
___ 5. In allen Städten gibt es Straßenbahnen, eine U-Bahn und eine S-Bahn.
___ 6. Mit öffentlichen Verkehrsmitteln kann man quer durch die Stadt fahren.
___ 7. Überall in Wäldern und Feldern gibt es Fahrradwege und Fußgängerzonen.
___ 8. In der Fußgängerzone kann man am Tag einkaufen, am Abend bummeln und manchmal Musik hören.
___ 9. Im amerikanischen Konsulat in München kann man picknicken.
___ 10. Wenn man ein Haus kaufen oder bauen möchte, muß man schwer arbeiten und sparen.

B. Haus oder Wohnung? Fill in the appropriate form.
1. Die meisten wohnen in ein____ Wohnung. **2.** In d____ Städten ist Bauland sehr teuer. **3.** Der Traum vom Häuschen mit Garten hat viele an d____ Stadtrand (*m.*) oder auf d____ Land gebracht. **4.** Zwischen d____ Wäldern und auf d____ Feldern stehen Reihenhäuser (*town houses*). **5.** Die Reihenhäuser stehen manchmal direkt an d____ Straße. **6.** Morgens fahren viele in d____ Stadt. **7.** Das Leben auf d____ Land kann unbequem sein. **8.** Viele bleiben in d____ Stadt, weil dort alles in d____ Nähe liegt. **9.** Nach d____ Arbeit fahren viele noch einmal in ____ Innenstadt. **10.** Mitten in d____ Zentrum (*n.*) ist immer etwas los.

C. In der Großstadt. You have never been to Munich before. Ask Margrit questions about the city, using **wo** or **wohin**.

BEISPIEL: In Großstädten gibt es eine U-Bahn. **Wo gibt es eine U-Bahn?**

1. Mit der U-Bahn kann man mitten in die Fußgängerzone fahren.
2. Dort kann man immer schön bummeln.
3. Abends kann man ins Kino gehen.
4. Man geht in den Park, wenn man ins Grüne will.
5. Dort gibt es überall Wege und Bänke.

D. kennen oder wissen?
1. _____ Sie den Spruch „Schaffen, sparen, Häuschen bauen"?
2. _____ Sie, wie viele Leute in Deutschland auf dem Land leben?
3. _____ Sie den Englischen Garten? _____ Sie, wo er ist?
4. _____ ihr, daß es überall Fahrradwege gibt?
5. Ich habe auch nicht _____ , daß es in der Stadt so viele Fußgängerwege gibt.
6. _____ du Herrn Jakob? Nein, aber Hans hat ihn _____ .
7. _____ du, daß er mit seinen 80 Jahren immer noch viel wandert?

To use exercise E as pre-reading activity, you may want to simplify some of the questions. Glossed in the text are:
1. die meisten
3. öffentliche Verkehrsmittel 5. pendeln.

E. Fragen

1. Leben die meisten Leute hier in Wohnungen oder in Häusern mit Gärten?
2. Wo ist Bauland teuer? Wo ist es nicht so teuer?
3. Was für öffentliche Verkehrsmittel gibt es hier?
4. Wie kommen die meisten Leute zur Arbeit? Wie kommen Sie zur Universität? Braucht man hier unbedingt ein Auto?
5. Gibt es hier Schlafstädte (*bedroom communities*), von wo die Leute morgens in die Stadt pendeln? Geben Sie Beispiele!
6. Wohin gehen oder fahren die Leute hier, wenn sie ins Grüne wollen?

F. Wo möchten Sie wohnen, und warum? Write three to four sentences describing where you would like to live and why. Include one phrase or word from each group below. After you have completed the exercise, your instructor polls the entire class to determine what choices others have made.

1	2
in einer Wohngemeinschaft	mitten in . . .
in einer Wohnung	in der Nähe von . . .
in einer Eigentumswohnung	am Stadtrand von . . .
in einem Reihenhaus	auf dem Land . . .
in einem Haus mit Garten	

BEISPIEL. Ich möchte in einem Reihenhaus mitten in San Francisco wohnen. Da komme ich schnell zur Arbeit und zum Ozean. Man braucht nicht unbedingt ein Auto.

„Der arme Poet" von Carl Spitzweg. So kann man auch wohnen.

Übrigens

1. German belongs to the Germanic branch of the Indo-European language family and is closely related to Dutch, English, and the Scandinavian languages. For various political, literary, and linguistic reasons, we speak of Germans and the German language as dating from around the year 800. At that time at least six major dialects and numerous variations of them were spoken. Not until the twelfth and thirteenth centuries was an effort made to write a standardized form of German; the period from 1170 to 1254 was one of great literary achievement. But afterwards this literary language declined and, with few exceptions, Latin was used in writing. (It remained the sole language of instruction at German universities until the 1700s!) Luther's translation of the Bible in the sixteenth century was a major influence on the development of a common written German language. However, because of political fragmentation, a standard language was slow to develop in Germany. As late as the beginning of this century, most people spoke only in dialect. First newspapers and magazines, and later radio and television, fostered the use of standard German, but regional accents are still very common, even among the highly educated.

2. People in the German-speaking countries are known for their hard work and thrift. Their per capita rate of savings is unusually high. Generous tax incentives encourage people to save in special savings institutions for the building of private homes and condominiums. Thrift is also reflected in the relatively low consumption of energy in spite of a high standard of living and industrial output.

SPRECHSITUATIONEN

Describing Locations

You have already learned many ways of describing the location of something, including the two-way prepositions in this chapter. Here are a few reminders:

im Norden / nördlich von	an der Ecke
bei	Ecke Schillerstraße
in der Nähe von	in der Schillerstraße
nicht weit von	da drüben
mitten in	hier / da / dort
rechts / links von	im Parterre / im ersten Stock
gegenüber von	

Offering Apologies

Entschuldigung!
Entschuldige! / Entschuldigen Sie!
Verzeih mir! / Verzeihen Sie mir! (*Forgive me.*)
Es tut mir (furchtbar) leid!
Leider . . .

Expressing Forgiveness

(Das) macht nichts.
Es ist schon gut.
Das ist kein Problem.

A. **Wo ist was?** Working with a classmate, look at the map of the former GDR in the front of the book and write at least ten different statements about the location of various cities.

   BEISPIEL: Halle liegt an der Saale, nordöstlich von Leipzig.

B. **Was sagen Sie?** Use the appropriate expression for each of the following situations.
   1. Sie haben den Pullover von einem Freund getragen. Der Pullover ist schmutzig geworden.
   2. Sie und ihr Zimmerkollege / ihre Zimmerkollegin haben am Samstag Plätzchen gekauft. Am Sonntag haben Sie alle Plätzchen gegessen. Ihr Zimmerkollege / Ihre Zimmerkollegin kann kein Plätzchen mehr finden.
   3. Sie haben bei einem Professor gegessen. Ihr Glas ist vom Tisch gefallen.
   4. Ihre Zimmerkollegin hat Ihre Flasche Cola getrunken.
   5. Ein Freund hat Ihnen nicht zum Geburtstag geschrieben, weil er zu viel zu tun hatte.

C. Wo genau ist das? Describe the location of ten places shown on the map.

BEISPIEL: Das Theater ist beim Park, gegenüber vom Hochhaus (*high-rise*).

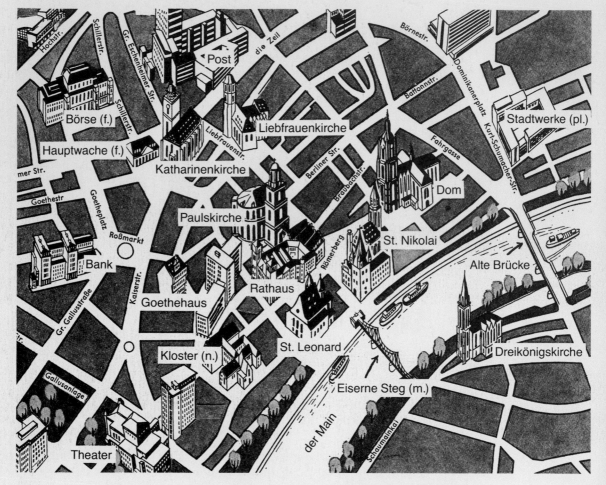

Frankfurt
am
Main

Das ist neu: der Eiserne Steg (*old bridge*), die Börse (*stock market*),
die Hauptwache (*old guard house*), die Stadtwerke (*utilities building*)

D. Kurzgespräche
1. In Munich you are looking for the well-known bookstore *Hugendubel.*
   You stop a woman to ask where it is. She tells you it is at the *Marien-platz,* across from city hall. She asks whether you see the *Frauenkirche* over there. You say yes; she says that the *Marienplatz* is quite (**ganz**) close. You thank her and say good-bye.
2. You have been invited to a classmate's house for dinner and you are quite late. You introduce yourself to her mother and apologize profusely for coming so late. She tells you that it doesn't matter. When you persist, she says it is no problem. After asking you to come in (**herein**), she tells you that dinner is ready.

7

Auf der Bank und im Hotel

Auf der Bank kann
man Geld um-
wechseln.

▮ LERNZIELE

Gespräche and **Wortschatz**. This chapter deals with banking and hotel
accommodations.

Struktur. You will learn about . . .

▪ **der-** and **ein-**words.

▪ separable-prefix verbs.

▪ gesture words.

Einblicke. Hotels, youth hostels, and other lodgings for travelers

Sprechsituationen

▪ Telling time

▪ Expressing disbelief

▪ Giving a warning

181

◆◆◆◆◆ GESPRÄCHE

Warm-ups: 1. **Was ist das Gegenteil von:** immer, oben, links, bequem, hell, nah, offen, schnell, Ausgang, Tag, mieten, zu Fuß gehen? 2. **Was für Zimmer gibt es in einem Haus?** Was gibt es im Wohnzimmer, in . . . ? 3. **Geben Sie den Plural von:** Bank, Fahrrad, Museum, Wald, Haus, Wohnung, Studentenheim, Bad, Bett, Ecke, Kommode, Regal, Schrank, Telefon, Teppich, Vorhang.

Auf der Bank[1]

TOURISTIN	Guten Tag! Können Sie mir sagen, wo ich Geld umwechseln kann?[2]
ANGESTELLTER	Am Schalter 2.
TOURISTIN	Vielen Dank! *(Sie geht zum Schalter 2.)* Guten Tag! Ich möchte Dollar in Franken[3] umwechseln. Hier sind meine Reiseschecks.
ANGESTELLTE	Darf ich bitte Ihren Paß sehen?
TOURISTIN	Bitte schön!
ANGESTELLTE	Unterschreiben Sie hier! Gehen Sie dort zur Kasse! Hier ist Ihre Nummer.
TOURISTIN	Danke! *(Sie geht zur Kasse.)*
KASSIERER	224 Franken 63 (Fr. 224,63): einhundert, zweihundert, zehn, zwanzig, vierundzwanzig Franken und dreiundsechzig Rappen. Bitte schön!
TOURISTIN	Danke schön! Auf Wiedersehen!

An der Rezeption im Hotel

HOTEL WOLF

Fragen: 1. Wer möchte Geld umwechseln? 2. Wo ist sie? 3. Wohin muß sie gehen? 4. Was muß sie der Angestellten zeigen? 5. Wo bekommt sie ihr Geld? 6. Wie viele Franken bekommt sie? 7. Was für ein Zimmer möchte der Gast? 8. Für wie lange braucht er es? 9. Was für ein Zimmer nimmt er, und wo liegt es? 10. Was gibt die Empfangsdame dem Gast? 11. Wo kann der Gast seinen Koffer lassen? 12. Wann macht das Hotel zu?

EMPFANGSDAME	Guten Abend!
GAST	Guten Abend! Haben Sie ein Einzelzimmer frei?
EMPFANGSDAME	Für wie lange?
GAST	Für zwei oder drei Nächte. Wenn möglich ruhig und mit Bad.
EMPFANGSDAME	Leider haben wir nur noch ein Doppelzimmer, und das nur für eine Nacht. Wollen Sie es sehen?
GAST	Ja, gern.
EMPFANGSDAME	Zimmer Nummer 12, im ersten Stock rechts. Hier ist der Schlüssel.
GAST	Sagen Sie, kann ich meinen Koffer einen Moment hier lassen?
EMPFANGSDAME	Ja, natürlich. Stellen Sie ihn da drüben in die Ecke!
GAST	Danke! Noch etwas, wann machen Sie abends zu?
EMPFANGSDAME	Um 24.00 Uhr. Wenn Sie später kommen, müssen Sie klingeln.

Übrigens

1. In 1990 the German central bank started to issue new bank notes which will be more difficult to counterfeit. Pictured on these notes are the poet Bettina von

Arnim (5 DM), the mathematician and astronomer Carl Friedrich Gauß (10 DM), the writer Annette von Droste-Hülshoff (20 DM), the architect Balthasar Neumann (50 DM), the pianist and composer Clara Schumann (100 DM), the physician Paul Ehrlich (200 DM), the artist Anna Maria Merian (500 DM), and the Grimm Brothers (1 000 DM).

If you have some German, Austrian, or Swiss money, bring it to class. Call a bank or look in a newspaper for the current exchange rates.

2. Currency can be exchanged and travelers' checks can be cashed in banks and post offices. Exchange offices (**Wechselstuben**) are open daily at all major railroad stations, airports, and border crossings.

3. Switzerland's basic monetary unit is the **Franken** (sFr). 1 sFr = 100 **Rappen.** Austria's basic monetary unit is the **Schilling** (öS), 1 öS = 100 **Groschen.**

In the Bank TOURIST: *Hello. Can you tell me where I can exchange money?* TELLER: *At counter 2.* TOURIST: *Thank you very much. (She goes to counter 2.) Hello. I'd like to change some dollars into francs. Here are my traveler's checks.* TELLER: *May I please see your passport?* TOURIST: *Here you are.* TELLER: *Sign here.—Go to the cashier over there. Here's your number.* TOURIST: *Thank you. (She goes to the cashier.)* CASHIER: *224 francs 63: one hundred, two hundred, ten, twenty, twenty-four francs and sixty-three rappen. Here you are.* TOURIST: *Thank you. Good-bye.*

At the Hotel Reception Desk RECEPTIONIST: *Good evening* GUEST: *Good evening. Do you have a single room available?* RECEPTIONIST: *For how long?* GUEST: *For two or three nights. If possible, quiet and with a bath.* RECEPTIONIST: *Unfortunately we have only one double room, and that for only one night. Do you want to see it?* GUEST: *Yes, I'd like to.* RECEPTIONIST: *Room number 12, on the second floor to the right. Here's the key.* GUEST: *Say, can I leave my suitcase here for a minute?* RECEPTIONIST: *Yes, of course. Put it in the corner over there.* GUEST: *Thank you. One more thing, when do you close at night?* RECEPTIONIST: *At midnight. If you come later, you'll have to ring the bell.*

WORTSCHATZ 1

DIE UHRZEIT *time (of the day)*

▪ The formal (official) time system is like the one used by the military. The hours are counted from 0 to 24, with 0 to 11 referring to a.m. and 12 to 24 referring to p.m. The system is commonly used in timetables for trains, buses, planes, etc., on radio and TV, and to state business hours of stores and banks.

16.05 Uhr = sechzehn Uhr fünf	*4:05 p.m.*
16.15 Uhr = sechzehn Uhr fünfzehn	*4:15 p.m.*
16.30 Uhr = sechzehn Uhr dreißig	*4:30 p.m.*
16.45 Uhr = sechzehn Uhr fünfundvierzig	*4:45 p.m.*
17.00 Uhr = siebzehn Uhr	*5:00 p.m.*

DIE BANK, -EN *bank*

der	Ausweis, -e	*identification card*	*das*	Geld	*money*
	Dollar,-	*dollar*		Bargeld	*cash*
	Paß, Pässe	*passport*		Kleingeld	*change*
	Schalter,-	*counter, ticket window*	*die*	Kasse, -n	*cashier's window (lit. cash register)*
	Scheck, -s	*check*			
	Reisescheck, -s	*traveler's check*			

DAS HOTEL, -S *hotel*

der	Ausgang, ⸚e	*exit*	*das*	Einzelzimmer,-	*single room*
	Eingang, ⸚e	*entrance*		Doppelzimmer,-	*double room*
	Gast, ⸚e	*guest*		Gepäck	*baggage, luggage*
	Koffer, -	*suitcase*	*die*	Nacht, ⸚e	*night*
	Schlüssel, -	*key*		Nummer, -n	*number*
				Tasche, -n	*bag; pocket*

WEITERES

frei	*free, available*
geöffnet / geschlossen	*open / closed*
möglich	*possible*
ruhig	*quiet(ly)*
Wann machen Sie auf / zu?	*When do you open / close?*

Einlösen and um-
wechseln are separable-
prefix verbs. Until dis-
cussed in the grammar
of this chapter, avoid
using these verbs in sep-
arated forms.

Wie steht . . . ?	*What's the exchange rate of . . .?*
einen Scheck einlösen	*to cash a check*
wechseln	*to make / get change (e.g., Mark >*
	Pfennige)
Geld (um)wechseln	*to (ex)change money (e.g., $ > DM)*
lassen (läßt), gelassen	*to leave (behind)*
unterschreiben, unterschrieben	*to sign*

PASSIVES VOKABULAR die Empfangsdame, -n *receptionist* **die Kreditkarte, -n einen Moment** *for / just a minute* **klingeln** *to ring the bell*

ZUM THEMA

A. Mustersätze
1. Geld wechseln: **Wo kann ich hier** Geld wechseln?
   Dollar umwechseln, einen Scheck einlösen, Reiseschecks einlösen
2. Paß: **Darf ich bitte Ihren** Paß **sehen?**
   Scheck, Reisecheck, Ausweis
3. Dollar: **Können Sie mir das in** Dollar **geben?**
   D-Mark, Franken, Schilling, Kleingeld, Bargeld
4. mein Auto: **Wo kann ich** mein Auto **lassen?**
   meinen Schlüssel, mein Gepäck, meinen Koffer, meine Tasche
5. 24.00 Uhr: **Wir machen um** 24.00 Uhr **zu.**
   22.00 Uhr, 22.15 Uhr, 22.30 Uhr, 22.45 Uhr, 23.00 Uhr

B. Was bedeuten die Wörter, und was ist der Artikel?

Ausgangstur, Gästeausweis, Geldwechsel, Gepäckstück, Handtasche, Hoteleingang, Kofferschlüssel, Nachtapotheke, Nachthemd, Nachtmensch, Paß-
nummer, Scheckbuch, Sparbuch, Taschengeld, Taschenlampe, Theater-
kasse

Have students act out
the dialogues.

C. Ich brauche Kleingeld. Ask for a place in which you can get change.
   x Ich habe kein Kleingeld. Kannst du mir _____ Mark wechseln?
   y Nein, _____
   x Schade!
   y Aber du kannst _____
   x Wo ist _____ ?
   y _____ .
   x Danke schön!
   y _____ !

Wer spart, kann große Sprünge machen.
BfG: Die Bank für Gemeinwirtschaft.

D. Im Hotel. Inquire about a room in a hotel in Basel.

x Guten _____ ! Haben Sie ein _____ mit _____ frei?

Y Wie lange wollen Sie bleiben?

x _____ .

Y Ja, wir haben ein Zimmer im _____ Stock.

x Was kostet es?

Y _____ .

x Kann ich es sehen?

Y _____ . Hier ist der Schlüssel. Zimmer Nummer _____ .

x Sagen Sie, wo kann ich _____ lassen?

Y _____ .

x Und wann machen Sie abends zu?

Y _____ .

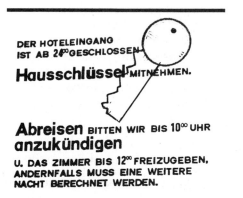

DER HOTELEINGANG
IST AB 24⁰⁰ GESCHLOSSEN

Hausschlüssel MITNEHMEN.

Abreisen BITTEN WIR BIS 10⁰⁰ UHR
anzukündigen

U. DAS ZIMMER BIS 12⁰⁰ FREIZUGEBEN,
ANDERNFALLS MUSS EINE WEITERE
NACHT BERECHNET WERDEN.

Frühstückszeiten

MONTAG u. SAMSTAG VON 7⁰⁰ – 10⁰⁰

DIENSTAG, MITTWOCH, DONNERSTAG
UND FREITAG   VON 6³⁰ – 10⁰⁰

Fußgängerzone

Sa 13 – 17 h
So 10 – 17 h
u. Feiertag
ausgenommen
Hotelübernachtungsgäste

E. Wie spät ist es? Ralf loves his new digital watch. Kurt prefers his old-fashioned one with hands. As Ralf says what time it is, Kurt confirms it in a more casual way. Work with a classmate. Take turns.

BEISPIEL: 14.15   Auf meiner Uhr ist es vierzehn Uhr fünfzehn.
        Ich habe Viertel nach zwei.

8.05 / 11.10 / 12.30 / 13.25 / 14.30 / 17.37 / 19.40 / 20.45 / 22.50 / 23.59 / 00.01

Dieser Bankautomat
ist immer offen.

F. Interview. Fragen Sie einen Nachbarn / eine Nachbarin, . . . !
1. wo man hier Bargeld oder Kleingeld bekommt
2. wie er / sie bezahlt, wenn er / sie einkaufen geht: bar, mit einem Scheck oder mit einer Kreditkarte
3. wie er / sie bezahlt, wenn er / sie reist *(travels)*
4. wo man hier D-Mark, Schillinge oder Franken bekommen kann
5. ob er / sie weiß, wie viele Mark (Schillinge, Franken) man für einen Dollar bekommt
6. was er / sie tut, wenn er / sie kein Geld mehr hat

G. Aussprache. See also 11.37, 40–41 in the pronunciation section of the Workbook.
1. [ei]   w**ei**l, w**ei**t, s**ei**t, s**ei**n, w**ei**ßt, bl**ei**bst, l**ei**der, b**ei**, fr**ei**
2. [ie]   w**ie**, w**ie**viel, n**ie**, l**ie**ben, l**ie**gen, m**ie**ten, l**ie**st, s**ie**hst, D**ie**nstag
3. B**ei**spiel, v**ie**ll**ei**cht, W**ie**n / W**ei**n, B**ei**ne / B**ie**ne, bl**ei**ben / bl**ie**ben, L**ie**der / l**ei**der, z**ei**gen / Z**ie**gen, h**ie**ßen / h**ei**ßen
4. Wortpaare
   a. See / Sie   c. biete / bitte   e. leider / Lieder
   b. beten / bieten   d. Miete / Mitte   f. Mais / mies

STRUKTUR

I. der- and ein-Words

1. **der**-Words

This small but important group of limiting words is called DER-words because their case endings are the same as those of the definite article **der, das, die.**

der, das, die	*the, that (when stressed)*
dieser, -es, -e	*this, these*
jeder, -es, -e	*each, every (sg. only, pl. **alle**)*
mancher, -es, -e	*many a (sg.); several, some (usually pl.)*
solcher, -es, -e	*such (usually pl.)*
welcher, -es, -e	*which*

CAUTION

The singular of **solcher** usually is **so ein,** which is not a **der-**word but an **ein-**word: **so ein Hotel** (*such a hotel*) BUT **solche Hotels** (*such hotels*).

COMPARE:

	masc.	neut.	fem.	pl.
nom.	der dieser welcher	das dieses welches	die diese welche	die diese welche
acc.	den diesen welchen			
dat.	dem diesem welchem	dem diesem welchem	der dieser welcher	den diesen welchen

nom.	Wo ist **der** Schlüssel?—**Welcher** Schlüssel? **Dieser** Schlüssel?
acc.	Hast du **den** Kofferschlüssel gesehen?—Wie soll ich **jeden** Schlüssel kennen?
dat.	Kannst du ihn mit **dem** Schlüssel öffnen?—Mit **welchem** Schlüssel?
pl.	Gib mir **die** Schlüssel!—Hier sind **alle** Schlüssel. **Manche** Schlüssel sind vom Haus, **solche** Schlüssel zum Beispiel.
BUT	**Der** Kofferschlüssel ist **so ein** Schlüssel. Hast du **so einen** Schlüssel?

2. **ein**-Words

POSSESSIVE ADJECTIVES are called **ein**-words because their case endings are the same as those of the indefinite article **ein** and the negative **kein**.

mein	*my*	**unser**	*our*
dein	*your (sg. fam.)*	**euer**	*your (pl. fam.)*
sein	*his / its*	**ihr**	*their*
ihr	*her / its*	**Ihr**	*your (sg. / pl. formal)*

COMPARE:

	masc.	neut.	fem.	pl.
nom.	ein mein unser	ein mein unser	eine meine unsere	keine meine unsere
acc.	einen meinen unseren			
dat.	einem meinem unserem	einem meinem unserem	einer meiner unserer	keinen meinen unseren

NOTE: The **-er** of **unser** and **euer** is not an ending!

- **Ein**-words have no endings in the masc. sing. nominative and in the neut. sing. nominative and accusative.

nom.   Hier ist **ein** Paß. Ist das **mein** Paß oder **dein** Paß?

acc.   Braucht er **keine** Kreditkarte?—Wo ist **seine** Kreditkarte? Hat sie **einen** Ausweis?—Natürlich hat sie **ihren** Ausweis. Haben Sie **Ihren** Ausweis?

dat.   In **welcher** Tasche sind die Schlüssel?—Sie sind in **meiner** Tasche. Oder sind die Schlüssel in **einem** Koffer?—Sie sind in **Ihrem** Koffer.

pl.   Wo sind **die** Schecks?—Hier sind **unsere** Schecks, und da sind **euere** Schecks.

ÜBUNGEN

A. Ersetzen Sie die Artikel!

1. **der-Wörter**

BEISPIEL: die Tasche *(this)* **diese Tasche**

a. das Gepäck *(every, which, this)* **b.** der Ausweis *(this, every, which)*
c. die Nummer *(which, every, this)* **d.** die Nächte *(some, such, those)*

Margin notes (left column):

If students need help in telling whether **ihr** is a dative pronoun or a possessive adjective (and which one of the three), write a few exercises like the following:
1. Ich gebe ihr das Buch. Ich habe ihr Buch. 2. Sie bringen ihr Blumen. Sie bringen ihre Blumen. 3. Das ist Ruth. Ich habe ihr Heft. 4. Wir fahren zu Müllers. Wo ist ihre Adresse? 5. Guten Tag, Herr Fiedler! Wie geht es Ihrer Frau?

When **unser** and **euer** have an ending, the **-e-** is often dropped (**unsre, eure**), especially in colloquial speech. For simplicity's sake we use uncontracted forms.

Translate into English! This can be used in reverse (or as a quiz) in the next period.

A.1–2: Use variations of these exercises during several class periods until students have mastered the **der-** and **ein-**words.

A.2: To make the practice of the possessive adjective more meaningful, do it with some of your own and the students' belongings: e.g., Ist das Ihr Bleistift? Nein, das ist sein Bleistift.

e. an dem Schalter *(this, which, each)*   **f.** an der Kasse *(this, every, which)*
g. mit den Schecks *(these, some, all)*

2. **ein-Wörter**

BEISPIEL: die Gäste *(your / 3×)*   **deine / euere / Ihre Gäste**

a. der Paß *(my, her, no, his)*   **b.** das Bargeld *(our, her, their)*   **c.** die Wohnung *(my, our, your / 3×)*   **d.** neben den Koffer *(your / 3×, our, their)*
e. in dem Doppelzimmer *(no, his, your / 3×)*   **f.** mit den Schlüsseln *(your / 3×, my, her)*

3. **der- und ein-Wörter**

BEISPIEL: Das Bad ist klein. *(our)*   **Unser Bad ist klein.**

a. **Das** Zimmer hat einen Fernseher. *(each, my, his, our)*
b. Bitte bringen Sie **den** Koffer zum Auto! *(this, her, our, my)*
c. Ich kann **die** Schlüssel nicht finden. *(your / 3×, our, some, my)*
d. Darf ich **das** Gepäck hier lassen? *(her, his, this, our)*
e. Der Ober kennt **den** Gast. *(each, our, this, your / 3×)*
f. **Die** Taschen sind schon vor dem Ausgang. *(our, all, some, my)*
g. **Den** Leuten gefällt das Hotel nicht. *(these, some, such)*
h. Du kannst **den** Scheck auf der Bank einlösen. *(this, my, every, such a, your / sg. fam.)*

Optional practice: Bilden Sie Sätze! z.B. *except for our bag* **Wir haben alles außer unserer Tasche.** e.g., *for his guest, after every meal, around their house, to your (pl. fam.) apartment, without my money, since that day, out of our suitcase, through this exit, from some people, into which restaurant, near this bridge, with your (sg. fam.) ID.*

B. Dias *(slides)* **von einer Deutschlandreise**

1. Auf _____ Bild seht ihr _____ Freunde aus Holland.   **2.** Das
            this   *my*

sind _____ Sohn Heiko und _____ Tochter Anke.   **3.** In
       their   *their*

_____ Stadt ist _____ Kirche?   **4.** _____ Kirchen gibt es in
which   *this*   *such*

Norddeutschland.   **5.** _____ Haus ist sehr alt, aber nicht _____
                         this   *every*

Haus in Bremen ist so alt.   **6.** Ich finde _____ Häuser sehr schön;
                                              such

Müllers wohnen in _____ Haus.   **7.** Und hier sind _____ Onkel
                    such a   *my*

Thomas und _____ Tante Hilde.   **8.** Ist das nicht _____ Auto da
             my   *your*

vor _____ Hotel?
      this

II. Separable-Prefix Verbs

1. English has a number of two-part verbs that consist of a verb and a preposition or an adverb.

   Watch out! Get up! Buzz off!

In German such verbs are called SEPARABLE-PREFIX verbs. You are already familiar with two of them:

Passen Sie auf! Hören Sie zu!

Their infinitives are **aufpassen** and **zuhören**. The prefixes **auf** and **zu** carry the main stress: **auf'passen, zu'hören**. From now on we will identify such separable-prefix verbs by placing a raised dot (·) between the prefix and the verb in vocabulary lists: **auf·passen, zu·hören**.

Tell students to kick the separable prefix to the end of the sentence or clause, just like the soccer player.

- These verbs are SEPARATED from the prefixes when the inflected part of the verb is the first or second sentence element: in imperatives, questions, and statements.

Hören Sie bitte **zu!**
Hören Sie jetzt **zu?**
Warum **hören** Sie nicht **zu?**
Wir **hören** immer gut **zu.**
V1   V2

- These verbs are NOT SEPARATED from the prefix when the verb stands at the end of a sentence or clause: with modals, in the present perfect, and in subordinate clauses. But watch, in the present perfect the **ge-** of the past participle is inserted BETWEEN the stressed prefix and the participle.

Ich soll immer gut **zuhören.**
Ich habe immer gut **zugehört.**
Ich weiß, daß ich immer gut **zuhöre.**
Ich weiß, daß ich immer gut **zuhören** soll.
Ich weiß, daß ich immer gut **zugehört** habe.

*You may want to point out that there are numerous compounds with **hin-** and **her-**: Ich gehe **hinaus** (**hinauf, hinein, hinüber**). Er kommt **heraus** (**herauf, herein, herüber**). In colloquial speech: **raus, rauf, rein, rüber.***

2. Knowing the basic meanings of some of the most frequent separable prefixes will help you derive the meanings of some of the separable-prefix verbs.

ab-	*away, off*	**mit-**	*together with, along with*
an-	*to, up to*	**nach-**	*after, behind*
auf-	*up, open*	**vor-**	*ahead, before*
aus-	*out, out of*	**vorbei-**	*past, by*
ein-	*into*	**zu-**	*closed*
her-	*toward (the speaker)*	**zurück-**	*back*
hin-	*away from (the speaker)*		

BEISPIEL: **an**·kommen   *to arrive (come to)*
her·kommen   *to come (toward the speaker)*
herein·kommen   *to come in (toward the speaker)*
heraus·kommen   *to come out (toward the speaker)*
hin·kommen   *to get there (away from the point of reference)*
mit·kommen   *to come along*
nach·kommen   *to follow (come after)*
vorbei·kommen   *to come by*
zurück·kommen   *to come back*

You will need to learn these common separable-prefix verbs.

an·rufen, angerufen	*to call, phone*
auf·machen	*to open*
auf·passen	*to pay attention, watch out*
auf·schreiben, aufgeschrieben	*to write down*
auf·stehen, ist aufgestanden	*to get up*
aus·gehen, ist ausgegangen	*to go out*
ein·kaufen	*to shop*
ein·lösen	*to cash (in)*
mit·bringen, mitgebracht	*to bring along*
mit·gehen, ist mitgegangen	*to go along*
mit·kommen, ist mitgekommen	*to come along*
mit·nehmen, mitgenommen	*to take along*
um·wechseln	*to exchange*
vorbei·gehen, ist vorbeigegangen (an, bei)	*to pass by*
zu·hören *(+ dat.)*	*to listen*
zu·machen	*to close*
zurück·kommen, ist zurückgekommen	*to come back*

Point out that **vorbei-gehen** uses the preposition **bei** or **an** if followed by an object: **Kommt ihr vorbei?** BUT **Ich gehe an der Uni vorbei. Kommst du bei der Drogerie vorbei?**

CAUTION

Not all verbs with prefixes are separable, e.g., **unterschreiben, wiederholen.** Here the main stress is on the verb, not on the prefix: **unterschrei′ben, wiederho′len.** Remember also the inseparable prefixes **be-, ent-, er-, ge-, ver-,** etc. They never stand alone.

ÜBUNGEN

C. Was bedeuten diese Verben? Knowing the meanings of the basic verbs and the prefixes, can you tell what these separable-prefix verbs mean?

abgeben, abnehmen
ansprechen
aufbauen, aufgeben, aufstehen, aufstellen
ausarbeiten, aushelfen, aus(be)zahlen
heraufkommen, herauskommen, herüberkommen, herunterkommen
hinaufgehen, hinausgehen, hineingehen, hinuntergehen
mitgehen, mitfahren, mitfeiern, mitsingen, mitspielen
nachkommen, nachlaufen
vorbeibringen, vorbeifahren, vorbeikommen
zuhalten
zurückbekommen, zurückbleiben, zurückbringen, zurückgeben, zurücknehmen, zurücksehen

D. Noch einmal. Wiederholen Sie die Sätze ohne Modalverb!

BEISPIEL: Sie soll ihm zuhören. **Sie hört ihm zu.**

1. Wir dürfen am Wochenende ausgehen. **2.** Wann mußt du morgens aufstehen? **3.** Wollt ihr mit mir einkaufen? **4.** Ich soll Wein mitbringen. **5.** Er will morgen zurückkommen. **6.** Ich möchte dich gern mitnehmen. **7.** Du kannst das Geld umwechseln. **8.** Er will an der Universität vorbeigehen. **9.** Können Sie bitte die Fenster aufmachen! **10.** Ihr sollt gut aufpassen.

E. Am Telefon. Report to your husband / wife what your mother-in-law is telling or asking you about tomorrow's family reunion.

BEISPIEL: Sie möchte wissen, ob Rainer und Wolfgang die Kinder mitbringen.
 Bringen Rainer und Wolfgang die Kinder mit?

1. Sie sagt, daß wir abends alle zusammen ausgehen.
2. Sie möchte wissen, ob du deine Kamera mitbringst.
3. Sie sagt, daß sie morgen noch ein paar Geschenke einkauft.
4. Sie möchte wissen, wann die Bank aufmacht.
5. Sie sagt, daß sie noch etwas Geld umwechselt.
6. Sie sagt, daß sie dann hier vorbeikommt.

F. Das tut man. Say what things one needs to do before checking out of a hotel.

BEISPIEL: früh aufstehen **Man steht früh auf.**

1. die Koffer zumachen **2.** das Gepäck zur Rezeption mitnehmen **3.** den Schlüssel zurückgeben **4.** vielleicht ein Taxi anrufen **5.** einen Reisescheck einlösen

G. Vor der Reise. Before leaving for your trip, make sure that everything is under control.

BEISPIEL: Macht ihr die Fenster zu? **Habt ihr die Fenster zugemacht?**

1. Machst du die Garagentür wieder zu? **2.** Macht ihr das Licht aus *(turn off the light)*? **3.** Geht Anke bei der Post vorbei? **4.** Wechselt Kurt Dollar in Schilling um? **5.** Nehmen wir genug Geld mit? **6.** Bringt ihr eu(e)re

Pässe mit?   **7.** Rufst du die Pension noch an?   **8.** Schreibst du die Telefonnummer auf?   **9.** Nimmst du ein paar Bücher mit?   **10.** Kaufen wir etwas zu essen ein?

H. Auf deutsch, bitte!

1. You (*sg. fam.*) didn't close your book.   **2.** Listen! (*formal*).   **3.** They came back on the weekend.   **4.** Are you (*pl. fam.*) going out?   **5.** I don't know if he's coming along.   **6.** Do you (*sg. fam.*) know when she went out?   **7.** I exchanged our money.   **8.** Whom did you (*formal*) bring along?

I. Geben Sie alle vier Imperative!

BEISPIEL: Die Tür aufmachen   **Machen Sie die Tür auf!**
Macht die Tür auf!
Mach die Tür auf!
Machen wir die Tür auf!

1. jetzt aufstehen
2. in der Stadt einkaufen
3. den Scheck noch nicht einlösen
4. genug Bargeld mitbringen

5. das Gepäck mitnehmen
6. mit uns mitkommen
7. bei der Bank vorbeigehen
8. trotzdem zuhören
9. wieder zurückkommen

J. Interview. Fragen Sie einen Nachbarn / eine Nachbarin, . . . !
1. wann er / sie heute aufgestanden ist
2. wann er / sie gewöhnlich am Wochenende aufsteht
3. wohin er / sie gern geht, wenn er / sie ausgeht
4. wo er / sie einkauft
5. was er / sie heute mitgebracht hat (drei Beispiele, bitte!)

III. Gesture Words

In everyday speech, German uses many gesture (or flavoring) words to convey what English often expresses through gestures or intonation, e.g. surprise, admiration or curiosity. When used in these contexts, gesture words have no exact English equivalent. Here are some examples:

aber	*expresses admiration*
denn	*expresses curiosity, interest*
doch	*expresses concern, impatience, assurance*
ja	*adds emphasis*

Euer Haus gefällt mir **aber**!
Du bist **aber** heute hübsch!

I <u>do</u> like your house.
Don't <u>you</u> look pretty today!

Das kann **doch** nicht richtig sein.
Paß **doch** auf!
Sie haben **doch** eine Wohnung zu vermieten?

That <u>can't</u> be right.
Why <u>don't</u> you watch out!
You <u>do</u> have an apartment for rent, don't you?

Optional practice: Wissen Sie, . . . ? 1. wo man Schecks einlösen kann 2. was man alles aufmachen kann (z.B. einen Schrank) 3. wo man aufpassen muß (z.B. auf der Straße) 4. was man aufschreibt 5. was man auf eine Reise mitnimmt, etc.

At this level, do not expect students to use gesture words actively.

Read these examples with varying intonations and gestures and make students aware how in English this expresses admiration, curiosity, impatience, assurance, or emphasis.

Was ist **denn** das?	*What (on earth) is that?*
Wieviel Geld brauchst du **denn**?	*How much money <u>do</u> you need?*
Euer Garten ist **ja** phantastisch!	*(Wow,) your garden is fantastic!*
Morgen hast du **ja** Geburtstag!	*(Hey,) tomorrow is your birthday!*

ÜBUNGEN

K. Im Hotel. Auf englisch, bitte!

BEISPIEL: Haben Sie denn kein Einzelzimmer mehr frei?
   Don't you have any single room available?

1. Hier ist ja der Schlüssel!
2. Das Zimmer ist aber schön!
3. Es hat ja sogar einen Balkon!
4. Hat es denn keine Dusche?
5. Wir gehen doch noch aus?
6. Hast du denn keinen Hunger?
7. Komm doch mit!
8. Ich komme ja schon!
9. Laß doch den Mantel hier!
10. Wohin gehen wir denn?

ZUSAMMENFASSUNG

L. Bilden Sie Sätze! Use the tenses suggested.

BEISPIEL: Eva / gestern / ausgehen / mit Willi *(present perfect)*
   Eva ist gestern mit Willi ausgegangen.

1. man / umwechseln / Geld / auf / eine Bank *(present tense)*
2. welch- / Koffer *(sg.)* / du / mitnehmen? *(present tense)*
3. einkaufen / ihr / gern / in / euer / Supermarkt? *(present tense)*
4. unser / Nachbarn *(pl.)* / zurückkommen / vor einer Woche *(present perfect)*
5. wann / ihr / aufstehen / am Sonntag? *(present perfect)*
6. ich / mitbringen / dir / mein / Stadtplan *(present perfect)*
7. vorbeigehen / noch / schnell / bei / Apotheke! *(imperative / sg. fam.)*
8. zumachen / Schalter / um 17.30 Uhr! *(imperative / formal)*
9. umwechseln / alles / in Schilling! *(imperative / pl. fam.)*

M. An der Rezeption. Auf deutsch, bitte!
1. All (the) hotels are full **(voll)**.   2. Look, there's another hotel.   3. Let's ask once more.   4. Do you *(formal)* still have a room available?   5. Yes, one room without (a) bath on the first floor and one room with shower **(Dusche)** on the second floor.   6. Excellent! Which room would you *(sg. fam.)* like?   7. Give *(formal)* us the room on the second floor.   8. Where can I leave these suitcases?   9. Over there. But don't go yet.   10. May I see your ID, please?   11. Gladly. Do you cash traveler's checks?—Of course   12. Did you see our restaurant?—Which restaurant?   13. This restaurant. From each table you can see the mountains.   14. A restaurant like this (such a restaurant) you don't find everywhere.

M: 1. Alle Hotels sind voll. 2. Sieh, da ist noch ein Hotel! 3. Fragen wir noch einmal! 4. Haben Sie noch ein Zimmer frei? 5. Ja, ein Zimmer ohne Bad im Parterre und ein Zimmer mit Dusche im ersten Stock. 6. Ausgezeichnet! Welches Zimmer möchtest du? 7. Geben Sie uns das Zimmer im ersten Stock. 8. Wo kann ich diese Koffer lassen? 9. Da drüben. Aber gehen Sie noch nicht! 10. Darf ich bitte Ihren Ausweis sehen? 11. Gern. Lösen Sie Reiseschecks ein?—Natürlich! 12. Haben Sie unser Restaurant gesehen?—Welches Restaurant? 13. Dieses Restaurant. Von jedem Tisch können Sie die Berge sehen. 14. So ein Restaurant finden Sie nicht überall.

EINBLICKE ◆◆◆◆◆◆◆◆◆◆◆

Pre-reading activity:
1. Wo kann man in den USA / in Kanada gut übernachten? 2. Wie heißen ein paar Hotels oder Motels? 3. Was gibt es in einem Hotelzimmer? 4. Was kostet ein Zimmer in einem Luxushotel in New York oder San Francisco? 5. Wo kann man frühstücken? Kostet das Frühstück extra? 6. Haben Sie schon einmal in einer Jugendherberge übernachtet? Wenn ja, wo? 7. Gehen Sie gern campen? Wenn ja, warum; wenn nein, warum nicht?

Ein Gasthof kann sehr gemütlich sein.

Names of small hotels (**Gasthöfe** or **Gasthäuser**), which first sprang up around monasteries toward the end of the Middle Ages, often referred to the Bible: **Gasthof Engel** (*angel*), **Gasthof Drei Könige** (the Kings were symbols of travel), **Gasthof Rose** or **Lilie** (both flowers representing the Virgin Mary), and **Gasthof Lamm** (the Lamb of God). In the 1400s when a postal system was developing, names like **Gasthof Goldenes Posthorn, Alte Post, Neue Post,** and **Zur Post** appeared.

WORTSCHATZ 2

der	Gasthof, ¨e	*small hotel*
die	Jugendherberge, -n	*youth hostel*
	Pension, -en	*boarding house; hotel*
	Reise, -n	*trip*
	einfach	*simple, simply*
	fast	*almost*
	meistens	*mostly*
	an·kommen, ist angekommen[1]	*to arrive*
	bedeuten	*to mean, signify*

1 Two-way prepositions take the dative with **an·kommen**: Er ist am Bahnhof (in der Stadt) angekommen.

kennen·lernen[2]	to get to know, meet
Glück (Pech) haben	to be (un)lucky
packen	to pack
reisen, ist gereist	to travel
reservieren	to reserve
übernachten	to spend the night

2 The verb **kennen** functions as a separable prefix in this combination: Er hat sie hier kennengelernt. *(He met her here.)*

WAS IST DAS? der Campingplatz, Evangelist, Preis; das Symbol; die Adresse, Bibel, Gruppe, Möglichkeit, Übernachtung, Übernachtungsmöglichkeit, Touristeninformation; ausfüllen, campen, diskutieren, Karten spielen; extra, international, luxuriös, modern, privat, voll

Übernachtungsmöglichkeiten

well / that depends

Wo kann man gut übernachten? Nun°, das kommt darauf an°, ob das Hotel elegant oder einfach, international oder typisch deutsch sein soll, ob es zentral liegen muß, oder ob es weiter draußen° sein darf.

farther out

same

. . . chain

In Amerika gibt es viele Hotels mit gleichen° Namen, weil sie zu einer Hotelkette° gehören, z.B. „Holiday Inn" oder „Hilton". Bei diesen Hotels   5
weiß man immer, was man findet, wenn man hineingeht. In Deutschland gibt es auch Hotels mit gleichen Namen, z.B. „Hotel zur Sonne" oder „Gast-

inside

on the contrary / different

Middle Ages / about

location / other

lion / eagle / bear / bull

hof Post". Aber das bedeutet nicht, daß solche Hotels innen° gleich sind. Im Gegenteil°, sie sind meistens sehr verschieden°, weil sie privat sind. Ihre Namen gehen oft bis ins Mittelalter° zurück. Oft sagen sie etwas über° ihre   10
Lage°, z.B. Berghotel, Pension Waldsee. Andere° Namen, wie z.B. Gasthof zum Löwen°, zum Adler°, zum Bären° oder zum Stier° sind aus der Bibel genommen. Sie sind Symbole für die vier Evangelisten.

form

Manche Hotels sind sehr luxuriös und teuer, andere sind einfach und billig. Sprechen wir von einem normalen Hotel, einem Gasthof oder Gast-   15
haus! Wenn Sie ankommen, gehen Sie zur Rezeption! Dort müssen Sie ein Formular° ausfüllen[1] und bekommen dann Ihr Zimmer: ein Einzelzimmer oder Doppelzimmer, ein Zimmer mit oder ohne Bad. Für Zimmer ohne Bad gibt es auf dem Flur eine Toilette und meistens auch eine Dusche.[2] Das

included

day off

accept

attractions

careful / exchange rate

better

Frühstück ist gewöhnlich im Preis inbegriffen°. Übrigens hat jeder Gasthof   20
seinen Ruhetag°. Dann ist das Restaurant geschlossen, und man nimmt keine neuen Gäste an°. Der Herr oder die Dame an der Rezeption kann Ihnen auch Geschäfte und Sehenswürdigkeiten° empfehlen, manchmal auch Geld umwechseln. Aber Vorsicht°! Auf der Bank ist der Wechselkurs° fast immer besser°.   25

Wenn Sie nicht vorher reservieren können, dann finden Sie auch Übernachtungsmöglichkeiten durch die Touristeninformation am Bahnhof.[3]

An der Rezeption

Hier gibt es Adressen von Privatfamilien und Pensionen. So eine Übernachtung ist gewöhnlich nicht sehr teuer, aber doch sauber und gut.

Haben Sie schon einmal in einer Jugendherberge[4] oder einem Jugendgästehaus übernachtet? Wenn nicht, tun Sie es einmal! Aber was Sie dann brauchen, ist ein Jugendherbergsausweis. So einen Ausweis können Sie aber schon vorher° in Amerika oder Kanada bekommen. Fast jede Stadt hat eine Jugendherberge, manchmal in einem modernen Gebäude°, manchmal in einer Burg° oder in einem Schloß. Jugendherbergen und Jugendgästehäuser sind in den Ferien meistens schnell voll, denn alle Gruppen reservieren schon vorher. Das Übernachten in einer Jugendherberge kann ein Erlebnis° sein, weil man immer wieder interessante Leute kennenlernt. Abends sitzt man gern gemütlich zusammen und diskutiert, macht ein bißchen Musik oder spielt Karten. Jugendherbergen haben nur einen Nachteil°: Sie machen gewöhnlich abends um 22.00 Uhr zu. Wenn Sie später zurückkommen, haben Sie Pech gehabt. In fast allen Großstädten gibt es Jugendgästehäuser. Wenn Sie schon vorher wissen, daß Sie fast jeden Abend ausgehen und spät nach Hause kommen, dann übernachten Sie lieber° in so einem Jugendgästehaus, denn diese machen erst° um 23.00 oder 24.00 Uhr zu, und in manchen Gästehäusern kann man sogar einen Hausschlüssel bekommen.

Man kann natürlich auch anders° übernachten, z.B. auf dem Campingplatz, aber da braucht man ein Zelt° oder einen Wohnwagen°. Campen gefällt nicht jedem°. Ob im Hotel oder auf dem Campingplatz, in einer Pension oder Jugendherberge, überall brauchen Sie etwas Glück. Und das wünschen° wir Ihnen auf Ihrer Reise durch Europa.

in advance
building
castle

experience

disadvantage

rather
not until

differently
tent / camper
everybody
wish

30

35

40

45

50

Jugendherberge
»15. August«
5300 Weimar
Humboldtstraße 17
Telefon 4021

Gästeausweis

Aushändigung des Zimmerschlüssels nur
gegen Vorlage dieses Ausweises.

Zimmernummer: 14
Name: Bean   Vorname: Margaret
Anschrift:
Paß/PA-Nr.:
Reiseroute:
Anreisetag: Abreisetag:

ZUM TEXT

Optional practice: Was
ist das? 1. eine Ho-
telkette 2. die Rezep-
tion 3. ein Einzelzim-
mer 4. der Flur
5. eine Sehenswürdig-
keit 6. ein Gasthof
7. eine Jugendher-
berge 8. eine Pension
9. ein Hausschlüssel
10. Glück

A. Was paßt? Indicate the correct answer.
1. Deutsche Hotels mit gleichen Namen sind . . .
    a. immer alle gleich
    b. innen meistens nicht gleich
    c. alle aus dem Mittelalter
    d. Symbole
2. Wenn Sie in einem Gasthof ankommen, gehen Sie erst . . . .
    a. ins Bad
    b. ins Restaurant
    c. zur Rezeption
    d. in Ihr Zimmer

Das Frühstück ist
gewöhnlich im Preis
inbegriffen.

3. Im Hotel kann man Geld umwechseln, aber ....
   a. nur an der Rezeption
   b. nicht an der Rezeption
   c. der Wechselkurs ist meistens nicht sehr gut
   d. der Wechselkurs ist oft eine Sehenswürdigkeit
4. Wenn Sie jung sind, können Sie auch in ... übernachten.
   a. einem Luxushotel billig
   b. einer Jugendherberge oder einem Jugendgästehaus
   c. einem Café
   d. einem Schloß
5. Das Übernachten in einer Jugendherberge kann sehr interessant sein, weil ....
   a. Jugendherbergen in den Ferien schnell voll sind
   b. sie gewöhnlich abends um 22.00 Uhr zumachen
   c. man oft interessante Leute kennenlernt
   d. sie immer auf einer Burg sind
6. Übernachten Sie in einem Jugendgästehaus, wenn Sie ...!
   a. spät nach Hause kommen wollen
   b. Pech gehabt haben
   c. es gern primitiv haben wollen
   d. Karten spielen wollen
7. Auf dem Campingplatz ....
   a. gibt es eine Toilette auf dem Flur
   b. ist das Frühstück im Preis inbegriffen
   c. gibt es viele Zelte und Wohnwagen
   d. darf man nicht früh ankommen

B. Wo sollen wir übernachten? Match each lodging with the corresponding description.

Campingplatz, Gasthof, Jugendgästehaus, Jugendherberge, Luxushotel, Pension

1. Diese Übernachtungsmöglichkeit ist meistens nicht teuer, aber doch gut. Man kann sie z.B. durch die Touristeninformation am Bahnhof finden.
2. Hier ist es besonders billig, aber wenn es viel regnet, kann es sehr ungemütlich sein.
3. Wenn man viel Geld hat, ist es hier natürlich wunderbar.
4. Diese Möglichkeit ist für junge Leute. Sie ist nicht teuer, und man kann abends spät zurückkommen oder einen Schlüssel bekommen.
5. Das Übernachten kann hier sehr bequem und gemütlich sein; das Frühstück kostet nichts extra. Am Ruhetag kann man dort nicht essen.
6. Hier können Leute mit Ausweis billig übernachten, aber man darf abends nicht nach zehn zurückkommen.

C. Übernachtungsmöglichkeiten. Was fehlt?
1. In _____ Hotel kann man gut übernachten, aber das kann man nicht von _____ Hotel sagen. *(this, every)*
2. Bei _____ Hotel wissen Sie immer, wie es innen aussieht. *(such a)*

C: 1. diesem, jedem 2. so einem 3. Manche, dieses 4. Unser 5. dieser 6. euerer 7. Unsere 8. dieser 9. diesem 10. Welchen

3. _____ Hotels sind sehr luxuriös und teuer, _____ Hotel zum Beispiel. *(some, this)*

4. _____ Hotel ist sehr schön gewesen. *(our)*

5. Hast du schon einmal von _____ Pension gehört? *(this)*

6. Wie gefällt es euch in _____ Jugendherberge? *(your)*

7. _____ Jugendherberge ist in einer Burg. *(our)*

8. In _____ Jugendherberge gibt es noch Platz. *(this)*

9. Wollen wir auf _____ Campingplatz übernachten? *(this)*

10. _____ Campingplatz meinst du *(do you mean)*? *(which)*

D. In der Jugendherberge. Sagen Sie die Sätze noch einmal ohne Modalverb, (a) im Präsens und (b) im Perfekt!

BEISPIEL: Du kannst in den Ferien vorbeikommen.
Du kommst in den Ferien vorbei.
Du bist in den Ferien vorbeigekommen.

1. Wann möchtet ihr ankommen?
2. In der Jugendherberge könnt ihr Leute kennenlernen.
3. Du mußt natürlich einen Jugendherbergsausweis mitbringen.
4. Wollt ihr abends spät ausgehen?
5. Die Jugendherberge soll um zehn zumachen.
6. Wer spät zurückkommen möchte, kann Pech haben.

E. Ruckzuck! Wem gehört das? One person claims to own everything. Quickly correct him / her and tell whose property it is.

BEISPIEL: Das ist mein Buch.
Quatsch! Das ist nicht dein Buch; das ist mein (ihr, sein) Buch.

F. Kofferpacken

1. **Europareise.** Was packen Sie in den Koffer, wenn Sie einen Monat unterwegs sind?

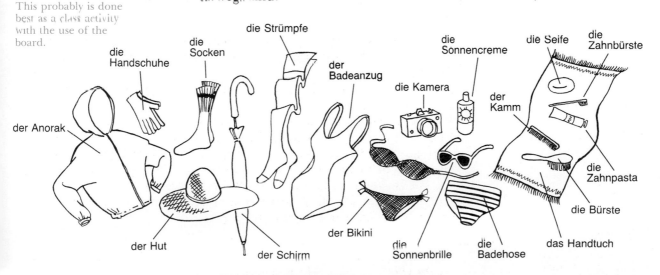

Und was noch? Machen Sie eine Liste!

2. **Was haben Sie mitgenommen?** Tell what you took along. One student starts, the next one repeats and adds to it, etc. When your memory fails, you're out.

BEISPIEL: Ich habe eine Sonnenbrille mitgenommen.
Ich habe eine Sonnenbrille und meine Kamera mitgenommen.

G. **Schriftliche Übung.** Using the questions as a guideline, write a brief paragraph.
1. Wohin geht Ihre nächste *(next)* Reise? Wann? Wo übernachten Sie dann, und warum dort?
2. Wo sind Sie das letzte Mal *(the last time)* gewesen? Wann? Wo haben Sie übernachtet, und wie hat es Ihnen gefallen?

Optional practice:
Geben Sie alle vier Imperative! (bei der Information fragen, die Namen lesen, in einer Pension übernachten, ein Zimmer reservieren, ein Formular ausfüllen, einen Scheck einlösen, Geld umwechseln, jetzt Frühstück essen, Ihre Tasche nehmen)

Übrigens

1. When registering in a hotel, all guests are required by law to fill out forms providing home address, date of birth, nationality, etc., in the interest of public safety.

2. If you intend to stay in a moderately priced hotel, take your own soap and shampoo. All hotels supply towels, but only the more expensive ones supply soap.

3. The Tourist Information Office has a room-referral service (**Zimmernachweis**). It usually charges a small fee for locating a room in the price range you indicate. **Pensionen,** by the way, usually have no rooms with bath. **Fremdenzimmer** are rooms in private homes.

4. Youth hostels (**Jugendherbergen**) can be found in almost every city and many small towns throughout Europe. They are particularly popular with students.

SPRECHSITUATIONEN

Telling and Asking About Time

You have now learned both the formal and the informal (see pre-unit 6) ways of telling time.

Meine Vorlesung beginnt um Viertel nach eins.
Meine Vorlesung beginnt um 13.15 Uhr.

Sie dauert von Viertel nach eins bis um drei.
Sie dauert von 13.15 Uhr bis 15.00 Uhr.

Wie spät ist es?
Wieviel Uhr ist es?
Wann beginnt . . . ?
Können Sie mir sagen, wie spät / wieviel Uhr es ist?

Expressing Disbelief

What can you say when someone tells you something that is hard to believe?

Wirklich?
Das gibt's doch nicht!   *That's not possible.*
Das ist doch nicht möglich!
Das kann doch nicht (wahr) sein!   *That can't be (true).*
Das kann ich nicht glauben.   *I can't believe that.*
Das ist wirklich unglaublich!   *That's truly unbelievable.*

Ach du Schreck!   *My goodness!*
Ach du liebes bißchen!   *Good grief!*
Quatsch!   *Nonsense.*
Du spinnst (wohl)!   *You're crazy.*
Du machst wohl Witze.   *You must be joking.*
Mach (doch) keine Witze!   *Stop joking.*
Das ist ja Wahnsinn!   *That's crazy.*

Giving a Warning

Here are a few ways to caution someone:

Also: **Achtung!** *Pay attention!*

Paß auf! / Paßt auf! / Passen Sie auf!
Warte! / Wartet! / Warten Sie! *(Wait!)*
Vorsicht! *(Careful!)*
Halt! *(Stop!)*

A. Öffnungszeiten.
Wann sind diese Restaurants und Kunstgalerien offen?

Gasthaus BAUER
1., Schottenbastei 4, Tel.: 533 6128
Mo-Fr 9-24 Uhr, warme Küche bis 21 Uhr,
Café MUSEUM 1., Friedrichstraße 6,
Tel.: 56 52 02
tgl. 7-23 Uhr; Alt-Wiener Kaffeehaus

ZUR WEINPERLE
9., Alserbachstraße 2, Tel.: 34 32 52
Mo-Fr 9-21.30 Uhr, Sa 9-14.30 Uhr
Café CENTRAL, 1., Herrengasse 14 (im/
inside Palais Ferstel), Tel.: 535 41 76
Mo-Sa 10-22 Uhr.

SCHNITZELWIRT
7., Neubaugasse 52, Tel.: 93 37 71
Mo-Sa 10-22 Uhr, warme Küche 11.30-
14.30 Uhr und 17.30-22 Uhr.
SCHWEIZERHAUS 2., Prater, Straße des
1. Mai 116, Tel.: 218 01 52
tgl. 10-24 Uhr, mitten im Wurstelprater

GALERIE NÄCHST ST. STEPHAN
1., Grünangergasse 1, Tel.: 512 12 66
Mo-Fr 10-18 Uhr, Sa 11-14 Uhr,
GALERIE HUMMEL
1., Bäckerstraße 14, Tel.: 512 12 96
Di-Fr 15-18 Uhr, Sa 10-13 Uhr;

GALERIE PETER PAKESCH
1., Ballgasse 6, Tel.: 52 48 14 und
3., Ungargasse 27, Tel.: 713 74 56
Di-Fr 14-19 Uhr, So 11-14 Uhr,
GALERIE STEINEK
1., Himmelpfortgasse 22, Tel: 512 87 59
Di-Fr 13-18 Uhr, Sa 10-12 Uhr;

B: Have students come up with a few examples of their own.

B. Was sagen Sie? Use the appropriate expression for each of the following situations.
1. Hier kostet ein Hotelzimmer 225 Mark.
2. Ich habe ein Zimmer für 200 Mark im Monat gefunden.
3. Du, die Vorlesung beginnt um 14.15 Uhr, und es ist schon 14.05 Uhr!
4. Sie bummeln mit einem Freund in der Stadt. Ihr Freund will bei Rot *(at a red light)* über die Straße laufen.
5. Sie sind auf einer Party, und es macht Ihnen viel Spaß. Aber morgen ist eine Prüfung, und Sie hören, daß es schon zwei Uhr ist.
6. Sie lernen auf einer Party einen Studenten kennen. Sie hören, daß sein Vater und Ihr Vater als Studenten Freunde gewesen sind.
7. Sie stehen mit einer Tasse Kaffee an der Tür. Die Tür ist zu. Ein Freund möchte hereinkommen.
8. Ein Freund aus Deutschland will die Kerzen auf seinem Weihnachtsbaum anzünden *(light)*. Sie sind sehr nervös.

C. Kurzgespräche
1. You are making your first excursion to Vienna and the university. You stop someone and ask if this is the foreign student office (**Auslandsstudentendienst**). It is, but you are told that it's only open until 4:00 in the afternoon, and it is 4:15 now. You say that you'll come back tomorrow, and thank the student.

Österr. Auslandsstudentendienst
1., Universität Wien, Dr. Karl-Lueger-Ring
Öffnungszeiten: Mo-Fr 9-12 Uhr, Di und Do
auch 14-16 Uhr

2. You are in the pedestrian area, the *Getreidegasse*, in Salzburg. Somebody calls your name. It turns out to be someone you went to high school with. You express your disbelief that he / she would be in Salzburg. Your friend then tells you he / she is studying in Munich. You say you're studying in Passau. Your friend expresses disbelief, too. You say you'd like to have a Coke; your friend agrees.

I. Verbs

1. **wissen**

   wissen, like the modals below, is irregular in the singular of the present tense.

singular	plural
ich weiß	wir wissen
du weißt	ihr wißt
er weiß	sie wissen

2. Modals

	dürfen	können	müssen	sollen	wollen	mögen	
ich	darf	kann	muß	soll	will	mag	möchte
du	darfst	kannst	mußt	sollst	willst	magst	möchtest
er	darf	kann	muß	soll	will	mag	möchte
wir	dürfen	können	müssen	sollen	wollen	mögen	möchten
ihr	dürft	könnt	müßt	sollt	wollt	mögt	möchtet
sie	dürfen	können	müssen	sollen	wollen	mögen	möchten

   The modal is the second sentence element (V1); the infinitive of the main verb (V2) stands at the end of the sentence.

   Sie **sollen** ihr den Kaffee **bringen**.   *You're supposed to bring her the coffee.*
      V1   V2

3. The Imperative

   The forms of the familiar imperative have no pronouns; the singular familiar imperative has no **-st** ending.

Schreiben Sie!	Schreibt!	Schreib(e)!	Schreiben wir . . . !
Antworten Sie!	Antwortet!	Antworte!	Antworten wir . . . !
Fahren Sie!	Fahrt!	**Fahr(e)!**	Fahren wir . . . !
Nehmen Sie!	Nehmt!	**Nimm!**	Nehmen wir . . . !

4. The Present Perfect

a. Past Participles

t-verbs (weak and mixed verbs)	n-verbs (strong verbs)
(ge) + stem (change) + (e)t	(ge) + stem (change) + en
gekauft gearbeitet gebracht	geschrieben
eingekauft verkauft reserviert	mitgeschrieben unterschrieben

b. Most verbs use **haben** as the auxiliary. Those that use **sein** are intransitive (take no object) and imply a change of place or condition. (**bleiben** and **sein** are exceptions to the rule.)

Wir haben Wien gesehen.
Wir sind viel gelaufen.
Abends sind wir müde gewesen.

5. Verbs with Inseparable and Separable Prefixes

a. Inseparable-prefix verbs (verbs with the unstressed prefixes **be-, emp-, ent-, er-, ge-, ver-** and **zer-**) are never separated.

Was bedeutet das?
Das verstehe ich nicht.
Was empfehlen Sie?
Wer bezahlt das Mittagessen?

über-, unter-, and **wieder-** can be used as separable or inseparable prefixes.

Übernachtet ihr in der Jugendherberge?
Unterschreiben Sie bitte hier!
Wiederholen Sie, bitte!

b. Separable-prefix verbs (verbs where the prefix is stressed) are separated in statements, questions, and imperatives.

Du **bringst** deine Schwester **mit**.
Bringst du deine Schwester **mit**?
Bring doch deine Schwester **mit**!

They are not separated when used with modals, in the present perfect, or in dependent clauses.

Du sollst deine Schwester **mitbringen**.
Hast du deine Schwester **mitgebracht**?
Sie will wissen, ob du deine Schwester **mitbringst**.

II. Cases

1. Two-Way Prepositions: Accusative or Dative?

> an, auf, hinter, in, neben, über, unter, vor, zwischen

The nine two-way prepositions take either the dative or the accusative, depending on the verb.

> wo?   LOCATION, activity within a place → dative
> wohin?   DESTINATION, motion to a place → accusative

Remember the difference between these two sets of verbs:

to put (upright)	Er **stellt** den Koffer neben den Ausgang.
to stand	Der Koffer **steht** neben dem Ausgang.
to put (flat), lay	**Legen** Sie den Ausweis auf den Tisch!
to lie (flat)	Der Ausweis **liegt** auf dem Tisch.

2. **der**-Words and **ein**-Words

   a. **der**-words have the same endings as the definite article **der** (see pp. 188 and 208).

   > dieser   solcher (so ein)
   > jeder   welcher
   > mancher   alle

   b. **ein**-words (or possessive adjectives) have the same endings as **ein** and **kein** (see charts on pp. 189 and 208).

   > mein   unser
   > dein   euer
   > sein, sein, ihr   ihr, Ihr

3. Pronouns

   a. Personal Pronouns

	singular					plural			sg. / pl.
nom.	ich	du	er	es	sie	wir	ihr	sie	Sie
acc.	**mich**	**dich**	**ihn**	**es**	**sie**	**uns**	**euch**	**sie**	**Sie**
dat.	**mir**	**dir**	**ihm**	**ihm**	**ihr**	**uns**	**euch**	**ihnen**	**Ihnen**

Don't confuse these pronouns with the **ein**-words (or possessive adjectives), which are always followed by a noun:

   > mein dein sein sein ihr   unser euer ihr   Ihr

b. Interrogative Pronouns

nom.	wer?	was?
acc.	wen?	was?
dat.	wem?	—

4. Summary of the Three Cases

	use	follows . . .	masc.	neut.	fem.	pl.
nom.	Subject, Predicate noun	heißen, sein, werden	der dieser ein mein	das dieses ein mein	die diese eine meine	die diese keine meine
acc.	Direct object	durch, für, gegen, ohne, um	den diesen einen meinen			
		an, auf, hinter, in neben, über, unter, vor, zwischen				
dat.	Indirect object	aus, außer, bei, mit, nach, seit, von, zu	dem diesem einem meinem	dem diesem einem meinem	der dieser einer meiner	den diesen keinen meinen
		antworten, danken, gefallen, gehören, helfen, zuhören				

III. Sentence Structure

1. Verb Position

a. V1—V2

In declarative sentences, yes / no questions, and imperatives, two-part verb phrases are split: the inflected part (V1) is the first or second sentence element; the other part (V2) appears at the end of the clause.

Er **ist** hier an der Uni **Student**.
Er **ist** wirklich sehr **interessant**.
    Hast du ihn schon **kennengelernt**?
Ich **kann** jetzt nicht lange **sprechen**.
    Komm doch später bei uns **vorbei**!
    V1   V2

b. Subordinate Clauses

▪ Subordinate clauses are introduced by subordinating conjunctions or interrogatives:

> **bevor, daß, ob, obwohl, weil, wenn**

> **wer? wen? wem? was? was für ein(e)? wohin? woher? wo? wann? warum? wie? wie lange? wieviel? wie viele?**

- In subordinate clauses the subject usually comes right after the conjunction and the inflected verb (V1) is at the end of the clause.

  Sie sagt, **daß** sie das Einzelzimmer **nimmt**.
  Er sagt, **daß** er den Zimmerschlüssel **mitbringt**.

- Two-part verb phrases appear in the order V2 V1.

  Sie sagt, **daß** er den Koffer **mitbringen soll**.

- If a subordinate clause is the first sentence element, then the inflected part of the verb in the main clause comes right after the comma.

  Ich habe den Schlüssel mitgenommen, **weil** das Hotel um 24.00 Uhr zumacht.
  Weil das Hotel um 24.00 Uhr zumacht, **habe ich** den Schlüssel mitgenommen.

2. Sequence of Objects

The indirect object usually precedes the direct object unless the direct object is a pronoun.

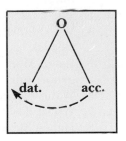

Sie gibt **dem Herrn** den Reisescheck.
Sie gibt **ihm** den Reisescheck.
Sie gibt ihn **dem Herrn**.
Sie gibt ihn **ihm**.

3. **sondern** vs. **aber**

sondern must be used when the first clause is negated AND the meaning *but on the contrary* is implied.

Er wohnt hier, **aber** er ist gerade nicht zu Hause.
Heinz ist nicht hier, **aber** er kommt in zehn Minuten zurück.
Heinz ist nicht hier, **sondern** bei Freunden.

WORTSCHATZWIEDERHOLUNG

A. Geben Sie das Gegenteil von . . . !
Ausgang, Tag, antworten, fahren, Glück haben, mieten, zumachen, bequem, furchtbar, geöffnet, hier, immer, links, ruhig, unten, weit

B. Was ist der Artikel und der Plural?
Ausweis, Bank, Bibliothek, Fest, Garten, Gast, Gasthof, Haus, Hotel, Jugendherberge, Koffer, Lied, Mann, Nacht, Radio, Regal, Reise, Schlüssel, Sessel, Tasche, Taxi, Universität, Wald, Weg

C. Welche Wörter kommen Ihnen in den Sinn?

BEISPIEL: aufmachen   **die Tür, das Fenster, der Schlüssel**

baden, bekommen, bummeln, einkaufen, feiern, Geld einlösen, halten, kochen, packen, singen, sitzen, sparen, Spaß machen, übernachten

D. Was für Wortkombinationen gibt es?

BEISPIEL: Telefon   **Telefonnummer, Telefonbuch**

1. Ausweis   4. Flasche   7. Haltestelle
2. Eingang   5. Gast   8. Scheck
3. Ferien   6. Geld   9. Schrank

E. Was paßt?

_____ 1. Können Sie mir sagen, wo das Hotel ist?
_____ 2. Wie komme ich dorthin *(to it)*?
_____ 3. Wie lange dauert das?
_____ 4. Wo kann ich das Gepäck lassen?
_____ 5. Einen Moment! Das gehört mir!
_____ 6. Wann machen Sie zu?
_____ 7. Wo ist das Zimmer?
_____ 8. Haben Sie kein Zimmer mit Bad?
_____ 9. Das Zimmer ist zu klein.

a. An der Rezeption.
b. Da drüben.
c. Das macht nichts.
d. Das tut mir leid.
e. Doch!
f. Ein paar Minuten.
g. Entschuldigen Sie!
h. Fahren Sie immer geradeaus!
i. Ich weiß nicht.
j. Im Parterre.
k. In ein paar Minuten.
l. Ja, gern.
m. Leider nicht.
n. Mit dem Bus.
o. Neben dem Rathaus.
p. Sind Sie sicher?
q. Um 23.00 Uhr.
r. Wirklich?
s. Zu Fuß!

STRUKTURWIEDERHOLUNG

F. Verben

1. **wissen oder kennen?**

   a. Ich möchte _____ , für wen das Geschenk ist.

   b. _____ du einen Herrn Mayerhofer?

   c. _____ ihr euere Nachbarn nicht?

   d. Nein, ich _____ sie nicht, aber ich _____ , daß sie aus Österreich sind.

   e. _____ du, wann sie zurückkommen sollen?

2. **Geben Sie alle Imperative!**

   BEISPIEL: Überraschen wir ihn!
   Überraschen Sie ihn!
   Überrascht ihn!
   Überrasch(e) ihn!

   a. Tun wir die Milch in den Kühlschrank! **b.** Stellen wir die Teller auf den Tisch! **c.** Gehen wir ins Wohnzimmer! **d.** Sprechen wir ein bißchen! **e.** Lassen wir alles liegen und stehen! **f.** Nehmen wir ein paar Gläser mit! **g.** Essen wir ein paar Kartoffelchips! **h.** Bleiben wir noch ein bißchen! **i.** Fahren wir später!

3. **Sagen Sie es im Perfekt!**

   a. Wohin geht ihr?—Wir fahren zum Museum.

   b. Was machst du heute?—Ich packe meinen Koffer.

   c. Wie feiert ihr seinen Geburtstag?—Wir überraschen ihn mit einer Party.

   d. Wie gefällt Ihnen die Landshuter Fürstenhochzeit?—Sie macht mir viel Spaß.

   e. Vermieten Sie die Wohnung?—Ja, eine Studentin nimmt sie.

   f. Weißt du, wo der Scheck ist?—Ja, er liegt auf dem Schreibtisch.

   g. Wie lange dauert die Party?—Sie ist um 12.00 Uhr vorbei.

   h. Wo sind Paula und Robert?—Sie kaufen ein.

4. **Variieren Sie die Sätze!**

   a. **Ihr dürft das Geschenk aufmachen.**
   May we open the present? We want to open it. I can't open it. He has to open it. Why am I not supposed to open it? Wouldn't you (3 ×) like to open it?

   b. **Wir kommen morgen an.**
   I arrived yesterday. She's arriving today. When are they arriving? When did he arrive? Is he arriving, too? I know that they're not arriving tomorrow. They're supposed to arrive the day after tomorrow. Has she arrived yet (**schon**)?

G. Personalpronomen. Variieren Sie die Sätze!

1. **Ich frage sie.**
   He's asking you (*formal*). She's asking him. Are they asking us? Yes, they are asking you (*sg. fam.*) We're asking you (*pl. fam.*). Don't ask them! Did you (*sg. fam.*) ask them? Weren't they asking you (*sg. fam.*)? Have you asked me?

2. **Dieses Museum gefällt mir.**

He likes our museum. Do you (*formal*) like this museum? They don't like their museum. Which museum do you (*sg. fam.*) like? I like such a museum. Don't you (*pl. fam.*) like any museum (Do you like no museum)? I don't like museums. I never liked such museums. He likes each museum.

3. **Das tut mir leid.**

She's sorry. Are you (*3 ×*) sorry? He isn't sorry. I was sorry. They were sorry.

H. Präpositionen. Bilden Sie Sätze wie in den Beispielen!

1. BEISPIEL: Wo ist der Koffer? Der Koffer steht an der Tür.
   Wohin soll ich den Koffer stellen? Stellen Sie ihn an die Tür!

   vor / Haus; in / Gästezimmer; neben / Sofa; hinter / Sessel; unter / Tisch; zwischen / Stuhl / und / Bett

2. BEISPIEL: Wohin soll ich das Messer legen? Legen Sie es auf den Tisch!
   Wo liegt das Messer? Es liegt auf dem Tisch.

   neben / Gabel; auf / Teller; zwischen / Butter / und / Käse; in / Küche; in / Eßzimmer

I. Konjunktionen

1. **Verbinden Sie die Sätze!** Note that both coordinating and subordinating conjunctions are used.
   a. Ich lerne Deutsch. Meine Großeltern sind aus Deutschland (*because*).
   b. Sie möchte wissen. Bist du schon einmal in Deutschland gewesen? (*whether*)
   c. Ich sage (es) ihr. Ich bin im Sommer dort gewesen. (*that*)
   d. Braucht man Hotelreservierungen? Man fährt nach Deutschland. (*when*)
   e. (*although*) Man braucht keine Reservierung. Es hat manchmal lange gedauert, bis ich ein Zimmer gefunden habe.
   f. Man muß alles gut planen. Man möchte nach Deutschland fahren. (*if*)

2. **sondern oder aber?**
   a. Momentan habe ich kein Kleingeld, _____ später gehe ich zur Bank.
   b. Die Bank ist um diese Zeit geschlossen, _____ sie macht in einer Stunde wieder auf.
   c. Wir möchten nicht in die Stadt gehen, _____ hier bleiben.
   d. In der Stadt kann man viel sehen, _____ wir haben schon alles gesehen.
   e. Das bedeutet nicht, daß die Stadt mir nicht gefällt, _____ es bedeutet nur, daß ich müde bin.

8 *Post und Reisen*

In Europa sind Züge bequem, pünktlich und schnell.

▌LERNZIELE

Gespräche and **Wortschatz**. This chapter deals with the postal service and traveling.

Struktur. You will learn about . . .

- the genitive case.

- time expressions.

- sentence structure (adverbs and the position of **nicht**).

Einblicke. Tourists' views of Switzerland

Sprechsituationen

- Expressing sympathy

- Expressing empathy

- Expressing relief

213

◆◆◆◆◆ # GESPRÄCHE

Fragen: 1. Wo ist die Post? 2. Wohin will Annemarie ihr Paket schicken? 3. Wie schickt sie es? 4. Wie lange soll das dauern? 5. Was muß man bei einem Paket ins Ausland *(abroad)* ausfüllen? 6. Was fehlt auf der Paketkarte? 7. Was muß Annemarie noch tun? 8. Wohin will sie fahren? 9. Wann fährt der Zug ab, und wann kommt sie in Interlaken an? 10. Wo muß sie umsteigen? 11. Was für eine Karte kauft sie?

Auf der Bahnhofspost

ANNEMARIE	Ich möchte dieses Paket nach Amerika schicken.
POSTBEAMTER	Normal oder mit Luftpost?
ANNEMARIE	Mit Luftpost. Wie lange dauert das denn?
POSTBEAMTER	Ungefähr zehn Tage. Füllen Sie bitte diese Paketkarte aus! Moment, hier fehlt noch Ihr Absender!
ANNEMARIE	Ach ja! Noch etwas. Ich muß telefonieren.
POSTBEAMTER	Wohin?
ANNEMARIE	Nach Basel. Hier ist die Telefonnummer.
POSTBEAMTER	Gehen Sie da drüben in Zelle vier![1]
ANNEMARIE	Danke!

Am Fahrkartenschalter

ANNEMARIE	Wann fährt der nächste Zug nach Interlaken[2]?
BEAMTIN	In einer Viertelstunde. Abfahrt 11.28 Uhr, Gleis 2.
ANNEMARIE	Und wann kommt er dort an?
BEAMTIN	Ankunft in Interlaken 14.16 Uhr.
ANNEMARIE	Muß ich umsteigen?
BEAMTIN	Ja, in Bern[3]. Aber Sie haben Anschluß zum InterCity[4] mit nur vierundzwanzig Minuten Aufenthalt.
ANNEMARIE	Prima. Dann geben Sie mir bitte eine Rückfahrkarte nach Interlaken!
BEAMTIN	Erster oder zweiter Klasse?
ANNEMARIE	Zweiter Klasse.

Zug	IC 118	518	1720		IC 120	1520	1822	
	◢4◣ ✗	✗			◢4◣ ✗	⚍	⚍	◢4◣
Zürich HB	10 03	10 07	10 28		11 03	11 07	11 28	
Baden			10 45				11 45	
Brugg (Aargau)			10 53				11 53	
Aarau		10 35	11 07			11 35	12 07	
Olten 24016 ○		10 44	11 15			11 44	12 15	
Olten 24000 ○		10 47				11 47		
Biel/Bienne ○		11 33				12 33		
Lausanne ○						13 48		
Genève ○		13 05						

Zug	IC 721	2521	EC 73	1866			IC 725
	⚍		7 ✗	◢4◣ ⚍			🛏
Basel SBB	10 00	10 11	10 29	11 00		11 29	12 00
Liestal		10 21	10 46			11 46	
Olten ○	10 26	10 43	11 11	11 26		12 11	12 26
Olten	10 28	10 48	11 17	11 28		12 17	12 28
Langenthal		11 00	11 29			12 29	
Herzogenbuchsee		11 06	11 35			12 35	
Burgdorf		11 18	11 47			12 47	
Bern ○	11 10	11 14	11 35	12 04	12 10 12 14	13 04	13 10
Bern 24004 ○	11 28 ←		12 28	↙	12 28		13 28 ◀
Interlaken West ○	12 16		13 16		13 16		14 16

1. Post offices in Germany provide a far greater range of services than in the United States or Canada. You can, for example, open a checking or savings account, get traveler's checks, arrange for money transfers, or send a telegram. Post offices usually have several booths from which long-distance calls can be made and then paid for at the counter. This is useful if you stay in a hotel, since many hotels impose a considerable surcharge on long-distance calls. Until recently, the post office had a monopoly on telephone and postal services. In 1989 the postal service was divided into three separate enterprises, administered by the **Bundesministerium für Post und Telekommunikation,** one for each function: telecommunications (**Telekom**), banking (**Postbank**), and postal service (**Postdienst**).

2. **Interlaken** (pop. 13,000), located between lakes Thun and Brienz, is one of the oldest and most popular summer resorts in Switzerland. Tourists enjoy the endless variety of hikes, climbs, and other excursions, especially into the mountains of the **Berner Oberland,** accessible also by mountain railroads and cablecars.

3. **Bern** (pop. 141,000) is the capital of Switzerland. Founded in 1191, the old section of Bern sits one hundred feet above a bend in the Aare River, which surrounds the city on three sides. Gray stone buildings, red tiled roofs, scenic paths, and fountains preserve the medieval charm of old Bern, which is linked by several bridges to its modern counterpart on the opposite side of the river.

4. Train travel in Europe is very popular. An extensive network of rail lines serves commuters as well as long-distance travelers. Trains are comfortable, clean, punctual, and fast. The **IC** (InterCity) and **EC** (EuroCity) trains connect all major European cities. Non-European travelers can buy a Eurail-Pass that permits unlimited train and some bus and boat travel in Germany and most other European countries.

At the Post Office in the Train Station ANNEMARIE: *I'd like to send this package to the United States.* CLERK: *By surface mail or by airmail?* ANNEMARIE: *By airmail. How long will it take?* CLERK: *About ten days. Please fill out this parcel form.—Just a minute. Your return address is missing.* ANNEMARIE: *Oh yes.—One more thing. I have to make a phone call.* CLERK: *Where to?* ANNEMARIE: *To Basel. Here's the phone number.* CLERK: *Go over there to booth four.* ANNEMARIE: *Thank you.*

At the Ticket Counter ANNEMARIE: *When does the next train for Interlaken leave?* CLERK: *In a quarter of an hour. Departure at 11:28, track 2.* ANNEMARIE: *And when will it arrive there?* CLERK: *Arrival in Interlaken at 14:16.* ANNEMARIE: *Do I have to change trains?* CLERK: *Yes, in Bern. But you have a connection to the InterCity Express with only a twenty-four minute stopover.* ANNEMARIE: *Great. Then give me a round-trip ticket to Interlaken, please.* CLERK: *First or second class?* ANNEMARIE: *Second class.*

WORTSCHATZ 1

DIE POST *post office, mail*

der	Absender, -	*return address*
	Brief, -e	*letter*
	Briefkasten, ⸚	*mailbox*
das	Paket, -e	*package, parcel*
die	Adresse, -n	*address*
	Briefmarke, -n	*stamp*
	(Post)karte, -n	*(post)card*

DIE REISE, -N *trip*

der	Aufenthalt	*stopover*	*das*	Flugzeug, -e	*plane*
	Bahnsteig, -e	*platform*		Gleis, -e	*track*
	Fahrplan, ⸚e	*schedule*	*die*	Abfahrt, -en	*departure*
	Flug, ⸚e	*flight*		Ankunft, ⸚e	*arrival*
	Flughafen, ⸚	*airport*		Bahn, -en	*railway, train*
	Wagen, -	*car; railroad car*		Fahrt, -en	*trip, drive*
	Zug, ⸚e	*train*		Fahrkarte, -n	*ticket*
				Rückfahr-	*round-trip ticket*
				karte, -n	

das Auto BUT *der* **Wagen!**

WEITERES

in einer Viertelstunde	*in a quarter of an hour*
in einer halben Stunde	*in half an hour*
in einer Dreiviertelstunde	*in three quarters of an hour*
ab·fahren (fährt ab), ist abgefahren (von)	*to leave (from), depart*
ab·fliegen, ist abgeflogen (von)	*to take off, fly (from)*
aus·steigen, ist ausgestiegen	*to get off*
ein·steigen, ist eingestiegen	*to get on (in)*
um·steigen, ist umgestiegen	*to change (trains etc.)*
aus·füllen	*to fill out*
besuchen	*to visit*
fliegen, ist geflogen	*to fly, go by plane*
landen, ist gelandet	*to land*
schicken	*to send*
telefonieren	*to call up, phone*
mit dem Zug / der Bahn fahren	*to go by train*

PASSIVES VOKABULAR **der Anschluß, ⸚sse** *connection* **der nächste Zug nach** *the next train to* **die Klasse, -n die Paketkarte, -n** *parcel form* **Telefonzelle, -n** *phone booth* **Einen Moment!** *One moment! Just a minute!* **mit Luftpost** *by airmail* **noch etwas** *one more thing, something else*

Im Hauptbahnhof
von Luzern

ZUM THEMA

A. Was paßt nicht?
1. der Absender, der Briefkasten, die Adresse, die Briefmarke
2. der Bahnhof, der Bahnsteig, das Gleis, der Flugkartenschalter
3. die Luftpost, die Ankunft, die Abfahrt, der Fahrplan
4. fliegen, fahren, schicken, fehlen
5. abfahren, abfliegen, ausfüllen, ankommen
6. hinaufsteigen, aussteigen, einsteigen, umsteigen

B. Was bedeutet das, und was ist der Artikel?
Adressbuch, Abfahrtszeit, Ankunftsfahrplan, Bahnhofseingang, Briefträger, Busbahnhof, Busfahrt, Flugkarte, Flugschalter, Flugsteig, Gepäckkarte, Landung, Zwischenlandung, Mietwagen, Nachtzug, Paketschalter, Rückflugkarte, Speisewagen, Telefonrechnung

C. Was tun sie?

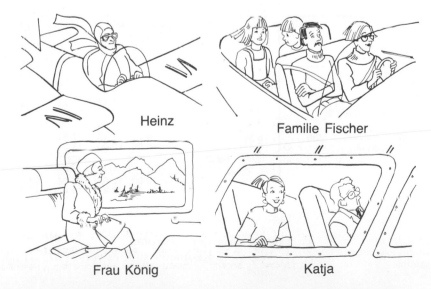

Heinz

Familie Fischer

Frau König

Katja

D: Have students prepare answers in small groups, then ask the class some of these questions, or let some students report their partners' answers.

D. Fragen

1. Was kostet es, wenn man einen Brief innerhalb *(inside)* von Amerika / Kanada schicken will? Wie lange braucht ein Brief innerhalb der Stadt? nach Europa?
2. Was muß man auf alle Briefe, Postkarten und Pakete schreiben? Schreiben Sie oft Briefe? Wem?
3. In Deutschland sind die Briefkästen gelb. Welche Farbe haben die Briefkästen hier?
4. Wo kann man hier telefonieren? Kann man hier auch auf der Post telefonieren?
5. Wie kann man reisen? Wie reisen Sie gern? Warum?
6. Wo sind Sie das letzte Mal *(the last time)* gewesen? Sind Sie geflogen oder mit dem Wagen gefahren?
7. Wie heißt der Ort *(place)*, wo Züge abfahren und ankommen? wo Flugzeuge abfliegen und landen? wo Busse halten?
8. Was ist das Gegenteil von abfahren? abfliegen? einsteigen? Abfahrt? Abflug?

E: Have students act out the dialogue. Reverse roles. If time permits, suggest another dialogue (e.g., calling someone from a train station, saying that you're coming, and giving details).

E. Am Flugschalter. Was sagen Sie?

x Wann gehen Flüge nach _____ ?

y Zu welcher Tageszeit möchten Sie denn fliegen?

x Ich muß um _____ in _____ sein.

y Es gibt einen Flug um _____ .

x Hat er eine Zwischenlandung?

y Ja, in _____ . Dort haben Sie _____ Aufenthalt.

x Muß ich umsteigen?

y _____ .

x _____ . Dann geben Sie mir eine Rückflugkarte nach _____ !

y Erster oder zweiter Klasse?

x _____ .

km	Stuttgart–Zürich	Zug	E 3504	D 83 [R]3)	D 381 [R]3)	D 383	D 85 [R]4)	D 389 [R]2)	D 87	D 385 [R]1) ◆1)	E 3309 [R]1) ◆1)	D 387 [R]1) ◆1)
0	**Stuttgart** Hbf 740			6 48	7 31	9 34	12 44	14 26	17 32	18 26	20 06	
26	Böblingen				7 53	9 56	13 06	14 48	17 55	18 48	20 29	
67	Horb			7 34	8 20	10 24	13 33	15 15	18 21	19 15	21 00	
110	Rottweil			8 05	8 59	10 54	14 02	15 52	18 51	19 45	21 36	
138	Tuttlingen			8 26	9 17	11 13	14 21	16 11	19 09	20 11	21 55	
172	Singen (Hohentwiel) ⊞	O		8 49	9 42	11 37	14 45	16 35	19 32	20 35	22 22	
		Zug										
	Singen (Hohentwiel) 730	O	6 31	8 55	9 49	11 44	14 51	16 44	19 37	20 44		22 44
192	Schaffhausen ⊞	O	6 49	9 10	10 05	12 00	15 07	17 00	19 52	21 00		23 00
		Zug	1559	(*EC* 83)			(*EC* 85)		(*IC* 87)			
	Schaffhausen 24032	O	7 02	9 12	10 09	12 09	15 09	17 09	19 55	21 09		23 09
238	**Zürich** HB	O	7 47	9 47	10 47	12 47	15 47	17 47	20 31	21 47		23 47

F: As in D, let students prepare this exercise in small groups.

F. Fragen über den Fahrplan

1. Wie viele Kilometer sind es von Stuttgart nach Zürich? *(1 km = 0.62 miles)*

2. Wann fährt der erste Zug morgens? der letzte *(last)* Zug abends?
3. In welchem Zug kann man Speisen und Getränke *(food and beverages)* kaufen? Welcher Zug hat einen Gepäckwagen oder Liegewagen?
4. Welcher Zug ist ab Schaffhausen ein EC-Zug? ein IC-Zug?
5. Wann ist man in Zürich, wenn man um 6.48 Uhr von Stuttgart abfährt? Ungefähr wie lange dauert die Fahrt?

G. Aussprache. See also II.8–10 in the pronunciation section of the Workbook.
   1. [ə]   Adresse, Briefe, Pakete, Flüge, Züge, Wagen, Ecke, Haltestelle, bekommen, besuchen, eine halbe Stunde
   2. [ʌ]   aber, sauber, euer, unser, Zimmer, Absender, Koffer, Nummer, Uhr, wir, vier, vor, nur, unter, über, hinter, außer, feiern, wiederholen, verkaufen
   3. Wortpaare
      a. Studenten / Studentin
      b. Touristen / Touristin
      c. diese / dieser
      d. arbeiten / Arbeitern
      e. lese / Leser
      f. mieten / Mietern

STRUKTUR

I. The Genitive Case

The genitive case has two major functions: it expresses possession or another close relationship between two nouns, and it follows certain prepositions.

1. The English phrases *the son's letter* and *the date of the letter* are expressed in German by phrases in the genitive.

Das ist **der Brief des Sohnes**.	*That's the son's letter.*
Was ist **das Datum des Briefes**?	*What's the date of the letter?*

   a. The genitive form of the INTERROGATIVE PRONOUN **wer** is **wessen** *(whose)*. The chart of interrogative pronouns is now complete.

	persons	things and ideas
nom.	wer?	was?
acc.	wen?	was?
dat.	wem?	—
gen.	**wessen?**	—

The interrogative pronoun **wessen** is always followed (eventually) by a noun: **Wessen Sohn? Wessen (furchtbar langer) Brief?**

Wessen Brief ist das? **Der Brief des Sohnes.**
Whose letter is that? The son's letter.

b. The genitive forms of the DEFINITE and INDEFINITE ARTICLES complete this chart of articles:

	masc.	singular neut.	fem.	plural
nom.	der ein kein	das ein kein	die eine keine	die — keine
acc.	den einen keinen			
dat.	dem einem keinem	dem einem keinem	der einer keiner	den — keinen
gen.	**des eines keines**	**des eines keines**		**der — keiner**

c. The genitive case is signaled not only by the special forms of the articles but also by a special ending for MASCULINE and NEUTER nouns in the singular.

- Most one-syllable nouns and nouns ending in **-s, -ß, -z, -tz,** or **-zt,** add **-es**:

der Zug	das Geld	das Gleis	der Paß	der Platz
des Zug**es**	**des** Geld**es**	**des** Gleis**es**	**des** Pass**es**	**des** Platz**es**

- Proper names and nouns with more than one syllable add an **-s**:

Annemaries Flug	*Annemarie's flight*
Frau Strobels Fahrt	*Ms. Strobel's trip*
Wiens Flughafen	*Vienna's airport*
des Flughafen**s**	*of the airport, the airport's*

Note that German uses NO apostrophe (') for the genitive!

The genitive of names ending in **-s, -, -tz, -x, -z** frequently takes the ending **-ens** in written language (**Schulzens Auto**); in colloquial speech, **von** or an apostrophe is used: **die Adresse von Hans, Hans' Adresse**.

- N-nouns have an **-n** or **-en** ending in ALL CASES except in the nominative singular. A very few n-nouns have a genitive -s.

der Herr, **-n,** -en	des Herr**n**
Junge, **-n,** -n	Jungen
Mensch, **-en,** -en	Menschen
Nachbar, **-n,** -n	Nachbarn
Student, **-en,**-en	Studenten
Tourist, **-en,** -en	Touristen
Name, **-n(s),** -n	Namen**s**

Note how they are listed in vocabularies and dictionaries: the first ending usually refers to the accusative, dative and genitive singular; the second one to the plural.

d. FEMININE NOUNS and PLURAL nouns have no special endings.

die Reise	**der** Reise
die Reisen	**der** Reisen

e. Nouns in the genitive NORMALLY FOLLOW the nouns they modify, while PROPER NAMES PRECEDE them.

Er liest **den Brief der Tante.**
Er liest **Annemaries Brief.**
Er liest **Herrn Müllers Brief.**

CAUTION

Don't confuse the use of the possessive adjectives **mein, dein,** etc., with that of the genitive case.

Das ist **mein** Onkel.	*That's my uncle.*
Das ist der Koffer **meines Onkels.**	*That's my uncle's suitcase (the suitcase of my uncle).*

2. These prepositions are followed by the genitive case:

(an)statt	*instead of*	Ich nehme oft den Bus **statt der Straßenbahn.**
trotz	*in spite of*	**Trotz des Wetters** bummele ich gern durch die Stadt.
während	*during*	**Während der Mittagspause** gehe ich in den Park.
wegen	*because of*	Heute bleibe ich **wegen des Regens** (*rain*) hier.

Den Fahrer während der Fahrt nicht ansprechen

ÜBUNGEN

A. Wissen Sie, wer das ist?

BEISPIEL: Wer ist der Vater Ihrer Mutter?   **Das ist mein Großvater.**

1. Wer ist der Sohn Ihres Vaters?   **2.** Wer ist die Mutter Ihrer Mutter?   **3.** Wer ist die Tochter Ihrer Mutter?   **4.** Wer ist der Großvater Ihrer Mutter?   **5.** Wer ist die Schwester Ihrer Mutter?   **6.** Wer ist der Mann Ihrer Tante?   **7.** Wer ist die Tochter Ihres Großvaters?   **8.** Wer ist der Sohn Ihres Urgroßvaters?

Simple introductory exercise: z.B. das Buch: des Buches 1. das Heft, der Stuhl, das Haus, der Paß, die Reise, der Scheck, das Taxi, die Tasche, der Koffer, der Ausweis, die Nacht, der Name 2. welche Bank, dieses Hotel, jeder Wagen, alle Flughäfen, manche Studenten, solche Leute 3. mein Großvater, deine Brüder, ihre Tante, unser Auto, euer Haus, ihre Nummern, Ihr Onkel, sein Telefon, so ein Wagen, so eine Bahn

während is also used as a subordinating conjunction: **Während ich hier bin, lerne ich viel Deutsch.**

A: There are various ways to handle this exercise in addition to, or instead of, the way it's presented: **Der Vater meiner Mutter ist mein Großvater.** OR **Der Vater meiner Mutter heißt Hermann.** When students are familiar with the genitive, you can reverse this exercise: Wer ist Ihr Großvater? Er ist der Vater meines Vaters.

B. Im Reisebüro. *(At the travel agency.)* Make sure that your assistant followed all the necessary steps to organize the tour leaving for Bern tomorrow.

BEISPIEL: Wo ist die Liste der Touristen? (Hotel / *pl.*)
Wo ist die Liste der Hotels?

1. Was ist der Name des Reiseführers *(tour guide)*? (Schloß, Dom, Museum, Straße, Platz, Tourist, Touristin)
2. Wo ist die Adresse der Jugendherberge? (Theater, Studentenheim, Universität, Restaurant)
3. Wo ist die Telefonnummer des Hotels? (Gästehaus, Pension, Gasthof, Jugendherbergen)
4. Wo ist die Adresse dieser Dame? (Gast, Mädchen, Junge, Herr, Herren, Student, Studenten / *pl.*)
5. Wann ist die Ankunft unserer Gruppe? (Bus, Zug, Flugzeug, Reiseführerin, Gäste)
6. Haben Sie wegen der Reservierung *(reservation)* angerufen? (Zimmer, Schlüssel, Gepäck, Adresse, Theaterkarten / *pl.*)
7. Wir fahren trotz des Gewitters *(thunderstorm)*. (Wetter, Regen / *m.*, Eis, Feiertag, Ferien)
8. Christiane Binder kommt statt ihrer Mutter mit. (Vater, Bruder, Onkel, Nachbar, Nachbarin, Großeltern)

C: Use anything students have with them or on them to ask these and similar questions.

C. Wem gehört das?

BEISPIEL: Gehört die Jacke Ihrem Freund?
Nein, das ist nicht die Jacke meines Freundes. Das ist meine Jacke.

Gehört das Hemd Ihrem Bruder? die Uhr Ihrer Mutter? das Buch Ihrem Professor? die Tasche Ihrer Freundin? das Papier Ihrem Nachbarn? der Kuli Fräulein _____ *(name a student)*? das Heft Herrn _____ *(name a student)*? der Platz Peter _____ *(add another name)*?

D: Have each student write 5 sentences (e.g., **Die Farbe des Autos ist rot**) and then share them with the class. Column 5 can be various things: an adjective, noun, name, pronoun, or a phrase.

D. Bilden Sie Sätze mit dem Genitiv!

BEISPIEL: Die Abfahrt des Zuges ist um 19.05 Uhr.

1	2	3	4	5
die Farbe	d-	Auto	Gasthof	ist	_____
der Name	dies-	Bus	Ausweis	gefällt	
die Adresse	mein-	Zug	Paß		
die Nummer	unser-	Bahnsteig	Reisescheck		
das Zimmer		Koffer	Flug		
das Gepäck		Tasche	Frau		
die Abfahrt		Haus	Herr		
der Preis		Wohnung	Freund(in)		
die Lage		Hotel	Tourist(in)		
(location)		Pension	Gäste		
		Berge			

E. Bahnfahrt. Auf deutsch, bitte! **1.** Is that Eva's train? **2.** Do you know the number of the platform? **3.** No. Where's the train schedule (schedule of the trains)? **4.** The departure of her train is in a few minutes (her train leaves in a few minutes). **5.** Take along Kurt's package. **6.** Kurt is a student and a friend of my friend (*f.*). **7.** Eva, do you have the address of the student? **8.** No, but I know the name of the dorm. **9.** I'll take it to him during the holidays. **10.** Because of the exams I don't have time now. **11.** I'll send you a postcard instead of a letter.

II. Time Expressions

1. Adverbs of Time

Point out capitalization rules with nouns: **der Morgen, Mittag, Nachmittag, Abend, die Nacht**; BUT with adverbs: **gestern morgen (mittag, nachmittag, abend), heute nacht**.

a. To refer to SPECIFIC TIMES, such as *yesterday evening* or *Monday morning*, combine one word from group A with one from group B. The words in group A can be used alone, while those in group B must be used in combinations: **gestern abend, Montag morgen, Sonntag nachmittag**.

A

vorgestern	*the day before yesterday*
gestern	*yesterday*
heute	*today*
morgen	*tomorrow*
übermorgen	*the day after tomorrow*

B

Montag	**früh[1], morgen**	*early, morning*
Dienstag	**vormittag**	*midmorning (9 to 12 a.m.)[2]*
Mittwoch	**mittag**	*noon (12 to 2 p.m.)*
Donnerstag	**nachmittag**	*afternoon (2 to 6 p.m.)*
Freitag	**abend**	*evening (6 to 10 p.m.)*
Samstag	**nacht**	*night (after 10 p.m.)*
Sonntag		

Heute fliege ich von New York ab.
Dann bin ich morgen früh in Frankfurt.
Übermorgen fahre ich nach Bonn.
Montag abend besuche ich Krauses.
Dann fahre ich Dienstag nachmittag mit dem Zug zurück.

[1] *Tomorrow morning* is always **morgen früh**.
[2] The times may vary somewhat, but these are reasonable guidelines.

b. Such familiar adverbs as **montags** and **morgens** don't refer to specific time (a specific Monday or morning), but rather imply that events occur USUALLY (more or less regularly) for example, *on Mondays* or *in the morning, most mornings:*

montags, dienstags, mittwochs, donnerstags, freitags, samstags, sonntags; morgens, vormittags, mittags, nachmittags, abends, nachts

> Sonntags tue ich nichts, aber montags arbeite ich schwer.
> Morgens und nachmittags gehe ich zur Universität.
> Mittags spiele ich eine Stunde Tennis.

2. Other Time Expressions

a. The Accusative of Time

To refer to a DEFINITE point of time (**wann?**) or length of time (**wie lange?**), German often uses time phrases in the accusative, without any prepositions. Here are some of the most common expressions:

wann?		wie lange?	
jeden Tag	*every day*	zwei Wochen	*for two weeks*
diese Woche	*this week*	einen Monat	*for one month*

Haben Sie diese Woche Zeit?	*Do you have time this week?*
Die Fahrt dauert zwei Stunden.	*The trip takes two hours.*
Ich bleibe zwei Tage in Frankfurt.	*I'll be in Frankfurt for two days.*

b. The Genitive of Time

To refer to an INDEFINITE point of time (in the past or future), German uses the genitive:

eines Tages	*one day*

Eines Tages ist ein Brief gekommen.	*One day a letter came.*
Eines Tages fahre ich in die Schweiz.	*One day I'll go to Switzerland.*

c. Prepositional Time Phrases

You are already familiar with the phrases below:

an	am Abend, am Wochenende, am Montag, am 1. April
bis	bis morgen, bis 2.30 Uhr, bis (zum) Freitag, bis (zum) Januar
für	für morgen, für Freitag, für eine Nacht
in	im Juli, im Sommer, im Monat; in zehn Minuten, in einer Viertelstunde, in einer Woche, in einem Jahr
nach	nach dem Essen, nach einer Stunde
seit	seit einem Jahr, seit September

um	um fünf (Uhr)
von ... bis	vom 1. Juni bis (zum) 25. August; von Juli bis August
vor	vor einem Monat, vor ein paar Tagen
während	während des Sommers, während des Tages

- Two-way prepositions usually use the dative in time expressions: Wir fahren **in einer Woche** in die Berge. **Am Freitag** fahren wir ab.

- German uses **seit** plus the present tense to describe an action or condition that began in the past and is still continuing in the present. English uses the present perfect progressive to express the same thing: **Er wohnt seit zwei Jahren hier.** (*He has been living here for two years.*)

ÜBUNGEN

F. Ein Besuch. Was fehlt?

1. Erich ist _____ angekommen. (*one week ago*)
2. Wir sind _____ abgefahren. (*Thursday evening at 7 o'clock*)
3. Er ist _____ geflogen. (*for nine hours*)
4. Ich habe ihn schon _____ nicht mehr gesehen. (*for one year*)
5. Er schläft _____ gewöhnlich nicht lange. (*in the morning*)
6. Aber er hat _____ geschlafen. (*Friday morning until 11 a.m.*)
7. Er bleibt noch ungefähr _____ bei uns. (*for one week*)
8. _____ sind wir bei meiner Tante gewesen. (*the day before yesterday*)
9. _____ gehen wir ins Kino. (*this evening*)
10. _____ kommen Erika und Uwe vorbei. (*tomorrow midmorning*)
11. _____ gehen wir alle essen. (*tomorrow at noon*)
12. _____ bummeln wir etwas durch die Stadt. (*in the afternoon*)
13. Was wir _____ tun, weiß ich noch nicht. (*the day after tomorrow*)
14. _____ machen wir etwas Besonderes. (*every day*)
15. _____ wollen wir an den See fahren. (*on the weekend*)
16. Was machst du _____ ? (*this weekend*)
17. Komm doch _____ mit! (*Friday afternoon*)
18. Du tust doch _____ und _____ nichts. (*on Saturdays / Sundays*)
19. _____ fahren wir ab. (*on Saturday morning*)
20. Wir bleiben _____ dort. (*for two days*)
21. _____ ist der See wunderbar. (*in the summer*)
22. Schade, daß Erich _____ schon wieder zu Hause sein muß. (*in one week*)

G. Was hat er / sie gemacht? You've been asked to escort a visiting German politician (musician, professor) who will lecture on your campus. The dean asks you to report, indicating what he / she did.

BEISPIEL: Morgens um acht ist er / sie am Flughafen angekommen. Wir sind zuerst zum Hotel gefahren, und dann . . .

III. Sentence Structure

1. Types of Adverbs

   You have already encountered various adverbs and adverbial phrases. They are usually divided into three major groups.

   a. ADVERBS OF TIME, answering the questions **wann? wie lange?**

      am Abend, am 1. April, eines Tages, heute, im Juni, immer, jetzt, manchmal, meistens, montags, morgens, nie, oft, um zwölf, vor einer Woche, während des Winters, bis Mai, eine Woche, stundenlang, ein paar Minuten, usw.

   b. ADVERBS OF MANNER, answering the question **wie?**

      gemütlich, langsam, laut, mit der Bahn, ohne Geld, schnell, zu Fuß, zusammen, usw.

   c. ADVERBS OF PLACE, answering the questions **wo? wohin? woher?**

      auf der Post, bei uns, da, dort, hier, im Norden, zu Hause, mitten in der Stadt, überall, nach Berlin, nach Hause, auf die Post, zur Uni, aus Kanada, von Amerika, aus dem Flugzeug, usw.

2. Sequence of Adverbs

   If two or more adverbs or adverbial phrases occur in one sentence, they usually follow the sequence TIME, MANNER, PLACE.

   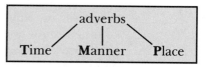

   Er kann das Paket **morgen mit dem Auto zur Post** bringen.
   　　　　　　　　　　T　　　　　M　　　　　P
   Like other sentence elements, adverbs and adverbial phrases may precede the verb.

   Morgen kann er das Paket mit dem Auto zur Post bringen.
   Mit dem Auto kann er das Paket morgen zur Post bringen.
   Zur Post kann er das Paket morgen mit dem Auto bringen.

3. Position of **nicht**

   As you already know, **nicht** usually comes after adverbs of time but before adverbs of manner.

   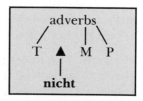

Er bringt das Paket ▲.
Er bringt das Paket ▲ mit.
Er kann das Paket ▲ mitbringen.

Er kann das Paket **morgen** ▲ mitbringen.
Er kann das Paket **morgen** ▲ **mit dem Auto** mitbringen.
Er kann das Paket **morgen** ▲ **mit dem Auto zur Post** bringen.

ÜBUNGEN

H. Sagen Sie das noch einmal! Use the adverbial expressions in the proper order.

BEISPIEL: Ich kaufe die Briefmarken. (auf der Post, morgen)
  Ich kaufe die Briefmarken morgen auf der Post.

1. Er kommt an. (heute abend, in Wien, mit dem Bus)
2. Sie reist. (nach Deutschland, ohne ihre Familie)
3. Dein Pullover liegt auf dem Sofa. (seit drei Tagen)
4. Wir fahren. (zu meiner Tante, am Sonntag, mit der Bahn)
5. Gehst du? (zu Fuß, in die Stadt, heute nachmittag)
6. Ich kaufe die Fier. (samstags, auf dem Markt, billig)
7. Wir wollen ins Kino gehen. (zusammen, morgen abend)
8. Ihr müßt umsteigen. (in einer Viertelstunde, in den Zug nach Nürnberg)
9. Sie läßt die Kinder in Salzburg (bei den Großeltern, ein paar Tage)

I. **Ferienwünsche.** Verneinen Sie die Sätze mit **nicht!**

I: nicht in die Berge / die Berge nicht / nicht gesagt, nicht diesen Winter (diesen Winter nicht), nicht sehr teuer / weiß nicht / nicht so müde / nicht gern / nicht mit dem Auto / nicht lange / nicht so heiß / nicht so langweilig / nicht nach Spanien, nicht mit

If students need more practice, have them negate: Hast du die Paketkarte ausgefüllt? Haben Sie Petras Telefonnummer? Sie hat den Brief mit Luftpost geschickt. Wollen wir zu Fuß zum Bahnhof gehen? Sie fahren gern mit dem Bus. Er kann morgen kommen. Olaf hat Tante Irma besucht. Dieser Zug fährt nach Basel.

GISELA Ich möchte diesen Winter in die Berge fahren.
OTTO Gefallen dir die Berge?
GISELA Das habe ich gesagt. Warum fliegen wir diesen Winter nach Spanien? 479,—DM ist sehr teuer.
OTTO Ich weiß.
GISELA Im Flugzeug wird man so müde.
OTTO Ich fliege gern.
GISELA Ich möchte mit dem Auto fahren.
OTTO Mittags kannst du lange in der Sonne liegen.
GISELA Morgens und nachmittags ist die Sonne so heiß.
OTTO In den Bergen ist es so langweilig.
GISELA Gut. Wenn wir nach Spanien fliegen, komme ich mit.

J. **So kann man's auch sagen.** Start each sentence with the expression in boldface. How does this change the meaning?

BEISPIEL: Wir bleiben **während der Ferien** gewöhnlich zu Hause.
Während der Ferien bleiben wir gewöhnlich zu Hause.
During the vacation we usually stay home.

1. Wir geben nicht viel Geld **für Reisen** aus.
2. Manfred hat **gerade** mit seiner Schwester in Holland gesprochen.
3. Sie ist **seit einer Woche** bei ihrem Bruder in Florida.
4. Wir wollen sie alle **am Wochenende** besuchen (*visit*).
5. Das finde ich **schön.**

ZUSAMMENFASSUNG

K: 1. Die Tante unserer Freunde lebt hier in Bern. 2. Leider weiß ich die Adresse dieser Tante nicht. 3. Der Name der Dame ist Köchli. 4. Wegen dieses Namens kann ich Frau Köchli nicht finden. 5. Statt eines Köchlis (einer Köchli) sind da viele Köchlis. 6. Weißt du die Telefonnummer eurer Freunde nicht? 7. Die Nummer steht im Adressbuch meiner Frau. 8. Ich kann Inges Adressbuch nicht finden. 9. Eines Tages findet Inge es sicher wieder. 10. Könnt ihr mir den Namen eines Hotels empfehlen? 11. Trotz der Preise brauchen wir ein Hotelzimmer. 12. Während der Feiertage hast du Probleme wegen der Touristen.

K. **Frau Köchli.** Bilden Sie Sätze!

BEISPIEL: Hauptstadt / Schweiz / sein / Bern
Die Hauptstadt der Schweiz ist Bern.

1. Tante / unsere Freunde / leben / hier in Bern
2. leider / ich / nicht / wissen / die / Adresse / diese Tante
3. Name / Dame / sein / Köchli
4. wegen / dieser Name / ich / nicht / können / finden / Frau Köchli
5. statt / ein Köchli (*m.*) / da / sein / viele Köchlis
6. du / nicht / wissen / Telefonnummer / euere Freunde?
7. Nummer / stehen / in / Adressbuch / meine Frau
8. ich / nicht / können / finden / Inge / Adressbuch
9. ein Tag / Inge / es / sicher / wieder / finden
10. können / ihr / mir / empfehlen / Name / ein Hotel?
11. trotz / Preise (*pl.*) / wir / brauchen / Hotelzimmer
12. während / Feiertage / du / haben / Probleme (*pl.*) / wegen / Touristen

L. **Schriftliche Übung.** Write eight to ten sentences describing a typical week, i.e., when you get up; when you eat; when you leave for class; what classes you have when; what you do in the evening and on the weekend. Use as many time expressions as possible.

BEISPIEL: Ich bin fast jeden Tag an der Uni. Morgens stehe ich um sechs auf . . .

EINBLICKE ◆◆◆◆◆◆◆◆◆◆

Zürich, Blick auf den
Limmat und das
Rathaus

Switzerland, a country less than half the size of Indiana, is a confederation of 26 cantons, including the half cantons. These cantons maintain considerable autonomy, having their own constitutions and legislatures. In 1838 a new constitution merged the old confederation into a single state, eliminating all commercial barriers and establishing a common postal service, army, legislature, and judiciary. Although women won the right to vote in federal elections in 1971, one half-canton (Appenzell-Innerrhoden) still withholds the vote from women in its local elections. The capital of Switzerland is Bern. Geneva (**Genf**) is the European headquarters for the United Nations and the home of the International Committee of the Red Cross. In a population of approximately 6.4 million, 70 percent speak German (**Schweizerdeutsch / Schwyzerdütsch**, the spoken dialect, as well as standard German), 20 percent speak French, and 9 percent Italian. These are the official languages of the country. A small minority (1 percent) speaks Romansh (**Rätoromanisch**), a variant of Latin. Most Swiss people understand two if not all three of the official languages.

WORTSCHATZ 2

Exercise F, p. 235, can
be used as a pre-read-
ing activity.

das	Dorf, ⸚er	*village*
die	Gegend, -en	*area, region*
	Geschichte, -n	*history; story*
	sofort	*immediately, right away*
	Geld aus·geben (gibt aus), ausgegeben	*to spend money*
	erzählen	*to tell*

Since **weiterfahren** means *to drive on, to keep on driving*, let students guess what these words mean: **weitergehen, weitergeben, weiterfliegen, weiterlesen, weiterschlafen, weitererzählen**.

Have students ask each other when they were born, e.g., **Wann bist du geboren? Ich bin 1966 geboren.** For further practice with dates, see B in "Zum Text."

Point out that **im Jahre** is more or less limited to historical dates.

hinauf·fahren (fährt hinauf), ist hinaufgefahren	*to go or drive up (to)*
weiter·fahren (fährt weiter), ist weitergefahren	*to drive on, keep on driving*
1291 (zwölfhunderteinundneunzig)[1]	*(in) 1291*
im Jahre . . .	*in the year . . .*

1 German does not use a preposition when simply naming a year: **Er ist 1972 geboren.** *(He was born in 1972.)*

WAS IST DAS? der Film, Hollywoodstar, Kanton, Kurzkommentar, Meter, Sessellift, Wintersport; das Ferienhaus, Schiff, Uhrengeschäft; die Alpenblume, Arkade, Bergbahn, Konferenz, Nation, Rückseite; bergsteigen, faszinieren, filmen, interessieren, wandern, Ski laufen; autofrei, natürlich, phantastisch

Reise in die Schweiz

(Kurzinterviews mit Touristen in der Schweiz)

Felix

wooden . . .

Swiss Confederation

confederacy

monument
outdoor performances /
* national holiday*
parades / fireworks

Wegen ihrer Geschichte finde ich die Gegend hier um den Vierwaldstätter See so interessant. Gestern bin ich in Luzern gewesen und über die alte Holzbrücke° gelaufen, wo man in Bildern die Geschichte der Eidgenossenschaft° sehen kann. Heute früh bin ich mit dem Schiff von Luzern zum Rütli[1] gefahren, wo 1291 die drei Kantone Uri, Schwyz und Unterwalden ihren Bund° gemacht haben und die Schweiz als eine Nation begonnen hat. Dann bin ich weitergefahren nach Altdorf. Hier in Altdorf steht ja Wilhelm Tells Denkmal°[2]. Heute abend gehe ich zu den Wilhelm Tell Freilichtspielen°. Dieses Wochenende ist außerdem noch Bundesfeier° mit Umzügen° und Feuerwerk°. Das möchte ich einmal sehen.

5

10

Bern, die Kramgasse bei Nacht

Yvonne

narrow streets
fountains / Middle Ages

last
namely
view of
snow scenes

as an aside
world

Bern, die Hauptstadt der Schweiz, gefällt mir be- 15
sonders gut wegen seiner alten Gassen°, Arkaden und
Brunnen°, viele noch aus dem Mittelalter°. Meine
Freundin und ich fahren fast jedes Jahr zum Wintersport in die Schweiz. Auf unserer Fahrt kommen wir
gewöhnlich durch Bern und bleiben dort einen Tag.
Letztes° Jahr sind wir ins Berner Oberland gefahren, 20
und zwar° nach Wengen. Wir sind auch mit der Berg-
bahn zum Jungfraujoch[3] hinaufgefahren. Der Blick auf° die Berge ist phantastisch. Haben Sie übrigens gewußt, daß man fast alle Schneeszenen° der
James Bond Filme im Berner Oberland gefilmt hat und daß viele Holly-
woodstars im Berner Oberland Ferienhäuser haben? Aber das nur nebenbei°. 25
Was mich fasziniert, ist die Welt° der Berge. Trotz der vielen Touristen ist
alles relativ natürlich geblieben. Eines Tages möchte ich die Gegend um
Kandersteg und Adelboden besser kennenlernen.

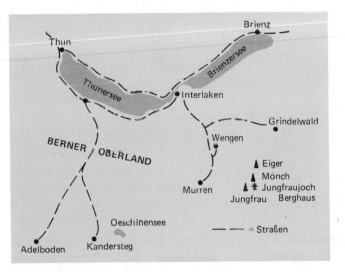

glaciers
all around
altitude
mountain goats / directions
cable cars
Alpine metro / underground
altitude

Hansruedi

Ich fahre gern nach Saas-Fee, weil das Dorf auto- 30
frei ist und man auf den Bergen und Gletschern°
ringsum° schön wandern und bergsteigen kann. Wegen
der Höhenlage° gibt es hier viele Alpenblumen und
Gemsen°. In alle Richtungen° gehen Sessellifte und
Seilbahnen°. Und wenn ich im Juli Ski laufen möchte,
fahre ich mit der Metro Alpin° unterirdisch° bis auf eine 35
Höhe° von 3500 Metern. Dort oben auf den Gletschern
kann man auch während des Sommers wunderbar Ski laufen.

Im Winter gehen
viele in den Bergen
Ski laufen.

numbered bank accounts

easily

this time

carnival

Frau Weber

Mein Mann hat oft in Zürich[4] und Basel[5] mit den
Schweizer Banken zu tun. Zürich ist eine schöne Stadt
am Zürichsee, mit einer Bank neben der anderen. Viele   40
Ausländer haben hier Nummernkonten°. Während der
Konferenzen meines Mannes bummele ich gern durch
die Bahnhofstraße mit ihren eleganten Uhrengeschäf-
ten und Boutiquen. Hier kann man leicht° viel Geld
ausgeben. Auf der Rückreise bleiben wir dieses Mal°   45
vielleicht ein paar Tage länger in Basel wegen der Basler Fasnacht°.

ZUM TEXT

Wie geht's weiter?
1. Felix findet . . . interessant 2. 1291 haben
drei Schweizer Kantone
einen Bund geschlossen,
und zwar am . . . 3. In
Bern gibt es viele . . .
4. Im Berner Oberland
kann man gut . . .

A. Richtig oder falsch? Wenn falsch, sagen Sie warum!

  R   1. Felix findet die Gegend um den Bodensee so interessant wegen ihrer
           Geschichte.

  F   2. Die Schweiz hat 1691 als Nation begonnen.

  R   3. Felix ist wegen des Wilhelm Tell Denkmals und der Freilichtspiele
           in Altdorf.

  F   4. Yvonne und ihre Freundin fahren jeden Sommer zum Sport in die
           Schweiz.

5. Dort haben viele
Filmstars . . .   6. In
Saas-Fee gibt es keine
. . .   7. Auf den Bergen
ringsum kann man . . .
8. Zürich liegt . . .
9. Dort gibt es . . .
10. Viele Ausländer . . .

R 5. Während ihrer Reise bleiben sie gewöhnlich einen Tag in Bern, weil ihnen die Stadt so gut gefällt.

F 6. Hansruedi besucht Saas-Fee so gern, weil er sein Auto mitbringen kann.

R 7. Oben auf den Gletschern kann man auch während des Sommers Ski laufen.

R 8. Frau Webers Mann muß oft nach Zürich oder Basel, weil er viel mit Schweizer Banken zu tun hat.

F 9. Zürich ist eine schöne Stadt am Genfer See.

F 10. Nummernkonten gibt es heute in der Schweiz nicht mehr.

Auch in SAAS FEE bieten
wir sämtliche Dienstleistungen
einer Grossbank

SCHWEIZERISCHER
BANKVEREIN

SOCIETE DE BANQUE SUISSE

SAAS FEE
Tel. 028 57 25 30

B: Since reading dates
like 1291 is new in this
chapter, this exercise is
merely meant as addi-
tional practice.

B. Etwas Geschichte. Lesen Sie laut!

1. 1291 machten Uri, Schwyz, und Unterwalden am Rütli einen Bund. **2.** Luzern ist 1332 dazu (*to it*) gekommen und Zürich 1351.   **3.** 1513 hat es dreizehn Kantone gegeben.   **4.** Heute, 19___   (*add present year*), sind es sechsundzwanzig Kantone.   **5.** 1848 ist die Schweiz ein Bundesstaat geworden.   **6.** Im 1. Weltkrieg (1914–1918) und im 2. Weltkrieg (1939–1945) ist die Schweiz neutral geblieben.

C. Die Eidgenossenschaft. Restate these sentences, using the suggested expressions. There may be more than one appropriate place for the expressions.

BEISPIEL: Viele Touristen fahren in die Schweiz. (jedes Jahr)
Viele Touristen fahren jedes Jahr in die Schweiz.
Jedes Jahr fahren viele Touristen in die Schweiz.

1. Felix findet die Gegend um den Vierwaldstätter See interessant. (wegen ihrer Geschichte)
2. Man kann die Geschichte der Eidgenossenschaft in Bildern auf einer alten Holzbrücke in Luzern sehen. (noch heute)
3. Felix ist mit einem Schiff zum Rütli gefahren. (von Luzern)
4. Wilhelm Tell ist aus Altdorf gewesen. (wie Sie wissen)
5. Viele Touristen wollen Wilhelm Tells Denkmal sehen. (natürlich)
6. In der Schweiz feiert man die Bundesfeier. (jedes Jahr am 1. August)
7. Felix ist noch einen Tag geblieben. (wegen dieses Festes)

D. Die Schweiz. Ersetzen Sie den Genitiv!

1. Kennst du die Geschichte der Schweiz? (Land, Eidgenossenschaft / *f.*, Kanton / *m.*)
2. Das ist das Land der Berge. (Wilhelm Tell, meine Großeltern, Banken)
3. Trotz der Touristen gefällt es mir dort. (Sprache, Wetter)
4. Ich finde unser Dorf interessant wegen seiner Lage (*f.*). (See, Häuser)

E. Welche Frage gehört zu welcher Antwort? Find the correct question for each of the responses below.

_____ 1. Geschichte ist mein Hobby.

_____ 2. Hier haben die drei Kantone Uri, Schwyz und Unterwalden ihren Bund gemacht, das heißt, hier hat die Schweiz als Nation begonnen.

_____ 3. Die Stadt gefällt uns so gut wegen ihrer alten Gassen, Arkaden und Brunnen.

_____ 4. Es ist trotzdem alles noch relativ natürlich geblieben.

_____ 5. Man kann hier wunderbar wandern, bergsteigen und Ski laufen.

_____ 6. Dort oben auf den Gletschern gibt es auch während des Sommers Schnee (snow).

_____ 7. Hier gibt es Nummernkonten.

_____ 8. Mir gefallen die Uhrengeschäfte und Boutiquen.

a. Warum bleiben Sie immer einen Tag in Bern?

b. Warum haben so viele Ausländer ein Bankkonto in der Schweiz?

c. Warum kommen Sie so gern nach Saas-Fee?

d. Warum finden Sie die Gegend um den Vierwaldstätter See so interessant?

e. Finden Sie die vielen Touristen nicht furchtbar?

f. Warum bummeln Sie gern auf der Bahnhofstraße in Zürich?

g. Warum haben Sie jetzt, im Juli, Skier (skis) mitgebracht?

h. Warum sind Sie mit dem Schiff zum Rütli gefahren?

F. Etwas Geographie. Answer the following questions, then write a paragraph about Switzerland, using the questions as guidelines.

1. Wie heißen die Nachbarländer der Schweiz? Wo liegen sie?
2. Wie heißt die Hauptstadt der Schweiz?
3. Nennen Sie ein paar Schweizer Flüsse, Seen und Berge! Welcher Fluß fließt weiter *(flows on)* nach Deutschland? nach Frankreich? Welcher See liegt zwischen der Schweiz und (a) Deutschland? (b) Italien? (c) Frankreich?
4. Wo liegt Bern? Basel? Zürich? Luzern? Genf ? Zermatt? Locarno? St. Moritz? Davos?
5. Wo spricht man Deutsch? Französisch? Italienisch? Rätoromanisch?

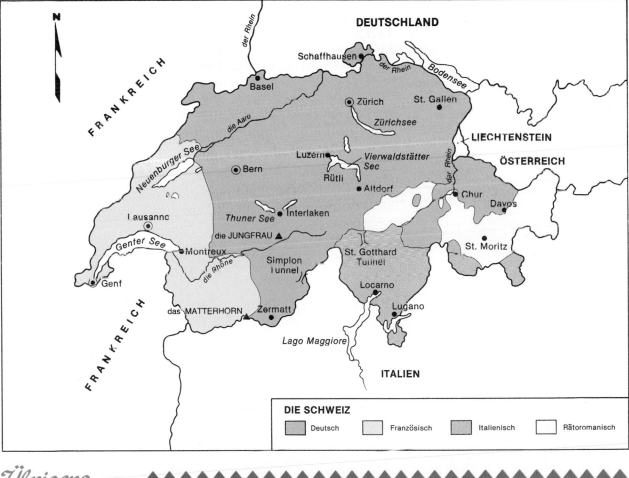

Übrigens

◆◆◆◆◆◆◆◆◆◆◆◆◆◆◆◆◆◆◆◆◆◆◆◆◆◆◆◆◆

1. The pact at the **Rütli** meadow, at the southern tip of Lake Lucerne (**Vierwaldstätter See**), marks the birth of modern Switzerland. Each year on August 1, the Swiss national holiday (**Bundesfeier**) is commemorated with bonfires, parades, and fireworks.

2: This story inspired Friedrich Schiller's drama *Wilhelm Tell* (1804) and Rossini's opera *Guillaume Tell* (1829).

2. According to legend, the tyrannical bailiff Geßler forced the Swiss folk hero **Wilhelm Tell** to shoot an arrow through an apple on his son's head. Tell did, but later took revenge by killing Geßler. That was the beginning of a general uprising of the Swiss against Austria.

3. Besides the **Matterhorn** (4,505 meters above sea level), the most famous Swiss peaks are the **Jungfrau, Mönch,** and **Eiger,** all around 4,000 meters high. A tunnel, seven kilometers long, leads steeply up to the **Jungfraujoch** terminus (3,454 meters). Its observation terrace offers a superb view of the surrounding mountains and the lakes of central Switzerland, and sometimes even of the Black Forest in Germany.

4. **Zürich,** the industrial heart and largest city (pop. 370,000) of Switzerland, is built around the northern tip of Lake Zurich and is characterized by its many bridges over the Limmat River. The city is a center of international banking. Although banking is an old tradition in Switzerland, it expanded enormously after World War II. Even during the war, Switzerland had a stable government and a sound, freely convertible currency. These circumstances, along with a bank-secrecy law that allows numbered accounts without names (**Nummernkonten**), continue to attract capital from all over the world.

5. **Basel**, Switzerland's "northern gateway" to the Rhine, is the country's second-largest city (pop. 180,000). Basel is not only known as a center for international banking and insurance, but also for its pharmaceutical and chemical industry.

SPRECHSITUATIONEN

There are times when you want to sympathize or empathize with a friend. You may also feel the need to express relief when something turned out better than expected. Here are appropriate expressions.

Expressing Sympathy

(Ach, das ist aber) schade!
Das ist ja furchtbar!
So ein Pech!
Das tut mir (furchtbar) leid.
Ach du liebes bißchen! *(Good grief.)*
Ach du meine Güte! *(My goodness.)*
Um Gottes willen! *(For heaven's sake.)*
Das ist wirklich zu dumm! *(That's really too bad.)*

Expressing a Lack of Sympathy

Na und! *(So what?)*
Das ist doch nicht wichtig.
Das macht doch nichts.
Das ist doch egal. *(That doesn't matter. Who cares?)*
Das geschieht dir recht. *(That serves you right.)*
Das sieht dir ähnlich. *(That's typical of you.)*
Pech gehabt! *(Tough luck.)*

Expressing Empathy

Das ist ja prima (wunderbar, toll)!
Das freut mich (für dich). *(I'm happy [for you].)*
Du Glückspilz! *(You lucky thing [literally: mushroom].)*

Expressing Relief

Gut / prima / toll!	*Great.*
(Na,) endlich!	*(Well,) finally.*
Gott sei Dank!	*Thank God.*
Ich bin wirklich froh.	*I'm really glad.*
Da haben wir aber Glück gehabt!	*We were really lucky!*
(Da haben wir aber) Schwein gehabt!	*(We were really) lucky!*

A. Was sagen Sie? Your friend Daniel has his ups and downs. Respond appropriately to these events in his life.
1. Daniel hat von seinen Eltern zum Geburtstag ein Auto bekommen.
2. Das Auto ist nicht ganz neu.
3. Aber es fährt so schön ruhig und schnell, daß er gleich am ersten Tag einen Strafzettel *(ticket)* bekommen hat.
4. Am Wochenende ist er in die Berge gefahren, aber es hat immer nur geregnet.
5. Es hat ihm trotzdem viel Spaß gemacht, weil er dort eine nette *(nice)* Studentin kennengelernt hat.
6. Auf dem Weg zurück ist ihm jemand hinten in sein Auto gefahren. Totalschaden *(total wreck)*!
7. Daniel hat aber nur ein paar Kratzer *(scratches)* bekommen.
8. Er hat übrigens seit ein paar Tagen eine Wohnung mitten in der Stadt. Sie ist gar nicht teuer.
9. Er möchte das Mädchen aus den Bergen wiedersehen, aber er kann sein Adressbuch mit ihrer Telefonnummer nicht finden.
10. Momentan läuft alles falsch. Er kann sein Portemonnaie *(wallet)* auch nicht finden.
11. Noch etwas. Die Katze *(cat)* des Nachbarn hat seine Goldfische gefressen *(ate)*.
12. Sein Bruder hat übrigens eine Operation gehabt. Aber jetzt geht es ihm wieder gut, und er ist wieder zu Hause.

B. Jeder hat Probleme. Form small groups, and have each person name at least one problem he or she has. Take turns expressing sympathy or lack of it.

C. Kurzgespräche. Your classmate expresses his / her feelings after each statement you make.
1. Trip home: The weather was awful. Your plane arrived two hours late (**mit zwei Stunden Verspätung**) and departed five hours late. You arrived at two o'clock in the morning. Your suitcase wasn't there. There were no buses into town. You didn't have enough cash for a cab. You phoned your father. You got home at 4 a.m. You were very tired.
2. Staying overnight: You and your friend arrived in Unterschönau. You inquired at three hotels; they had no rooms available. They sent you to the *Gasthof zum Löwen*. There they had some rooms. You were very tired, so you went to bed early (**ins Bett**). There was a party in the hotel until midnight. Then cars drove by. It was very loud. At 2 a.m. you heard trains, too. You got up early and left. What a night!

KAPITEL **9** *Hobbys*

Familienausflug
(*. . . excursion*) mit
dem Fahrrad

▌ INHALT

Gespräche and **Wortschatz**. This chapter deals with sports and hobbies.

Struktur. You will learn about . . .

▪ endings of preceded adjectives.

▪ reflexive verbs.

▪ the infinitive with **zu**.

Einblicke. Leisure time in the German-speaking countries.

Sprechsituationen

▪ Making a phone call

▪ Extending, accepting, and declining an invitation

239

◆◆◆◆◆ GESPRÄCHE

Am Telefon[1]

FRAU SCHMIDT	Hier Frau Schmidt.[2]
BÄRBEL	Guten Tag, Frau Schmidt! Ich bin's, Bärbel. Ist Karl-Heinz da?
FRAU SCHMIDT	Nein, er ist gerade zur Post gegangen.
BÄRBEL	Bitte sagen Sie ihm, daß ich heute abend nicht mit ihm ausgehen kann!
FRAU SCHMIDT	Ach, was ist denn los?
BÄRBEL	Ich bin krank. Mir tut der Hals weh, und ich habe Kopfschmerzen.
FRAU SCHMIDT	Das tut mir aber leid. Gute Besserung!
BÄRBEL	Danke. Auf Wiederhören!
FRAU SCHMIDT	Auf Wiederhören!

Gute Idee!

YVONNE	Hier bei Mayer.
DANIELA	Hallo, Yvonne! Ich bin's, Daniela.
YVONNE	Tag, Daniela! Was gibt's Neues?
DANIELA	Nichts Besonderes. Hast du Lust, Squash zu spielen oder schwimmen zu gehen?
YVONNE	Squash? Nein, danke. Ich habe noch Muskelkater von vorgestern. Mir tun alle Knochen weh.
DANIELA	Lahme Ente![3] Willst du dann Schach spielen?
YVONNE	Ja, gute Idee! Komm rüber!

Übrigens

CATS

Karten täglich von 9 bis 21 Uhr über 040 - 270 75 270
OPERETTENHAUS HAMBURG

1. Compared to the United States and Canada, telephoning in the German-speaking countries is expensive. One pays for every call according to length of time and distance. There is no call waiting, and teenagers do not have their own lines. Most calls from public booths are paid for with coins, but calling with a phone card (**Telefonkarte**) is becoming popular. These cards can be bought at any post office and allow you to make calls up to a certain pre-paid value.

Point out that Germans usually identify themselves when they answer the phone.

2. If Mrs. Schmidt answers her own phone, she says **Hier Schmidt**. If someone else answers, he / she would say **Hier bei Schmidt** (*Schmidt residence*).

3. As in the case of **lahme Ente** (*lit. lame duck*), names of animals are frequently used in everyday speech to characterize people, usually in a derogatory way: **Du Esel! Du Affe!** (*donkey, monkey*) for someone who made a mistake or behaves silly; **Du hast einen Vogel! Bei dir piept's!** (*You're cuckoo*) for someone crazy; **Fauler Hund!** (*dog*) for someone lazy; **So ein Brummbär!** (*bear*) for someone grumpy; **(Das ist) alles für die Katz'!** (*That's all for nothing, i.e., useless*); **Du Schwein!** (*pig*) for someone messy or for a scoundrel. **Schwein haben**, however, has quite a different meaning: *to be lucky*. In addition, names of food are used in special expressions: **Das ist Käse!** (*That's nonsense*) or **(Das) ist doch Wurst!** (*It doesn't matter*).

On the Telephone MRS. SCHMIDT: *This is Mrs. Schmidt.* BÄRBEL: *Hello, Mrs. Schmidt. It's me, Bärbel. Is Karl-Heinz there?* MRS. SCHMIDT: *No, he just went to the post office.* BÄRBEL: *Please tell him that I can't go out with him tonight.* MRS. SCHMIDT: *Oh, what's the matter?* BÄRBEL: *I'm sick. My throat hurts and I have a headache.* MRS. SCHMIDT: *I'm sorry. I hope you get better.* BÄRBEL: *Thank you. Good-bye.* MRS. SCHMIDT: *Good-bye.*

A good idea YVONNE: *Mayer residence.* DANIELA: *Hello, Yvonne! It's me, Daniela.* YVONNE: *Hi, Daniela! What's up?* DANIELA: *Nothing special. Do you feel like playing squash or going swimming?* YVONNE: *Squash? No thanks. I'm still sore from the day before yesterday. All my bones ache.* DANIELA: *Poor baby! Do you want to play chess then?* YVONNE: *Yes, (that's a) good idea! Come on over.*

WORTSCHATZ 1

DAS HOBBY,-S *hobby*

der	Fußball	*soccer*	*die*	Gitarre, -n	*guitar*
das	Klavier, -e	*piano*		Karte, -n	*card*
	Spiel, -e	*game*		Kassette, -n	*cassette*
				(Schall)platte, -n	*record*

fern·sehen (sieht fern), ferngesehen	to watch TV
photographieren	to take pictures
sammeln[1]	to collect
schwimmen, geschwommen	to swim
schwimmen gehen, ist schwimmen gegangen[2]	to go swimming
Ski laufen gehen, ist Ski laufen gegangen[2]	to go skiing
spazieren·gehen, ist spazierengegangen	to go for a walk
(Schach) spielen[2]	to play (chess)
wandern, ist gewandert	to hike
wünschen	to wish

DER KÖRPER,- *body*

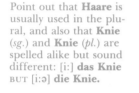

Point out that **Haare** is usually used in the plural, and also that **Knie** (*sg.*) and **Knie** (*pl.*) are spelled alike but sound different: [i:] **das Knie** BUT [i:ə] **die Knie.**

Optional vocabulary: die Augenbraue, -n *eyebrow*; **die Augenwimper, -n** *eyelash*; **die Backe, -n** *cheek*; **die Stirn** *forehead*; **die Zunge, -n** *tongue*; **das Kinn** *chin*; **die Brust,** *chest, breast*; **der Busen,-** *bosom*; **der Rücken,-** *back*; **die Schulter,-n** *shoulder*; **der Popo** *bottom*; **der Fingernagel,-** *fingernail*; **der Fuß-nagel,-** *toenail*; **der Daumen,-** *thumb*; **der Zeigefinger,-** *index finger*; **die Zehe, -n** *toe*

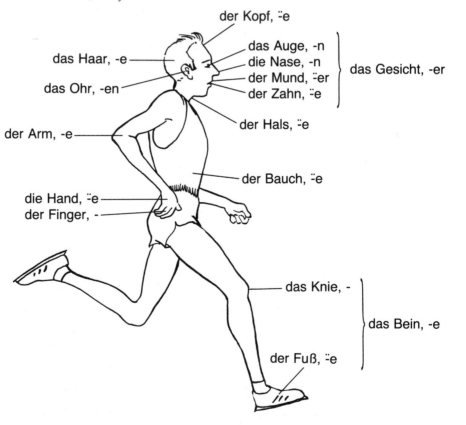

der Kopf, -̈e
das Auge, -n
die Nase, -n
der Mund, -̈er
der Zahn, -̈e
das Haar, -e
das Ohr, -en
das Gesicht, -er
der Hals, -̈e
der Arm, -e
der Bauch, -̈e
die Hand, -̈e
der Finger, -
das Knie, -
das Bein, -e
der Fuß, -̈e

Also like **bummeln: angeln, wechseln, tun.**

1 Like **bummeln: ich samm(e)le, du sammelst, er sammelt, wir sammeln, ihr sammelt, sie sammeln.**

2 In each of these combinations, **gehen** and **spielen** function as V1, while the other word, the verb complement, functions as V2: **Ich gehe heute schwimmen** (Ski laufen, wandern . . .). **Sie spielen Schach** (Karten, Klavier, Platten, Tennis . . .).

WEITERES

die	Freizeit	*leisure time*
	Idee, -n	*idea*

gesund / krank	*healthy / sick, ill*
phantastisch	*fantastic, great, super*
Ich habe (Kopf)schmerzen.	*I have a (head)ache.*
Ich habe (keine) Lust, Tennis zu spielen.	*I (don't) feel like playing tennis.*
Mir tut der Hals weh.	*My throat hurts.*
Was gibt's Neues?[3]	*What's new?*
nichts Besonderes[3]	*nothing special*
Was ist los?	*What's the matter?*

3 Similarly **etwas B**esonderes, **etwas** Interessantes, **etwas S**chönes and **nichts** Neues, **nichts G**utes, **nichts S**chlechtes

PASSIVES VOKABULAR **der Knochen,-** *bone*   **der Muskelkater** *sore muscles, charley horse*   **Gute Besserung!** *Get well soon.*   **Gute Idee!** *Good idea.* **Hallo! Hier bei . . .** *. . . residence.*   **Ich bin's.** *It's me.*   **Komm 'rüber!** *Come on over.*

ZUM THEMA

A: Rather than giving students the cue words, you could make gestures or have students supply their own words.

A. Mustersätze
1. Hals: **Mir tut** der Hals **weh.**
   Kopf, Zahn, Bauch, Fuß, Knie, Hand
2. Hände: **Mir tun die** Hände **weh.**
   Füße, Finger, Ohren, Beine, Augen
3. Kopf: **Ich habe** Kopf**schmerzen.**
   Hals, Zahn, Bauch, Ohren
4. Squash: **Hast du Lust,** Squash **zu spielen?**
   Tennis, Fußball, Klavier, Platten, Karten, Schach

B: Sport und Gymnastik **treibt** man.

B. Was tust du gern in deiner Freizeit? Read through the list below. Then ask classmates what they like to do during their leisure time. Poll the class to see which activities are most popular.

BEISPIEL: Ich lese gern, und du?   **Ich spiele gern Klavier, und du?**

backen, joggen / laufen, kochen (*to cook*), lesen, malen (*to paint*), nähen (*to sew*),
gehen: angeln, bergsteigen, campen, joggen, reiten (*horseback riding*), Rollschuh laufen (*rollerskating*), Schlittschuh laufen (*ice-skating*), Ski laufen, Wasserski laufen, segeln (*sailing*), turnen (*exercising*), wandern
spielen: Basketball, Federball (*badminton*), Fußball, Volleyball, Golf, Hockey, Squash, Tennis, Tischtennis; Monopoly; Cello, Geige (*violin*), Flöte (*recorder*), Querflöte (*flute*), Trommel, Trompete

**Schachspiel auf der
Straße**

C. Interview. Fragen Sie einen Nachbarn / eine Nachbarin, . . .!
1. ob er / sie als Kind ein Instrument gelernt hat, und wenn ja, welches
   Instrument; seit wann er / sie spielt und ob er / sie das heute noch
   spielt
2. ob er / sie gern singt, und wenn ja, was und wo (in der Dusche oder
   Badewanne [*bathtub*], im Auto, im Chor . . .)
3. was für Musik er / sie schön findet (klassische Musik, moderne Musik,
   Jazz, Rock-, Pop-, Country-, Volksmusik . . .)
4. ob er / sie viel fernsieht, und wenn ja, wie lange pro Tag; was er / sie
   gestern abend gesehen hat
5. ob er / sie oft lange am Telefon spricht, und wenn ja, mit wem

D. Mir tut 'was weh. Complete each sentence with one of the responses supplied
or with one of your own.

    _____ 1. Wenn ich
          Kopfschmerzen
          habe . . .

    _____ 2. Wenn mir die Füße
          weh tun . . .

    _____ 3. Wenn mir der Bauch
          weh tut . . .

    _____ 4. Wenn ich
          Halsschmerzen
          habe . . .

    _____ 5. Wenn ich Augen-
          schmerzen habe . . .

    _____ 6. Wenn ich krank bin . . .

a. mache ich die Augen zu.
b. gurgele (*gargle*) ich.
c. sehe ich nicht fern.
d. nehme ich Aspirin.
e. trinke ich Cola.
f. esse ich nichts.
g. rufe ich Doktor Schmidt an.
h. gehe ich ins Bett.
i. gehe ich nicht spazieren.
j. trinke ich Tee.

Strandkörbe (*beach shelters*) an der Nordsee

E: Have students act out the dialogue.

E. Während der Freizeit. Was sagen Sie?

x Hallo, _____ ! Hast du Lust _____

y Nein, ich kann nicht mit dir _____ .

x Warum? Was ist los?

y Ich bin krank. Mir tut / tun _____ weh.

x _____ . Wie lange hast du schon _____schmerzen?

y Seit _____ .

x _____ . Ich wünsche dir gute Besserung.

y _____.

x Hast du Lust _____ ?

y _____ .

F. Aussprache. See also III. 8–10 in the pronunciation section of the Workbook.

1. [l]   laut, lustig, leben, liegen, leider, Lampe, Luft, Hals, Geld, Platte, malen, spielen, fliegen, stellen, schnell, Schlüssel, Teil, Ball, hell

2. [ts] zählen, zeigen, zwischen, ziemlich, zurück, Zug, Zahn, Schmerzen, Kerzen, Einzelzimmer, bezahlen, erzählen, tanzen, ausgezeichnet, jetzt, schmutzig, trotz, kurz, schwarz, Salz, Schweiz, Sitzplatz

3. Wortpaare

   a. *felt* / Feld   c. *plots* / Platz   e. seit / Zeit
   b. *hotel* / Hotel   d. Schweiß / Schweiz   f. so / Zoo

STRUKTUR

I. Endings of Adjectives Preceded by der- and ein-words

1. PREDICATE ADJECTIVES and ADVERBS do not have endings.

Willi fährt schnell.	*Willi drives fast.*
Willi ist schnell.	*Willi is quick.*

You could go through the whole declension using these examples: der lange Hals, das lange Bein, die lange Nase; der junge Mann, das junge Mädchen, die junge Frau; der große Fernseher, das große Radio, die große Gitarre

2. However, ADJECTIVES MODIFYING A NOUN do have an ending that varies with the noun's case, gender, and number, and the preceding articles. As in English, these adjectives always precede the noun they modify.

Er ist ein schnell**er** Fahrer (m.).	*He's a fast driver.*
Er hat ein schnell**es** Auto (n.).	*He has a fast car.*

If you compare the tables below, you will readily see that there are only four DIFFERENT endings: **-en, -e, -er, -es**.

	masculine	neuter	feminine	plural
nom.	der neue Wagen	das neue Auto	die neue Nummer	die neu**en** Farben
acc.	den neu**en** Wagen	das neue Auto	die neue Nummer	die neu**en** Farben
dat.	dem neu**en** Wagen	dem neu**en** Auto	der neu**en** Nummer	den neu**en** Farben
gen.	des neu**en** Wagens	des neu**en** Autos	der neu**en** Nummer	der neu**en** Farben
nom.	ein neu**er** Wagen	ein neu**es** Auto	eine neue Nummer	keine neu**en** Farben
acc.	einen neu**en** Wagen	ein neu**es** Auto	eine neue Nummer	keine neu**en** Farben
dat.	einem neu**en** Wagen	einem neu**en** Auto	einer neu**en** Nummer	keinen neu**en** Farben
gen.	eines neu**en** Wagens	eines neu**en** Autos	einer neu**en** Nummer	keiner neu**en** Farben

As you can tell from the left table below, adjectives preceded by the definite article or any **der**-word have either an **-e** or **-en** ending. The table on the right shows that adjectives preceded by the indefinite article or any **ein**-word have two different adjective endings WHENEVER **ein** HAS NO ENDING: **-er** for masculine nouns and **-es** for neuter nouns. The **-en** ending predominates and is used in all plural cases and in the dative and genitive singular.

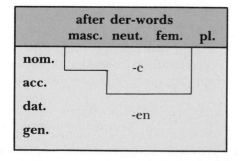

Or, to put it another way, the endings are:

a. in the NOMINATIVE and ACCUSATIVE singular

- after **der, das, die,** and **eine** ─────────────→ **-e**

                               with masc. nouns → **-er**
- after **ein** <
                               with neut. nouns → **-es**

b. in ALL OTHER CASES (including the masc. accusative sg., all datives, genitives and plurals) → **-en**

Der schwarz**e** Wagen ist prima.
Das rot**e** Auto hat auch eine schön**e** Form.
Solche klein**en** Wagen sind sehr bequem.
Das ist ein gut**er** Preis für so ein schön**es** Auto.

3. If a noun is modified by more than one adjective, all the adjectives have the same ending.

Das ist ein klein**es**, schnell**es**, aber teuer**es** Auto.
Haben Sie keinen ander**en**, gut**en**, aber nicht so teuer**en** Wagen?

ÜBUNGEN

A. Das Jubiläum. (*The anniversary.*) Comment on each photo you took at your grandparents' 40th anniversary.

BEISPIEL: Das ist mein Onkel Max mit seinen drei Kindern. (wild, klein)
             Das ist mein Onkel Max mit seinen drei wilden Kindern.
             Das ist mein Onkel Max mit seinen drei kleinen Kindern.

1. Das ist Tante Jutta mit ihrem Freund aus London. (verrückt, englisch)
2. Hier sitzen wir alle an einem Tisch und spielen Monopoly. (groß, rund)
3. Das ist Oma (*grandma*) mit ihrem Porsche (*m.*). (teuer, rot)
4. Die Farbe dieses Autos gefällt mir. (toll, schnell)
5. Das ist wirklich ein Geschenk! (wunderbar, phantastisch)
6. Opa hat ein Fahrrad bekommen. (schön, neu)
7. Jetzt kann er mit seinen Freunden Fahrrad fahren. (viel, alt)
8. Das hier ist unser Hund (*dog, m.*). (klein, braun)
9. Das ist wirklich ein Hündchen (*n.*). (lieb, klein)
10. Wegen des Wetters haben wir nicht im Garten gefeiert. (schlecht, kalt)

B. Die neue Wohnung. Lesen Sie den Dialog mit den Adjektiven!

BEISPIEL: Ist der Schrank neu? (groß)   **Ist der große Schrank neu?**

x Ist dieser Sessel bequem? (braun)
y Ja, und das Sofa auch. (lang)
x Die Lampe gefällt mir. (klein)
   Woher hast du diesen Teppich? (phantastisch)
   Und wo hast du dieses Bild gefunden? (supermodern)

Y In einem Geschäft. (alt)
   Wenn du willst, kann ich dir das Geschäft mal zeigen. (interessant)
X Ist es in der Müllergasse (*f.*)? (klein)
Y Ja, auf der Seite. (link-)
X Während der Woche habe ich keine Zeit. (nächst-)
Y Sind diese Möbel teuer gewesen? (schön)
X Natürlich nicht. Für solche Möbel gebe ich nicht viel Geld aus. (alt)

C. Inge zeigt Jens ihr Zimmer. Jens stellt Fragen und macht Kommentare (*comments*). Bilden Sie aus zwei Sätzen einen Satz!

BEISPIEL: Woher kommt dieses Schachspiel? Es ist interessant.
        Woher kommt dieses interessante Schachspiel?

1. Weißt du, was so ein Schachspiel kostet? Es ist chinesisch (*Chinese*).
2. Bist du Schachspielerin? Spielst du gut?
3. Ich bin kein Schachspieler (*m.*). Ich spiele nicht gut.
4. Woher hast du diese Briefmarkensammlung? Sie ist alt.
5. Mein Vater hat auch eine Sammlung. Sie ist groß.
6. Sammelst du solche Briefmarken auch? Sie sind normal (*regular*).
7. Was machst du mit so einer Briefmarke? Sie ist doppelt (*double*).
8. Darf ich diese Briefmarke haben? Sie ist ja doppelt!
9. Hast du diese Bilder gemacht? Sie sind groß.
10. Wer ist der Junge? Er ist klein.
11. Ich habe nicht gewußt, daß du einen Bruder hast. Er ist noch so klein!
12. Was für ein Gesicht! Es ist phantastisch!
13. Die Augen gefallen mir! Sie sind dunkel.
14. Mit meiner Kamera ist das nicht möglich. Sie ist billig.
15. Und das hier ist ein Tennisspieler, nicht wahr? Er ist bekannt und kommt aus Deutschland.
16. Weißt du, daß wir gestern trotz des Wetters Fußball gespielt haben? Das Wetter ist schlecht gewesen.
17. Leider kann ich wegen meines Knies nicht mehr mitspielen. Das Knie ist kaputt.

D: To simplify, divide the class into two groups, one giving the first response and the other the second.

D. Ist das nicht schön? Your friend Alex is very insecure and continuously needs positive reinforcement. Show agreement and ask according to the model.

1. BEISPIEL: Ist der Pullover nicht warm?
        Ja, das ist ein warmer Pullover.
        Woher hast du den warmen Pullover?

   a. Ist das Hemd nicht elegant?
   b. Ist die Uhr nicht phantastisch?
   c. Ist der Hut (*hat*) nicht verrückt?

2. BEISPIEL: Ist das Hotel nicht gut?
        Ja, das ist ein gutes Hotel.
        Wo hast du von diesem guten Hotel gehört?

   a. Ist die Pension nicht wunderbar?

b. Ist der Gasthof nicht billig?

c. Ist das Restaurant nicht gemütlich?

3. BEISPIEL: Ist das alte Schloß nicht schön?
   Ja, das ist ein altes, schönes Schloß.
   Ich gehe gern in solche alten, schönen Schlösser.

a. Ist der neue Supermarkt nicht modern?

b. Ist das kleine Café nicht gemütlich?

c. Sind die alten Kirchen nicht interessant?

E. Beschreibung (*description*) **einer Wohnung**

1. **Petras Wohnung.** Fill in the missing adjective endings.
   Petra wohnt in einem alt_____ Haus im neu_____ Teil unserer schön_____ Stadt. Ihre klein_____ Wohnung liegt im neunt_____ Stock eines modern_____ Hochhauses (*high-rise*). Sie hat eine praktisch_____ Küche und ein gemütlich_____ Wohnzimmer. Von dem groß_____ Wohnzimmerfenster kann sie unsere ganz_____ Stadt und die viel_____ Brücken über dem breit_____ (*wide*) Fluß sehen. Petra liebt ihre Wohnung wegen des schön_____ Blickes (*view, m.*) und der billig_____ Miete. In ihrem hell_____ Schlafzimmer stehen ein einfach_____ Bett und ein klein_____ Nachttisch mit einer klein_____ Nachttischlampe. An der Wand steht ein braun_____ Schreibtisch, und über dem braun_____ Schreibtisch hängt ein groß_____ Regal mit ihren viel_____ Büchern. Petra findet ihr Zimmer schön_____ .

2. **Ihre Wohnung.** Write a paragraph about your own place. Use at least one adjective with an ending in each sentence.

II. Reflexive Verbs

If the subject and one of the objects of a sentence are the same person or thing, a reflexive pronoun must be used for the object. In the English sentence, *I see myself in the picture,* the reflexive pronoun *myself* is the accusative object. (*Whom do I see?—Myself.*) In the sentence, *I am buying myself a record,* the pronoun *myself* is the dative object. (*For whom am I buying the record?—For myself.*)

In German only the third-person singular and plural have a special reflexive pronoun: **sich.** The other persons use the accusative and dative forms of the personal pronouns, which you already know.

COMPARE: Ich sehe meinen Bruder auf dem Bild.
Ich sehe **mich** auf dem Bild.

Ich kaufe meinem Bruder eine Platte.
Ich kaufe **mir** eine Platte.

nom.	ich	du	er / es / sie	wir	ihr	sie	Sie
acc.	mich	dich	**sich**	uns	euch	**sich**	**sich**
dat.	mir	dir					

1. Many familiar verbs CAN BE USED REFLEXIVELY. (Note that the English equivalent may not include a reflexive pronoun.)

- The reflexive pronoun used as the direct object (ACCUSATIVE): sich fragen (*to wonder*), sich legen (*to lie down*), sich sehen (*to see oneself*) usw.

Since only the 1st and 2nd person sg. distinguish between dative and accusative by FORM, they are stressed in examples and exercises.

Ich frage **mich,** ob das richtig ist.	*I wonder (ask myself) whether that's right.*
Ich lege **mich** aufs Sofa.	*I lie down on the sofa.*
Ich sehe **mich** im Spiegel.	*I see myself in the mirror.*

- The reflexive pronoun used as the indirect object (DATIVE): sich bestellen, sich kaufen, sich kochen, sich nehmen, sich wünschen (*to wish*) usw.

Ich bestelle **mir** ein Eis.	*I order an ice cream (for myself).*
Ich koche **mir** ein Ei.	*I'm cooking an egg (for myself).*
Ich wünsche **mir** ein Auto.	*I'm wishing for a car (for myself).*

2. Some verbs are ALWAYS REFLEXIVE, or are reflexive when they express a certain meaning. Here are some important verbs that you need to know.

It is important for students to realize that reflexive pronouns play exactly the same role as nouns or personal pronouns in a sentence, i.e., they function as accusative (direct) objects, dative (indirect) objects, or objects of prepositions.

sich an·hören	*to listen to*
sich an·sehen, angesehen	*to look at*
sich an·ziehen, angezogen	*to put on (clothing), get dressed*
sich aus·ziehen, ausgezogen	*to take off (clothing), get undressed*
sich beeilen	*to hurry*
sich duschen	*to take a shower*
sich erkälten	*to catch a cold*
sich (wohl) fühlen	*to feel (well)*
sich (hin·)legen	*to lie down*
sich kämmen	*to comb one's hair*
sich (die Zähne / Nase) putzen	*to clean (brush one's teeth / blow one's nose)*
sich rasieren	*to shave*
sich (hin·)setzen	*to sit down*
sich waschen (wäscht), gewaschen	*to wash (oneself)*

Setz dich (hin)!	*Sit down.*
Warum müßt ihr **euch beeilen?**	*Why do you have to hurry?*
Ich **fühle mich** nicht wohl.	*I don't feel well.*
Sie hat **sich erkältet.**	*She caught a cold.*

- With some of these verbs, the reflexive pronoun may be EITHER THE ACCUSATIVE OR THE DATIVE OBJECT. If there are two objects, then the person (the reflexive pronoun) is in the dative and the thing is in the accusative.

Ich wasche **mich.**	*I wash myself.*
Ich wasche **mir** die Haare.	*I wash my hair.*

Ich ziehe **mich** an.	*I'm getting dressed.*
Ich ziehe **mir** einen Pullover an.	*I'm putting on a sweater.*

3. In English we use possessive adjectives when referring to parts of the body: *I'm washing my hands*. In German the definite article is frequently used together with the reflexive pronoun in the dative.

Ich wasche **mir die** Hände.   *I'm washing **my** hands.*
Sie kämmt **sich die** Haare.   *She's combing **her** hair.*
Putz **dir die** Zähne!   *Brush **your** teeth.*

▪ Remember that when there are two object pronouns, the accusative precedes the dative!

Ich wasche mir **die Hände**.   Ich wasche **sie** mir.
Du kämmst dir **die Haare**.   Du kämmst **sie** dir.
　　　　　acc.   　　　　acc.

Du kannst dir auch mal wieder die Ohren waschen.

ÜBUNGEN

Optional practice: Was wünschst du dir zum Geburtstag? z.B. **Ich wünsche mir eine Uhr. Und du?**

F. Antworten Sie mit ja!

1. **Singular** *(formal and familiar)*

   BEISPIEL: Soll ich mir die Hände waschen?
   Ja, waschen Sie sich die Hände!
   Ja, wasch dir die Hände!

   a. Soll ich mich warm anziehen?
   b. Soll ich mir die Haare kämmen?
   c. Soll ich mir ein Auto kaufen?
   d. Soll ich mich jetzt setzen?
   e. Soll ich mir die Bilder ansehen?

2. **Plural** *(formal and familiar)*

   BEISPIEL: Sollen wir uns die Hände waschen?
   Ja, waschen Sie sich die Hände!
   Ja, wascht euch die Hände!

   a. Sollen wir uns ein Zimmer mieten?
   b. Sollen wir uns ein Haus bauen?
   c. Sollen wir uns in den Garten setzen?
   d. Sollen wir uns die Kassetten anhören?
   e. Sollen wir uns die Briefmarken ansehen?

G. Antworten Sie mit ja!

BEISPIEL: Fühlen Sie sich wohl? **Ja, ich fühle mich wohl.**

1. Legen Sie sich aufs Sofa?
2. Möchten Sie sich die Jacke ausziehen?
3. Haben Sie sich wieder erkältet?
4. Haben Sie sich zu elegant angezogen?
5. Haben Sie sich die Bilder angesehen?
6. Haben Sie sich auf dem Bild gefunden?

H. Was fehlt?

1. Kinder, zieht _____ schnell an!
2. Ich muß _____ noch die Haare kämmen.
3. Wir haben _____ ein Klavier gekauft.
4. Setzen Sie _____ bitte!
5. Peter, putz _____ die Nase!
6. Kinder, erkältet _____ nicht!
7. Karin hat _____ einen Fernseher gewünscht.
8. Ich will _____ etwas im Radio anhören.
9. Fühlst du _____ nicht wohl, Dieter?
10. Möchten Sie _____ die Hände waschen?

I. Was machst du den ganzen Tag? In pairs, ask each other what you do at certain hours of the day, using reflexive verbs whenever possible. Take notes and then report back to the class.

BEISPIEL: Was machst du abends um zehn?
Ich höre mir die Nachrichten (*news*) **an. Und du?**
Um diese Zeit lege ich mich ins Bett.

1. 6.00 Uhr	5. 11.00 Uhr	9. 16.00 Uhr
2. 6.30 Uhr	6. 11.30 Uhr	10. 17.30 Uhr
3. 9.00 Uhr	7. 13.00 Uhr	11. 20.00 Uhr
4. 9.30 Uhr	8. 13.30 Uhr	12. 22.00 Uhr

J. Auf deutsch, bitte! Mrs. Brockmann is a healthnut. She's determined to get her whole family up early and out on the exercise trail, but they aren't too eager.
1. Otto, get dressed. **2.** Christian, hurry. **3.** Lotte and Ulle, are you putting on sweaters? **4.** We still have to brush our teeth. **5.** Peter, comb your hair. **6.** I don't feel well. **7.** Then lie down. **8.** Otto, have you shaved? **9.** Yes, but I've caught a cold. **10.** Nonsense (**Quatsch**)! Today we're all going jogging.

J: 1. Otto, zieh dich an! 2. Christian, beeil(e) dich! 3. Lotte und Ulle, zieht ihr euch Pullover an? 4. Wir müssen uns noch die Zähne putzen. 5. Peter, kämm(e) dir die Haare! 6. Ich fühle mich nicht wohl. 7. Dann leg(e) dich hin! 8. Otto, hast du dich rasiert? 9. Ja, aber ich habe mich erkältet. 10. Quatsch! Heute gehen wir alle joggen.

III. The Infinitive with zu

English and German use infinitives in much the same way.

Es ist interessant **zu** reisen.	*It's interesting to travel.*
Ich habe keine Zeit gehabt **zu** essen.	*I didn't have time to eat.*

1. If the infinitive is combined with other sentence elements, a COMMA separates the infinitive phrase from the main clause.

Haben Sie Zeit, eine Reise **zu machen**? *Do you have time to take a trip?*

Note that in German the infinitive comes at the end of the phrase.

2. If a separable-prefix verb is used, the **-zu-** is inserted between the prefix and the verb.

> prefix + **zu** + verb

Es ist Zeit ab**zu**fahren. *It's time to leave.*

CAUTION

No **zu** after modals! Wir müssen jetzt abfahren. (*We have to leave now.*)

3. Infinitive phrases beginning with **um** explain the purpose of the action described in the main clause.

Wir fahren in die Schweiz, **um** unsere   (*in order to visit*)
Großeltern **zu** besuchen.
Rudi geht ins Badezimmer, **um** sich **zu**   (*in order to take a shower*)
duschen.

„Die Menschen
haben gelernt,
    zu schwimmen wie die Fische
und zu fliegen wie die Vögel,
    aber wie Brüder
        zusammenzuleben
haben sie nicht
        gelernt"
                M. L. King

ÜBUNGEN

K: The present perfect isn't used very often in such constructions; the simple past is much more common.

K. Wie geht's weiter?

BEISPIEL: Hast du Lust . . .? (sich Kassetten anhören)
Hast du Lust, dir Kassetten anzuhören?

1. Dort gibt es viel . . . (sehen, tun, photographieren, zeigen, essen)
2. Habt ihr Zeit . . .? (vorbeikommen, die Nachbarn kennenlernen, ein Glas Apfelsaft trinken, euch ein paar Bilder ansehen)

3. Es ist wichtig . . . (aufpassen, Sprachen lernen, einmal etwas anderes tun, Freunde haben)
4. Es ist interessant . . . (ihm zuhören, Briefmarken sammeln, mit der Bahn fahren, mit dem Flugzeug fliegen)
5. Es hat Spaß gemacht . . . (reisen, wandern, singen, spazierengehen, ins Grüne fahren, Freunde anrufen)

L. Bilden Sie Sätze!
1. heute / wir / haben / nicht viel / tun
2. es / machen / ihm / Spaß / Fußball spielen
3. sie (*sg.*) / müssen / einlösen / Scheck
4. ich / haben / keine Zeit / / Geschichte / fertig / erzählen (*pres. perf.*)
5. du / haben / keine / Lust / / auf den Stephansdom / hinauffahren? (*pres. perf.*)
6. möchten / du / fernsehen / bei uns?
7. wir / wollen / kaufen / neu / Auto
8. es / sein / sehr bequem / / hier / sitzen
9. ich / sein / zu müde / / Tennis spielen
10. du / sollen / anrufen / dein- / Mutter

Drachenflieger (*hang gliders*) vor dem Abflug

M. Jobinterview. Tell your interviewer about your hobbies and leisure time.
1. Ich habe keine Lust . . .
2. Ich habe nie Zeit . . .
3. Mir macht es Spaß . . .
4. Ich finde es wichtig . . .
5. Ich finde es langweilig . . .
6. Als (*as*) Kind hat es mir Spaß gemacht . . .
7. Ich brauche das Wochenende gewöhnlich, um . . .
8. Ich lerne Deutsch, um . . .

ZUSAMMENFASSUNG

N. Rotkäppchen und der Wolf. Was fehlt?
1. Es hat einmal ein_____ gut_____ Mutter mit ihr_____ klein_____ Mädchen in ein_____ ruhig_____ Dorf gewohnt. **2.** Sie hat zu ihr_____ klein_____ Tochter gesagt: „Geh zu dein_____ alt_____ Großmutter, und bring ihr dies_____ gut_____ Flasche Wein und dies_____ frisch_____ Kuchen! **3.** Aber du mußt in d_____ dunkl_____ Wald aufpassen, weil dort d_____ bös_____ (bad) Wolf (m.) wohnt." **4.** D_____ klein_____ Mädchen ist mit sein_____ groß_____ Tasche in d_____ grün_____ Wald gegangen. **5.** Auf d_____ dunkl_____ Weg ist d_____ bös_____ Wolf gekommen und hat d_____ klein_____ Mädchen gefragt, wo sein_____ alt_____ Großmutter lebt. **6.** Er hat d_____ gut_____ Kind auch d_____ wunderbar_____ Blumen am Weg gezeigt. **7.** Dann hat d_____ furchtbar_____ Wolf d_____ arm_____ (poor) Großmutter gefressen (swallowed) und hat sich in d_____ bequem_____ Bett d_____ alt_____ Frau gelegt. **8.** D_____ müd_____ Rotkäppchen (n.) ist in d_____ klein_____ Haus gekommen und hat gefragt: „Großmutter, warum hast du solch_____ groß_____ Ohren? Warum hast du solch_____ groß_____ Augen? Warum hast du so ein_____ groß_____ Mund?" **9.** Da hat d_____ bös_____ Wolf geantwortet: „Daß ich dich besser fressen (eat) kann!" **10.** Nun (well), Sie kennen ja das Ende dies_____ bekannt_____ Geschichte (story, f.)! **11.** D_____ Jäger (hunter) hat d_____ dick_____ Wolf getötet (killed) und d_____ klein_____ Mädchen und sein_____ alt_____ Großmutter aus d_____ Bauch d_____ tot_____ (dead) Wolfes geholfen.

O. Hallo, Max! Auf deutsch, bitte!
1. What have you been doing today? **2.** Oh, nothing special. I listened to my old records. **3.** Do you feel like going swimming? **4.** No, thanks. I don't feel well. I have a headache and my throat hurts. Call Stephan. **5.** Hello, Stephan! Do you have time to go swimming? **6.** No, I have to go to town (**in die Stadt**) in order to buy (myself) a new pair of pants and a warm coat. Do you feel like coming along? **7.** No, I already went shopping this morning. I bought (myself) a blue sweater and a white shirt. **8.** Too bad. I've got to hurry. I want to put on my trunks (**die Badehose**) and go swimming. Bye!

O: 1. Was hast du heute gemacht (getan)? 2. O, nichts Besonderes. Ich habe mir meine alten Platten angehört. 3. Hast du Lust, schwimmen zu gehen? 4. Nein, danke. Ich fühle mich nicht wohl. Ich habe Kopfschmerzen, und mein Hals tut mir weh. Ruf (doch) Stephan an! 5. Hallo, Stephan! Hast du Zeit, schwimmen zu gehen? 6. Nein, ich muß in die Stadt (fahren / gehen), um mir eine neue Hose und einen warmen Mantel zu kaufen. Hast du Lust mitzukommen? 7. Nein, ich bin heute früh (morgen) schon einkaufen gegangen (gewesen). Ich habe mir einen blauen Pullover und ein weißes Hemd gekauft. 8. Schade! Ich muß mich beeilen. Ich will mir die Badehose anziehen und schwimmen gehen. Auf Wiederhören! (Tschüß!)

EINBLICKE ◆◆◆◆◆◆◆◆◆◆◆

Whereas many Americans view their summer vacations as a short break from the grind, a chance to unwind for a few days, Germans are more likely to view their annual vacations as the year's major event. In fact, vacation planning and saving generally starts in September, just after people go back to work. With relatively high incomes and a minimum of three weeks paid vacation (**Urlaub**) each year, Germans have a wide range of interesting options to choose from. Many head south, to the beaches of Spain, France, and Yugoslavia. Others opt for educational experiences, including language courses abroad, other adventures, and alternative life styles. The important thing is that a vacation be interesting.

Throughout the year, sports are very popular with those who want to keep fit. One citizen out of three belongs to a sports club. Soccer is a national pastime, but tennis, skiing, gymnastics, swimming, and windsurfing are also very popular. In addition to sports clubs, there are associations (**Vereine**) for all sorts of leisure activities, from rabbit breeding and pigeon racing to gardening, crafts, music, dancing, hiking, and mountain climbing, e.g., with the **Alpenverein**. Clubs devoted to regional traditions and costumes (**Trachtenvereine**) and centuries-old rifle clubs (**Schützenvereine**), each with their own banners, badges, uniforms, and ceremonial meetings, keep some of the old traditions alive and draw thousands to their annual fairs and festivities.

WORTSCHATZ 2

der Sport		*sport(s)*
das Leben[1]		*life*

1 In German **Leben** is used only in the singular: **ihr Leben** (*their lives*).

die Musik	*music*
ander- *(adj.)*	*other, different*
anders *(adv.)*	*different(ly)*
etwas anderes	*something different*
ganz	*whole, entire(ly)*
(genauso) wie . . .	*(just) like . . .*
aus·geben (gibt aus), ausgegeben	*to spend [money]*
sich aus·ruhen	*to relax*
sich fit halten (hält), gehalten	*to keep in shape*
sich langweilen	*to get (or be) bored*
vor·ziehen, vorgezogen	*to prefer*

WAS IST DAS? der Arbeiter, Farbfernseher, Ferientag, Freizeitboom, Musik-club, Nationalsport, Streß; das Gartenhäuschen, Gartenrestaurant, Gartenstück, Musikfest, Privileg, Problem, Schwimmbad, Windsurfen, Zusehen; die Auto-bahn, Disco, Kulturreise, Stadtwohnung; *(pl.)* die Aktivitäten, Industrieländer; planen; aktiv, deutschsprachig, frustriert, nämlich, populär, täglich, überfüllt

Freizeit: Lust° oder Frust°?

fun / frustration

was / rich

Vor hundert Jahren noch war° es das Privileg der reichen° Leute, nicht arbeiten zu müssen. Die Arbeiter in den deutschsprachigen Ländern haben aber zu der Zeit oft noch 75 Stunden die Woche gearbeitet. Urlaub° für

[paid] vacation

first

Arbeiter gibt es erst seit 1919: zuerst° nur drei Tage im Jahr! Heute ist das anders. Die Deutschen zum Beispiel arbeiten nur ungefähr 180 Tage im 5 Jahr—weniger als° die Menschen in fast allen anderen Industrieländern.

less than

soon

Außer den vielen Feiertagen haben sehr viele Leute fünf oder sechs Wochen Urlaub im Jahr; und es ist gut möglich, daß die Deutschen bald° nur 35 Stunden in der Woche arbeiten.[1] So wird die Freizeit ein sehr wichtiger Teil

more than

des Lebens: mehr als° nur Zeit, sich vom täglichen Streß auszuruhen. 10

Reiten macht Spaß.

Was tun die Menschen mit der vielen Freizeit? Natürlich ist das Fernsehen sehr wichtig: Viele sitzen über zwei Stunden am Tag vor ihrem
Farbfernseher. Aber auch Sport ist sehr populär, und nicht nur das Zusehen,
sondern auch das aktive Mitmachen°, um sich fit zu halten. Heute sind solche
neuen Sportarten° wie Aerobics, Squash oder Windsurfen „in", genauso wie   15
Tennis und Golf. Fußball ist besonders bei den Deutschen und Österreichern
Nationalsport, aber auch Handball und Volleyball sind in den deutschsprachigen Ländern sehr beliebt°.

Die Leute sind gern draußen°. An Wochenenden fahren sie oft mit dem
Zug oder mit dem Auto ins Grüne° und gehen spazieren, fahren Rad oder   20
wandern. Dann setzt man sich gern in ein schönes Gartenrestaurant und
ruht sich aus. Im Sommer gehen sie oft ins öffentliche Schwimmbad oder
fahren an einen schönen See. Sie sind auch viel im Garten. Wenn sie in einer
Stadtwohnung leben, können sie sich ein kleines Gartenstück pachten°² und
dort Blumen und Gemüse ziehen°. Viele bauen sich dort auch ein Garten-   25
häuschen, wo sie sich duschen, umziehen oder ausruhen können.

Die Deutschen sind besonders reiselustig°³. Sie geben fast ein Sechstel°
des Touristikumsatzes° der ganzen Welt aus! Manche machen Kulturreisen,
um Land und Leute kennenzulernen, in Museen zu gehen oder sich auf

participation
. . . types

popular
outdoors
out into nature

lease
raise

love traveling / one sixth
here: travel expenditures

Windsurfen und
Bergsteigen ist nicht
für jeden.

others

nicely tanned

above mentioned
pubs

traffic jams
well
last / on the road
peace and quiet / main season
... spots

einem der vielen Musikfestspiele Musik anzuhören. Andere° reisen, um 30
Sprachen zu lernen oder einmal etwas ganz anderes zu tun. Viele fahren in
den warmen Süden, um sich in die Sonne zu legen und schön braun gebrannt°
wieder nach Hause zu kommen.

Und die jungen Leute? Außer den oben genannten° Aktivitäten macht
es ihnen besonders Spaß, mit Freunden in Kneipen°, Discos, Cafés, Musik- 35
clubs oder ins Kino zu gehen. Auch gehen sie gern bummeln oder einkaufen.

Dieser ganze Freizeitboom bringt aber auch Probleme mit sich: Manche
langweilen sich, weil sie nicht wissen, was sie mit ihrer Freizeit machen sollen.
Andere sind frustriert, wenn sie auf der Autobahn in lange Staus° kommen
oder die Züge überfüllt sind. Nun°, manchmal muß man etwas planen. Man 40
muß ja nicht am ersten oder letzten° Ferientag unterwegs° sein. Und wenn
man seine Ruhe° haben will, darf man nicht in der Hauptsaison° zu den
bekannten Ferienorten° fahren. Dann ist nämlich die Freizeit nicht Lust,
sondern Frust!

ZUM TEXT

A. Was paßt? Complete the sentences with one of the words or phrases from the list below.

a. im Garten
b. vorm Fernseher
c. Staus auf den Autobahnen
d. den vielen Feiertagen
e. mit ihrer freien Zeit
f. sich da richtig wohl fühlen
g. sich ein kleines Gartenstück zu pachten

h. auszuruhen
i. anzuhören
j. arbeiten zu müssen
k. schön braun gebrannt zurückzu-kommen
l. 35 Stunden in der Woche

1. Vor hundert Jahren noch war es das Privileg der reichen Leute, nicht _____. **2.** Heute haben sehr viele Leute außer _____ auch noch fünf oder sechs Wochen Urlaub im Jahr. **3.** Es kann sein, daß die Deutschen bald nur noch _____ arbeiten. **4.** Die Freizeit ist mehr als nur Zeit, sich von der Arbeit _____ und sich hinzulegen. **5.** Viele Leute sitzen über zwei Stunden am Tag _____. **6.** Man arbeitet auch gern _____. **7.** Wer keinen Garten hat, hat die Möglich-keit, _____. **8.** Wenn das Wetter schön ist, kann man _____. **9.** Manche machen Kulturreisen, um sich zum Beispiel auf einem der vielen Musikfeste Musik _____. **10.** Andere fahren in den warmen Süden, um _____. **11.** Weil zu viele Leute zur gleichen (*same*) Zeit in die Ferien fahren, ist oft alles überfüllt und es gibt _____. **12.** Für manche Leute ist Freizeit ein Problem, weil sie nicht wissen, was sie _____ tun sollen.

B. Ich ziehe es vor... You and your roommate can never agree on anything, especially when it comes to leisure activities. Follow the model.

BEISPIEL: Ich habe Lust, . . . (baden gehen // hier bleiben)
Ich habe Lust, baden zu gehen. Und du?
Ich ziehe es vor, hier zu bleiben.

1. Nach der Vorlesung habe ich Zeit, . . . (Tennis spielen // mein Buch lesen)
2. Mir gefällt es, . . . (durch Geschäfte bummeln und einkaufen // nichts ausgeben)
3. Ich habe Lust, diesen Sommer . . . (in den Süden fahren // nach Norwegen reisen)
4. Ich finde es schön, abends . . . (in einen Musikclub gehen // sich Musik im Radio anhören)
5. Meine Freunde und ich haben immer Lust, . . . (Windsurfen gehen // in den Bergen wandern)
6. Mir ist es wichtig, . . . (viel reisen und Leute kennenlernen // sich mit Freunden gemütlich hinsetzen)

C. Mal etwas anderes in den Ferien!
1. Wo gibt es Sprachkurse in Französisch? Wie viele Stunden sind Sie da in der Klasse, und wie viele Stunden Praxis (*practice*) bekommen Sie in der Woche?
2. Was für Ferien kann man in der Südschweiz machen? Was kann man da auch pflegen (*cultivate*)?

3. Wohin kann man in den Osterferien fliegen? Wo fliegt man ab? Wie viele Tage braucht man für die Rundreise, und was kann man nach der Rundreise tun?

4. Wo kann man Segelfliegen lernen? Wie lange braucht ein Anfänger (*beginner*), bevor er / sie allein fliegen kann? Von wann bis wann gibt es Intensivkurse?

5. Was für eine Farm ist Hotel Tannenhof? Was kann man da wohl (*probably*) tun?

6. Welche Ferienidee finden Sie besonders interessant? Warum?

D. Welches Hobby hast du? Geben Sie die Adjektivendungen!

1. Du fragst mich, was ich in meiner frei_____ Zeit mache.   **2.** Ich gehe gern mit meinen gut_____ Freunden ins Kino und sehe mir einen neu_____ Film an, oder wir gehen in eine toll_____ Disco und tanzen.   **3.** Manchmal gehen wir auch in das gemütlich_____ Café neben dem alt_____ Dom und essen ein gut_____ Stück Kuchen.   **4.** Wenn es heiß ist, setzen wir uns gern in ein schön_____ Gartenrestaurant und trinken eine kalt_____ Limo(nade).   **5.** Im Sommer fahren wir oft zusammen an einen schön_____ See und baden.   **6.** Mein Freund Manfred ist ein fanatisch_____ Fußballspieler.   **7.** Er sieht sich jedes wichtig_____ Fußballspiel an, und wir müssen uns immer die neu_____ Fußballresultate anhören.   **8.** Wenn ich allein bin, lese ich gern ein interessant_____ Buch oder höre mir eine neu_____ Kassette an.   **9.** Wenn ich Zeit habe, gehe ich in unser ausgezeichnet_____ Fitness-Center (*n.*).   **10.** Und du, welches interessant_____ Hobby hast du?

 *Übrigens*

1. In the late 1980s there was great debate in the Federal Republic about the length of the workweek. The unions fought for shorter hours and businesses insisted on flex time. Especially controversial were weekend work and late store hours. In 1989, work hours in the public service sector were reduced from 40 to 39, and in the metals industry from 37.5 to 37. The metals industry union later reached an agreement about the gradual reduction to 35 work hours per week with full compensation.

2. People who don't have a garden of their own can lease one from the city. These small gardens (**Schrebergärten**) not only supplement the family menu with fresh fruit and vegetables, but also provide outdoor recreation for many apartment dwellers.

3. Before the Berlin Wall was opened on November 9, 1989, the inability to travel freely, especially to the West, was among the most important causes of frustration and restlessness among the people of East Germany. The restrictions were especially irritating, since the East Germans were well-informed via television about the extensive travels of the West Germans.

SPRECHSITUATIONEN

Speaking on the Telephone

Speaking on the telephone in a foreign language may seem scary, but with a little practice it is no more difficult than conversing in person.

When answering the phone, Germans identify themselves.

Hier Schmidt. (*This is [Mr. / Mrs.] Schmidt.*)
Hier bei Schmidt. (*Schmidt residence.*)

When calling a business, you may hear:

Guten Tag! Photo Albrecht, Margit (*Margit speaking*). Wen möchten Sie sprechen?

To ask for your party, say:

Kann ich mit . . . sprechen?
Ich möchte gern mit . . . sprechen.
Ist . . . zu sprechen (*available to speak*)?

The answer might be:

Einen Moment / Augenblick, bitte! (*Just a minute, please.*)
. . . ist nicht da. Kann ich etwas ausrichten (*take a message*)?

At the end of a conversation you often hear:

Auf Wiederhören!
Also, mach's gut! (*Well, take care.*)
Tschüß! (*colloquial*)

Extending an Invitation*

Wir möchten euch am . . . zu einer Party einladen.
Darf ich Sie zum Essen einladen?
Möchtest du mit uns . . . (ins Kino) gehen?
Wir gehen . . . Willst / kannst du mitkommen?
Wir gehen . . . Komm doch mit!
Wir gehen . . . Wir nehmen Sie gern mit.
Habt ihr Lust, mit uns . . . zu gehen?

* The forms of the pronouns and verbs depend, of course, on who the addressed person is.

Accepting an Invitation

Danke für die Einladung (*invitation*)!
Das ist aber nett (*nice*). Vielen Dank!
Ja, gern.
Gute Idee!
Prima! Wann denn?
Sicher (*sure*)!
Das klingt gut. (*That sounds good.*)

Declining an Invitation

Nein, danke. Heute kann ich nicht.
Nein, das geht heute nicht. (*No, that won't work today.*)
Nein, ich kann leider nicht.
Ach, es tut mir leid . . .
Schade, aber ich habe schon etwas vor (*planned*).
Nein, ich habe keine Zeit / Lust.
Nein, ich bin zu müde.
Nein, ich fühle mich nicht wohl.
Nein, ich habe Kopfschmerzen.

A. Hast du Lust . . . ? Working with a classmate, take turns extending invitations. Decline or accept them, depending on how they appeal to you. Use as many different expressions as you can.
1. ins Kino gehen
2. eine Vorlesung über deutsche Literatur anhören
3. ein Ballett ansehen
4. in ein Kunstmuseum gehen
5. am Wochenende mit dem Zug aufs Land fahren und wandern
6. während der Semesterferien eine Reise in die Schweiz machen
7. Ski laufen gehen
8. zu einem Fußballspiel gehen
9. in ein Restaurant gehen
10. eine Party für ein paar Freunde geben
11. Tennis oder Squash spielen
12. in den Park gehen und sich in die Sonne legen, usw.

B. Kurzgespräche
1. Your Aunt Elisabeth, who lives in Leipzig, calls. You answer the phone, greet her and ask how she and Uncle Hans are doing. She says they are fine and asks how you are. You tell her you've caught a cold and aren't feeling very well. She expresses her sympathy and asks if you'd like to visit them during Christmas break. You say that that's very nice and you'd like to accept. Your aunt says she's glad and to tell her when you are going to arrive. You both say good-bye.

2. You call a travel agency, *Reisebüro Eckhardt*. An employee answers the phone and connects you with an agent. You ask the agent about trains to Leipzig. She wants to know when you want to go. You tell her on December 22. She says you need to reserve a seat (**einen Platz reservieren**). There is a train that leaves at 8 a.m. and another at 11 a.m. You ask what time you will arrive and whether you have to change trains. You find out that the first train arrives at 1:50 p.m. with a change of trains in Hannover, and the second one arrives at 4:14 p.m. with a change of trains in Braunschweig or Magdeburg. You also ask her about the return schedule and how much a round-trip ticket costs. She says it costs DM 280, and you tell her to reserve a seat. She asks when you want the tickets, and you tell her that you'll come by on Wednesday. You both say good-bye.

C. Was tue ich gern?

The class divides into two teams. One team thinks of a hobby, the other may ask ten (or fifteen) questions to determine what the hobby might be. The teams alternate roles.

KAPITEL

10

Unterhaltung

Szene aus *Mutter Courage* von Bertolt Brecht

▮ LERNZIELE

Gespräche and **Wortschatz**. This chapter deals with entertainment.

Struktur. You will learn about . . .

- verbs with prepositional objects.
- **da-** and **wo-**compounds.
- endings of unpreceded adjectives.

Einblicke. The influence of the mass media in German-speaking countries.

Sprechsituationen

- Expressing satisfaction and dissatisfaction
- Expressing anger

265

◆◆◆◆◆ GESPRÄCHE

Blick in die Zeitung

SONJA	Sag mal, Stephan, was gibt's denn heute abend im Fernsehen?
STEPHAN	Keine Ahnung! Bestimmt nichts Besonderes.
SONJA	Laß mich mal sehen!—*Familie Feuerstein,* einen Dokumentarfilm und einen Krimi.
STEPHAN	Ach, dazu habe ich keine Lust.
SONJA	Vielleicht gibt's was im Kino?
STEPHAN	Ja, *Zurück in die Zukunft* und *Valmont.*
SONJA	Hab' ich schon gesehen.
STEPHAN	Im Theater[1] gibt's *Mutter Courage.*[2]
SONJA	Nicht schlecht! Hast du Lust?
STEPHAN	Ja, das klingt gut. Gehen wir!

18:05

Familie Feuerstein

Fred macht einen Fehler

An der Theaterkasse

SONJA	Haben Sie noch Karten für heute abend?
FRÄULEIN	Ja, erste Reihe erster Rang rechts und Parkett Mitte.
STEPHAN	Zwei Plätze im ersten Rang! Hier sind unsere Studentenausweise.
FRÄULEIN	18 DM, bitte!
SONJA	Wann fängt die Vorstellung an?
FRÄULEIN	Um 20.15 Uhr.

Während der Pause

STEPHAN	Möchtest du eine Cola?
SONJA	Ja, gern. Aber laß mich zahlen! Du hast schon die Programme gekauft.
STEPHAN	Na gut. Wie hat dir der erste Akt gefallen?
SONJA	Prima! Ich habe *Mutter Courage* mal in der Schule gelesen, aber noch nie auf der Bühne gesehen.
STEPHAN	Ich auch. Brecht[2] ist doch immer noch aktuell.

1. Was spielt wo?
2. Wer spielt in *Zurück in die Zukunft* die Hauptrollen? 3. Von wem ist der Film *Valmont*? 4. Welche anderen Filme hat Milos Forman gemacht?
5. Haben Sie *Amadeus* gesehen? Wie hat Ihnen der Film gefallen?
6. Wann laufen die Filme? 7. Wann ist die letzte Vorstellung *(performance)*? 8. Wie lange laufen die beiden Filme schon? 9. Wie alt muß man (mindestens) sein für die beiden Filme?
10. Kennen Sie diese Filme? Wenn ja, wie haben Sie sie gefunden?

Übrigens

◆◆◆◆◆◆◆◆◆◆◆◆◆◆◆◆◆◆◆◆◆◆◆◆◆◆◆◆◆◆

1. Germany, Austria, and Switzerland have a large number of theaters, the majority of them heavily subsidized by public funds. Most are repertory theaters with resident actors who present a number of different plays each season. Most municipal theaters in medium-sized cities also offer ballets, musicals, and operas as part of their regular repertoire. Senior citizens and students are usually able to purchase tickets at a discount. This is also true for museums and galleries, so be sure to take your student ID along when you go to Europe.

2. Bertolt Brecht (1898–1956) was one of the most important German playwrights of the 20th century. His theory of "epic theater" has had a considerable impact on German as well as non-German drama. By using various visual techniques and stylized acting, such as letting performers read their lines in a deliberately expressionless way, he tried to prevent the audience from identifying with the characters and increase the awareness of the play's moral and political message. Brecht's works include *Die Dreigroschenoper*, *Mutter Courage und ihre Kinder*, and *Der kaukasische Kreidekreis*.

A Glance at the Newspaper SONJA: *Say Stephan, what's on TV tonight?* STEPHAN: *I have no idea. Nothing special for sure.* SONJA: *Let me check.*—The Flintstones, *a documentary, and a detective story.* STEPHAN: *Oh, I don't feel like (watching) that.* SONJA: *Maybe there's something at the movies.* STEPHAN: *Yes,* Back to the Future *and* Valmont. SONJA: *I already saw that.* STEPHAN: Mother Courage *is playing in the theater.* SONJA: *Not bad. Do you feel like going?* STEPHAN: *Yes, that sounds good. Let's go.*

At the Ticket Window STEPHAN: *Do you have any tickets for tonight?* YOUNG LADY: *Yes, in the first row of the first balcony on the right and in the middle of the orchestra.* STEPHAN: *Two seats on the first balcony. Here are our student ID's.* YOUNG LADY: *18 marks, please.* SONJA: *When does the performance start?* YOUNG LADY: *At 8.15 p.m.*

During the Intermission STEPHAN: *Would you like a coke?* SONJA: *Yes, I'd love one. But let me pay. You've already bought the programs.* STEPHAN: *OK. How did you like the first act?* SONJA: *Great. I once read* Mother Courage *at school, but I've never seen it on stage.* STEPHAN: *Me neither. Brecht is still relevant today.*

WORTSCHATZ 1

Optional vocabulary: der Dirigent, -en, -en *conductor;* das Ballett, -e; die Ballerina, Ballerinen, Operette, -n; pfeifen, gepfiffen *to whistle, boo.* Note the cultural difference: in Europe whistling is generally a sign of disapproval!

DIE UNTERHALTUNG *entertainment*

der	Anfang, ̈e	*beginning, start*
	Autor, -en	*author*
	Chor, ̈e	*choir*
	Film, -e	*film*
	Komponist, -en, -en	*composer*
	Krimi, -s	*detective story*
	Plattenspieler, -	*record player*
	Roman, -e	*novel*
	Schauspieler, -	*actor*
das	Ende	*end*
	Konzert, -e	*concert*
	Orchester, -	*orchestra*
	Programm, -e	*program; channel*
	Stück, -e	*play*
die	Oper, -n	*opera*
	Pause, -n	*intermission, break*
	Vorstellung, -en	*performance*
	Werbung	*advertisement*
	Zeitschrift, -en	*magazine*
	Zeitung, -en	*newspaper*
	dumm	*stupid, silly*
	komisch	*funny (strange, comical)*
	langweilig	*boring*
	spannend	*exciting, suspenseful*
	traurig	*sad*
	an·fangen (fängt an), angefangen	*to start, begin*
	an·machen / aus·machen	*to turn on / to turn off*
	klatschen	*to clap, applaud*
	lachen / weinen	*to laugh / to cry*

WEITERES

am Anfang / am Ende	*in the beginning / at the end*
letzt-	*last*
Was gibt's im Fernsehen?	*What's (playing) on TV?*

PASSIVES VOKABULAR der Akt, -e der Blick *glance* die Reihe, -n *row* bestimmt *certainly* Das klingt gut. *That sounds good.* Dazu habe ich keine Lust. *I don't feel like (doing) that.* Keine Ahnung! *I've no idea.* im Parkett *in the orchestra* im Rang *on the balcony*

ZUM THEMA

A: Have students act out the dialogue.

A. Was sagen Sie? Inquire about tonight's movies.

x Was gibt's heute abend im Kino?

y _____ .

x Hast du Lust, ins Kino zu gehen?

y Ja / nein, _____ .

x Hast du schon _____ (*name of a movie*) gesehen?

y Ja / nein, _____ , aber _____ .

x Das ist ein _____ Film!

y Wieso (*how come*)?

x _____ .

y Wo läuft dieser Film?

x _____ .

B: Students first ask each other, then they report to the class.

B. Interview. Fragen Sie einen Partner / eine Partnerin . . .!
1. ob er / sie viel fernsieht
2. welche Sendungen (*programs*) ihm / ihr gefallen
3. ob er / sie ein Bücherwurm (*bookworm*) ist
4. welche Zeitschrift oder Zeitung er / sie interessant findet

C: Consult the newspaper for current offerings in your area. Also come prepared with names of composers and titles of plays and / or operas.

C. Fragen
1. Was kann man hier zur (*for*) Unterhaltung tun? Gehen Sie gern tanzen? Wo kann man hier tanzen?
2. Gehen Sie oft ins Kino? Was haben Sie in der letzten Zeit gesehen? Was möchten Sie gern sehen?

Zeitungskiosk

3. Wo kann man hier Theaterstücke sehen? Haben Sie dieses Jahr ein interessantes Stück gesehen? Welches? Wie heißen ein paar Autoren von guten Theaterstücken?

4. Gehen Sie oft ins Konzert? Wohin? Welche Komponisten hören Sie gern?

5. Kann man hier Opern sehen / hören? Welche Opern haben Sie schon gesehen?

6. Wer von Ihnen singt gern? Wer singt im Chor? Wer spielt im Orchester? Wer hat schon einmal eine Rolle *(role)* in einem Theaterstück gespielt? Was für eine Rolle?

7. Wie heißen ein paar gute amerikanische Zeitungen? Nennen *(name)* Sie ein paar interessante Zeitschriften!

8. Wer kann einen guten Roman empfehlen? Wie dick ist er (wie viele Seiten hat er)? Wie oft haben Sie das Buch schon gelesen? Welche Autoren finden Sie besonders gut?

D. Wie geht's weiter?

1. Auf diesem Bild gehört zu einem guten Frühstück die _____ Zeitung.   **2.** Das ist natürlich _____ für diese Zeitung.   **3.** Ich kenne diese Zeitung _____ .   **4.** Auf dem Frühstückstisch stehen _____ .   **5.** Ich esse morgens gern _____ und trinke _____ .   **6.** Wenn ich Zeit habe, lese ich _____ .   **7.** Diese Woche liest man in den Zeitungen viel über (*about*) _____ .   **8.** Ich interessiere mich besonders für (*am interested in*) _____ .   **9.** Am _____ ist die Zeitung immer sehr dick.

E. Aussprache. See also II.9 and III.11 in the pronunciation section of the Workbook.

1. [r]   **r**ot, **r**osa, **r**uhig, **r**echts, **R**adio, **R**egal, **R**eklame, **R**oman, P**r**ogramm, A**r**m, Ame**r**ika, Do**r**f, Konze**r**t, Fah**r**t, Gita**rr**e, t**r**aurig, k**r**ank, wäh**r**end, mo**r**gens, He**rr**.

2. [ʌ]   Absend**er**, Fing**er**, Koff**er**, Orchest**er**, Tocht**er**, Theat**er**, Mess**er**, Tell**er**, v**er**rückt, ab**er**, hint**er**, unt**er**, üb**er**, wied**er**, weit**er**

3. [ʌ / r]   U**hr** / U**hr**en; O**hr** / O**hr**en; Tü**r** / Tü**r**en; Cho**r** / Chö**r**e; Auto**r** / Auto**r**en; Klavie**r** / Klavie**r**e; saub**er** / saub**er**e

4. Wortpaare
   a. *ring* / Ring
   b. *Rhine* / Rhein
   c. *fry* / frei
   d. *brown* / braun
   e. *tear* / Tier
   f. *tour* / Tour

STRUKTUR

I. Verbs with Prepositional Objects

In both English and German a number of verbs are used together with certain prepositions. These combinations have special idiomatic meanings.

I'm thinking of my vacation. I'm waiting for my flight.

Since the German combinations differ from English, they must be memorized.

denken an (+ acc.)	*to think of*
schreiben an (+ acc.)	*to write to*
warten auf (+ acc.)	*to wait for*
sich freuen auf (+ acc.)	*to look forward to*
sich ärgern über (+ acc.)	*to get annoyed (upset) about*
sich interessieren für (+ acc.)	*to be interested in*
erzählen von (+ dat.)	*to tell about*
halten von (+ dat.)	*to think of, be of an opinion*
sprechen von (+ dat.)	*to talk about*

Remind students that the preposition **von** after **erzählen** and **halten** is not a two-way preposition but is always followed by the dative. Refer students to the summary chart in part III of the "Rückblick" (Chapters 7–11).

NOTE: In these idiomatic combinations, two-way prepositions most frequently take the accusative.

Er denkt an seine Reise.	*He's thinking of his trip.*
Sie schreibt an ihre Eltern.	*She's writing to her parents.*

Ich warte auf ein Telefongespräch.   *I'm waiting for a call.*
Freut ihr euch aufs Wochenende?   *Are you looking forward to the weekend?*
Ich ärgere mich über den Brief.   *I'm upset about the letter.*
Interessierst du dich für Sport?   *Are you interested in sports?*
Erzählt von euerem Flug!   *Tell about your flight.*
Was hältst du denn von dem Film?   *What do you think of the movie?*
Sprecht ihr von *Valmont?*   *Are you talking about Valmont?*

CAUTION

In these idiomatic combinations, **an, auf, über,** etc., are not separable prefixes, but prepositions followed by nouns or pronouns in the appropriate cases:

Ich **rufe** dich morgen **an.**   BUT   Ich **denke an** dich.
I'll call you tomorrow.   *I'm thinking of you.*

Note also these two different uses of **auf**:

Ich warte **auf den** Zug.   BUT   Ich warte **auf dem** Zug.
For what? For the train.   *Where? On (top of) the train.*

ÜBUNGEN

A. Sagen Sie es noch einmal! Replace the nouns following the prepositions with the words suggested.

BEISPIEL: Sie warten auf den Zug. (Telefongespräch)
       Sie warten auf das Telefongespräch.

1. Wir interessieren uns für Kunst. (Sport, Musik)
2. Er spricht von seinen Ferien. (Bruder, Hobbys)
3. Sie erzählt von ihrem Flug. (Familie, Geburtstag)

You may need to point out the difference between a separable-prefix verb (**aufstehen**) and verbs commonly used in combination with a preposition (**warten auf**). **Er steht früh auf.** (Nothing follows **auf**; it's a V2, i.e., part of the verb infinitive.) BUT **Ich warte auf dem Bahnsteig auf den Zug.** (**auf** is followed by an object of the preposition; the infinitive is **warten.**)

A: These sentences can be used with different objects or in a quick English-German drill:
1. **sich interessieren für:** Sprachen, Philosophie, Bücher, Theater . . . 2. **sprechen von** Geld, Land, Politik, Autos . . . 3. **erzählen von:** Universität, Schweiz, Ferien, Museum . . . 4. **denken an:** Blumen, Prüfung, Werbung, Wochenende . . . 5. **warten auf:** Student, Antwort, Rechnung, Freund . . . 6. **sich freuen auf:** Schiffsreise, Fußballspiel, Postkarte . . . 7. **sich ärgern über:** Konzert, Film, Fernsehprogramm . . . 8. **schreiben an:** Bruder, Schwester, Tante, Onkel . . . 9. **halten von:** Werbung, Autor, Theaterstück . . .

4. Ich denke an seinen Brief. (Postkarte, Name)
5. Wartest du auf deine Familie? (Gäste, Freundin)
6. Freut ihr euch auf das Volksfest? (Vorstellung, Konzert)
7. Ich habe mich über das Wetter geärgert. (Junge, Kinder)
8. Haben Sie an Ihre Freunde geschrieben? (Frau, Vater)
9. Was haltet ihr von der Idee? (Krimi, Leute)

B. Afrikareise. Was fehlt?

1. Meine Tante hat _____ mein____ Vater geschrieben.   **2.** Sie will uns _____ ihr____ Reise durch Afrika erzählen.   **3.** Wir freuen uns _____ ihr____ Besuch *(m.)*.   **4.** Meine Tante interessiert sich sehr _____ Afrika.   **5.** Sie spricht hier im Museum ____ ihr____ Fahrten.   **6.** Sie denkt nie _____ ihr____ Gesundheit *(f.)*.   **7.** Wir können kaum *(hardly)* _____ sie warten.

C. Was tun Sie?

1. Ich denke oft _____ .   **2.** Ich warte _____ .   **3.** Ich schreibe gern _____ .   **4.** Ich interessiere mich _____ .   **5.** Ich freue mich _____ .   **6.** Ich ärgere mich manchmal _____ .   **7.** Ich spreche gern _____ .   **8.** Ich halte nicht viel _____ .

D. Auf deutsch, bitte!

1. Don't wait for me (3×).   **2.** I'm writing to the newspaper.   **3.** He didn't think of the family.   **4.** Why do you (3×) always get upset about every performance?   **5.** I'm looking forward to the concert.   **6.** He isn't interested in such music.   **7.** We don't think much of his letter.

II. da- and wo-Compounds

1. **da-**Compounds

In English, pronouns following prepositions can refer to people, things, and ideas:

I'm coming with him.
I'm coming with it.

Ask students why this is so. (In English, most objects are referred to as *it*; in German, objects come in all genders.)

In German, this is not the case; pronouns following prepositions refer only to people:

Ich komme **mit ihm (mit meinem Freund).**

If you wish to refer to a thing or an idea, you must use a **da-**COMPOUND.

Ich komme **damit (mit unserem Auto).**

Most accusative and dative prepositions (except **außer, ohne** and **seit**) can be made into **da-**compounds. If the preposition begins with a vowel (**an, auf, in,** etc.), it is used with **dar-**:

dafür	*for it (them)*	**darauf**	*on it (them)*
dagegen	*against it (them)*	**darin**	*in it (them)*
damit	*with it (them)*	**darüber**	*above it (them)*
danach	*after it (them)*	usw.	

Können Sie mir sagen, wo ein Briefkasten ist?—Ja, sehen Sie die Kirche dort? **Daneben** ist eine Apotheke, **dahinter** ist die Post, und **davor** ist ein Briefkasten.

2. **wo-**Compounds

The interrogative pronouns **wer, wen,** and **wem** refer to people.

Von wem sprichst du?	*About whom are you talking? (Who are you talking about?)*
Auf wen wartet ihr?	*For whom are you waiting? (Who are you waiting for?)*

When asking about things or ideas, **was** is used. But if a preposition is involved, you must use a **wo-**compound. Again, if the preposition begins with a vowel, it is combined with **wor-**.

wofür?	*for what?*	**worauf?**	*on what?*
wogegen ?	*against what?*	**worüber?**	*above what?*
womit?	*with what?*	usw.	

Wovon sprichst du?	*About what are you talking? (What are you talking about?)*
Worauf wartet ihr?	*For what are you waiting? (What are you waiting for?)*

**Wer weiß
schon genau,
woraus ein
Hamburger
besteht?**

ÜBUNGEN

E. Wo ist die Brille? Remind your roommate, who is very careless, where he / she can find his / her glasses. Use a **da-**compound.

BEISPIEL: auf dem Sofa   **Sie liegt darauf.**

neben dem Bett, vor dem Telefon, hinter der Lampe, auf dem Plattenspieler, in der Tasche, unter den Photos, zwischen den Zeitungen und Zeitschriften

F. Noch einmal, bitte! Replace the phrases in boldface with a preposition and a pronoun or with a **da-**compound. Always consider whether the sentence deals with a person or with an object or idea.

BEISPIEL: Hans steht **neben Christa**.   **Hans steht neben ihr.**
Die Lampe steht **neben dem Klavier**.   **Die Lampe steht daneben.**

1. Was machst du **nach den Ferien**?
2. Bist du auch **mit dem Bus** gefahren?
3. Er hat die Gitarre **für seine Freundin** gekauft.
4. Was hast du **gegen Skilaufen**?
5. Das Paket ist **von meinen Eltern** gewesen.
6. Die Karten liegen **auf dem Tisch**.
7. Die Kinder haben **hinter der Garage** gespielt.
8. Anja hat **zwischen Herrn Fiedler und seiner Frau** gesessen.
9. Was sagen Sie **zu dem Haus**?
10. Ist die Nummer **im Telefonbuch**?
11. Er hat sich furchtbar **über diese Idee** geärgert.
12. Wir denken oft **an unseren kranken Freund**.
13. Freust du dich auch so **auf unsere Fahrt**?
14. Der Koffer ist **auf dem Schrank**.
15. Ich habe diese Theaterkarten **für meine Großeltern** gekauft.

G. Das Klassentreffen. *(The class reunion.)* You were not able to participate at the last high school reunion, but you are dying to know what has become of your ex-classmates. Ask one of the participants by referring to the phrases in boldface.

BEISPIEL: Horst interessiert sich **für Sport**.   **Wofür interessiert er sich?**
Horst interessiert sich **für eine junge Lehrerin**.   **Für wen interessiert er sich?**

1. Jutta hat **von ihrem Mann** erzählt.
2. Gerd und Martina interessieren sich immer noch **für Politik**.
3. Ernst hält nicht viel **von Politik**.
4. Er ärgert sich oft **über die Politiker**.
5. Sebastian und Nicole sind **mit ihrem neuen Mercedes** gekommen.
6. Natürlich hat Sebastian **von seinen Hobbys** gesprochen.
7. Daniel wohnt jetzt in Kanada, aber er schreibt jede Woche **an seine Familie**.
8. Toni und Evelyn freuen sich **auf ihr erstes Baby**.
9. Wir haben oft **an die Vergangenheit** *(past)* gedacht.

For additional practice, use exercise C (p. 273) as a chain drill by letting students make up questions and answers: **Woran** ODER **an wen denkst du?** (Ich denke an das Mittagessen. Ich denke an meine Freundin.)

H. Auf deutsch, bitte!
1. **a.** She's sitting next to them (i.e., their friends).   **b.** They have two presents, one (**eins**) for her and one for him.   **c.** Do you see the chair? The presents are lying on it.   **d.** What's in them?   **e.** Who are they for?   **f.** Is this for me?   **g.** What does one do with it?   **h.** Don't *(sg. fam.)* sit down on it.
2. **a.** With whom is he coming?   **b.** What are they talking about?   **c.** What are you *(sg. fam.)* thinking of?   **d.** For whom is he waiting?   **e.** What are you *(pl. fam.)* annoyed about?   **f.** What is she interested in?   **g.** To whom are you *(formal)* writing?   **h.** For whom is this present?   **i.** What do you *(sg. fam.)* think of it?

III. Endings of Unpreceded Adjectives

You already know how to deal with adjectives preceded by either **der-** or **ein-** words. But occasionally adjectives are preceded by neither; these are called UNPRECEDED ADJECTIVES. The equivalent in English would be adjectives preceded by neither *the* nor *a(n)*:

We bought fresh fish and fresh eggs.

1. Unpreceded adjectives have the endings that the definite article would have if it were used:

der	frische	Fisch	**das**	frische	Obst	**die**	frische	Wurst	**die**	frischen	Eier
	frisch**er**	Fisch		frisch**es**	Obst		frische	Wurst		frische	Eier
nom.	frisch**er**	Fisch		frisch**es**	Obst		frische	Wurst		frische	Eier
acc.	frisch**en**	Fisch		frisch**es**	Obst		frische	Wurst		frische	Eier
dat.	frisch**em**	Fisch		frisch**em**	Obst		frisch**er**	Wurst		frisch**en**	Eiern
gen.[1]	(frisch**en**	Fisches)		(frisch**en**	Obstes)		(frisch**er**	Wurst)		(frisch**er**	Eier)

1 The genitive singular forms are irregular and relatively rare.

Heute abend gibt es heiß**e** Suppe, holländisch**en** Käse, frisch**e** Brötchen und verschieden**es** Obst.

▪ If there are several unpreceded adjectives, all have the same ending.

Ich wünsche dir schön**e**, interessant**e** Ferien.

2. Several important words are often used as unpreceded adjectives in the plural:

einige	*some, a few (pl. only)*
mehrere	*several (pl. only)*
viele	*many*
wenige	*few*

Wir haben uns mehrer**e** neu**e** Filme angesehen.
Sie haben einig**en** jung**en** Leuten gefallen, aber mir nicht.

▪ Usually neither **viel** *(much)* nor **wenig** *(little, not much)* has an ending in the singular. But the words are often used as unpreceded adjectives in the plural.

Viele Studenten haben **wenig** Geld, aber nur **wenige** Studenten haben viel Zeit.

*The adjective **prima** also never has an ending.*

▪ Numerals, **mehr,** and **ein paar** have no endings. The same holds true for a few colors, such as purple and pink (**lila, rosa**), and adjectives like **Frankfurter, Berliner,** etc.

Da sind **drei** junge **Wiener** Studenten mit **ein paar** kurzen Fragen.
Haben Sie noch **mehr** graues oder blaues Papier?
Was soll ich mit diesem alten **rosa** Pullover?

ÜBUNGEN

1.1: schwarzen Kaffee is an apposition to **eine Tasse.** Appositions are in the same case as the noun they refer to.

I. Ersetzen Sie die Adjektive!

BEISPIEL: Das sind nette Leute. (verrückt) **Das sind verrückte Leute.**

1. Geben Sie mir eine Tasse schwarzen Kaffee. (heiß, frisch)
2. Sie braucht ein Paket dünnes Papier. (billig, weiß)
3. Er schreibt tolle Bücher. (spannend, lustig)
4. Heute haben wir wunderbares Wetter. (ausgezeichnet, furchtbar)
5. Dort gibt es gutes Essen. (einfach, gesund)
6. Hier bekommen wir frischen Fisch. (wunderbar, gebacken)
7. Er hat oft verrückte Ideen. (dumm, phantastisch)

J. Sagen Sie es noch einmal! Omit the **der-** or **ein-**word preceding the adjective.

BEISPIEL: Der holländische Käse ist ausgezeichnet.
Holländischer Käse ist ausgezeichnet.

1. Die deutschen Zeitungen haben auch viel Werbung.
2. Der Mann will mit dem falschen Geld bezahlen.
3. Sie hat das frische Brot gekauft.
4. Er hat den schwarzen Kaffee getrunken.
5. Wir haben die braunen Eier genommen.
6. Er ist mit seinen alten Tennisschuhen auf die Party gegangen.
7. Sie trinken gern das dunkle Bier.
8. Auf der Party haben sie diese laute Musik gespielt.
9. Er erzählt gern solche traurigen Geschichten.
10. Sie hat Bilder der bekannten Schauspieler.

K: Have students do this individually in class or at home.

K. Was fehlt?

1. Geben Sie mir bitte ein paar— rote Äpfel!
2. Wir haben einige bekannte Autoren kennengelernt.
3. Ich habe nur wenig— amerikanisches Geld.
4. Viele neue Studenten sind heute gekommen.
5. Trinkst du gern warme Milch?
6. Wir wünschen Ihnen schöne und interessante Ferien.
7. Sie haben mit mehreren anderen Ausländern an einem Tisch gesessen.
8. Regensburg und Landshut sind zwei hübsche alte Städte.
9. In der Prüfung habe ich ein paar— dumme Fehler (mistakes) gemacht.
10. Trink nicht so viel— kaltes Bier!
11. Liebe Bettina, lieber Hans, liebe Freunde!
12. Lieber Onkel Max, liebe Tante Elisabeth!

L. Was ich gern mache. Include an unpreceded adjective.

BEISPIEL: Ich singe ... **Ich singe alte Lieder.**

1. Ich esse gern ...
2. Ich trinke meistens ...

3. Ich samm(e)le . . .
4. Ich lese gern . . .
5. Ich trage . . .
6. Ich sehe gern . . .
7. Ich finde . . . prima.
8. Ich möchte . . .

ZUSAMMENFASSUNG

M. Bilden Sie ganze Sätze!

1. wie lange / du / warten / — / ich? *(pres. perf.)*
2. ich / sich freuen / — / Reise nach Spanien *(pres.)*
3. er / sich ärgern / — / Film *(pres. perf.)*
4. wo- / ihr / sich interessieren? *(pres.)*
5. wollen / sich kaufen / du / einig- / deutsch / Zeitschriften? *(pres.)*
6. in London / wir / sehen / mehrer- / interessant / Stücke *(pres. perf.)*
7. während / Pause / wir / trinken / billig / Sekt *(pres. perf.)*
8. Renate / schon / lesen / ein paar / spannend / Krimi *(pres. perf.)*
9. am Ende / viel / modern / Stücke / Leute / nicht / klatschen / lange *(pres.)*

N. Ein interessanter Mensch. Auf deutsch, bitte!

1. Two weeks ago an old friend of my father's visited us. **2.** He is the author of several plays. **3.** I'm very interested in the theater. **4.** He knows many interesting people, also several well-known actors. **5.** He spoke about them. **6.** He also told us some exciting stories. **7.** He has just been to (**in**) Vienna. **8.** He saw several performances of his new play and he bought a few interesting books. **9.** He's coming back in the summer. **10.** We all look forward to that.

N: 1. Vor zwei Wochen hat uns ein alter Freund meines Vaters besucht. 2. Er ist der Autor mehrerer Stücke. 3. Ich interessiere mich sehr fürs Theater. 4. Er kennt viele interessante Leute, auch mehrere bekannte Schauspieler. 5. Er hat von ihnen gesprochen. 6. Er hat uns auch ein paar (einige) spannende Geschichten erzählt. 7. Er ist gerade in Wien gewesen. 8. Er hat mehrere Vorstellungen seines neuen Stückes gesehen, und er hat einige interessante Bücher gekauft. 9. Er kommt im Sommer zurück. 10. Wir alle freuen uns darauf.

EINBLICKE ◆◆◆◆◆◆◆◆◆◆◆◆

Aktuelles Sport-Studio im Fernsehen

Pre-reading activity:
1. Nennen Sie die Massenmedien auf deutsch! Welche sind hier besonders wichtig?
2. Wovon leben die Massenmedien hier?
3. Gibt es hier Radio und Fernsehen ohne Werbung? 4. Lebt das Kabelfernsehen auch nur von Werbung?
5. Wie finden Sie das Fernsehen hier?
6. Was für Sendungen sehen die Leute hier besonders gern? 7. Was für Programme gibt's im öffentlichen Fernsehen? 8. Wie viele Stunden am Tag sehen die Menschen hier fern? 9. Wie ist das bei Kindern? 10. Wie finden Sie das?

German public radio and television are run by independent public corporations. The main nationwide television channels are called ARD (or **1. Programm**) and ZDF (or **2. Programm**); together they produce a third regional channel (**3. Programm**) which is primarily educational. Since 1985 the public corporations have been participating in additional ventures, e.g., "3-Sat" (a joint venture of ZDF, the Austrian broadcasting corporation ORF, and the Swiss corporation SRG) and "1-Plus". The public broadcasting corporations get most of their funds from fees which every owner of a radio or television set has to pay, but revenues from advertising are increasingly important. The two major private television networks operating in Germany are "RTL-plus" (based in Cologne) and "Sat 1" (based in Mainz). Their transmissions are beamed via satellite.

WORTSCHATZ 2

der	Bürger, -	*citizen*
	Zuschauer, -	*viewer, spectator*
das	Fernsehen	*television (the medium)*
die	Nachricht, -en	*news (usually pl. in radio and TV)*
	Sendung, -en[1]	*(particular) program*
	amerikanisch	*American*

1 Note the difference between **das Programm** and **die Sendung** as they refer to television: **das Programm** generally refers to *a channel* (Es gibt auch private Programme). **Die Sendung** refers to *a particular program* (Ich sehe mir gern diese Sportsendung an).

leicht / schwer	*light, easy / heavy, difficult*
monatlich (täglich, wöchentlich)	*monthly (daily, weekly)*
öffentlich / privat	*public / private*
verschieden	*different (kinds of)*
vor allem	*mainly, especially*
weder . . . noch	*neither . . . nor*

WAS IST DAS? der Haushalt, Kritiker, Regen, Sex; das Hauptprogramm, Kabelprogramm, Nachbarland, Osteuropa, Problem, Satellitenprogramm; die Diskussion, Droge, Fernsehsendung, Interessengruppe, Kolonialisierung, Kreativität, Kultursendung, Rolle, Serie; *(pl.)* die Kommunikationsmedien, Massenmedien, Statistiken; etwas Positives; finanzieren, ignorieren, registrieren, warnen; ausländisch, experimentell, finanziell, informativ, international, kulturell, lokal, passiv, politisch, staatlich kontrolliert

Die Macht° des Fernsehens

power

Wie überall spielen die Massenmedien, vor allem das Fernsehen, auch in Deutschland eine wichtige Rolle. Ungefähr fünf Stunden jeden Tag nutzen° *use* die Deutschen im Durchschnitt° Fernsehen, Radio, Zeitungen und Zeitschrif- *on the average* ten. Fast jeder Haushalt hat heute einen Fernseher. Die Auswahl an° Sen- *selection of* dungen ist groß und wird jedes Jahr größer°. Zu den Hauptprogrammen 5 *bigger* kommen Programme aus Nachbarländern und seit kurzer Zeit auch privates Fernsehen, Kabel- und Satellitenprogramme.

Die privaten Sender° leben natürlich von der Werbung. Aber um das *stations* öffentliche Fernsehen zu finanzieren, müssen die Deutschen ihre Fernseher und Radios bei der Post registrieren und monatliche Gebühren° zahlen. 10 *fees* Werbung gibt es da auch, aber nie während einer Sendung, sondern nur zu festgesetzten° Zeiten. *fixed*

Das öffentliche Fernsehen ist weder staatlich noch privat kontrolliert, sondern finanziell und politisch unabhängig°. Darum° kann es auch leicht *independent / therefore* Sendungen für kleine Interessengruppen bringen, z.B. Nachrichten[1] in 15 verschiedenen Sprachen, Sprachunterricht° für ausländische Gastarbeiter°[2], *. . . instruction / foreign workers* experimentelle Musik, politische Diskussionen und lokales Kabarett[3]. Das deutsche Fernsehen bietet° eigentlich eine gute Mischung° von aktuellem° *offers / mixture / current* Sport und leichter Unterhaltung, von informativen Reiseberichten°, interna- *. . . reports* tionalen Filmen und kulturellen Sendungen (z.B. Theaterstücke, Opern und 20 Konzerte).

Manche Kritiker halten nicht viel vom Fernsehen. Sie ärgern sich zum Beispiel darüber, daß so viele amerikanische Filme und Serien laufen, obwohl die Statistiken zeigen, daß sich die Zuschauer dafür interessieren. Sie wollen nicht nur gute und informative Kultursendungen, sondern auch viel Sex 25 und Gewalt°. Aber nicht nur darin sehen die Kritiker Probleme, sondern *violence* auch in der passiven Rolle der Zuschauer. Manche Menschen, vor allem

let themselves be showered
lose
against
acid
damaged / visible

less dangerous

developments
GDR / could
FRG
more / than

bring closer

Kinder, lassen sich täglich stundenlang vom Fernsehen „berieseln°". Sie werden dadurch passiv und verlieren an° Kreativität. Zeitungen und Zeitschriften warnen heute vor° der „Kolonialisierung der Köpfe" durch Fernsehen und Radio, und man spricht von der Musik als Droge: „Was der saure° Regen in den Wäldern angerichtet° hat, ist sichtbar° geworden. Was die Massenmedien in unseren Köpfen anrichten, ist nicht sichtbar, aber trotzdem nicht weniger gefährlich°!" 30

Auf der anderen Seite darf man nicht ignorieren, was für eine wichtige Rolle Radio und Fernsehen bei den politischen Entwicklungen° in Osteuropa gespielt haben. In der DDR° zum Beispiel konnte° man fast überall Fernsehsendungen aus der Bundesrepublik° sehen, und die Bürger haben sich oft mehr° für westliche Nachrichten, Filme und auch Werbung interessiert, als° für die Sendungen ihres staatlich kontrollierten Fernsehens. So sind Radio und Fernsehen auch wichtige Kommunikationsmedien, weil sie Menschen verschiedener Nationen miteinander verbinden°. Und das ist doch etwas Positives! 35 40

ZUM THEMA

Was ist das? 1. die Massenmedien 2. Fernsehgebühren 3. Werbung 4. leichte Unterhaltung 5. die Kolonialisierung der Köpfe

A. Richtig oder falsch? Wenn falsch, erklären Sie *(explain)* warum!

F   1. In Deutschland spielt das Fernsehen keine wichtige Rolle.

F   2. Die Menschen dort sehen sich ungefähr fünf Stunden am Tag Fernsehen an.

R   3. Jetzt gibt es in Deutschland auch privates Fernsehen.

F   4. Weil die Deutschen monatliche Gebühren zahlen, gibt es im öffentlichen Fernsehen keine Werbung.

(R)   5. Werbung läuft im öffentlichen Fernsehen nie während einer Sendung.

R   6. Manche Kritiker finden es nicht gut, daß im deutschen Fernsehen so viele amerikanische Filme und Serien laufen.

F   7. Aber die passive Rolle der Zuschauer findet mancher Kritiker gut.

R   8. Ein paar Kritiker denken, daß die Massenmedien in unseren Köpfen tun, was der saure Regen in den Wäldern tut.

F   9. Das westliche Fernsehen hat im Osten keine wichtige Rolle gespielt.

R   10. Radio und Fernsehen können Nationen miteinander verbinden.

B. Was fehlt? Geben Sie die fehlenden *(missing)* Präpositionen!

1. Der Artikel spricht _____ deutschen Fernsehen.   **2.** Viele denken bei Qualitätssendungen _____ internationale Nachrichten.   **3.** Manche Kritiker ärgern sich _____ die vielen amerikanischen Filme.   **4.** Sie interessieren sich nicht _____ amerikanische Serien.   **5.** Andere warten jede Woche _____ diese Serien.   **6.** Sie freuen sich schon _____ die nächste Woche.   **7.** Die Kritiker sprechen _____ einer Kolonialisierung der Köpfe durch die Massenmedien.   **8.** Wenn Sie das Quatsch finden, schreiben Sie bitte _____ die *Frankfurter Rundschau*!

C. Womit? Damit! Stellen Sie Fragen mit einem wo-Wort, und antworten Sie mit einem da-Wort!

BEISPIEL: Das deutsche Fernsehen ist unabhängig **von der Werbung.**
Wovon ist das deutsche Fernsehen unabhängig?
Davon! Von der Werbung!

1. Einige Kritiker halten nicht viel **vom Fernsehen.** **2.** Vor allem ärgern sie sich **über die vielen amerikanischen Serien.** **3.** Manche Zuschauer lassen sich täglich stundenlang **vom Fernsehen oder von moderner Musik** berieseln. **4. Durch zu viel Fernsehen und zu viel Musik** verlieren sie an Kreativität. **5. Fürs Hobby** haben sie oft keine Zeit.

D. Deutsches Fernsehen. Geben Sie die Adjektivendungen, wo nötig (necessary)!
1. Das deutsch _e_ Fernsehen ist eine gut _e_ Mischung von kulturell _en_ Sendungen und leicht _er_ Unterhaltung. **2.** Man bekommt auch viel _e_ interessant _e_ Sendungen (pl.) aus verschieden _en_ Nachbarländern. **3.** Das öffentlich _e_ Fernsehen finanziert man durch monatlich _e_ Gebühren. **4.** Öffentlich _e_ Sender (pl.) haben natürlich auch öffentlich _e_ Aufgaben. **5.** Sie können leicht verschieden _e_ Sendungen für klein _e_ Interessengruppen bringen, z.B. international _e_ Nachrichten in verschieden _en_ Sprachen oder auch lokal _es_ Kabarett (n.). **6.** Privat _es_ Fernsehen gibt es noch nicht lange. **7.** Diese klein _en_ Sender sind natürlich abhängig von viel _/_ Werbung; und sie bringen sie oft noch zu spät _er_ Stunde. **8.** Beim privat _en_ Fernsehen kann man auch viel _e_ amerikanisch _e_ Filme sehen. **9.** Kritiker sprechen von schlecht _er_ Qualität beim privat _en_ Fernsehen. **10.** Sie ärgern sich auch über das Berieseln durch modern _e_ Musik. **11.** Sie denken, daß das schwer _e_ Konsequenzen (consequences) bringt. **12.** Wie wir in der letzt _en_ Zeit in Osteuropa gesehen haben, haben Fernsehen und Radio auch eine sehr positiv _e_ Seite. **13.** Sie sind nämlich ein wichtig _es_ Kommunikationsmittel (n.) **14.** Denn sie verbinden die Menschen verschieden _er_ Nationen miteinander.

E. Was gibt's im Fernsehen? Sehen Sie aufs Programm auf Seite 283, und beantworten Sie die Fragen darüber!
1. Wann beginnt das gemeinsame (shared) Vormittagsprogramm von ARD und ZDF? Bis wann läuft es?
2. Wann gibt es Nachrichten im ersten Program (die Tagesschau)? im 2. Programm (Heute)? Wie lange sind diese Nachrichten? In welchen anderen Sprachen gibt es Nachrichten im 3. Programm?
3. Wo und wann gibt es eine Sendung über Sport oder Freizeit? über Kunst oder Musik?
4. Was ist vor allem für Kinder? für Schüler und Studenten?
5. Worüber diskutieren Frauen in der Sendung um halb acht im 2. Programm? **(der Beruf** profession, work)
6. Worüber ist die Sendung um elf Uhr im 3. Programm? Um Viertel vor sechs im RTL plus?

7. Womit beginnt das Tagesprogramm von SAT 1? Was für ein Film ist das bestimmt?
8. Was für amerikanische Filme und Serien finden Sie auf dem Programm? Wann und wo laufen sie?

1. PROGRAMM 1   **2. PROGRAMM ZDF**   **10. April**

1. PROGRAMM

Das gemeinsame Programm von ARD und ZDF bis 13.45 Uhr:
- **9.00** Tagesschau
- **9.03** Unter der Sonne Kaliforniens
  Eine neue Familie (Wh. v. 1989)
- **9.45** Sport treiben – fit bleiben
- **10.00** Tagesschau
- **10.03** Gesundheitsmagazin Praxis
  Zum Weltgesundheitstag: „Ich landele Sie jetzt!" Wo denn, wie denn, was denn? / Der unnötige Schmerz. Von Marlene Linke (Wh. vom 5. April)
- **10.50** Mosaik-Ratschläge
  Ostereier aus aller Welt – Färbemittel / Hasentreffen in Stuttgart
- **11.00** Tagesschau
- **11.03** Fantomas
  2. Teil: Tödliche Umarmung (Wh.) Ist Doktor Chaleck der geheimnisumwitterte Serienmörder Fantomas? Inspektor Juvè findet im Haus des Arztes die Leiche einer Frau.
  3. Teil: nächsten Dienstag
- **12.30** Umschau
- **12.55** Presseschau
- **13.00** Tagesschau
- **13.05** ARD Mittagsmagazin

3. PROGRAMM

- **9.50** Tele-Gymnastik (27)
- **10.00** News of the week
- **10.15** Actualités
- **10.30** Avanti! Avanti!
  Italienisch-Kurs (16)
- **11.00** Wer hat Angst vorm kleinen Chip?
  Mikroelektronik; Verwandelt
- **11.30** Computerclub (5)
- **12.15** Reiseführer Die Borinage: Auf den Spuren des niederländischen Malers Vincent van Gogh
- **13.00** Telekolleg II
  Deutsch (31): Das Buch des Lebens – Der Roman
- **13.30** Telekolleg II
  Mathematik, Trigonometrie
- **17.00** Ferntourismus am Beispiel Kenias
  Bericht. Letzter Teil: Hakuna Matata: Schönes Kenia – Keine Probleme?
- **17.30** Schüler machen Filme

RTL PLUS

- **16.25** Snoopy Zeichentrickfilm
- **17.45** Kunst und Botschaft Rembrandt »Josephs Traum im Stall« (1645)
- **17.50** Dirty Dancing Serie
  Gefährliche Gefühle
- **18.18** Bi. Wild Serie
  Delta und die Bannermänner
- **18.45** RTL aktuell Nachrichten, Sport
- **19.00** Airwolf Serie
  Dem Wolf eine Falle stellen
- **19.50** Der Hammer Serie

SAT 1

- **21.00** Der junge Löwe
  Die Lebensgeschichte des Politikers Winston Churchill (1874–1965)
- **23.15** SAT 1-Blick Berichte vom Tage

2. PROGRAMM ZDF

- **13.00** Tennis:
  Grand-Prix-Turniere
  Grand-Prix der Damen in Hamburg. Reporter: Hans-Jürgen Pohmann
- **18.00** Sooomstraße
  Für Kinder im Vorschulalter
- **18.30** flicflac
  Magazin für Freizeit
- **19.00** heute
- **19.30** Doppelpunkt
  „Baby oder Beruf?"
  Junge Frauen diskutieren über ihre Entscheidungen und Erfahrungen Moderation. Barbara Stöckl
  ► Siehe auch rechts
- **20.15** Und das am Montagmorgen
  Deutsche Filmkomödie von 1959
  Nach dem Bühnenstück von John Boynton Priestley

  Alois Kessel ...... O. W. Fischer
  Delia Mond ..... Ulla Jacobsson
  Herbert Acker ...... Robert Graf
  Monika ...... Vera Tschechowa
  Professor Gross ... Werner Finck
  Müller ..... Reinhard Kolldehoff
  Frau Mutz .... Lotte Stein
  Frau Präfke . Blandine Ebinger
  v. Schmitz . Siegfried Schürenberg
  Wegeleben .. Herbert Weissbach
  Regie: Luigi Comencini (Wh. v. 83)
  „Der englische Romancier, Buch- und Bühnenautor John Boynton Priestley lieferte den Stoff zu dieser reizenden Komödie, einem Brevier für Managerkranke. Wenn O. W. Fischer bisweilen auch reichlich theatralisch wird, so ist das Stück doch ein einziges Schmunzelvergnügen." (Hamburger Abendblatt)
  ► Siehe auch rechts
- **21.45** Magnum US-Serie
  Hinter Gittern
  Thomas Magnum ..Tom Selleck
  Jonathan Higgins . John Hillerman
  Rick .... Larry Manetti
  TC ....Roger E. Mosley
  Carol .... Kathleen Lloyd
  Darryl Jacobs ... Asher Brauner
  Jack Damon ...... Matt Clark
  Becky Damon .. Linda Grovenor
  Regie: Bernie Kowalski
- **22.40** Gottes eigenes Land
  US-Dokumentarfilm von 1979/85
  Kamera, Buch, Regie: Louis Malle
  Der zweite Dokumentarfilm „... und das Streben nach Glück" folgt am 24. Mai.
  ► Siehe auch rechts
- **0.05** Europas Jugend musiziert
  Auszüge aus dem fünften internationalen Konzert junger Solisten Ha Young Soul (Schweden), Klavier; Emer McDonough (England), Flöte; Koh Gabriel Kameda (Deutschland), Violine; Velgko Klenkovski (Jugoslawien), Klarinette. Werke von Haydn, Pergolesi und Weber. Das Orchester des belgischen Rundfunks und Fernsehens Leitung: Aleksander Rahbari
- **0.50** heute

17.45 Hotel Paradies Lisa bekommt ihr Traumhaus

Vor dem Glück der Lindemanns gibt's erst mal Streß· Max hat Magenbeschwerden und ohrfeigt seinen Sohn Michael. Lisa bekommt einen Schwächeanfall. Das ist zuviel für Max: Er will das Hotel aufgeben! Zwischen Renate und ihrem Freund, dem Schiffsmakler Rowalt, gibt es Spannungen.

Max (Klaus Wildbolz) macht seine Frau (Grit Boettcher) überglücklich: Er hat ihr heimlich das Traumhaus gekauft

19.30 Doppelpunkt Junge Frauen diskutieren: Baby oder Beruf?

Wie sie es macht, ist's verkehrt: Entscheidet sich eine junge Frau für die Familie, gilt sie als „naives Dümmchen", räumt sie dem Beruf Vorrang ein, muß sie mit dem Vorwurf „Karrierefrau" leben. Beides unter einen Hut bringen kann nur eine „Rabenmutter". Gibt es Auswege aus dem Dilemma? Barbara Stöckl diskutiert heute live mit Betroffenen.

20.15 Und das am Montagmorgen Filmkomödie mit O. W. Fischer als „Aussteiger"

Korrekt und pflichtbewußt bis in die Knochen – Bankdirektor Kessel ist ohne Tadel. Das einzige Vergnügen, das sich der Junggeselle gönnt, ist die Mitarbeit in einem Kunstverein. Zwar findet er das hübsche Mitglied Dr. Delia Mond reizend, aber schließlich ist sie verlobt ... An einem trüben Morgen reitet den Direktor offenbar der Teufel. Er will nicht mehr zur Bank gehen, sondern nur noch tun, was ihm Spaß macht! 88 Min.

Verliebt schmiegt sich Delia (Ulla Jacobsson) an Bankdirektor Kessel (O. W. Fischer)

21.45 Magnum ... als Häftling auf einer Gefängnisfarm

Diese Art von Aufträgen haßt Magnum besonders: das Aufspüren durchgebrannter Teenager. Doch als seine Freundin Carol ihn bittet, ihre vermißte Cousine Becky zu suchen, muß er ran. Er findet heraus, daß Becky mit einem gewissen Darryl zusammen war. Der ist inzwischen auf einer Gefängnisfarm gelandet. Um mehr zu

F. Wofür interessieren Sie sich im Fernsehen? Together as a class, create a ratings chart on various types of television programs. Use: 1 = sehr interessant; 2 = manchmal interessant; 3 = uninteressant.

___ 1. Nachrichten
___ 2. Reiseberichte (. . . *reports*)
___ 3. Freizeitmagazin (. . . *feature*)
___ 4. Gesundheitsmagazin
___ 5. Sportmagazin
___ 6. Wirtschaftsmagazin (*economic* . . .)
___ 7. politische Diskussionen
___ 8. Sprachunterricht
___ 9. Ballett
___ 10. Konzerte
___ 11. Theaterstücke
___ 12. Opern
___ 13. Liebesfilme (*love* . . .)
___ 14. Kriminalfilme
___ 15. Horrorfilme
___ 16. Science Fiction Film
___ 17. Geschichtsfilme (*historical* . . .)
___ 18. Western
___ 19. Zeichentrickfilme (*cartoons*)
___ 20. Fernsehspiele

G. Schriftliche Übung. Compare the German and American / Canadian TV systems by writing brief statements of two to four sentences for each of the points below. Use the reading text and the TV program as references.

1. Popularität
2. Anzahl *(number)* der Programme
3. Art *(type)* der Programme
4. Werbung und Fernsehgebühren
5. Qualität
6. Rolle von Radio und Fernsehen im politischen Leben

Übrigens

1. News reports are quite frequent throughout the day. The ARD calls them **Tagesschau**, and the ZDF calls them **Heute**. They are generally much shorter and have much less on-the-spot reporting than in the United States.

2. During the economic boom of the FRG, especially in the 1960s after the Berlin Wall had halted the flow of people from the East, German industry needed additional workers. These "guest workers" (**Gastarbeiter**) came from countries like Spain, Italy, Yugoslavia, and Turkey. With automation and economic slowdown, the need for such workers has diminished. But there are still over four million foreign workers in Germany. Although they have equal rights before the law, many have not been integrated into society because of language and cultural differences.

You might want to explain the play on words in the names of these cabarets: **Lach- und Schießgesellschaft** (a company that provokes laughter through sharpshooting with words) derived from **Wach- und Schließ- gesellschaft** (a security firm); **Floh de Cologne** (*literally: a flea from Cologne*) derived from **Eau de Cologne; Mausefalle** (*a mouse trap*); **Stachelschweine** (*porcupines*), **Distel** (*thistle*), **Sündikat** (**Sünde** = *sin*) derived from **Syndikat**.

3. The term cabaret **(Kabarett)** describes both a form of theatrical entertainment and the dance halls and taverns in which the genre emerged at the turn of the century. Performers satirized contemporary culture and politics through skits, pantomimes, poems, and songs (chansons). This type of variety show flourished during the Weimar Republic but was banned during the last years of the Nazi regime because of the political satire. Since the end of World War II cabaret has reemerged as a popular form of entertainment. Some of Germany's most frequented cabarets are the *Lach- und Schießgesellschaft* in Munich, the *Floh de Cologne* in Cologne, the *Mausefalle* in Hamburg, and in Berlin the *Stachelschweine*, the *Distel*, and the *Sündikat*. The *Kabarett der Komiker* was one of Berlin's most popular cabarets during the 1920s.

Sa./So., 1. und 2. Dezember, 15 Uhr, Philharmonie
WEIHNACHTSKONZERTE der weltberühmten
WIENER SÄNGERKNABEN
Mit kleiner Spieloper, Motetten und Weihnachtsliedern

1. bis 5. Dezember, jew. 20 Uhr, URANIA-THEATER
Münchner Lach- und Schiessgesellschaft
Das neue Programm: "Altes oder nichts"
Mit Renate Küster, Rainer Basedow, Jochen Busse, Henning Venske

SPRECHSITUATIONEN

There are times when you want or need to express satisfaction or dissatisfaction with something. You may even be pushed to the point of anger. Here are phrases to deal with such situations.

Expressing Satisfaction

Optional vocabulary: einmalig *unique;* herrlich *beautiful;* ganz große Klasse, Spitze *super*

Das ist gut (prima, toll, wunderbar, phantastisch, super, ausgezeichnet).
Das ist praktisch (bequem, interessant, spannend, nicht schlecht).
Das ist genau das Richtige *(exactly the right thing).*
Das gefällt mir (gut).
Das schmeckt (gut).
Das finde ich . . .

Expressing Dissatisfaction

Optional vocabulary: schrecklich or scheußlich *awful;* ekelhaft *disgusting;* geschmacklos or kitschig *tacky*

Das ist schlecht (furchtbar, unpraktisch, unbequem, langweilig).
Das finde ich (nicht) . . .
Das ist zu *(too)* . . .
Das ist nicht . . . genug.
Das gefällt mir nicht.
Das schmeckt mir nicht.
Das paßt mir nicht. *(That doesn't fit / suit me.)*

Expressing Anger

Optional vocabulary: Jetzt langt's aber! *That's enough now!* Das stinkt mir! *That stinks!* Verdammt noch mal! *Darn it!* So ein Blödsinn! *Such stupidity!* Jetzt schlägt's dreizehn! *That's it! That goes too far!*

Das ist doch die Höhe!	*That's the limit.*
Das ist doch unglaublich!	*That's hard to believe.*
Das ist doch ärgerlich!	*That's annoying.*
Das ärgert mich wirklich.	*That really makes me mad.*
Jetzt habe ich aber genug.	*That's enough. I've had it.*
Ich habe die Nase voll.	*I'm fed up (with it).*
Das hängt mir zum Hals heraus.	*I'm fed up (with it).*
(So eine) Unverschämtheit!	*Such impertinence.*

A. Weißt du . . . Working with a classmate, describe three situations that caused you satisfaction, dissatisfaction, or anger. Describe very briefly the cause, and then state your reaction.

BEISPIEL.   Weißt du, das Autohaus hat mein Auto schon dreimal repariert. Ich habe schon über 400 Dollar dafür bezahlt, und es läuft immer noch nicht richtig. Jetzt habe ich aber die Nase voll!

B. Kurzgespräche

1. You are in a department store. As the clerk approaches you, tell him / her you need a new raincoat. He / she shows you one that he / she says is very nice. You try it on but soon realize that it is too big and the color is not practical. The next one also doesn't fit, and it's too expensive. The third one is just right: it fits, you like it, it's practical and comfortable, and the price is right. You take it.

2. You are waiting in line to get some tickets for a rock concert, and someone cuts in front of you. You express your irritation to your friend. Then a whole group of people joins the "intruder." You and your friend tell them that you're annoyed. When they get the last available tickets, you really blow your top. You try to convince the ticket clerk that those should be your tickets, but it's too late.

C. Was, wo and wann? Telephone the cinema information, ask what films are showing in which theaters, and when the shows begin. Talk to your friend(s) and decide what you want to see and why.

11 Eigenschaften

Junges Paar *(couple)* im Park

▌LERNZIELE

Gespräche and **Wortschatz**. This chapter deals with love and with character traits.

Struktur. You will learn about . . .

- the simple past.
- the conjunctions **als**, **wann**, **wenn**.
- the past perfect.

Einblicke. The fairy tale *King Thrushbeard (König Drosselbart)*.

Sprechsituationen

- Expressing admiration
- Telling a story
- Encouraging a speaker

◆◆◆◆◆ # ANZEIGEN

Heiratswünsche

♀

♂

Gesucht wird[1]: charmanter, unternehmungslustiger, zärtlicher ADAM. Belohnung: hübsche, temperamentvolle EVA, Mitte 20, mag Antiquitäten, alte Häuser, schnelle Wagen, Tiere, Kinder.

Es gibt, was ich suche. Aber wie finden? Akademikerin, Ende 20 / 153[2], schlank, musikalisch, sucht sympathischen, gebildeten Mann mit Humor.

Welcher Mann mit Herz, bis 45 Jahr jung, mag reisen, tanzen, schwimmen, Ski laufen und mich? Attraktiv, dunkelhaarig, unternehmungslustig und schick. Geschieden, Anfang 30, zwei nette Jungen.

Warum sind Männer immer dann so zurückhaltend, wenn eine Frau selbständig, gutaussehend und selbstbewußt ist? Gehören Sie auch zu diesen Männern? Sind Sie kinderlieb, bis 55 Jahre alt und lieben das Leben, dann schreiben Sie mir doch, mit Photo!

Millionär bin ich nicht! Will mir ja auch kein Glück kaufen, sondern verdienen. Ich, 28 / 170[2], suche keine Modepuppe oder Disco-Queen, sondern ein nettes, natürliches Mädchen, das auch hübsch sein darf.

Tanzen, Segeln, und Reisen sind meine drei großen Leidenschaften. Welche sympathische Frau mit Phantasie will mitmachen? Ich bin Journalist (Wassermann), optimistisch und unkonventionell.

Liebe gemeinsam erleben . . . zu Hause, im Konzert, beim Tanzen, in den Bergen, auf dem Tennis- oder Golfplatz, im und auf dem Wasser, wo auch immer, wünsche ich mir eine junge, schlanke, beruflich engagierte Vierzigerin mit viel Charme und Esprit, die auch gern liest und schreibt.

Einsamer Waschlappen, Ende 30, sucht wohlriechende Seife für gemeinsames Schaumbad. Hobbys: Kinder, Tiere, ein gemütliches Zuhause und gute Küche.

Übrigens

◆◆◆◆◆◆◆◆◆◆◆◆◆◆◆◆◆◆◆◆◆◆◆◆◆◆◆◆◆

1. Advertising for marriage partners is generally accepted and not at all unusual in the German-speaking countries. Many newspapers and magazines carry such ads.

2. In Europe the metric system is standard. Is someone who has a height of 180 cm short or tall? Figure it out yourself. Since 1 inch = 2.54 cm, divide the height by 2.54 to get the number of inches. How tall are you in metric terms? Multiply your height in inches by 2.54.

Fragen: 1. Wie soll der Partner / die Partnerin sein? (Make a list of the qualities wanted.) 2. Wie sehen die Leute sich? (Make a list of what these people stress about themselves.) 3. Was sagen sie nicht? 4. Finden Sie Beispiele mit Adjektiv-endungen, mit und ohne Artikel! (Group them as preceded and unpreceded adjectives.)

Wanted: *charming, enterprising, affectionate ADAM. Reward: pretty, dynamic EVA, mid 20s, likes antiques, old houses, fast cars, animals, (and) children.*

What I'm looking for *exists. But how to find it? Woman with university degree, late 20s / 1 meter 53 (5 feet), slim, musical, artistic, is looking for congenial, educated man with a sense of humor.*

Which man *with feelings, up to 45 years young, likes traveling, dancing, swimming, skiing and (likes) me? Attractive, dark-haired enterprising and chic. Divorced, early 30s, two nice boys.*

Why are men *always so reticent when a woman is independent, good-looking and self-confident? Are you one of them? If you like children, are you up to 55 years old and love life, then write me, with a picture enclosed.*

I'm not *a millionaire. I don't want to buy my happiness but earn it. I, 28, 1 meter 70 (5 feet 7), am not looking for a fashion doll or disco queen, but (rather) a nice, natural girl, who may also be pretty*

Dancing, *sailing, and traveling are my three great passions. What congenial woman with imagination wants to join me? I'm a journalist (Aquarius), optimistic and unconventional.*

To experience *love together . . . at home, in a concert, while dancing, in the mountains, on the tennis court or golf course, in or on the water, wherever, I wish for a young, slender, professionally active woman in her 40s with a lot of charm and esprit, who also likes to read and write.*

Lonely washcloth *(fig., wimp), late 30s, is looking for a fragrant soap to share a bubble bath with. Hobbies: children, animals, a cozy home and fine cuisine.*

WORTSCHATZ 1

DIE LIEBE *love*

der Partner, -	*partner*	suchen	*to look for*
Wunsch, ⁻e	*wish*	sich wünschen	*to wish*
die Ehe, -n	*marriage*	sich verlieben (in)	*to fall in love (with)*
Hochzeit, -en	*wedding*	sich verloben (mit)	*to get engaged (to)*
Scheidung, -en	*divorce*	heiraten	*to marry, get married (to)*
ledig	*single*		
geschieden	*divorced*		
verliebt (in)	*in love (with)*		
verlobt (mit)	*engaged (to)*		
(un)verheiratet	*(un)married*		

Optional vocabulary: abstoßend *repulsive;* **schrecklich** *awful;* **dumm, einfach** *plain;* **lahm** *lame, lacking enthusiasm;* **ruhig** *quiet;* **schüchtern** *shy;* **verständnislos** *lacking empathy*

DIE EIGENSCHAFT, -EN *attribute*

attraktiv	*attractive*	(un)freundlich	*(un)friendly*
charmant	*charming*	(un)gebildet	*(un)educated*
fleißig / faul	*industrious / lazy*	(un)musikalisch	*(un)musical*

hübsch / häßlich	*pretty / ugly*	(un)sportlich	*(un)athletic*
intelligent	*intelligent*	(un)sympathisch	*(un)congenial,*
jung	*young*		*(un)likable*
nett	*nice*	(un)talentiert	*(un)talented*
reich / arm	*rich / poor*		
schick	*chic, neat*		
schlank	*slim*		
temperamentvoll	*dynamic*		
unternehmungs-	*enterprising*		
lustig			
verständnisvoll	*understanding*		

WEITERES

auf diese Weise	*this way*
beid-	*both*
bestimmt	*surely, for sure; certain(ly)*
Du hast recht / unrecht.	*You're right / wrong.*
jemand	*someone, somebody*
einladen (lädt ein), lud ein, eingeladen	*to invite*
setzen[1]	*to put, place*
träumen (von)	*to dream (of)*
vergessen (vergißt), vergessen	*to forget*
verlieren, verloren	*to lose*
versuchen	*to try*

1 Compare **Ich setze das Paket auf den Stuhl.** AND **Ich setze mich auf den Stuhl.** Also remember that **sich setzen** means *to sit down* and **sitzen** means *to be sitting.* Don't confuse **setzen** with **sitzen.**

PASSIVES VOKABULAR

beruflich engagiert *professionally active* **einsam** *lonely* **gutaussehend** *good-looking* **kinderlieb** *loves children* **optimistisch** **selbständig** *independent* **selbstbewußt** *self-confident* **unkonventionell** **wohlriechend** *fragrant* **zärtlich** *affectionate* **zurückhaltend** *reticent* **gute Küche** *fine cuisine* **Mitte . . .** *mid . . .* **mit Charme** **mit Esprit** **mit Herz** *with feelings* **mit Humor** *with a sense of humor* **mit Phantasie** *with imagination* **erleben** *to experience* **die Anzeige, -n** *ad* **die Leidenschaft** *passion* **das Tier, -e** *animal* **der Waschlappen** *washcloth (fig. wimp)*

ZUM THEMA

A. Was ist das Adjektiv dazu?
der Charme, Freund, Optimismus, Reichtum, Sport, Verstand
das Glück, Selbstbewußtsein, Temperament, Unternehmen
die Attraktion, Bildung, Gemütlichkeit, Intelligenz, Liebe für Kinder, Natur, Musik, Scheidung, Selbständigkeit, Sympathie
heiraten, sich verlieben, sich verloben

Optional vocabulary:
der Bekannte (ein Be-
kannter) *acquaintance;*
die Verlobung, -en *en-
gagement;* die Flit-
terwochen *(pl.),* honey-
moon; s. scheiden lassen
to get divorced; s. tren-
nen *to separate;* geduldig
patient; geizig *stingy.*

B. Partnersuche. Machen Sie mit, und beantworten Sie die Fragen!

1. **Persönliche Angaben** *(information)*

   Name: _____

   Adresse: _____

   _____

   Telefon: _____

   Geburtstag: _____ Größe: _____ Haarfarbe: _____

   Familienstand: ledig ☐   getrennt ☐   geschieden ☐   verwitwet ☐
   (separated) *(widowed)*

   Eigene Kinder: Ja ☐   Nein ☐

   Wenn ja, wie viele leben in Ihrem Haushalt? _____

   Nationalität: ____ _____

   Muttersprache: _____

   Fremdsprachen: _____

   Beruf: _____

   Unterschrift *(signature):* _____

2. **Das macht mir besonders Spaß.**

   ☐ Autos   ☐ Film und Theater   ☐ Photographie
   ☐ Basteln *(crafts)* ☐ Handarbeit *(needlework)*   ☐ Politik
   ☐ Blumen   ☐ Kochen, Essen   ☐ Reisen
   ☐ Computer   ☐ Literatur   ☐ Sport
   ☐ Diskutieren   ☐ Musik, Kunst   ☐ Tiere

   Weiteres _____

3. **So bin ich.**

ja	nein	manchmal	nie	
☐	☐	☐	☐	Sprechen Sie gern über Probleme?
☐	☐	☐	☐	Können Sie über sich lachen?
☐	☐	☐	☐	Können Sie anderen lange zuhören?
☐	☐	☐	☐	Ärgern Sie sich manchmal?
☐	☐	☐	☐	Machen Sie viele Pläne für Ihre Zukunft *(future)?*
☐	☐	☐	☐	Finden Sie, daß Sex etwas Wichtiges ist?
☐	☐	☐	☐	Sind Sie spontan und flexibel?

4. **Partnerwünsche**

   Alter *(age):*   von _____ bis _____ Jahre
   Größe *(height):* von _____ bis _____ cm

Haar: ☐ schwarz   ☐ blond   ☐ braun   ☐ grau
              ☐ rötlich   ☐ unwichtig

Familienstand: ☐ ledig   ☐ geschieden   ☐ verwitwet
              ☐ getrennt ☐ unwichtig

5. **Eigenschaften des Partners / der Partnerin.**

☐ zärtlich   ☐ ruhig   ☐ temperamentvoll
☐ häuslich   ☐ tolerant   ☐ verständnisvoll
☐ treu   ☐ sportlich   ☐ unternehmungslustig
☐ natürlich   ☐ musikalisch   ☐ kinderlieb
☐ reich   ☐ lustig   ☐ tierlieb
☐ ehrlich *(honest)*   ☐ sparsam *(thrifty)* ☐ religiös

Es ist ganz einfach . . .

. . . mit einer Anzeige in der
FRANKFURTER RUNDSCHAU

C. Fragen
1. Was machen Sie und Ihre Freunde in der Freizeit? Worüber sprechen Sie?
2. Was für Eigenschaften finden Sie bei Freunden wichtig? Wie dürfen sie nicht sein?
3. Waren Sie schon einmal in einen Schauspieler / eine Schauspielerin verliebt? In wen?
4. Was halten Sie vom Zusammenleben mit einem Freund / einer Freundin vor dem Heiraten?
5. Was halten Sie vom Heiraten? Wie alt sollen Leute wenigstens *(at least)* sein, wenn sie heiraten? Finden Sie eine lange Verlobung wichtig? Warum? Warum nicht?

D. Gesucht wird. Schreiben Sie Ihre eigene *(own)* Anzeige!

E. Charakterisierung *(characterization)*. Schreiben Sie 8 bis 10 Sätze!
1. So bin ich.
2. Ein Freund / eine Freundin von mir *(or anybody else you would like to write about)*.

F. Aussprache. See also III. 1, 4, and 5 in the pronunciation section of the Workbook.
1. [f]   **f**ür, **f**ast, **f**rei, **f**rüh, **f**ertig, **f**it, **f**ühlen, **f**ehlen, **f**reundlich, **F**ilm, **F**ernsehen, öf**f**nen, Brie**f**, el**f**, au**f**
2. [f]   **v**erliebt, **v**erlobt, **v**erheiratet, **v**erständnisvoll, **v**ergessen, **v**erlieren, **v**ersuchen, **v**erschieden, **v**orbei, **v**ielleicht, **ph**antastisch, **ph**otographieren, Geogra**ph**ie, wie**v**iel

3. [v] **Vanille, Vision, Video, Klavier, reservieren, Silvester, Pullover, Uni**versität
4. [v] **wer, wen, wem, wessen, warum, werden, wünschen, Waldweg,** schwimmen, schwarz, schwer, Schwester, zwischen
5. Wortpaare

   a. *wine* / Wein
   b. *when* / wenn
   c. *oven* / Ofen
   d. *veal* / viel
   e. Vetter / Wetter
   f. vier / wir

STRUKTUR

I. The Simple Past (Imperfect, Narrative Past)

The past tense is often referred to as the SIMPLE PAST because it is a single verb form in contrast to the perfect tenses (also called "compound past tenses"), which consist of two parts, an auxiliary and a past participle

We spoke German.   Wir **sprachen** Deutsch.

In spoken German the present perfect is the preferred tense, especially in Southern Germany, Austria, and Switzerland. Only the simple past of **haben, sein,** and the modals are common everywhere.

The simple past is used primarily in continuous narratives such as novels, short stories, newspaper reports, and letters relating a sequence of events. Therefore, it is often also called the "narrative past."

Again, one German verb form corresponds to several in English.

Sie **sprachen** Deutsch.
$\begin{cases} \textit{They spoke German.} \\ \textit{They were speaking German.} \\ \textit{They did speak German.} \\ \textit{They used to speak German.} \end{cases}$

1. t-Verbs (*weak verbs*)

   t-Verbs can be compared to such regular English verbs as *love* / *loved* and *work* / *worked,* which form the past tense by adding *-d* or *-ed* to the stem. To form the simple past of t-verbs, add **-te, -test, -te, -ten, -tet, -ten** to the STEM of the verb.

ich lernte	wir lernten
du lerntest	ihr lerntet
er lernte	sie lernten

   Verbs that follow this pattern include: fragen, freuen, hören, interessieren, lachen, machen, sagen, sammeln, setzen, spielen, suchen, träumen, wandern, weinen, wohnen, wünschen.

a. Verbs with stems ending in **-d, -t** or certain consonant combinations add an **-e-** before the simple past ending.

ich arbeitete	wir arbeiteten
du arbeitetest	ihr arbeitetet
er arbeitete	sie arbeiteten

Verbs that follow this pattern include: antworten, baden, bedeuten, heiraten, kostcn, landen, mieten, öffnen, übernachten, warten.

b. Irregular t-verbs (sometimes called *mixed verbs*) usually have a stem change. Compare the English *bring / brought* and the German **bringen / brachte.**

ich br**ach**te	wir br**ach**ten
du br**ach**test	ihr br**ach**tet
er br**ach**te	sie br**ach**ten

Here is a list of the PRINCIPAL PARTS of all the irregular t-verbs that you have used up to now. Irregular present-tense forms are noted. You already know all the forms of these verbs except their simple past. Verbs with prefixes have the same forms as the corresponding simple verbs (**brachte mit**). If you know the principal parts of a verb, you can derive all the verb forms you need!

INFINITIVE	PRESENT	SIMPLE PAST	PAST PARTICIPLE
bringen		**brachte**	gebracht
denken		**dachte**	gedacht
haben	hat	**hatte**	gehabt
kennen		**kannte**	gekannt
wissen	weiß	**wußte**	gewußt

Modals also belong to this group. (The past participles of these verbs are rarely used.)

dürfen	darf	**durfte**	(gedurft)
können	kann	**konnte**	(gekonnt)
müssen	muß	**mußte**	(gemußt)
sollen	soll	**sollte**	(gesollt)
wollen	will	**wollte**	(gewollt)

NOTE: The simple past of irregular t-verbs has the same stem change as the past participle.

2. n-Verbs *(strong verbs)*

n-Verbs correspond to such English verbs as *write / wrote* and *speak / spoke*. They usually have a stem change in the simple past which is difficult to predict and must therefore be memorized. (Overall they fall into a number of groups with the same changes. For a listing by group, see p. 428 in the Appendix.)

To form the simple past, add **-, -st, -, -en, -t, -en** to the (IRREGULAR) STEM of the verb.

ich sprach	wir sprach**en**
du sprach**st**	ihr sprach**t**
er sprach	sie sprach**en**

Below is a list of the PRINCIPAL PARTS of n-verbs that you have used up to now. You already know all the forms except the simple past. Irregular present-tense forms and the auxiliary **sein** are specially noted.

INFINITIVE	PRESENT	SIMPLE PAST	PAST PARTICIPLE
an·fangen	fängt an	**fing an**	angefangen
an·ziehen		**zog an**	angezogen
beginnen		**begann**	begonnen
bleiben		**blieb**	ist geblieben
ein·laden	lädt ein	**lud ein**	eingeladen
empfehlen	empfiehlt	**empfahl**	empfohlen
essen	ißt	**aß**	gegessen
fahren	fährt	**fuhr**	ist gefahren
fallen	fällt	**fiel**	ist gefallen
finden		**fand**	gefunden
fliegen		**flog**	ist geflogen
geben	gibt	**gab**	gegeben
gefallen	gefällt	**gefiel**	gefallen
gehen		**ging**	ist gegangen
halten	hält	**hielt**	gehalten
heißen		**hieß**	geheißen
helfen	hilft	**half**	geholfen
kommen		**kam**	ist gekommen
lassen	läßt	**ließ**	gelassen
laufen	läuft	**lief**	ist gelaufen
lesen	liest	**las**	gelesen
liegen		**lag**	gelegen
nehmen	nimmt	**nahm**	genommen
rufen		**rief**	gerufen
schlafen	schläft	**schlief**	geschlafen
schreiben		**schrieb**	geschrieben
schwimmen		**schwamm**	ist geschwommen
sehen	sieht	**sah**	gesehen
sein	ist	**war**	ist gewesen
singen		**sang**	gesungen
sitzen		**saß**	gesessen
sprechen	spricht	**sprach**	gesprochen
stehen		**stand**	gestanden
steigen		**stieg**	ist gestiegen
tragen	trägt	**trug**	getragen
trinken		**trank**	getrunken

tun	tut	**tat**	getan
vergessen	vergißt	**vergaß**	vergessen
verlieren	verliert	**verlor**	verloren
waschen	wäscht	**wusch**	gewaschen
werden	wird	**wurde**	ist geworden

3. Sentences in the simple past follow familiar word-order patterns.

Der Zug **kam** um acht.
Der Zug **kam** um acht **an**.
Der Zug **sollte** um acht **ankommen**.
       V1   V2

Er wußte, daß der Zug um acht **kam**.
Er wußte, daß der Zug um acht **ankam**.
Er wußte, daß der Zug um acht **ankommen sollte**.
                              V2   V1

ÜBUNGEN

A: Only practice those verbs for which students have mastered the forms (items 1 and 2: t-verbs; item 3: modals and irregular t-verbs; item 4: n-verbs).

A. Geben Sie das Imperfekt (*simple past*)!

BEISPIEL: feiern   **feierte**

1. fragen, fehlen, erzählen, klatschen, lachen, legen, bummeln, wechseln, photographieren, schicken, putzen, sich kämmen, sich rasieren, sich setzen, versuchen
2. arbeiten, baden, bedeuten, kosten, antworten, übernachten, öffnen
3. haben, müssen, denken, wissen, können, kennen
4. geben, nehmen, essen, sehen, lesen, finden, singen, sitzen, liegen, kommen, tun, sein, schreiben, heißen, einsteigen, schlafen, fallen, lassen, fahren, tragen, waschen, werden, einladen

B: As in A, we suggest that each day you do only those sentences that the students can handle and add the others later.

B. Ersetzen Sie die Verben!

BEISPIEL: Sie schickte das Paket. (mitbringen)
           Sie brachte das Paket mit.

1. Sie schickten ein Taxi. (suchen, bestellen, mieten, warten auf)
2. Das hatte ich nicht. (wissen, kennen, denken, mitbringen)
3. Wann solltet ihr zurückkommen? (müssen, wollen, dürfen, können)
4. Wir fanden es dort. (sehen, lassen, verlieren, vergessen)
5. Ich dankte seiner Mutter. (antworten, zuhören, helfen, schreiben)
6. Du empfahlst den Sauerbraten. (nehmen, wollen, bringen)

C. Wiederholen Sie die Texte im Imperfekt!
1. **Weißt du noch?** A brother and sister reminisce. Repeat in the simple past.

BEISPIEL: Großvater erzählt stundenlang von seinen jungen Jahren.
           Großvater erzählte stundenlang von seinen jungen Jahren.

a. Ich setze mich aufs Sofa und höre ihm zu.   **b.** Seine Geschichten interessieren mich.   **c.** Vater arbeitet im Garten.   **d.** Du telefonierst oder besuchst die Nachbarn.   **e.** Karin und Jörg spielen stundenlang Karten.   **f.** Mutter kauft ein oder bezahlt Rechnungen.   **g.** Großmutter legt sich nachmittags ein Stündchen hin und freut sich danach auf ihre Tasse Kaffee.   **h.** Das wiederholt sich oft am Wochenende. Richtig?

2. **Haben Sie das nicht gewußt?** Two neighbors gossip about Lothar and Ute.

   BEISPIEL: Hat Ute ihren Mann schon lange gekannt?
   Kannte Ute ihren Mann schon lange?

   a. Wie hat sie ihn kennengelernt?   **b.** Der Postbote *(mailman)* hat ihr einen Brief von einem jungen Herrn gebracht.   **c.** Hast du nichts von ihrer Anzeige gewußt?   **d.** Sie hat Lothar durch die Zeitung kennengelernt.   **e.** Gestern haben sie Hochzeit gehabt.   **f.** Sie hat Glück gehabt.   **g.** Das habe ich mir auch gedacht.

3. **Schade!** Bärbel talks to her friend about plans that didn't materialize.

   BEISPIEL: Was willst du denn machen?   **Was wolltest du denn machen?**

   a. Ich will mit Karl-Heinz ins Kino gehen, aber ich kann nicht.   **b.** Warum, darfst du nicht?   **c.** Doch, aber meine Kopfschmerzen wollen einfach nicht weggehen.   **d.** Mußt du im Bett bleiben?   **e.** Nein, aber ich darf nicht schon wieder krank werden.   **f.** Leider kann ich nicht mit Karl-Heinz sprechen.   **g.** Aber seine Mutter will es ihm sagen.   **h.** Er soll mich anrufen.

4. **Wo wart ihr?** Caroline tells about a short trip to Switzerland.

   BEISPIEL: Wir sind eine Woche in Saas-Fee gewesen.
   Wir waren eine Woche in Saas-Fee.

   Von unserem Zimmer haben wir einen Blick auf *(view of)* die Alpen gehabt. Die Pension hat natürlich „Alpenblick" geheißen. Morgens haben wir lange geschlafen, dann haben wir gemütlich Frühstück gegessen. Später bin ich mit dem Sessellift auf die Berge gefahren und bin den ganzen Nachmittag Ski laufen gegangen. Wolfgang ist unten geblieben, hat Bücher gelesen und Briefe geschrieben.

D. Schriftliche Übung. Write eight to ten sentences on one of the topics below. Write in the simple past without using any verb more than once.
   1. **Als ich sechzehn war . . .** Tell where you went to school, and how and why you liked or didn't like it. You may also pick any other age.
   2. **Eine interessante Party.** Tell where the party was, who was there, what was so special about it, etc.
   3. **Eine schöne Reise.** Tell where you went, who you traveled with, what you saw, etc.

II. The Conjunctions als, wann, wenn

Care must be taken to distinguish between **als, wann,** and **wenn,** all of which correspond to the English *when.* **Als** refers to a SINGLE EVENT IN THE PAST *(When*

I came home at 6 p.m., he wasn't back yet). **Wann** introduces direct or indirect questions REFERRING TO TIME *(I wonder when he'll return).* **Wenn** covers all other situations, including repeated events in the past *(When he came, he always brought flowers. We'll call you, when he comes in).*

at the time when	→	**als**
when — *at what time*	→	**wann**
whenever, if	→	**wenn**

Als ich nach Hause kam, war er noch nicht zurück.
When I came home (referring to a particular event in the past) . . .

Ich frage mich, **wann** er nach Hause kommt.
. . . when (at what time) he's going to come home.

Wenn er kam, brachte er immer Blumen.
When(ever) he came (referring to repeated events in the past) . . .

Wenn es nicht regnet, gehen wir spazieren.
If it doesn't rain (stating a condition) . . .

ÜBUNGEN

E. Was fehlt: als, wann oder wenn?
1. _____ ihr kommt, zeigen wir euch die Bilder von unserer Reise.
2. Können Sie mir sagen, _____ der Zug aus Köln ankommt?
3. _____ wir letzte Woche im Theater waren, sahen wir Stephan und Sonja.
4. Sie freute sich immer sehr, _____ wir sie besuchten.
5. Sie bekommen diese Möbel, _____ sie heiraten. Wer weiß, _____ sie heiraten!
6. _____ ich ein Kind war, habe ich nur Deutsch gesprochen.

F. Verbinden Sie *(link)* **die Sätze mit als, wann oder wenn!** If "when" stands at the beginning, make the first sentence the dependent clause. Watch the position of the verb.

BEISPIEL: Sie riefen an. Ich duschte mich. *(when)*
     Sie riefen an, als ich mich duschte.
     (when) Ich duschte mich. Sie riefen an.
     Als ich mich duschte, riefen sie an.

1. Wir sahen Frau Loth heute früh. Wir gingen einkaufen. *(when)*
2. *(when)* Sie spricht von Liebe. Er hört nicht zu.
3. Sie möchte (es) wissen. Die Weihnachtsferien fangen an. *(when)*
4. *(when)* Ich stand gestern auf. Es regnete.
5. *(when)* Das Wetter war schön. Die Kinder spielten immer im Park.
6. Er hat mir nicht geschrieben. Er kommt. *(when)*

III. The Past Perfect

Students often find it difficult to remember to use the past perfect since in English this is often replaced by the simple past. *After we saw the movie we had a hamburger.* It might be helpful to study newspaper or magazine articles or literary texts to show proper usage.

1. Like the present perfect, the PAST PERFECT in both English and German is a compound form consisting of an auxiliary and a past participle. However, the AUXILIARY IS IN THE SIMPLE PAST.

Ich **hatte** das gut **gelernt.**　　　　*I had learned that well.*
Er **war** um zehn Uhr nach Hause　　*He had come home at ten o'clock.*
gekommen.

ich	**hatte**	... gelernt	**war**	... gekommen
du	**hattest**	... gelernt	**warst**	... gekommen
er	**hatte**	... gelernt	**war**	... gekommen
wir	**hatten**	... gelernt	**waren**	... gekommen
ihr	**hattet**	... gelernt	**wart**	... gekommen
sie	**hatten**	... gelernt	**waren**	... gekommen

Reviewing the past perfect presents an excellent opportunity to review the use of **haben** and **sein** as auxiliaries of the perfect tenses.

2. The past perfect is used to refer to events *preceding* other events in the past.

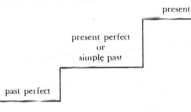

Er hat mich gestern angerufen.　　*He called me yesterday.*
Ich **hatte** ihm gerade **geschrieben**.　*I had just written to him.*

Wir kamen zu spät am Bahnhof an.　*We arrived too late at the station.*
Der Zug **war** schon **abgefahren**.　　*The train had already left.*

The conjunction **nachdem** *(after)* is usually followed by the past perfect in the subordinate clause, whereas the main clause is in the present perfect or simple past.

Nachdem er mich **angerufen hatte**, schickte ich den Brief nicht mehr ab.
Nachdem der Zug **abgefahren war**, ging ich ins Bahnhofsrestaurant.

ÜBUNGEN

G. Ersetzen Sie das Subjekt!

BEISPIEL:　Sie hatten uns besucht. (du)
　　　　　Du hattest uns besucht.

1. Du hattest den Schlüssel gesucht. (ihr, Sie, sie / *sg.*)
2. Sie hatten das nicht gewußt. (wir, ihr, sie / *sg.*)
3. Ich war nach Dresden gereist. (sie / *pl.*, du, wir)
4. Sie waren auch in der Dresdener Oper gewesen. (er, du, ich)

H. Auf englisch, bitte! Last night Stephan and Sonja looked at the video *Männer.* Now they are talking about when the movie first appeared.

1. Ich hatte den Film schon einmal gesehen.   **2.** Er war eine Sensation gewesen.   **3.** Man hatte den Film zur gleichen Zeit in sieben Kinos gezeigt.   **4.** Ich hatte Glück gehabt.   **5.** Durch Walter hatte ich noch Karten für die Premiere bekommen.   **6.** Die Regisseurin Doris Dörrie war sogar da gewesen.   **7.** Ich hatte schon lange nicht mehr so gelacht.

I. Am Flughafen. Auf deutsch, bitte!
1. We got to the airport after the plane had landed.   **2.** When I arrived, they had already picked up (**holen**) their luggage.   **3.** After I had found them, we drove home.   **4.** My mother had been looking forward to this day.   **5.** When she had shown them the house, we sat down in the living room and talked about the family.

J.1: You could have students add to this list by telling about other events during the day.

J. Und dann?
1. **Zu Hause.** Mrs. Schneider recounts a typical day at home. Find out what happened next by asking **Und dann?** Note how she'll switch from the present perfect to the past perfect.

    BEISPIEL: Ich bin aufgestanden.—Und dann?
    Nachdem ich aufgestanden war, habe ich mir die Zähne geputzt.

    a. Ich habe mir die Zähne geputzt.
    b. Ich habe mich angezogen.
    c. Ich habe Frühstück gemacht.
    d. Alle haben sich an den Tisch gesetzt.
    e. Das Telefon hat geklingelt (*rang*).
    f. Ich bin aufgestanden.
    g. Helmut hat die Zeitung gelesen.
    h. Er ist zur Arbeit gegangen.
    i. Ich habe die Betten gemacht.

Schick sein, reich sein, cool sein – und sonst nichts?

J.2: This could be done in small groups or individually. Tell students not to use any verbs from the previous exercise.

2. **Was haben Sie am Wochenende gemacht?** Write five sentences in the simple past, then follow the pattern in exercise 1 (**Nachdem ich . . .**).

ZUSAMMENFASSUNG

K. Wiederholen Sie die Sätze im Imperfekt!
1. Lothar denkt an Sabine. Er will ein paar Wochen segeln gehen. Aber sie hat keine Lust dazu. Er spricht mit Holger. Die beiden setzen eine Anzeige in die Zeitung. Ute liest die Anzeige und antwortet darauf. Durch die Anzeige finden sie sich. Jetzt hat Holger für Sabine keine Zeit mehr. Er träumt nur noch von Ute. Am 24. Mai heiraten die beiden. Sie laden Holger zur Hochzeit ein. Die Trauung (*ceremony*) ist in der lutherischen Kirche. Ute heißt vorher (*before*) Kaiser. Jetzt wird sie Ute Müller.

2. Weil es im Fernsehen nichts Besonderes gibt, gehen Sonja und Stephan ins Theater. Sie haben keine Lust, einen Krimi zu sehen. Aber *Mutter Courage* gefällt ihnen gut. Sonja kennt das Stück schon, aber sie sieht es gern noch einmal. Während der Pause lädt Stephan sie zu einer Cola ein. Leider haben sie nur ein paar Minuten, weil die Pause kurz ist.

Verliebt...
...Verlobt...
...Verheiratet

Lothar Müller
Ute Müller
ge b. Kaiser

Vahrenwalder Str. 93
Hannover 1

Kirchliche Trauung am 24. Mai 1991, 15⁰⁰ Uhr in der Ev.-luth.
Vahrenwalder Kirche

L. 1. Arthur hatte an die Hochzeit seiner Tochter gedacht.
2. Als wir sie im Dezember sahen, war sie in einen charmanten, reichen Mann verliebt.
3. Sie sollten im April heiraten. 4. Ich hatte schon ein schönes Geschenk gekauft.
5. Vor zwei Wochen verlobte sie sich mit einem anderen Mann.
6. Er ist ein armer Student an ihrer Universität. 7. Sie sagten nicht, wann sie heiraten wollten. 8. Am Wochenende rief sie ihre Eltern an. 9. Sie und der Student hatten gerade geheiratet.
10. Sie hatten ihre Eltern nicht zur Hochzeit eingeladen. 11. Arthur ärgert sich, wenn er daran denkt.

L. Auf deutsch, bitte! Use the simple past unless another tense is clearly required.
1. Arthur had been thinking of his daughter's wedding. **2.** When we saw her in December, she was in love with a charming, well-to-do man. **3.** They were supposed to get married in April. **4.** I had already bought a beautiful present. **5.** Two weeks ago she got engaged to another man. **6.** He's a poor student at (**an**) her university. **7.** They didn't say when they wanted to get married. **8.** On the weekend she called her parents. **9.** She and the student had just gotten married. **10.** They hadn't invited their parents to (**zu**) the wedding. **11.** Arthur gets annoyed when he thinks about it.

HALTET MIT HUMOR UND CHARME
EURE JUNGE LIEBE WARM!
MIT ALLEN GUTEN WÜNSCHEN

EINBLICKE ◆◆◆◆◆◆◆◆◆◆◆◆

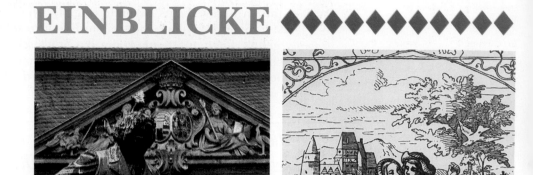

Das Brüder Grimm-Denkmal in Hanau

Your students' response to a fairy tale as a reading text will depend on your attitude. You might discuss the genre, typical style, and features. Our students enjoyed occasional telling of familiar tales because they could understand them quite easily.

The brothers Grimm, Jacob (1785–1863) and Wilhelm (1786–1859), are well remembered for their collection of fairy tales, including **Hänsel und Gretel**, **Schneewittchen** (*Snow-White*), **Rotkäppchen** (*Little Red Riding Hood*), **Aschenputtel** (*Cinderella*), **Dornröschen** (*Sleeping Beauty*), **Rumpelstilzchen, Rapunzel, König Drosselbart** (*King Thrushbeard*), and many others. Jacob Grimm also wrote the first historical German grammar in which he compared fifteen different Germanic languages and analyzed their stages of development. The brothers' work on the **Deutsches Wörterbuch** was a pioneering effort that served as a model for later lexicographers. In 1840 the brothers became members of the German Academy of Sciences in Berlin.

WORTSCHATZ 2

der König, -e		*king*
	bald	*soon*
	böse	*angry, mad*
	endlich	*finally*
	niemand	*nobody, no one*
	plötzlich	*sudden(ly)*
	stolz	*proud*

Pre-reading: 1. Was ist ein Märchen? 2. Wie beginnen viele Märchen im Englischen? 3. Wo spielen Märchen? 4. Was für Personen sind typisch in einem Märchen? 5. Was für Märchen kennen Sie? 6. Haben Sie als Kind gern Märchen gelesen? Warum (nicht)?

auf·hören (zu + *inf.*)	*to stop (doing something)*
geschehen (geschieht), geschah, ist geschehen	*to happen*
herein·kommen, kam herein, ist hereingekommen	*to enter, come in*
kaputt·gehen, ging kaputt, ist kaputtgegangen	*to get broken, break*
sich lustig machen über (+ acc.)	*to make fun of*
rennen, rannte, ist gerannt	*to run*
ziehen, zog, gezogen	*to pull*

WAS IST DAS? der Rest, Ton; das Unglück; die Ware; eine Weile; betrunken, delikat, golden, hart, nobel; aufessen, verdammen, vorbei sein

König Drosselbart

once upon a time / he
eager to marry
far

Es war einmal° ein König. Der° hatte eine schöne, aber sehr stolze Tochter. Eines Tages gab er ein großes Fest, wozu er alle heiratslustigen° noblen Männer von nah und fern° einlud. Aber niemand war der Tochter gut genug. Der eine war zu dick, der andere zu dünn, der dritte zu lang, der vierte zu kurz und so weiter. Besonders aber machte sie sich über einen guten König   5

crooked chin
a thrush's beak / . . .beard

mit einem krummen Kinn° lustig. „O", rief sie und lachte, „er hat ein Kinn wie ein Drosselschnabel°!" Seit dieser Zeit hieß er nur noch Drosselbart°.

first beggar who comes along

Als der König sah, daß seine Tochter sich über alle Leute nur lustig machte, wurde er böse. Jetzt sollte sie den ersten besten Bettler° heiraten. Als ein paar Tage später ein Bettler kam, mußte sie ihn heiraten. Da half   10

begging
leave

kein Betteln° und Weinen. Der Bettler nahm sie bei der Hand, und sie mußte mit ihm zu Fuß das Schloß verlassen°.

Als sie in einen großen Wald kamen, fragte sie: „Wem gehört der schöne Wald?" „Dem König Drosselbart", antwortete er. Bald kamen sie über ein Feld. Da fragte sie wieder: „Wem gehört das schöne Feld?" „Dem König   15
Drosselbart", war wieder seine Antwort. Danach kamen sie durch eine große Stadt, und sie fragte: „Wem gehört diese schöne, große Stadt?" „Dem König Drosselbart", hörte sie wieder. Endlich kamen sie an ein kleines Häuschen,

Wälder und Felder
in Süddeutschland

da sprach sie: „Ach, wem gehört dieses kleine Häuschen?" „Das gehört mir und dir", antwortete der Bettler. Sie mußte sich bücken°, um durch die Tür zu kommen. „Und wo sind die Diener°?" fragte die Königstochter. „Was für Diener? Hier mußt du alles tun. Koch mir jetzt mein Essen, ich bin müde!" 20

Die Königstochter konnte aber gar nicht kochen, und der Bettler mußte ihr dabei helfen. Als sie das bißchen° Essen gegessen hatten, gingen sie zu Bett. Am nächsten Morgen mußte sie schon früh aufstehen und kochen, 25 waschen und putzen. Nach ein paar Tagen sagte der Mann: „Das geht nicht, daß wir alles aufessen und nichts verdienen°. Du sollst Körbe flechten°." Er ging hinaus und brachte Weiden°. Da machte sie den ganzen Tag Körbe, aber die harten Weiden taten ihren zarten° Händen weh.

„Ich sehe, das geht nicht", sprach der Mann. „Vielleicht kannst du 30 spinnen°." So setzte sie sich hin und spann, aber der harte Faden° tat ihren zarten Fingern weh. „Siehst du", sprach der Mann, „nichts kannst du. Vielleicht kannst du Töpfe° auf dem Markt verkaufen." Ach, dachte sie, wenn mich da die Leute aus dem Reich° meines Vaters sehen, machen sie sich bestimmt über mich lustig. Aber es half alles nichts°. Sie mußte es tun, wenn 35 sie nicht verhungern° wollte.

Das erst Mal° ging es gut. Weil die Frau so schön war, kauften die Leute gern ihre Ware. Manche schenkten ihr sogar Geld. Davon lebten sie eine Weile. Das zweite Mal setzte sie sich an die Ecke des Marktes. Plötzlich kam ein betrunkener Husar° und ritt° mitten durch ihre Töpfe. Alles ging kaputt. 40 Sie weinte sehr, lief nach Hause und erzählte alles ihrem Mann. „Wer setzt sich auch an eine Ecke des Marktes!" sprach der Mann. „Hör auf zu weinen! Ich sehe, du kannst wirklich nichts. Ich bin heute auf dem Schloß unseres Königs gewesen. Dort wollen sie dich als Küchenmagd° nehmen. Dafür bekommst du freies Essen." So wurde die Königstochter Küchenmagd und 45 mußte alle schmutzige Arbeit tun. Sie machte sich in beiden Taschen ein Töpfchen fest°. Darin brachte sie täglich Überreste° nach Hause, wovon sie lebten.

Eines Tages war auf dem Schloß ein großes Fest, die Hochzeit des Königssohnes. Da ging die arme Frau hin, stellte sich an die Tür und wollte 50 alles sehen. Als alles so wunderschön war, da dachte sie mit traurigem Herzen° an ihr Leben und verdammte ihren Stolz°, der° ihr soviel Unglück gebracht hatte. Manchmal gaben ihr die Diener Reste von den delikaten Speisen°. Sie tat sie in ihre Töpfchen und wollte sie nach Hause tragen. Plötzlich kam der Königssohn herein. Er trug elegante Kleider und hatte 55 goldene Ketten° um den Hals. Als er die schöne Frau an der Tür stehen sah, nahm er sie bei der Hand und wollte mit ihr tanzen. Aber sie wollte nicht, denn sie sah, daß es König Drosselbart war. Aber es half alles nichts; er zog sie in den Saal°. Plötzlich fielen die Töpfchen auf den Boden°: Suppe, Überreste, alles lag da. Als die Leute das sahen, machten sie sich über sie 60 lustig. Die arme Königstochter rannte, so schnell sie konnte, aber im Flur war ein Mann, und er brachte sie zurück. Als sie ihn ansah, war es wieder

stoop
servants

little bit of

earn / weave baskets
willow twigs
tender

spin (yarn) / thread

pots
kingdom
she had no choice
starve
time

cavalryman / rode

. . . maid

fastened / leftovers

heart / pride / which

delicious foods

chains

ballroom / floor

don't be afraid

König Drosselbart. „Fürchte dich nicht°!" sagte er in freundlichem Ton. „Ich und der Bettler sind eins. Und der Husar, das bin ich auch gewesen. Das alles ist aus Liebe zu dir geschehen, weil du so stolz warst." Da weinte sie sehr 65

wrong / worthy

und sagte: „Ich habe großes Unrecht° getan und bin nicht wert°, deine Frau zu sein."

Er aber sprach: „Deine schlechten Tage sind vorbei. Jetzt wollen wir

ladies in waiting

unsere Hochzeit feiern." Bald kamen die Kammerfrauen° und zogen ihr

court

wunderschöne Kleider an. Und ihr Vater, der ganze Hof°, alle wünschten 70

died

ihr Glück mit König Drosselbart. Und wenn sie nicht gestorben° sind, dann leben sie noch heute.

fairy tale / adapted

Märchen° der Brüder Grimm (nacherzählt°)

Schloß Neuschwanstein von Ludwig II. stammt aus *(dates back to)* dem 19. Jahrhundert.

ZUM TEXT

A. Erzählen Sie die Geschichte vom König Drosselbart! Retell the story in your own words, using the simple past and the following key words.

König, Tochter, Fest, sich lustig machen, Bettler heiraten, Wald, Feld, Stadt, Häuschen, arbeiten, Körbe flechten, spinnen, Töpfe verkaufen, Husar, Küchenmädchen, Fest, Königssohn, tanzen, Hochzeit

B. Ein böses Spielchen. Read what Drosselbart's wife tells her son. Underline the past perfect tense.

Bevor wir heirateten, spielten dein Großvater und dein Vater ein böses Spielchen mit mir. Weil ich mich über deinen Vater lustig gemacht hatte, hat Großvater mich mit dem ersten besten Bettler weggeschickt. Er hatte mir natürlich nicht gesagt, daß der Bettler König Drosselbart, dein Vater, war. Nachdem wir eine Weile in einer alten Gartenhütte (. . . hut) gelebt hatten, fand ich Arbeit im Schloß. Eines Tages feierte man dort Hochzeit, wozu dein Vater viele noble Gäste eingeladen hatte. Ich hatte mich erst ein paar Minuten an die Tür gestellt, als dein Vater mich zum Tanzen holte. Vor Schreck (out of shock) waren mir meine Töpfchen hingefallen. Er und der Bettler waren der gleiche gewesen. Erst hatte ich mich sehr darüber geärgert, aber dann war ich sehr glücklich. Nachdem ich mich umgezogen hatte, feierten wir Hochzeit.

C. Als, wenn oder wann?
1. _____ die Prinzessin das hörte, fing sie an zu weinen.
2. Ich weiß nicht genau, _____ sie geheiratet haben, aber _____ sie nicht gestorben sind, dann leben sie noch heute.
3. _____ ich Märchen lese, suche ich immer nach einer Moral.

D. Fragen
1. Aus welcher Zeit kommen solche Märchen wie *König Drosselbart*?
2. Was ist die Rolle *(role)* des Mannes in diesem Märchen? die Rolle der Frau? Wie ist die Frau hier? Sieht man die Frau auch heute so?
3. In welchem Märchen gibt es starke *(strong)* Frauenfiguren? Was für Frauen sind das oft? Warum?

E. Rollenwechsel. Erzählen Sie die Geschichte noch einmal, aber dieses Mal wechseln Sie die Rollen!

BEISPIEL: Es war einmal eine Königin. Sie hatte einen schönen, aber sehr stolzen Sohn. Eines Tages gab sie ein großes Fest . . .

F. Mischmasch. Following are three famous fairy tales all mixed together. In each numbered item, select one of the three phrases and retell one of these stories in its familiar form or, if you prefer, with a different twist. Or you can create an original fairy tale by supplying your own phrases.

1. Es war einmal . . .
    a. ein junger Prinz. Der . . .
    b. ein kleines Mädchen. Das . . .
    c. ein kleiner Junge. Der . . .
    d. _____

2. a. hatte eine alte Großmutter.
    b. war nicht besonders attraktiv.
    c. hatte immer Hunger.
    d. _____

3. Eines Tages . . .
    a. lud ihn / es der Nachbarkönig zu einem Ball ein.
    b. wurde die Großmutter krank.
    c. war wieder nichts im Kühlschrank.
    d. _____

4. Da ging er / es / sie . . .
    a. in den dunklen Wald.
    b. mit einem Kuchen und etwas Wein hin.
    c. natürlich hin.
    d. _____

5. a. um ihr zu helfen.
    b. um die Prinzessin kennenzulernen.
    c. um etwas Essen zu finden.
    d. _____

6. Aber er / es / sie . . .
    a. machte sich nur über alle lustig.
    b. verlief sich (got lost) im Wald.
    c. dachte nicht an den bösen Wolf.
    d. _____

7. Plötzlich . . .
    a. wurde es dem Vater zuviel, und er sagte . . .
    b. sah er / sie ein paar schöne Blumen und sagte . . .

    c. war da ein Häuschen aus Kuchen und Plätzchen, und jemand sagte . . .
    d. _____

8. a. „Jetzt heiratest du den ersten besten Bettler."
    b. „Wer knuspert (nibbles) an meinem Häuschen?"
    c. „Sie freut sich bestimmt über ein paar Blumen."
    d. _____

9. Da kam . . .
    a. der Prinz als Bettler zurück und sagte . . .
    b. eine alte Frau und sagte . . .
    c. der böse Wolf und fragte . . .
    d. _____

10. a. „Bleib bei mir, . . .
    b. „Jetzt mußt du mit mir kommen, . . .
    c. „Wohin gehst du? . . .
    d. _____

11. a. und ich will alles für dich tun."
    b. weil du so stolz warst."
    c. Ich habe Hunger."
    d. _____

12. Später . . .
    a. wollte er / sie / es wieder nach Hause und sagte . . .
    b. erzählte er / es / sie, wer er / es / sie wirklich war und sagte . . .
    c. fragte er / es / sie . . .
    d. _____

13. a. „Vergiß alles, und laß uns neu anfangen!"
    b. „Warum hast du so ein großes Maul (mouth)?"
    c. „Ich habe genug und möchte nach Hause."
    d. _____

14. Da . . .
   a. warf *(threw)* sie ihm die Töpfe vor die Füße.
   b. freute er / es / sie sich und war glücklich.
   c. wurde er / es / sie furchtbar böse.
   d. _____

15. Die Moral von der Geschicht':
   a. Spiele mit der Liebe nicht!
   b. Traue *(trust)* einem Wolf nicht!
   c. Geh zu fremden Leuten *(strangers)* nicht!
   d. _____

SPRECHSITUATIONEN

Expressing Admiration

You have now learned enough adjectives to express admiration for people as well as for objects. Remember that the gesture word **aber** also expresses admiration (see p. 194).

Was für ein netter Mann / eine sympathische Frau!
So ein interessantes Buch!
Das ist aber nett!
Wie nett!
Das gefällt mir aber!
Das finde ich sehr schön!

Telling a Story

As you have seen in the reading text, many fairy tales start with the phrase **Es war einmal** . . . Here are some common expressions to catch a listener's attention when beginning to relate a story:

Weißt du, was mir passiert ist *(happened)*?
Du, mir ist heute / gestern 'was passiert!
Ich muß dir 'was erzählen.
Mensch, du glaubst gar nicht *(won't believe)*, was . . .
Ich vergesse nie . . .
Hast du gewußt, daß . . .
Hast du schon gehört, daß . . .

Encouraging a Speaker

Wirklich?	Was hast du dann gemacht?
Natürlich! Klar!	Und wo warst du, als . . .?
Und dann?	Und wie geht's weiter?

A: Could also be used as a small group activity. Have students bring to class actual photos and let others comment on them.

A. Was sagen Sie? Express your admiration.
1. Sie haben einen besonders guten Film gesehen.
2. Sie haben einen sehr netten Mann / eine sehr nette Dame kennengelernt.
3. Sie haben ein besonders interessantes Museum besucht.
4. Sie sind auf den Turm *(tower)* eines großen Domes gestiegen und haben einen wunderbaren Blick.

5. Ein Freund hat einen sehr schönen, neuen Pullover.
6. Freunde haben Sie zum Essen eingeladen. Sie haben nicht gewußt, daß Ihre Freunde so gut kochen können.
7. Ihre Freunde haben ihre neue Wohnung sehr schick eingerichtet (*furnished*).
8. Sie besuchen eine Professorin. She hat wunderschöne Blumen in ihrem Garten.
9. Eine junge Frau mit einem sehr hübschen und freundlichen Baby sitzt neben Ihnen im Flugzeug.
10. Sie sehen sich zusammen ein Photoalbum an. Dabei sehen Sie einige interessante Bilder. (Phantasieren Sie etwas!)

B. Es tut mir leid, aber . . . Use your imagination to make excuses.
1. Sie sollten heute Ihrem Professor Ihren Aufsatz (*paper*) geben, aber Sie sind noch nicht damit fertig, weil . . .
2. Statt um elf zu Hause zu sein, kommen Sie erst nachts um eins zurück, weil . . .
3. Sie haben Ihren Eltern schon wochenlang nicht mehr geschrieben oder sie angerufen, weil . . .
4. Sie hatten versprochen, mit Ihrem Freund / Ihrer Freundin auszugehen, aber sie haben es vergessen, weil . . .

C. Ich muß dir 'was erzählen. Briefly tell a classmate something interesting that happened to you on your last vacation, during a plane trip, at work, or on a visit to your family. Your partner comments as you tell your story.

 **KAPITEL 8–11**

1. Verbs

1. Reflexive Verbs

If the subject and object of a sentence are the same person or thing, the object is a reflexive pronoun. The reflexive pronouns are as follows:

	ich	du	er / es / sie	wir	ihr	sie	Sie
acc.	mich	dich	sich	uns	euch	sich	sich
dat.	mir	dir	sich	uns	euch	sich	sich

a. Many verbs can be used reflexively.

Ich habe (mir) ein Auto gekauft. *I bought (myself) a car.*

b. Other verbs must be used reflexively, even though their English counterparts are often not reflexive.

Ich habe mich erkältet. *I caught a cold.*

c. With parts of the body, German normally uses the definite article together with a reflexive pronoun in the dative.

Ich habe mir die Haare gewaschen. *I washed my hair.*

You are familiar with the following: sich anhören, sich ansehen, sich anziehen, sich ausruhen, sich ausziehen, sich beeilen, sich duschen, sich erkälten, sich fit halten, sich (wohl) fühlen, sich (hin)legen, sich kämmen, sich langweilen, sich (die Nase / Zähne) putzen, sich rasieren, sich (hin)setzen, sich waschen, sich wünschen (see also 2 below).

2. Verbs with Prepositional Objects

Combinations of verbs and prepositions often have a special idiomatic meaning. These patterns cannot be translated literally but must be learned.

Er denkt an seine Reise. *He's thinking of his trip.*

You are familiar with the following: denken an, erzählen von, halten von, schreiben an, sprechen von, warten auf; sich ärgern über, sich freuen auf, sich interessieren für, sich lustig machen über, träumen von.

3. Infinitive with **zu**

In German the use of the infinitive is much like that of English.

Ich habe viel zu tun.
Ich habe keine Zeit, eine Reise zu machen.

If the infinitive is combined with other sentence elements, a COMMA separates the infinitive phrase from the main clause. If a separable prefix is used, **zu** is inserted between the prefix and the verb.

Hast du Lust, heute nachmittag mit**zu**kommen?
Sie sind ins Kino gegangen, um sich einen neuen Film an**zu**sehen.

REMEMBER: Don't use **zu** with modals! (Möchtest du heute nachmittag **mitkommen**?)

Die feine englische Art
Tee zu trinken

1. Summary of Past Tenses

Be sure to learn the principal parts of verbs. If you know that a verb is a regular t-verb, all its forms can be predicted, but the principal parts of irregular t-verbs and n-verbs must be memorized. You must also memorize those verbs that take **sein** as the auxiliary verb in the perfect tense.

a. The Perfect Tense

▪ Past participles:

t-verbs (weak verbs)	n-verbs (strong verbs)
(ge) + stem (change) + (e)t	(ge) + stem (change) + en
gekauft	gestanden
geheiratet	
gedacht	
eingekauft	aufgestanden
verkauft	verstanden
telefoniert	

▪ When used as auxiliaries in the PRESENT PERFECT, **haben** and **sein** are in the present tense. In the PAST PERFECT, **haben** and **sein** are in the simple past.

Er **hat** eine Flugkarte gekauft.   Er **ist** nach Kanada geflogen.
Er **hatte** eine Flugkarte gekauft.   Er **war** nach Kanada geflogen.

▪ In conversation, past events are usually reported in the present perfect. (The modals, **haben**, and **sein** may be used in the simple past.) The past perfect is used to refer to events happening BEFORE other past events.

Nachdem wir den Film gesehen hatten, haben wir eine Tasse Kaffee getrunken.

b. The Simple Past

▪ Forms:

t-verbs (weak verbs)		n-verbs (strong verbs)	
ich			—
du			st
er	(e)te		—
	(e)test		
	(e)te		
stem (change) +		stem (change) +	
wir	(e)ten		en
ihr	(e)tet		t
sie	(e)ten		en
kaufte		stand	
heiratete			
dachte			
kaufte ein		stand auf	
verkaufte		verstand	
telefonierte			

▪ In writing, the simple past is used to describe past events. However, in dialogues within narration the present perfect is correct.

5. Sentence Structure in the Past Tenses

Er **brachte** einen Freund.
Er **brachte** einen Freund **mit**.
Er **wollte** einen Freund **mitbringen**.
Er **hat** einen Freund **mitgebracht**.
Er **hatte** einen Freund **mitgebracht**.
　V1　　　　　　　　　V2

　　　..., weil er einen Freund **brachte**.
　　　..., weil er einen Freund **mitbrachte**.
..., weil er einen Freund **mitbringen wollte**.
　　..., weil er einen Freund **mitgebracht hat**.
..., weil er einen Freund **mitgebracht hatte**.
　　　　　　　　　　　V2　　　V1

II. The Conjunctions als, wann, wenn

when	at the time when	→	**als**
	at what time	→	**wann**
	whenever, if	→	**wenn**

III. Cases

1. Genitive

    a. Masculine and neuter nouns have endings in the genitive singular.

        -es: for one-syllable nouns and nouns ending in **-s, -ß, -z, -tz, -zt** (des Kopfes, Halses, Fußes, Salzes, Platzes, Arztes / *physician's*).

        -s: for nouns of more than one syllable and proper nouns (des Bahnhofs, Lothars, Lothar Müllers).

    b. n-Nouns usually end in **-(e)n**; **der Name** is an exception (des Herrn, Studenten BUT des Namens).

2. Summary of the Four Cases

    a. Interrogative Pronouns

nom.	wer?	was?
acc.	wen?	was?
dat.	wem?	—
gen.	wessen?	—

    b. Use of the Four Cases and Forms of **der-** and **ein-**Words

	use	follows ...	masc.	neut.	fem.	pl.
nom.	Subject, Predicate noun	**heißen, sein, werden**	der dieser ein mein	das dieses ein mein	die diese eine meine	die diese keine meine
acc.	Direct object	**durch, für, gegen, ohne, um**	den diesen einen meinen			
		an, auf, hinter, in, neben, über, unter, vor, zwischen				
dat.	Indirect object	**aus, außer, bei, mit, nach, seit, von, zu**	dem diesem einem meinem	dem diesem einem meinem	der dieser einer meiner	den diesen keinen meinen
		antworten, danken, gefallen, gehören, helfen, zuhören				
gen.	Possessive	**(an)statt, trotz, während, wegen**	des dieses eines meines	des dieses eines meines		der dieser keiner meiner

IV. Da- and wo-Compounds

Pronouns following prepositions refer to people; **da-** and **wo**-compounds refer to objects and ideas. Most accusative and dative prepositions, and all two-way prepositions, can be part of such compounds. Prepositions beginning with a vowel are preceded by **dar-** and **wor-**.

Er wartet auf einen Brief.
Worauf wartet er? Er wartet **dar**auf.

V. Adjective Endings

1. Preceded Adjectives

   Predicate adjectives and adverbs have no endings. However, adjectives followed by nouns do have endings.

   a. In the nominative and accusative singular:

   - preceded by **der, das, die,** and **eine:**   **-e**

   - preceded by **ein** ⎰ with masculine nouns: **-er**
                         ⎱ with neuter nouns: **-es**

   b. In all other cases: **-en**

	masc.	neut.	fem.	pl.
nom.	-e -er	-e	-e	
acc.		-es		
dat.				
gen.		-en		

   Der alt**e** Fernseher und das alt**e** Radio sind kaputt.
   Mein alt**er** Fernseher und mein alt**es** Radio sind kaputt.

2. Unpreceded Adjectives

   a. Unpreceded adjectives have the endings that the definite article would have if it were used.

       Heiß**e** Suppe und heiß**er** Tee schmecken bei kalt**em** Wetter prima.

   b. The following words are often used as unpreceded adjectives: **einige, mehrere, viele,** and **wenige. Viel** and **wenig** in the singular, **mehr** and **ein paar,** numerals, colors like **rosa** and **lila,** and adjectives like **Frankfurter** and **Wiener** have no endings.

       Er hat mehrere interessante Theaterstücke und ein paar kurze Fernsehfilme geschrieben.

VI. Sentence Structure

1. Sequence of Adverbs

If two or more adverbs or adverbial phrases occur in one sentence, they usually follow the sequence time, manner, place. The negative **nicht** usually comes after the adverbs of time but before adverbs of manner or place.

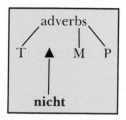

Er fährt morgens gern mit dem Wagen zur Arbeit.
Er fährt morgens **nicht** gern mit dem Wagen zur Arbeit.

2. Summary Chart

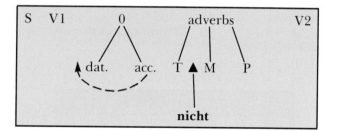

3. Time Expressions

   a. Specific time

   To refer to specific time, a definite point in time or length of time, German uses the ACCUSATIVE: **jeden Tag, nächstes Jahr, eine Woche, einen Monat.**

   Other familiar phrases referring to specific time are:

   - gerade, am Abend, am 1. Mai, im Mai, in einer Viertelstunde, um zwei Uhr, von Juni bis September, vor einer Woche

   - vorgestern, gestern, heute, morgen, übermorgen, Montag, Dienstag, Mittwoch, usw.

   - früh (morgen), vormittag, mittag, nachmittag, abend, nacht; gestern früh, heute morgen, morgen vormittag, Montag nachmittag, usw.

   b. Indefinite and nonspecific time

   - To refer to an indefinite point in time, the GENITIVE is used: **eines Tages.**

   - Familiar time expressions referring to nonspecific times are:
     montags, dienstags, mittwochs, usw.

morgens, mittags, abends, usw.
bald, manchmal, meistens, monatlich, oft, stundenlang, täglich, usw.

WORTSCHATZWIEDERHOLUNG

A. Fragen
1. **Welches Hauptwort** *(noun)* **kennen Sie dazu?**

anfangen, fahren, fliegen, schenken, sprechen, amerikanisch, deutsch, freundlich, glücklich, monatlich, musikalisch, sportlich, verliebt

2. **Was ist ein Synonym dazu?**

BEISPIEL: mit der Bahn   **mit dem Zug**

mit dem Auto, in 30 Minuten, in einer Viertelstunde, beginnen, laufen, telefonieren, schön

3. **Was ist das Gegenteil davon?**

abfliegen, sich anziehen, aufhören, ausmachen, einsteigen, finden, gewinnen, weinen, böse, dick, dumm, furchtbar, gesund, glücklich, hübsch, jung, leicht, lustig, nett, nie, privat, reich, verheiratet

Ask students when they were born: **Wann sind Sie geboren?**

4. **Wann wurden** *(were)* **sie geboren?** Antworten Sie mündlich *(orally)*!

BEISPIEL: Hermann Hesse (1877)
Hermann Hesse wurde 1877 geboren.

a. Johann Sebastian Bach (1685) **b.** Johann Wolfgang von Goethe (1749) **c.** Friedrich Schiller (1759) **d.** Franz Liszt (1811) **e.** Thomas Mann (1875) **f.** Bertolt Brecht (1898) **g.** Friedrich Dürrenmatt (1921)

B. Welches Wort paßt nicht?
1. wandern, gewinnen, spazierengehen, laufen
2. häßlich, gemütlich, sympathisch, charmant
3. die Autorin, der Komponist, der Schauspieler, der Plattenspieler
4. die Tochter, der Sohn, der Nachbar, die Tante
5. täglich, wöchentlich, monatlich, gewöhnlich

C. Was kommt Ihnen dabei in den Sinn?

BEISPIEL: Koffer **packen, Reise, Ferien, . . .**

Wunsch, Hochzeit, Plattenspieler, Zeitung, Fernsehpause, Hobby, Nase, Auge, Bauch

D. Bilden Sie eine Worttreppe. Wie weit kommen Sie in einer Minute?

BEISPIEL: charmant
        treu
            ungemütlich

STRUKTURWIEDERHOLUNG

E. Reflexivverben. Variieren Sie die Sätze!

1. **Willi hält sich fit.**

   Do you *(formal)* keep fit? They're not keeping fit. How did she keep fit? Keep fit (3 ×). I'd like to keep fit. We must keep fit. We had to keep fit.

2. **Sie erkälten sich wieder.**

   We'll get a cold again. Don't catch a cold again (3 ×). They've caught a cold again. She doesn't want to get a cold again. We had caught a cold again. Why do you *(sg. fam.)* always get a cold? They always caught a cold.

F. Am Morgen. Auf deutsch, bitte!

   a. You've *(sg. fam.)* got to get dressed.   **b.** First I want to take a shower and wash my hair.   **c.** And you *(sg. fam.)* need to shave.   **d.** Why don't you *(pl. fam.)* hurry up?   **e.** Listen *(pl. fam.)* to that.   **f.** He got annoyed and sat down.

G. Verben mit Präpositionen. Bilden Sie Sätze!

BEISPIEL: schreiben   **Ich muß an meine Eltern schreiben.**

denken, erzählen, sich freuen, sich interessieren, sich lustig machen, sprechen, träumen, warten

H. Infinitiv mit zu. Bilden Sie Sätze!

1. **Es ist zu spät . . .**

   in die Oper gehen, ein Geschenk kaufen, an ihn schreiben, mit dem Krimi anfangen, alle einladen

2. **Es ist nicht leicht . . .**

   so früh aufstehen, immer aufpassen, Zeit zum Sport finden, moderne Musik verstehen, einen Roman schreiben, eine Sprache lernen

I. Sagen Sie es im Perfekt!

1. Wohin geht ihr?—Wir besuchen Onkel Erich.
2. Was machst du heute?—Ich gehe schwimmen.
3. Wie gefällt Ihnen der Film?—Er ist wirklich ausgezeichnet.
4. Warum beeilt sie sich so?—Die Vorstellung fängt um acht an.
5. Weißt du, daß er ein sehr guter Schwimmer ist?—Nein, er spricht nicht viel von sich.
6. Wen ladet ihr ein?—Ein paar Freundinnen und Freunde kommen.

J. Bilden Sie Sätze im Plusquamperfekt *(past perfect)*!

1. wir / nicht / denken / daran
2. Daniela und Yvonne / gehen / zum Schwimmbad
3. wir / sich anziehen / warm
4. er / sich lustig machen / über uns
5. Auto / kaputtgehen / plötzlich
6. das / sein / nicht so lustig
7. aber / das / verdienen / er

K. Die Trappfamilie. Was fehlt?

1. Gestern abend haben sie in d____ zweit____ Programm d____ deutsch____ Fernsehens d___ bekannt____ Film über d___ österreichisch____ Familie Trapp gespielt. **2.** Erst ist es ein____ deutsch____ Theaterstück gewesen, und dann ist daraus ein____ amerikanisch____ Film geworden. **3.** Eigentlich kannte ich dies____ interessant____ Film schon von d____ amerikanisch____ Kino. **4.** Aber ich sehe mir gern amerikanisch____ Stücke in deutsch____ Sprache an. **5.** D____ ganz____ Film spielt rings um d____ hübsch____ Stadt Salzburg. **6.** Am Anfang ist Maria in ein____ alt____ Kloster *(convent, n.)*, aber sie fühlt sich bei d____ streng____ *(strict)* Nonnen *(nuns, pl.)* nicht richtig____ wohl. **7.** Eines Tages schickt d____ verständnisvoll____ Oberin *(mother superior)* sie zu d___ groß Familie ein____ reich____, verwitwet____ *(widowed)* Kapitäns *(m.)*. **8.** Sein____ sieben____ klein____ Kinder sind anfangs nicht gerade nett____, aber d____ temperamentvoll____ Maria hat viel____ gut____ Ideen, womit sie die sieben Kinder unterhalten kann. **9.** Später heiratet d____ verwitwet____ Kapitän d____ jung____ Fräulein Maria. **10.** Kurz nach ihr____ phantastisch____ Hochzeit kommt d____ deutsch____ Militär *(n.)* nach Österreich. **11.** Weil d____ österreichisch____ Kapitän nicht zu d____ deutsch____ Marine *(f.)* will, verlassen *(leave)* sie nach kurz____ Zeit ihr____ schön____ groß____ Haus und fliehen *(escape)* über d____ hoh____ *(high)* Berge in d____ neutral____ Schweiz. **12.** Heute hat d____ bekannt____ Trappfamilie ein____ neu____, groß____ Haus in d____ amerikanisch____ Staat Vermont. **13.** Wie in viel____ der sogenannt____ *(so-called)* wahr____ *(true)* Geschichten, ist in d____ amerikanisch____ Film *The Sound of Music* nicht alles wahr____. **14.** Aber es ist ein____ nett____ Film mit viel____ schön____ Musik.

Blick auf Salzburg

L. Ein Rendez-vous. Sagen Sie es im Imperfekt!

1. Sonja und Stephan gehen am Samstag abend aus. **2.** Zuerst versuchen sie, Opernkarten zu bekommen, aber alle Karten sind schon ausverkauft *(sold out)*. **3.** Dann wollen sie mit einem Taxi zum Theater fahren, aber sie können kein Taxi finden. **4.** Als sie zum Theater kommen, gibt es auch keine Karten mehr. **5.** Aber in der Nähe des Theaters ist ein Kino. **6.** Dort läuft ein neuer Film. **7.** Der Film gefällt ihnen prima, weil er sehr komisch ist. **8.** Die Zuschauer lachen oft so laut, daß man nichts hören kann. **9.** Als sie aus dem Kino kommen, sehen sie plötzlich Jürgen und Barbara. **10.** In einem kleinen Restaurant essen sie ein paar Würstchen und trinken dazu ein Glas Bier. **11.** Dann bummeln sie gemütlich durch die Stadt nach Hause.

M: 1. als 2. wann
3. wenn 4. als 5. wenn
6. wann

M. Als, wann oder wenn?

1. _____ das Stück zu Ende war, klatschten die Leute.
2. Weißt du, _____ die Party anfängt?
3. Könnt ihr mir die Zeitschrift geben, _____ ihr damit fertig seid?
4. _____ ich den Roman vor zwei Jahren las, gefiel er mir nicht so gut.
5. Ich muß immer an euch denken, _____ ich dieses Lied im Radio höre.
6. Er wußte auch nicht, _____ seine Nachbarn zurückkommen sollten.

N. Der Genitiv. Verbinden Sie die zwei Wörter wie in den Beispielen!

BEISPIEL: der Sender / der Brief   **der Sender des Briefes**
der Brief / Annette   **Annettes Brief**

1. das Ende / der Krimi
2. der Genitiv / der Satz
3. die Farbe / unser Auto
4. der Flughafen / diese Stadt
5. der Sohn / mein Onkel
6. der Eingang / euer Haus
7. der Name / der Komponist
8. der Anfang / der Name
9. der Wunsch / alle Kinder
10. die Taschen / manche Frauen
11. die Musik / Beethoven
12. das Stück / Bertolt Brecht
13. die Geschichten / Herr Keuner

O. wo- und da-Wörter

1. **Kombinieren Sie!**

   BEISPIEL: mit **womit? damit**

   durch, in, vor, zu, für, von, über, an, auf, bei

O.2: a. Woran / An meine b. Wovon / Von einem c. Über wen / Über d. Wovon / Von meinen e. Worauf / Auf einen / darauf f. von ihren / Davon g. an deine / an sie h. über den / worüber i. für / dafür

2. **Was fehlt?**

   a. _____ denkst du? _____ Reise. *(of what, of my)*

   b. _____ spricht Professor Schulz heute? _____ spannenden Roman. *(about what, about a)*

   c. _____ macht er sich jetzt lustig? _____ uns. *(of whom, of)*

   d. _____ hast du geträumt? _____ Ferien. *(about what, about my)*

   e. _____ wartest du? _____ Brief von Paul. Warte nicht _____ ! *(for what, for a, for that)*

   f. Trudi erzählt immer gern _____ Partys. _____ hat sie gerade erzählt. *(about her, about that)*

   g. Hast du schon _____ Eltern geschrieben? Ja, ich habe am Wochenende _____ geschrieben. *(to your, to them)*

   h. Er hat sich furchtbar _____ Brief geärgert, aber _____ ärgert er sich nicht? *(about the, about what)*

   i. Interessiert Jürgen sich _____ Sport? Nein, _____ interessiert er sich nicht. *(in, in that)*

EC EuroCity: Das neue europäische Zugsystem.

Deutsche Bundesbahn   **DB**

P. Wann und wie lange?

1. **Er fährt morgen.**

   the day after tomorrow, after supper, Sundays, tomorrow morning, at 4:30, in 15 minutes, Monday morning, on Tuesday, in February, on the weekend, in the evening, in the fall, most of the time, sometimes, each year, now, never, one day

2. **Er bleibt zwei Tage.**

   from March to May, until Wednesday, until Friday afternoon, until 10:45, for months, one day

Q. Die Musikschule. Expand the sentences by including the phrases in parentheses.

BEISPIEL: Renate geht zur Musikschule in Dresden. (seit ein paar Jahren)
Renate geht seit ein paar Jahren zur Musikschule in Dresden.

1. Ihre Eltern leben in der Nähe von Meißen. (schon lange)
2. Aber Renate wohnt in einem Schülerheim in Dresden. (mit vielen Mädchen)
3. Sie kann am Wochenende einfach schnell nach Hause fahren. (nicht)
4. Sie hat keine Zeit, jeden Tag mit der Bahn zu fahren. (stundenlang)
5. Dafür ist sie während der Ferien zu Hause. (gewöhnlich)
6. Ihre Schule soll leicht sein. (nicht)
7. Sie muß jeden Tag arbeiten. (schwer)
8. Sie spielt manchmal stundenlang Klavier. (mit ihrer Freundin)
9. Renate interessiert sich für klassische Musik. (besonders)
10. Wir haben uns letztes Jahr kennengelernt. (bei einem Musikwettbewerb in Weimar)

12

Beruf und Arbeit

Um Zahnärztin zu werden, muß man lange studieren.

▌ LERNZIELE

Gespräche and **Wortschatz.** This chapter deals with the world of work.

Struktur. You will learn about . . .

- the comparison of adjectives.
- the future.
- nouns with special features.

Einblicke. Reader commentaries about the future.

Sprechsituationen

- Expressing agreement and disagreement
- Expressing hesitation

◆◆◆◆◆ GESPRÄCHE

Weißt du, was du werden willst?

TRUDI   Sag mal Fränzi, weißt du schon, was du werden willst?
FRANZISKA   Ja, Tischlerin.
TRUDI   Ist das nicht sehr anstrengend?
FRANZISKA   Ach, daran gewöhnt man sich. Vielleicht mache ich mich eines Tages selbständig.
TRUDI   Du hast ja große Pläne!
FRANZISKA   Warum nicht? Ich habe keine Lust, immer nur im Büro zu sitzen und für andere Leute zu arbeiten.
TRUDI   Glaubst du, du bekommst eine Lehrstelle?[1]
FRANZISKA   Ja, meine Tante hat ihre eigene Firma. Sie hat mir schon einen Platz angeboten.
TRUDI   Da hast du aber Glück!
FRANZISKA   Und wie ist es denn mit dir? Weißt du, was du machen willst?
TRUDI   Vielleicht werde ich Zahnärztin. Gute Zahnärzte[2] braucht man immer, und außerdem verdient man gut.
FRANZISKA   Da mußt du aber lange studieren.
TRUDI   Ich weiß, aber ich freue mich eigentlich schon darauf.

1. Training through apprenticeships (**Lehrstellen**) is widespread in commerce, trade, and industry. This tradition dates back to the Middle Ages when apprentices served for three years under one or several masters (**Meister**) in order to learn a trade. Apprentices combine practical training with several days of schooling per week.

2. The German language, just like English, often works to the disadvantage of women: words which are supposedly inclusive (e.g., **Wissenschaftler**, **Ärzte**, **Lehrer**) reinforce the old notion that such professions are only for men. A recent report by a government-supported working group suggested using both masculine and feminine forms in official communications to break out of this pattern (e.g., **Ärzte und Ärztinnen**).

Do You Know What You Want to Be? TRUDI: *Say, Fränzi, do you know yet what you want to be?* FRANZISKA: *Yes, a carpenter.* TRUDI: *Isn't that very strenuous?* FRANZISKA: *Oh, you get used to it. Perhaps someday I'll open my own business.* TRUDI: *You have big plans.* FRANZISKA: *Why not? I don't feel like always sitting in an office and working for other people.* TRUDI: *Do you think you can get an apprenticeship?* FRANZISKA: *Yes, my aunt has her own business. She's already offered me a place (as an apprentice).* TRUDI: *Boy, are you lucky!* FRANZISKA: *And how about you? Do you know what you want to do?* TRUDI: *Perhaps I'll be a dentist. Good dentists are always needed and, besides, it pays well.* FRANZISKA: *But then you have to study for a long time.* TRUDI: *I know, but I'm actually looking forward to it.*

WORTSCHATZ 1

DER BERUF, -E *profession*

der	Arzt, ⸚e	*physician*
	Beamte, -n (ein Beamter)[1]	*civil servant*
	Geschäftsmann, -leute	*businessman*
	Ingenieur, -e[2]	*engineer*
	Journalist, -en, -en	*journalist*
	Lehrer, -	*teacher*
	Polizist, -en, -en	*policeman*
	Rechtsanwalt, ⸚e	*lawyer*
	Verkäufer, -	*salesman*
	Wissenschaftler, -	*scientist*
	Zahnarzt, ⸚e	*dentist*
die	Geschäftsfrau, -en	*businesswoman*
	Hausfrau, -en	*housewife*
	Krankenschwester, -n	*nurse*
	Sekretärin, -nen	*secretary*

Karl-Heinz Lehmann
Rechtsanwalt

Elisabeth Landgraf
Rechtsanwältin

There appears to be no male equivalent to **Krankenschwester.** The term **Krankenpfleger** refers to a position requiring less training, somewhat like our practical nurse. The male equivalent of **die Sekretärin** is **der Sekretär,** but **Sekretäre** are a distinct minority.

DIE ARBEIT *work*
DIE STELLE, -N *job, position, place*

der	Arbeiter, -	*(blue-collar) worker*	anstrengend	*strenuous*
	Haushalt	*household*	eigen-	*own*
	Plan, ⸚e	*plan*	gleich	*equal, same*
das	Büro, -s	*office*	hoch (hoh-)[3]	*high*
	Einkommen	*income*	selbständig	*self-employed,*
	Geschäft, -e	*business*		*independent*
die	Ausbildung	*training, education*	sicher	*safe, secure*
	Firma, Firmen	*company, business*		
	Zukunft	*future*		

WEITERES

sich gewöhnen an (+ acc.)	*to get used to*
glauben (an + acc.)	*to believe (in); to think*
verdienen	*to earn, make money*
Ich will . . . werden.	*I want to be a(n) . . .*
Was willst du werden?	*What do you want to be?*

1 See "Struktur" III in this chapter, p. 337.
2 In most cases the feminine forms can be derived by adding **-in** (der Ingenieur / die Ingenieurin; der Polizist / die Polizistin). Some require an umlaut in the feminine form (der Arzt / die **Ärztin**; der Rechtsanwalt / die Rechtsanwältin) or other small changes (der Beamte / die Beam**tin**).
3 **hoh-** is the adjective; **hoch** is the predicate adjective and adverb: die **hohen** Berge BUT Die Berge sind **hoch.**

Pfarrer / Pfarrerin refers to a Protestant minister. A Catholic priest is **der Priester, -,** and a Jewish rabbi is **der Rabbiner, -.**

Optional vocabulary:
Dachdecker,- *roofer;*
Klempner, - *plumber;*
Maler,- *painter;*
Maurer, - *bricklayer;*
Schornsteinfeger, - *chimney sweep*

PASSIVES VOKABULAR **der Angestellte, -n (ein Angestellter)**

employee, clerk **Apotheker,- Dirigent, -en, -en** *music conductor* **Elektriker,- Künstler,-** *artist* **Landwirt, -e** *farmer* **Makler, -** *real-estate agent* **Mechaniker, - Pfarrer,-** *minister* **Pilot, -en, -en Professor, -en Programmierer, - Schriftsteller,-** *writer* **Techniker, - Tischler,-** *carpenter* **die Lehrstelle, -n** *apprenticeship* **anbieten, bot an, angeboten** *to offer*

ZUM THEMA

A. Kurze Fragen

1. Was ist die feminine Form von Lehrer? Ingenieur? Arzt? Verkäufer? Arbeiter?
2. Was ist die maskuline Form von Rechtsanwältin? Sekretärin? Geschäftsfrau? Journalistin? Beamtin?
3. Wo arbeitet die Apothekerin? die Professorin? der Pfarrer? die Beamtin? der Bäcker? der Verkäufer?

B. Was bin ich?

1. In meinem Beruf habe ich es mit vielen jungen Menschen zu tun. Viele denken, daß mein Beruf leicht ist, weil ich so viele Ferien habe. Aber mein Beruf ist manchmal sehr anstrengend. Meine Arbeit geht zu Hause weiter, weil ich viel lesen und korrigieren *(correct)* muß. Was bin ich?
2. Viele Leute kommen zu mir nur, wenn ihnen etwas weh tut. Meistens kommen sie nicht gern, weil sie denken, daß ich ihnen noch mehr weh tue. Aber da haben sie unrecht. Sie kommen mit Schmerzen, setzen sich in meinen gemütlichen Stuhl, öffnen ihren Mund, und bald sind die Schmerzen weg *(gone)*. Was bin ich?
3. Ich bin viel unterwegs. Wenn es eine Katastrophe oder etwas Besonderes gibt, bin ich da. Ich spreche mit Politikern, Wissenschaftlern, Rechtsanwälten, Polizisten, Menschen aus allen Berufen, mit den Leuten auf der Straße. Ich hoffe *(hope)*, daß Sie dann meine Artikel in der Zeitung oder in einer Zeitschrift lesen. Was bin ich?
4. Ich bin Mädchen für alles: Putzfrau, Köchin *(cook)*, Lehrerin, Beraterin *(counselor)*, Sekretärin und Chauffeur. Meine Arbeit hat kein Ende, sie fängt immer wieder neu an. Dabei verdiene ich nichts, nur ab und zu ein Dankeschön. Was bin ich?
5. Schreiben Sie Ihr eigenes **Was bin ich?**, und lassen Sie die anderen raten *(guess)*, was Sie sind!

C. Zu welchem Arzt / welcher Ärztin geht man?

1. Wenn man Zahnschmerzen hat, geht man zu . . .
2. Wenn man schlechte Augen hat, geht man zu . . .
3. Mit kranken Kindern geht man zu . . .
4. Wenn man Hals-, Nasen- oder Ohrenprobleme hat, geht man zu . . .
5. Frauen gehen zu . . .

D. Berufspläne. Was sagen Sie?

x Weißt du schon, was du werden willst?

y Ich werde _____ .

x Und warum?

y _____ . Und wie ist es denn mit dir? Weißt du, was du machen willst?

x _____ .

y Ist das nicht sehr _____ ?

x _____ .

E. Was sind das für Berufe? Sagen Sie's auf englisch, und erklären Sie dann auf deutsch, was die Leute tun!

Zahntechniker/in   Uhrmacher (Meister)

Gebrauchtwagenverkäufer **Putzfrau**

Fernfahrer   **Koch**

Chemie-Laboranten(innen)

Bankangestellter

Damen- und Herrenfriseur **Telefonistin** Sozialpädagogin

Phonotypistinnen   **Arztsekretärin**

Industriekaufmann

Rechtsanwaltsgehilfin

Diplom-Ingenieur **Krankengymnast(in)**

REISELEITER/-INNEN **Systemberater(in)** **Repräsentanten** Bäcker

Haushälterin   **Zahnarzthelferin**

Buchhalter/in **PSYCHOLOGE/IN**

Kassiererin **Fremdsprachenkorrespondentin** Hausmeister

F. Ein interessanter Beruf

1. **Was ist Ihnen im Beruf wichtig?** Poll each other as to the sequence of importance of the points below; then report to the class.

☐ interessante Arbeit   ☐ Sicherheit *(security)*
☐ ruhige Arbeit   ☐ Selbständigkeit *(independence)*
☐ saubere Arbeit   ☐ Verantwortung *(responsibility)*
☐ hohes Einkommen   ☐ Gleichberechtigung *(equality)*
☐ viel Prestige   ☐ Abwechslung *(variety)*

☐ viel Reisen   ☐ Aufgabe *(challenge)*
☐ viel Freizeit   ☐ Risiken *(risks)*
☐ viel Fahrerei *(driving)*   ☐ nette Kollegen
☐ viel Papierkrieg *(paper work)* ☐ ein Geschäftsauto

2. **In welchen Berufen finden Sie das?** Tell which professions best meet the criteria mentioned above.

Arbeiter in einer Fabrik *(factory)*

G. Aussprache. See also III.3 in the pronunciation section of the Workbook.
1. [p] A**b**fahrt, A**b**sender, O**b**st, Her**b**st, Er**b**se, hü**b**sch, o**b**, hal**b**, gel**b**
   BUT [p / b] verlie**b**t / verlie**b**en; blei**b**t / blei**b**en; ha**b**t / ha**b**en
2. [t] un**d**, gesun**d**, spannen**d**, anstrengen**d**, Gel**d**, Han**d**, währen**d**, sin**d**, sei**d**, aben**d**s
   BUT [t / d] Freun**d** / Freun**d**e; Ba**d** / Bä**d**er; Kin**d** / Kin**d**er; wir**d** / wer**d**en
3. [k] mitta**g**s, unterwe**g**s, Ta**g**, Zu**g**, We**g**, Bahnstei**g**, Flugzeu**g**, Ber**g**
   BUT [k / g] fra**g**st / fra**g**en; flie**g**st / flie**g**en; trä**g**st / tra**g**en; le**g**st / le**g**en

STRUKTUR

I. The Comparison of Adjectives and Adverbs

In English and German adjectives have three forms:

POSITIVE	COMPARATIVE	SUPERLATIVE
cheap	*cheaper*	*cheapest*
expensive	*more expensive*	*most expensive*

Whereas there are two ways to form the comparative and the superlative in English, there is only ONE WAY in German; it corresponds to the forms of *cheap* above.

NOTE: In German there is no equivalent to such forms as *more* and *most expensive*.

1. In the COMPARATIVE adjectives add **-er**; in the SUPERLATIVE they add **-(e)st**.

> **billig   billiger   billigst-**

a. Some one-syllable adjectives with the stem vowel **a**, **e**, or **u** have an umlaut in the comparative and superlative, which is shown in the end vocabulary as follows: warm **(ä)**, groß **(ö)**, jung **(ü)**.

warm	wärmer	wärmst-
groß	größer	größt-
jung	jünger	jüngst-

Other adjectives that take an umlaut include: alt, arm, kalt, krank, lang, nah, schwarz, rot, dumm, gesund, kurz.

b. Most adjectives ending in **d** or **-t**, in an **s**-sound, or in vowels add **-est** in the superlative.

kalt	kälter	käl**test-**
heiß	heißer	heiß**est-**
neu	neuer	neu**est-**

Adjectives that follow this pattern include: alt (ä), bekannt, charmant, gesund (ü), intelligent, interessant, laut, leicht, nett, oft (ö), rot (ö), schlecht, talentiert, verrückt; hübsch, weiß, kurz (ü), schwarz (ä), stolz; frei.

A few adjectives ending in **-el** (e.g., **dunkel**) drop the **-e** in the comparative: **dunkler**; **teuer** frequently does the same: **teu(e)rer**.

c. A few adjectives and adverbs have irregular forms in the comparative and / or superlative

gern	**lieber**	**liebst-**
groß	**größer**	**größt-**
gut	**besser**	**best-**
hoch (hoh-)	**höher**	**höchst-**
nah	**näher**	**nächst-**
viel	**mehr**	**meist-**

Big Mäc-Esser fahren besser

2. The comparative of PREDICATE ADJECTIVES (after **sein, werden** and **bleiben**) and of ADVERBS is formed as described above. The superlative is preceded by **am** and ends in **-sten**.

> **billig   billiger   am billigsten**

Die Wurst ist billig.	*The sausage is cheap.*
Der Käse ist billig**er**.	*The cheese is cheaper.*
Das Brot ist **am** billig**sten**.	*The bread is the cheapest.*

Ich fahre **gern** mit dem Bus.	*I like to go by bus.*
Ich fahre **lieber** mit dem Fahrrad.	*I prefer to (I'd rather) go by bike.*
Ich gehe **am liebsten** zu Fuß.	*Best of all I like (I like best) to walk.*
Ich laufe **viel**.	*I walk a lot.*
Theo läuft **mehr**.	*Theo walks more.*
Katrin läuft **am meisten**.	*Katrin walks the most (i.e., more than Theo and I).*

CAUTION

Point out that **meisten** in **die meisten Leute** is an adjective, **am meisten** is an adverb of manner, and **meistens** an adverb of time.

Die **meisten** Leute gehen gern spazieren.	*Most people love to walk.*
Mein Vater geht **am meisten** spazieren.	*My father walks the most.*
Mein Vater geht **meistens** in den Park.	*My father goes mostly to the park.*

3. Adjectives in the comparative and superlative forms that describe nouns (e.g., *the better wine*) have the same endings as preceded and unpreceded adjectives in the positive forms (see Chapters 9 and 10).

der gut**e** Käse	der besser**e** Käse	der best**e** Käse
Ihr gut**er** Käse	Ihr besser**er** Käse	Ihr best**er** Käse
gut**er** Käse	besser**er** Käse	best**er** Käse

Haben Sie keinen besser**en** Käse? Doch, aber besser**er** Käse ist teuer**er**.

4. There are four special phrases frequently used in comparisons:

a. When you want to say that one thing is like another or not quite like another, use **(genau)so . . . wie** or **nicht so . . . wie**.

Ich bin **(genau)so alt wie** sie.	*I'm (just) as old as she is.*
Sie ist **nicht so fit wie** ich.	*She is not as fit as I am.*

b. If you want to bring out a difference, use the **comparative + als**.

Ich bin **älter als** Helga.	*I'm older than Helga.*
Er ist **jünger als** sie.	*He is younger than she (is).*

c. If you want to express that something is getting continually more so, use **immer + comparative**.

Die Tage werden **immer länger**.	*The days are getting longer and longer.*
Ich gehe **immer später** ins Bett.	*I'm getting to bed later and later.*

d. If you are dealing with a pair of comparatives, use **je + comparative . . . desto + comparative**.

If you prefer: **je . . . desto = je . . . um so.**

Je länger, **desto** besser.	*The longer, the better.*
Je länger ich arbeite, **desto** müder bin ich.	*The longer I work, the more tired I am.*
Je früher ich ins Bett gehe, **desto** früher stehe ich morgens auf.	*The earlier I go to bed, the earlier I get up in the morning.*

Note that **je** is followed by dependent word order, while **desto** is a coordinating conjunction.

ÜBUNGEN

A. Komparative und Superlative. Geben Sie den Komparativ und den Superlativ, und dann die Formen des Gegenteils!

BEISPIEL: schnell **schneller, am schnellsten**
langsam, langsamer, am langsamsten

billig, sauber, gesund, groß, gut, hübsch, intelligent, jung, kalt, lang, laut, nah, neu, viel

B. Ersetzen Sie die Adjektive!

BEISPIEL: Diese Zeitung ist so langweilig wie die andere Zeitung. (interessant)
Diese Zeitung ist so interessant wie die andere Zeitung.

1. Axel ist so groß wie Horst. (alt, nett)
2. Hier ist es kühler als bei euch. (kalt, heiß)
3. Fernsehsendungen werden immer langweiliger. (verrückt, dumm)
4. Je länger das Buch ist, desto besser. (spannend, interessant)

C. Antworten Sie mit nein! Use the new adjective or adverb in your response, as shown in the example.

BEISPIEL: Ist dein Großvater auch so alt? (jung) **Nein, er ist jünger.**

1. Waren euere Schuhe auch so schmutzig? (sauber)
2. Verdient Jutta auch so wenig? (viel)
3. Ist seine Wohnung auch so toll? (einfach)
4. Sind die Geschäftsleute dort auch so unfreundlich? (freundlich)
5. Ist es bei Ihnen auch so laut? (ruhig)
6. Ist die Schule auch so weit weg? (nah)
7. Ist Ihre Arbeit auch so anstrengend? (leicht)

D. Wie geht's weiter? Complete each sentence, first with a comparative and then with a superlative.

BEISPIEL: Inge spricht schnell, aber . . .
Maria spricht schneller. Peter spricht am schnellsten.

1. Willi hat lange geschlafen, aber . . .
2. Brot zum Frühstück schmeckt gut, aber . . .
3. Ich trinke morgens gern Tee, aber . . .
4. Die Montagszeitung ist dick, aber . . .
5. Ich spreche viel am Telefon, aber . . .
6. Deutsch ist schwer, aber . . .
7. Hier ist es schön, aber . . .

E. Ersetzen Sie die Adjektive!

BEISPIEL: Peter ist der sportlichste Junge. (talentiert)
Peter ist der talentierteste Junge.

1. Da drüben ist ein moderneres Geschäft. (gut)

2. Mein jüngster Bruder ist nicht verheiratet. (alt)
3. Das ist die interessanteste Nachricht. (neu)
4. Zieh dir einen wärmeren Pullover an! (dick)
5. Die besten Autos sind sehr teuer. (viel)

F. Vergleiche. Complete the following sentence fragments by comparing different professions.

BEISPIEL: ... verdienen viel, aber ...
Professoren und Professorinnen verdienen viel, aber Ärzte und Ärztinnen verdienen mehr.

1. ... verdienen wenig, aber ...
2. ... haben viel Freizeit, aber ...
3. ... haben viel Papierkrieg *(paper work)*, aber ...
4. ... haben viel Fahrerei *(driving)*, aber ...
5. ... zu sein ist interessant, aber ...
6. ... zu sein ist anstrengend, aber ...

G. Eine bessere Stelle. Was fehlt?
1. Möchtest du nicht _____ Postbeamter werden? *(rather)*
2. Der Staat *(state)* bezahlt _____ deine Firma. *(better than)*
3. Da hast du _____ Sicherheit *(f.)*. *(the greatest)*

Students need time to think about these comparisons; so you might want to assign this as homework.

Verkehrspolizistin in Zürich

4. Bei der Post hast du _____ Freizeit _____ bei deiner Firma. (*just as much . . . as*)

5. Vielleicht hast du sogar _____ Zeit _____ jetzt. (*more . . . than*)

6. Es ist auch nicht _____ anstrengend _____ jetzt. (*as . . . as*)

7. _____ Leute arbeiten für den Staat. (*more and more*)

8. _____ Leuten gefällt es. (*most*)

9. Ich finde es bei der Post _____ und _____. (*the most interesting, the safest*)

10. Eine _____ Stelle gibt es nicht. (*nicer*)

11. _____ du wirst, _____ ist es zu wechseln. (*the older . . . the harder*)

12. Wenn du eine _____ Stelle haben willst, dann wechsele bald! _____ früher, _____ besser. (*better, the . . . the*)

13. Beamter ist für mich _____ Beruf. (*the most beautiful*)

14. Vielleicht verdienst du etwas _____. (*less*)

15. Aber dafür hast du _____ _____ Probleme (*pl.*) (*mostly, few*)

H. Interview. Fragen Sie einen Nachbarn / eine Nachbarin, . . .!

1. ob er / sie größer als die Eltern oder Großeltern ist

2. ob er / sie jüngere Brüder oder Schwestern hat, und wer am jüngsten und ältesten ist

3. was er / sie am liebsten ißt und trinkt, und ob er / sie abends meistens warm oder kalt ißt

4. wo er / sie am liebsten essen geht, und wo es am billigsten und am teuersten ist

5. welche Fernsehsendung ihm / ihr am besten gefällt, und was er / sie am meisten sieht

6. was er / sie am liebsten in der Freizeit macht, und was er / sie am nächsten Wochenende tut

7. welche amerikanische Stadt er / sie am schönsten und am häßlichsten findet und warum

8. wo er / sie jetzt am liebsten sein möchte und warum

PORSCHE
FAHREN IN SEINER SCHÖNSTEN FORM.

II. The Future

As you know, future events are often referred to in the present tense in both English and German, particularly when a time expression points to the future.

Wir **gehen** heute abend ins Kino.

{ *We're going to the movies tonight.*
We will go to the movies tonight.
We shall go to the movies tonight.

In German conversation this is the preferred form. However, German does have a future tense. It is used when there is no time expression and under somewhat formal circumstances.

1. The FUTURE consists of **werden** as the auxiliary plus the infinitive of the verb.

werden . . . + infinitive	
ich **werde** . . . gehen	wir **werden** . . . gehen
du **wirst** . . . gehen	ihr **werdet** . . . gehen
er **wird** . . . gehen	sie **werden** . . . gehen

Ich **werde** ins Büro **gehen**.   *I'll go to the office.*
Wirst du mich **anrufen**?   *Will you call me?*

2. If the future sentence also contains a modal, the modal appears as an infinitive at the very end.

werden . . . + verb infinitive + modal infinitive

Ich **werde** ins Büro **gehen müssen**.   *I'll have to go to the office.*
Wirst du mich **anrufen können**?   *Will you be able to call me?*

3. Sentences in the future follow familiar word-order rules.

Er **wird** auch **kommen**.
Er **wird** auch **mitkommen**.
Er **wird** auch **mitkommen wollen**.
  V1   V2

Ich weiß, daß er auch **kommen wird**.
Ich weiß, daß er auch **mitkommen wird**.
                    V2   V1

4. The future form can also express PRESENT PROBABILITY especially when used with the word **wohl**.

Er wird wohl auf dem Weg sein.   *He is probably on the way (now).*
Sie wird wohl krank sein.   *She is probably sick (now).*

5. Don't confuse the modal **wollen** with the future auxiliary **werden**!

Er **will** auch mitkommen.   *He wants to (intends to) come along, too.*
Er **wird** auch mitkommen.   *He will come along, too.*

And remember that **werden** is also a full verb in itself, meaning *to get, to become*!

Es **wird** kalt.   *It's getting cold.*

ÜBUNGEN

I. Sagen Sie die Sätze in der Zukunft!

BEISPIEL: Gute Zahnärzte braucht man immer.
          Gute Zahnärzte wird man immer brauchen.

1. Dabei verdiene ich auch gut. **2.** Aber du studierst einige Jahre auf der Universität. **3.** Ich gehe nicht zur Uni. **4.** Meine Tischlerarbeit ist anstrengend. **5.** Aber daran gewöhnst du dich. **6.** Fängst du bei deiner Tante an? **7.** Dieser Beruf hat bestimmt Zukunft. **8.** Ihr seht das schon. **9.** Eines Tages mache ich mich selbständig. **10.** Als Chefin *(boss)* in einem Männerberuf muß ich besonders gut sein. **11.** Das darfst du nicht vergessen. **12.** Aber ich kann vielen Leuten helfen.

J. Beginnen Sie jeden Satz mit Wissen Sie, ob . . .?

BEISPIEL: Er wird bald zurückkommen.
Wissen Sie, ob er bald zurückkommen wird?

1. Wir werden in Frankfurt umsteigen.
2. Sie wird sich die Sendung ansehen.
3. Zimmermanns werden die Wohnung mieten.
4. Willi und Eva werden bald heiraten.
5. Müllers werden in Zürich bleiben.
6. Wir werden fahren oder fliegen.

K. Was bedeutet das auf englisch?

BEISPIEL: Martina wird Journalistin.
Martina is going to be a journalist.

1. Walter will Polizist werden. **2.** Die Kinder werden zu laut. **3.** Ich werde am Bahnhof auf Sie warten. **4.** Petra wird wohl nicht kommen. **5.** Wir werden Sie gern mitnehmen. **6.** Sie wird Informatik studieren wollen. **7.** Oskar wird wohl noch im Büro sein. **8.** Wirst du wirklich Lehrer?

L. Eine moderne Familie. Auf deutsch, bitte!
1. Children, I want to tell you something. **2.** Your mother is going to be a lawyer. **3.** I'll have to stay home. **4.** I'll (do the) cook(ing). **5.** Helga, you will (do the) wash(ing). **6.** Karl and Maria, you will (do the) clean-(ing). **7.** We'll (do the) shop(ping) together. **8.** We'll have to work hard. **9.** But we'll get used to it. **10.** When we get tired, we'll take a break **(eine Pause machen)**. **11.** Your mother will make a lot of money (earn well). **12.** And we will help her.

L: 1. Kinder, ich will euch (et)was sagen. 2. Eure Mutter wird Rechtsanwältin. 3. Ich werde zu Hause bleiben müssen. 4. Ich werde kochen. 5. Helga, du wirst waschen. 6. Karl und Maria, ihr werdet putzen. 7. Wir werden zusammen einkaufen. 8. Wir werden schwer arbeiten müssen. 9. Aber wir werden uns daran gewöhnen. 10. Wenn wir müde werden, werden wir eine Pause machen. 11. Eure Mutter wird gut verdienen. 12. Und wir werden ihr helfen.

III. Nouns with Special Features

1. As you already know, German, unlike English, does NOT use the indefinite article before predicate nouns denoting professions, nationalities, religious preference, or political adherence:

Er ist **Amerikaner**.	*He is an American.*
Sie ist **Rechtsanwältin**.	*She's a lawyer.*

However, when an adjective precedes that noun, **ein** is used.

Er ist **ein** typischer Amerikaner.	*He's a typical American.*
Sie ist **eine** gute Rechtsanwältin.	*She's a good lawyer.*

You might want to point out that these are also called *adjectival nouns.*

2. German has a few nouns that are derived from adjectives and therefore change their endings with the preceding article and case.

| | singular | | plural |
	masc.	fem.	
nom.	der Deutsche ein Deutscher	die Deutsche	die Deutschen
acc.	den Deutschen einen Deutschen	eine Deutsche	keine Deutschen
dat.	dem Deutschen einem Deutschen	der Deutschen einer Deutschen	den Deutschen keinen Deutschen
gen.	des Deutschen eines Deutschen	der Deutschen einer Deutschen	der Deutschen keiner Deutschen

Also: **der Angestellte** *employee, clerk*; **Bekannte** *acquaintance*; **Kranke, Verlobte** *fiancé*; **Verwandte** *relative*

Also: der Beamte (ein Beamter)   BUT   die Beamtin (eine Beamtin)

Have students translate these examples.

Karl ist Beamter, und seine Frau ist Beamtin.
Ein Beamter hat das gesagt. Wie heißt der Beamte?
Hast du den Beamten da drüben gefragt? Ich sehe keinen Beamten.

ÜBUNGEN

M. Auf deutsch, bitte!
1. He's a composer.
2. Is she a housewife?
3. She's a very good scientist.
4. He's going to be a policeman.
5. He was a bad teacher but a good car salesman.
6. She is Austrian.

N. Was fehlt?
1. Ein Deutsch_____ hat mir das erzählt.
2. Hast du den nett_____ Deutsch _____ kennengelernt?
3. Geben Sie dem Beamt_____ die Papiere!
4. Auch viele Deutsch_____ sind heute ohne Arbeit.
5. Der Deutsch_____ ist Journalist.
6. Zeigen Sie den Deutsch_____ die Büros!
7. Was hat der Beamt_____ Ihnen gesagt?
8. In Deutschland verdient ein Beamt_____ sehr gut.

ZUSAMMENFASSUNG

O. Was ich einmal werden möchte / wollte. Write eight to ten sentences explaining what you would like to be, or once wanted to be, and why.

P. Zukunftspläne. Auf deutsch, bitte!

1. Did you *(pl. fam.)* know that Volker wants to become a journalist?   **2.** He doesn't want to be a teacher.   **3.** There are only a few teaching positions (**Lehrerstellen**).   **4.** I've gotten used to it.   **5.** Trudi is as enterprising as he is.   **6.** She was my most talented student (**Schülerin**).   **7.** If she wants to become a dentist, she will become a dentist.   **8.** She's smarter, more independent, and more likable than her brother.   **9.** She says she will work hard.   **10.** I know that she'll be self-employed one day.   **11.** I'll go to her rather than to another dentist.   **12.** The more I think of it, the better I like the idea.

P: 1. Habt ihr gewußt (Wußtet ihr), daß Volker Journalist werden will? 2. Er will kein (nicht) Lehrer werden. 3. Es gibt nur wenige Lehrerstellen. 4. Ich habe mich daran gewöhnt. 5. Trudi ist so unternehmungslustig wie er. 6. Sie war meine talentierteste Schülerin. 7. Wenn sie Zahnärztin werden will, wird sie Zahnärztin. 8. Sie ist intelligenter, selbständiger (unabhängiger) und sympathischer als ihr Bruder. 9. Sie sagt, daß sie fleißig arbeiten wird. 10. Ich weiß, daß sie eines Tages selbständig sein wird (sich selbständig machen wird). 11. Ich werde lieber zu ihr als zu einem anderen Zahnarzt gehen. 12. Je mehr ich daran denke, desto besser gefällt mir die Idee.

EINBLICKE ◆◆◆◆◆◆◆◆◆◆◆

Gleichberechtigung *(equal rights)* zu Hause

The merger of the two Germanies will stand as the major event in German history in the second half of this century. While the economic and political unification proceeded very quickly, the joining of two very different economic and social systems, sets of laws, and especially attitudes will cause debate for years to come.

The role of women is one such issue. In the GDR over 90% of the women were in the work force; in the FRG only about 50%. Only since 1976 have women had equal rights with men according to the Basic Law of the Federal Republic. The clause that women could work only if it was compatible with their obligations toward marriage and family was eliminated at that time.

Women have had equal access to schools, universities, and other training facilities in both countries for a long time, and women have increasingly taken advantage of these opportunities. On the whole, however, men are still better paid and women tend to work in areas that are undervalued and therefore pay less. Although German women won full voting rights in 1918, the number of women at the upper levels of business, government, and politics is still small. In recent years there have been clear signs that women as well as men are changing their attitudes about their roles; eventually, full equality may be achieved.

Point out the difference between **sich vorstellen** *(to introduce oneself)* and **sich vorstellen** *(to imagine);* **Darf ich mich vorstellen? Mein Name ist Schmidt. Darf ich vorstellen? Das ist Herr Schmidt!** BUT **Ich kann mir nicht vorstellen, wie ich fertig werden soll. (Stell dir das vor!** *Just imagine!* **Wie hast du dir das vorgestellt?** *How did you think that would work?)*

Pre-reading activity: **Was denken Sie?** 1. Was für Berufe haben Zukunft? 2. Wo wird es immer Arbeitsplätze geben? 3. Wie sehen Sie die Rolle von Mann und Frau in der Zukunft? 4. Werden die Computer unser Leben leichter machen, oder sind sie eine Gefahr? Geben Sie Beispiele! 5. Glauben Sie an eine bessere Zukunft? Warum (nicht)?

WORTSCHATZ 2

die Erde	earth
Gefahr, -en	danger
Luft	air
Umwelt	environment
Welt	world
darum	therefore
breit	broad; wide
früher	earlier; formerly
verantwortungsvoll	responsible
so daß	so that (subord. conj.)
gewinnen, gewann, gewonnen	to win
hoffen	to hope
teilen	to share
sich vor·stellen	to imagine
Ich stelle mir vor, daß . . .	I imagine that . . .

WAS IST DAS? der Arbeitsplatz, Biochemiker, Elektromechaniker, Leserbrief, Roboter; das Jahrhundert, Umweltproblem; die Berufsmöglichkeit, Bezahlung, Dritte Welt, Flexibilität, Freiheit, Geschäftswelt, Hoffnung, Kultur, Qualifikation, Rolle, Sicherheit, Spezialisierung; *(pl.)* die Medien, Mitmenschen; Gott sei Dank; halbtags, hoffnungsvoll, klar, kreativ, problematisch, zukunftssicher; integrieren, registrieren, übernehmen

Was wird werden?

(Leserbriefe über die Zukunft)

choice of . . .

at least

Ganz klar, die Berufswahl° wird immer problematischer. Sicher werden viele wenigstens° einmal ihren Beruf wechseln müssen. Darum wird eine breite Ausbildung wichtiger sein als eine Spezialisierung. Neben guten Fach-

special and (foreign) language skills
ability

und Sprachkenntnissen° wird man andere Qualifikationen suchen, z.B. die ⁵
Fähigkeit°, dazu zu lernen, kreativ zu denken und verantwortungsvoll zu
sein. Auf die Frage nach zukunftssicheren Berufen kann man nur schwer
eine Antwort geben. Aber bestimmt können Männer und Frauen als Biochemiker, Programmierer, Elektromechaniker, Ingenieure, Ärzte und Wissenschaftler immer Arbeit finden. Auch Handwerker° wird man nie genug ¹⁰
haben. Im Hotel- und Restaurantgeschäft, im Verkauf° und in hauswirt-
schaftlichen° Berufen wird es immer Arbeitsplätze geben. Eins ist sicher: eine
gute Ausbildung ist auch in der Zukunft die beste Sicherheit.

craftsmen
in sales
domestic

counselor

Lilo Friedrich, Berufsberaterin°

Im Labor

legally

Ich hoffe, daß die Frauen den Männern in der Zukunft nicht nur gesetz-
lich° gleich sind, sondern auch im wirklichen Leben; daß sie gleiche Berufsmöglichkeiten haben; und daß sie für gleiche Arbeit gleiche Bezahlung bekommen. Die Rollen der Männer und Frauen sind heute nicht mehr so klar
getrennt° wie früher; aber es wird bestimmt noch Jahre dauern, bis niemand ²⁰
es mehr° komisch findet, wenn der Mann zu Hause bleibt und auf die Kinder
aufpaßt und die Frau das Geld verdient. Ich hoffe, daß es dann auch leichter
sein wird, halbtags zu arbeiten oder eine Stelle zu teilen, so daß Arbeit und
Familie für Mann und Frau leichter zu integrieren sind.

separated
anymore

Marianne Dreesen, Studentin   25

change

Ich stelle mir vor, daß Computer und Roboter unsere Welt noch mehr
verändern° werden, als sie es schon getan haben. Nichts wird mehr ohne sie
gehen. Auf der einen Seite besteht die Gefahr, daß wir immer mehr zur

Nummer werden, weil die Computer alles registrieren—zu viel Information 30
in falscher Hand ist eine Gefahr für Freiheit. Auf der anderen Seite wird
der Computer immer mehr Arbeiten übernehmen, und der Mensch wird
dadurch größere Flexibilität und mehr Freizeit gewinnen.

Karl-Heinz Wendland, Beamter

35

destroy themselves

government / pressure

opinion / report

there is

cleaner / breathe

Kranke Wälder, kranke Kinder—kranke Kinder, kranke Zukunft. Wenn
die Menschen nicht verantwortungsvoller für ihre Erde werden, sehe ich die
Gefahr, daß sie sich eines Tages selbst vernichten°. Gott sei Dank ist schon
viel geschehen. Die Regierung° und Geschäftswelt stehen unter dem Druck°
der öffentlichen Meinung°. Die Medien berichten° täglich über Umweltpro- 40
bleme. Ja, es besteht° Hoffnung, daß unsere Kinder saubereres Wasser trinken und reinere° Luft atmen° werden.

Stephan Motsch, Wissenschaftler

united

development / affluence

understanding / peace /
  nations

mainly / armament

education

until now

Ein vereintes° Deutschland in einem vereinten Europa ist für mich die 45
hoffnungsvollste Entwicklung° in diesem Jahrhundert. Wohlstand°, Verstän-
digung° und Frieden° unter den Völkern° Europas werden es möglich machen, daß wir unser Geld nicht mehr hauptsächlich° für die Rüstung° ausgeben, sondern für Bildung°, Kultur und Umwelt. Auch unseren
Mitmenschen der Dritten Welt werden wir mehr helfen können als bisher°. 50
Ich glaube an eine bessere Zukunft.

Elke Wiegand, Journalistin

Wie geht's weiter?
1. Einige zukunftssi-
chere Berufe sind . . .
2. Qualifikationen
wie . . . sind wichtig.
3. Manche Leute finden
es immer noch komisch,
wenn . . . 4. Die Stu-
dentin hofft, daß . . .
5. Der Beamte sieht
eine Gefahr, daß wir
durch den Computer
. . . 6. Auf der ande-
ren Seite gewinnen
wir . . . 7. Der Wis-
senschaftler findet, daß
wir verantwortungs-
voller für . . . 8. In
den Medien hören wir
täglich über . . . 9. Die
Journalistin hofft, daß
ein vereintes Europa
. . . 10. Sie glaubt
an . . .

ZUM TEXT

A. Blick in die Zukunft

1. Die Berufsberaterin glaubt, in der Zukunft brauchen die Leute vor allem . . . .
   a. berufliche Spezialisierung
   b. weniger Sprachkenntnisse
   c. Qualifikationen wie die Fähigkeit, Verantwortung zu tragen
2. Die Studentin hofft, daß die Frauen in der Zukunft . . . .
   a. das Geld verdienen und die Männer zu Hause bleiben
   b. für gleiche Arbeit gleiche Bezahlung bekommen
   c. bessere Berufsmöglichkeiten haben als die Männer
3. Der Beamte stellt sich vor, daß wir in der Zukunft . . . .
   a. alle zum Computer werden
   b. alle Computer registrieren
   c. durch den Computer Freizeit gewinnen

4. Der Wissenschaftler denkt, daß die Leute . . . .
   a. verantwortungsvoller für ihre Umwelt werden müssen
   b. nichts für die Umwelt tun
   c. die öffentliche Meinung der Umwelt nicht hilft
5. Die Journalistin glaubt nicht besonders an . . . .
   a. ein vereintes Europa
   b. Kultur und Bildung
   c. Rüstung

B. Im nächsten Jahrhundert. Wiederholen Sie die Sätze in der Zukunft!

BEISPIEL: Im nächsten Jahrhundert ist alles anders.
   Im nächsten Jahrhundert wird alles anders sein.

1. Auf die Frage nach zukunftssicheren Berufen kann man nur schwer eine Antwort geben. **2.** Krankenschwestern und Wissenschaftler hat man nie genug. **3.** Eine gute Ausbildung ist die beste Sicherheit. **4.** Wir müssen verantwortungsvoller sein. **5.** Ohne Verantwortung helfen die besten Pläne nichts. **6.** Dann vernichten wir uns eines Tages selbst.

C. Vielleicht. Was fehlt?

1. Vielleicht können _____ Leute in der Zukunft nicht mehr ohne Computer sein. *(most)*
2. Der Computer wird aber nie _____ kreativ sein _____ ein Mensch. *(as . . . as)*
3. Aber er kann viel _____ denken _____ wir. *(faster . . . than)*
4. In der Zukunft wird die Berufswahl _____ problematischer werden. *(more and more)*
5. Darum wird eine breite Ausbildung _____ sein _____ eine Spezialisierung. *(more important . . . than)*
6. _____ Geld wir für die Rüstung ausgeben, _____ haben wir für Bildung und Umwelt. *(the less . . . the more)*
7. _____ wir jetzt für unsere Umwelt tun, _____ wird es uns und unsren Kindern in der Zukuft gehen. *(the more . . . the better)*

C: 1. die meisten
2. so . . . wie
3. schneller . . . als
4. immer 5. wichtiger
. . . als 6. je weniger
. . . desto mehr 7. je
mehr . . . desto besser

Ohne Worte
Dick Lucas, Masters Agency

Optional practice:
1. **Geben Sie den Komparativ und Superlativ!** z.B. einfach: einfacher, am einfachsten (breit, neu leicht, problematisch, klar, sicher, viel, gut wenig)
2. **Ersetzen Sie die Adjektive!** z.B. eine schönere Zukunft (gut, sicher) / die Frage nach sichereren Berufen (spannend, verantwortungsvoll) / die beste Sicherheit (groß, viel, hoch), unsere schönsten Pläne (neu, nah)

D. Stellenangebot (*job offer*). Write down a list of five to six questions you would ask during an interview for the advertised position.

Das McDonald's Hauptbüro für Europa in Frankfurt sucht zum baldmöglichsten Eintritt eine

Fremdsprachensekretärin

mit sehr gutem bzw. muttersprachlichem Italienisch sowie perfekten Deutsch- und Englischkenntnissen zur Unterstützung unserer Abteilungssekretärin für die Real Estate, Licensing und Legal Departments.

Wenn Sie eine bewegliche und umsichtige Kollegin sind, die Spaß an viel Arbeit in einem jungen Team hat, sollten Sie sich umgehend bei uns melden.

Bewerbungen für diese Position senden Sie bitte an:

McDonald's System of Europe, Inc.
z. Hd. Frau Mohib
Kennedyallee 109
6000 Frankfurt/Main 70

Das etwas andere Restaurant

E. In zehn / zwanzig / dreißig Jahren. Write a paragraph of eight to ten sentences telling how you picture your life or life on this earth ten, twenty, or thirty years from now.

BEISPIEL: In zehn Jahren werde ich dreißig sein. Dann werde ich . . .
          In zehn Jahren wird nichts mehr ohne den Computer gehen . . .

SPRECHSITUATIONEN

When you participate in a discussion of a controversial topic, you need to be able to express agreement or disagreement.

Expressing Agreement

Richtig!
Genau! *(Exactly.)*
Das stimmt. / Das ist wahr! *(That's true.)*
Natürlich. / (Na) klar. *(Of course.)*
Sie haben recht.
Das finde / glaube ich auch.

Expressing Disagreement

Also: **Da irrst du dich!**
There you are wrong!

Das stimmt nicht.   Unsinn! / Quatsch! *(Nonsense.)*
(Das ist) gar nicht wahr!   Ach was! *(Oh, come on!)*
Im Gegenteil. *(On the contrary.)*   Das ist doch lächerlich *(ridiculous).*
Das finde ich (gar) nicht.   Auf der anderen Seite *(hand)* . . .
Das glaube ich (aber) nicht.

Expressing Hesitation

If you don't know how you feel about a topic or what to say—which might happen when conversing in a foreign language—you can use one of these phrases to bridge the gap.

Nun / na ja / tja / also . . .   *Well . . .*
Mal sehen . . .   *Let's see . . .*
Ich weiß nicht.   *I don't know.*
(Ich habe) keine Ahnung.   *(I have) no idea.*
Gute Frage.   *Good question.*
Das kommt darauf an.   *That depends.*

A. **Was hältst du davon?** Working with a classmate, take turns expressing your feelings about the statements below.
   1. Die Schweiz ist keine Reise wert.
   2. Wir haben heute schon viel zu viel Freizeit.
   3. Wir leben heute gesünder als unsere Eltern und Großeltern.
   4. Es ist heute noch wichtiger als früher, Fremdsprachen zu lernen.
   5. Wir sitzen alle zu viel vor dem Fernseher.
   6. Fernsehen macht dumm.

7. Kinder interessieren sich heute nicht mehr für Märchen.
8. Es ist doch komisch, wenn der Mann zu Hause bleibt und auf die Kinder aufpaßt, während die Frau arbeitet.

B. Was denkst du? Take turns with a classmate asking each other questions. Express hesitation before you answer.
1. Was willst du einmal werden? Warum? (Warum bist du . . . geworden?)
2. Wohin möchtest du am liebsten reisen? Warum?
3. Möchtest du gern für den Staat arbeiten? Warum (nicht)?
4. Was für Sendungen siehst du am liebsten im Fernsehen? Warum?
5. Wie hältst du dich am liebsten fit? Warum?
6. Welche Eigenschaft ist dir am wichtigsten bei einem Freund / einer Freundin oder einem Partner / einer Partnerin?

C. An wen denke ich? Work in groups of four to five students. One thinks of a famous person, the others may ask up to twenty questions to figure out who it is.

13

Das Studium

DEM LEBENDIGEN GEIST

An der Heidelberger
Universität

▮ LERNZIELE

Gespräche and **Wortschatz**. This chapter deals with universities and student life.

Struktur. You will learn about . . .

- the subjunctive mood.
- the present-time general subjunctive.
- the past-time general subjunctive.

Einblicke. Talking about a possible year abroad

Sprechsituationen

- Giving advice
- Asking for permission
- Granting or denying permission

347

◆◆◆◆◆◆ GESPRÄCHE

Warm-ups: 1. **Welche Adjektive beginnen mit** a, b, c, f, g, h, k, l, n, r, s, v? Was ist der Komparativ und der Superlativ dazu? z.B. neu: neuer, am neuesten 2. **Wofür geben Sie viel Geld aus?** Was ist billig / teuer? 3. **Was tun Sie,** wenn Sie keine Lust haben zu lernen, d.h., wenn Sie faul sind? wenn Sie sich erkältet haben? wenn es regnet? wenn es sehr heiß ist? 4. **Was für Berufe kennen Sie?**

Bei der Immatrikulation

PETRA   Tag, David! Wie geht's?
DAVID   Danke, gut. Und dir?
PETRA   Prima! Was machst du denn da?
DAVID   Ich muß diese Antragsformulare hier ausfüllen.
PETRA   Soll ich dir helfen?
DAVID   Wenn du Zeit hast.
PETRA   Hast du deinen Paß dabei?
DAVID   Nein, wieso?
PETRA   Darin ist deine Aufenthaltserlaubnis[1]. Die brauchen wir.
DAVID   Ich kann ihn ja schnell holen.
PETRA   Tu das! Ich warte hier auf dich.

Etwas später

DAVID   Hier ist mein Paß. Ich muß mich jetzt auch bald entscheiden, was ich belegen soll. Kannst du mir da auch ein bißchen helfen?
PETRA   Na klar. Was ist denn dein Hauptfach? Wofür interessierst du dich?
DAVID   Mein Hauptfach ist moderne Geschichte. Ich möchte Kurse über deutsche Geschichte und Literatur belegen.
PETRA   Hier ist mein Vorlesungsverzeichnis. Sehen wir mal . . .!

Am Schwarzen Brett *(bulletin board)* gibt's Information über die Kurse.

◆◆◆◆◆◆◆◆◆◆◆◆◆◆◆◆◆◆◆◆◆◆◆◆◆◆◆◆◆◆◆◆

Übrigens

1. Everyone in Germany has to be registered with the **Einwohnermeldeamt** at his or her place of residence. Non-Germans who wish to reside in Germany longer than two months must get a residence permit (**Aufenthaltserlaubnis**).

During Registration PETRA: *Hi, David. How are you?* DAVID: *Fine thanks. And how are you?* PETRA: *Very well. What are you doing there?* DAVID: *I've got to fill out these application forms.* PETRA: *Do you want me to help you?* DAVID: *If you have time.* PETRA: *Do you have your passport with you?* DAVID: *No, why?* PETRA: *In it is your residence permit. We need it.* DAVID: *I can get it quickly.* PETRA: *Do that. I'll wait for you here.*

A Little Later DAVID: *Here is my passport. I'll also have to decide soon what to take. Can you help me a little with that, too?* PETRA: *Sure. What's your major? What are you interested in?* DAVID: *My major is modern history. I'd like to take some courses in German history and literature.* PETRA: *Here's my course catalog. Let's see . . .*

WORTSCHATZ 1

DAS STUDIUM *(course of) study*

der	Hörsaal, -säle	*lecture hall*	das	Seminar, -e	*seminar*
	Kurs, -e	*course*		Stipendium,	*scholarship*
	Professor, -en	*professor*		Stipendien	
	Zimmerkollege, -n, -n	*roommate*	die	Arbeit, -en	*(term) paper*
das	Fach, ¨er	*subject*		Note, -n	*grade*
	Hauptfach, ¨er	*major (field)*		Prüfung, -en	*exam*
	Nebenfach, ¨er	*minor (field)*		Vorlesung, -en	*lecture*
	Labor, -s	*lab*		Wissenschaft, -en	*science*
	Semester, -	*semester*		Zimmerkollegin, -nen	*roommate*

belegen	*to sign up for, take (a course)*
bestehen, bestand, bestanden	*to pass (an exam)*
sich entscheiden, entschied, entschieden	*to decide*
holen	*to get (fetch)*
lehren	*to teach*
eine Prüfung schreiben	*to take an exam*

WEITERES

wieso?	*why? how come?*

PASSIVES VOKABULAR der Antrag, ¨e *application*   das Formular, -e das System, -e   das Quartal, -e *quarter*   das Vorlesungsverzeichnis, -se *course catalog*   die Aufenthaltserlaubnis *residence permit*   dabei *with / on you*

Universität in
Hildesheim

ZUM THEMA

A. Was sagt Ihnen der Schein? What does this certificate tell you about Miriam
and her studies? Make five statements in German.

While freedom of reli-
gion is guaranteed, the
German government
nonetheless collects
church taxes and pro-
vides financial support
to churches, mainly the
Catholic and Protestant
Churches. Religion is
taught in primary and
secondary schools, al-
though not obligatory.
Questions about religion
may be asked to provide
appropriate services, if
necessary, and for statis-
tical purposes (as in the
application on page
351).

Optional vocabulary: A
(**sehr gut** = 1), B (**gut** =
2), C (**befriedigend** =
3), D (**ausreichend** =
4), E (**mangelhaft** = 5),
F (**ungenügend** = 6).

Universität Regensburg
Deutsch als Fremdsprache

~~Herrn~~
~~Frau~~/Frl. .... Miriam Burton ....

aus .... den USA ....
wird hiermit bescheinigt, daß $\frac{\text{er}}{\text{sie}}$ an dem DEUTSCHKURS

.... Landeskunde - Oberstufe I ....

im ~~Sommer~~/Winter Semester 19 90/91..... teilgenommen hat.

~~Er~~
Sie hat die Abschlußprüfung mit .... sehr gut ....

bestanden.

Regensburg, den ...... 25.2.91 ....

(Dr. Armin Wolff, Akad. Direktor)

Bewertung: sehr gut (1); gut (2); befriedigend (3); ausreichend (4)

B. Füllen Sie den Antrag aus!

A N T R A G

für die Aufnahme als ordentliche(r) Studierende(r) an der Universität

I. Angaben zur Person

Familienname: | 01 |

Geburtsname
(z. B. bei Frauen Mädchenname)

Vornamen: | 02 |

Geburtsort: | 03 | / _____ (Ort) / (Bundesland oder Staat)

Geburtstag:
z. B. [0 1 0 6 5 6] = 1. 6. 6 | 04 | Tag Mon. Jahr

Geschlecht: Männlich (1)   Weiblich (2) ──────────► | 05 |

Familienstand: Ledig (1) Verheiratet (2) Verwitwet (0) Geschieden (4) ──────► | 06 |

Zahl der Kinder: (Ohne = 0) ──────────────────► | 07 |

Religionszugehörigkeit: Röm.-Kath. (1) Evangelisch (0) Jüdisch (3) Muslemisch (4)
Orthodox (5) Sonstige (6) Keine (7) ────────── | 08 |

Staatsangehörigkeit: | 09 |

| 10 a | (Bundesland)   (Kreis)

Ständiger Wohnsitz: | 10 b | Postleitzahl / Ort / Kreis / Bundesland, bei Ausländern Staat

| 11 | Straße und Hausnummer

Semesteranschrift: | 12 | Postleitzahl / Ort

| 13 | Straße und Hausnummer

| 14 | Name des Vermieters   Telefon:

Bonner Universität

C. Fragen übers Studium. Fragen Sie einen Nachbarn / eine Nachbarin, . . .!

1. was er / sie studiert (hat) und warum
2. wie viele Kurse er / sie dieses Semester belegt hat und welche
3. welche Kurse er / sie besonders gut findet, und worin er / sie die besten Noten hat
4. ob er / sie viele Arbeiten schreiben muß; wenn ja, in welchen Fächern
5. ob er / sie außer Deutsch noch andere Sprachen spricht oder lernt
6. wie lange er noch studieren muß (studiert hat)
7. was er / sie danach macht (gemacht hat)

Anglistik[1]	Informatik[5]	Pharmazie
Archäologie	Krankenpflege[6]	Philologie
Architektur	Kunstgeschichte	Philosophie
Bergbau[2]	Landwirtschaft[7]	Physik
Betriebswirtschaft[3]	Lebensmittelchemie	Politik(wissenschaft)
Biochemie	Linguistik	Psychologie
Biologie	Maschinenbau[8]	Romanistik[10]
Chemie	Mathematik	Slawistik
Elektrotechnik	Medizin	Soziologie
Forstwirtschaft[4]	Mineralogie	Theologie
Geologie	Musikwissenschaft	Tiefbau[11]
Germanistik	Naturwissenschaften	Volkswirtschaft[12]
Hauswirtschaft	Pädagogik[9]	Zahnmedizin

1 English   **2** mining   **3** business administration   **4** forestry   **5** computer science   **6** nursing   **7** agriculture   **8** mechanical engineering   **9** education   **10** Romance languages   **11** civil engineering   **12** economics

D. Aussprache. See also III. 6 and 12 in the pronunciation section of the Workbook.

1. [z]   so, sauber, sicher, Saal, Semester, Seminar, Musik, Physik, Reise, Pause, lesen

2. [s]   bis, eins, Ausweis, Kurs, Professor, Adresse, wissen, lassen, vergessen, interessant, außerdem, fleißig, häßlich, Fuß, Fluß, Grüße, Paß

3. [št]   statt, stolz, Studium, Stipendium, Student, Stück, Staat, Stunde, bestehen, studieren, anstrengend, bestimmt

4. [st]   erste, beste, meistens, desto, Journalist, Komponist, Kunst, Lust, Prost

5. [šp]   Spiel, Sport, Spaß, Speisekarte, Sprache, spät, spanisch, sportlich, spannend

STRUKTUR

1. The Subjunctive Mood

Assure students that there is nothing extraordinary about the subjunctive. It is used all the time in everyday speech.

Until now, almost all sentences in this book have been in the INDICATIVE MOOD. Sentences in the indicative mood are assumed to be based on reality. Sometimes, however, we want to speculate on matters that are unreal, uncertain, or unlikely, or we wish for something that cannot be, or we want to approach other people less directly, more discreetly and politely. These things are done in the SUBJUNCTIVE MOOD.

1. Polite Requests or Questions

   Would you like a cup of coffee?
   Would you pass me the butter?
   Could you help me for a moment?

2. Hypothetical Statements and Questions

   He should be here any moment.
   What would you do?
   You should have been there.

3. Wishes

   If only I had more time.
   I wish you would hurry up.
   I wish I had known that.

4. Unreal Conditions

   If I had time, I'd go to a movie. (But I don't have time, so I'm not going.)
   If the weather were good, we'd go for a walk. (But it's raining, so we won't go.)
   If you had told me, I could have helped you. (But you didn't tell me, so I couldn't help you.)

Contrast the sentences above with real conditions:

If I have time, I'll go to a movie.
If the weather is good, we'll go for a walk.

In real conditions the possibility exists that the events will take place. In unreal conditions this possibility does not exist or is highly unlikely.

NOTE: The forms of the present-time subjunctive are derived from the simple past: *If I told you (now)* . . . Those of the past-time subjunctive are derived from the past perfect: *If you had told me (yesterday)* . . . Another very common way to express the subjunctive mood is the form *would. I'd go, I would not stay home.*

ÜBUNG

A: This exercise is intended to give students a feeling for the subjunctive vs. the indicative. You might ask them to look for such sentences in conversation or in assignments for other subjects. You also can bring similar sentences to class until the students are confident about the subjunctive. They MUST become aware of this in English before trying to cope with it in German.

A. Indikativ oder Konjunktiv (*subjunctive*)? Indicate whether sentences are in the indicative or in the subjunctive, and whether they refer to the present, future, or past.

BEISPIEL: If you don't ask, you won't know.   **indicative, present / future**
What would you do?   **subjunctive, present-time**

1. If she can, she'll write.
2. If only he'd study more.
3. If only I had known that.
4. They could be here any minute.
5. Will you take the bike along?
6. Would you please hold this?
7. Could they help us for a minute?
8. I had known that all along.
9. We should really be going.
10. I wish you had told me that.
11. If you were a student, you could fly for a lower fare.
12. I wish I could buy that car.
13. Could you take the children along?
14. You shouldn't go barefoot in this weather.
15. What would she have done if you hadn't come along?
16. If it rains, we won't go.
17. If we had had the money, we'd have bought it.
18. I couldn't come yesterday because I was ill.
19. If she has the money, she'll give it to us.
20. You could have told me.

II. The Present-Time General Subjunctive

German has two subjunctives. The one most commonly used is often referred to in grammar books as the GENERAL SUBJUNCTIVE or SUBJUNCTIVE II. (The SPECIAL SUBJUNCTIVE or SUBJUNCTIVE I, primarily found in written German, is explained in Chapter 15.)

1. Forms

The PRESENT-TIME SUBJUNCTIVE refers to the present *(now)* or the future *(later)*. Its forms are derived from the forms of the simple past. You already know the verb endings from having used the **möchten**-forms of **mögen,** which are actually subjunctive forms. All verbs in the subjunctive have these endings:

ich möch**te**	wir möch**ten**
du möch**test**	ihr möch**tet**
er möch**te**	sie möch**ten**

a. t-Verbs

The present-time subjunctive forms of regular t-verbs cannot be distinguished from those of the simple past. Their use usually becomes clear from context.

Wenn Sie mir nur **glaubten!**   *If only you would believe me.*
Wenn er mir nur **antwortete!**   *If only he would answer me.*

b. Irregular t-Verbs

Most of the irregular t-verbs, which include the modals, have an umlaut in the present-time subjunctive. Exceptions are **sollen** and **wollen**.

	haben **hatte**	wissen **wußte**	bringen **brachte**	müssen **mußte**	sollen **sollte**
ich	hätte	wüßte	brächte	müßte	sollte
du	hättest	wüßtest	brächtest	müßtest	solltest
er	hätte	wüßte	brächte	müßte	sollte
wir	hätten	wüßten	brächten	müßten	sollten
ihr	hättet	wüßtet	brächtet	müßtet	solltet
sie	hätten	wüßten	brächten	müßten	sollten
	had, would have	*knew, would know*	*brought, would bring*	*had to, would have to*	*should, ought to*

Hättest du Zeit?　　　　　　*Would you have time?*
Könntest du kommen?　　　　*Could you come?*

c. n-Verbs

The present-time subjunctive forms of n-verbs add the subjunctive endings to the past stem. If the past stem vowel is an **a, o,** or **u,** the subjunctive forms have an umlaut.

	gehen **ging**	bleiben **blieb**	sein **war**	kommen **kam**	fliegen **flog**	werden **wurde**
ich	ginge	bliebe	wäre	käme	flöge	würde
du	gingest	bliebest	wärest	kämest	flögest	würdest
er	ginge	bliebe	wäre	käme	flöge	würde
wir	gingen	blieben	wären	kämen	flögen	würden
ihr	ginget	bliebet	wäret	kämet	flöget	würdet
sie	gingen	blieben	wären	kämen	flögen	würden
	went, would go	*stayed, would stay*	*were, would be*	*came, would come*	*flew, would fly*	*got / became would get / become*

Wenn ich du **wäre, ginge** ich nicht.　　　*If I were you, I wouldn't go.*

d. würde-form

In conversation speakers of German commonly use the subjunctive forms of **haben, sein, werden, wissen,** and the modals.

Hättest du Zeit?	*Would you have time?*
Das wäre schön.	*That would be nice.*
Was möchtest du tun?	*What would you like to do?*

Wenn ich das nur wüßte!   *If only I knew that.*
Wir könnten ins Kino gehen.   *We could go to the movies.*

For the subjunctive forms of other verbs, however, German speakers frequently substitute a simpler verb phrase which closely corresponds to the English *would + infinitive.*

Was **würde** dir Spaß **machen?**   *What would amuse you?*
Ich **würde** lieber tanzen **gehen.**   *I'd rather go dancing.*

Due to its simplicity the **würde**-form is very common in everyday speech. It's the preferred form when the subjunctive is identical to the indicative (t-verbs) and especially where there are irregular subjunctive forms (**kennte, nennte; begönne, hülfe, stünde,** etc.) which we avoid in this text. It's also frequently used in the conclusion clause of a contrary-to-fact condition: **Wenn ich könnte, würde ich . . .**

2. Uses

You are already familiar with the most common uses of the subjunctive in English. Here are examples of these uses in German.

a. Polite Requests or Questions

Möchtest du eine Tasse Kaffee?   *Would you like a cup of coffee?*
Würdest du mir die Butter geben?   *Would you pass me the butter?*
Könntest du mir einen   *Could you help me for a minute?*
Moment helfen?

b. Hypothetical Statements and Questions

Er sollte jeden Moment hier sein.   *He should be here any minute.*
Das wäre schön.   *That would be nice.*
Was würdest du tun?   *What would you do?*
Ich würde spazierengehen.   *I'd go for a walk.*

c. Wishes

▪ Wishes starting with **Wenn** . . . usually add **nur** after the subjunctive or any pronoun object.

Wenn ich nur mehr Zeit hätte!   *If only I had more time.*
Wenn er mir nur glaubte!   *If only he'd believe me.*

▪ Wishes starting with **Ich wünschte,** . . . have BOTH CLAUSES in the subjunctive.

Ich wünschte, ich hätte mehr Zeit.   *I wish I had more time.*
Ich wünschte, du würdest   *I wish you'd hurry.*
dich beeilen.

d. Unreal Conditions

Wenn ich Zeit hätte, würde ich   *If I had time, I'd go to a movie.*
ins Kino gehen.
Wenn ihr mitkommen wolltet,   *If you wanted to come along, you'd*
müßtet ihr euch beeilen.   *have to hurry.*
Wenn wir euch helfen könn-   *If we could help you, we would do it.*
ten, würden wir das tun.

Contrast the preceding sentences with real conditions.

Wenn ich Zeit habe, gehe ich   *If I have time, I'll go to a movie.*
ins Kino.

Wenn ihr mitkommen wollt, müßtet ihr euch beeilen.

*If you want to come along, you'll have
to hurry.*

Wenn wir euch helfen können,
tun wir es.

If we can help you, we'll do it.

Translating these songs
might help clarify the
difference between the
indicative and the sub-
junctive. You could sing
them, too. **Mein Hut . . .**
can be a lot of fun as
you leave out one word
in each round and re-
place it with a gesture.

Wenn ich ein Vöglein° wär',   *little bird*
und auch zwei Flügel° hätt',   *wings*
flög' ich zu dir.
Weil's aber nicht kann sein,
weil's aber nicht kann sein,
bleib' ich allhier°.   *right here*

    Mein Hut°, der hat drei Ecken.   *hat*
    Drei Ecken hat mein Hut.
    Und hätt' er nicht drei Ecken,
    dann wär' es nicht mein Hut.

ÜBUNGEN

B. Was tun? Auf englisch, bitte!

1. Wohin möchtest du gehen?
2. Wir könnten uns einen Film ansehen.
3. Wir sollten in die Zeitung sehen.
4. Ich würde lieber zu Hause bleiben.
5. Ich wünschte, ich wäre nicht so müde.
6. Hättest du morgen abend Zeit?
7. Ich ginge heute lieber früh ins Bett.
8. Morgen könnte ich länger schlafen.

Peter

Wenn ich meinen Eltern alles erzählen würde, na dann gute Nacht!

C. Geben Sie das Imperfekt und die Konjunktivform!

BEISPIEL: ich hole   **ich holte / ich holte**
             du bringst   **du brachtest / du brächtest**
             er kommt   **er kam / er käme**

1. ich frage, mache, belege, studiere, lehre, versuche
2. du arbeitest, antwortest, wartest, öffnest, heiratest
3. er muß, kann, darf, soll, mag
4. wir bringen, denken, wissen, haben
5. ihr bleibt, fliegt, seid, werdet, seht, gebt, eßt, schlaft, fahrt, singt, sitzt, tut

Throughout these exer-
cises ask students what
the sentences mean in
English to monitor their
comprehension of the
use of the subjunctive.

D. Reisepläne. Was fehlt?

1. **Bauers würden nach Wien fahren.** Use the **würde**-form.

    x Dort _____ wir erst eine Stadtrundfahrt machen.
    y Dann _____ Dieter sich sicher den Stephansdom ansehen.
    Und du _____ dann durch die Kärntnerstraße bummeln.
    Natürlich _____ ihr auch in die Hofburg gehen.

x Ja, und einen Abend _____ wir in Grinzing feiern.

y Das _____ euch bestimmt gefallen.

2. **Ute führe in die Schweiz.** Use the suggested verb in the subjunctive.

a. Ich _____ mit ein paar Freunden in die Schweiz fahren. (können)

b. Erst _____ wir an den Bodensee. (fahren)

c. Von dort _____ es weiter nach Zürich und Bern. (gehen)

d. In Zürich _____ ich mir gern das Thomas-Mann-Archiv (*archives*) _____ . (ansehen)

e. Ihr _____ auch nach Genf fahren. (sollen)

f. Dort _____ du Französisch sprechen. (müssen)

g. Das _____ keine schlechte Idee! (sein)

E. Sagen Sie es höflicher (*more politely*)!

1. BEISPIEL: Können Sie uns die Mensa zeigen?
   Könnten Sie uns die Mensa zeigen?

   a. Darf ich kurz mit Ihnen sprechen? **b.** Haben Sie Lust mitzukommen? **c.** Können wir uns an einen Tisch setzen? **d.** Haben Sie etwas Zeit?

2. BEISPIEL: Rufen Sie mich morgen an!
   Würden Sie mich morgen anrufen?

   a. Erzählen Sie uns von der Reise! **b.** Bringen Sie die Bilder mit!
   c. Machen Sie mir eine Tasse Kaffee! **d.** Geben Sie mir die Milch!

F. Wünsche

F.1: When converting these German statements into wishes, **nicht so** is added immediately AFTER the verb. If this switch from statement to wish creates a problem, have students give the equivalent English first.

1. **Beginnen Sie mit Ich wünschte . . . !** Was bedeutet das auf englisch?

   BEISPIEL: Der Kurs ist schwer.
   Ich wünschte, der Kurs wäre nicht so schwer.
   I wish the course weren't so hard.

   a. Ich muß viel lesen. **b.** Das braucht viel Zeit. **c.** Ich bin müde.
   d. Ihr seid faul.

F.2: When converting these wishes into the **wenn**-form, **nur** is added AFTER the subject and any pronoun object. Again, you might have students give the English equivalents first.

2. **Beginnen Sie mit Wenn nur . . . !** Was bedeutet das auf englisch?

   BEISPIEL: Ich wünschte, ich könnte schlafen.
   Wenn ich nur schlafen könnte!
   If I could only sleep!

   a. Ich wünschte, wir hätten keine Prüfungen.
   b. Ich wünschte, ich könnte das verstehen.
   c. Ich wünschte, du könntest mir helfen.
   d. Ich wünschte, diese Woche wäre schon vorbei.

G. Wechseln Sie vom Indikativ zum Konjunktiv!

   BEISPIEL: Wenn das Wetter schön ist, kann man die Berge sehen.
   Wenn das Wetter schön wäre, könnte man die Berge sehen.

1. Wenn es möglich ist, zeige ich euch das Schloß.
2. Wenn du das Schloß sehen willst, mußt du dich beeilen.
3. Wenn ihr zu spät kommt, ärgert ihr euch.
4. Wenn das Schloß zu ist, können wir wenigstens in den Schloßpark gehen.
5. Wenn ihr mehr sehen wollt, müßt ihr länger hier bleiben.

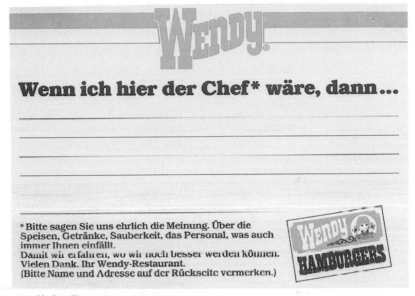

Wenn ich hier der Chef* wäre, dann...

* Bitte sagen Sie uns ehrlich die Meinung. Über die Speisen, Getränke, Sauberkeit, das Personal, was auch immer Ihnen einfällt.
Damit wir erfahren, wo wir noch besser werden können. Vielen Dank. Ihr Wendy-Restaurant.
(Bitte Name und Adresse auf der Rückseite vermerken.)

H: Students can do these orally with a partner or in writing.

II. Persönliche Fragen
1. Was würden Sie gern lernen?
2. Wo würden Sie gern leben?
3. Würden Sie lieber in einem Haus oder in einer Wohnung wohnen?
4. Welchen Film würden Sie sich gern ansehen?
5. Was für ein Auto würden Sie sich am liebsten kaufen?
6. Was würden Sie jetzt am liebsten essen? trinken?

I. Was wäre, wenn . . . ?
1. Wenn das Wetter heute schön wäre, . . .
2. Wenn ich jetzt in Florida (Alaska, usw.) wäre, . . .
3. Wenn ich morgen Geburtstag hätte, . . .
4. Wenn ich jetzt ein paar Tage frei hätte, . . .
5. Wenn ich eine Million Dollar hätte, . . .
6. Wenn ich Präsident (Professor, usw.) wäre, . . .
7. Wenn ich eine Frau (ein Mann) wäre, . . .

Wie wär's denn mal mit **SURFEN**

J. Wie geht's weiter?

BEISPIEL: Ich wäre stolz, wenn
Ich wäre stolz, wenn ich gut Deutsch sprechen könnte.

1. Ich wäre froh, wenn . . .
2. Ich fände es prima, wenn . . .
3. Es wäre furchtbar, wenn . . .
4. Ich würde mich ärgern, wenn . . .
5. Ich würde sparen, wenn . . .

K. Eine Einladung. Auf deutsch, bitte!

1. Would you like to come on Saturday?   **2.** It would be nice.   **3.** We could swim in the lake.   **4.** We wish we had time.   **5.** If Walter didn't have to work, we would come.   **6.** Could you come on Sunday?   **7.** Yes, I believe we can come.

III. The Past-Time General Subjunctive

You already know that a simple-past form in English can express the present-time subjunctive (referring to *now* or *later*). The past-perfect form, or *would have* + participle, expresses the same thought in the PAST-TIME SUBJUNCTIVE (referring to *earlier*).

NOW OR LATER: If I *had* time, I *would* come along.
EARLIER: If I *had had* time, I *would have* come along.

1. Forms

   a. In German the forms of the past-time subjunctive are based on the forms of the past perfect. The past-time subjunctive is very easy to learn because it simply consists of a form of **hätte** or **wäre** plus the past participle:

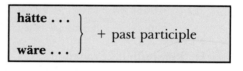

$$\left.\begin{array}{l}\textbf{hätte . . .}\\[1em]\textbf{wäre . . .}\end{array}\right\} + \text{past participle}$$

Wenn ich das **gewußt hätte, wäre** ich froh **gewesen.**   *If I had known that, I would have been happy.*

Ich wünschte, du **hättest** mir das **gesagt!**   *I wish you had told me that.*

   b. All modals follow this pattern in the past-time subjunctive:

hätte . . . + verb infinitive + modal infinitive

Ich **hätte** dich **anrufen sollen.**   *I should have called you.*

For now, avoid using these forms in dependent clauses.

2. Uses

   The past-time subjunctive is used for the same purpose as the present-time subjunctive. Note that there are no polite requests in the past.

   a. Hypothetical Statements and Questions

   Ich wäre zu Hause geblieben.   *I would have stayed home.*
   Was hättet ihr gemacht?   *What would you have done?*
   Hättet ihr mitkommen wollen?   *Would you have wanted to come along?*

b. Wishes

Wenn ich das nur gewußt hätte!	*If only I had known that.*
Ich wünschte, du wärest da gewesen.	*I wish you had been there.*

c. Unreal Conditions

Wenn du mich gefragt hättest, hätte ich es dir gesagt.	*If you had asked me, I would have told you.*
Wenn du da gewesen wärest, hättest du alles gehört.	*If you had been there, you would have heard everything.*

ÜBUNGEN

L. Wechseln Sie von der Gegenwart zur Vergangenheit! Change from the present to the past, using the past-time subjunctive.

1. BEISPIEL: Sie würde das tun.
   Sie hätte das getan.

   a. Sie würde euch anrufen.   **b.** Ihr würdet ihr helfen.   **c.** Ihr würdet sofort kommen.   **d.** Du würdest alles für sie tun.

2. BEISPIEL: Hansi sollte nicht so viel Schokolade essen.
   Hansi hätte nicht so viel Schokolade essen sollen.

   a. Wir dürften ihm keine Schokolade geben.   **b.** Das sollten wir wissen.
   c. Er könnte auch Obst essen.   **d.** Wir müßten besser aufpassen.

M. Was wäre gewesen, wenn . . .?

1. **Wechseln Sie von der Gegenwart zur Vergangenheit!**

   BEISPIEL: Wenn ich es wüßte, würde ich nicht fragen.
   Wenn ich es gewußt hätte, hätte ich nicht gefragt.

   a. Wenn wir eine Theatergruppe hätten, würde ich mitmachen.
   b. Wenn das Radio billiger wäre, würden wir es kaufen.
   c. Wenn ich Hunger hätte, würde ich mir etwas kochen.
   d. Wenn sie fleißiger arbeitete, würde es ihr besser gehen.

*M.2: Follow up with at least two **Und dann?** questions.*

2. **Und dann?** Ask each other what you would have done or what might have been if . . . ! Follow up with **Und dann?**

   BEISPIEL: Ich hatte keinen Hunger. Wenn ich Hunger gehabt hätte, . . .
   wäre ich in die Küche gegangen.
   Und dann?
   Dann hätte ich mir ein Wurstbrot gemacht.

   a. Gestern hat es geregnet. Wenn das Wetter schön gewesen wäre, . . .
   b. Ich bin nicht lange auf der Party gewesen. Wenn ich zu lange gefeiert hätte, . . .
   c. Natürlich hatten wir letzte Woche Vorlesungen. Wenn wir keine Vorlesungen gehabt hätten, . . .

N. Schade! Auf deutsch, bitte!

1. We should have stayed at home.   **2.** If the weather had been better, we could have been swimming in the lake.   **3.** But it rained all day.   **4.** I wish they hadn't invited us.   **5.** If only we hadn't visited him.

ZUSAMMENFASSUNG

O. Indikativ oder Konjunktiv? Was bedeutet das auf englisch?

1. Wenn er uns besuchte, brachte er immer Blumen mit.
2. Können Sie mir Horsts Telefonnummer geben?
3. Wenn du früher ins Bett gegangen wärest, wärest du jetzt nicht so müde.
4. Gestern konnten sie nicht kommen, aber sie könnten uns morgen besuchen.
5. Er sollte gestern anrufen.
6. Ich möchte Architektur studieren.
7. Sie waren schon um 6 Uhr aufgestanden.
8. Ich wünschte, er ließe nicht immer alles auf dem Sofa liegen.
9. Er ließ seine Bücher zu Hause.
10. Wenn ich könnte, was du kannst, dann wäre ich glücklich.

Betten, zu **Preisen,** wie Sie's gern hätten

P. Guter Rat (Good advice)

1. **Was soll ich tun?** In small groups, give each other advice. One person mentions a problem, real or invented, and the others give advice as to what to do.

   BEISPIEL: Ich bin immer so müde.
   Wenn ich du wäre, würde ich früher ins Bett gehen.

2. **Was hätte ich tun sollen?** This time give advice as to what one should have done or not done.

   BEISPIEL: Ich habe meine Schlüssel verloren.
   Du hättest besser aufpassen sollen.

Q. Kommst du mit? Auf deutsch, bitte!

1. Would you *(sg. fam.)* like to go **(fahren)** with us to Salzburg?   **2.** We could go by train.   **3.** It ought to be quieter now than in the summer.   **4.** That would be nice.   **5.** I'd come along, if I could find my passport.   **6.** I wish you *(pl. fam.)* had thought of it earlier.   **7.** Then I could have looked for it.   **8.** If I only knew where it is.   **9.** I'd like to see the churches, the Mozart house, and the castle **(die Burg).**   **10.** The city is supposed to be wonderful.   **11.** Without my passport I'd have to stay home.—Here it is!   **12.** If you *(sg. fam.)* hadn't talked **(reden)** so much, you'd have found it faster.

Q: 1. Möchtest du mit uns nach Salzburg fahren? 2. Wir könnten mit dem Zug (mit der Bahn) fahren. 3. Es sollte jetzt ruhiger sein als im Sommer. 4. Das wäre schön. 5. Ich käme mit (würde mitkommen), wenn ich meinen Paß finden könnte. 6. Ich wünschte, ihr hättet früher daran gedacht. 7. Dann hätte ich ihn suchen können. 8. Wenn ich nur wüßte, wo er ist! 9. Ich möchte die Kirchen, das Mozarthaus und die Burg sehen. 10. Die Stadt soll wunderbar sein. 11. Ohne meinen Paß müßte ich zu Hause bleiben.—Hier ist er! 12. Wenn du nicht so viel geredet hättest, hättest du ihn schneller gefunden.

EINBLICKE

Heidelberg am Neckar, Blick auf die Altstadt und das Schloß

The oldest universities in the German-speaking countries date back to the late Middle Ages: the University of Vienna was founded in 1365 and the University of Heidelberg in 1385. Over the last twenty-five years, many new universities and technical colleges have been founded. Practically all universities are state supported and require no tuition payments from students except for certain activity fees and mandatory health insurance. There is no tradition of private universities in the German-speaking countries.

The system varies considerably from that of the United States. When entering the university, students come prepared with a broad general education and therefore can focus right away on a major field of study. They are basically responsible for their own progress and take only a few required courses with exams at the end of each year, for which they receive a certificate **(Schein)** and a grade. After collecting a certain number of certificates over four to five semesters, they are eligible to take the intermediate qualifying exam **(Zwischenprüfung)** and eventually the very comprehensive and demanding final exam. There is no such thing as a Bachelor's degree. Instead, students complete their studies with the equivalent of an M.A., called **Magister** in the arts and humanities and **Diplom** in the natural or social sciences and in engineering. Those who wish to become teachers, doctors, or lawyers need to pass a comprehensive academic exam in their field **(1. Staatsexamen)**, to be followed by a second state exam **(2. Staatsexamen)** after a practical internship.

WORTSCHATZ 2

Extra practice with "in your shoes"; e.g., **ich: an meiner Stelle** (du, er, sie / *sg.*, wir, ihr, sie / *pl.*, Bernd, Margaret, Margaret und Tina, Frau Meier).

das	Problem, -e	*problem*
	an deiner / seiner Stelle	*in your / his shoes; if I were you / he*
	ausländisch	*foreign*
	erst	*first of all; not before, not until*
	gar nicht	*not at all*
	jedenfalls	*in any case*
	sowieso	*anyhow*
	teil·nehmen (nimmt teil), nahm teil, teilgenommen (an + *dat.*)	*to participate (in), take part (in)*

Pre-reading activity:
1. Würden Sie gern in Europa studieren? Wo? Wann? Wie lange?
2. Worauf würden Sie sich freuen? 3. Denken Sie, es würde mehr oder weniger kosten, drüben zu studieren?
4. Was würden Sie in den Ferien tun?
5. Hat Ihre Uni ein Austauschprogramm? Wenn ja, mit welcher Uni?

WAS IST DAS? der Grammatikkurs, Intensivkurs, Lesesaal, Semesteranfang; das Archiv, Sommersemester, System, Wintersemester; die Sprachprüfung; teil-möbliert

Ein Jahr drüben wäre super!

(Gespräch an einer amerikanischen Universität)

TINA	Hallo, Margaret!	
MARGARET	Tag, Tina! Kennst du Bernd? Er ist aus Heidelberg und studiert ein Jahr bei uns.	5
TINA	Guten Tag! Wie gefällt es dir hier?	
BERND	Sehr gut. Meine Kurse und Professoren sind ausgezeichnet. Ich wünschte nur, es gäbe nicht so viele Prüfungen!	
TINA	Habt ihr keine Prüfungen?	
BERND	Doch, aber weniger. Dafür° haben wir nach ungefähr vier Semestern eine große Zwischenprüfung und dann am Ende des Studiums das Staatsexamen.	10
TINA	Ich würde gern einmal in Europa studieren.	
MARGARET	Das solltest du wirklich tun.	
TINA	Es ist bestimmt sehr teuer.	15
MARGARET	So teuer ist es gar nicht! Mein Jahr in München hat auch nicht mehr gekostet als ein Jahr hier.	
TINA	Wirklich?	
BERND	Ja, bestimmt. Unsere Studentenheime und die Mensa sind viel billiger als bei euch, und unsere Studiengebühren° sind viel niedriger°. Ohne mein Stipendium könnte ich hier nicht studieren.	20
TINA	Ist es schwer, dort drüben einen Studienplatz zu bekommen?	
BERND	Als Deutsche wäre es vielleicht nicht so einfach,[1] aber als Ausländerin und mit einem Auslandsprogramm wäre das gar kein Problem.	25

instead

tuition
lower

	TINA	Ich muß noch mal mit meinen Eltern sprechen. Sie meinen, daß ich ein Jahr verlieren würde.
foreign study . . .	MARGARET	Wieso denn? Wenn du mit einem Auslandsprogramm° nach Deutschland gingest, würde das genauso wie ein Jahr hier zählen.
	TINA	Ich weiß nicht, ob ich genug Deutsch kann.

30

	MARGARET	Bestimmt! Viele Studenten können weniger Deutsch als du. Du lernst es ja schon seit vier Jahren. Außerdem haben die meisten Programme vor Semesteranfang einen Intensivkurs für ausländische Studenten. Damit würdest du dich auch auf die Sprachprü-

prepare   fung am Anfang des Semesters vorbereiten°. Wenn du die Prü- 35

fung wirklich nicht bestehen solltest—was ich mir nicht vorstellen

just   kann, denn dein Deutsch ist gut—, dann müßtest du eben° einen

Grammatikkurs belegen und sie am Ende des Semesters wieder-

holen.

That's OK.	TINA	Das geht°. Vielleicht kann ich im Herbst ein Semester nach 40 Deutschland.
	MARGARET	Nur im Herbst ginge nicht, weil das Wintersemester erst Ende Februar aufhört.
	TINA	Im Februar? Und wann ist das Frühlingssemester?
	BERND	Bei uns gibt es ein Wintersemester und ein Sommersemester. Das 45 Wintersemester läuft von November bis März, das Sommerseme-

therefore   ster von April bis Ende Juli[2]. Du müßtest also° ein ganzes Jahr

bleiben oder nur für das Sommersemester kommen. Aber ein

ganzes Jahr wäre sowieso besser, denn dann hättest du zwischen

den Semestern Zeit zu reisen.   50

	MARGARET	Stimmt. Da bin ich auch viel gereist. Ich war in Italien, Griechen- land und danach noch in der Tschechoslowakei und in Ungarn.
	TINA	Wunderbar! Was für Kurse sollte ich belegen?
	BERND	Im ersten Semester würde ich nur Vorlesungen[3] belegen, keine

takes notes   Seminare. Da hört man nur zu und macht Notizen°. Im zweiten 55

Semester könntest du dann auch ein Seminar belegen. Bis dann

ist dein Deutsch jedenfalls gut genug, daß du auch eine längere

give a report   Seminararbeit schreiben oder ein Referat halten° könntest.

	TINA	Seminararbeiten und Referate auf deutsch?
	MARGARET	Am Anfang geht's langsam, aber man lernt's.

60

	BERND	Ich tue's ja auch auf englisch. Übrigens, was bei euch viel besser ist, sind die Bibliotheken. Wir müssen Bücher immer erst bestel- len, was oft Tage dauert. Man kann nicht einfach in die Archive

lend out   wie hier. Und die Fachbibliotheken[4] leihen keine Bücher aus°,

außer am Wochenende.   65

	TINA	Ich kann mir ja die Bücher kaufen.
	BERND	Das wäre furchtbar teuer! Dann würde ich schon lieber im Lese- saal sitzen.
	TINA	Und wie ist das mit Studentenheimen?

MARGARET	Wenn du an einem Auslandsprogramm teilnimmst, hast du keine Probleme.	70
BERND	An deiner Stelle würde ich versuchen, ein Zimmer im Studentenheim zu bekommen. Auf diese Weise würdest du leichter andere Studenten kennenlernen. Die Zimmer sind oft sehr schön, teilmöbliert und mit Bad. Dazu müßtest du auf deinem Flur die Küche mit fünf oder sechs anderen Studenten teilen.	75
TINA	Da habe ich nichts dagegen. Meint ihr Heidelberg wäre besser als Berlin oder München?	
BERND	Ach, das ist schwer zu sagen.	
MARGARET	Wenn ich Berlin gekannt hätte, hätte ich vielleicht dort studiert. Mir hat es dort sehr gut gefallen. Aber erst mußt du wissen, ob du wirklich nach Deutschland fahren willst. Wenn du das weißt, dann kann ich dir weiterhelfen.	80
TINA	Danke!	
MARGARET	An deiner Stelle würde ich erst mal mit deinen Eltern sprechen! Denk mal, was du alles lernen und sehen würdest!	85
TINA	Ja, das wäre super!	

ZUM TEXT

A. Ein Jahr im Ausland. Was fehlt?

Europa, ein Jahr, eine Küche, München, Prüfungen, Sommersemester, Sprachprüfung, andere Studenten, Vorlesungen, Heidelberg, Wintersemester

1. Bernd ist aus _____ und studiert _____ in Amerika.
2. Ihm gefallen nur die vielen _____ nicht.
3. Tina möchte gern in _____ studieren.
4. Margarets Jahr in _____ hat nicht viel mehr gekostet als ein Jahr zu Hause.
5. Ausländische Studenten müssen vor Semesteranfang eine _____ schreiben.
6. Das _____ ist von November bis Ende Februar, das _____ von April bis Ende Juli.
7. Im ersten Semester sollte Tina nur _____ belegen.
8. In einem Studentenheim kann man leichter _____ kennenlernen.
9. In einem deutschen Studentenheim muß man _____ mit anderen Studenten teilen.

B. Das Studium hier und dort. In brief statements compare what Bernd says about studying in Heidelberg and what you know about studying here.
1. Prüfungen   **2.** Studiengebühren   **3.** Semesterkalender   **4.** Kurse
5. Bibliotheken

Staatsbibliothek in
München

C. An der Uni. Was fehlt?
1. Bernd _____ , es _____ nicht so viele Prüfungen. *(wishes, there were)*
2. Wenn Bernd kein Stipendium _____ , _____ , _____ er nicht hier studieren können. *(had gotten, could have)*
3. Wenn Tina mit einem Austauschprogramm nach Deutschland _____ , _____ das wie ein Jahr hier zählen. *(would go, would)*
4. Tina _____ ein ganzes Jahr bleiben, oder sie _____ nur für das Sommersemester gehen. *(would have to, could)*
5. Ein ganzes Jahr drüben _____ besser. *(would be)*
6. Dann _____ Tina zwischen den Semestern Zeit zu reisen. *(would have)*
7. In einem Studentenheim _____ Tina leichter deutsche Studenten kennenlernen. *(would)*
8. Wenn Margaret Berlin _____ _____ , _____ sie dort studiert. *(had known, would have)*
9. Wenn sie nicht an einer deutschen Uni _____ _____ , _____ sie nicht so gut Deutsch sprechen. *(had studied, could)*

D. Am liebsten würde ich . . .
1. Wenn ich könnte, würde ich einmal in . . . studieren.
2. Am liebsten würde ich in . . . wohnen, weil . . .
3. Am Anfang des Semesters . . .
4. Am Ende des Semesters . . .
5. Während der Semesterferien . . .

E. Das wäre schön! Write a paragraph of six to eight sentences on one of the topics below, using the subjunctive.
1. Ein Jahr drüben wäre super!   4. Das würde mir gefallen.
2. Ein Traumhaus.   5. Das hätte mir gefallen.
3. Eine Traumfamilie.

Übrigens

1. In many disciplines, especially in the fields of medicine and pharmacy, admission to college is limited under a system called **Numerus clausus,** and openings **(Studienplätze)** are filled on the basis of high school grades. Sometimes would-be students have to wait up to five years before being accepted.

2. The exact dates for the beginning and end of each semester differ in various parts of Germany since each state **(Land)** is autonomous in regard to education.

3. The registration process at German universities permits students to attend lectures and seminars for three weeks before making a final decision to enroll. That allows them to select only those courses that are suited to their needs and likes.

4. Besides the large university library **(Universitätsbibliothek),** there is a separate library **(Fachbibliothek)** with a reading room for each of the major disciplines, usually located in the building that houses these departments.

Freiburger Universität

SPRECHSITUATIONEN

As you know, the subjunctive can express politeness. It is used therefore quite frequently when giving advice or asking for permission.

Giving Advice

Sie sollten / könnten . . .
Es wäre besser, wenn . . .
Wie wär's, wenn . . . ?
Ich würde . . .
An deiner / Ihrer Stelle, würde ich . . .
Wenn ich du / Sie wäre, würde ich . . .
Ich empfehle dir / Ihnen . . .
Ich rate dir / Ihnen . . . *(I advise you . . .)*
Du mußt unbedingt *(absolutely)* . . .
Du kannst / darfst nicht . . .

Asking for Permission

Darf / dürfte ich . . . ?	*May / might I . . . ?*
Kann / könnte ich . . . ?	*Can / could I . . . ?*
Ist / wäre es Ihnen recht, wenn . . . ?	*Is / would it be all right with you, if . . . ?*
Ist es erlaubt, (. . . zu + *infinitive*)?	*Is it permitted, to . . . ?*
Haben / hätten Sie etwas dagegen, wenn . . . ?	*Do / would you mind, if . . . ?*
Stört es Sie / würde es Sie stören, wenn . . . ?	*Does / would it bother you, if . . . ?*

Granting or Denying Permission

Ja, natürlich. Gern.
Es ist mir recht.
Ich habe nichts dagegen.
Es stört mich nicht. *(It doesn't bother me.)*
Nein, natürlich nicht.
Es tut mir leid, aber . . .
Hier darf man nicht . . .
Es ist nicht erlaubt (. . . zu + *infinitive*). *(It is forbidden to . . .)*
Es ist verboten (. . . zu + *infinitive*). *(It is forbidden to . . .)*
Es wäre mir lieber, wenn . . . *(I would prefer it if . . .)*

Have students think of real or imaginary problems they need to resolve. They should then ask classmates for advice.

A. Was tun? Take turns asking for or giving advice in the following situations.
  1. Sie wissen nicht, was Sie werden wollen (oder welche Arbeitsmöglichkeiten es gibt).

2. Sie wissen nicht, was Sie als Hauptfach studieren wollen (oder was Sie tun müssen, um einen besseren Arbeitsplatz zu finden).
3. Sie möchten eigentlich gern Lehrer(in) werden, aber wenn Sie . . . studierten, könnten Sie bei Ihrem (Schwieger)vater arbeiten und mehr verdienen.
4. Sie möchten in Deutschland studieren / arbeiten, aber Ihre Familie ist dagegen.
5. Sie sollen heute abend mit einem Freund in ein Konzert gehen; er hat auch schon Karten. Aber Sie haben keine Lust dazu.

Ask students to come up with other requests.

B. Darf ich . . . ? Working with a classmate, take turns asking for permission and granting or denying it.
1. mal kurz dein Buch haben
2. deine Hausaufgaben sehen / abschreiben *(copy)*
3. mein Radio anmachen / eine neue Kassette spielen
4. deinen Kuli / deinen Pullover . . . borgen *(borrow)*
5. für dich bezahlen / dir die Rechnung geben
6. deine Kreditkarte / dein Auto . . . borgen

C. Schont die Parkanlangen! Protect the park. You have just arrived in Germany and can't quite make out what the sign says. Your partner explains.
1. Im Park darf man nicht . . .
2. Es ist nicht erlaubt, . . .
3. Es ist verboten, . . .
4. Man soll . . .

SCHONT DIE PARKANLAGEN
Es wird gebeten:
Auf den Wegen zu bleiben
Blumen u. Sträucher nicht abzupflücken
Gebäude u. Denkmäler sauber zu halten
Hunde an der Leine zu führen
Fahrräder nicht in den Park mitzunehmen

es wird gebeten *please; lit., it is requested* **der Strauch, ¨er** *bush* **ab·pflücken** *to pick, break off* **das Gebäude,-** *building* **das Denkmal, ¨er** *monument* **die Leine, -n** *leash* **führen** *to lead*

D. Kurzgespräch
You call up Margaret, who has been to Germany. Introduce yourself and ask if you might ask her some questions. You are told to go ahead, and you ask whether you should study in Germany. She says that she would do it if she were you. You ask for how long you should go. She suggests you go (for) a year. You would learn more German and see more of Europe. You ask if you could have lunch together the next day. She says she would prefer it if you could have supper. You agree and say good-bye.

14

Damals und jetzt

Blick auf die Ge-
dächtniskirche
in Berlin

■ LERNZIELE

Gespräche and **Wortschatz**. This chapter deals with Berlin then and now.

Struktur. You will learn about . . .

▪ relative clauses.

▪ indirect speech.

Einblicke. Berlin yesterday and today

Sprechsituationen

▪ Making descriptions

◆◆◆◆◆ GESPRÄCHE

Hier ist immer etwas los

HEIKE   Und das ist die Gedächtniskirche mit ihren drei Gebäuden. Wir nennen sie den „Hohlen Zahn", den „Lippenstift" und die „Puderdose[1]".

MARTIN   Ihr Berliner habt doch für alles einen witzigen Namen!

HEIKE   Der alte Turm der Gedächtniskirche soll kaputt bleiben als Erinnerung an den Krieg. Die neue Gedächtniskirche mit dem neuen Turm ist eben modern.

MARTIN   Und sie sieht wirklich ein bißchen aus wie ein Lippenstift und eine Puderdose! Sag mal, wie ist das Leben hier?

HEIKE   Phantastisch! Einmalig! Berlin hat sehr viel zu bieten, nicht nur historisch, sondern auch kulturell[2].

MARTIN   Das stimmt schon. Hier ist immer etwas los. Außerdem habt ihr eine wunderschöne Umgebung.

HEIKE   Ja, ohne die Seen und Wälder wäre es bestimmt nicht so schön!

MARTIN   Sag mal, du warst doch bestimmt dabei, als sie die Mauer[3] durchbrochen haben, oder?

HEIKE   Na klar! Das werde ich nie vergessen.

MARTIN   Ich auch nicht, obwohl ich's nur im Fernsehen gesehen habe.

HEIKE   Wir haben die ganze Nacht gewartet, und es war ganz schön kalt. Aber vom Roten Kreuz haben wir heißen Tee bekommen. Als das erste Stück Mauer kippte, haben wir alle laut gesungen „So ein Tag, so wunderschön wie heute, so ein Tag, der dürfte nie vergehen."

MARTIN   Ich sehe immer noch die Leute oben auf der Mauer tanzen und Sekt trinken.

HEIKE   Ja, das war schon einmalig. Wer hätte gedacht, daß das alles so schnell käme!

MARTIN   Und vor allem so friedlich.

HEIKE   Stimmt.

Übrigens

1. Berliners are known for their humor and "big mouth" (**freche Schnauze**), as seen in the amusing names they have given to various places. Besides the nicknames mentioned above, there are: the **Schwangere Auster** (*pregnant oyster*), a cultural center; the **Hungerkralle** (*hunger claw*), the monument to the Berlin airlift of 1948–1949; or the **Mauerspechte** (*wall [wood]peckers*), the souvenir hunters who chipped away at the Berlin Wall after it was opened.

Mauerdurchbruch
am 9.11.1989

2. Berlin is now returning to the cultural preeminence it had before World War II. It has around thirty major art museums, two important symphony orchestras, three opera houses, numerous theaters and cabarets, and well over one hundred educational institutions.

3. During the first years after the war, the open border between the Soviet and Western occupation zones was fairly easy to cross. By 1952, however, the increasing flight of the population had become so alarming that the GDR began to surround itself with a "protective strip" of barbed wire, armed guards, and a three-mile-deep "forbidden zone" along its border with the West. When the Berlin Wall was built in 1961, the entire border was massively reinforced with minefields, shrapnel-scattering trap guns, parallel steel fences, guard dogs, and watchtowers. Such devices were not designed to keep the enemy out, but to keep people in. For twenty-eight years the Wall was the symbol of a "divided Berlin in a divided Germany in a divided Europe." On November 9, 1989, television viewers around the world witnessed the dramatic end to the artificial division of the city as hundreds of jubilant Berliners danced atop the breached Wall. On the following weekend three million East Germans (close to a fifth of the population) flooded through open checkpoints to the West. Berlin was suddenly no longer an island. And that, said West Berlin's Mayor Walter Momper, was "the nicest Christmas news for all Berliners."

There's Always Something Happening Here HEIKE: *And that's the Memorial Church with its three buildings. We call them the "Hollow Tooth," the "Lipstick," and the "Compact."* MARTIN: *You Berliners have a witty name for everything.* HEIKE: *The old tower of the Memorial Church is to stay in ruins as a reminder of the war. The new Memorial Church with the new tower is modern.* MARTIN: *And it does look a little like a lipstick and a compact. Tell me, what's life like here?* HEIKE: *Fantastic! Unique! Berlin has a lot to offer, not only historically but also culturally.* MARTIN: *That's true. There's always something happening here. Besides, you also have beautiful surroundings.* HEIKE: *Yes, without the lakes and forests it certainly* *wouldn't be as nice. MARTIN: Say, you probably were there when they broke through the Wall, right? HEIKE: Of course, I'll never forget that. MARTIN: I won't either, although I only saw it on TV. HEIKE: We waited all night, and it was pretty cold. But we got some hot tea from the Red Cross. When the first piece of wall tipped over, we all sang "Such a beautiful day as today, such a day should never end." MARTIN: I still see the people dancing on top of the Wall and drinking champagne. HEIKE: Yes, that really was incredible (lit. unique). Who would have thought that all would come so fast. MARTIN: And especially so peacefully. HEIKE: True.*

WORTSCHATZ 1

DAMALS UND JETZT *then (in those days) and now*

der	Frieden	*peace*	*die*	Grenze, -n	*border*
	Krieg, -e	*war*		Mauer, -n	*wall*
	Turm, ⸚e	*tower*		Umgebung	*surrounding(s)*
das	Gebäude, -	*building*			
	Volk, ⸚er	*people*			

WEITERES

aus·sehen (sieht aus), sah aus, ausgesehen	*to look, appear*
aus·sehen wie (+ *nom.*)	*to look like something or someone*
bieten, bot, geboten	*to offer*
erinnern (an + *acc.*)[1]	*to remind (of)*
sich erinnern (an + *acc.*)[1]	*to remember*
nennen, nannte, genannt	*to name, call*
stören	*to bother, disturb*
teilen	*to divide*
eben	*after all, just (gesture word)*
einmalig	*unique*
historisch	*historical(ly)*
kulturell	*cultural(ly)*
mitten durch	*right through (the middle of)*
rings um (+ *acc.*)	*all around*
witzig	*witty, funny*
wunderschön	*beautiful*

Examples with **erinnern**: Peter, please remind me of the exam. Why do I always have to remind you? Can't you remember anything? I remember the vacation!

1 Ich werde **dich** an die Karten erinnern. (*I'll remind you of the tickets.*) BUT Ich kann **mich** nicht daran erinnen. (*I can't remember it.*)

PASSIVES VOKABULAR **der Lippenstift, -e** *lipstick* **die Puderdose, -n** *compact* **als Erinnerung an** *as a reminder of* **durchbrochen** *broken through* **(um)kippen** *to tip over* **vergehen, verging, ist vergangen** *to pass, end* **friedlich** *peaceful(ly)* **dabei** *there* **hohl** *hollow* **na klar** *of course*

Der Mauerspecht
holt sich ein Souvenir.

*Offene Grenzen
offene Herzen
die Deutschen
ein Volk*

ZUM THEMA

A. Wie geht's weiter? Use the phrases below in complete sentences. Use your imagination.

BEISPIEL: . . . sieht gut aus.   **Heike sieht gut aus.**

1. . . . sieht . . . aus.
2. . . . sieht aus wie ein(e) . . .
3. . . . hat viel zu bieten.
4. . . . ist immer etwas los.
5. Ich erinnere mich gern an . . .

6. Ich kann mich noch gut erinnern an die Zeit, als . . .
7. Bitte erinnere mich nicht an . . . !
8. Es stört mich, wenn . . .

B. Stadtbesichtigung. What would you say if you were taking a foreign visitor through your own city?

x Und das ist _____ .
y _____ .
x Ja, wir sind sehr stolz darauf.
y Wie ist das Leben _____ ?
x _____ .
y Ist hier kulturell viel los?
x _____ .
y Die Umgebung ist _____ .
x Wie findest du / finden Sie _____ ?
y _____ .

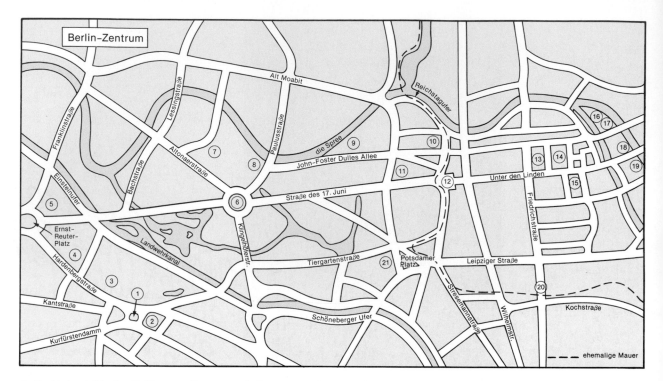

1. Gedächtniskirche 2. Europa-Zentrum 3. Zoo 4. Hochschule für Musik 5. Technische Universität 6. Siegessäule 7. Akademie der Künste 8. Schloß Bellevue 9. Kongreßhalle 10. Reichstaggebäude 11. Sowjetisches Denkmal 12. Brandenburger Tor 13. Staatsbibliothek 14. Humboldt Universität 15. Staatsoper 16. Pergamonmuseum 17. Nationalgalerie 18. Dom 19. alter Palast der Republik 20. früherer *(former)* Checkpoint Charlie 21. Philharmonie

C. Stadtplan vom Berliner Zentrum. Complete these sentences with one of the words from the list below.

a. Berlin	e. Humboldt	i. Reichstag
b. Brandenburger	f. Juni	j. sowjetische
c. Europa	g. Musik	k. Spree
d. Gedächtniskirche	h. Pergamon	l. Unter den Linden

1. Dieser Stadtplan zeigt nur einen Teil von _____ , aber er gibt einen kleinen Eindruck *(impression)*, wo die verschiedenen Straßen und wichtigen Gebäude sind.   **2.** Im Südwesten sehen Sie den Kurfürstendamm und die _____ .   **3.** Gegenüber davon ist das _____ -Zentrum.   **4.** In der Nähe der Gedächtniskirche ist auch die Technische Universität und die Hochschule für _____ .   **5.** Von dort geht eine lange Straße zur Siegessäule *(Victory Column)* und weiter bis zum _____ Tor *(Gate)*. **6.** Diese lange Straße erinnert an den 17. _____ 1953, als die Ost-Berliner und die Deutschen in der DDR gegen die Sowjetunion rebellierten.   **7.** Kurz vor dem Brandenburger Tor, auf der linken Seite, steht das _____ Denkmal *(monument)*. Die Panzer *(tanks)* daneben sollen 1945 als erste Berlin erreicht *(reached)* haben.   **8.** Ganz in der Nähe ist auch das alte _____ gebäude.   **9.** Östlich vom Brandenburger Tor ist die alte

Optional practice:
1. Welcher Fluß fließt mitten durchs Zentrum von Berlin? 2. Welcher Kanal fließt am Tiergarten *(zoo)* entlang? 3. Wie heißt die alte Repräsentationsstraße Berlins? 4. Was ist ihr Gegenstück *(counterpart)* im Südwesten? 5. Wo ist das Brandenburger Tor? usw. 6. Welche historischen Gebäude liegen auf der Spreeinsel? 7. Wo lief die Mauer entlang? Finden Sie die Grenzlinie! Wo war der internationale Checkpoint Charlie?

You may want to point out how easy it is to form adjectives from the names of cities (e.g., Brandenburger, Berliner, Wiener) and that these adjectives don't have the usual endings: das alte Tor / das Brandenburger Tor; ein neues Gebäude / ein Berliner Gebäude

Repräsentationsstraße Berlins: _____ .   **10.** Sie führt *(leads)* ins alte Zentrum von Berlin und zur _____ Universität.   **11.** Nicht weit davon ist auch der Dom und das bekannte _____museum.   **12.** Das Pergamonmuseum und der Dom sind auf einer Insel *(island)*. Auf beiden Seiten der Insel fließt *(flows)* die _____ .

D. Aussprache. See also III. 19, 21, and 22 in the pronunciation section of the Workbook.

1. [pf]   **Pf**arrer, **Pf**effer, **Pf**efferminz, **Pf**ennig, **Pf**und, A**pf**el, Ko**pf**, em**pf**ehlen

2. [ps]   **Ps**ychologe, **Ps**ychiater, **Ps**ychologie, **ps**ychologisch, **Ps**alm, **Ps**eudonym, Ka**ps**el

3. [kv]   **Qu**atsch, **Qu**alität, **Qu**antität, **Qu**artal, **Qu**ote, be**qu**em

STRUKTUR

I. Relative Clauses

Point out that relative clauses in German work the same way as in formal English.

RELATIVE CLAUSES supply additional information about a noun in a sentence.

There is the professor **who** *teaches the course.*
He taught the course **(that)** *I enjoyed so much.*
He teaches a subject **in which** *I'm very interested (I'm very interested in).*
He's the professor **whose** *course I took last semester.*

English relative clauses may be introduced by the relative pronouns *who, whom, whose, which,* or *that.* The noun to which the relative pronoun "relates" is called the ANTECEDENT. The choice of the relative pronoun depends on the antecedent (is it a person or a thing?) AND on its function in the relative clause. The relative pronoun may be the subject *(who, which, that)*, an object or an object of a preposition *(whom, which, that)*, or it may indicate possession *(whose)*. German relative clauses work essentially the same way. However, while in English the relative pronouns are frequently omitted (especially in conversation), IN GERMAN THEY MUST ALWAYS BE USED.

To be more precise, relative pronouns in English are omitted only if they're objects or objects of prepositions.

Ist das der Roman, **den** ihr gelesen habt?   *Is that the novel you read?*

1. Forms

The German relative pronouns have the same forms as the definite article, EXCEPT FOR THE GENITIVE FORMS AND THE DATIVE PLURAL.

	masc.	neut.	fem.	pl.
nom.	der	das	die	die
acc.	den	das	die	die
dat.	dem	dem	der	denen
gen.	dessen	dessen	deren	deren

The form of the relative pronoun is determined by two factors:

a. its ANTECEDENT.

Decide whether the antecedent is singular or plural AND whether it is masculine, neuter, or feminine.

b. its FUNCTION in the relative clause.

Determine whether the relative pronoun is the subject, an accusative or dative object, an object of a preposition, or whether it indicates possession.

> ... ANTECEDENT, (preposition) RP _____ V1, ...
> gender? number?   function?

Das ist der Professor. Er lehrt an meiner Universität.
Das ist **der Professor, der** an meiner Universität lehrt.
*That's **the professor who** teaches at my university.*
antecedent: der Professor; sg. / masc.
function: subject > nom.

Wie heißt der Kurs? Du findest ihn so interessant.
Wie heißt **der Kurs, den** du so interessant findest?
*What's the name of **the course (that)** you find so interesting?*
antecedent: der Kurs; sg. / masc.
function: object of **finden** > acc.

Da ist der Student. Ich habe ihm mein Buch gegeben.
Da ist **der Student, dem** ich mein Buch gegeben habe.
*There's **the student to whom** I gave my book (I gave my book to).*
antecedent: der Student; sg. / masc.
function: object of **geben** > dat.

Kennst du den Professor? Erik hat sein Seminar belegt.
Kennst du **den Professor, dessen Seminar** Erik belegt hat?
*Do you know **the professor whose seminar** Erik is taking?*
antecedent: den Professor; sg. / masc.
function: related possessively to **Seminar** > gen.

Das Buch ist von einem Autor. Ich interessiere mich sehr für ihn.
Das Buch ist von **einem Autor, für den** ich mich sehr interessiere.
*The book is by **an author in whom** I'm very interested.*
antecedent: von einem Autor; sg. / masc.
function: object of **für** > acc.

Die Autoren sind aus Leipzig. Der Professor hat von ihnen gesprochen.
Die Autoren, von denen der Professor gesprochen hat, sind aus Leipzig.
***The authors of whom** the professor spoke are from Leipzig.*
antecedent: die Autoren; pl.
function: object of **von** > dat.

Relative clauses require regular practice. Give students two simple German sentences to connect with a relative pronoun, or a few easy English sentences or phrases to express in German:
1. **Da ist das Restaurant:** Es ist so teuer. Wir haben in dem Restaurant gegessen. Seine Weine sind bekannt. Sie wollen es kaufen. Wir möchten in das Restaurant gehen.
2. **Ich habe das Buch gekauft:** Ich habe viel von dem Buch gehört. Du hast über das Buch gesprochen. Erika hat es mir empfohlen. Sein Titel ist *Krieg und Frieden.* Die Geschichte spielt in Rußland.

CAUTION

Don't use the interrogative pronoun in place of the relative pronoun!

Wer hat das Seminar gegeben?
Das ist der Professor, **der** das Seminar gegeben hat.

Who gave the seminar?
That's the professor who gave the seminar.

2. Word order

a. Relative pronouns can be the objects of prepositions. If that is the case, the preposition will always precede the relative pronoun.

Das Buch ist von einem Autor, **für den** ich mich sehr interessiere.
The book is by an author in whom I'm very interested.

b. The word order in the RELATIVE CLAUSE is like that of all SUBORDINATE clauses: the inflected part of the verb (V1) comes last. Always separate the main clause from the relative clause by a COMMA.

> ..., RP _____ V1, ...

Der Professor, **der** den Prosakurs **lehrt**, ist sehr nett.
V1

c. Relative clauses immediately follow the antecedent unless the antecedent is followed by a prepositional phrase that modifies it, a genitive, or a V2.

Das Buch von Dürrenmatt, **das wir lesen sollen,** ist leider ausverkauft.
Das Buch des Autors, **das wir lesen sollen,** ist teuer.
Ich kann **das Buch** nicht bekommen, **das wir lesen sollen.**

ÜBUNGEN

A: Do this exercise in class. A close analysis of each sentence will help students understand relative clauses.

A. Analysieren Sie die Sätze! Find the antecedent and state the function of the relative pronoun in each relative clause.

BEISPIEL: Renate Berger ist eine Arbeiterin, die für gleiche Arbeit gleiches Einkommen möchte.
antecedent: eine Arbeiterin, sg. / fem.
function: subject > nom.

1. Der Mann, der neben ihr arbeitet, verdient pro Stunde 1,80 DM mehr.
2. Es gibt leider noch viele Frauen, deren Kollegen ein höheres Einkommen bekommen.
3. Und es gibt Frauen, denen schlecht bezahlte Arbeit lieber ist als keine Arbeit.
4. Was denken die Männer, deren Frauen weniger Geld bekommen als ihre Kollegen?

5. Der Mann, mit dem Renate Berger verheiratet ist, findet das nicht so schlecht.
6. Aber die Frauen, die bei der gleichen Firma arbeiten, ärgern sich sehr darüber.
7. Es ist ein Problem, das die meisten Firmen haben.
8. Es gibt Berufe, in denen Männer für gleiche Arbeit mehr verdienen.
9. Und die Berufe, in denen fast nur Frauen arbeiten, sind am schlechtesten bezahlt.
10. Wir leben in einer Welt, in der Gleichberechtigung noch nicht überall Realität (reality) ist.

B. Rundfahrt in Berlin. While Sepp shows slides from his visit to Berlin, his Austrian friends ask questions. Answer according to the model, using relative pronouns.

B.1: Nominative

1. BEISPIEL: Ist das der Alexanderplatz?
Ja, das ist der Alexanderplatz, der so bekannt ist.

a. Ist das der Dom? **b.** Ist das das Pergamonmuseum? **c.** Ist das die Staatsbibliothek? **d.** Ist das der Fernsehturm? **e.** Sind das die Universitätsgebäude?

B.2: Accusative

2. BEISPIEL: Ist das der Potsdamer Platz?
Ja, das ist der Potsdamer Platz, den du da siehst.

a. Ist das die Philharmonie? **b.** Ist das der Landwehrkanal? **c.** Ist das die Gedächtniskirche? **d.** Ist das der Kurfürstendamm? **e.** Ist das das Europa-Zentrum?

B.3: Dative

3. BEISPIEL: Ist das die Hochschule für Musik?
Ist das die Hochschule für Musik, zu der wir jetzt kommen?

a. Ist das der Zoo? **b.** Ist das die Siegessäule? **c.** Ist das die Kongreßhalle? **d.** Ist das das Reichstaggebäude? **e.** Sind das die sowjetischen Panzer?

B.4: Genitive

4. BEISPIEL: Wo ist der Student? Sein Vater lehrt an der Universität.
Da ist der Student, dessen Vater an der Universität lehrt.

Point out the change in pattern, which combines two sentences into one.

a. Wo ist die Studentin? Ihre Eltern wohnten früher (formerly) in Berlin. **b.** Wo ist das Mädchen? Ihr Bruder war so witzig. **c.** Wo ist der Herr? Seine Frau sprach so gut Englisch. **d.** Wo sind die alten Leute? Ihre Kinder sind jetzt in Amerika.

C. Was gefällt Ihnen? Geben Sie Beispiele!

BEISPIEL: Stück   **Ein Stück, das mir gefällt, ist Goethes *Faust*.**

1. Buch   **2.** Film   **3.** Fernsehsendung   **4.** Zeitschrift   **5.** Schlagersänger(in) (*pop singer*)   **6.** Komponist(in)   **7.** Restaurant   **8.** Auto   **9.** Stadt

Leute, über die man spricht

D: Assign this as home-work or give students a few minutes in class to complete it. Each student should deal with it individually.

D. Kein Wiedersehen. Geben Sie die fehlenden Relativpronomen!

1. Der junge Mann, _der_ da steht, heißt David.
2. Das Mädchen, mit _dem (der)_ er spricht, heißt Tina.
3. Das andere Mädchen, _das (die)_ daneben steht, heißt Margaret.
4. Sie sprechen über einen Film, _der_ momentan im Kino läuft.
5. Der Film, über _den_ sie sprechen, spielt in Berlin.
6. Die Geschichte spielt kurz vor dem Bau der Mauer, _die_ von 1961 bis 1989 Berlin geteilt hat.
7. In den fünfziger Jahren, in _denen_ man mit der S-Bahn von Ost-Berlin nach West-Berlin fahren konnte, war es relativ leicht zu fliehen.
8. Ein junger Mann, _dessen_ Freundin auch weg wollte, fuhr mit der S-Bahn nach West-Berlin und blieb da.
9. Die Freundin, _deren_ Eltern in Weimar wohnten, wollte noch ein-mal ihre Eltern sehen.
10. Das war aber gerade an dem Tag, an _dem_ man die Mauer baute.
11. Das bedeutete, daß sie den Freund, _den_ sie in West-Berlin zu-rückgelassen hatte und _der_ dort auf sie wartete, nie wieder-sehen würde.
12. Am Ende des Filmes, _der_ sehr spannend war, blieb nur die Er-innerung an den Freund.

E: Ku'damm is what Berliners would say for Kurfürstendamm. Use whatever you prefer.

Optional practice: Have students make up rela-tive clauses for each of the nouns below, e.g., die Universität; die Universität, an der er studiert, . . . (1. der Kurs 2. die Professorin 3. das Austauschpro-gramm 4. die Studenten 5. das Stipendium 6. der Hörsaal 7. der Beruf 8. die Leute)

E. Kombinieren Sie! Bilden Sie aus zwei Sätzen einen Satz mit Hilfe eines Relativpronomens!

BEISPIEL: Der Ku(rfüsten)damm ist eine bekannte Berliner Straße. Jeder kennt sie.
   Der Ku'damm ist eine bekannte Berliner Straße, die jeder kennt.

1. Die Gedächtniskirche gefällt mir. Ihr habt schon von der Gedächtnis-kirche gehört.
2. Der alte Turm soll kaputt bleiben. Die Berliner nennen ihn den „Hohlen Zahn".
3. Die Berliner nennen den neuen Turm „Lippenstift". Die Berliner ha-ben für alles einen Namen.
4. Der Ku'damm beginnt bei der Gedächtniskirche. Am Ku'damm gibt es viele schöne Geschäfte.
5. Die Geschäfte sind nicht billig. Sie sind sehr elegant.
6. Da gibt es auch viele Cafés. Man kann in den Cafés gemütlich sitzen.
7. Das Café war prima. Ich habe seinen Namen vergessen.
8. Heike hat mir alles gezeigt. Ihre Eltern wohnen in Berlin.
9. Ihr Bruder war auch sehr nett. Ich bin mit ihm am Abend in einen Jazzkeller gegangen.
10. In dem Jazzkeller konnte man auch tanzen. Ich fand den Jazzkeller übrigens einmalig.

F: 1. Wo ist der Hörsaal, in dem Professor Schulz liest? 2. Der Kurs, den er lehrt, ist moderne deutsche Geschichte. 3. Die Studenten, die seine Kurse belegen, müssen schwer (fleißig) arbeiten. 4. Geschichte ist ein Fach, das ich sehr interessant finde. 5. Aber ich habe einen Zimmerkollegen, der nichts interessant findet. 6. Er ist ein Mensch, den ich nicht verstehe. 7. Er studiert Fächer, die ihm nicht gefallen (die er nicht mag). 8. Die Freunde, mit denen er ausgeht, sind langweilig. 9. Er macht sich über seinen Vater lustig, dessen Geld er jeden Monat bekommt. 10. Aber das Mädchen, mit dem er verlobt ist, ist sehr nett.

If you feel that indirect speech is not necessary in the first year, or that your students can't deal with it at this time, LEAVE IT OUT! Ignore exercises G to J, L in the "Zusammenfassung," and E in "Zum Text."

It might help to translate these and the following examples.

F. An der Uni. Auf deutsch, bitte!

1. Where's the lecture hall in which Professor Schulz is lecturing (reading)? **2.** The course he teaches is modern German history. **3.** The students who take his courses must work hard. **4.** History is a subject that I find very interesting. **5.** But I have a roommate who finds nothing interesting. **6.** He's a person (**Mensch**) I don't understand. **7.** He studies subjects he doesn't like. **8.** The friends he goes out with (with whom he goes out) are boring. **9.** He makes fun of his father, whose money he gets every month. **10.** But the girl he's engaged to (to whom he is engaged) is very pleasant.

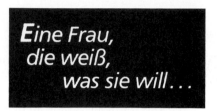

Eine Frau, die weiß, was sie will...

II. Indirect Speech

When reporting what someone else has said, you can use DIRECT SPEECH with quotation marks, or INDIRECT SPEECH without quotation marks.

Heike said, "Berlin has a lot to offer."
Heike said (that) Berlin has a lot to offer.

Often, corresponding direct and indirect speech will require different personal pronouns and possessive adjectives, depending on who reports the conversation.

- If Heike says to Martin *"I'll bring my map,"* and she reports the conversation, she will say: *I told him I would bring my map.*

- If Martin reported the conversation, he would say: *She told me she would bring her map.*

- If a third person reported, he or she would say: *She told him she would bring her map.*

In spoken German such indirect reports are generally in the INDICATIVE when the opening verb is in the present (**Sie sagt, . . .**). However, when the opening verb is in the past (**Sie sagte, . . .**), the SUBJUNCTIVE usually follows. We will focus on the latter.

> „Ich bringe meinen Stadtplan mit."
> Sie sagt, sie bringt ihren Stadtplan mit.
> Sie sagte, sie **würde** ihren Stadtplan **mitbringen.**

NOTE: In German opening quotation marks are placed at the bottom of the line.

1. Statements

   The tense of the indirect statement is determined by the tense of the direct statement.

   a. Direct statements in the present or future are reported indirectly in the present-time subjunctive or the **würde**-form.

   > present tense ⎱
   > future tense ⎰ → present-time subjunctive or **würde**-form

„Ich **komme** später."	Sie sagte, sie **käme** später.
	Sie sagte, sie **würde** später **kommen.**
„Ich **kann** dich anrufen."	Sie sagte, sie **könnte** ihn **anrufen.**
„Ich **werde** dir Berlin zeigen."	Sie sagte, sie **würde** ihm Berlin **zeigen.**

   b. Direct statements IN ANY PAST TENSE are reported indirectly in the past-time subjunctive.

   > present perfect ⎫
   > simple past   ⎬ → past-time subjunctive
   > past perfect   ⎭

„Sie **ist** nicht **gekommen."**	Sie sagte, sie **wäre** nicht **gekommen.**
„Sie **hatte** keine Zeit."	Sie sagte, sie **hätte** keine Zeit **gehabt.**
„Sie **hatte** aber **angerufen."**	Sie sagte, sie **hätte** aber **angerufen.**

   c. The conjunction **daß** may or may not be used. If it is not used, the sentence is in the original word order. If **daß** is used, the inflected part of the verb comes last.

   Sie sagte, sie **käme** morgen.
   Sie sagte, **daß** sie morgen **käme.**

   Sie sagte, sie **hätte** andere Pläne gehabt.
   Sie sagte, **daß** sie andere Pläne gehabt **hätte.**

2. Questions

   The tense of an indirect question is also determined by the tense of a direct question. Indirect YES / NO QUESTIONS are introduced by **ob,** and indirect INFORMATION QUESTIONS by the question word.

Er fragte: „Hast du jetzt Zeit?"	*He asked, "Do you have time now?"*
Er fragte, **ob** sie jetzt Zeit hätte.	*He asked if she had time now.*
Er fragte: „Wo warst du?"	*He asked, "Where were you?"*
Er fragte, **wo** sie gewesen wäre.	*He asked where she had been.*

3. Imperatives

Direct requests in the imperative are expressed indirectly with the auxiliary **sollen.**

Sie sagte: „Frag(e) nicht so viel!"	*She said, "Don't ask so much."*
Sie sagte, er **sollte** nicht so viel **fragen.**	*She said he shouldn't ask so much.*

ÜBUNGEN

Remind students not to use the **würde**-form with **haben, sein, werden, wissen,** and the modals unless you want to introduce the double infinitive.

G. Was haben die Studenten gesagt? Convert from indirect to direct speech. Be sure to change the pronouns accordingly.

BEISPIEL: Phillip sagte, er wäre im Theater gewesen.
Phillip sagte: „Ich bin im Theater gewesen."

1. Phillip sagte, er hätte das Stück sehr gut gefunden.
2. Stephan sagte, er wollte es sich auch ansehen.
3. Sonja sagte, sie würde mit Stephan ins Theater gehen.
4. Sonja sagte, sie würde heute nachmittag die Karten dafür kaufen.
5. Stephan sagte, er würde lieber Freitag abend ins Theater gehen.
6. Stephan sagte, er wollte das Stück erst lesen.

H. Wiederholen Sie die Sätze als indirekte Aussagen (*statements*)!
   1. **Aussagen in der Gegenwart oder Zukunft** (*referring to now or later*). Trudi's friend reports what Trudi told her. Now report what the friend said.

BEISPIEL: „Trudi will Zahnärztin werden."
Sie sagte, Trudi wollte Zahnärztin werden.
(Sie sagte, daß Trudi Zahnärztin werden wollte.)

„Gute Zahnärzte braucht man immer. Sie kann leicht kürzere Stunden arbeiten, wenn sie mal kleine Kinder hat. Außerdem verdient man gut. Natürlich muß man lange studieren. Aber darauf freut sie sich schon."

   2. **Aussagen in der Vergangenheit** (*referring to earlier*). Margaret's friend reports what Margaret told him about her year abroad. Now write what the friend said.

BEISPIEL: „Margaret hat letztes Jahr in Deutschland studiert."
Er sagte, Margaret hätte letztes Jahr in Deutschland studiert.

„Es hat ihr gut gefallen. Sie hat die Sprachprüfung leicht bestanden. Während der Semesterferien ist sie in die Schweiz gefahren. Im Winter ist sie Ski laufen gegangen. Sie ist erst vor drei Wochen zurückgekommen."

I: Tell students to watch out for changes in pronouns.

I. Martin und Heike im Gespräch. Wiederholen Sie die Fragen indirekt!
   1. **Ja / nein-Fragen.** Beginnen Sie mit Martin fragte, . . .!

BEISPIEL: „Hast du Freunde im östlichen Teil Berlins?"
Martin fragte, ob sie Freunde im östlichen Teil Berlins hätte?

a. „Sind sie auch Studenten?" **b.** „Studieren sie auch Kunst?"
c. „Geht ihr manchmal zusammen aus?" **d.** „Seht ihr euch viel?"
e. „Gefällt dir Berlin jetzt besser?" **f.** „Warst du beim Mauerdurchbruch dabei?" **g.** „Freust du dich, daß Berlin wieder die Hauptstadt von Deutschland ist?"

2. **Informationsfragen.** Beginnen Sie mit Martin fragte, . . . !

BEISPIEL: „Wie lange bist du schon in Berlin?"
Martin fragte, wie lange sie schon in Berlin wäre?

a. „Wo ist das Brandenburger Tor?" **b.** „Wie kommt man dorthin?"
c. „Was für andere Sehenswürdigkeiten (attractions) gibt es hier?"
d. „Wofür interessierst du dich?" **e.** „Wann gehst du mal ins Theater?" **f.** „Was hast du das letzte Mal (time) gesehen?"

3. **Imperative.** Beginnen Sie mit Heike sagte ihm, . . . !

BEISPIEL: „Komm doch einmal mit!"
Heike sagte ihm, er sollte doch einmal mitkommen.

a. „Nimm die U-Bahn!" **b.** „Sieh dir die Museen an!" **c.** „Geh auch ins Potsdamer Schloß!" **d.** „Hör dir ein Konzert an!" **e.** „Besuche die Filmfestspiele!" **f.** „Erinnere mich daran!"

J. Was hat er / sie gesagt? Ask your classmate five questions about himself / herself and then report to the class, using indirect speech.

BEISPIEL: Er / sie hat mir erzählt, er / sie wäre aus Chicago, er / sie hätte zwei Brüder . . .

ZUSAMMENFASSUNG

3rd stanza of the *Deutschlandlied:* Einigkeit und Recht und Freiheit für das deutsche Vaterland. Danach laßt uns alle streben, brüderlich mit Herz und Hand. Einigkeit und Recht und Freiheit sind des Glückes Unterpfand. Blüh im Glanze dieses Glückes, blühe deutsches Vaterland!

K. Ein toller Tag. Geben Sie das fehlende Relativpronomen!
1. Christa Grauer ist eine junge Frau, _____ mit einem Computer die Anzeigetafeln (scoreboards) in einem Kölner Fußballstadion bedient (takes care of). **2.** Sie erzählt von einem Tag, _____ sie nie vergessen wird. **3.** Eine Woche nach dem 9. November, einem Tag, _____ Geschichte gemacht hat, spielte die deutsche Fußball-Nationalmannschaft (. . . team) gegen Wales. **4.** Vor dem Spiel, zu _____ 60 000 Menschen gekommen waren, schrieb Christa wie immer die dritte Strophe (stanza) des Deutschlandliedes auf die Anzeigetafeln. **5.** Das hatte sie schon 14 Jahre lang getan. Aber es gab wenige Spiele, bei _____ die Leute wirklich mitsangen. **6.** Aber diesmal sangen Tausende mit, denn die Strophe, _____ Text ihnen bisher nicht viel bedeutet hatte, bedeutete ihnen plötzlich sehr viel.

L. Was Bürger aus Ost und West an den Tagen im November 1989 sagten.
Convert from direct to indirect speech, with and without the conjunction **daß.**
Be sure to change the pronouns accordingly.

BEISPIEL: „West-Berlin war wie Chicago für uns ein schwarzes Loch *(hole)*
auf der Landkarte." (Ost-Berlinerin)
**Sie sagte, West-Berlin wäre wie Chicago für sie ein schwarzes
Loch auf der Landkarte gewesen.**
**Sie sagte, daß West-Berlin wie Chicago für sie ein schwarzes
Loch auf der Landkarte gewesen wäre.**

1. „So viel Fernsehen haben wir noch nie gesehen. Ich werde ganz
   nervös, wenn ich mal aufs Klo *(toilet)* muß." (Ost-Berliner Taxifahrer)
2. „Wir feiern jede Nacht. Geschlafen haben wir schon 28 Jahre."
   (Mecklenburger in Hamburg)
3. „Wir zählen nicht mehr. Sie kommen von überall wie die Ameisen
   (ants)." (West-Berliner Polizistin)
4. „Wir haben uns jeden Tag gesehen, jetzt will ich ihm mal die Hand
   schütteln *(shake)*." (West-Polizist über seinen Kollegen aus Ost-Berlin)
5. „Die einzige *(only)* Chance, die wir haben, den Sozialismus zu retten
   (save), ist richtiger Sozialismus." (DDR-Autor Stephan Heym)
6. „Ich bin Gott dankbar, daß ich das noch erleben *(experience)* darf."
   (Willy Brandt)
7. „Ich dachte, ihr Deutschen könnt nur Fußball spielen oder
   Stechschritt *(goose-step)*, aber jetzt könnt ihr sogar Revolutionen machen." (Afrikanischer Diplomat)
8. „Vor meinen Augen tanzte die Freiheit." (NBC-Korrespondent)
9. „Mauern sind nicht für ewig gebaut . . . In Berlin habe ich für mein
   Herz gespielt." (Cellist Mstislaw Rostropowitsch)

Cellist Mstislaw Ro-
stropowitsch am
11.11.1989 vor der
Mauer

M: 1. Brecht, der aus Augsburg war, studierte erst Medizin. 2. Aber es war das Theater, für das er sich wirklich interessierte. 3. Kurt Weill war ein Komponist, mit dem Brecht oft arbeitete. 4. *Die Drei-groschenoper* ist ein Stück, das Brecht und Weill zusammen geschrieben haben. 5. *Mutter Courage* und *Der kaukasische Kreide-kreis* sind zwei Stücke, die er 1938 schrieb. 6. Das Theater, das Brecht nach 1948 leitete, ist in Berlin. 7. Berlin ist auch die Stadt, in der er 1956 starb. 8. *Der Augsburger Kreidekreis* ist eine Geschichte von Brecht, die viele Studenten lesen.

M. Bertolt Brecht. Auf deutsch, bitte!

1. Brecht, who was from Augsburg, studied medicine **(Medizin)** at first.   **2.** But it was the theater in which he was really interested.   **3.** Kurt Weill was a composer with whom Brecht often worked.   **4.** *Die Dreigroschenoper* is a play that Brecht and Weill wrote together.   **5.** *Mutter Courage* and *Der kaukasische Kreidekreis* are two plays he wrote in 1938.   **6.** The theater that Brecht directed **(leiten)** after 1948 is in Berlin.   **7.** Berlin is also the city in which he died **(starb)** in 1956.   **8.** *Der Augsburger Kreidekreis* is a story by Brecht that many students read.

EINBLICKE ◆◆◆◆◆◆◆◆◆◆◆

Blick auf Berlin mit Fernsehturm

First mentioned in a document in 1237, Berlin became the seat of the electors **(Kurfürsten)** of Brandenburg in 1486 and later, after 1701, of the Prussian kings. After 1871 it gained political, economic, and cultural prominence as the capital of the German nation. At the beginning of World War II, Berlin was the sixth-largest city in the world, with over four million inhabitants. More than a third did not survive the war. In 1945, at the Yalta conference, Berlin was put under the four-power administration of the Allies: Great Britain, France, the United States, and the Soviet Union. But differences among the occupation powers brought about the 1948 Soviet blockade and the division of the city. In 1949 East Berlin became the capital of the GDR. On August 13, 1961, the GDR began to build the Berlin Wall, a symbol for the division of Germany as a whole. Ironically, the Wall was opened for the same reason for which it had been built: a mass exodus of the population, this time through the open borders of Hungary. Once the Wall was open, the reunification of the city and the country could not be stopped; now Berlin has a new future as the capital of Germany.

> ## „Möge diese Welt mit Gottes Hilfe eine Wiedergeburt der Freiheit erleben."

WORTSCHATZ 2

der	Gedanke, -ns, -n	*thought*
die	Heimat	*homeland, home*
	Insel	*island*
	Jugend	*youth*
	Macht, ⸚e	*power*
	Mitte	*middle*
	berühmt	*famous*
	kaum	*hard(ly)*
	nun	*well; now*
	aus·tauschen	*to exchange*
	erkennen, erkannte, erkannt	*to recognize*
	scheinen, schien, geschienen	*to seem, appear like*
	verlassen (verläßt), verließ, verlassen	*to leave (a place)*

WAS IST DAS? der Bomber, Einmarsch, Jeep, Sonderstatus; das Gefühl, System, Transportflugzeug, Turmcafé; die Blockade, Elektrizität, Industriestadt, Metropole, Olympiade, Paßkontrolle, Rote Armee, Teilung, Viereinhalbmillionenstadt; *(pl.)* Industriefirmen, Medikamente, Westmächte; reagieren; britisch, enorm viel, grenzenlos, kapitalistisch, sowjetisch, sozialistisch, teils, total blockiert, ummauert, (un)freiwillig, vital, zentral

„Berlin bleibt doch Berlin!"

for a long time

raves / shaped

Da saßen wir nun, Vater und Tochter, im Flugzeug auf dem Weg zu der Stadt, die er eigentlich nie vergessen konnte: Berlin. "Ich bin schon lange° in Amerika, aber Berlin . . . Nun, Berlin ist eben meine Heimat." Und dann wanderten seine Gedanken zurück zu den zwanziger bis vierziger Jahren, als er dort gelebt hatte. Die Viereinhalbmillionenstadt, von deren Charme und Esprit er heute noch schwärmt°, hätte seine Jugend geprägt°. Und er erzählte mir von dem, was er dort so geliebt hatte; von den Wäldern und Seen in der Umgebung und von der berühmten Berliner Luft; von den Museen, der   5

offerings
big mouth

economically
administration

university

dominated / . . .scene

air raids / rubble

victorious allies

fuel

raisin . . .
made

Oper und den Theatern, deren Angebot° damals einmalig gewesen wäre;
vom Kabarett mit seiner „frechen Schnauze"° und den Kaffeehäusern, in   10
denen immer etwas los war. „In Berlin kamen eben alle Fäden zusammen,
nicht nur kulturell, sondern auch politisch und wirtschaftlich°. Es war damals
die größte Industriestadt Europas. Die zentrale Verwaltung° aller deutschen
Industriefirmen war in Berlin. Und man kannte sich, tauschte Gedanken
aus, auch mit der Hochschule°. Einfach phantastisch! . . ."   15

„Und dann kam 1933[1]. Viele verließen Berlin, teils freiwillig, teils unfrei-
willig. Die Nazis beherrschten° das Straßenbild°. Bei der Olympiade 1936 sah
die ganze Welt nicht nur Berlins moderne S-Bahn und schöne Straßen,
sondern auch Hitler. Und drei Jahre später war Krieg!" Nun sprach er von
den schweren Luftangriffen° und den Trümmern°, die diese hinterlassen   20
hätten, vom Einmarsch der Roten Armee, der Teilung Deutschlands unter
den vier Siegermächten° (1945) und auch von der Luftbrücke[2], mit der die
Westmächte auf die sowjetische Blockade reagiert hätten. „Plötzlich waren
wir total blockiert, eine Insel. Es gab nichts zu essen, keine Kleidung, kein
Heizmaterial°, keine Medikamente, kaum Wasser und Elektrizität. An guten   25
Tagen landeten in den nächsten zehn Monaten alle paar Minuten britische
und amerikanische Transportflugzeuge—wir nannten sie die Rosinenbom-
ber°—und brachten uns, was wir brauchten. Ohne die Westmächte hätten
wir es nie geschafft°!"

Ein „Rosinen-
bomber" während
der Blockade

wide-open space

Dann kamen wir in West-Berlin an. Erst machten wir eine Stadtrund-   30
fahrt. „Es ist wieder schön hier, und doch, die Weite° ist weg. Berlin schien
früher grenzenlos, und jetzt . . . überall diese Grenze." Immer wieder stand

view of

man vor der Mauer, die seit 1961 mitten durch Berlin lief. Besonders traurig machte ihn der Blick auf° das Brandenburger Tor[3], das auf der anderen Seite der Mauer stand. Und doch gefiel mir diese ummauerte Insel. West- 35 Berlin war wieder eine vitale Metropole, die enorm viel zu bieten hatte.

GDR police (Volkspolizei)

Der Besuch in Ost-Berlin, der Hauptstadt der DDR, war wie eine Reise in eine andere Welt. Allein schon die Gesichter der Vopos° am Checkpoint Charlie[4] und das komische Gefühl, das man bei der Paßkontrolle hatte! Berlin-Mitte war für meinen Vater schwer wiederzuerkennen. Der Pots- 40 damer Platz, der früher voller Leben gewesen war, war leer. Leichter zu erkennen waren die historischen Gebäude entlang „Unter den Linden": die Staatsbibliothek, die Humboldt Universität[5] und die Staatsoper. Interessant waren auch das Pergamonmuseum, der Dom und gegenüber der Palast der Republik, den die Berliner „Palazzo Prozzo"° nannten, und in dem 45 die Volkskammer° saß. Dann natürlich überall der Fernsehturm, dessen Turmcafé sich dreht°. Wir sahen auch einen britischen Jeep, der „Unter den Linden" Streife fuhr°, was uns an den Sonderstatus Berlins erinnerte. Hier trafen die kapitalistische und die sozialistische Welt aufeinander°, und für beide Welten waren Ost- und West-Berlin Schaufenster° zweier gegensätz- 50 licher° Systeme.

Braggarts' Palace
GDR house of representatives
turns
patrolled
came together
display windows
opposite

Heute ist das alles Geschichte. Die Berliner können wieder reisen, wohin sie wollen, denn Berlin ist keine Insel mehr. Als mein Vater das Öffnen der Mauer im Fernsehen sah, sagte er immer wieder: „Daß ich das noch erleben° durfte!" Und unsere Gedanken gingen zurück zu Präsident Kennedys Wor- 55 ten 1963 an der Mauer: „Alle freien Menschen sind Bürger Berlins . . . Ich bin ein Berliner!" Und wir mußten ihm zustimmen°.

experience

agree

He really should have said **„Ich bin Berliner."** **ein Berliner** is a jelly-filled donut!

John F. Kennedy in Berlin am 26.6.1963

ZUM TEXT

Was ist das? 1. die vierziger Jahre 2. eine Olympiade 3. eine Metropole 4. die Luftbrücke 5. ein Rosinenbomber 6. die Westmächte 7. Vopos 8. ein Schaufenster 9. ein Fernsehturmcafé 10. Unter den Linden

A. Richtig oder falsch?

____ 1. Der Vater und die Tochter fliegen nach Amerika.

____ 2. Der Vater hatte 40 Jahre in Berlin gelebt.

____ 3. Er hatte Berlin sehr geliebt.

____ 4. In Berlin war damals nicht viel los gewesen.

____ 5. 1939 hatte der Krieg begonnen.

____ 6. 1945 teilten die Siegermächte Deutschland und Berlin.

____ 7. Die Luftbrücke brachte den Berlinern nur Rosinen.

____ 8. Von 1961 bis 1989 teilte die Mauer Berlin.

____ 9. Ein Vopo war ein ostdeutsches Auto.

____ 10. Der Potsdamer Platz war der „Palazzo Prozzo" Ost-Berlins.

____ 11. „Unter den Linden" ist eine berühmte alte Straße in Berlin.

____ 12. Ost-Berlin war ein Schaufenster des Kapitalismus.

____ 13. Der Vater ist beim Öffnen der Mauer in Berlin gewesen.

____ 14. Präsident Nixon sagte 1963: „Ich bin ein Berliner."

B. Suchen Sie die Relativpronomen im Text! Working in groups of two to four students, underline all the relative pronouns and their antecedents that you can find in the text. Which group can find the greatest number?

C. Bilden Sie Relativsätze! Make up two relative clauses for each pronoun; then compare results with the rest of the class.

1. Berlin ist eine Stadt, die . . .   4. Berlin ist eine Stadt, von der . . .
2. Berlin ist eine Stadt, in der . . .   5. Berlin ist eine Stadt, um die . . .
3. Berlin ist eine Stadt, deren . . .

D. Was fehlt?

D: 1. der 2. das 3. deren 4. den 5. dessen 6. dem 7. der 8. deren 9. dessen 10. die (2 ×)

1. Mir gefällt diese Stadt, in _____ mehr als drei Millionen Menschen wohnen.   **2.** Es ist ein Kulturzentrum (*n.*), _____ enorm viel zu bieten hat.   **3.** Die Filmfestspiele, _____ Filme wirklich einmalig sind, muß man einmal gesehen haben.   **4.** Der letzte Film, _____ ich mir angesehen habe, war sehr witzig.   **5.** Ein anderer Film, an _____ Titel (*m.*) ich mich nicht erinnern kann, war etwas traurig.   **6.** Es war ein Film, in _____ mehrere berühmte Schauspieler mitspielten.   **7.** Der Hauptschauspieler, _____ am Ende seine Heimat verläßt, hieß Humphrey Bogart.   **8.** Morgen abend gehe ich mit Heike, _____ Vater Extrakarten hat, ins Kabarett.   **9.** Das Kabarett, _____ Name nicht nur in Berlin bekannt ist, heißt „Die Stachelschweine" (*The Porcupines*).   **10.** Die Leute, über _____ sie sich lustig machen, sind meistens Politiker oder andere berühmte Persönlichkeiten (*pl.*), _____ jeder kennt.

E. Vater und Tochter. Lesen Sie das Gespräch, und erzählen Sie dann indirekt, was sie gesagt oder gefragt haben!

TOCHTER   Wie lange hast du dort gewohnt?

VATER   Ungefähr 25 Jahre.

TOCHTER   Waren deine Eltern auch aus Berlin?

VATER   Nein, aber sie sind später nachgekommen.
TOCHTER   Hast du dort studiert?
VATER   Ja, an der Humboldt Universität.
TOCHTER   Hast du dort Mutti kennengelernt?
VATER   Ja, das waren schöne Jahre!
TOCHTER   Und wann seid ihr von dort weggegangen?
VATER   1949.
TOCHTER   Erzähl mir davon!
VATER   Ach, das ist eine lange Geschichte. Setzen wir uns in ein Café!
          Dann werde ich dir davon erzählen.

F. Schriftliche Übung. Wenn Sie die Wahl *(choice)* hätten, würden Sie in Berlin leben wollen? Warum oder warum nicht? Schreiben Sie acht bis zehn Sätze!

1. In 1933 Adolf Hitler became chancellor of Germany. This began a twelve-year dictatorship that included World War II and ended in the total defeat and division of Germany in 1945, and the loss of millions of lives.

2. On June 24, 1948, at the height of the Cold War, Soviet troops tried to force the integration of West Berlin into the GDR by blocking all vital supply lines—roads, railroads, and canals leading into the city. The West then sustained the more than two million West Berliners through the famous airlift **(Luftbrücke).** The Russians finally ended their blockade on May 12, 1949.

3. When King Wilhelm II of Prussia built the Brandenburg Gate **(Brandenburger Tor)** 200 years ago, he intended it to be a "Gate of Peace." Instead, it has witnessed two centuries of war and revolution. The Brandenburg Gate, inspired by the Propylaea of the Parthenon, is an arch surmounted by the reconstructed Victory Quadriga (1793). In 1963 Communist soldiers dropped huge red drapes over the gate to prevent President Kennedy from looking into East Berlin during his visit to the western part of the city.

4. From 1945 to 1990, all of Berlin was officially governed by the four Allies, and only the British, French, Russians, and Americans had access to and patrolled it regularly. The one East-West crossing reserved exclusively for non-German visitors was "Checkpoint Charlie."

5. Humboldt University, named after the German scientist and geographer Alexander von Humboldt (1769–1859), was founded in the mid-1770s. Its Western counterpart, the Free University of Berlin, was founded in 1948.

SPRECHSITUATIONEN

Making Descriptions

When you are abroad, you may have to describe something you want to buy or something for which you don't know the appropriate German word. How do you do that? What are some useful descriptive adjectives or phrases?

Wie ist es?

groß / klein	(hell)rot . . .
dick / dünn	(dunkel)rot . . .
schwer / leicht	bunt *(multi-colored, colorful)*
hoch / niedrig *(low)*	gestreift *(striped)*
breit / eng *(narrow)*	getüpfelt *(polka-dotted)*
rund / (vier)eckig	kariert *(checkered)*
kurz / lang	
hart / weich *(soft)*	
süß / sauer *(sweet / sour)*	
salzig *(salty)*	
so groß wie	
größer als	

Woraus ist es?

Optional vocabulary: das Eisen iron; die Seide silk

der	Kunststoff	*synthetics*	*die*	Baumwolle	*cotton*
	Stahl	*steel*		Pappe	*cardboard*
das	Holz	*wood*		Wolle	*wool*
	Leder	*leather*			
	Metall	*metal*			
	Papier	*paper*			
	Plastik	*plastic*			
	Porzellan	*porcelain*			

Was macht man damit?	Man schreibt damit.
Wozu gebraucht *(use)* man es?	Man gebraucht es, um besser zu sehen.

Often a sentence with a relative pronoun will be helpful in describing people or things.

x Kennst du die Leute, die in dem neuen Gebäude an der Ecke wohnen?
y Ist das nicht das Gebäude, in dem Alfred arbeitet?

A. Woran denke ich? Working in small groups, one thinks of an object, the others have twenty questions to figure out what it is. The German word for the object should be one that has been used in the course.

B. Wie bitte? Pretend you are in a store and need to purchase something, but you don't know the German word for it. Describe it as best as you can, using gestures if necessary.†

1. towel
2. soap
3. deodorant stick
4. shampoo
5. suntan lotion
6. scissors
7. bandaid
8. needle
9. hair dryer
10. iron
11. umbrella
12. clothes hanger
13. checkered shirt
14. polka-dot bikini
15. round table cloth

You could easily add to this list.

C. Kurzgespräche. Describe to a classmate . . .
1. a favorite car you (would like to) drive.
2. a favorite place where you once lived or would like to live.
3. a favorite food.
4. something you need to buy (e.g., in a supermarket, bookstore, department store, furniture store, etc.).
5. what you would do if you had $5,000.

†1. ein Handtuch 2. Seife 3. einen Deo-Stift 4. Shampoo 5. Sonnencreme 6. eine Schere 7. Pflaster 8. eine Nadel 9. einen Fön 10. ein Bügeleisen 11. einen Schirm 12. einen Kleiderbügel 13. ein kariertes Hemd 14. einen getüpfelten Bikini 15. eine runde Tischdecke

15

Wo ein Wille ist, ist auch ein Weg

Das Schiller-Goethe
Denkmal vor dem
Theater in Weimar

▌LERNZIELE

Gespräche and **Wortschatz**. This chapter deals with the Germans and historical developments in Germany.

Struktur. You will learn about . . .

▪ the passive voice.

▪ the different uses of **werden.**

▪ the special subjunctive (or Subjunctive I).

Einblicke. The question of German identity since 1945

Sprechsituationen

▪ Expressing doubt and uncertainty

▪ Expressing probability and possibility

▪ Making deductions

◆◆◆◆◆ GESPRÄCHE

Warm-ups: 1. **Defi-
nieren Sie! z.B. Sekre-
tärin: Eine Sekretärin
ist eine Frau, die in
einem Büro arbeitet.**
(Verkäufer, Hausfrau,
Geburtstag, Silvester,
Ferien, Bibliothek,
Kaufhaus, Jugendher-
berge, Ausweis, Platten-
spieler) 2. **Geben Sie
die Verbformen, z.B.
aussehen, sah aus, aus-
gesehen** (bestehen, bie-
ten, erkennen, haben,
nennen, scheinen, teil-
nehmen, verlassen,
wachsen, werden)!
3. **Geben Sie den Kon-
junktiv! Das sieht schön
aus. Was habt ihr zu
bieten? Erinnerst du
dich daran? Das er-
kenne ich sofort.**

Zu Besuch in Weimar

THOMAS   Komisch. Dieses Denkmal kommt mir bekannt vor. Ich glaube,
          ich habe es schon irgendwo gesehen.

DANIELA   Warst du schon mal in San Francisco?

THOMAS   Natürlich! Im Golden Gate Park!

DANIELA   Genau! Vor ein paar Jahren war es noch leichter für uns, das
          Denkmal dort zu sehen, als hierher nach Weimar[1] zu kommen.

THOMAS   Und dabei ist es nur eine Fahrt von zwei Stunden!

DANIELA   Du kennst ja das Goethe-Denkmal[2] in Frankfurt. In Stuttgart gibt
          es ein Schiller-Denkmal[3]. Aber hier sind die beiden vereint.

THOMAS   Das ist eigentlich ein schönes Symbol für die deutsche Einheit.
          Die gemeinsame Kultur konnte man ja nicht teilen.

DANIELA   Die alten Häuser hier sind wirklich hübsch.

THOMAS   Ja, sie sind vor ein paar Jahren gut restauriert worden. Da hat
          der Staat hier ganz schön viel Geld dafür ausgegeben.

DANIELA   Ist ja auch gut, daß hier keine Autos fahren.

THOMAS   Gott sei Dank! Die Fassaden hätten die Abgase der Trabis[4] nicht
          lange überlebt! Bei uns gibt es jetzt eine Bürgerinitiative, alle
          Autos in der Altstadt zu verbieten, um die alten Gebäude zu
          retten.[5]

DANIELA   Das finde ich prima.

THOMAS   Ja, wo ein Wille ist, ist auch ein Weg.

Übrigens

1. Weimar is a center of German culture where two of Germany's greatest
writers, Goethe and Schiller, lived. In 1919 the National Assembly, meeting in
Weimar to symbolize the new republic's ties to the German humanist tradition,
adopted the democratic constitution that established the Weimar Republic. The
republic came to an end soon after Hitler was appointed chancellor in 1933.
Today Weimar remains a quiet little town with many literary associations.

2. Johann Wolfgang von Goethe (1749–1832) was one of Germany's greatest
poets, novelists, and playwrights. He was also a leading thinker and scientist.
Because of his vast scope of knowledge and his comprehensive interest in the
world of human experience, he is often referred to as "the last universal man."
His works include *Die Leiden des jungen Werther*, *Wilhelm Meister*, and *Faust*.

3. Friedrich von Schiller (1759–1805) ranks second only to Goethe among the
leading figures of classical German literature. His dramas, often pleas for human
freedom and dignity, inspired liberals in their fight for liberty during the early

Richtig oder falsch?
1. Thomas und Daniela sind in Weimar. (R)
2. Das Denkmal, das sie sehen, gibt es auch in Stuttgart. (F) 3. Das Denkmal zeigt Goethe und Nietzsche. (F)
4. Thomas findet das Denkmal ein schönes Symbol für ein vereintes Deutschland, dessen Kultur man nicht teilen konnte. (R) 5. Leider sind die Gebäude, vor denen sie stehen, alle alt und grau. (F) 6. Zum Glück gibt es hier im Zentrum keine Autos. (R) 7. Ein Trabi ist ein kleines Auto, das viele Abgase hat. (R)
8. Thomas kommt aus einer Stadt, in deren Altstadt Autos fahren dürfen (R) 9. Viele möchten aber auch dort Autos verbieten. (R)
10. Man will die Altstadt, deren Gebäude sehr alt sind, retten. (R)

1800s and during the Revolution of 1848. His works include *Don Carlos, Die Jungfrau von Orleans, Maria Stuart,* and *Wilhelm Tell.*

4. The old, smoke-belching East German Trabant („Trabi") with its two-stroke engine emitted roughly nine times more hydrocarbons and five times more carbon dioxide than conventional cars with four-stroke engines.

5. German cities in both East and West have made a special effort to restore and protect historical buildings from the effects of acid rain and air pollution.

A Visit to Weimar THOMAS: *That's funny. This monument seems so familiar to me. I think I've seen it somewhere before.* DANIELA: *Have you been in San Francisco?* THOMAS: *Of course! In the Golden Gate Park!* DANIELA: *Exactly. A few years ago it was still easier for us to see the monument there than to come here to Weimar.* THOMAS: *And yet it's only a two-hour trip.* DANIELA: *You know the Goethe-Monument in Frankfurt. In Stuttgart there is a Schiller-Monument. But here the two are united.* THOMAS: *That's actually a nice symbol for German unity. They couldn't divide the culture we had in common.*

DANIELA: *The old houses here are really pretty.* THOMAS: *Yes, a few years ago they were thoroughly renovated. The state spent quite a bit of money for this.* DANIELA: *It's also good that there are no cars here.* THOMAS: *Thank God. The façades wouldn't have survived the exhaust fumes of the Trabis. In our city they now have a citizens' initiative to prohibit all cars in the old part of town in order to save the old buildings.* DANIELA: *I think that's great.* THOMAS: *Yes, where there's a will, there's a way.*

WORTSCHATZ 1

DIE UMWELT *environment, surroundings*

ab·reißen, riß ab, abgerissen	*to tear down*
erklären	*to explain*
erlauben	*to allow, permit*
finanzieren	*to finance*
garantieren	*to guarantee*
gebrauchen[1]	*to use, utilize*
parken	*to park*
planen	*to plan*
reden (mit, über)	*to talk (to about)*
renovieren	*to renovate*
restaurieren	*to restore*
retten	*to save, rescue*
(sich) verändern	*to change*

1 Don't confuse **brauchen** *(to need)* with **gebrauchen** *(to use);* Ich **brauche** einen Kuli. BUT Ich kann diesen Kuli nicht **gebrauchen,** weil er kaputt ist.

verbieten, verbot, verboten	*to forbid*
(wieder)auf·bauen	*to (re)build*
zerstören	*to destroy*

WEITERES

| *der* Staat, -en | *state* |
| *das* Denkmal, ⸚er | *monument* |

gemeinsam	*together, (in) common*
vereint	*united*
Wo ein Wille ist, ist auch ein Weg.[2]	*Where there's a will, there's a way.*

2 For other proverbs, see "Zum Thema," exercise C.

PASSIVES VOKABULAR **das Symbol, -e** **die Abgase** *(pl.) exhaust fumes* **die Einheit** *unity* **die Fassade, -n** *façade* **die Initiative, -n** **die Kultur -en** **dabei** *yet* **Das kommt mir bekannt vor.** *That seems familiar to me.* **ganz schön viel** *quite a bit* **überleben** *to survive*

ZUM THEMA

A. Reporter im Rathaus. You're a radio reporter attending a meeting of the city-planning commission. Read what one man says, then report to YOUR listeners.

BEISPIEL: **Er hat gesagt, wir sollten nicht auf die Bürger hören, die immer . . .**

„Hören Sie nicht auf die Bürger, die immer wieder alles, ja die ganze Altstadt, retten wollen. Viele alte Innenhöfe *(inner courts)* sind dunkel und häßlich. Abreißen ist viel billiger und einfacher als renovieren! Wenn man die alten Gebäude abreißt und die Innenstadt schön modern aufbaut, dann kommt bestimmt wieder Leben in unser Zentrum. Auf diese Weise kann man auch die Straßen verbreitern *(widen)* und alles besser planen. Fußgängerzonen sind schön und gut, aber nicht im Zentrum, denn alle wollen ihr Auto in der Nähe haben. Das ist doch klar, weil's viel bequemer und sicherer ist! Ich kann Ihnen garantieren, wenn Sie aus dem Zentrum eine Einkaufszone machen, zu deren Geschäften man nur zu Fuß hinkommt *(gets to)*, dann verlieren Sie alle, meine Damen und Herren, viel Geld!"

B. Altbau oder Neubau? Wo würden Sie lieber wohnen? Was spricht dafür und was dagegen? Stellen Sie eine Liste auf! Machen Sie eine Meinungsumfrage *(opinion poll)*!

C. Ein paar Sprichwörter *(proverbs)*.
1. **Was bedeuten diese Sprichwörter?** Was ist die englische Version?

    a. Ohne Fleiß kein Preis.
    b. Es ist noch kein Meister° vom Himmel° gefallen.

(margin note) C.1: a. No pain, no gain. b. No man is born a master of his craft. c. Rome wasn't build in a day. d. Tomorrow, tomorrow, not today, all the lazy people say. e. If you don't learn it when you're young, you'll never learn it. f. Too many cooks spoil the broth. g. Lies have short legs. h. The early bird catches the worm. i. Everyone is the architect of his own future. j. All's well that ends well.

master / sky

c. Rom ist nicht an einem Tag gebaut worden.
d. Morgen, morgen, nur nicht heute, sagen alle faulen Leute.

nevermore

e. Was Hänschen nicht lernt, lernt Hans nimmermehr°.

cooks / spoil / porridge

f. Viele Köche° verderben° den Brei°.

lies

g. Lügen° haben kurze Beine.
h. Morgenstund' hat Gold im Mund.

blacksmith

i. Jeder ist seines Glückes Schmied°.
j. Ende gut, alles gut.

2. **Schriftliche Übung.** Tell an anecdote or describe a situation demonstrating one of the proverbs. Write about eight to ten sentences.

D. **Aussprache: Glottal Stops.** See also II. 42 in the pronunciation section of the Workbook.
1. +Erich +arbeitet +am +alten Dom.
2. Die +Abgase der +Autos machen +einfach +überall +alles kaputt.
3. +Ulf +erinnert sich +an +ein +einmaliges +Abendkonzert +im +Ulmer Dom.
4. +Otto sieht +aus wie +ein +alter +Opa.
5. +Anneliese +ist +attraktiv +und +elegant.

STRUKTUR

I. The Passive Voice

English and German sentences are in one of two voices: the active or the passive. In the ACTIVE VOICE the subject of the sentence is doing something; it's "active."

The students ask the professor.

In the PASSIVE VOICE the subject is not doing anything, rather, something is being done to it; it's "passive."

The professor is asked by the students.

Note what happens when a sentence in the active voice is changed into the passive voice. The direct object of the active becomes the subject of the passive.

    subj.   obj.
The students ask the professor.

The professor is asked by the students.
    subj.   obj. of prep.

In both languages the active voice is used much more frequently than the passive voice, especially in everyday speech. The passive voice is used when the focus is on the person or thing at whom the action is directed, rather than on the agent who is acting.

The passive is treated only briefly because by now many students will be saturated with verb forms. If you want your students to use the passive, elaborate on the explanations; there are plenty of exercises for active mastery of the passive. Otherwise, teach the passive for recognition only. In that case, use exercises C and D for translation into English and omit exercises E to G, H.2, 4, 7, K, and L.

1. Forms
   a. In English the passive is formed with the auxiliary *to be* and the past participle of the verb. In German it is formed with the auxiliary **werden** and the past participle of the verb.

werden . . . + past participle			
ich	**werde**	. . . gefragt	*I am (being)*
du	**wirst**	. . . gefragt	*you are (being)*
er	**wird**	. . . gefragt	*he is (being)*
wir	**werden**	. . . gefragt	*we are (being)*
ihr	**werdet**	. . . gefragt	*you are (being)*
sie	**werden**	. . . gefragt	*they are (being)*

   asked

   Der Professor **wird** von den Studenten **gefragt.**

   b. The passive voice has the same tenses as the active voice. They are formed with the various tenses of **werden** + the past participle of the verb. Note, however, that in the perfect tenses of the passive voice, the past participle of **werden** is **worden!** When you see or hear **worden,** you know immediately that you are dealing with a sentence in the passive voice.

Remind students that they are back in the indicative here.

PRESENT	Er **wird** . . . gefragt.	*He is being asked . . .*
SIMPLE PAST	Er **wurde** . . . gefragt.	*He was asked . . .*
FUTURE	Er **wird** . . . gefragt **werden.**	*He'll be asked . . .*
PRES. PERF.	Er **ist** . . . gefragt **worden.**	*He has been asked . . .*
PAST PERF.	Er **war** . . . gefragt **worden.**	*He had been asked . . .*

Die Altstadt wird renoviert.	*The old part of town is being renovated.*
Die Pläne wurden letztes Jahr gemacht.	*The plans were made last year.*
Alles wird finanziert werden.	*Everything will be financed.*
Alles ist entschieden worden.	*Everything has been decided.*
Manche Gebäude waren im Krieg zerstört worden.	*Some buildings had been destroyed during the war.*

   c. Modals themselves are not put into the passive voice. Rather, they follow this pattern:

   modal . . . + past participle + **werden**

   In this book only the present and simple-past tense of the modals will be used.

PRESENT	Er **muß** . . . gefragt **werden.**	*He must (has to) be asked . . .*
SIMPLE PAST	Er **mußte** . . . gefragt **werden.**	*He had to be asked . . .*

Das Gebäude muß renoviert werden.	*The building must be renovated.*
Die Pläne sollten letztes Jahr gemacht werden.	*The plans were supposed to be made last year.*

2. Expression of the Agent

If the AGENT who performs the act is expressed, the preposition **von** is used.

Alles wird **vom Staat** finanziert. *Everything is financed by the state.*

3. Impersonal Use

In German the passive voice is frequently used without a subject or with **es** functioning as the subject.

Hier darf nicht gebaut werden. *You can't build here.*
Es darf hier nicht gebaut werden. *Building is not permitted here.*

4. Alternative to the Passive Voice

One common substitute for the passive voice is a sentence in the active voice with **man** as the subject.

Hier darf nicht gebaut werden.

Es darf hier nicht gebaut werden.

→ **Man** darf hier nicht bauen.

There are three other substitutes for the passive that we chose not to include: a. the reflexive; b. **sein . . . zu** + infinitive; c. **sich lassen** + infinitive. (**Hier verändert sich nichts.** *Nothing changes here.* **Hier ist nichts zu verändern.** *Nothing is to be changed here.* **Hier läßt sich nichts verändern.** *Nothing can be changed here.*)

ÜBUNGEN

A. Trier. Aktiv oder Passiv? Decide whether statements are in the active or passive voice.
1. The city of Trier on the Moselle River recently celebrated its 2000th anniversary.
2. Trier was founded by the Romans in 15 B.C.
3. Its original name was *Augusta Treverorum.*
4. Under Roman occupation, *Germania* along the Rhine and Danube had been transformed into a series of Roman provinces.
5. The names of many towns go back to Latin.
6. Remnants from Roman times can still be seen today.
7. New discoveries are made from time to time.
8. Beautiful Roman museums have been built.
9. One of them is located in the former *Colonia Agrippina* (**Köln**).

B. Köln. Was bedeutet das auf englisch?
1. a. Köln wurde während des Krieges schwer zerstört.
   b. 80 Prozent *(percent)* der Innenstadt war zerbombt *(destroyed by bombs)* worden.
   c. Heute wird Köln wieder von vielen Touristen besucht.
   d. Vieles ist wieder aufgebaut und restauriert worden.
   e. Und vieles wird noch renoviert werden.

2. a. Erst sollten natürlich neue Wohnungen gebaut werden.
   b. Manche alten Gebäude konnten gerettet werden.
   c. Der Dom mußte restauriert werden.
   d. Aber die alten Kirchen aus dem zwölften Jahrhundert dürfen auch nicht vergessen werden.

Köln am Rhein

e. Das kann natürlich nicht ohne Geld gemacht werden.

f. Durch Bürgerinitiativen soll genug Geld für die Restaurierung gesammelt werden.

3. a. In der Altstadt wird in Parkgaragen geparkt.

b. Es wird viel mit dem Bus gefahren.

c. In der Fußgängerzone wird nicht Auto gefahren.

d. Dort wird zu Fuß gegangen.

e. Dort wird gern eingekauft.

C: Remind students to retain the tense of the original sentence.

C. Ein schönes altes Haus. Sagen Sie die Sätze im Aktiv!

1. BEISPIEL: Nicht alle Gebäude waren vom Krieg zerstört worden.
   Der Krieg hatte nicht alle Gebäude zerstört.

   a. Viele Gebäude sind von Baggern *(bulldozers)* zerstört worden.

   b. Dieses Haus wurde von den Bürgern gerettet.

   c. Viele Unterschriften *(signatures)* wurden von Studenten gesammelt.

   d. Das Haus ist von der Uni gekauft worden.

   e. Die Fassade wird von Spezialisten renoviert werden.

   f. Die Hauspläne werden von Architekten gemacht.

2. BEISPIEL: Der Hausplan darf von den Architekten nicht sehr verändert werden.
   Die Architekten dürfen den Hausplan nicht sehr verändern.

   a. Ein Teil soll von der Stadt finanziert werden.

   b. Der Rest muß von der Uni bezahlt werden.

   c. Das Haus konnte von der Universität als Gästehaus ausgebaut werden.

   d. Das Parterre darf von den Studenten als Café gebraucht werden.

3. BEISPIEL: Das Gästehaus wird viel besucht.
Man besucht das Gästehaus viel.

a. Dort werden Gedanken ausgetauscht.
b. Es wird auch Englisch und Französisch gesprochen.
c. Heute abend wird ein Jazzkonzert gegeben.
d. Letzte Woche wurde ein Film gezeigt.
e. Hier werden auch Seminare gehalten werden.

D. Ein alter Film. Wiederholen Sie die Sätze im Passiv, aber in einer anderen Zeitform!

BEISPIEL: Ein alter Film wird gespielt. *(simple past)*
Ein alter Film wurde gespielt.

1. Er wird von den Studenten sehr empfohlen. *(present perfect)*
2. Während des Krieges wird er nicht gezeigt. *(simple past)*
3. Er wird verboten. *(past perfect)*
4. Es wird viel darüber geredet. *(future)*
5. Daraus kann viel gelernt werden. *(simple past)*
6. Er soll übrigens wiederholt werden. *(simple past)*

E. Post und Geld. Wiederholen Sie die Sätze im Passiv, aber mit einem Modalverb! Was heißt das auf englisch?

BEISPIEL: Das Paket wird zur Post gebracht. (sollen)
Das Paket soll zur Post gebracht werden.

1. Die Postkarte wird noch ausgefüllt. (müssen)
2. Dann wird es am ersten Schalter abgegeben. (können)
3. Auf der Post werden auch Telefongespräche gemacht. (dürfen)
4. Dollar werden auf der Bank umgewechselt. (sollen)
5. Nicht überall wird mit Reiseschecks bezahlt. (können)
6. Taxifahrer werden mit Bargeld bezahlt. (wollen)

F: Remind students not to express the agent.

Additional practice from *"Gespräche"*: Man hat die Häuser in den letzten Jahren renoviert. Durch Bürgerinitiativen hat man sie gerettet. Man restauriert auch den Dom. Die Abgase haben viel zerstört.

G: Encourage students to add sentences of their own.

F. Im Restaurant. Sagen Sie die Sätze im Passiv!

BEISPIEL: Hier spricht man Deutsch. **Hier wird Deutsch gesprochen.**

1. Am anderen Tisch spricht man Französisch.
2. Mittags ißt man warm.
3. Dabei redet man gemütlich.
4. Natürlich redet man nicht mit vollem Mund.
5. Übrigens hält man die Gabel in der linken Hand.
6. Und vor dem Essen sagt man „Guten Appetit!"

G. Wir geben eine Party.
1. **Was wird auf der Party gemacht?**

BEISPIEL: Man tanzt. Es wird getanzt.

a. Man spielt Spiele. **b.** Man ißt Pizza. **c.** Man trinkt etwas dazu.
d. Man erzählt Witze *(jokes).* **e.** Man lacht viel. **f.** Man hört Platten an. **g.** Man redet über Politik oder das Wetter.

2. **Was muß noch gemacht werden?** Answer by saying that things have already been done.

BEISPIEL: Fritz und Frieda müssen noch angerufen werden.
Fritz und Frieda sind schon angerufen worden!

a. Die Wohnung muß noch geputzt werden.   **b.** Der Tisch muß noch in die Ecke gestellt werden.   **c.** Die Gläser müssen noch gewaschen werden.   **d.** Das Bier muß noch kalt gestellt werden.   **e.** Die Kartoffelchips müssen noch in die Schüssel *(bowl)* getan werden.

> **„Je weniger die Leute darüber wissen, wie Würste und Gesetze gemacht werden, desto besser schlafen sie nachts."**
>
> Otto von Bismarck

II. Review of the Uses of werden

Distinguish carefully between the various uses of **werden.**

1. **werden** + predicate noun / adjective = a FULL VERB

Er wird Arzt.	*He's going to be a doctor.*
Es wird dunkel.	*It's getting dark.*

2. **werden** + infinitive = auxiliary of the FUTURE TENSE

Ich werde ihn fragen.   *I'll ask him.*

3. **würde** + infinitive = auxiliary in the PRESENT-TIME SUBJUNCTIVE

Ich würde ihn fragen.   *I would ask him.*

4. **werden** + past participle = auxiliary in the PASSIVE VOICE

Er wird von uns gefragt.   *He's (being) asked by us.*

ÜBUNG

H. Analysieren Sie, wie *werden* gebraucht wird! Was bedeutet das auf englisch?

BEISPIEL: Leonie ist nach Amerika eingeladen worden.
werden + past participle = passive voice
Leonie was invited (to go) to America.

1. Jutta möchte Lehrerin werden.
2. Das Studium dort mußte von ihr bezahlt werden.
3. Es ist teuerer geworden, als sie dachte.

4. Das wurde ihr nie erklärt.
5. Was würdest du an ihrer Stelle tun?
6. Ich würde ein Semester arbeiten.
7. Das wird nicht erlaubt werden.
8. Übrigens wird ihr Englisch schon viel besser.

May be omitted if desired.

III. The Special Subjunctive

German has another subjunctive, often called the SPECIAL SUBJUNCTIVE or SUBJUNCTIVE I. English only has a few remnants of this subjunctive.

So be it. Long live the Queen. Be that as it may.

In German, too, the special subjunctive is rarely used, and then primarily in formal writing and indirect speech. It is most frequently encountered in critical literary or scientific essays, in news reports, and in literature.

In general, the forms of the third person singular are the ones used most often because they clearly differ from those of the indicative. When the forms of the special subjunctive are identical with those of the indicative, the general subjunctive is used. At this point, you only need to be able to recognize the forms of the special subjunctive and know why they are used.

1. Here are the PRESENT-TIME forms of the special subjunctive for the most common verbs as well as examples of all the verb types you have learned. They have the same endings as the general subjunctive, **-e, -est, -e, -en, -et, -en,** and are added to the stem of the INFINITIVE.

	können	haben	sein	werden	lernen	bringen	kommen
ich	**könne**	habe	**sei**	werde	lerne	bringe	komme
du	**könnest**	**habest**	**seiest**	**werdest**	**lernest**	**bringest**	**kommest**
er	**könne**	habe	**sei**	werde	lerne	bringe	komme
wir	können	haben	**seien**	werden	lernen	bringen	kommen
ihr	**könnet**	**habet**	**seiet**	**werdet**	**lernet**	**bringet**	**kommet**
sie	können	haben	**seien**	werden	lernen	bringen	kommen

Er sagte, er **habe** keine Zeit.   *He said he had no time.*
Er sagte, sie **sei** nicht zu Hause.   *He said she wasn't home.*

If referring to the future *(to later)*, the special subjunctive of **werden** is combined with an infinitive.

werde . . . + infinitive

Er sagte, er **werde** bald fertig **sein.**   *He said he'd be finished soon.*

2. The PAST-TIME special subjunctive is formed by using the special subjunctive of **haben** or **sein** with a past participle.

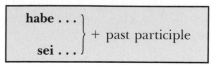

Er sagt, er **habe** keine Zeit **gehabt.**　　*He says he didn't have time.*
Er sagte, sie **sei** nicht zu Hause **gewesen.**　　*He said she hadn't been home.*

ÜBUNGEN

I. Finden Sie den Konjunktiv! Underline all subjunctive forms in the following texts.
  1. **Ein Gedicht *(poem)* von Johann Wolfgang von Goethe (1828)**

I don't worry

among each other

"dollar" / "dime"
here: *country*
value

here: *travel*

Mir ist nicht bange°,
Daß Deutschland nicht eins werde,
Vor allem
Sei es eins in Liebe untereinander°—
Und immer sei es eins,
Daß der deutsche Thaler° und Groschen°
Im ganzen Reiche°
Gleichen Wert° habe—
Eins, daß mein Reisekoffer
Durch alle deutschen Länder ungeöffnet
Passieren° könnte.

  2. **Städte deutscher Kultur**
  Er schrieb, daß Weimar, Leipzig, Halle, Wittenberg und Eisenach wichtige deutsche Kulturstädte seien. In Weimar sei Goethe Theaterdirektor und Staatsminister gewesen, und dort habe Schiller seine wichtigsten Dramen geschrieben. In Leipzig habe Bach 27 Jahre lang Kantaten und Oratorien für den Thomanerchor komponiert. Dieser Knabenchor *(boys choir)* sei heute noch sehr berühmt. Nicht weit von Leipzig liege Halle, wo Händel geboren worden sei. In Wittenberg, das man heute die Lutherstadt nenne, habe Luther mit seinen 95 Thesen die Reformation begonnen. Sein Zimmer auf der Wartburg bei Eisenach, wo er die Bibel ins Deutsche übersetzt habe, sei heute noch zu besichtigen. Man könne auch heute noch sehen, wo er dem Teufel ein Tintenfaß nachgeworfen habe *(had thrown an inkpot after the Devil).* Er wisse nicht, woher diese Geschichte komme. Er glaube sie jedenfalls nicht.

Die Wartburg bei
Eisenach

For additional ACTIVE
practice, you may ask students to report exercise
A from "Zum Thema" or
any of the previous dia-
logues / readings indi-
rectly with the special
subjunctive.

J: 1. Gestern war ein
schlechter Tag. 2. Erst
habe ich meinen Paß
verloren. 3. Dann wur-
den meine Tasche und
mein Geld gestohlen. 4.
Ich versuchte, mit Rei-
seschecks zu bezahlen.
5. Aber ohne meinen
Paß wurden meine
Schecks nicht ange-
nommen. 6. Es war
gut, daß Anne da war.
7. Die Rechnung wurde
von Anne bezahlt.
8. Heute morgen (heute
früh) wurde ich von der
Polizei angerufen.
9. Man hatte (sie hatten)
meine Tasche gefun-
den. 10. Aber mein Paß
ist noch nicht gefunden
worden. 11. Ich
wünschte, ich wüßte, was
ich damit gemacht
habe. 12. Ich hoffe, er
wird bald gefunden (daß
er bald gefunden wird).

3. **In der Vorlesung**

Der Professor erzählte von dem Archäologen Heinrich Schliemann.
Schliemann habe sich schon als achtjähriges Kind für die Geschichte
von dem Trojanischen Krieg interessiert und habe gesagt, er wollte
später Troja *(Troy)* finden. Er sei als junger Mann sehr arm gewesen,
aber er habe in Rußland und Amerika viel Geld verdient. Erst mit vierzig Jahren habe er angefangen, Archäologie zu studieren, und er habe
später auch Troja gefunden. Besonders interessant sei, daß Schliemann
etwa zwölf bis vierzehn Sprachen gelernt habe. Er habe eine besondere
Methode entwickelt *(developed)*: z.B. habe er jeden Tag zwanzig Seiten
von *Vikar of Wakefield* und *Ivanhoe* gelernt und habe nach sechs Monaten gut Englisch gesprochen. Später habe er Fremdsprachen in etwa
sechs Wochen gelernt!

ZUSAMMENFASSUNG

J. **Wo ist mein Paß?** Auf deutsch, bitte!
1. Yesterday was a bad day. **2.** First I lost my passport. **3.** Then my
handbag and my money were stolen (**gestohlen**). **4.** I tried to pay with
traveler's checks. **5.** But without my passport, my checks weren't accepted
(**angenommen**). **6.** It was good that Anne was there. **7.** Anne paid the
bill (The bill was paid by Anne). **8.** This morning I was called by the police
(**die Polizei**). **9.** They had found my handbag. **10.** But my passport
hasn't been found yet. **11.** I wish I knew what I did with it. **12.** I hope
it'll be found soon.

EINBLICKE ◆◆◆◆◆◆◆◆◆◆◆

Brief Chronicle of German History since 1945

1945 Unconditional surrender of Germany (May 9). The Allies assume supreme power. Germany and Greater Berlin divided into four zones of occupation. German territories east of the Oder-Neisse rivers ceded to Poland. Potsdam Conference concerning democratization, decentralization and demilitarization of Germany.

1947 The American Marshall Plan provides comprehensive aid for the rebuilding of Europe, including Germany. Plan is rejected by the Soviet Union and Eastern Europe.

1948 Introduction of separate new currencies in Western and Eastern zones. Introduction of D-Mark into West Berlin leads to Berlin Blockade and Berlin Airlift (June 1948).

1949 Founding of the FRG (May 23) and the GDR (October 7).

1952 The GDR begins to seal the border with the FRG (May 27).

1953 Uprising in the GDR (June 17) is suppressed by Soviet military power.

1954 The FRG becomes a member of NATO.

1955 The GDR becomes a member of Warsaw Pact. The FRG becomes sovereign; the occupation is ended.

1961 Construction of the Berlin Wall and extensive fortification of East German borders.

1970 New **Ostpolitik**: FRG Chancellor Willy Brandt meets with GDR Minister-President Willi Stoph.

1971 Four-Power Agreement on Berlin guarantees unhindered traffic between West Berlin and the FRG. De facto recognition of the GDR.

1973 Bundestag approves Basic Treaty between the FRG and the GDR in which both states recognize each other's sovereignty and promise to keep "good neighborly" relations. The opposition in Bonn rejects the treaty and refers to the constitutional mandate to reestablish German unity.

1989 Opening of Austro-Hungarian borders (September 10) brings stream of refugees from the GDR to the FRG. Demonstrations all across the GDR. Opening of the Berlin Wall (November 9) and the Brandenburg Gate (December 22).

1990 Economic union of both German states (July 2). German reunification (October 3). First joint elections (December 2).

WORTSCHATZ 2

die Bevölkerung		*population*
Hilfe		*help, aid*
Landschaft		*landscape, scenery*
(Wieder)vereinigung		*(re)unification*
Wirtschaft		*economy*

sich (auseinander·)entwickeln	*to develop (apart)*
sich ein·setzen für	*to support actively*
eine Frage stellen	*to ask (literally; pose) a question*

geteilt	*divided*
schließlich	*after all, in the end*
typisch	*typical(ly)*
wirtschaftlich	*economic(ally)*

Pre-reading activity: Typisch deutsch. List on the board what your students consider typical of Germans and their lifestyle.

WAS IST DAS? der Bau, Dialekt, Europagedanke, kalte Krieg, Sozialismus, Weltkrieg, Wiederaufbau; das Regime, System, Wirtschaftswunder; die Demokratie, Hoffnung, Lebensqualität, (Protest)demonstration, Umweltpartei, Zone; *(pl.)* die Atomwaffen, Reparationen; sich identifizieren, sich organisieren, reagieren, verhindern; dankbar, informiert, jahrelang, kritisch, massiv, militärisch, nämlich, parlamentarisch, regional, sogenannt, weltoffen

Wer sind wir?

Wer sind wir? Diese Frage wurde besonders nach 1945 in Deutschland immer wieder gestellt. Nach der furchtbaren Zeit des Krieges und des Nazi-Regimes suchte man neue Antworten. Das Land war in vier Zonen geteilt worden. Während in den drei westlichen Zonen von Anfang an eine parlamentarische Demokratie gefördert° wurde, wurde in der östlichen Zone das sowjetische 5
System eingeführt°. Der kalte Krieg, der sich nun schnell entwickelte, verhinderte die Wiedervereinigung mit der sowjetischen Zone. 1949 wurden die Bundesrepublik und die Deutsche Demokratische Republik gegründet°, und wir waren plötzlich Ost-Deutsche und West-Deutsche. Aber die Menschen auf beiden Seiten der Grenze fanden es schwer, sich mit diesen 10
Staaten zu identifizieren. So setzte man große Hoffnung auf internationale Ideen, im Westen auf die Idee eines vereinten Europas und im Osten auf den Sozialismus.

So entwickelten sich die zwei Teile getrennt°. Der Westen, unterstützt durch die massive finanzielle Hilfe des Marshall-Planes, erlebte° einen schnel- 15
len Wiederaufbau, während im Osten ein großer Teil der Industrie als Reparationen demontiert° wurde. Die Einführung° von zwei verschiedenen Währungen° brachte 1948 die endgültige° wirtschaftliche Trennung°. In den nächsten Jahren erlebte die BRD ein wahres „Wirtschaftswunder", während das sozialistische System in der DDR große wirtschaftliche Probleme mit sich 20
brachte. Diese führten° schließlich zu dem Arbeiteraufstand° vom 17. Juni 1953 und zu einer jahrelangen Fluchtwelle° über die offene Grenze in den Westen. Am 13. August 1961 reagierte die DDR mit dem Bau der Mauer und der militärischen Abriegelung° der Grenze, die ja nun bis 1989 gedauert hat. 25

Durch die politischen und wirtschaftlichen Umstände° haben wir uns in mancher Weise auseinanderentwickelt, und doch sind wir uns nicht fremd°. Wir haben ja schließlich eine gemeinsame Sprache und gemeinsame Geschichte. Gemeinsames in Kunst, Musik und Literatur findet man überall.

encouraged

introduced

founded

separately

experienced

dismantled / introduction
currencies / final / separation

led / . . . uprising
mass exodus

closing off

circumstances
no strangers to each other

social
clubs

who love to travel
grew up
ethnic group

stressed / understandable
consisted of

believing in authority

leather pants

gets involved / constant
. . . weapons / . . . power

fight for environmental protection

seriously

consciously

Aber wer sind wir nun, die Deutschen? Da ist eigentlich wenig, was charakteristisch wäre für uns alle: Vielleicht sind wir gesellig°, sitzen gern in Straßencafés oder in Gartenrestaurants, organisieren uns in Vereinen° und lieben Fußball. Die Familie und die Freizeit bedeuten uns meistens mehr als der Staat. Vielleicht sind wir auch ein reiselustiges° Volk. Aber wir lieben auch unsere Heimat: die Landschaft, in der wir aufgewachsen sind°, die Stadt oder das Dorf. Viele sind wieder stolz auf ihren Volksstamm°; regionale Dialekte werden wieder mehr gesprochen und auch im Radio und im Theater betont°. Das ist auch verständlich°, denn unsere Bevölkerung bestand schon immer aus° verschiedenen Volksstämmen. Wir waren nur kurze Zeit EIN Staat, nämlich von Bismarcks[1] Reichsgründung 1871 bis zum Ende des Zweiten Weltkrieges 1945.

Wenn es schon schwer zu sagen ist, wie wir sind, so kann man doch sehen, daß wir uns verändert haben. Wir sind weltoffener, informierter und kritischer geworden und sind nicht mehr so autoritätsgläubig° wie am Anfang dieses Jahrhunderts. Das sogenannte typisch Deutsche ist nicht mehr so wichtig; das Ausländische ist interessanter geworden. Es werden Jeans statt Lederhosen° getragen. Man ißt besonders gern chinesisch oder italienisch; und französischer Wein wird genauso gern getrunken wie deutsches Bier. Ja, und man engagiert sich° wieder. Denken wir nur an die ständigen° Demonstrationen gegen Atomwaffen° und Atomkraft°, die Bürgerinitiativen und die Protestdemonstrationen in der DDR, ohne die die Grenze nicht so schnell geöffnet worden wäre. Der Kampf für den Umweltschutz° ist auch sehr wichtig geworden. Es gibt sogar eine Umweltpartei, die Grünen[2]. Lebensqualität ist uns allen sehr wichtig geworden.

Wir sind dankbar, wieder EIN Volk[3] zu sein. Das ändert aber nichts daran, daß wir den Europagedanken sehr ernst° nehmen und uns dafür einsetzen. Ja, wir sind Deutsche, lieben unser Land, unsere Sprache und Kultur, aber zur gleichen Zeit sind wir auch bewußt° Europäer und glauben an eine gemeinsame Zukunft.

30

35

40

45

50

55

ZUM TEXT

Was ist das? 1. die sowjetische Zone 2. die DDR 3. die BRD 4. der Marshall-Plan 5. das Wirtschaftswunder 6. der Mauerbau 7. eine Grenze 8. die Heimat 9. die Grünen 10. Europagedanke

A. Was paßt?

1. Nach dem 2. Weltkrieg war Deutschland in . . . Zonen geteilt worden.
   a. zwei b. drei c. vier

2. Die Menschen auf beiden Seiten der Grenze fanden es schwer, sich mit . . . zu identifizieren.
   a. der BRD b. der DDR c. diesen neuen Staaten

3. Der Westen erlebte einen schnellen Wiederaufbau, wegen der . . . .
   a. verschiedenen Währungen b. amerikanischen Wirtschaftshilfe c. Reparationen

4. Die DDR baute die Berliner Mauer, weil . . . .
   a. zu viele Menschen in den Westen gingen   b. die Arbeiter 1953
   protestierten   c. die BRD große wirtschaftliche Probleme hatte

5. Die Deutschen in Ost und West haben sich etwas auseinanderentwickelt, weil . . . haben.
   a. sie nichts gemeinsam gehabt   b. sie keine Zeit gehabt
   c. die politischen Umstände sie getrennt

6. Vielleicht kann man allgemein (in general) von den Deutschen sagen,
   daß sie . . . .
   a. keine Fragen stellen   b. reiselustig sind   c. alle Dialekt sprechen

7. Deutschland war . . . EIN Staat.
   a. vor kurzer Zeit   b. von Bismarcks Reichsgründung bis 1939
   c. nicht lange

8. Die Deutschen sind . . . geworden.
   a. weltfremder   b. autoritätsgläubiger   c. europäischer

9. Sie setzen sich sehr für . . . ein.
   a. den sauren Regen   b. die Umwelt   c. Atomkraft

10. Die Deutschen sind dankbar, daß es keine . . . mehr gibt.
    a. innerdeutsche Grenze   b. Umweltprobleme   c. deutsche Wäh-
    rung

B. Was fehlt?

1. Die Frage nach der deutschen Identität _____ besonders nach 1945 immer wieder _____ . *(was asked)*
2. 1945 _____ Deutschland _____ . *(was divided)*
3. 1989 _____ die Grenze wieder _____ . *(was opened)*
4. Ohne die Protestdemonstrationen _____ die Grenze nicht so schnell _____ _____ . *(would have been opened)*
5. Seit der Zeit _____ viel _____ _____ . *(has been done)*
6. Aber viel _____ noch _____ _____ . *(must be done)*
7. Umweltprobleme _____ wichtig _____ *(are taken)*
8. Die Deutschen _____ weltoffener _____ . *(have become)*
9. Französischer Wein _____ genauso gern wie deutsches Bier _____ . *(is being drunk)*
10. Zur gleichen Zeit _____ wieder mehr Dialekte _____ . *(are being spoken)*

C. Typisch deutsch! Write a list of the points the author makes about "the Germans." How do they compare to your picture of them?

D. Typisch amerikanisch / kanadisch!

1. Was finden Sie typisch für die Amerikaner / Kanadier?
2. Worauf ist man hier stolz?
3. Wofür setzt man sich hier besonders ein?
4. Gibt es hier auch regionale Dialekte? Wo?
5. Stellen Sie sich vor, Sie hätten in ein anderes Land geheiratet. Was würde Ihnen als typisch amerikanisch / kanadisch dort fehlen? Oder glauben Sie, daß Sie überall gleich *(equally)* zu Hause wären?

Wenn man die Frage über Ihr Land stellen würde, was wäre Ihre Antwort?

Was sich die Deutschen wünschen

Umfragen in der Bundesrepublik Deutschland brachten es an den Tag:

1 Gesundheit

2 Umweltschutz

3 Flexible Altersgrenze

Rentner

Übrigens

1. **Otto Graf von Bismarck** was instrumental in the founding of the Second German Empire in 1871, when the Prussian king was made emperor (**Kaiser Wilhelm** I). Bismarck served as chancellor until 1890, when he was dismissed by the young **Kaiser Wilhelm II**.

2. One of the most interesting phenomena in the postwar political scene in the FRG is the emergence of the **Partei der Grünen**. Somewhat resented by the traditional parties, the Greens represent an alliance of dissenting forces, such as radical peace and antinuclear groups, as well as people of all ages and walks of life who are deeply concerned about the mounting ecological problems of densely populated Central Europe.

3. The initial euphoria over reunification gave way to frustration as Germans in the east were faced with a crumbling economy and high unemployment, and Germans in the west saw billions of D-marks flow into a seemingly bottomless pit. Collapsing cities, ownership problems, and primitive telephone, interstate and postal systems hindered a speedy recovery in the east. Though Berlin once again became the official capital of Germany, there was heated debate over the actual seat of parliament. Real unity will take time.

Fußball ist in Europa Nationalsport.

SPRECHSITUATIONEN

Expressing Doubt and Uncertainty

If you are unsure of your response, you can use any of the following expressions:

Vielleicht . . .
Ich bin mir nicht sicher, aber . . .
Es ist möglich, daß . . .
Ich glaube (nicht), daß . . .
So viel ich weiß *(as far as I know)*, . . .
Ich nehme an *(I suppose)*, . . .

If you don't know at all, use:

Ich weiß nicht.
Ich habe keine Ahnung *(no idea)*.

Expressing Probability and Possibility

You know that the future can be used to express probability. There are also other ways to express this.

Bestimmt.
Sicher(lich).
Vielleicht.
Wahrscheinlich *(probably)*.

Es ist möglich, daß . . .
Ich bin sicher, daß . . .
Ich glaube, . . .

Drawing Conclusions

Darum / daher / deshalb / deswegen . . .   *Therefore . . .*
Aus dem / diesem Grund . . .   *For that / this reason . . .*
Das (End)resultat ist . . .   *The (end) result is . . .*
Im ganzen . . .   *On the whole . . .*

A. Was nun? Work in small groups of two to four students. Take turns in asking a classmate many questions about his / her future plans. He / she is not at all certain about details, and expresses this uncertainty in the responses.

1. He / she is going to study in one of the German-speaking countries.
2. He / she is about to graduate and has no definite plans for the future.
3. He / she has just applied to join the Peace Corps.

B. Warum? Darum! Work in pairs. Your partner asks you questions about your future plans. This time you have a pretty good idea of what you are planning to do. Express the probability in your responses.

1. You are taking time off from your studies.
2. You are travelling in Europe for two and a half months.
3. During the summer you will be working as an intern for an American bank in Frankfurt.

I. Comparison

1. The COMPARATIVE is formed by adding **-er** to an adjective, and the SUPERLATIVE by adding **-(e)st.** Many one-syllable adjectives and adverbs with the stem vowel **a, o,** or **u** have an umlaut.

schnell	lang	kurz
schneller	länger	kürzer
schnellst-	längst-	kürzest-

A few adjectives and adverbs have irregular forms in the comparative and superlative.

gern	groß	gut	hoch	nah	viel
lieber	größer	besser	höher	näher	mehr
liebst-	größt-	best-	höchst-	nächst-	meist-

2. With predicate adjectives and adverbs, the comparative ends in **-er.** The superlative is preceded by **am** and ends in **-sten.**

Ich esse schnell. Du ißt schnell**er.** Er ißt **am** schnell**sten.**

3. In the comparative and superlative, adjectives preceding nouns have the same endings under the same conditions as adjectives in the positive form.

der gut**e** Wein	der besser**e** Wein	der best**e** Wein
Ihr gut**er** Wein	Ihr besser**er** Wein	Ihr best**er** Wein
gut**er** Wein	besser**er** Wein	best**er** Wein

4. Here are four important phrases used in comparisons:

Gestern war es nicht **so heiß wie** heute. *(as hot as)*
Heute ist es **heißer als** gestern. *(hotter than)*
Es wird **immer heißer.** *(hotter and hotter)*
Je länger du wartest, **desto heißer** wird es. *(the longer, the hotter)*
Je heißer, desto besser. *(the hotter, the better)*

II. Relative Clauses

1. Relative clauses are introduced by RELATIVE PRONOUNS.

	masc.	neut.	fem.	plural
nom.	der	das	die	die
acc.	den	das	die	die
dat.	dem	dem	der	denen
gen.	dessen	dessen	deren	deren

The form of the relative pronoun depends on the NUMBER AND GENDER OF THE ANTECEDENT and on the FUNCTION of the relative pronoun WITHIN THE RELATIVE CLAUSE.

> ... ANTECEDENT, (preposition) RP _____ V1, ...
> gender? number?   function?

2. The word order in the relative clause is like that of all subordinate clauses: the inflected part of the verb (V1) comes last.

> ..., RP _____ V1, ...

Der junge Mann, **der** gerade hier **war,** studiert Theologie. Die Universität, **an der** er **studiert,** ist schon sehr alt.

III. The Future

1. The future consists of a present-tense form of

werden... + infinitive	
ich werde ... gehen	wir werden ... gehen
du wirst ... gehen	ihr werdet ... gehen
er wird ... gehen	sie werden ... gehen

Er **wird** es dir **erklären.**

2. The future of a sentence with a modal consists of

> **werden** ... + verb infinitive + modal infinitive

Er **wird** es dir **erklären können.**

IV. The Subjunctive

English and German follow very similar patterns in the subjunctive:

If he came ...   Wenn er käme, ...
If he would come ...   Wenn er kommen würde, ...
If he had come ...   Wenn er gekommen wäre, ...

German, however, has two subjunctives, the GENERAL SUBJUNCTIVE (SUBJUNCTIVE II) and the SPECIAL SUBJUNCTIVE (SUBJUNCTIVE I), of which the latter is primarily used in writing. The endings of both subjunctives are the same.

ich **-e**	wir **-en**
du **-est**	ihr **-et**
er **-e**	sie **-en**

1. Forms

    a. GENERAL SUBJUNCTIVE (II)

present time or future time		past time
Based on the forms of the simple past; refers to *now*	Based on the forms of **werden** + inf.; refers to *later*	Based on the forms of the past perf.; refers to *earlier*

er **lernte**	er **würde lernen**	er **hätte gelernt**
brächte	würde bringen	hätte gebracht
hätte	würde haben	hätte gehabt
wäre	würde sein	wäre gewesen
nähme	würde nehmen	hätte genommen
käme	würde kommen	wäre gekommen

      • In conversation the **würde**-form is commonly used when referring to present time. However, avoid using the **würde**-form with **haben, sein, wissen,** and the modals. When referring to past time, the **würde**-form is hardly ever used.

      Er **würde** es dir **erklären**.

      • Modals in the past-time subjunctive follow this pattern:

hätte . . . + verb infinitive + modal infinitive

      Er **hätte** es dir **erklären können**.

    b. The SPECIAL SUBJUNCTIVE (I)

If you did not cover the special subjunctive, omit part IV. 1.b and 2.b. Also omit special-subjunctive forms, given in parentheses, in section V, INDIRECT SPEECH.

present time	future time	past time
Based on the forms of the infinitive; refers to *now*	Based on the forms of the future; refers to *later*	Based on the forms of the pres perf; refers to *earlier*

er **lerne**	er **werde lernen**	er **habe gelernt**
bringe	werde bringen	habe gebracht
habe	werde haben	habe gehabt
sei	werde sein	sei gewesen
nehme	werde nehmen	habe genommen
komme	werde kommen	sei gekommen

2. Use

    a. The GENERAL SUBJUNCTIVE is quite common in everyday speech and is used in:

      • Polite Requests or Questions

Könnten Sie mir sagen, wo die Universität ist?	*Could you tell me where the university is?*

▪ Hypothetical Statements or Questions

Er sollte bald hier sein.	*He should be here soon.*
Was würdest du tun?	*What would you do?*
Was hättest du getan?	*What would you have done?*

▪ Wishes

Wenn ich das nur wüßte!	*If only I knew that!*
Wenn ich das nur gewußt hätte!	*If only I had known that!*
Ich wünschte, ich hätte das gewußt!	*I wish I had known that!*

▪ Unreal Conditions

Wenn wir Geld hätten, würden wir fliegen.	*If we had the money, we'd fly.*
Wenn wir Geld gehabt hätten, wären wir geflogen.	*If we had had the money, we would have flown.*

▪ Indirect Speech (see below)

b. The SPECIAL SUBJUNCTIVE is used primarily in formal WRITING and in indirect speech, unless the form of the indicative is the same as the subjunctive, in which case the general subjunctive is used (ich komme = **ich komme** > **ich käme**; ich frage = **ich frage** > **ich würde fragen**).

V. Indirect Speech

The tense of the indirect statement is determined by the tense of the direct statement.

direct statement	indirect statement
present tense future tense	→ present-time subjunctive or **würde**-form
present perfect simple past past perfect	→ past-time subjunctive

The forms in parentheses refer to the special subjunctive; they can be omitted.

„Ich komme nicht."	Sie sagte, sie käme (komme) nicht.
„Ich werde nicht kommen."	Sie sagte, sie würde (werde) nicht kommen.
„Ich bin nicht gegangen."	Sie sagte, sie wäre (sei) nicht gegangen.
„Ich hatte keine Lust."	Sie sagte, sie hätte (habe) keine Lust gehabt.

This is also true of questions. Remember to use **ob** when the question begins with the verb.

„Kommst du mit?"   Er fragte, ob ich mitkäme (mitkomme).
„Wirst du mitkommen?"   Er fragte, ob ich mitkommen würde (werde).
„Wann seid ihr zurück-   Sie fragte, wann wir zurückgekommen wären
gekommen?"   (seien).

Indirect requests require the use of **sollen.**

„Frag nicht so viel!"   Er sagte, sie sollte (solle) nicht so viel fragen.

VI. The Passive Voice

In the active voice the subject of the sentence is doing something. In the passive voice the subject is not doing anything; rather, something is being done to it.

1. Forms

werden . . . + past participle	
ich werde . . . gefragt	wir werden . . . gefragt
du wirst . . . gefragt	ihr werdet . . . gefragt
er wird . . . gefragt	sie werden . . . gefragt

2. The tenses in the passive are formed with the various tenses of **werden** + past participle.

er **wird** . . . gefragt	er **ist** . . . gefragt **worden**
er **wurde** . . . gefragt	er **war** . . . gefragt **worden**
er **wird** . . . gefragt **werden**	

Das ist uns nicht erklärt worden.

3. Modals follow this pattern:

modal . . . + past participle + infinitive of **werden**

Das muß noch einmal erklärt werden.

4. In German the passive is often used without a subject or with **es** functioning as the subject.

Hier wird renoviert.
Es wird hier renoviert.

5. Instead of using the passive voice, the same idea may be expressed in the active voice with the subject **man.**

Man hat alles noch einmal erklärt.

VII. Review of the uses of werden

1.	FULL VERB	Er **wird** Arzt.	*He's going to be a doctor.*
2.	FUTURE	Ich **werde** danach **fragen.**	*I'll ask about it.*
3.	SUBJUNCTIVE	Ich **würde** danach **fragen.**	*I'd ask about it.*
4.	PASSIVE	Er **wird** danach **gefragt.**	*He's (being) asked about it.*

WORTSCHATZWIEDERHOLUNG

A. Fragen
 1. **Verschiedene Berufe.** Wie viele Berufe kennen Sie auf deutsch? Sie haben eine Minute.
 2. **Woran denken Sie dabei?**
    Zahnarzt, Hausfrau, Note, sich fühlen, parken, gewinnen
 3. **Was ist der Artikel dieser Wörter?** Was bedeuten sie auf englisch?
    Haushaltsgeld, Chemielabor, Weltkrieg, Zwischenprüfungsnote, Rechtsanwaltsfirma, Universitätsparkplatz, Liebesgeschichte, Berglandschaft, Hals-Nasen-Ohrenarzt

B. Was paßt?
 1. **Nennen Sie das passende Verb!**
    der Gedanke, Plan, Traum, Verkäufer, Versuch, Wunsch; das Gebäude; die Erklärung
 2. **Nennen Sie das passende Hauptwort!**
    beruflich, frei, sportlich, verlobt; arbeiten, leben, lehren, studieren, teilen, trennen

C. Geben Sie das Gegenteil davon!
 arm, dick, faul, furchtbar, gleich, häßlich, hell, langweilig, leicht, privat, schmutzig, vereint; damals, nie; rennen, suchen, verbieten, vergessen, verlieren, zerstören; der Krieg, das Nebenfach

STRUKTURWIEDERHOLUNG

D. Vergleiche *(comparisons)*
 1. **Geben Sie den Komparativ und den Superlativ!**

    BEISPIEL: lang   **länger, am längsten**

    berühmt, dumm, faul, gern, groß, gut, heiß, hoch, hübsch, kalt, kurz, sauber, typisch, viel, warm
 2. **Ersetzen Sie das Adjektiv!**
    a. Rolf ist nicht so alt wie Heinz. (charmant, freundlich, bekannt, witzig)
    b. Heinz ist älter als Rolf. (sympathisch, nett, talentiert, ruhig)
    c. Die Stadt wird immer schöner. (groß, reich, interessant, international)
 3. **Was fehlt?**
    a. Wir wohnen jetzt in _____ Stadt. *(a prettier)*

D.3: a. einer schöneren
b. schöner c. interessan-
tere d. die anstregend-
ste e. das höchste f. die
meisten und besten
g. netteren h. die größte
i. je länger, desto besser
j. genausoviel wie
k. weniger als

b. Die Umgebung ist noch _____ als vorher. (*more beautiful*)

c. Es gibt keine _____ Umgebung. (*more interesting*)

d. Peter hat _____ Arbeit. (*the most strenuous*)

e. Aber er hat _____ Einkommen. (*the highest*)

f. Er hat immer _____ Ideen. (*the most and the best*)

g. Es gibt keine _____ Kollegen (*pl., nicer*)

h. Sie geben ihm _____ Freiheit (*freedom*). (*the greatest*)

i. _____ er hier ist, _____ gefällt es ihm. (*the longer, the better*)

j. Die Lebensmittel kosten _____ bei euch. (*just as much as*)

k. Aber die Häuser kosten _____ bei euch. (*less than*)

E. Bilden Sie Relativsätze!

BEISPIEL: die Dame, _____ , . . . Sie wohnt im dritten Stock.
    Die Dame, die im dritten Stock wohnt, . . .

1. **der Freund,** _____ , . . .
   a. Er war gerade hier. **b.** Du hast ihn kennengelernt. **c.** Ihm gehört das Büchergeschäft in der Goethestraße. **d.** Seine Firma ist in Stuttgart.

2. **die Ärztin,** _____ , . . .
   a. Ihre Sekretärin hat uns angerufen. **b.** Sie ist hier neu. **c.** Wir haben durch sie von dem Programm gehört.

3. **das Gebäude,** _____ , . . .
   a. Ihr werdet es bald sehen. **b.** Du bist an dem Gebäude vorbeigefahren. **c.** Es steht auf der Insel. **d.** Man hat von dem Gebäude so einen wunderschönen Blick (*m*).

4. **die Leute,** _____ , . . .
   a. Sie sehen aus wie Amerikaner. **b.** Dort steht ihr Bus. **c.** Die Landschaft gefällt ihnen so gut. **d.** Du hast dich für sie interessiert. **e.** Du hast mit ihnen geredet.

F. Sagen Sie die Sätze in der Zukunft!
   1. Ich nehme an einer Gruppenreise teil. **2.** Das ist billiger. **3.** Du mußt ihnen bald das Geld schicken. **4.** Meine Tante versucht, uns in Basel zu sehen. **5.** Wie kann sie uns finden? **6.** Das erklärst du ihr bestimmt.

G. Bilden Sie ganze Sätze im Konjunktiv!
   1. **Konjunktiv der Gegenwart oder würde-Form**
      a. ich / mich / fühlen / besser / / wenn / die / Arbeit / sein / fertig
      b. das / sein / wunderschön
      c. ihr / können / uns / dann / besuchen
      d. ich wünschte / / Rolf / haben / mehr Zeit
      e. wenn / ich / nur / können / sich gewöhnen / daran!
      f. erklären / du / mir / das?
      g. ich wünschte / / er / nicht / reden / so viel am Telefon
      h. was / du / tun?
   2. **Konjunktiv der Vergangenheit**
      a. wir / nicht / sollen / in / Berge / fahren
      b. ich wünschte / / sie (*sg.*) / zu Hause / bleiben
      c. das / sein / einfacher

    d. wenn / wir / nur / nicht / wandern / so viel!
    e. wenn / du / mitnehmen / bessere Schuhe / / die Füße / weh tun / dir / nicht
    f. du / sollen / mich / erinnern / daran
    g. ich / es / finden / schöner / / bleiben / zu Hause

3. **Ich studiere dort.** Variieren Sie den Satz!
   I'll study here. I'd study there. Would you (*sg. fam.*) like to study there? I wish I could study there. She could have studied there. If I study there, my German will get better. If I were to study there, I could visit you (*pl. fam.*). I should have studied there.

H: This exercise can also be done in the special subjunctive: z.B. 1. Er schrieb, er habe eine nette Wohnung. Sein Zimmerkollege sei aus New York. 2. Er schrieb, er habe eine nette Wohnung gehabt. Sein Zimmerkollege sei aus New York gewesen.

H. Indirekte Rede (*indirect speech*). Lesen Sie erst, was David aus Amerika geschrieben hat, und erzählen Sie es dann indirekt!

„Ich habe eine nette Wohnung. Mein Zimmerkollege ist aus New York. Ich lerne viel von ihm. Ich spreche nur Englisch. Manchmal gehe ich auch zu Partys. Ich kenne schon viele Studenten. Viele wohnen im Studentenheim. Aber das ist mir zu teuer. Die Kurse und Professoren sind ausgezeichnet. Aber ich muß viel lesen. Eigentlich habe ich keine Probleme. Nur gibt es zu viele Prüfungen. Ich kann mehr Geld gebrauchen. Ich muß etwas nebenher (*on the side*) verdienen. Ich will mir eine Stelle als Ober suchen."

1. **Erzählen Sie, was David geschrieben hat!**

   BEISPIEL: David schrieb, er hätte eine nette Wohnung. Sein Zimmerkollege wäre aus New York . . .

2. **Was schrieb David damals über seine Zeit in Amerika?**

   BEISPIEL: David schrieb, er hätte eine nette Wohnung gehabt. Sein Zimmerkollege wäre aus New York gewesen . . .

J: 1. Jetzt bin ich mit meinem ersten Jahr Deutsch fertig geworden. 2. Ich habe wirklich viel gelernt. 3. Ich hätte nie gedacht, daß es soviel Spaß machen könnte. 4. Nicht alles ist leicht gewesen. 5. Ich mußte viele Wörter lernen. 6. Viele Übungen mußten gemacht werden. 7. Bald haben wir unsere letzte Prüfung (werden . . . haben). 8. Weil ich mich immer gut vorbereitet habe, muß ich jetzt nicht so schwer arbeiten (viel lernen). 9. Am Tag nach der Prüfung wird gefeiert (werden). 10. Ich bin von ein paar Freunden zu einer (auf eine) Party eingeladen worden. 11. Wenn ich das Geld hätte, würde ich jetzt nach Europa fliegen. 12. Dann könnte ich viele der Städte sehen, über die wir gelesen haben, und ich könnte mein Deutsch gebrauchen.

I. Sagen Sie die Sätze im Passiv! Do not express pronoun agents.
   1. Viele Studenten besuchen diese Universität.
   2. Man renoviert dieses Gebäude.
   3. In den Hörsälen gibt man Vorlesungen.
   4. Wir müssen viel für die Kurse lesen.
   5. Am Wochenende zeigte man hier einen Film.
   6. Man hat Marlene Dietrich oft photographiert.
   7. Diesen Film soll man wiederholen.
   8. Man muß den Hörsaal noch einmal reservieren.

J. Ein Jahr Deutsch! Auf deutsch, bitte!
   1. Now I have finished (**fertig werden mit**) my first year of German.   **2.** I've really learned a lot.   **3.** I never would have thought that it could be so much fun.   **4.** Not everything has been easy.   **5.** I had to learn many words.   **6.** Many exercises had to be done.   **7.** Soon we'll have our last exam.   **8.** Because I've always prepared (myself) well, I don't have to work so much now.   **9.** On the day after the exam there will be celebrating.   **10.** I've been invited to a party by a couple of friends.   **11.** If I had the money, I'd fly to Europe now.   **12.** Then I could see many of the cities we read about, and I could use my German.

◆◆◆◆◆◆ APPENDIX

1. Predicting the Gender of Some Nouns

As a rule, nouns must be memorized with their articles because their genders are not readily predictable. However, here are a few hints to help you determine the gender of some nouns in order to eliminate unnecessary memorizing.

a. Most nouns referring to males are MASCULINE.

der Vater, der Bruder, der Junge

- Days, months, and seasons are masculine, too.

    der Montag, der Juni, der Winter

b. Most nouns referring to females are FEMININE.

die Mutter, die Schwester, die Frau

- Many feminine nouns can be derived from masculine nouns. Their plurals always end in **-nen:**

    sg.: der Schweizer / die Schweizerin; der Österreicher / die Österreicherin
    pl.: die Schweizerinnen, Österreicherinnen

- All nouns ending in **-heit, -keit, -ie, -ik, -ion, -schaft, -tät,** and **-ung** are feminine. Their plurals end in **-en.**

    sg.: die Schönheit, Richtigkeit, Geographie, Musik, Religion, Nachbarschaft, Qualität, Rechnung
    pl.: die Qualitäten, Rechnungen usw.

- Most nouns ending in **-e** are feminine. Their plurals end in **-n.**

    sg.: die Sprache, Woche, Hose, Kreide, Farbe, Seite
    pl.: die Sprachen, Wochen usw.

There are exceptions, e.g., **der Affe, der Löwe, der Neffe, der Name, das Ende,** etc.

c. All nouns ending in **-chen** or **-lein** are NEUTER. These two suffixes make diminutives of nouns, i.e., they make them smaller. They often have an umlaut, but there is no special plural ending.

sg.: der Bruder / das Brüderchen; die Schwester / das Schwesterlein
pl.: die Brüderchen, Schwesterlein

- Because of these suffixes, two nouns referring to females are neuter.

    das Mädchen, das Fräulein

- Most cities and countries are neuter, too.

    (das) Berlin, (das) Deutschland BUT die Schweiz, die Tschechoslowakei

2. Summary Chart of the Four Cases

	use	follows ...	masc.	singular neut.	fem.	plural	personal pronouns and interrogative pronouns						
nom.	Subject, Predicate noun	**heißen** **sein** **werden**	der dieser[1] ein mein[2]	das dieses ein	die diese eine	die diese keine	ich wir	du ihr wer?	er	es was?		sie sie	Sie Sie
acc.	Direct object	**durch, für, gegen, ohne, um**	den diesen einen meinen	mein	meine	meine	mich uns	dich euch wen?	ihn	es was?		sie sie	Sie Sie
		an, auf, hinter, in neben, über, unter, vor, zwischen											
dat.	Indirect object	**aus, bei, mit, nach, seit, von, zu**	dem diesem einem meinem	dem diesem einem meinem	der dieser einer meiner	den diesen keinen meinen	mir uns	dir euch wem?	ihm	ihm ihnen —	ihr	Ihnen Ihnen
		antworten, danken, fehlen, gefallen, gehören, glauben,[3] gratulieren, helfen, schmecken usw.											
gen.	Possessive	**(an)statt, trotz, während, wegen**	des dieses eines meines	des dieses eines meines	der dieser keiner meiner	der dieser keiner meiner		wessen?		—		

NOTE: 1. The **der**-words are **dieser, jeder, welcher, alle, manche, solche.**
2. The **ein**-words are **kein, mein, dein, sein, sein, ihr, unser, euer, ihr, Ihr.**
3. Ich glaube **ihm.** BUT Ich glaube **es.**

3. Reflexive Pronouns

	ich	**du**	**er**	**es**	**sie**	**wir**	**ihr**	**sie**	**Sie**
acc.	mich	dich		sich		uns	euch	sich	sich
dat.	mir	dir		sich		uns	euch	sich	sich

4. Relative Pronouns

	masc.	neut.	fem.	plural
nom.	der	das	die	die
acc.	den	das	die	die
dat.	dem	dem	der	denen
gen.	dessen	dessen	deren	deren

5. Adjective Endings

a. Preceded Adjectives

	masc.	neut.	fem.	plural
nom.	der gute Käse	das gute Brot	die gute Wurst	die guten Säfte
	ein guter Käse	ein gutes Brot	eine gute Wurst	keine guten Säfte
acc.	den guten Käse	das gute Brot	die gute Wurst	die guten Säfte
	einen guten Käse	ein gutes Brot	eine gute Wurst	keine guten Säfte
dat.	dem guten Käse	dem guten Brot	der guten Wurst	den guten Säften
	einem guten Käse	einem guten Brot	einer guten Wurst	keinen guten Säften
gen.	des guten Käses	des guten Brotes	der guten Wurst	der guten Säfte
	eines guten Käses	eines guten Brotes	einer guten Wurst	keiner guten Säfte

b. Unpreceded Adjectives

	masc.	neut.	fem.	plural
nom.	guter Käse	gutes Brot	gute Wurst	gute Säfte
acc.	guten Käse	gutes Brot	gute Wurst	gute Säfte
dat.	gutem Käse	gutem Brot	guter Wurst	guten Säften
gen.	guten Käses	guten Brotes	guter Wurst	guter Säfte

6. n-Nouns

	singular	plural
nom.	der Student	die Studenten
acc.	den Studenten	die Studenten
dat.	dem Studenten	den Studenten
gen.	des Studenten	der Studenten

Other nouns are: Herr (-n, -en), Franzose, Gedanke (-ns, -n), Journalist, Junge, Komponist, Mensch, Nachbar, Name (-ns, -n), Polizist, Tourist, Zimmerkollege.

7. Adjectival Nouns

	masc.	fem.	plural
nom.	der Deutsche ein Deutscher	die Deutsche eine Deutsche	die Deutschen keine Deutschen
acc.	den Deutschen einen Deutschen		
dat.	dem Deutschen einem Deutschen	der Deutschen einer Deutschen	den Deutschen keinen Deutschen
gen.	des Deutschen eines Deutschen	der Deutschen einer Deutschen	der Deutschen keiner Deutschen

Other adjectival nouns are: der Beamte (BUT die Beamtin), der Angestellte

8. Comparison of Irregular Adjectives and Adverbs

	gern	groß	gut	hoch	nah	viel
Comparative	lieber	größer	besser	höher	näher	mehr
Superlative	liebst-	größt-	best-	höchst-	nächst-	meist-

9. Principal Parts of N-Verbs ("strong verbs") and Irregular T-Verbs ("irregular weak verbs"). Listed Alphabetically.

This list is limited to the active n-verbs and irregular t-verbs used in this text. Compound verbs like **ankommen** or **abfliegen** are not included, since their principal parts are the same as those of the basic verbs **kommen** and **fliegen.**

infinitive	present	simple past	past participle	meaning
anfangen	fängt an	fing an	angefangen	*to begin*
backen	bäckt	buk (backte)	gebacken	*to bake*
beginnen		begann	begonnen	*to begin*
bekommen		bekam	bekommen	*to receive*
bleiben		blieb	ist geblieben	*to remain*
bringen		brachte	gebracht	*to bring*
denken		dachte	gedacht	*to think*
einladen	lädt ein	lud ein	eingeladen	*to invite*

Continued

infinitive	present	simple past	past participle	meaning
empfehlen	empfiehlt	empfahl	empfohlen	*to recommend*
essen	ißt	aß	gegessen	*to eat*
fahren	fährt	fuhr	ist gefahren	*to drive, go*
fallen	fällt	fiel	ist gefallen	*to fall*
finden		fand	gefunden	*to find*
fliegen		flog	ist geflogen	*to fly*
geben	gibt	gab	gegeben	*to give*
gefallen	gefällt	gefiel	gefallen	*to please*
gehen		ging	ist gegangen	*to go*
geschehen	geschieht	geschah	ist geschehen	*to happen*
gewinnen		gewann	gewonnen	*to win*
haben	hat	hatte	gehabt	*to have*
halten	hält	hielt	gehalten	*to hold; stop*
hängen		hing	gehangen	*to be hanging*
heißen		hieß	geheißen	*to be called, named*
helfen	hilft	half	geholfen	*to help*
kennen		kannte	gekannt	*to know*
klingen		klang	geklungen	*to sound*
kommen		kam	ist gekommen	*to come*
lassen	läßt	ließ	gelassen	*to let, leave (behind)*
laufen	läuft	lief	ist gelaufen	*to run; walk*
lesen	liest	las	gelesen	*to read*
liegen		lag	gelegen	*to lie*
nehmen	nimmt	nahm	genommen	*to take*
nennen		nannte	genannt	*to name, call*
rennen		rannte	ist gerannt	*to run*
rufen		rief	gerufen	*to call*
scheinen		schien	geschienen	*to shine; seem*
schlafen	schläft	schlief	geschlafen	*to sleep*
schreiben		schrieb	geschrieben	*to write*
schwimmen		schwamm	geschwommen	*to swim*
sehen	sieht	sah	gesehen	*to see*
sein	ist	war	ist gewesen	*to be*
singen		sang	gesungen	*to sing*
sitzen		saß	gesessen	*to sit*
sprechen	spricht	sprach	gesprochen	*to speak*
stehen		stand	gestanden	*to stand*
steigen		stieg	ist gestiegen	*to climb*
tragen	trägt	trug	getragen	*to carry; wear*
trinken		trank	getrunken	*to drink*
tun	tut	tat	getan	*to do*
verlieren		verlor	verloren	*to lose*
waschen	wäscht	wusch	gewaschen	*to wash*
werden	wird	wurde	ist geworden	*to become; get*
wissen	weiß	wußte	gewußt	*to know*
ziehen		zog	gezogen	*to pull*

10. Principal Parts Listed in Groups

This is the same list as above, but this time it is divided in groups with the same stem changes.

I.	essen	(ißt)	aß	gegessen
	geben	(gibt)	gab	gegeben
	geschehen	(geschieht)	geschah	ist geschehen
	sehen	(sieht)	sah	gesehen
	lesen	(liest)	las	gelesen
	liegen		lag	gelegen
	sitzen		saß	gesessen
II.	empfehlen	(empfiehlt)	empfahl	empfohlen
	helfen	(hilft)	half	geholfen
	nehmen	(nimmt)	nahm	genommen
	sprechen	(spricht)	sprach	gesprochen
	beginnen		begann	begonnen
	gewinnen		gewann	gewonnen
	schwimmen		schwamm	geschwommen
	bekommen		bekam	bekommen
	kommen		kam	ist gekommen
III.	finden		fand	gefunden
	klingen		klang	geklungen
	singen		sang	gesungen
	trinken		trank	getrunken
IV.	bleiben		blieb	ist geblieben
	scheinen		schien	geschienen
	schreiben		schrieb	geschrieben
	steigen		stieg	ist gestiegen
V.	fliegen		flog	ist geflogen
	verlieren		verlor	verloren
	ziehen		zog	gezogen
VI.	einladen	(lädt ein)	lud ein	eingeladen
	fahren	(fährt)	fuhr	ist gefahren
	tragen	(trägt)	trug	getragen
	waschen	(wäscht)	wusch	gewaschen
VII.	fallen	(fällt)	fiel	ist gefallen
	gefallen	(gefällt)	gefiel	gefallen
	halten	(hält)	hielt	gehalten
	lassen	(läßt)	ließ	gelassen
	schlafen	(schläft)	schlief	geschlafen
	laufen	(läuft)	lief	ist gelaufen
	heißen		hieß	geheißen
	rufen		rief	gerufen

VIII. n-verbs that do not belong to any of the groups above:

anfangen	(fängt an)	fing an	angefangen
backen	(bäckt)	buk (backte)	gebacken
gehen		ging	ist gegangen
hängen		hing	gehangen
sein	(ist)	war	ist gewesen
stehen		stand	gestanden
tun	(tut)	tat	getan
werden	(wird)	wurde	ist geworden

IX. irregular t-verbs

bringen		brachte	gebracht
denken		dachte	gedacht
haben		hatte	gehabt
kennen		kannte	gekannt
nennen		nannte	genannt
rennen		rannte	gerannt
wissen	(weiß)	wußte	gewußt

11. Verb Forms in Different Tenses

a. Indicative

present

ich	frage	fahre
du	fragst	fährst
er	fragt	fährt
wir	fragen	fahren
ihr	fragt	fahrt
sie	fragen	fahren

simple past

fragte	fuhr
fragtest	fuhrst
fragte	fuhr
fragten	fuhren
fragtet	fuhrt
fragten	fuhren

present perfect

ich	habe		bin	
du	hast		bist	
er	hat	gefragt	ist	gefahren
wir	haben		sind	
ihr	habt		seid	
sie	haben		sind	

past perfect

hatte		war	
hattest		warst	
hatte	gefragt	war	gefahren
hatten		waren	
hattet		wart	
hatten		waren	

future

ich	werde	
du	wirst	
er	wird	fragen / fahren
wir	werden	
ihr	werdet	
sie	werden	

b. Subjunctive

● PRESENT-TIME

general subjunctive

ich	fragte	führe
du	fragtest	führest
er	fragte	führe
wir	fragten	führen
ihr	fragtet	führet
sie	fragten	führen

special subjunctive

frage	fahre
fragest	fahrest
frage	fahre
fragen	fahren
fraget	fahret
fragen	fahren

ich	würde	
du	würdest	
er	würde	fragen / fahren
wir	würden	
ihr	würdet	
sie	würden	

• PAST-TIME

general subjunctive

ich hätte
du hättest
er hätte ⎫
wir hätten ⎬ gefragt
ihr hättet
sie hätten ⎭

wäre
wärest
wäre ⎫
wären ⎬ gefahren
wäret
wären ⎭

special subjunctive

habe
habest
habe ⎫
haben ⎬ gefragt
habet
haben ⎭

sei
seiest
sei ⎫
seien ⎬ gefahren
seiet
seien ⎭

c. Passive Voice

present

ich werde
du wirst
er wird ⎫
wir werden ⎬ gefragt
ihr werdet
sie werden ⎭

simple past

wurde
wurdest
wurde ⎫
wurden ⎬ gefragt
wurdet
wurden ⎭

present perfect

ich bin
du bist
er ist ⎫
wir sind ⎬ gefragt worden
ihr seid
sie sind ⎭

past perfect

war
warst
war ⎫
waren ⎬ gefragt worden
wart
waren ⎭

future

ich werde
du wirst
er wird ⎫
wir werden ⎬ gefragt werden
ihr werdet
sie werden ⎭

VOCABULARIES

GERMAN-ENGLISH

The vocabulary includes all the ACTIVE AND PASSIVE vocabulary used in *Wie geht's?*
The English definitions of the words are limited to their use in the text. Each
active vocabulary item is followed by a number and a letter indicating the chapter
and section where it first occurs.

NOUNS Nouns are followed by their plural endings unless the plural is rare
or nonexistent. In the case of n-nouns the singular genitive ending is also given:
der Herr, -n, -en. Nouns that require adjective endings appear with two endings:
der Angestellte (ein Angestellter). Female forms of masculine nouns are not
listed if only **-in** needs to be added: **der Apotheker.**

VERBS For regular t-verbs ("weak verbs"), only the infinitive is listed. All
irregular t-verbs ("irregular weak verbs") and basic n-verbs ("strong verbs") are
given with their principal parts: **bringen, brachte, gebracht; schreiben, schrieb,
geschrieben.** Separable-prefix verbs are identified by a dot between the prefix
and the verb: **mit·bringen.** Compound mixed and n-verbs are asterisked to
indicate that the principal parts can be found under the listing of the basic verb:
mit·bringen*, beschreiben*. When **sein** is used as the auxiliary of the perfect
tenses, the form **ist** is given: **wandern (ist); kommen, kam, ist gekommen.**

ADJECTIVES and ADVERBS Adjectives and adverbs that have an umlaut in
the comparative and superlative are identified by an umlauted vowel in parentheses: **arm (ä) = arm, ärmer, am ärmsten.**

ACCENTUATION Stress marks are provided for all words that do not follow
the typical stress pattern. The accent follows the stressed syllable: **Balkon', Amerika'ner, wiederho'len.** The stress is not indicated when the word begins with an
unstressed prefix, such as **be-, er-, ge-.**

ABBREVIATIONS

~	repetition of the key word	*nom.*	nominative
abbrev.	abbreviation	*o.s.*	oneself
acc.	accusative	*pl.*	plural
adj.	adjective	*refl. pron.*	reflexive pronoun
adv.	adverb	*rel. pron.*	relative pronoun
comp.	comparative	*S*	Schritt
conj.	subordinate conjunction	*sg.*	singular
dat.	dative	*s.th.*	something
fam.	familiar	*W*	Wortschatz 1
gen.	genitive	*G*	Grammatik
inf.	infinitive	*E*	Einblicke(Wortschatz 2)
lit.	literally		

A

der **Aal, -e** eel
ab- away, off
der **Abend, -e** evening; **am ~** in the evening (6E); **Guten ~!** Good evening. (S1) **—abend** evening (8G); **gestern ~** yesterday evening (8G); **heute ~** this evening (8G)
das **Abendessen, -** supper, evening meal (3W); **zum ~** for supper (3W)
abends in the evening, every evening (S6)
aber but, however (S3,2G,5G); *gesture word expressing admiration* (7G)
ab·fahren* (von) to depart, leave (from) (8W)
die **Abfahrt, -en** departure (8W)
ab·fliegen* (von) to take off, fly (from) (8W)
die **Abgase** *(pl.)* exhaust fumes
ab·geben* to give up, hand over
abhängig (von) dependent (on)
die **Abhängigkeit** dependence
ab·holen to pick up
das **Abitur, -e** final comprehensive exam (at the end of the Gymnasium)
ab·nehmen* to take s.th. from, take off
abonnieren to subscribe
ab·pflücken to pick, break off
ab·reißen* to tear down (15W)
die **Abriegelung** closing off
der **Abschluß, ¨sse** diploma
die **Abschlußprüfung, -en** final exam
der **Absender, -** return address (8W)
absolut' absolute(ly)
die **Abwechslung, -en** distraction, variety
ach oh; **~ so!** Oh, I see; **~ was!** Oh, come on!
die **Achtung:** respect; **~!** Pay attention!
das **Adjektiv, -e** adjective
der **Adler, -** eagle
die **Adresse, -n** address (8W)
der **Advents'kranz, ¨e** Advent wreath
die **Advents'zeit** Advent season
das **Adverb', -ien** adverb
(das) **Ägy'pten** Egypt

der **Ägy'pter, -** the Egyptian
ägy'ptisch Egyptian
Aha'! There, you see. Oh, I see.
ähnlich similar; **Das sieht dir ~.** That's typical of you.
die **Ahnung: Keine ~!** I've no idea.
die **Akademie', -n** academy
der **Akade'miker, -** (university) graduate; professional
akade'misch academic
der **Akkusativ, -e** accusative
der **Akt, -e** act (play)
das **Aktiv** active voice
aktiv' active
die **Aktivität', -en** activity
aktuell' up to date, current
der **Akzent', -e** accent
all- all (7G); **vor ~em** above all, mainly (10E); **~e drei Jahre** every three years
allein' alone
alles everything (2E); **Das ist ~.** That's all.
allgemein (in) general; **im allgemeinen** in general
der **Alltag** everyday life
die **Alpen** *(pl.)* Alps
die **Alpenblume, -n** Alpine flower
das **Alphabet'** alphabet
als as; *(conj.)* (at the time) when (11G); *(after comp.)* than (12G)
also therefore, thus, so; well
alt (ä) old (S3); **ur~** ancient
das **Alter** age
die **Altstadt, ¨e** old part of town
der **Amateur', -e** amateur
die **Ameise, -n** ant
(das) **Ame'rika** America (1W)
der **Amerika'ner, -** the American (1W)
amerika'nisch American (10W)
die **Ampel, -n** traffic light
an- to, up to
an (+ *acc. / dat.*) to, at (the side of), on (vertical surface) (6G)
analysie'ren to analyze
an·bieten to offer
ander- other (9E)
andererseits on the other hand
anders different(ly) (9E); **etwas anderes** something else, something different (9E)
anerkannt recognized, credited
die **Anerkennung, -en** recognition
der **Anfang, ¨e** beginning, start

(10W): **am ~** in the beginning (10W)
an·fangen* to begin, start (10W)
der **Anfänger, -** beginner
die **Angabe, -n** information
das **Angebot, -e** offering
angeln to fish; **~ gehen*** to go fishing
angepaßt geared to
angeschlagen posted
der **Angestellte (ein Angestellter)** employee, clerk
die **Angestellte (eine Angestellte)** employee, clerk
die **Angli'stik** study of English
der **Angriff, -e** attack
die **Angst, ¨e** fear, anxiety; **~ haben* (vor** + *dat.*) to fear, be afraid (of)
sich **an·hören** to listen to (9G); **Hör dir das an!** Listen to that.
an·kommen* (in + *dat.*) to arrive (in) (7E); **Das kommt darauf an.** That depends.
die **Ankunft** arrival (8W)
an·machen to turn on (a radio, etc.) (10W)
die **Anmeldung** reception desk
die **Annahme, -n** hypothetical statement *or* question
an·nehmen* to accept; to suppose
der **Anorak, -s** parka
an·reden to address
an·richten to do (damage)
der **Anruf, -e** call
an·rufen* to call up, phone (7G)
an·schlagen* to post
der **Anschluß, ¨sse** connection
die **Anschrift, -en** address
(sich) **an·sehen*** to look at (9G)
an·sprechen* to address, speak to
(an)statt (+ *gen.*) instead of (8G)
anstrengend strenuous (12W)
die **Antiquität', -en** antique
der **Antrag, ¨e** application
die **Antwort, -en** answer
antworten to answer (S2)
die **Anzahl** number, amount
die **Anzeige, -n** ad
die **Anzeigetafel, -n** scoreboard
(sich) **an·ziehen*** to put on (clothing), get dressed (9G)
an·zünden to light
der **Apfel, ¨** apple (2W)
der **Apfelstrudel, -** apple strudel
die **Apothe'ke, -n** pharmacy (2E)

der **Apothe′ker, -** pharmacist
der **Appetit′** appetite; **Guten ~!** Enjoy your meal (food). (3W)
der **April′** April (S5); **im ~** in April (S5)
der **Äqua′tor** equator
das **Äquivalent′** equivalent
die **Arbeit, -en** work (12W); **~** (term) paper (13W); **bei der ~** at work; **Tag der ~** Labor Day
　arbeiten to work (4E)
der **Arbeiter, -** (blue-collar) worker (12W)
die **Arbeitserlaubnis** work permit
　arbeitslos unemployed
die **Arbeitslosigkeit** unemployment
der **Arbeitsplatz, ̈e** job; place of employment
das **Arbeitszimmer, -** study (6W)
die **Archäologie′** archeology
der **Architekt′, -en, -en** architect
die **Architektur′** architecture
das **Archiv′, -e** archive
　ärgerlich annoying
sich **ärgern über** (+ *acc.*) to get annoyed (upset) about (10G); **Das ärgert mich.** That makes me mad.
die **Arka′de, -n** arcade
　arm (ä) poor (11W)
der **Arm, -e** arm (9W)
die **Armbanduhr, -en** wristwatch
die **Armut** poverty
　arrogant′ arrogant
die **Arroganz′** arrogance
das **Arsenal′, -e** arsenal
die **Art, -en** kind, type
der **Arti′kel, - (von)** article (of)
der **Arzt, ̈e** physician (12W)
die **Ärztin, -nen** physician (12W)
　ästhe′tisch aesthetic
　atmen to breathe
die **Atmosphä′re** atmosphere
die **Atom′kraft** atomic power
der **Atom′müll** atomic waste
die **Atom′waffe, -n** atomic weapon
die **Attraktion′, -en** attraction
　attraktiv′ attractive (11W)
　auch also, too (S1)
　auf (+ *acc. / dat.*) on (top of) (6G); open (7W)
　auf- up, open
　auf·bauen to build up (15W)
　aufeinan′der·treffen* to come together
der **Aufenthalt, -e** stay, stopover (8W)
die **Aufenthaltserlaubnis** residence permit

　auf·essen* to eat up
die **Aufgabe, -n** assignment; task, challenge
　auf·geben* to give up
　auf·halten* to hold open
　auf·hören (**zu** + *inf.*) to stop (doing s.th.) (11E)
　auf·machen to open (7G)
die **Aufnahme** acceptance
　auf·nehmen* to take (a picture)
　auf·passen to pay attention, watch out (7G); **Passen Sie auf!** Pay attention.
　auf·stellen to put up
der **Aufsatz, ̈e** essay, composition, paper
　auf·schreiben* to write down (7G)
der **Aufstand, ̈e** uprising
　auf·stehen* to get up (7G)
　auf·stellen to put up
　auf·wachsen* to grow up
der **Aufzug, ̈e** elevator
das **Auge, -n** eye (9W)
der **Augenblick, -e** moment; **(Einen) ~!** Just a minute!
der **August′** August (S5); **im ~** in August (S5)
　aus (+ *dat.*) out of, from (a place of origin) (3G); **Ich bin ~ . . .** I'm from (a native of) . . . (1W)
　aus- out, out of
　aus·arbeiten to work out
　aus·(be)zahlen to pay out
die **Ausbildung** training, education (12W)
sich **auseinan′der·entwickeln** (15E) to develop apart
　aus·füllen to fill out (8W)
der **Ausgang, ̈e** exit (7W)
　aus·geben* to spend (money) (9E)
　aus·gehen* to go out (7G)
　ausgezeichnet excellent (6E)
　aus·helfen* to help out
das **Ausland** foreign country; **im ~** abroad
der **Ausländer, -** foreigner
　ausländisch foreign (13E)
das **Auslandsprogramm, -e** foreign-study program
　aus·leihen* to loan, lend out
　aus·machen to turn off (a radio etc.) (10W)
　aus·packen to unpack
　aus·richten to tell; **Kann ich etwas ~?** Can I take a message?
(sich) **aus·ruhen** to relax (9E)
die **Aussage, -n** statement

　aus·sehen* (**wie** + *nom.*) to look (like) (14W)
　außer (+ *dat.*) besides, except for (3G)
　äußer- outer
　außerdem (*adv.*) besides (6E)
　außerhalb outside (of)
die **Aussprache** pronunciation
　aus·steigen* to get off (8W)
der **Austausch** exchange; **das ~programm, -e** exchange program
　aus·tauschen to exchange (14E)
die **Auster, -n** oyster
　ausverkauft sold out
die **Auswahl (an** + *dat.*) choice, selection (of)
der **Ausweis, -e** ID, identification (7W)
　aus·zahlen to pay out
(sich) **aus·ziehen*** to take off (clothing), get undressed (9G)
　authen′tisch authentic
das **Auto, -s** car (5W)
die **Autobahn, -en** freeway
　autofrei free of cars
　automatisiert′ automated
der **Autor, -en** author (10W)
　autoritäts′gläubig believing in authority

B

　backen (bäckt), buk (backte), gebacken to bake
das **Backblech, -e** cookie sheet
der **Bäcker, -** baker
die **Bäckerei′, -en** bakery (2W)
das **Bad, ̈er** bath (6W)
der **Badeanzug, ̈e** swimsuit
die **Badehose, -n** swimming trunks
　baden to take a bath, swim (6W)
die **Badewanne, -n** bathtub
die **Bahn, -en** railway, train (8W); **~übergang, ̈e** railroad crossing
der **Bahnhof, ̈e** train station (5W)
der **Bahnsteig, -e** platform (8W)
　bald soon (11E)
der **Balkon′, -s** balcony (6W)
der **Ball, ̈e** ball
die **Bana′ne, -n** banana (2W)
　bange worried
die **Bank, -en** bank (7W)

die **Bank, ⸚e** bench
der **Bankier', -s** banker
der **Bann** ban
der **Bär, -en** bear; **Du bist ein Brumm~.** You're a grouch.
barfuß barefoot
das **Bargeld** cash (7W)
der **Bart, ⸚e** beard
basteln to do crafts
der **Bau, -ten** building, construction
der **Bauch, ⸚e** stomach, belly (9W)
bauen to build (6E)
der **Bauer, -n** farmer
der **Bauernhof, ⸚e** farm
das **Baugesetz, -e** building code
das **Bauland** building lots
der **Baum, ⸚e** tree (6W)
die **Baumwolle** cotton
der **Bayer, -n, -n** the Bavarian
(das) **Bayern** Bavaria (in southeast Germany)
bayrisch Bavarian
der **Beamte (ein Beamter)** civil servant (12W)
die **Beamtin, -nen** civil servant, clerk (12W)
beantworten to answer
bedeuten to mean, signify (7E)
die **Bedeutung, -en** meaning, significance
bedienen to take care of, serve
die **Bedienung** service, service charge
beherrschen to dominate, rule
sich **beeilen** to hurry (9G)
beeindrucken to impress
beeinflussen to influence
beenden to finish
der **Befehl, -e** instruction, request, command
beginnen, begann, begonnen to begin (S6)
die **Begrenzung, -en** limitation, limit
begrüßen to greet, welcome
die **Begrüßung, -en** greeting; **zur ~** as greeting
die **Behandlung, -en** treatment
bei (+ *dat.*) at, near, at the home of (3G); **Hier ~.** This is __'s office / residence.
beid- both (11W)
das **Bein, -e** leg (9W); **auf den Beinen** on the go
das **Beispiel, -e** example; **zum ~ (z.B.)** for example (e.g.)
bekannt well known (5E)
der **Bekannte (ein Bekannter)** acquaintance

die **Bekannte (eine Bekannte)** acquaintance
bekommen* (hat) to get, receive (4W)
belegen to sign up for, take (a course) (13W)
beliebt popular
die **Belohnung, -en** reward
benutzen to use
das **Benzin'** gas(oline)
beo'bachten to watch, observe
die **Beo'bachtung, -en** observation
bequem' comfortable, convenient (6W)
der **Berater, -** counselor
berauben to rob
der **Berg, -e** mountain (1W)
die **Bergbahn, -en** mountain train
der **Bergbau** mining
bergsteigen gehen* to go mountain climbing
der **Bericht, -e** report
berichten to report
berieseln *here:* to shower
der **Beruf, -e** profession (12W)
beruflich professional(ly); **~ engagiert'** professionally active
der **Berufstätige (ein Berufstätiger)** someone who has a job
berühmt famous (14E)
bescheinigen to verify, document
beschreiben* to describe
die **Beschreibung, -en** description
beschriftet labeled
besichtigen to visit (an attraction) (5W)
der **Besitz** property
besitzen* to own
besonders especially (3E); **nichts Besonderes** nothing special (9W)
besser better (12G)
die **Besserung** improvement; **Gute ~!** Get well soon.
best- best (12G); **am besten** it's best (12G)
bestätigen to verify
bestehen* to pass (an exam) (13W); **~ aus** (+ *dat.*) to consist of; **es besteht** there is
bestellen to order (3W)
die **Bestellung, -en** order
bestimmt surely, for sure, certain(ly) (11W)
der **Besuch, -e** visit, visitor
besuchen to visit (8W); attend
der **Besucher, -** visitor
beten to pray

der **Beton'** concrete
betonen to stress, emphasize
betreten* to enter, step on
die **Betriebswirtschaft** business administration
betrunken drunk
das **Bett, -en** bed (6W); **ins ~** to bed
betteln to beg
der **Bettler, -** beggar
die **Bevölkerung** population (15E)
bevor (*conj.*) before (4G)
die **Bewertung, -en** evaluation, grading
bewußt conscious(ly)
bezahlen to pay (for) (3W)
die **Bezahlung** pay
der **Bezirk, -e** district
die **Bibel, -n** Bible
die **Bibliothek', -en** library (5W)
die **Biene, -n** bee
das **Bier, -e** beer (2W)
bieten, bot, geboten to offer (11W)
der **Biki'ni, -s** bikini
das **Bild, -er** picture (S2)
bilden to form; **~ Sie einen Satz!** Make a sentence.
die **Bildung** education
billig cheap, inexpensive (2E)
die **Biochemie'** biochemistry
der **Bioche'miker, -** biochemist
der **Bio-Laden, ⸚** health-food store
die **Biologie'** biology
bis to, until (S4); **~ später!** See you later! So long!
bisher' until now
bißchen: ein ~ some, a little bit (4E); **Ach du liebes ~!** Good grief!, My goodness!, Oh dear!
bitte please (S1); **~ bitte! / ~ schön!** (S6) / **~ sehr!** You're welcome. **Hier ~!** Here you are.; **~ schön?** May I help you?; **Wie ~?** What did you say? Could you say that again? (S3)
die **Bitte, -n** request
das **Blatt, ⸚er** leaf; sheet
blau blue (S2)
das **Blei** lead
bleiben, blieb, ist geblieben to stay, remain (4E)
der **Bleistift, -e** pencil (S2)
der **Blick (auf** + *acc.*) view (of)
der **Blickpunkt, -e** focus
blind blind
blitzen to sparkle
der **Block, ⸚e** block
die **Blocka'de, -n** blockade

blockiert blocked
blond blond
blühen to flourish
die **Blume, -n** flower (2E)
die **Bluse, -n** blouse (S3)
der **Boden** ground, floor
die **Bohne, -n** bean (2W)
der **Bomber, -** bomber
der **Bonus, -se** bonus
das **Boot, -e** boat
borgen to borrow
böse angry, mad, upset (11E)
die **Bouti'que, -n** boutique
die **Bowle, -n** alcoholic punch
boxen to box
der **Braten, -** roast
die **Bratwurst, ⁻e** fried sausage
der **Brauch, ⁻e** custom
brauchen to need (S4)
braun brown (S2); **~ gebrannt** tanned
die **Braut, ⁻e** bride
das **Brautkleid, -er** wedding dress
die **BRD (Bundesrepublik Deutschland)** FRG (Federal Republic of Germany)
brechen (bricht), brach, gebrochen to break
der **Brei, -e** porridge
breit broad, wide (12E)
das **Brett, -er** board; **Schwarze ~** bulletin board
die **Brezel, -n** pretzel
der **Brief, -e** letter (8W)
der **Briefkasten, ⁻** mailbox (8W)
brieflich by letter
die **Briefmarke, -n** stamp (8W)
der **Briefträger, -** mailman
die **Brille, -n** glasses
bringen, brachte, gebracht to bring (3W)
das **Brot, -e** bread (2W)
das **Brötchen, -** roll (2W); **belegte ~** sandwich
der **Brotwürfel, -** small piece of bread, cube
die **Brücke, -n** bridge (5W)
der **Bruder, ⁻** brother (1W)
das **Brüderchen, -** little brother
brummig grouchy
der **Brunnen, -** fountain
das **Buch, ⁻er** book (S2)
der **Bücherwurm, ⁻er** bookworm
die **Buchführung** bookkeeping
die **Buchhandlung, -en** bookstore (2W)
das **Büchlein, -** booklet, little book
buchstabie'ren to spell
sich **bücken** to stoop
der **Buddha, -s** Buddha
die **Bude, -n** booth, stand; **Schieß~** shooting gallery

das **Büffet', -s** dining room cabinet
das **Bügeleisen, -** iron
die **Bühne, -n** stage; **auf der ~** on stage
bummeln (ist) to stroll (5E)
der **Bund, ⁻e** confederacy
der **Bundesbürger, -** citizen of the FRG
die **Bundesfeier, -n** Swiss national holiday
das **Bundesland, ⁻er** province
die **Bundespost** federal postal service
die **Bundesrepublik (BRD)** Federal Republic of Germany (FRG)
bunt colorful; multicolored
die **Burg, -en** castle
der **Bürger, -** citizen (10E)
der **Bürgersteig, -e** sidewalk
das **Bürgertum** citizenry
das **Büro', -s** office (12W)
die **Bürokratie'** bureaucracy
die **Bürste, -n** brush
der **Bus, -se** bus (5W); **mit dem ~ fahren*** to take the bus (5W)
der **Busbahnhof, ⁻e** bus depot
der **Busch, ⁻e** bush
die **Butter** butter (2W)

C

das **Café', -s** café (3W)
campen gehen* to go camping
der **Campingplatz, ⁻e** campground
der **Cellist, -en, -en** cello player
das **Cello, -s** cello
die **Charakterisie'rung, -en** characterization
charakteri'stisch characteristic
charmant' charming (11W)
der **Charme** charm
der **Chauffeur', -e** chauffeur
der **Chef, -s** boss
die **Chemie'** chemistry
der **Chor, ⁻e** choir (10W)
der **Christkindlmarkt, ⁻e** Christmas fair
der **Clown, -s** clown
der **Club, -s** club
die **Cola** Coke (2W)
das **College, -s** college
die **Combo, -s** (musical) band
der **Compu'ter, -** computer

computerisiert' computerized
cremig creamy, smooth

D

da there (S2); **~ drüben** over there (5W)
dabei' along; there; yet
das **Dach, ⁻er** roof
der **Dachdecker, -** roofer
dafür instead
dagegen against it; **Hast du etwas ~, wenn . . .?** Do you mind, if . . .?
daher therefore
die **Dahlie, -n** dahlia
damals then, in those days (14W)
die **Dame, -n** lady (5W)
der **Däne, -n, -n** the Dane
(das) **Dänemark** Denmark
dänisch Danish
der **Dank: Vielen~!** Thank you very much. (5W)
dankbar grateful
danke thank you (S1); **~ schön!** Thank you very much. (S6); **~ gleichfalls!** Thanks, the same to you. (3W)
danken (+ *dat*.) to thank (3G); **Nichts zu ~!** You're welcome. No need to thank me.
dann then (3E)
dar·stellen to portray
darum therefore (12E)
das that (S2)
daß (*conj*.) that (4G); **so ~** (*conj*.) so that (12E)
der **Dativ, -e** dative
das **Datum, Daten** date (calendar) (4W)
dauern to last (duration) (4W); **Wie lange dauert das?** How long does that take? (4W)
die **DDR (Deutsche Demokratische Republik)** German Democratic Republic (GDR)
dein (*sg. fam*.) your (1W)
die **Dekoration', -en** decoration
dekorie'ren to decorate
delikat' delicate
der **Demokrat', -en, -en** democrat
die **Demokratie'** democracy
demokra'tisch democratic
der **Demonstrant', -en, -en** demonstrator
demonstrie'ren to demonstrate
demontie'ren to dismantle
denken, dachte, gedacht to

think (4W); **~ an** (+ *acc.*) to think of (10G)

der **Denker, -** thinker

das **Denkmal, ⁻er** monument (15W)

denn because, for (2G); *gesture word expressing curiosity, interest* (7G)

der **Deostift, -e** deodorant stick

die **Depression', -en** (mental) depression

deshalb therefore

deswegen therefore

deutsch: auf ~ in German (S2)

(das) **Deutsch: Sprechen Sie ~?** Do you speak German? (1W)

der **Deutsche (ein Deutscher)** the German (1W,12G)

die **Deutsche (eine Deutsche)** the German (1W)

die **Deutsche Demokratische Republik (DDR)** German Democratic Republic (GDR)

(das) **Deutschland** Germany (1W)

deutschsprachig German-speaking

der **Dezem'ber** December (S5); **im ~** in December (S5)

d.h. (das heißt) that is (i.e.)

das **Dia, -s** slide

der **Dialekt', -e** dialect

der **Dialog', -e** dialogue

dick thick, fat (S3); **~ machen** to be fattening

dienen to serve

der **Diener, -** servant

der **Dienst, -e** service

der **Dienstag** Tuesday (S5); **am ~** on Tuesday

dienstags on Tuesdays (2E)

dies- this, these (7G)

das **Diktat', -e** dictation

die **Dimension', -en** dimension

das **Diplom', -e** diploma (e.g., in natural and social sciences, engineering), M.A.

der **Diplomat', -en, -en** diplomat

direkt' direct(ly)

der **Dirigent', -en, -en** (music) conductor

die **Diskothek', -en** discotheque

die **Diskussion', -en** discussion

diskutie'ren to discuss

sich **distanzie'ren** to keep apart

die **Disziplin'** discipline

die **DM (Deutsche Mark)** German mark

doch yes (I do), indeed, sure (2W); yet, however, but; *gesture word expressing concern, impatience, assurance* (7G)

der **Dokumentar'film, -e** documentary

der **Dollar, -** dollar (7W)

der **Dolmetscher, -** interpreter

der **Dom, -e** cathedral (5W)

dominie'ren to dominate

der **Donnerstag** Thursday (S5); **am ~** on Thursday

donnerstags on Thursdays (2E)

doppelt double

das **Doppelzimmer, -** double room (7W)

das **Dorf, ⁻er** village (8E)

dort (over) there (4E)

draußen outside, outdoors; **hier ~** out here; **weit ~** far out

drehen to turn

die **Droge, -n** drug

die **Drogerie', -n** drugstore (2E)

die **Drossel, -n** thrush (bird)

der **Druck** pressure

duften to smell good

dumm (ü) stupid, silly (10W); **Das ist zu ~.** That's too bad.

die **Dummheit, -en** stupidity

der **Dummkopf, ⁻e** dummy

dunkel dark (6W); **~haarig** dark-haired

dünn thin, skinny (S3)

durch (+ *acc.*) through (2G); **mitten ~** right through

durchbre'chen* to break through, penetrate

durcheinander mixed up, confused

durch·fallen* to flunk (an exam)

der **Durchschnitt** average; **im ~** on the average

dürfen (darf), durfte, gedurft to be allowed to, may (5W); **Was darf's sein?** May I help you?

der **Durst** thirst (2E); **Ich habe ~.** I'm thirsty. (2E)

die **Dusche, -n** shower

der **Duschvorhang, ⁻e** shower curtain

(sich) **duschen** to take a shower (9G)

das **Dutzend, -e** dozen

E

eben after all, just (*gesture word*) (14W)

die **Ebene, -n** plain

echt real, genuine

die **Ecke, -n** corner (6W)

die **EG (Europä'ische Gemeinschaft)** EC (European Community)

egal' the same; **Es ist ~.** It doesn't matter. Who cares?; **~ wie / wo** no matter how / where

die **Ehe, -n** marriage (11W)

ehemalig former

das **Ehepaar, -e** married couple

eher rather

die **Ehre** honor

ehrlich honest(ly)

das **Ei, -er** egg (2W)

die **Eidgenossenschaft** Swiss Confederation

das **Eigelb** egg yolk

eigen- own (12W)

die **Eigenschaft, -en** characteristic (11W)

eigentlich actual(ly) (4E)

die **Eigentumswohnung, -en** condo(minium)

eilig hurried; **es ~ haben*** to be in a hurry

ein a, an (16G,7G); **die einen** the ones; **einer** one

ein- into

einan'der each other

die **Einbahnstraße, -n** one-way street

der **Einblick, -e** insight

der **Eindruck, ⁻e** impression

einfach simple, simply (7E)

die **Einfahrt, -en** driveway; **Keine ~!** Don't enter.

der **Einfluß, ⁻sse** influence

ein·führen to introduce

die **Einführung, -en** introduction

der **Eingang, ⁻e** entrance (7W)

einig- (*pl. only*) some, a few (10G); **so einiges** all sorts of things

ein·kaufen to shop; **~ gehen*** to go shopping (2E,7G)

die **Einkaufsliste, -n** shopping list

das **Einkommen** income (12W)

ein·laden* (zu) to invite (to) (11W)

die **Einladung, -en** invitation

ein·lösen to cash (in) (7G); **einen Scheck ~** to cash a check (7W)

einmal once, (at) one time (5E); **auch ~** for once; **nicht ~** not even; **noch ~** once more, again (S3); **es war ~** once upon a time

einmalig unique (14W)

der **Einmarsch, ⁻e** marching in

ein·packen to pack (in a suitcase)
ein·richten to furnish
einsam lonely
sich **ein·schreiben*** to register
sich **ein·setzen (für)** to support actively (15E)
ein·steigen* to get on *or* in (8W)
der **Eintritt** entrance fee
der **Einwohner, -** inhabitant
das **Einwohnermeldeamt, ⁻er** resident registration office
das **Einzelzimmer, -** single room (7W)
einzig- only
das **Eis,** ice, ice cream (3W)
eisern (made of) iron
eisig icy
eiskalt ice-cold
der **Elefant', -en, -en** elephant
elegant' elegant
der **Elek'triker, -** electrician
elek'trisch electric
die **Elektrizität'** electricity
der **Elek'tromecha'niker, -** electrical mechanic
die **Elek'trotech'nik** electrical engineering
das **Element', -e** element
die **Eltern** (*pl.*) parents (1W); **Gross~** grandparents; **Stief~** step-parents; **Urgroß~** great-grandparents
die **Emanzipation'** emancipation
emanzipiert' emancipated
emotional' emotional(ly)
empfangen* to receive
die **Empfangsdame, -n** receptionist
empfehlen (empfiehlt), empfahl, empfohlen to recommend (3W)
die **Empfehlung, -en** recommendation
das **Ende** end (10W); **am ~** in the end (10W); **zu ~ sein*** to be finished
enden to end
endgültig finally
endlich finally (11E)
die **Energie'** energy
eng narrow
sich **engagie'ren** to get involved
der **Engel, -** angel
(das) **England** England (1W)
der **Engländer, -** the Englishman (1W)
englisch: auf ~ in English (S2)
(das) **Englisch: Sprechen Sie ~?** Do you speak English? (1W)

enorm' enormous
die **Ente, -n** duck; **Lahme ~!** Poor baby!
enthalten* to contain
der **Enthusias'mus** enthusiasm
entlang along; **die Straße ~** along the street
sich **entscheiden, entschied, entschieden** to decide (13W)
entschuldigen to excuse; **~ Sie bitte!** Excuse me, please. (5W)
die **Entschuldigung, -en** excuse
entsprechen* to correspond to
entstehen* (ist) to develop
(sich) **entwickeln** to develop (15E)
die **Entwicklung, -en** development
die **Erbse, -n** pea (2W)
die **Erdbeere, -n** strawberry (2W)
die **Erde** earth (12E); **unter der ~** underground
der **Erfolg, -e** success
ergänzen to supply, complete
ergreifen, ergriff, ergriffen to grab
erhalten* to keep up, preserve
die **Erholung** recuperation, relaxation
erinnern (an + *acc.*) to remind (of) (14W)
sich **erinnern (an + *acc.*)** to remember (14W)
die **Erinnerung, -en (an + *acc.*)** reminder, memory of
sich **erkälten** to catch a cold (9G)
die **Erkältung, -en** cold
erkennen* to recognize (14E)
erklären to explain (15W)
die **Erklärung, -en** explanation
erlauben to permit, allow (15W)
die **Erlaubnis** permit
erleben to experience
das **Erlebnis, -se** experience
die **Ermäßigung, -en** discount
die **Ernährung** nutrition
ernst serious(ly)
die **Ernte, -n** harvest
erreichen to reach
erscheinen* (ist) to appear
erschrecken (erschrickt), erschrak, ist erschrocken to be frightened
ersetzen to replace
erst- first (4W)
erst only, not until (13E)
erwärmen to heat (up)
erzählen (von + *dat.*) to tell (about) (8E,10G)

die **Erziehung** education
der **Esel, -** donkey; **Du ~!** You dummy!
der **Esprit'** esprit
eßbar edible
essen (ißt), aß, gegessen to eat (S6)
das **Essen, -** food, meal (2W); **beim ~** while eating
das **Eßzimmer, -** dining room (5W)
etwas (zu) something (to), a little (to) (2W); something (3W); **so ~ wie** s.th. like; **noch ~** one more thing, s.th. else; **Sonst noch ~?** Anything else?
euer (*pl. fam.*) your (7G)
(das) **Euro'pa** Europe
der **Europä'er, -** the European
europä'isch European
der **Evangelist', -en, -en** evangelist
ewig eternal(ly); **für ~** forever
exakt exact(ly)
das **Exa'men, -** exam
existie'ren to exist
experimentell' experimental
extra extra

F

das **Fach, ⁻er** subject (13W); **Haupt~** major (field) (13W); **Neben~** minor (field) (13W)
der **Fachbereich, -e** field (of study)
die **Fachrichtung, -en** specialization
das **Fachwerkhaus, ⁻er** half-timbered house
der **Faden, ⁻** thread
die **Fähigkeit, -en** ability
fahren (fährt), fuhr, ist gefahren to drive, go (by car, etc.) (3G)
die **Fahrerei'** driving
die **Fahrkarte, -n** ticket (8W)
der **Fahrplan, ⁻e** schedule (of trains, etc.) (8W)
das **Fahrrad, ⁻er** bicycle (6E); **mit dem ~ fahren*** to bicycle
der **Fahrradweg, -e** bike path
die **Fahrt, -en** trip, drive (8W)
fair fair
der **Fall, ⁻e** case; **auf jeden ~** in any case

fallen (fällt), fiel, ist gefallen
to fall (4E); **~ lassen*** to
drop

falsch wrong, false (S2)

die **Fami'lie, -en** family (1W)

fangen (fängt), fing, gefangen
to catch

die **Farbe, -en** color (S2); **Welche
~ hat . . .?** What's the color
of . . .? (S2)

der **Farbstoff, -e** dye, (artificial)
color

der **Fasching** carnival; **zum ~** for
carnival (Mardi Gras)

die **Fassa'de, -n** façade

fast almost (7E)

die **Fastenzeit** Lent

die **Faszination'** fascination

faszinie'ren to fascinate

faul lazy

die **Faulheit** laziness

der **Februar** February (S5); **im ~**
in February (S5)

**fechten (ficht), focht, gefoch-
ten** to fence

der **Federball, -̈e** badminton (ball)

fehlen to be missing, lacking

fehlend missing

der **Fehler, -** mistake

feierlich festive

feiern to celebrate (4W)

der **Feiertag, -e** holiday (4W)

die **Feind, -e** enemy

feindlich hostile

das **Feld, -er** field

das **Fenster, -** window (S2)

die **Ferien** (*pl.*) vacation (4W)

der **Ferienplatz, -̈e** vacation spot

fern far, distant

die **Ferne** distance

das **Ferngespräch, -e** long-distance call

fern·sehen* to watch TV
(9W)

das **Fernsehen** TV (the medium)
(10W); **im ~** on TV (10W)

der **Fernseher, -** TV set (6W)

fertig finished, done (S6)

fertig·machen to finish

das **Fest, -e** celebration (4W);
~spiel, -e festival

festgesetzt fixed

festlich festive

fest·machen to fasten

das **Feuer, -** fire

das **Feuerwerk, -e** firework(s)

die **Figur', -en** figure

der **Film, -e** film (10W)

die **Finan'zen** (*pl.*) finances

finanziell' financial(ly)

finanzie'ren to finance (15W)

finden, fand, gefunden to

find (S5); **Ich finde es . . .**
I think it's . . . (S5)

der **Finder, -** finder

der **Finger, -** finger (9W)

der **Finne, -n, -n** the Finn

finnisch Finnish

die **Firma, Firmen** company,
business (12W)

der **Fisch, -e** fish (2W); **ein kalter
~** a cold-hearted person

fit: sich ~ halten* to keep in
shape (9E)

die **Flasche, -n** bottle (3E); **eine ~
Wein** a bottle of wine (3E)

**flechten (flicht), flocht,
geflochten** to weave
(baskets)

das **Fleisch** (*sg.*) meat (2W)

der **Fleischer, -** butcher

die **Fleischerei', -en** butcher shop

fleißig industrious(ly), hard-
working (13W)

flexi'bel flexible

die **Flexibilität'** flexibility

fliegen, flog, ist geflogen to
fly (8W); **mit dem Flugzeug
~** to go by plane (8W)

fliehen, floh, ist geflohen to
flee, escape

fließen, floß, ist geflossen to
flow

fließend fluent(ly)

das **Floß, -̈e** raft

die **Flöte, -n** flute, recorder

die **Flucht** escape

der **Flüchtling, -e** refugee

die **Fluchtwelle, -n** mass exodus

der **Flug, -̈e** flight (8W)

der **Flügel, -** wing

die **Flugkarte, -n** plane ticket

der **Flughafen, -̈** airport (8W)

der **Flugsteig, -e** gate

das **Flugzeug, -e** airplane (8W)

der **Flur** hallway, entrance foyer
(6W)

der **Fluß, -̈sse** river (1W)

folgen (ist) (+ *dat.*) to follow

der **Fön, -e** hair dryer

das **Fondue', -s** fondue

fördern to encourage

die **Form, -en** form, shape

das **Formular', -e** form

formulie'ren to formulate

der **Förster, -** forest ranger

die **Forstwirtschaft** forestry

die **Frage, -n** question (1W); **eine
~ stellen** (15E) to ask a
question; **Ich habe eine ~.**
I have a question. (S6)

fragen to ask (S2); **sich ~** to
wonder (9G)

fraglich questionable

(das) **Frankreich** France (1W)

der **Franzo'se, -n, -n** Frenchman
(1W)

die **Franzö'sin, -nen** French-
woman (1W)

(das) **Franzö'sisch; Ich spreche ~.**
I speak French. (1W)

die **Frau, -en** Mrs., Ms. (S1);
woman; wife (1W)

die **Frauenbewegung** women's
movement

das **Fräulein, -** Miss, Ms.; young
lady (S1); **~!** Miss! Waitress!
(3W)

frech impudent, sassy, fresh

frei free, available (7W)

freigiebig generous

die **Freiheit** freedom

das **Freilichtspiel, -e** outdoor performance

frei·nehmen* to take time off

der **Freitag** Friday (S5); **am ~** on
Friday (S5)

freitags on Fridays (2E)

freiwillig voluntary

die **Freizeit** leisure time (9W)

fremd foreign

die **Fremdsprache, -n** foreign language

fressen (frißt), fraß, gefressen
to eat (like a glutton or an
animal)

die **Freude, -n** joy

sich **freuen auf** (+ *acc.*) to look
forward to (10G); **Freut
mich.** I'm glad to meet you.
(S1); **(Es) freut mich auch.**
Likewise. Glad to meet you,
too; **Das freut mich für
dich.** I'm happy for you.

der **Freund, -e** (boy)friend (3E)

die **Freundin, -nen** (girl)friend
(3E)

freundlich friendly (11W)

die **Freundlichkeit** friendliness

die **Freundschaft, -en** friendship

der **Frieden** peace (14W)

friedlich peaceful(ly)

frieren, fror, gefroren to
freeze

frisch fresh (2W)

froh glad, happy

fröhlich cheerful, merry

der **Frosch, -̈e** frog

früh early, morning (8G)

früher earlier, once, for-
mer(ly) (12E)

der **Frühling, -e** spring (S5)

das **Frühstück** breakfast (3W);
zum ~ for breakfast (3W)

frustriert' frustrated

die **Frustrie'rung** frustration

der **Fuchs, ̈e** fox; **ein alter ~** a sly person

sich **fühlen** to feel (a certain way) (9W)

führen to lead

die **Führung, -en** guided tour

füllen to fill

die **Funktion', -en** function

für (+ *acc.*) for (S2,2G); **was ~ ein?** what kind of a? (2W)

die **Furcht** fear, awe

furchtbar terrible, awful (S5)

sich **fürchten (vor)** to be afraid (of)

der **Fürst, -en, -en** sovereign, prince

der **Fuß, ̈e** foot (9W); **zu ~ gehen*** to walk (5W)

der **Fußball, ̈e** soccer (ball) (9W)

der **Fußgänger, -** pedestrian; **~überweg, -e** pedestrian crossing; **~weg, -e** pedestrian walkway; **~zone, -n** pedestrian area

G

die **Gabel, -n** fork (3W)

die **Galerie', -n** gallery

die **Gans, ̈e** goose; **eine dumme ~** a silly person (*fem.*)

ganz whole, entire(ly) (9E); very; **~ meinerseits.** The pleasure is all mine; **~ schön** quite (nice)

die **Gara'ge, -n** garage (6W)

garantie'ren to guarantee (15W)

gar nicht not at all (13E)

der **Garten, ̈** garden (6W)

die **Gasse, -n** narrow street

der **Gast, -ë** guest (7W)

der **Gastarbeiter, -** foreign worker

das **Gästezimmer, -** guest room

das **Gasthaus, ̈er** restaurant, inn

der **Gasthof, ̈e** small hotel (7E)

die **Gaststätte, -n** restaurant, inn

das **Gebäck** pastry

das **Gebäude, -** building (14W)

geben (gibt), gab, gegeben to give (3G); **es gibt** there is, there are (2W); **Was gibt's?** What's up?; **Was gibt's Neues?** What's new? (9W); **Was gibt's im . . . ?** What's (playing) on . . . ? (10W); **Das gibt's doch nicht!** That's not possible!

das **Gebiet, -e** area, region

gebildet well educated (11W)

geboren: Ich bin . . . ~ I was born . . . (S5); **Wann sind Sie ~?** When were you born? (S5); **Wann wurde . . . geboren?** When was . . . born?

gebrauchen to use, utilize (15W)

die **Gebühr, -en** fee

der **Geburtstag, -e** birthday (4W); **Wann haben Sie ~?** When is your birthday? (4W); **Ich habe am . . . (s)ten ~.** My birthday is on the . . . (*date*) (4W); **Ich habe im . . . ~.** My birthday is in . . . (*month*). (4W); **Herzlichen Glückwunsch zum ~!** Happy birthday!; **zum ~** at the / for the birthday (4W)

der **Gedanke, -ns, -n** thought (14E)

die **Gefahr, -en** danger (12E)

gefährlich dangerous

das **Gefälle, -** decline

gefallen (gefällt), gefiel, gefallen (+ *dat.*) to like, be pleasing to (3G); **Es gefällt mir.** I like it. (3G)

gefettet greased

der **Gefrierschrank, ̈e** freezer

das **Gefühl, -e** feeling

gegen (+ *acc.*) against (2G); toward (time)

die **Gegend, -en** area, region (8E)

gegensätzlich opposite

das **Gegenteil, -e** opposite (S3); **im ~** on the contrary

gegenüber (von + *dat.*) across (from) (5W)

die **Gegenwart** present (tense)

das **Gehalt, ̈er** salary

gehen, ging, ist gegangen to go (S3); **Es geht mir . . .** I am (feeling) . . . (S1); **Das geht nicht.** That's impossible. That doesn't work. You can't; **Es geht.** That's all right.; **So geht's.** That's the way it goes.; **Wie geht's? Wie geht es Ihnen?** How are you? (S1); **zu Fuß ~** to walk (5W)

gehören (+ *dat.*) to belong to (3G)

die **Geige, -n** violin

geistig mentally, intellectual(ly)

geizig stingy

das **Geländer, -** railing

gelb yellow (S2)

das **Geld** money (7W); **~ aus· geben*** to spend money (8E); **Bar~** cash (7W); **Klein~** change (7W)

die **Gelegenheit, -en** opportunity, chance

gelten (gilt), galt, gegolten to apply to, be valid for, be true

gemeinsam together, shared, (in) common (15W)

die **Gemeinschaft, -en** community

gemischt mixed

die **Gemse, -n** mountain goat

das **Gemüse, -** vegetable(s) (2W)

gemütlich cozy, pleasant, comfortable (5E)

die **Gemütlichkeit** nice atmosphere, coziness

genau exact(ly); **~so** the same; **~ wie** just like (9E)

die **Generation', -en** generation

generös' generous

genießen, genoß, genossen to enjoy

der **Genitiv, -e** genitive

genug enough (5E); **Jetzt habe ich aber ~.** That's enough. I've had it.

geöffnet open (7W)

die **Geographie'** geography

die **Geologie'** geology

das **Gepäck** baggage, luggage (7W)

gerade just, right now (4W); **~ als** just when

geradeaus' straight ahead (5W)

germa'nisch Germanic

die **Germani'stik** study of German language and literature

gern (lieber, liebst-) gladly (2W); **furchtbar ~** very much; **~ geschehen!** Glad to . . . ; **Ich hätte ~ . . .** I'd like to have . . .

das **Geschäft, -e** store (2W); business (12W)

geschäftlich concerning business

die **Geschäftsfrau, -en** businesswoman (12W)

der **Geschäftsmann, -leute** businessman (12W)

geschehen (geschieht), geschah, ist geschehen to happen (11E); **Das geschieht dir recht.** That serves you right.

das **Geschenk, -e** present (4W)

die **Geschichte, -n** story (10W); history (10E)

geschieden divorced (11W)

das **Geschlecht, -er** gender, sex

geschlossen closed (7W)

die **Geschwindigkeit, -en** speed

die **Geschwister** (*pl.*) brothers and sisters, siblings

gesellig social

die **Gesellschaft, -en** society

das **Gesetz, -e** law

gesetzlich legal(ly)

gesichert secure

das **Gesicht, -er** face (9W)

das **Gespräch, -e** conversation, dialogue

gestern yesterday (4W,8G)

gestreift striped

gesucht wird wanted

gesund (ü) healthy (9W)

die **Gesundheit** health

geteilt divided (15E); shared

das **Getränk, -e** beverage

getrennt separated

getüpfelt polka-dotted

die **Gewalt** violence

gewinnen, gewann, gewonnen to win (12E)

das **Gewitter, -** thunderstorm

sich **gewöhnen an** (+ *dat.*) to get used to (12W)

gewöhnlich usual(ly) (3E)

gießen, goß, gegossen to pour

die **Gitar're, -n** guitar (9W)

die **Gladio'le, -n** gladiola

das **Glas, -̈er** glass (2E); **ein ~** a glass of (2E)

glauben (an + *acc.*) to believe (in), think (12W); **Ich glaube es. Ich glaube ihm.** I believe it. I believe him. (12W)

gleich equal, same (12W); right away

gleichberechtigt with equal rights

die **Gleichberechtigung** equality, equal rights

gleichfalls: Danke ~! Thank you, the same to you. (3W)

das **Gleis, -e** track (8W)

der **Gletscher, -** glacier

die **Glocke, -n** bell

glorreich glorious

das **Glück** luck; **~ haben*** to be lucky (7E); **Viel ~!** Good luck.; **Du ~spilz!** You lucky thing!

glücklich happy (11W)

der **Glückwunsch, -̈e** congratulation; **Herzliche Glückwünsche!** Congratulations! Best wishes!

der **Glühwein** mulled wine

der **Gnom, -e** gnome, goblin

das **Gold** gold

golden golden

(das) **Golf** golf; **Mini~** miniature golf

der **Gott** God; **~ sei Dank!** Thank God!; **Um ~es willen!** For Heaven's sake! My goodness!

der **Grad, -e** degree

die **Gramma'tik** grammar

gramma'tisch grammatical(ly)

das **Gras, -̈er** grass

gratulie'ren (+ *dat.*) to congratulate (4W); **Wir ~!** Congratulations.

grau gray (S2)

die **Grenze, -n** border (14W)

grenzenlos unlimited

der **Grieche, -n, -n** the Greek

(das) **Griechenland** Greece

griechisch Greek

groß (größer, größt -) large, big (S3)

die **Größe, -n** size

die **Großeltern** (*pl.*) grandparents (1W); **Ur~** great-grandparents

die **Großmutter, -** grandmother (1W); **Ur~** great-grandmother

der **Großvater, -** grandfather (1W); **Ur~** great-grandfather

grün green (S2); **ins Grüne / im Grünen** out in(to) the country, out in(to) nature

der **Grund, -̈e** reason; **aus dem ~** for that reason

gründen to found

die **Gründung, -en** founding

die **Gruppe, -n** group

der **Gruß, -̈e** greeting; **Viele Grüße (an** + *acc.*) **. . .!** Greetings (to . . .)!

grüßen to greet; **Grüß dich!** Hi!; **Grüß Gott!** Hello! Hi! (*in southern Germany*)

der **Gummi** rubber

gurgeln to gargle

die **Gurke, -n** cucumber (2W); **saure ~** pickle

gut (besser, best -) good, fine (S1); **~aussehend** good-looking; **na ~** well, all right; **Mach's ~!** Take care.

das **Gute: Alles ~!** All the best.

die **Güte** goodness; **Ach du meine ~!** My goodness!

das **Gymna'sium, Gymna'sien** academic high school

H

das **Haar, -e** hair (9W)

haben (hat), hatte, gehabt to have (S6,2G); **Ich hätte gern . . .** I'd like to have . . .

der **Hafen, -̈** port

halb half (to the next hour) (S6); **~tags** part time; **in einer ~en Stunde** in half an hour (8W)

die **Hälfte, -n** half

die **Halle, -n** hall

Hallo! Hello! Hi!

der **Hals, -̈e** neck, throat (9W); **Das hängt mir zum ~ heraus.** I'm fed up (with it).

halten (hält), hielt, gehalten to stop (a vehicle) (5W); **~ von** to think of, be of an opinion (10G)

die **Haltestelle, -n** (bus, etc.) stop (5W)

das **Halterverbot, -e** no stopping *or* parking

die **Hand, -̈e** hand (3E,9W)

die **Handarbeit, -en** needlework

der **Handball, -̈e** handball

der **Handel** trade

der **Handschuh, -e** glove

das **Handtuch, -̈er** towel

der **Handwerker, -** craftsman

hängen to hang (up) (6G)

hängen, hing, gehangen to hang (be hanging) (6G)

harmo'nisch harmonious

hart (ä) hard

hassen to hate

häßlich ugly (11W)

die **Häßlichkeit** ugliness

das **Hauptfach, -̈er** major (field of study) (13W)

hauptsächlich mainly

die **Hauptsaison** (main) season

die **Hauptstadt, -̈e** capital (1W)

die **Hauptstraße, -n** main street

das **Hauptwort, -̈er** noun

das **Haus, -̈er** house (6W); **nach ~e** (toward) home (3W); **zu ~e** at home (3W); **das Zuhause** home

das **Häuschen, -** little house

die **Hausfrau, -en** housewife (12W)

der **Haushalt** household (12W)

die **Hauswirtschaft** home economics

hauswirtschaftlich domestic

das **Heft, -e** notebook (S2)

der **Heiligabend** Christmas Eve; **am ~** on Christmas Eve

der **Heimcomputer, -** home computer
die **Heimat** homeland, home (14E)
heiraten to marry, get married (11W)
heiratslustig eager to marry
heiß hot (S5)
heißen, hieß, geheißen to be called; **Ich heiße . . .** My name is . . . (S1); **Wie ~ Sie?** What's your name? (S1)
die **Heizung** heating
das **Heiz′material′** heating material, fuel
helfen (hilft), half, geholfen (+ *dat.*) to help (3G)
hell light, bright (6W)
das **Hemd, -en** shirt (S3)
die **Henne, -n** hen
heran′- up to
der **Herbst, -e** fall, autumn (S5)
der **Herd, -e** range
herein′- in(to)
herein′·kommen* to come in, enter (11E)
herein′·lassen~ to let in
der **Herr, -n, -en** Mr., gentleman (S1,2G); lord
herum′- around
herum′·laufen~ to run around
herum′·reisen (ist) to travel around
das **Herz, -ens, -en** heart
der **Heurige, -n** (*sg.*) new wine
die **Heurigenschänke, -n** Viennese wine-tasting inn
heute today (S4); **für ~** for today (S2); **~ morgen** this morning (8G)
heutig- of today
hier here (S2)
die **Hilfe, -n** help (15E)
der **Himmel** sky
hin und her back and forth
hinauf′·fahren~ to go *or* drive up (to)
hinein′·gehen~ to go in(to), enter
hin·legen to lay *or* put down; **sich ~** to lie down (9G)
sich **hin·setzen** to sit down (9G)
hinter (+ *acc. / dat.*) behind (6G)
hinterlassen* to leave behind
hinun′ter down
histo′risch historical(ly) (14W)
das **Hobby, -s** hobby (9W)
hoch (hoh-) (höher, höchst-) high(ly) (12W)
das **Hochhaus, ̈er** high-rise building

die **Hochschule, -n** university, college
die **Hochzeit, -en** wedding (11W)
(das) **Hockey** hockey
der **Hof, ̈e** court, courtyard
hoffen to hope (12E)
die **Hoffnung, -en** hope
hoffnungsvoll hopeful, promising
höflich polite(ly)
die **Höhe, -n** height, altitude; **Das ist doch die ~!** That's the limit!
der **Höhepunkt, -e** climax
hohl hollow
die **Höhle, -n** cave
holen to (go and) get, pick up, fetch (13W)
der **Holländer, -** the Dutchman
holländisch Dutch
die **Hölle** hell
das **Holz** wood
hörbar audible
hören to hear (S2)
der **Hörer, -** listener; receiver
der **Hörsaal, -säle** lecture hall (13W)
das **Hörspiel, -e** radio play
die **Hose, -n** slacks, pants (S3)
das **Hotel′, -s** hotel (5W,7W)
hübsch pretty (11W)
der **Hügel, -** hill
das **Hühnchen, -** chicken
der **Humor′** (sense of) humor
der **Hund, -e** dog
Hunderte von hundreds of
der **Hunger** hunger (2E); **Ich habe ~.** I'm hungry. (2E)
hungrig hungry
der **Husar′, -en** cavalryman
der **Hut, ̈e** hat
die **Hütte, -n** hut, cottage

I

ideal′ ideal
das **Ideal′, -e** ideal
der **Idealis′mus** idealism
die **Idee′, -n** idea (9W)
sich **identifizie′ren** to identify oneself
idyl′lisch idyllic
ignorie′ren to ignore
ihr her, its, their (7G)
Ihr (*formal*) your (1W,7G)
die **Imbißstube, -n** snack bar, fast-food stand
die **Immatrikulation′** enrollment (at university)
immer always (4E); **~ geradeaus** always straight ahead (5W); **~ länger** longer and longer

(12G); **~ noch** still; **~ wieder** again and again (12G)
der **Imperativ, -e** imperative
das **Imperfekt** imperfect, simple past
in (+ *acc. / dat.*) in, into, inside of (6G)
inbegriffen in (+ *dat.*) included in
der **India′ner, -** the Native American
der **In′dikativ** indicative
in′direkt indirect(ly)
die **Individualität′** individuality
individuell′ individual(ly)
die **Industrie′, -n** industry
industriell′ industrial
der **Infinitiv, -e** infinitive
die **Informa′tik** computer science
die **Information′, -en** information
informativ′ informative
(sich) **informie′ren** to inform, get informed
der **Ingenieur′, -e** engineer (12W)
die **Initiati′ve, -n** initiative
innen inside
der **Innenhof, ̈e** inner court
die **Innenstadt, ̈e** inner city, center (of town)
inner- inner
innerhalb within
die **Insel, -n** island (14E)
das **Institut′, -e** institute
das **Instrument′, -e** instrument
integrie′ren to integrate
intellektuell′ intellectual(ly)
intelligent′ intelligent (11W)
die **Intelligenz′** intelligence
intensiv′ intensive
interessant′ interesting (5E); **etwas Interessantes** s.th. interesting
das **Interes′se, -n an** (+ *dat.*) interest in
sich **interessie′ren für** to be interested in (10G)
international′ international
interpretie′ren to interpret
das **Interview, -s** interview
intervie′wen to interview
in′tolerant intolerant
das **Inventar′, -e** inventory
inzwi′schen in the meantime
irgendwo somewhere
(das) **Ita′lien** Italy (1W)
der **Italie′ner, -** the Italian (1W)
italie′nisch Italian (1W)

J

ja yes (S1); *gesture word expressing emphasis* (7G)

die **Jacke, -n** jacket, cardigan (S3)
der **Jäger, -** hunter
das **Jahr, -e** year (S5)
jahrelang for years
die **Jahreszeit, -en** season
das **Jahrhun'dert, -e** century
-jährig years old; years long
der **Januar** January (S5); **im ~** in January (S5)
je (+ comp.) **... desto** (+ comp.) ... the ... the ... (12G)
die **Jeans** (pl.) jeans
jed- (sg.) each, every (7G)
jedenfalls in any case (13E)
jeder everyone, everybody
jederzeit any time
der **Jeep, -s** jeep
jemand someone, somebody (11W)
jetzt now (S6)
der **Job, -s** job
joggen gehen* to go jogging
das **Joghurt** yogurt
(das) **Judo: ~ kämpfen** to do judo
der **Journalist', -en, -en** journalist (12W)
das **Jubilä'um, Jubiläen** anniversary
die **Jugend** youth (14E)
die **Jugendherberge, -n** youth hostel (7E)
der **Jugosla'we, -n, -n** the Yugoslav
der **Juli** July (S5); **im ~** in July (S5)
jung (ü) young (11W)
der **Junge, -n, -n** boy (1W,2G)
der **Junggeselle, -n, -n** bachelor
der **Juni** June (S5); **im ~** in June (S5)
die **Jurisprudenz, Jura: Er studiert ~.** He's studying law.

K

das **Kabarett', -e** or **-s** cabaret
das **Kabelfernsehen** cable TV
der **Kaffee** coffee (2W); **~ mit Schlag** coffee with whipped cream
der **Kaffeeklatsch** chatting over a cup of coffee (and cake)
der **Kaiser, -** emperor
das **Kalb, -er** calf; **Kalbsleber** calves' liver
der **Kalen'der, -** calendar
kalt (ä) cold (S5)
die **Kälte** cold(ness)
die **Kamera, -s** camera

der **Kamin', -e** fireplace
der **Kamm, -e** comb
(sich) **kämmen** to comb (o.s.) (9G)
die **Kammer, -n** chamber; **~frau, -en** chambermaid
der **Kampf, -e (um)** fight, struggle (for)
kämpfen to fight, struggle
(das) **Kanada** Canada (1W)
der **Kana'dier, -** the Canadian (1W)
kana'disch Canadian
der **Kanal', -e** channel
die **Kanti'ne, -n** cafeteria (at a workplace)
das **Kanu', -s** canoe
kapitalis'tisch capitalist
das **Kapi'tel, -** chapter
kaputt' broken
kaputt'·gehen* to get broken, break (11E)
kariert' checkered
der **Karneval** carnival
die **Karot'te, -n** carrot (2W)
die **Karte, -n** ticket (8W); card (9W); **~n spielen** to play cards (9W)
die **Kartof'fel, -n** potato (3W); **~brei** (sg.) mashed potatoes; **~mehl** cornstarch; **~salat** potato salad
der **Käse** cheese (2W); **Das ist (doch) ~!** That's nonsense.
die **Kasse, -n** cash register, cashier's window (7W)
die **Kasset'te, -n** cassette (9W)
die **Katze, -n** cat; **(Das ist) alles für die Katz'!** (That's) all for nothing! **ein ~nsprung zu** a stone's throw from
kaufen to buy (2W)
das **Kaufhaus, -er** department store (2W)
der **Kaufmann, -leute** merchant
kaum hardly (14E)
kein no, not a, not any (1G)
der **Keller, -** basement
der **Kellner, -** waiter (3W)
die **Kellnerin, -nen** waitress (3W)
kennen, kannte, gekannt to know, be acquainted with (6G)
kennen·lernen to get to know, meet (7E)
der **Kenner, -** connoisseur
die **Kenntnis, -se** knowledge, skill
der **Kerl, -e** guy
der **Kern, -e** core
die **Kerze, -n** candle (4E)
die **Kette, -n** chain; necklace
die **Kettenreaktion, -en** chain reaction
das **Kilo, -s (kg)** kilogram
der **Kilome'ter, - (km)** kilometer

das **Kind, -er** child (1W)
der **Kindergarten, -** kindergarten
kinderlieb fond of children
das **Kinn, -e** chin
das **Kino, -s** movie theater (5W)
die **Kirche, -n** church (5W)
die **Kirsche, -n** cherry
klappen to work out
klar clear; **~!** Sure! Of course!
die **Klasse, -n** class
das **Klassentreffen, -** class reunion
das **Klassenzimmer, -** classroom
klassisch classical
klatschen to clap (10W)
das **Klavier', -e** piano (9W)
das **Kleid, -er** dress (S3)
der **Kleiderbügel, -** clothes hanger
der **Kleiderschrank, -e** closet
die **Kleidung** clothing (s3)
der **Kleidungsartikel, -** article of clothing
klein small, little (S3)
das **Kleingeld** change (7W)
das **Klima, -s** climate
die **Klimaanlage, -n** air conditioning
klingeln to ring a bell
klingen, klang, geklungen to sound; **Das klingt gut.** That sounds good.
das **Klo, -s** toilet
klopfen to knock
der **Kloß, -e** dumpling
das **Kloster, -** monastery; convent
die **Knappheit** shortage
die **Kneipe, -n** pub
das **Knie, -** knee (9W)
der **Knirps, -e** little fellow, dwarf
der **Knoblauch** garlic
der **Knöd(e)l, -** dumpling (in southern Germany)
der **Knopf, -e** button
der **Knoten, -** knot
der **Koch, -e** cook
kochen to cook (6W)
die **Köchin, -nen** cook
der **Koffer, -** suitcase (7W)
der **Kolle'ge, -n, -n** colleague; **Zimmer~** roommate (13W)
die **Kolle'gin, -nen** colleague
die **Kolonialisie'rung** colonization
kombinie'ren to combine
der **Komfort'** comfort
ko'misch funny (strange, comical) (10W)
kommen, kam, ist gekommen to come (1W); **Komm' rüber!** Come on over!
der **Kommentar', -e** commentary
kommerziell' commercial
die **Kommo'de, -n** dresser (6W)

kommunis'tisch communist
der Kom'parativ, -e comparative
komponie'ren to compose
der Komponist', -en, -en composer (10W)
die Konditorei', -en pastry shop
der Kongreß', -sse conference
der König, -e king (11E)
die Königin, -nen queen
die Konjunktion', -en conjunction
der Kon'junktiv subjunctive
können (kann), konnte, gekonnt to be able to, can (5G)
die Konsequenz', -en consequence
das Konservie'rungsmittel, - preservative
das Konsulat', -e consulate
die Kontakt'linse, -n contact lense
das Konto, -s or Konten account
kontrollie'ren to control, check
die Konversation', -en conversation
konzentriert' concentrated
das Konzert', -e concert (10W)
der Kopf, ⸚e head (9W)
kopf·stehen* to stand on one's head
der Korb, ⸚e basket
der Korbball, ⸚e basketball
der Körper, - body (9W)
körperlich physical(ly)
der Korrespondent', -en, -en correspondent
korrigie'ren to correct
kosten to cost; Was ~ ...? How much are ...? (S4); Das kostet (zusammen) ... That comes to ... (S4)
die Kosten (pl.) cost
das Kostüm', -e costume
der Kracher, - firecracker
die Kraft, ⸚e strength, power
die Kralle, -n claw
krank (ä) sick, ill (9W)
das Krankenhaus, ⸚er hospital
die Krankenkasse, -n health insurance
die Krankenpflege nursing
die Krankenschwester, -n nurse (12W)
die Krankheit, -en sickness
der Kranz, ⸚e wreath
der Kratzer, - scratch
die Krawatte, -n tie
kreativ' creative
die Kreativität' creativity
die Kredit'karte, -n credit card
die Kreide chalk (S2)
der Kreis, -e circle; county

die Kreuzung, -en crossing
das Kreuzworträtsel, - crossword puzzle
der Krieg, -e war (14W)
der Kri'tiker, - critic
der Krimi, -s detective story (10W)
kritisch critical(ly)
kritisie'ren to criticize
die Krone, -n crown
krönen to crown
krumm (ü) crooked
die Küche, -n kitchen (6W); cuisine
der Kuchen, - cake (2W)
die Kugel, -n ball
kühl cool (S5)
der Kühlschrank, ⸚e refrigerator (6W)
der Kuli, -s pen (S2)
die Kultur', -en culture
kulturell' cultural(ly) (14W)
die Kunst, ⸚e art
der Künstler, - artist
der Kurfürst, -en, en elector
der Kurort, -e health resort, spa
der Kurs, -e cours (13W)
die Kurve, -n curve
kurz (ü) short (S3); ~ vor shortly before; vor ~em recently
die Kürze shortness, brevity
die Kusi'ne, -n (female) cousin
küssen to kiss

L

das Labor', -s or -e lab (13W)
lachen to laugh (10W)
lächerlich ridiculous
laden (lädt), lud, geladen to load
die Lage, -n location
lahm lame
das Lamm, ⸚er lamb
die Lampe, -n lamp (6W)
das Land, ⸚er country, state (1W); auf dem ~ in the country (6E); aufs ~ in(to) the country(side) (6E)
landen (ist) to land (8W)
die Landkarte, -n map (1W)
die Landschaft, -en landscape, scenery (15E)
die Landung, -en landing
der Landwirt, -e farmer
die Landwirtschaft agriculture
landwirtschaftlich agricultural

lang (ä) (adj.) long (S3)
lange (adv.) long; noch ~ nicht not by far; schon ~ for a long time; wie ~? how long? (4W)
langsam slow(ly) (S3)
sich langweilen to get (or be) bored (9E)
langweilig boring, dull (10W)
lassen (läßt), ließ, gelassen to leave (behind) (7W)
(das) Latein' Latin
laufen (läuft), lief, ist gelaufen to run, walk (3G)
laut loud(ly), noisy (4E); Sprechen Sie ~! Speak up. (S3)
läuten to ring
der Lautsprecher, - loudspeaker
leben to live (6E)
das Leben life (9E)
die Lebensfreude joy of living
die Lebensmittel (pl.) groceries (2W)
die Leber, -n liver
der Lebkuchen, - gingerbread
das Leder leather
die Lederhose, -n leather pants
ledig single (11W)
leer empty
legen to lay, put (flat) (6G); sich~ to lie down (9G)
die Lehre, -n apprenticeship
lehren to teach (13W)
der Lehrer, - teacher (12W)
die Lehrstelle, -n apprenticeship (position)
leicht light, easy (10E)
leid: Es tut mir ~ I'm sorry. (5W)
die Leidenschaft, -en passion
leider unfortunately (5E)
leihen, lieh, geliehen to lend
die Leine, -n leash
leise quiet(ly), soft(ly)
leiten to direct
die Leiter, - ladder
lernen to learn (S2)
der Lerntip, -s study suggestion
das Lernziel, -e learning objective
lesbar legible
lesen (liest), las, gelesen to read (S2)
der Leser, - reader
die Leseratte, -n bookworm
der Lesesaal, -säle reading room
letzt- last (10W)
die Leute (pl.) people (1W)
das Licht, -er light
lieb- dear (5E)
die Liebe love (11W)
lieben to love (6E)

lieber rather (12G); **Es wäre mir ~, wenn . . .** I would prefer it, if . . .

der **Liebling, -e** darling, favorite; **~sdichter** favorite poet; **~sfach** favorite subject

liebst-: am liebsten best of all (12G)

das **Lied, -er** song (4E); **Volks~** folk song

liegen, lag, gelegen to lie, be (located) (1W); be lying (flat) (6G)

der **Liegestuhl, ⸚e** lounge chair

die **Lilie, -n** lily, iris

die **Limona'de, -n** soft drink, lemonade (2W)

die **Lingui'stik** linguistics

link- left; **auf der ~en Seite** on the left

links left (5W); **erste Straße ~** first street to the left (5W)

die **Lippe, -n** lip

der **Lippenstift, -e** lipstick

der **Liter, -** liter

das **Loch, ⸚er** hole

der **Löffel, -** spoon (3W); **ein Eß~** one tablespoon (of)

logisch logical

lokal' local(ly)

los; ~·werden* to get rid of; **etwas ~ sein*** to be happening, going on; **Was ist ~?** What's the matter? (9W)

lösen to solve

die **Lösung, -en** solution

der **Löwe, -n, -n** lion

die **Luft** air (12W); **mit ~post** by airmail; **~brücke** airlift

die **Lüge, -n** lie

die **Lust** inclination, desire, fun; **Ich habe (keine) Lust (zu) . . .** I (don't) feel like (doing s.th.) . . . (9W)

lustig funny (4E); **sich ~ machen über** (+ acc.) to make fun of (11E); **reise~** eager to travel

luxuriös' luxurious

der **Luxus** luxury

M

machen to make, do (2W); **Spaß ~** to be fun (4E); **Mach's gut!** Take care!; **Was machst du Schönes?** What are you doing?; **Das macht nichts.** That doesn't

matter. (5E); **das macht zusammen.** that comes to

die **Macht, ⸚e** power (14E)

das **Mädchen, -** girl (1W)

das **Magazin', -e** magazine; feature (e.g., on TV)

die **Magd, ⸚e** maid

der **Magi'ster, -** M.A.

die **Mahlzeit, -en** meal; **~!** Enjoy your meal (food)!

der **Mai** May (S5); **im ~** in May (S5)

der **Mais** corn

der **Makler, -** (real-estate) agent, broker

mal times

das **Mal, -e: das erste~** the first time; **zum ersten ~** for the first time; **~ sehen!** Let's see.

malen to paint

der **Maler, -** painter

man one (they, people) (3E)

das **Management, -s** management

manch- many a, several, some (7G)

manchmal sometimes (3E)

manipuliert' manipulated

der **Mann, ⸚er** man, husband (1W)

männlich masculine, male

die **Mannschaft, -en** team

der **Mantel, ⸚** coat (S3)

das **Manuskript', -e** manuscript

das **Märchen, -** fairy tale

die **Margari'ne, -n** margarine

die **Mari'ne, -n** navy

die **Mark (DM)** mark (S4); **zwei Mark** two marks (S4)

der **Markt, ⸚e** market (2W)

die **Marmela'de, -n** marmalade, jam (2W)

der **März** March (S5); **im ~** in March (S5)

die **Maschi'ne, -n** machine

der **Maschi'nenbau** mechanical engineering

die **Maske, -n** mask

die **Massa'ge, -n** massage

die **Masse, -n** mass

die **Massenmedien** (pl.) mass media

die **Mathematik'** mathematics

die **Mauer, -n** wall (14W)

der **Maurer, -** bricklayer

die **Maus, ⸚e** mouse; **~efalle, -n** mousetrap

der **Mecha'niker, -** mechanic

die **Medien** (pl.) media

das **Medikament', -e** medicine, prescription

die **Medizin'** medicine

das **Mehl** flour

mehr more (12G); **immer ~** more and more (12G)

mehrer- (pl.) several (10G)

die **Mehrwertsteuer, -n** value-added tax

meiden, mied, gemieden to avoid

mein my (1W,7G)

meinen to mean, think (be of an opinion) (13E)

meinerseits as far as I'm concerned; **Ganz ~.** The pleasure is all mine.

die **Meinung, -en** opinion; **meiner ~ nach** in my opinion

die **Meinungsumfrage, -n** opinion poll

meist-: am meisten most (12G)

meistens mostly (7E)

der **Meister, -** master

die **Mensa** student cafeteria (3W)

der **Mensch, -en, -en** human being, person; people (pl.) (1E,2G); **~!** Man! Boy! Hey!; **Mit~** fellow man

die **Menschheit** mankind

das **Menü', -s** dinner, daily special

merken to notice

die **Messe, -n** (trade) fair

das **Messer, -** knife (3E); **ein Taschen~** pocket knife

das **Metall', -e** metal

der **Meter, -** meter

die **Metropo'le, -n** metropolis

die **Metzgerei', -en** butcher shop

mies miserable

mieten to rent (6W)

die **Miete, -n** rent

der **Mieter, -** renter, tenant

die **Mietwohnung, -en** apartment

der **Mikrowellenherd, -e** microwave oven

die **Milch** milk (2W)

das **Militär'** military

militä'risch military

die **Million', -en** million

der **Millionär', -e** millionaire

die **Mineralogie'** mineralogy

das **Mineral'wasser** mineral water

minus minus (S4)

die **Minu'te, -n** minute (S6)

mischen to mix; **darunter ~** to blend in

die **Mischung, -en** mixture

misera'bel miserable

die **Mission'** mission

mit (+ dat.) with (3G); along

mit·bringen* to bring along (7G)

mit·fahren* to drive along

mit·feiern to join in the celebration

mit·gehen* to go along (7G)

mit·kommen* to come along (7G)

mit·machen to participate

der **Mitmensch, -en, -en** fellow man

mit·nehmen* to take along (7G)

mit·schicken to send along

mit·singen* to sing along

mit·spielen to participate

der **Mittag, -e** noon

—**mittag** noon (8G); **heute ~** today at noon (8G)

das **Mittagessen, -** lunch, noontime meal (3W); **beim ~** at lunch; **zum ~** for lunch (3W)

mittags at noon (S6)

die **Mitte** middle, center (14E)

das **Mittel, -** means (of)

das **Mittelalter** Middle Ages; **im ~** in the Middle Ages (14W)

mittelalterlich medieval

(das) **Mitteleuropa** Central Europe

mittelgroß average size

mitten: ~ durch right through (14W); **~ in** in the middle of (6E)

die **Mitternacht: um ~** at midnight

der **Mittwoch** Wednesday (S5); **am ~** on Wednesday; **Ascher~** Ash Wednesday

mittwochs on Wednesdays (2E)

die **Möbel** (*pl.*) furniture (6W)

die **Mobilität'** mobility

möbliert' furnished

möchten *or* **möchte** (*see* **mögen**)

das **Modal'verb, -en** modal auxiliary

die **Mode** fashion; **~puppe, -n** fashion doll

modern' modern

mögen (mag), mochte, gemocht to like (5G); **Ich möchte . . .** I would like (to have) . . . (2W)

möglich possible (7W)

die **Möglichkeit, -en** possibility

der **Moment', -e** moment; **(Einen) ~!** One moment. Just a minute.

momentan' at the moment, right now

der **Monat, -e** month (S5); **im ~** a month, per month (6W)

monatelang for months

monatlich monthly (10E)

der **Mond, -e** moon

der **Montag** Monday (S5); **am ~** on Monday

montags on Mondays (2E)

die **Moral'** moral

der **Mörder, -** murderer

morgen tomorrow (S4,4W); **Bis ~!** See you tomorrow; **für ~** for tomorrow (S2)

der **Morgen** morning: **Guten ~!** Good morning. (S1)

—**morgen** early morning (8G); **heute ~** this morning (8G) **morgens** in the morning (S6), every morning

das **Motto, -s** motto

müde tired (S1); **tod~** dead tired

die **Müdigkeit** fatigue

der **Müll** garbage

der **Müller,-** miller

der **Müllschlucker, -** garbage disposal

der **Mund, ¨er** mouth (9W)

die **Mundharmonika, -s** harmonica

mündlich oral(ly)

das **Muse'um, Muse'en** museum (5W)

die **Musik'** music (9E)

musika'lisch musical (11W)

die **Musik'wissenschaft** study of music

(der) **Muskat'** nutmeg

der **Muskelkater** charley horse; **Ich habe ~.** I'm sore.

müssen (muß), mußte, gemußt to have to, must (5G)

das **Muster,-** sample

die **Mutter, ¨** mother (1W); **Groß~** grandmother; **Urgroß~** great-grandmother

mütterlich motherly

N

na well; **~ also** well; **~ gut** well, all right; **~ ja** well; **~ und!** So what?

nach (*+ dat.*) after (time), to (cities, countries, continents) (3G)

der **Nachbar, -n, -n** neighbor (1E, 2G)

die **Nachbarschaft, -en** neighborhood; neighborly relations

nachdem' (*conj.*) after (11G)

nacherzählt retold, adapted

nach·kommen* to follow

nach·laufen* to run after

nach·machen to imitate

der **Nachmittag, -e** afternoon; **am ~** in the afternoon

—**nachmittag** afternoon (8G); **heute ~** this afternoon (8G)

nachmittags in the afternoon (S6), every afternoon

der **Nachname, -ns, -n** last name

die **Nachricht, -en** news (10E)

nächst- next (12G)

die **Nacht, ¨e** night (7W); **Gute ~!** Good night!

—**nacht** night (8G); **heute ~** tonight (8G)

der **Nachteil, -e** disadvantage

die **Nachteule, -n** night owl

der **Nachtisch** dessert (3W); **zum ~** for dessert (3W)

nachts during the night, every night (8G)

der **Nachttisch, -e** nightstand

nach·werfen* to throw after

die **Nadel, -n** needle

nah (näher, nächst-) near (5W,12G)

die **Nähe** nearness, vicinity; **in der ~** nearby; **in der ~ von** (*+ dat.*) near (5W)

nähen to sew

der **Name, -ns, -n** name (8G); **Mein ~ ist . . .** My name is . . . (S1); **Mädchen~** maiden name; **Vor~** first name; **Nach~** last name; **Spitz~** nickname

nämlich namely

die **Nase, -n** nose (9W); **pro ~** per person; **Ich habe die ~ voll.** I'm fed up (with it).

national' national

der **Nationalis'mus** nationalism

die **Nationalität', -en** nationality

die **Natur'** nature

natür'lich natural(ly), of course (2W)

die **Natur'wissenschaft, -en** natural science

natur'wissenschaftlich scientific

neben (*+ acc. / dat.*) beside, next to (6G)

nebeneinander next to each other

das **Nebenfach, ¨er** minor (field of study) (14W)

der **Nebensatz, ¨e** subordinate clause

negativ negative(ly)

nehmen (nimmt), nahm, genommen to take (S4); to have (food) (3G)

nein no (S1)

nennen, nannte, genannt to name, call (14W); **ich nenne das** that's what I call

nett nice (11W)

neu new (S3); **Was gibt's Neues . . . ?** What's new? (9W)

neugierig curious

der **Neujahrstag** New Year's Day

nicht not (S1); **gar ~** not at all (13E); **~ nur . . . sondern auch** not only . . . but also (3E); **~ wahr?** isn't it? (S5)

nichts nothing (3W); **~ Besonderes** nothing special (9W)

nie never (4E); **noch ~** never before, not ever (4E)

niemand nobody, no one (11E)

nimmermehr never again

nobel noble

noch still (4W); **~ ein** another (3W); **~ einmal** once more, again (S2); **~ lange nicht** not by far; **~ nicht** not yet (6E); **~ nie** never (before), not ever (4E); **Sonst ~ etwas?** What else?; **weder . . . ~** neither . . . nor (10E)

der **Nominativ, -e** nominative

die **Nonne, -n** nun

der **Norden: im ~** in the north (1W)

nördlich (von) to the north, north (of) (1W)

normal normal; by regular mail

(das) **Nor'wegen** Norway

der **Nor'weger, -** the Norwegian

nor'wegisch Norwegian

die **Note, -n** grade (13W)

nötig necessary, needed

die **Notiz', -en** note; **~en machen** to take notes

der **Novem'ber** November (S5); **im ~** in November (S5)

nüchtern sober

die **Nudel, -n** noodle (3W)

null zero (S4)

die **Nummer, -n** number (7W)

nun well (14E); now (14E)

nur only (S4)

nutzen to use

O

ob (*conj.*) if, whether (4G)

oben upstairs (6W); up; **~ genannt** above mentioned

der **Ober, -** waiter (3W); **Herr ~!** Waiter! (3W)

die **Oberin, -nen** mother superior

die **Oberschule, -n** high school

das **Objekt', -e** object

das **Obst** (*sg.*) fruit (2W)

obwohl (*conj.*) although (4G)

oder or (S3,2G)

der **Ofen, ∺** oven

offen open (2E)

öffnen to open (S4)

öffentlich public

oft often (2E)

ohne (+ *acc.*) without (2G)

das **Ohr, -en** ear (9W)

der **Okto'ber** October (S5); **im ~** in October (S5)

das **Öl, -e** oil, lotion

die **Olympia'de, -n** Olympics

die **Oma, -s** grandma

das **Omelett', -s** omelet

der **Onkel, -** uncle (1W)

die **Oper, -n** opera (10W)

das **Opfer, -** victim

oran'ge orange (S2)

die **Oran'ge, -n** orange (2W)

das **Orche'ster, -** orchestra (10W)

ordentlich orderly; regular

die **Ordungszahl, -en** ordinal number

die **Organisation', -en** organization

(sich) **organisie'ren** to organize

das **Original', -e** original

der **Ort, -e** place, town

der **Osten: im ~** in the east (1W)

(das) **Ostern: zu ~** at / for Easter (4W); **Frohe ~!** Happy Easter.

(das) **Österreich** Austria (1W)

der **Österreicher, -** the Austrian (1W)

österreichisch Austrian

östlich (von) east (of), to the east (of) (1W)

der **Ozean, -e** ocean

P

paar: ein ~ a couple of, some (2E)

das **Paar, -e** couple, pair

pachten to lease

packen to pack (7E)

die **Päda'go'gik** education

das **Paddelboot, -e** canoe

paddeln to paddle

das **Paket', -e** package, parcel (8W)

die **Paket'karte, -n** parcel form

die **Palatschinken** (*pl.*) dessert crêpes

das **Panora'ma** panorama

der **Panzer, -** tank

das **Papier', -e** paper (S2)

der **Papierkrieg** paper work, red tape

die **Pappe** cardboard

der **Park, -s** park (5W)

parken to park (15W)

das **Parkett': im ~** in the orchestra

der **Parkplatz, -ë** parking lot

parlamenta'risch parliamentary

die **Partei', -en** (political) party

das **Parter're: im ~** on the first floor (ground level) (6W)

das **Partizip', -ien** participle

der **Partner, -** partner (11W)

die **Party, Parties** party (4W)

der **Paß, ∺sse** passport (7W)

passen to fit; **Das paßt mir nicht.** That doesn't suit me.

passend appropriate, suitable

passie'ren (ist) to happen

das **Passiv** passive voice

die **Pause, -n** intermission, break (10W); **eine ~ machen** to take a break

das **Pech** tough luck; **~ haben*** to be unlucky (7E); **~ gehabt!** Tough luck!

pendeln to commute

die **Pension', -en** boarding house; hotel (7E)

das **Perfekt** present perfect

permanent' permanent

persön'lich personal(ly)

die **Persön'lichkeit, -en** personality

der **Pfarrer, -** minister

der **Pfeffer** pepper (3W)

die **Pfefferminze** peppermint

die **Pfeife, -n** pipe

der **Pfennig, -e** German penny, pfennig (S4); **zwei ~** two pennies (S4)

das **Pferd, -e** horse

(das) **Pfingsten** Pentecost

das **Pflaster, -** bandaid

das **Pflichtfach, ∺er** required subject

das **Pfund, -e** pound (2W); **zwei ~** two pounds (of) (2W)

die **Phantasie', -n** fantasy, imagination

phantas'tisch fantastic (9W)

die **Pharmazie'** pharmaceutics
die **Philologie'** philology
der **Philosoph', -en, -en** philosopher
die **Philosophie'** philosophy
die **Photographie'** photography
photographie'ren to take pictures (9W)
die **Physik'** physics
der **Physiker, -** physicist
physisch physical(ly)
das **Picknick, -s** picnic
picknicken gehen* to go picnicking
der **Pilot', -en, -en** pilot
der **Plan, ̈e** plan (12W)
planen to plan (15W)
das **Plastik** plastic
die **Platte, -n** record (9W); platter
der **Plattenspieler, -** record player (10W)
der **Platz, ̈e** square, place (5W); seat
die **Platzanweiserin, -nen** usher
das **Plätzchen, -** cookie (2W)
plötzlich suddenly (11E)
der **Plural, -e (von)** plural of (S2)
plus plus (S4)
das **Plusquamperfekt** past perfect
die **Politik'** politics
die **Politik'(wissenschaft)** political science, politics
poli'tisch political(ly)
die **Polizei'** (*sg.*) police
der **Polizist', -en, -en** policeman (12W)
der **Pole, -n, -n** the Pole
(das) **Polen** Poland
polnisch Polish
die **Pommes frites** (*pl.*) French fries
der **Pool, -s** pool
populär' popular
das **Portemonnaie, -s** wallet
der **Portier', -s** desk clerk
das **Porto** postage
(das) **Portugal** Portugal
der **Portugie'se, -n, -n** the Portuguese
die **portugie'sisch** Portuguese
das **Porzellan'** porcelain
die **Post** post office (5W); mail (8W)
der **Postdienst** postal service
das **Postfach, ̈er** P.O. box
das **Posthorn, ̈er** bugle
die **Postkarte, -n** postcard (8W)
die **Postleitzahl, -en** zip code
prägen to shape
praktisch practical(ly) (6W)
die **Präposition', -en** preposition
der **Präsident', -en, -en** president

die **Praxis** practical experience
der **Preis, -e** price; prize
die **Presse** press
das **Presti'ge** prestige
prima great, wonderful (S5)
der **Prinz, -en, -en** prince
die **Prinzes'sin, -nen** princess
privat' private
das **Privat'gefühl, -e** feeling for privacy
das **Privileg', Privilegien** privilege
pro per
probie'ren to try
das **Problem', -e** problem (13E)
problema'tisch problematic
das **Produkt', -e** product
die **Produktion'** production
produzie'ren to produce
der **Profes'sor, -en** professor (13W)
das **Programm', -e** program, channel (10W)
der **Programmie'rer, -** programmer
das **Prono'men, -** pronoun
proportional' proportional(ly)
Prost! Cheers!
protestie'ren to protest
protzen to brag
das **Proviso'rium** provisional state
die **Prüfung, -en** test, exam (1W); **eine ~ schreiben*** to take an exam (13W)
der **Psalm, -e** psalm
das **Pseudonym', -e** pseudonym
der **Psychia'ter, -** psychiatrist
die **Psy'choanaly'se** psychoanalysis
der **Psycholo'ge, -n, -n** psychologist
die **Psychologie'** psychology
psycholo'gisch psychological(ly)
das **Publikum** audience
die **Puderdose, -n** compact
der **Pudding, -s** pudding (3W)
der **Pullo'ver, -** pullover, sweater (S3)
pünktlich on time
die **Puppe, -n** doll
putzen to clean; **sich die Zähne ~** to brush one's teeth (9G)

Q

die **Qualifikation', -en** qualification

die **Qualität'** quality
die **Quantität'** quantity
das **Quartal', -e** quarter (university)
das **Quartett', -e** quartet
das **Quartier', -s** lodging
der **Quatsch** nonsense
die **Quelle, -n** source
die **Querflöte, -n** flute
das **Quintett', -s** quintet
die **Quote, -n** quota

R

rad·fahren (fährt Rad), fuhr Rad, ist radgefahren to bicycle
das **Radio, -s** radio (6W)
der **Rand, ̈er** edge
der **Rang, ̈e** theater balcony; **im ersten ~** in the first balcony
der **Rasen** lawn
sich **rasie'ren** to shave o.s. (9G)
der **Rat** advice, counsel
raten (rät), riet, geraten to advise, guess
das **Rathaus, ̈er** city hall (5W)
die **Ratte, -n** rat
rauchen to smoke
der **Raum** space
reagie'ren to react
die **Reaktion', -en** reaction
rebellie'ren to rebel
rechnen to calculate
die **Rechnung, -en** check, bill (3W)
recht: Du hast ~. You're right. (11W); **Das geschieht dir ~.** That serves you right.
recht-: auf der ~en Seite on the right side
das **Recht, -e** right
rechts right (5W); **erste Straße ~** first street to the right (5W)
der **Rechtsanwalt, ̈e** lawyer (12W)
die **Rechtsanwältin, -nen** lawyer (12W)
die **Rechtswissenschaft** study of law
die **Rede, -n** speech
reden (mit / über) to talk (to / about), chat (15W)
die **Redewendung, -en** idiom, saying
das **Referat', -e** report; **ein ~ halten*** to give a report
reflexiv' reflexive

das **Reform'haus, ⁻er** healthfood store

das **Regal', -e** shelf (6E)

der **Regen** rain

der **Regenschirm, -e** umbrella

die **Regie'rung, -en** government

das **Regime', -s** regime

die **Region', -en** region
regional regional(ly)

der **Regisseur', -e** director (film)
registrie'ren to register
regnen to rain; **Es regnet.** It's raining. (S5).
regulie'ren to regulate
reiben, rieb, gerieben to rub
reich rich (11W)

das **Reich, -e** empire, kingdom

der **Reichtum, ⁻er** wealth
reif ripe; mature

die **Reihe, -n** row
rein pure

der **Reis** rice (3W)

die **Reise, -n** trip (7E); **eine ~ machen** to take a trip, travel

das **Reisebüro, -s** travel agency

der **Reiseführer,-** tour guide
reiselustig fond of traveling
reisen (ist) to travel (7E)

der **Reisescheck, -s** traveler's check
reißen, riß, ist gerissen to tear
reiten, ritt, ist geritten to ride (on horseback)

die **Reitschule, -n** riding academy
relativ' relative(ly)

das **Relativ'pronomen, -** relative pronoun

der **Relativ'satz, ⁻e** relative clause

die **Religion', -en** religion

das **Rendez-vous** date
rennen, rannte, ist gerannt to run (11E)
renovie'ren to renovate (15W)
repräsentativ' representative
reservie'ren to reserve (7E)

die **Reservie'rung, -en** reservation

die **Residenz', -en** residence
resignie'ren to resign, give up

der **Rest, -e** rest

das **Restaurant', -s** restaurant (3E)
restaurie'ren to restore (15W)

die **Restaurie'rung** restoration

das **Resultat', -e** result
retten to save, rescue (15W)

die **Rezeption', -en** reception (desk)

das **R-Gespräch, -e** collect call
richtig right, correct (S2); **Das ist genau das Richtige.** That's exactly the right thing.

die **Richtigkeit** correctness

die **Richtung, -en** direction; **in ~** in the direction of
riechen, roch, gerochen to smell

das **Riesenrad, ⁻er** ferris wheel
riesig huge

die **Rindsroulade, -n** stuffed beef roll

der **Ring, -e** ring
rings um (+ *acc.*) all around (14W)

das **Risiko, Risiken** risk

der **Ritter, -** knight

der **Roboter, -** robot

der **Rock, ⁻e** skirt (S3)

die **Rolle, -n** role

der **Roman', -e** novel (10W)

die **Romani'stik** study of Romance languages

die **Roman'tik** romanticism
roman'tisch romantic
rosa pink (S2)

die **Rose, -n** rose

die **Rosi'ne, -n** raisin
rot (ö) red (S2); **bei Rot** at a red light

das **Rotkäppchen** Little Red Riding Hood

das **Rotkraut** red cabbage
rötlich reddish

die **Roula'de, -n** stuffed beef roll

der **Rückblick, -e** review

die **Rückfahrkarte, -n** round-trip ticket (8W)

der **Rückgang** decline

der **Rucksack, ⁻e** backpack
Ruckzuck! Quickly!

das **Ruderboot, -e** rowboat
rudern to row
rufen, rief, gerufen to call

die **Ruhe** peace and quiet

der **Ruhetag, -e** holiday, day off
ruhig quiet (7W)

der **Ruhm** fame
rühren to stir

der **Rum** rum
rund round

die **Rundfahrt, -en** sightseeing trip

der **Rundfunk** radio, broadcasting

der **Russe, -n, -n** the Russian
russisch Russian

(das) **Rußland** Russia

die **Rüstung** armament

S

der **Saal, Säle** large room, hall

die **Sache, -n** thing, matter

der **Saft, ⁻e** juice (2W)
sagen to say, tell (S3); **Sag mal!** Say. Tell me (us etc.); **wie gesagt** as I (you etc.) said

die **Saison', -s** season

der **Salat', -e** salad, lettuce (2W)

das **Salz** salt (3W)
salzig salty

die **Salzstange, -n** pretzel stick
sammeln to collect (9W)

der **Sammler, -** collector

der **Samstag** Saturday (S5); **am ~** on Saturday (S5)
samstags on Saturdays (2E)

der **Samt** velvet

der **Sand** sand

der **Sängerknabe, -n, -n** choir boy

der **Satellit', -en** satellite

der **Satz, ⁻e** sentence (1W); **Bilden Sie einen ~!** Make a sentence.
sauber clean, neat (S3)

die **Sauberkeit** cleanliness
sauber·machen to clean
sauer sour; acid

der **Sauerbraten** marinated pot roast

das **Sauerkraut** sauerkraut

die **Säule, -n** column

die **S-Bahn, -en** commuter train

das **Schach: ~ spielen** to play chess (9W)
schade too bad (5W)

das **Schaf, -e** sheep
schaffen to work hard
schaffen, schuf, geschaffen to create

der **Schaffner, -** conductor

die **Schale, -n** shell, peel

die **(Schall)platte, -n** record (9W)

der **Schalter, -** ticket window, counter (7W)

der **Schaschlik, -s** shish kebab

das **Schaufenster, -** display window

das **Schaumbad, ⁻er** bubble bath

der **Schauspieler, -** actor (10W)

der **Scheck, -s** check (7W)

die **Scheidung, -en** divorce (11W)

der **Schein, -e** certificate
scheinen, schien, geschienen to shine (S5); to seem (like), appear (to be) (14E)
schenken to give (as a present) (4W)

die **Schere, -n** scissors
schick chic, neat (11W)
schicken to send (8W)

die **Schießbude, -n** shooting gallery

das **Schiff, -e** ship, boat; **mit dem ~ fahren*** to go by boat

das **Schild, -er** sign

der **Schinken, -** ham

der **Schirm, -e** umbrella

schlafen (schläft), schlief, geschlafen to sleep (3E)

der **Schlafsack, ‐e** sleeping bag

die **Schlafstadt, ‐e** bedroom community

das **Schlafzimmer, -** bedroom (6W)

schlagen (schlägt), schlug, geschlagen to hit

der **Schlager, -** popular song, hit

der **Schlagersänger, -** pop singer

die **Schlagsahne** whipped cream

die **Schlange, -n** snake

schlank slim, slender (11W)

schlecht bad(ly) (S1)

schließen, schloß, geschlossen to lock, close

schließlich after all, in the end (15E)

schlimm bad, awful

das **Schloß, ‐sser** palace (5W)

der **Schlüssel, -** key (7W)

schmecken to taste; **Das schmeckt gut.** That tastes good. (3W)

schmelzen (schmilzt), schmolz, geschmolzen to melt

der **Schmerz, -en** pain, ache; **Ich habe (Kopf)schmerzen.** I have a (head)ache. (9W)

der **Schmied, -e** blacksmith

der **Schmutz** dirt

schmutzig dirty (S3)

der **Schnee** snow

schneiden, schnitt, geschnitten to cut

schneien to snow; **es schneit** it's snowing (S5)

schnell quick(ly), fast (S3)

die **Schnellimbißstube, -n** fast food stand

der **Schnellweg, -e** express route

das **Schnitzel, -** veal cutlet

die **Schokola'de** chocolate

schon already (5E)

schön fine, nice, beautiful (S5)

die **Schönheit** beauty

der **Schrank, ‐e** closet, cupboard (6W); **Gefrier~** freezer; **Kleider~** closet; **Küchen~** kitchen cabinet; **Kühl~** refrigerator

der **Schrebergarten, ‐** leased garden

der **Schreck** shock; **Ach du ~!** My goodness.

schreiben, schrieb, geschrieben to write (S3); **~ an** (+ *acc.*) to write to (10G); **eine Prüfung ~** to take an exam (13W)

der **Schreibtisch, -e** desk (6W)

schriftlich written; in writing

der **Schriftsteller, -** writer, author

der **Schritt, -e** step; pre-unit

der **Schuh, -e** shoe (S3); **Sport~** gym shoe, sneaker

die **Schule, -n** school (5W)

der **Schüler, -** pupil, student

die **Schüssel, -n** bowl

schütteln to shake

der **Schütze, -n, -n** rifleman, marksman, Sagittarius

schützen to protect

der **Schwabe, -n, -n** the Swabian

(das) **Schwaben(land)** Swabia

schwäbisch Swabian

die **Schwäche, -n** weakness

schwanger pregnant

schwärmen to rave

schwarz (ä) black (S2)

das **Schwarzbrot, -e** rye bread

der **Schwede, -n, -n** the Swede

(das) **Schweden** Sweden

schwedisch Swedish

das **Schwein, -e** pig, pork; scoundrel; **~ haben*** to be lucky; **~ gehabt!** You were lucky!

die **Schweinshaxe, -n** pigs' knuckles

die **Schweiz** Switzerland (1W)

der **Schweizer, -** the Swiss (1W)

Schweizer / schweizerisch Swiss

schwer heavy; difficult, hard (10E)

die **Schwester, -n** sister (1W)

das **Schwesterchen, -** little sister

schwimmen, schwamm, geschwommen to swim (9W); **~ gehen*** to go swimming (9W)

das **Schwimmbad, ‐er** swimming pool

der **Schwimmer, -** swimmer

ein Sechstel one sixth

der **See, -n** lake (1W)

die **See** sea, ocean

das **Segelboot, -e** sailboat

segelfliegen gehen* to go gliding

segeln to sail; **~ gehen*** to go sailing (9W)

sehen (sieht), sah, gesehen to see, look (3G); **Mal ~!** Let's see!

die **Sehenswürdigkeit, -en** sight (worth seeing)

sehr very (S5)

die **Seide, -n** silk

die **Seife, -n** soap

die **Seilbahn, -en** cable car

sein his, its (7G)

sein (ist), war, ist gewesen to be (S1,S2,2G); **Wie wär's mit . . .?** How about . . .?; **Ich bin's.** It's me.

seit (+ *dat.*) since, for (time) (3G)

die **Seite, -n** page; **auf ~** on page, to page (S4); **auf der anderen ~** on the other hand

die **Sekretä'rin, -nen** secretary (12W)

der **Sekt** champagne (4W)

die **Sekun'de, -n** second (S6)

selbst -self; **~ wenn** even if

selbständig self-employed, independent (12W)

die **Selbständigkeit** independence

selbstbewußt self-confident

das **Selbstbewußtsein** self-confidence

selten seldom

das **Seme'ster, -** semester (13W)

das **Seminar', -e** seminar (13W)

die **Seminar'arbeit, -en** term paper

der **Sender, -** (radio or TV) station

die **Sendung, -en** (part of) TV or radio program (10E)

das **Sendungsbewußtsein** sense of mission

der **Septem'ber** September (S5); **im ~** in September (S5)

die **Serie, -n** series

servie'ren to serve (food)

die **Serviet'te, -n** napkin (3W)

die **Sesamstraße** Sesame Street

der **Sessel, -** armchair (6W)

der **Sessellift, -e** chairlift

setzen to set (down), put (11W); **sich ~** to sit down (9G)

das **Shampoo', -s** shampoo

die **Show, -s** show

sicher sure, certain (4W); safe, secure (12W)

die **Sicherheit** safety, security

sicherlich surely, certainly, undoubtedly

sichern to secure

sichtbar visible

die **Siedlung, -en** settlement, subdivision

der **Sieg, -e** victory

der **Sieger, -** victor

das **Silber** silver

(das) **Silve'ster: zu ~** at / for New Year's Eve (4W)

singen, sang, gesungen to sing (4W)

der **Sinn, -e** mind, sense
die **Situation', -en** situation
sitzen, saß, gesessen to sit (be sitting) (6G)
die **Sitzecke, -n** corner bench
Ski laufen gehen* to go skiing (9W); **Wasserski laufen gehen*** to go waterskiing
der **Skiläufer, -** skier
die **Slawi'stik** study of Slavic language and literature
so so, like that; this way; **~ daß** (*conj.*) so that (12E); **~ ein** such a (7G); **~ so** fair; **~ ... wie** as ... as (12G)
die **Socke, -n** sock
das **Sofa, -s** sofa, couch (6W)
sofort' immediately, right away (8E)
sogar' even (6W)
sogenannt so-called
der **Sohn, ̈-e** son (1W)
solch - such (7G)
der **Soldat', -en, -en** soldier
sollen (soll), sollte, gesollt to be supposed to (5G)
der **Sommer, -** summer (S5); **im ~** in the summer (S5)
das **Sonderangebot, -e: im ~** on sale, special
sondern but (on the contrary) (5W,5G); **nicht nur ... ~ auch** not only ... but also (3E)
der **Sonderstatus** special status
die **Sonne** sun; **Die ~ scheint.** The sun is shining. (S5)
die **Sonnenbrille, -n** sunglasses
die **Sonnencreme, -n** suntan lotion
das **Sonnenöl** suntan lotion
der **Sonnenuntergang, ̈-e** sunset
der **Sonntag** Sunday (S5); **am ~** on Sunday (S5); **Toten~** Memorial Day
sonntags on Sundays (2E)
sonst otherwise; **~ noch etwas?** Anything else?
die **Soße, -n** sauce, gravy
sowieso' anyway, anyhow (13E)
sowje'tisch Soviet
sowohl ... als auch as well as
der **Sozialis'mus** socialism
die **Sozial'kunde** social studies
die **Soziologie'** social studies, sociology
(das) **Spanien** Spain (1W)
der **Spanier, -** the Spaniard (1W)
spanisch Spanish (1W)
spannend exciting, suspenseful (10W)
sparen to save (money) (6E)

sparsam thrifty
sparta'nisch Spartan, frugal
der **Spaß, ̈-e** fun; **~ machen** to be fun (4E)
spät late; **Wie ~ ist es?** How late is it? (S6)
später later; **Bis ~!** See you later! (4W)
spazie'ren·gehen* to go for a walk (9W)
der **Spazier'gang, ̈-e** walk
die **Speise, -n** food, dish
die **Speisekarte, -n** menu (3W)
die **Spekulation', -en** speculation
das **Spezial'geschäft, -e** specialty shop
die **Spezialisie'rung** specialization
der **Spezialist', -en, -en** specialist
die **Spezialität', -en** specialty
der **Spiegel, -** mirror
das **Spiel, -e** game, play (9W)
spielen to play; **Tennis ~** to play tennis (S6)
der **Spielplan, ̈-e** program, schedule
der **Spielplatz, ̈-e** playground
das **Spielzeug** toys
der **Spieß, -e** spit; spear
spinnen, spann, gesponnen to spin (yarn); **Du spinnst wohl!** You're crazy!
der **Spitzname, -ns, -n** nickname
spontan' spontaneous
der **Sport** sport(s) (9E); **~ treiben*** to be active in sports
der **Sportler, -** athlete
sportlich athletic, sporty (11W)
die **Sprache, -n** language (1W)
-sprachig -speaking
sprechen (spricht), sprach, gesprochen to speak (S3); **~ Sie laut!** Speak up. (S3); **Man spricht ...** They (people) speak ...; **~ von** to speak about (10G)
der **Sprecher, -** speaker
die **Sprechsituation, -en** (situation for) communication
das **Sprichwort, ̈-er** saying, proverb
springen, sprang, ist gesprungen to jump
das **Spritzgebäck** cookies shaped with a cookie press
der **Spruch, ̈-e** saying
die **Spülmaschine, -n** dishwasher
der **Staat, -en** state (15W)
staatlich public
die **Staatsangehörigkeit** citizenship
der **Staatsbürger, -** citizen
die **Stadt, ̈-e** city, town (1W)

das **Stadtbild, -er** character of a town
das **Städtchen, -** small town
der **Stadtplan, ̈-e** city map (5W)
der **Stahl** steel
der **Stamm, ̈-e** tribe, clan
der **Stammbaum, ̈-e** family tree
stammen (aus + *dat.*) to stem (from), originate
der **Standard, -s** standard
das **Standesamt, ̈-er** marriage registrar
ständig permanent(ly), constant(ly)
stark (ä) strong
die **Station', -en** station (bus stop)
die **Stati'stik, -en** statistic
statt instead of (8G)
der **Stau, -s** traffic jam
stehen, stand, gestanden to stand (or be standing) (6W); **Wie steht der Dollar?** What's the exchange rate of the dollar? (7W)
stehen·bleiben* to come to a stop, remain standing
stehlen, stahl, gestohlen to steal
steif stiff
steigen, stieg, ist gestiegen to go up, rise, climb
steigern to increase
steil steep
der **Stein, -e** stone
die **Stelle, -n** job, position, place (12W); **an deiner ~** in your shoes, if I were you (13E)
stellen to stand (upright), put (6G); **eine Frage ~** to ask a question (15E)
sterben (stirbt), starb, ist gestorben to die
der **Stern, -e** star
die **Stereoanlage, -n** stereo set
die **Steuer, -n** tax
Stief: die ~eltern stepparents; **die ~mutter** stepmother; **der ~vater** stepfather
der **Stier, -e** bull
der **Stil, -e** style
still quiet
stimmen: (Das) stimmt. (That's) true. (That's) right.
das **Stipen'dium, Stipen'dien** scholarship (13W)
der **Stock, ~werke: im ersten ~** on the second floor (6W)
stolz proud (11E)
der **Stolz** pride
das **Stopschild, -er** stop sign
stören to bother, disturb (14W)

der **Strafzettel, -** (traffic violation) ticket

die **Straße, -n** street (5W)

die **Straßenbahn, -en** streetcar (5W)

strate′gisch strategic

der **Strauch, ⸚er** bush

der **Stre′ber, -** grind

streng strict

das **Stroh** straw

die **Strophe, -n** stanza

die **Struktur′, -en** structure, grammar

der **Strumpf, ⸚e** stocking

das **Stück, -e,** piece; **ein ~** a piece of (2W); **zwei ~** two pieces of (2W); (theater) play (10W)

der **Student′, -en, -en** student (2G)

die **Studen′tin, -nen** student (2E)

die **Studiengebühr, -en** tuition

der **Studienplatz, ⸚e** opening to study at the university

studie′ren (an + dat.) to study a particular field, be a student at a university (4E)

der **Studie′rende (ein Studie-render)** student

das **Studium, Studien** study (13W)

der **Stuhl, ⸚e** chair (S2)

die **Stunde, -n** hour, class lesson (S6); **in einer halben ~** in half an hour (8W); **in einer Viertel~** in 15 minutes (8W); **in einer Dreiviertel~** in 45 minutes (8W)

stundenlang for hours (5E)

der **Stundenplan, ⸚e** schedule (of classes)

das **Subjekt′, -e** subject

die **Suche** search

suchen to seek, look for (11W); **gesucht wird** wanted

der **Süden: im ~** in the south (1W)

südlich (von) south (of), to the south (of) (1W)

der **Su′perlativ, -e** superlative

der **Supermarkt, ⸚e** supermarket (2W)

su′permodern′ very modern

die **Suppe, -n** soup (3W)

süß sweet

das **Symbol′, -e** symbol

die **Sympathie′** congeniality

sympa′thisch congenial, likable (11W)

die **Symphonie′, -en** symphony

synchronisiert′ dubbed

das **System′, -e** system

die **Szene, -n** scene

T

die **Tafel, -n** (black)board (S2); **Gehen Sie an die ~!** Go to the (black)board. (S3)

der **Tag, -e** day (S5); **am ~** during the day (6E); **eines Tages** (*gen.*) one day (8G); **Guten ~!** Hello. (S1); **jeden ~** every day (8G); **~ der Arbeit** Labor Day

tagelang for days

-tägig days long

täglich daily (10E)

das **Tal, ⸚er** valley

das **Talent′, -e** talent

talentiert′ talented (11W)

die **Tante, -n** aunt (1W)

der **Tanz, ⸚e** dance

tanzen to dance (4W)

die **Tasche, -n** bag, pocket (7W); handbag

die **Tasse, -n** cup (2E); **eine ~** a cup of (2E)

die **Tatsache, -n** fact

tauchen (in + acc.) to dip (into)

tauschen to trade

das **Taxi, -s** taxi (5W)

der **Techniker, -** technician

technisch technical

der **Tee, -s** tea (2W)

der **Teenager, -** teenager

der **Teil, -e** part (1E)

teilen to divide (14W), to share

teilmöbliert partly furnished

die **Teilnahme** participation

teil·nehmen* (an + dat.) to participate (in), take part (in) (13E)

teils partly

die **Teilung, -en** division

das **Telefon′, -e** telephone (6W)

telefonie′ren to call up, phone (8W)

der **Teller, -** plate (3W)

das **Temperament′, -e** temperament

temperament′voll dynamic (11W)

die **Temperatur′, -en** temperature

das **Tennis: ~ spielen** to play tennis (S6)

der **Teppich, -e** carpet (6W)

die **Terras′se, -n** terrace

teuer expensive (2E)

der **Teufel, -** devil

der **Text, -e** text

das **Thea′ter, -** theater (5W)

das **Thema, Themen** topic

der **Theolo′ge, -n, -n** theologian

die **Theologie′** theology

die **Theorie′, -n** theory

das **Thermome′ter, -** thermometer

der **Tiefbau** civil engineering

das **Tier, -e** animal

tierlieb fond of animals

das **Tierzeichen, -** sign of the zodiac

das **Tintenfaß, ⸚sser** inkpot

der **Tip, -s** hint

der **Tisch, -e** table (S2); **Nacht~** nightstand

die **Tischdecke, -n** tablecloth

der **Tischler, -** carpenter

das **Tischtennis: ~ spielen** to play Ping-Pong

der **Titel, -** title

tja well

die **Tochter, ⸚** daughter (1W)

der **Tod** death

Toi, toi, toi! Good luck!

die **Toilet′te, -n** toilet (6W)

tolerant′ tolerant

toll great, terrific (5E)

die **Toma′te, -n** tomato (2W)

der **Ton, ⸚e** tone

der **Topf, ⸚e** pot

das **Tor, -e** gate

die **Torte, -n** (fancy) cake

tot dead

total′ total

der **Total′schaden** total wreck

töten to kill

die **Tour, -en** tour

der **Touris′mus** tourism

der **Tourist′, -en, -en** tourist (5W)

der **Touri′stikumsatz** spending on travel

die **Touri′stin, -nen** tourist (5W)

die **Tournee, -s** tournament

die **Tracht, -en** (traditional) costume

traditionell′ traditional(ly)

tragen (trägt), trug, getragen to carry (3G); to wear (3G)

die **Tragetasche, -n** tote bag

der **Trainer, -** coach

das **Training** training

das **Transport′flugzeug, -e** transport plane

der **Traum, ⸚e** dream

träumen (von) to dream (of) (11W)

der **Träumer, -** dreamer

traurig sad (10W)

die **Traurigkeit** sadness

die **Trauung, -en** wedding ceremony
treffen (trifft), traf, getroffen to meet
das **Treffen, -** meeting, reunion
treiben, trieb, getrieben to push
die **Trennung** separation
die **Treppe, -n** stairs, stairway
treten (tritt), trat, ist getreten to step
treu faithful, true
trinken, trank, getrunken to drink (2W)
das **Trinkgeld, -er** tip
der **Trockner, -** dryer
die **Trommel, -n** drum
die **Trompe'te, -n** trumpet
trotz (+ *gen.*) in spite of (8G)
trotzdem nevertheless, in spite of that (6E)
der **Tscheche, -n, -n** the Czech
die **Tschechoslowakei'** Czechoslovakia
tschechisch Czech
Tschüß! So long; (Good)bye! (4W)
tun (tut), tat, getan to do (4W)
die **Tür, -en** door (S2)
der **Türke, -n -n** the Turk
die **Türkei'** Turkey
türkisch Turkish
der **Turm, -e** tower (14W); steeple
turnen to do sports *or* gymnastics
typisch typical(ly) (15E)

U

die **U-Bahn, -en** subway (5W)
über (+ *acct. / dat.*) over, above (6G); about (10G)
überall' everywhere (3E)
überein'·stimmen to agree
überfüllt' overcrowded
das **Überhol'verbot, -e** no passing
überle'ben to survive
übermorgen the day after tomorrow (4W)
übernach'ten to spend the night (7E)
überneh'men* to take over
überra'schen to surprise (4W)
die **Überra'schung, -en** surprise (4W)
die **Überreste** (*pl.*) leftovers
überset'zen to translate
die **Überset'zung, -en** translation

üblich usual, customary
übrigens by the way; **die übrigen** the rest
die **Übung, -en** exercise, practice
das **Ufer, -** riverbank
die **Uhr, -en** watch, clock; o'clock (S6); **Wieviel ~ ist es?** What time is it? (S6); **~zeit** time of the day (7W)
um (+ *acc.*) around (the circumference) (2G); at . . . o'clock (S6); **~ . . . zu** in order to (9G)
umge'ben (von) surrounded by
die **Umge'bung** (*sg.*) surroundings (14W)
umgekehrt vice versa
(um·)kippen (ist) to tip over
ummau'ert surrounded by a wall
der **Umsatz** sales, spending
der **Umstand, -e** circumstance
um·steigen* (ist) to change (trains etc.) (8W)
um·wechseln to exchange (7W)
die **Umwelt** environment, surroundings (12W)
der **Umzug, -e** parade; move
unabhängig (von) independent (of)
unattraktiv unattractive
unbedingt definitely, necessarily
unbegrenzt unlimited
unbequem uncomfortable, inconvenient (6W)
und and (S1,2G)
unfreundlich unfriendly (11W)
der **Ungar, -n, -n** the Hungarian
(das) **Ungarn** Hungary
ungebildet uneducated (11W)
ungeduldig impatient
ungefähr about, approximately (1E)
ungemütlich unpleasant, uncomfortable
ungestört unhindered
unglaublich inbelievable, incredible
das **Unglück** bad luck
unglücklich unhappy (11W)
die **Uni, -s** (*abbrev.*) university (5W)
die **Universität', -en** university (5W)
unmöbliert unfurnished
unmöglich impossible
unmusikalisch unmusical (11W)

das **Unrecht** wrong
unrecht haben* to be wrong (11W)
uns us, to us (5G); **bei ~** at our place (3G)
unser our (7G)
der **Unsinn** nonsense
unsportlich unathletic (11W)
unsympathisch uncongenial, unlikable (11W)
untalentiert untalented (11W)
unten downstairs (6W)
unter (+ *acc. / dat.*) under, below (6G); among; **~einander** among each other
der **Untergang** fall, downfall
die **Unterhal'tung** entertainment (10W)
das **Unternehmen, -** enterprise, business
unterneh'mungslustig enterprising (11W)
der **Unterricht** instruction, lesson, class
der **Unterschied, -e** difference
unterschrei'ben* to sign (7W)
die **Unterschrift, -en** signature
unterstüt'zen to support
unterwegs' on the go, on the road
untreu unfaithful
unverheiratet unmarried, single (11W)
die **Unverschämtheit** impertinence
die **Unwahrscheinlichkeit** unreal condition
unzerstört intact
unzufrieden discontent
Urgroß: die ~eltern great-grandparents; **die ~mutter** great-grandmother; **der ~vater** great-grandfather
der **Urlaub, -e** paid vacation
ursprünglich original(ly)
die **USA (Vereinigten Staaten von Amerika)** (*pl.*) USA
u.s.w. (und so weiter) etc. (and so on)

V

die **Vanil'le** vanilla
die **Variation', -en** variation
variie'ren to vary
die **Vase, -n** vase
der **Vater, -** father (1W); **Groß~** grandfather (1W); **Urgroß~**

great-grandfather; **Stief~** step-father

verallgemei′nern to generalize

(sich) **verändern** to change (15W)

verantwortlich responsible

die **Verantwortung, -en** responsibility

verantwortungsvoll responsible

das **Verb, -en** verb

verbannen to ban

verbessern to improve

verbieten, verbot, verboten to forbid, prohibit (15W)

verbinden, verband, verbunden to link, connect, combine, tie together

das **Verbot, -e** restriction

verboten forbidden (15W)

der **Verbraucher, -** consumer

verbreiten to distribute, spread

die **Verbreitung, -en** distribution

verbrennen, verbrannte, verbrannt to burn

verbunden in touch, close

die **Verbundenheit** closeness

verdammen to curse

verderben (verdirbt), verdarb, verdorben to spoil

verdienen to deserve; earn; make money (12W)

der **Verein, -e** club, association; **Turn~** athletic club

die **Vereinigten Staaten (U.S.A.)** (*pl.*) United States (U.S.)

die **Vereinigung** unification (15E)

vereint united (15E)

Verflixt! Darn it.

die **Vergangenheit** past; simple past

vergehen* (ist) to pass (time), end

vergessen (vergißt), vergaß, vergessen to forget (11W)

der **Vergleich, -e** comparison

vergleichen, verglich, verglichen to compare

das **Verhältnis, -se** relationship

verheiratet married (11W)

verhindern to prevent

verhungern to starve

die **Verkabelung** connecting everything by cable

verkaufen to sell (2W)

der **Verkäufer, -** salesman, sales clerk (12W)

der **Verkehr** traffic

das **Verkehrsmittel, -** means of transportation

verlassen (verläßt), verließ, verlassen to leave (behind) (14E)

sich **verlieben (in +** *acc.***)** to fall in love (with) (11W)

verliebt (in + *acc.***)** in love (with) (11W)

verlieren, verlor, verloren (an + *dat.***)** to lose (in) (11W)

sich **verloben (mit)** to get engaged (to)

verlobt (mit) engaged (to) (11W)

die **Verlobung, -en** engagement

verlockend tempting

vermieten to rent out (6W)

der **Vermieter, -** landlord

verneinen to negate

(sich) **vernichten** to (self-)destruct

die **Vernichtung** destruction

verrückt crazy (4E)

verschenken to give away

verschieden various, different (10E)

verschlechtern to deteriorate

die **Verschmutzung** pollution

verschönern to beautify

die **Verspätung** delay; **Der Zug hat ~.** The train is late.

versprechen* to promise

der **Verstand** reasoning, logic

die **Verständigung** understanding, communication

verständlich understandable

verständnisvoll understanding (11W)

verstecken to hide

verstehen* (hat) to understand (S3)

versuchen to try (11W)

die **Verteidigung** defense

der **Vertrag, ¨e** contract

die **Verwaltung, -en** administration

der **Verwandte (ein Verwandter)** relative

verwitwet widowed

verwöhnen to spoil

das **Verzeichnis, -se** index, catalog

verzeihen, verzieh, verziehen to forgive; **~ Sie (mir)!** Forgive me. Pardon (me)!

der **Vetter, -n** cousin

die **Videoanlage, -n** VCR

viel- (mehr, meist-) much, many (3W,10G,12G); **ganz schön ~** quite a bit

vielleicht′ perhaps (3E)

viereckig square

das **Viertel, -:** (**um**) **~ nach** (at) a quarter past (S6); (**um**) **~ vor** (at) a quarter to (S6); **in einer ~stunde** in a quarter of an hour (8W); **in einer**

Dreiviertelstunde in three quarters of an hour (8W)

die **Vision′, -en** vision

vital′ vital

der **Vogel, ¨** bird

die **Voka′bel, -n** (vocabulary) word

das **Vokabular′** vocabulary

das **Volk, ¨er** folk; people, nation (14W)

das **Volkslied, -er** folk song

der **Volksstamm, ¨e** ethnic tribe

der **Volkswagen, -** VW

die **Volkswirtschaft** economics

voll full

der **Volleyball, ¨e** volleyball

von (**+** *dat.*) of, from, by (3G); **~ ... bis** from ... until (S4); **vom ... bis zum** from the ... to the (4W)

vor (**+** *acc. / dat.*) in front of, before (6G); **~ einer Woche** a week ago (4W); **~ allem** mainly (10E)

voran′·kommen* to advance

vorbei′·bringen* to bring over

vorbei′·fahren* to drive by, pass

vorbei′·gehen* (bei + *dat.*) to pass by (7G)

vorbei·kommen* to come by, pass by

vorbei sein* to be over, finished

(sich) **vor·bereiten (auf +** *acc.*) to prepare (for)

die **Vorbereitung, -en** preparation

die **Vorbeugung, -en** prevention

die **Vorfahrt** right of way

vorgestern the day before yesterday (4W)

vor·haben* to plan (to), intend (to)

der **Vorhang, ¨e** curtain (6W)

vorher ahead (of time), in advance, before

vor·kommen* (in) to appear (in); **Das kommt mir ... vor.** That seems ... to me.

die **Vorlesung, -en** lecture, class (university) (S6)

—vormittag midmorning (8G); **heute ~** this (mid)-morning (8G)

der **Vorname, -ns, -n** first name

die **Vorsicht: ~!** Careful!

vor·stellen: Darf ich ~? May I introduce?

sich **vor·stellen** to imagine (12E)

die **Vorstellung, -en** performance (10W)

der **Vorteil, -e** advantage
der **Vortrag, ⁻e** talk, speech, lecture
vorüb'ergehend temporary
vor·wärmen to preheat
vor·ziehen* (hat) to prefer (9E)

W

das **Wachs** wax
wachsen (wächst), wuchs, ist gewachsen to grow
die **Waffe, -n** weapon
wagen to dare
der **Wagen, -** car (8W); railroad car (8W)
die **Wahl** choice, selection
wählen to choose; elect
das **Wahlfach, ⁻er** elective (subject)
der **Wahnsinn** insanity; **Das ist ja ~!** That's crazy.
wahnsinnig crazy
während (+ gen.) during (8G); while (conj.)
wahr true; **nicht ~?** isn't it? (S5)
wahrschein'lich probably
die **Währung, -en** currency
der **Wald, ⁻er** forest, woods (6E)
der **Walzer, -** waltz
die **Wand, ⁻e** wall (S2)
der **Wanderer, -** hiker
wandern (ist) to hike (9W)
der **Wanderweg, -e** hiking trail
wann? when?, at what time? (S5, 11G)
die **Ware, -n** goods, wares, merchandise
warm (ä) warm (S5)
warnen (vor) to warn (against)
warten to wait; **~ auf (+ acc.)** to wait for (10G)
warum? why? (2E)
was? what? (S2, 2G); **~ für (ein)?** what kind of (a)? (2W)
das **Waschbecken, -** sink
die **Wäsche** laundry
die **Waschecke, -n** corner reserved for washing
(sich) **waschen (wäscht), wusch, gewaschen** to wash (o.s.) (9G)
der **Waschlappen, -** washcloth (fig., wimp)
die **Waschmaschi'ne, -n** washing machine
das **Wasser** water (2W)

der **Wassermann, ⁻er** Aquarius
Wasserski laufen* to water ski
der **Wasserstoff** hydrogen
der **Wechsel** change
der **Wechselkurs, -e** exchange rate
wechseln to change (7W)
die **Wechselstube, -n** exchange office
weder ... noch neither ... nor (10E)
weg away
der **Weg, -e** way, path, trail (5W); route; **nach dem ~ fragen** to ask for directions
wegen (+ gen.) because of (8G)
weh tun* to hurt; **Mir tut (der Hals) weh.** My (throat) hurts. (9W)
weich soft
die **Weide, -n** willow
(das) **Weihnachten: zu ~** at / for Christmas (4W); **Fröhliche ~!** Merry Christmas!
der **Weihnachtsbaum, ⁻e** Christmas tree
das **Weihnachtslied, -er** Christmas carol
der **Weihnachtsmann, ⁻er** Santa Claus
weil (conj.) because (4G)
die **Weile: eine ~** for a while
der **Wein, -e** wine (2W)
der **Weinberg, -e** vineyard
weinen to cry (10W)
die **Weinstube, -n** inn, restaurant
weise wise
die **Weise: auf diese ~** (in) this way (11W); **in vieler ~** in many ways
weiß white (S2)
weit far (5W)
die **Weite** distance; wide-open feeling
weiter: und so ~ (usw.) and so on (etc.): **~ draußen** farther out; **Wie geht's ~?** How does it go on?
Weiteres additional words and phrases
weiter·fahren* (ist) to drive on (8E); continue the trip
weiter·geben* to pass on
weiter·gehen* (ist) to continue, go on
welch- which (7G); **Welche Farbe hat ...?** What's the color of ...? (S2)
die **Welle, -n** wave
die **Welt, -en** world (12E)
weltoffen cosmopolitan

wem? (to) whom? (3G)
wen? whom? (2G)
wenig- little (not much), few (10G)
wenigstens at least
wenn (conj.) if, (when)ever (4G, 11G); **selbst ~** even if
wer? who? (1G); who(so)ever
die **Werbung** advertisement (10W)
werden (wird), wurde, ist geworden to become, get (3G); **Was willst du ~?** What do you want to be? (12W); **Ich will ... ~.** I want to be a ... (12W)
werfen, (wirft), warf, geworfen to throw
der **Wert, -e** value
wert worth
wertvoll valuable
wessen? (gen.) whose? (8G)
der **Westen: im ~** in the west (1W)
westlich von west of
der **Wettbewerb, -e** contest
das **Wetter** weather (S5)
wichtig important (1E)
widersteh'en* (+ dat.) to withstand
wie? how? (S1); like, as; **~ bitte?** What did you say? Could you say that again? (S3); **so ... ~ as ... as** (1E); **~ lange?** how long? (4W); **~ gesagt** as I (you, etc.) said
wieder again (S5); **immer ~** again and again, time and again (12G); **Da sieht man's mal ~!** That just goes to show you. (15W)
der **Wiederaufbau** rebuilding
wieder·erkennen* to recognize again
wiederho'len to repeat (S2)
die **Wiederho'lung, -en** repetition, review
wieder·hören: Auf Wiederhören! Good-bye. (on the phone)
wieder·sehen*: Auf Wiedersehen! Good-bye. (S1)
die **Wiedervereinigung** reunification (15E)
der **Wiener, -** the Viennese
Wieso' (denn)? How come? Why? (13W)
wieviel? how much? (3W); **Der wievielte ist ...?** What is the date ...? (4W)
wie viele? how many? (3W)
wild wild
die **Wildwest'-Serie, -n** Western series

der **Wille, -ns, -n** will; **Wo ein ~ ist, ist auch ein Weg.** Where there's a will, there's a way. (15W)
der **Wind, -e** wind
der **Winter, -** winter (S5); **im ~** in (the) winter (S5)
das **Winzerfest, -e** vintage festival
wirken to appear
wirklich really, indeed (S5)
die **Wirklichkeit** reality
die **Wirtschaft** economy (15E)
wirtschaftlich economical(ly) (15E)
das **Wirtschaftswunder** economic miracle
wissen (weiß), wußte, gewußt to know (a fact) (6G); **Ich weiß nicht.** I don't know. (S3); **soviel ich weiß** as far as I know
die **Wissenschaft, -en** science, academic discipline (13W)
der **Wissenschaftler, -** scientist (12W)
der **Witz, -e** joke; **Mach (doch) keine Witze!** Stop joking!
witzig witty, funny (14W)
wo? where? (S2,6G)
die **Woche, -n** week (S5)
das **Wochenende** weekend; **am ~** on the weekend (4W)
wochenlang for weeks
wöchentlich weekly (10E)
-wöchig weeks long
woher'? where from? (1W)
wohin'? where to? (6G)
wohl probably
wohlriechend fragrant
der **Wohlstand** affluence
die **Wohngemeinschaft, -en** group sharing a place to live
wohnen to live, reside (1E)
das **Wohnsilo, -s** high-rise apartment (cluster)
der **Wohnsitz, -e** residence
die **Wohnung, -en** apartment (6W)
der **Wohnwagen, -** camper
das **Wohnzimmer, -** living room (6W)
der **Wolf, ⸚e** wolf
die **Wolke, -n** cloud
die **Wolle** wool
wollen (will), wollte, gewollt to want to (5G)
das **Wort, -e** (connected) word; **mit anderen Worten** in other words
das **Wort, ⸚er** (individual) word
das **Wörtchen, -** little word

das **Wörterbuch, ⸚er** dictionary
der **Wortschatz** vocabulary
das **Wunder,-** wonder, miracle
wunderbar wonderful(ly) (S1)
sich **wundern: ~ Sie sich nicht!** Don't be surprised.
wunderschön beautiful (14W)
der **Wunsch, ⸚e** wish (11W); **~traum, ⸚e** ideal dream
(sich) **wünschen** to wish (11W)
die **Wunschwelt** ideal world
der **Würfel, -** small piece of, cube
die **Wurst, ⸚e** sausage (2W); **Das ist doch ~!** That doesn't matter.
würzen to season

Z

die **Zahl, -en** number (S4)
zählen to count (S4)
der **Zahn, ⸚e** tooth (9W); **sich die Zähne putzen** to brush one's teeth (9G)
der **Zahnarzt, ⸚e** dentist (12W)
die **Zahnärztin, -nen** dentist (12W)
die **Zahnbürste, -n** toothbrush
die **Zahnmedizin'** dentistry
die **Zahnpaste, -n** toothpaste
zart tender
zärtlich affectionate
z.B. (zum Beispiel) e.g. (for example)
das **Zeichen, -** signal, sign
der **Zeichentrickfilm, -e** cartoon, animated film
die **Zeichnung, -en** drawing
zeigen to show (5W); **Zeig mal!** Show me (us, etc.)!
die **Zeit, -en** time (S6); tense; **die gute alte ~** the good old days
die **Zeitschrift, -en** magazine (10W)
die **Zeitung, -en** newspaper (10W); **Wochen~** weekly newspaper
die **Zelle, -n** cell, booth
das **Zelt, -e** tent
zentral' central(ly)
das **Zentrum, Zentren** center; **im ~** downtown
zerstören to destroy (15W)
die **Zerstörung** destruction
ziehen, zog, gezogen to pull (11E); to raise (vegetables, etc.)

ziemlich quite, fairly (6W)
die **Zigeu'nerin, -nen** gypsy
das **Zimmer, -** room (S2)
der **Zim'merkolle'ge, -n, -n** roommate (13W)
die **Zimmerkolle'gin, -nen** roommate (13W)
der **Zimmernachweis, -e** room-referral service
der **Zirkel, -** club, circle
das **Zitat', -e** quote
die **Zitro'ne, -n** lemon (2W)
der **Zoll** customs; toll
die **Zone, -n** zone, area
der **Zoo, -s** zoo
zu (+ *dat.*) to, in the direction of, at, for (purpose) (3G); too (S3); closed (2); (+ *inf.*) to (9G)
zu·bleiben* (ist) to stay closed
der **Zucker** sugar (3W)
zuerst' first (of all)
zufrie'den satisfied, content
der **Zug, ⸚e** train (8W); **mit dem ~ fahren*** to go by train (8W)
zu·halten* to hold closed
zu·hören* to listen (7G); **Hören Sie gut zu!** Listen well.
die **Zukunft** future (12W)
zu·machen to close (7G)
zurück'- back
zurück'·bleiben (ist) to stay behind
zurück·bringen to bring back
zurück'fliegen (ist) to fly back
zurück'·geben* to give back, return
zurück'·halten* to hold back
zurück'·kommen* (ist) to come back, return (7G)
zurück'·nehmen* to take back
zurück'·sehen* to look back
sich **zurück'·ziehen* (hat)** to withdraw
zusam'men together; **alle ~** all together; **~gewürfelt** thrown together
die **Zusam'menfassung, -en** summary
die **Zusam'mengehörigkeit** affiliation; solidarity
zu'sehen* to watch; see to it
zu·stimmen to agree
zuvor' previously; **wie nie ~** as never before
zwischen (+ *acc. / dat.*) between (6G); **~durch** in between
die **Zwischenlandung, -en** stopover

ENGLISH-GERMAN

Except for numbers, pronouns, **da-** and **wo-**compounds, this vocabulary includes all active words used in this book. If you are looking for certain idioms, feminine equivalents, or other closely related words, look at the key word given and then check it in the German-English vocabulary. Irregular t-verbs ("irregular weak verbs") and n-verbs ("strong verbs") are indicated by an asterisk (*); check their forms and auxiliaries in the list of principal parts (pp. 426–29)

A

able; to be ~ können*
about (approximately) ungefähr
above über (+ *dat. / acc.*)
academic discipline die Wissenschaft, -en
ache: I have a (head)~. Ich habe (Kopf)schmerzen.
across (from) gegenüber (von + *dat.*)
actor der Schauspieler, -
actual(ly) eigentlich
address die Adresse, -n; **return ~** der Absender, -
advertising die Werbung
after (time) nach (+ *dat.*); **~** (+ *past perf.*) nachdem; **~ all** (*gesture word*) eben, schließlich
afternoon der Nachmittag, nachmittag; **in the ~** nachmittags
afterward danach
again wieder, noch einmal; **Could you say that ~?** Wie bitte?; **~ and ~** immer wieder
against gegen (+ *acc.*)
ago vor (+ *dat.*); **a week ~** vor einer Woche
ahead: straight ~ geradeaus
aid die Hilfe
air die Luft; **by ~mail** mit Luftpost
airplane das Flugzeug, -e
airport der Flughafen, ¨
all all-, alles (*sg.*); **after ~** (*gesture word*) eben
to **allow** erlauben
allowed: to be ~ to dürfen*
almost fast
already schon
also auch
although (*conj.*) obwohl
always immer
America (das) Amerika
American (*adj.*) amerikanisch; (**person**) der Amerikaner, -

among unter (+ *dat. / acc.*)
and und
angry böse; **to get ~ about** sich ärgern über (+ *acc.*)
another noch ein
to **answer** antworten
answer die Antwort, -en
anyhow sowieso
anyway sowieso
apart auseinander
apartment die Wohnung, -en
to **appear (to be)** scheinen*
to **applaud** klatschen
apple der Apfel, ¨
approximately ungefähr
April der April; **in ~** im April
area die Gegend, -en
arm der Arm, -e
armchair der Sessel, -
around um (+ *acc.*); **all ~** rings um (+ *acc.*)
arrival die Ankunft
to **arrive (in)** an·kommen* (in + *dat.*)
art die Kunst, ¨e
as wie; **~ . . . ~** so . . . wie
to **ask** fragen; **to ~ a question** eine Frage stellen
at an (+ *dat.*); (**o'clock**) um . . . (Uhr); (**the place of**) bei (+ *dat.*)
athletic sportlich; **un~** unsportlich
attention: to pay ~ auf·passen
attractive attraktiv, hübsch
August der August; **in ~** im August
aunt die Tante, -n
Austria (das) Österreich
Austrian (person) der Österreicher, -
author der Autor, -en
available frei

B

bad(ly) schlecht; schlimm; **too ~** schade

bag die Tasche, -n
baggage das Gepäck
bakery die Bäckerei, -en
balcony der Balkon, -e *or* -s
banana die Banane, -n
bank die Bank, -en
bath das Bad, ¨er; **to take a ~** baden
to **be** sein*; (**become**) werden*; **Be . . .!** Sei (Seid, Seien Sie) . . .!
bean die Bohne, -n
beautiful (wunder)schön
because (*conj.*) weil, denn; **~ of** wegen (+ *gen.*)
to **become** werden*
bed das Bett, -en; **~room** das Schlafzimmer, -
beer das Bier
before vor (+ *acc. / dat.*); (*conj.*) bevor; **not ~** (*time*) erst; (*adv.*) vorher
to **begin** beginnen*, an·fangen*
beginning der Anfang, ¨e, **in the ~** am Anfang
behind hinter (+ *acc. / dat.*)
to **believe (in)** glauben (an + *acc.*); (**things**) Ich glaube es.; (**persons**) Ich glaube ihm.
belly der Bauch, ¨e
to **belong to** gehören (+ *dat.*)
below unter (+ *acc. / dat.*)
beside neben (+ *acc. / dat.*)
besides (*adv.*) außerdem
best best-, am besten
better besser
between zwischen (+ *acc. / dat.*)
bicycle das Fahrrad, ¨er
to **bicycle** mit dem Fahrrad fahren*
big groß (ö)
bill die Rechnung, -en
birthday der Geburtstag, -e; **on / for ~** zum Geburtstag
bit: a little ~ ein bißchen
black schwarz (ä)
blackboard die Tafel, -n
blouse die Bluse, -n
blue blau

457

boarding house die Pension, -en
body der Körper, -
book das Buch, ̈er
bookstore die Buchhandlung, -en
border die Grenze, -n
bored; to get (or be) ~ sich langweilen
boring langweilig
born geboren (ist); **I was ~ May 3, 1968, in Munich.** I bin am 3.5.68 in München geboren.
both (things, sg.) beides; (pl.) beide
to **bother** stören
bottle die Flasche, -n; **a ~ of . . .** eine Flasche . . .
boy der Junge, -n, -n
bread das Brot,- e
break (intermission) die Pause, -n
to **break** kaputt·gehen*
breakfast das Frühstück; **for ~** zum Frühstück
bridge die Brücke, -n
bright (light) hell
to **bring** bringen*; **to ~ along** mit·bringen*
broad weit
broken: to get ~ kaputt·gehen*
brother der Bruder, ̈
brown braun
to **brush (one's teeth)** sich (die Zähne) putzen
to **build** bauen; **to re~** wieder·auf·bauen
building das Gebäude, -
bus der Bus, -se
business das Geschäft, -e
businessman der Geschäftsmann, -leute
businesswoman die Geschäftsfrau, -en
but aber; doch; **not only . . . ~ also** nicht nur . . . sondern auch
butter die Butter
to **buy** kaufen
by von (+ dat.)

C

café das Café, -s
cafeteria (student) die Mensa
cake der Kuchen, -

to **call** rufen*; **to ~ (up)** an·rufen*, telefonieren; **to ~ (name)** nennen*; **to be called** heißen*
campground der Campingplatz, ̈e
can können*
Canada (das) Kanada
Canadian (adj.) kanadisch; **(person)** der Kanadier, -
candle die Kerze, -n
capital die Hauptstadt, ̈e
car das Auto, -s; der Wagen,-; **(railroad)** der Wagen, -
card die Karte, -n; **post~** die Postkarte, -n
cardigan die Jacke, -n
carpet der Teppich, -e
carrot die Karotte, -n
to **carry** tragen*
case: in any ~ jedenfalls
cash das Bargeld; **~ register** die Kasse, -n
to **cash (in) (a check)** ein·lösen
cassette die Kassette, -n
cathedral der Dom, -e
to **celebrate** feiern
celebration das Fest, -e
center die Mitte
certain(ly) bestimmt
chair der Stuhl, ̈e; **arm~** der Sessel, -
chalk die Kreide
champagne der Sekt
change das Kleingeld
to **change** (sich) verändern; **(money: DM > Pfennige)** wechseln; **(money: $ > DM)** (um)wechseln: **(trains)** um·steigen*
channel das Programm, -e
charming charmant
cheap billig
check der Scheck, -s; **traveler's ~** der Reisescheck, -s
cheese der Käse
chic schick
child das Kind, -er
choir der Chor, ̈e
Christmas (das) Weihnachten; **at / for ~** zu Weihnachten
church die Kirche, -n
citizen der Bürger, -
city die Stadt ̈e; **~ hall** das Rathaus, ̈er; **~ map** der Stadtplan, ̈e
to **clap** klatschen
class (group) die Klasse, -n; **(time)** die Stunde, -n; **(instruction, school)** der Unterricht; **(instruction, university)** die Vorlesung, -en

clean sauber
to **clean** putzen
clerk: (civil servant) der Beamte (ein Beamter); **(salesman)** der Verkäufer, -
clock die Uhr, -en; **o'clock** Uhr
to **close** zu·machen
closed zu, geschlossen
closet der Schrank, ̈e
clothing die Kleidung
coat der Mantel, ̈
coffee der Kaffee
Coke die Cola
cold kalt (ä)
cold: to catch a ~ sich erkälten
to **collect** sammeln
color die Farbe, -n; **What's the ~ of . . .?** Welche Farbe hat . . .?
colorful bunt
to **comb** (sich) kämmen
to **come** kommen*; **to ~ along** mit·kommen*; **to ~ back** zurück·kommen*; **to ~ in** herein·kommen*; **That comes to . . . (altogether).** Das kostet (zusammen) . . .
comfortable bequem
comical komisch
common gemeinsam
company die Firma, Firmen
composer der Komponist, -en, -en
concert das Konzert, -e
congenial sympathisch; **un~** unsympathisch
to **congratulate** gratulieren
to **continue** weiter·gehen*, weiter·machen
convenient bequem
to **cook** kochen
cookie das Plätzchen, -
cool kühl
corner die Ecke, -n
correct richtig
to **cost** kosten
to **count** zählen
counter der Schalter, -
country das Land, ̈er; **in(to) the ~(side)** aufs Land
couple: a ~ of ein paar
course der Kurs, -e; **of ~** natürlich
cozy gemütlich
crazy verrückt
to **cry** weinen
cucumber die Gurke, -n
cup die Tasse, -n; **a ~ of . . .** eine Tasse . . .
cupboard der Schrank, ̈e

cultural(ly) kulturell
curtain der Vorhang, ⸚e

D

daily täglich
to **dance** tanzen
danger die Gefahr, -en
dark dunkel
date das Datum, Daten;
  What's the ~ today? Der
  wievielte ist heute?
daughter die Tochter, ⸚
day der Tag, -e; **during the ~**
  am Tag; **one ~** eines Tages;
  all ~ long, the whole ~ den
  ganzen Tag; **each ~** jeden
  Tag; **in those days** damals
dear lieb-
December der Dezember; **in**
  ~ im Dezember
to **decide** sich entscheiden*
desk der Schreibtisch, -e
dessert der Nachtisch
to **destroy** zerstören
to **develop** (sich) entwickeln; **~**
  apart sich auseinander·ent·
  wickeln
difference der Unter-
  schied, -e
different(ly) verschieden, anders; **something ~** etwas anderes
difficult schwer
dining room das Eßzimmer, -
dinner das Mittagessen; das
  Abendessen
dirty schmutzig
to **disturb** stören
to **divide** teilen
divided geteilt
divorce die Scheidung, -en
divorced geschieden
to **do** tun*, machen
doctor der Arzt, ⸚e, die Ärztin, -nen
dollar der Dollar, -
door die Tür, -en
dorm das Studentenheim, -e
downstairs unten
to **dream (of)** träumen (von)
dress das Kleid, -er
dressed: to get ~ (sich) an·zie-
  hen*; **to get un~** (sich) aus·-
  ziehen*
dresser die Kommode, -n
to **drink** trinken*
to **drive** fahren*; **to ~ on (keep**
  on driving) weiter·fahren*;
  to ~ up hinauf·fahren*

drugstore die Drogerie, -n
dull langweilig
during während (+ *gen.*)
dynamic temperamentvoll

E

each jed-
ear das Ohr, -en
earlier früher
early früh
to **earn** verdienen
earth die Erde
east der Osten; **~ of** östlich
  von
Easter Ostern; **at / for ~** zu
  Ostern
easy leicht
to **eat** essen*
economy die Wirtschaft
educated gebildet
egg das Ei, -er
end das Ende; **in the ~** am
  Ende, schließlich
engaged verlobt; **to get ~ (to)**
  sich verloben (mit)
engineer der Ingenieur, -e
England (das) England
English (*adj.*) englisch; **in ~**
  auf englisch; **(language)**
  Englisch; **Do you speak ~?**
  Sprechen Sie Englisch?;
  (person) der Engländer, -
enough genug
to **enter** herein·kommen*
entertainment die Unterhaltung
entire(ly) ganz
entrance der Eingang, ⸚e
environment die Umwelt
equal gleich
especially besonders
etc. usw., und so weiter
even sogar
evening der Abend, -e;
  abend; **Good ~.** Guten
  Abend! **in the ~** abends,
  am Abend
every jed-
everything alles
everywhere überall
exact(ly) genau
exam die Prüfung, -en; **to**
  take an ~ eine Prüfung
  schreiben*
excellent ausgezeichnet
to **exchange** aus·tauschen;
  (money) um·wechseln;
  What's the ~ rate of the

dollar? Wie steht der
  Dollar?
exciting spannend
to **excuse** sich entschuldigen;
  ~ me! Entschuldigen Sie!
exit der Ausgang, ⸚e
expensive teuer
to **explain** erklären
eye das Auge, -n

F

face das Gesicht, -er
fairly ziemlich
to **fall** fallen*; **to ~ in love**
  (with) sich verlieben (in +
  acc.)
fall der Herbst, -e; **in (the) ~**
  im Herbst
false falsch
family die Familie, -n
famous berühmt
fantastic phantastisch, toll
far weit
fast schnell
fat dick
father der Vater, ⸚
February der Februar; **in ~**
  im Februar
to **feel (a certain way)** sich fühlen; **How are you (feeling)?**
  Wie geht es Ihnen? Wie
  geht's?; **I'm (feeling) . . .** Es
  geht mir . . .; **to ~ like (do-**
  ing something) Lust haben*
  zu (+ *inf.*)
few wenig-; ein paar
to **fill out** aus·füllen
film der Film, -e
finally endlich
to **finance** finanzieren
to **find** finden*
fine gut (besser, best-), schön
finger der Finger, -
finished fertig
firm die Firma, Firmen
first erst-; **~ of all** (zu)erst
fish der Fisch, -e
flight (plane) der Flug, ⸚e
to **fly** fliegen*
floor; on the first ~ im Parterre; **on the second ~** im
  ersten Stock
flower die Blume, -n
to **follow** folgen (ist) (+ *dat.*)
food das Essen; **Enjoy your ~.**
  Guten Appetit!
foot der Fuß, ⸚e

for für (+ *acc.*); **(since)** seit (+ *dat.*)

to **forbid** verbieten*
forbidden verboten
foreign ausländisch
forest der Wald, -̈er

to **forget** vergessen*
fork die Gabel, -n
foyer der Flur
France (das) Frankreich
free frei
French *(adj.)* französisch; **in ~** auf französisch; **(language)** Französisch; **Do you speak ~?** Sprechen Sie Französisch?; **(person)** der Franzose, -n, die Französin, -nen
fresh frisch
Friday (der) Freitag; **on Fridays** freitags
friend der Freund, -e
friendly freundlich; **un~** unfreundlich
from von (+ *dat.*); **(a native of)** aus (+ *dat.*); **I'm ~ . . .** Ich bin aus . . . . Ich komme aus . . .; **(numbers) ~ . . . to** von . . . bis; **(place) ~ . . . to** von . . . nach
front: in ~ of vor (+ *acc.* / *dat.*)
fruit das Obst
fun der Spaß; **to be ~** Spaß machen; **to make ~ of** sich lustig machen über (+ *acc.*)
funny lustig, witzig; komisch
furniture die Möbel *(pl.)*
future die Zukunft

G

game das Spiel, -e
garage die Garage, -n
garden der Garten, -̈
gentleman der Herr, -n, -en
German *(adj.)* deutsch; **in ~** auf deutsch; **(language)** Deutsch; **Do you speak ~?** Sprechen Sie Deutsch?; **(person)** der Deutsche (ein Deutscher)
Germany (das) Deutschland

to **get (become)** werden*; **(fetch)** holen; **(receive)** bekommen* (hat); **to ~ off** aus·steigen*; **to ~ on** *or* **in** ein·steigen*; **to ~ up** auf·stehen*; **to ~ to know** kennen·lernen; **to ~ used to** sich gewöhnen an

girl das Mädchen, -

to **give** geben*; **(as a present)** schenken
glad froh
gladly gern (lieber, liebst-)
Glad to meet you. Freut mich.
glass das Glas, -̈er, **a ~ of . . .** ein Glas . . .

to **go** gehen*; **to ~ by (bus)** fahren* mit; **to ~ by plane** fliegen*; **to ~ out** aus·gehen*; **to ~ up** hinauf·fahren*
good gut (besser, best-)
Good-bye! Auf Wiedersehen! Tschüß!
grade die Note, -n
grandfather der Großvater, -̈
grandmother die Großmutter, -̈
grandparents die Großeltern *(pl.)*
gray grau
great (size) groß; **(terrific)** prima, toll
green grün
greeting der Gruß, -̈e
groceries die Lebensmittel *(pl.)*

to **grow** wachsen*

to **guarantee** garantieren
guest der Gast, -̈e
guitar die Gitarre, -n

H

hair das Haar, -e
half halb; **in ~ an hour** in einer halben Stunde
hallway der Flur
hand die Hand, -̈e

to **hang (up)** hängen

to **hang, be hanging** hängen*

to **happen** geschehen*
happy glücklich, froh
hard (difficult) schwer
hardly kaum

to **have** haben*; **to ~ to** müssen*
head der Kopf, -̈e
healthy gesund (ü)

to **hear** hören
heavy schwer
Hello! Guten Tag!
help die Hilfe

to **help** helfen* (+ *dat.*)
her ihr
here hier
Hi! Guten Tag! Hallo!

high hoch (hoh-) (höher, höchst)

to **hike** wandern (ist)
his sein
historical(ly) historisch
history die Geschichte
hobby das Hobby, -s
holiday der Feiertag, -e
home: at ~ zu Hause; **(toward) ~** nach Hause; **at the ~ of** bei (+ *dat.*); **(homeland)** die Heimat

to **hope** hoffen
hot heiß
hotel das Hotel, -s, der Gasthof, -̈e, die Pension, -en
hour die Stunde, -n; **for hours** stundenlang
house das Haus, -̈er
household der Haushalt
housewife die Hausfrau, -en
how wie; **~ much?** wieviel?; **~ many?** wie viele?; **~ much is . . .?** Was kostet . . .?; **~ much are . . .?** Was kosten . . .? **~ are you?** Wie geht's? Wie geht es Ihnen?; **~ come?** Wieso?
however aber; doch
human being der Mensch, -en, -en
hunger der Hunger
hungry: I'm ~. Ich habe Hunger.

to **hurry** sich beeilen

to **hurt** weh tun*; **My (throat) hurts.** Mir tut (der Hals) weh.
husband der Mann, -̈er

I

ice, ice cream das Eis
idea die Idee, -n
identification der Ausweis, -e
if *(conj.)* wenn; ob
ill krank (ä)

to **imagine** sich vor·stellen
immediately sofort
important wichtig
in in (+ *dat.* / *dat.*)
income das Einkommen
independent selbständig
inexpensive billig
indeed wirklich, doch
industrious(ly) fleißig
inn der Gasthof, -̈e
inside in (+ *dat.* / *acc.*)
in spite of trotz (+ *gen.*)

instead of (an)statt (+ *gen.*)
intelligent intelligent
interest (in) das Interesse (an + *dat.*)
interested: to be ~ in sich interessieren für
interesting interessant
intermission die Pause, -n
to **invite (to)** ein·laden* (zu)
island die Insel, -n
isn't it? nicht wahr?
Italian (*adj.*) italienisch; **in ~** auf italienisch; **(language)** Italienisch; **Do you speak ~?** Sprechen Sie Italienisch?; **(person)** der Italiener, -
Italy (das) Italien
its sein, ihr

J

jacket die Jacke, -n
jam die Marmelade, -n
January der Januar; **in ~** im Januar
job die Arbeit; **(position)** die Stelle, -n
juice der Saft, -e
July der Juli; **in ~** im Juli
June der Juni,; **in ~** im Juni
just gerade; **~ like** genau(so) wie; **~ when** gerade als

K

keep: to ~ in shape sich fit halten*
key der Schlüssel, -
kind nett; **what ~ of (a)?** was für (ein)?
king der König, -e
kitchen die Küche, -n
knee das Knie, -
knife das Messer, -
to **know (be acquainted with)** kennen*; **(a fact)** wissen*; **(a skill)** können*
known bekannt

L

lab das Labor, -s (*or* -e)
lady die Dame, -n; **young ~ (Miss, Ms.)** das Fräulein, -

lake der See, -n
lamp die Lampe, -n
to **land** landen (ist)
landscape die Landschaft
language die Sprache, -n
large groß (ö)
last letzt-
late spät; **How ~ is it?** Wie spät ist es? Wieviel Uhr ist es?
later später; **See you ~.** Bis später!
to **laugh** lachen
lawyer der Rechtsanwalt, ⸚e, die Rechtsanwältin, -nen
lazy faul
to **learn** lernen
to **leave (behind)** lassen*; **(~ from)** ab·fahren* von, ab·fliegen* von; **(~ a place)** verlassen*
lecture die Vorlesung, -en; **~ hall** der Hörsaal, -säle
left links; **link-**
leg das Bein, -e
leisure time die Freizeit
lemonade die Limonade, -n
to **let** lassen*
letter der Brief, -e
lettuce der Salat
library die Bibliothek, -en
to **lie (to be located)** liegen*; **(to be lying flat)** liegen*; **to ~ down** sich (hin·)legen
life das Leben
light leicht; **(bright)** hell
likable sympathisch; **un~** unsympathisch
like wie; **just ~** genau(so) wie; **s.th. ~** so etwas wie
to **like** gefallen*; **I would ~ (to have)** ... Ich möchte ...; mögen*
to **listen** zu·hören (+ *dat.*); **to ~ to** sich an·hören
little klein; **(amount)** wenig, ein bißchen; **(some)** etwas
to **live** leben; **(reside)** wohnen
living room das Wohnzimmer, -
long (*adj.*) lang (ä); (*adv.*) lange; **how ~?** wie lange?; **So ~!** Tschüß!
to **look** sehen*; **to ~ (like)** aus·sehen* (wie + *nom.*); **to ~ at** sich an·sehen*; **to ~ for** suchen; **to ~ forward to** sich freuen auf (+ *acc.*)
to **lose** verlieren*
loud(ly) laut
love die Liebe; **to be in ~ (with)** verliebt sein (in + *acc.*)

to **love** lieben; **to fall in ~ (with)** sich verlieben (in + *acc.*)
luck das Glück; **to be lucky** Glück haben*; **to be unlucky** Pech haben*
luggage das Gepäck
lunch das Mittagessen, -; **for ~** zum Mittagessen

M

mad böse
magazine die Zeitschrift, -en
mail die Post; **~box** der Briefkasten, ⸚; **by air~** mit Luftpost
mainly vor allem
major (field of study) das Hauptfach, ⸚er
to **make** machen
man der Mann, ⸚er; **(human being)** der Mensch, -en, -en; **gentle~** der Herr, -n, -en
many viele; **how ~?** wie viele?; **~ a** manch-
map die Landkarte, -n; **city ~** der Stadtplan, ⸚e
March der März; **in ~** im März
mark (German) die Mark (DM)
market der Markt, ⸚e
marmalade die Marmelade, -n
marriage die Ehe, -n
married verheiratet
to **marry, get married** heiraten
matter: What's the ~? Was ist los?
may dürfen*
May der Mai; **in ~** im Mai
meal das Essen, -; **Enjoy your ~.** Guten Appetit!
to **mean (signify)** bedeuten; **(think)** meinen
meanwhile inzwischen
meat das Fleisch
meet (get to know) kennen·lernen; **Glad to ~ you.** Freut mich (sehr, Sie kennenzulernen).
menu die Speisekarte, -n
middle die Mitte; **in the ~ of** mitten in / auf(+ *dat.*)
milk die Milch
minor (field of study) das Nebenfach, ⸚er
minute die Minute, -n
Miss Fräulein

Monday (der) Montag; **on Mondays** montags
money das Geld; **to earn ~** Geld verdienen; **to spend ~** Geld aus·geben*
month der Monat, -e; **per ~** im Monat, pro Monat; **for one ~** einen Monat
monthly monatlich
monument das Denkmal, -̈er
more mehr; **once ~** noch einmal
morning der Morgen; **Good ~.** Guten Morgen!; **in the ~** morgens; **early ~** früh, morgen; **mid~** der Vormittag, vormittag
most meist-; am meisten
mostly meistens
mother die Mutter, -̈
mountain der Berg, -e
mouth der Mund, -̈er
movie (film) der Film, -e; **(theater)** das Kino, -s
Mr. Herr
Mrs. Frau
Ms. Frau
much viel (mehr, meist-); **how ~?** wieviel?
museum das Museum, Museen
music die Musik
musical musikalisch; **un~** unmusikalisch
must müssen*
my mein

N

name der Name, -ns; -n; **What's your ~?** Wie heißen Sie?; **My ~ is . . .** Ich heiße . . . Mein Name ist . . .
to **name** nennen*
napkin die Serviette, -n
nation das Volk, -̈er
near (distance) nah (näher, nächst-); **(vicinity)** bei (+ dat.), in der Nähe von (+ dat.)
neat prima; schick
neck der Hals, -̈e
to **need** brauchen
neighbor der Nachbar, -n, -n
neither . . . nor weder . . . noch

never nie
nevertheless trotzdem
new neu; **s.th. ~** etwas Neues; **nothing ~** nichts Neues; **What's ~?** Was gibt's Neues?
New Year's Eve Silvester; **at / for ~** zu Silvester
news die Nachricht, -en
newspaper die Zeitung, -en
next nächst-; **~ to** neben (+ dat. / acc.)
nice schön, nett
night die Nacht, -̈e, nacht; **at ~** nachts; **to spend the ~** übernachten
no nein
nobody niemand
noisy laut
no one niemand
noodle die Nudel, -n
noon der Mittag, -e, mittag; **at ~** mittags; **after~** der Nachmittag, nachmittag
north der Norden; **in the ~** im Norden; **~ of** nördlich von
nose die Nase, -n
not nicht; **~ any** kein; **~ only . . . but also** nicht nur . . . sondern auch; **~ yet** noch nicht; **~ at all** gar nicht
notebook das Heft, -e
nothing (to) nichts (zu); **~ special** nichts Besonderes
novel der Roman, -e
November der November; **in ~** im November
now jetzt, nun; **just ~** gerade
number die Nummer; -n; die Zahl, -en
nurse die Krankenschwester, -n

O

o'clock Uhr
October der Oktober; **in ~** im Oktober
of course natürlich; doch
to **offer** bieten*
office das Büro, -s
often oft
old alt (ä)
on auf (+ acc./dat.); **~ the first of July** am ersten Juli

once einmal; **~ more** noch einmal; **~ in a while** manchmal; **(formerly)** früher
one (people, they) man
only nur; **(not before)** erst; **not ~ . . . but also** nicht nur . . . sondern auch
open auf, offen, geöffnet
to **open** öffnen, auf·machen
opposite das Gegenteil, -e
or oder
orange die Orange, -n; **(color)** orange
orchestra das Orchester, -
order: in ~ to um . . . zu (+ inf.)
to **order** bestellen
other ander-
our unser
out of aus (+ dat.)
over (location) über (+ acc. / dat.); **(finished)** vorbei; **~ there** da drüben
own (adj.) eigen-

P

to **pack** packen
package das Paket, -e
page die Seite, -n; **on / to ~** auf Seite
to **paint** malen
palace das Schloß, -̈sser
pants die Hose, -n
paper das Papier, -e; **(term paper)** die Arbeit, -en
parcel das Paket, -e
parents die Eltern (pl.)
park der Park, -s
to **park** parken
part der Teil, -e; **to take ~ (in)** teil·nehmen* (an + dat.)
to **participate (in)** teil·nehmen* (an + dat.)
party die Party, -s
to **pass (an exam)** bestehen*; **to ~ by** vorbei·gehen*, vorbei·kommen*, vorbei·fahren*
passport der Paß, -̈sse
past: in the ~ früher
to **pay** bezahlen
pea die Erbse, -n
peace der Frieden
pen der Kuli, -s
pencil der Bleistift, -e
penny der Pfennig, -e; **two pennies** zwei Pfennig

people die Leute (*pl.*); **(human beings)** der Mensch, -en, -en; **(nation)** das Volk, ̈er
pepper der Pfeffer
per pro
performance die Vorstellung, -en
perhaps vielleicht
person der Mensch, -en, -en
pharmacy die Apotheke, -n
to **phone** an·rufen*, telefonieren
piano das Klavier, -e; **to play the ~** Klavier spielen
picture das Bild, -er; **to take ~s** photographieren
piece das Stück, -e
pink rosa
place (location) der Platz, ̈e; **at our ~** bei uns; **in your ~** an deiner Stelle
plan der Plan, ̈e
to **plan** planen, vor·haben*
plane das Flugzeug, -e
plate der Teller, -
platform der Bahnsteig, -e
to **play** spielen
play (theater) das Stück, -e
pleasant gemütlich; **un~** un-gemütlich
to **please** gefallen*
please bitte, bitte schön
pocket die Tasche, -n
policeman der Polizist, -en, -en
policewoman die Polizistin, -nen
poor arm (ä)
population die Bevölkerung
position die Stelle, -n
possible möglich; **im~** un-möglich
(post)card die(Post)karte, -n
post office die Post
potato die Kartoffel, -n
pound das Pfund, -e
power die Macht, ̈e
praktisch practical(ly)
to **prefer** lieber tun*; vor·ziehen*
present (gift) das Geschenk, -e
pretty hübsch
problem das Problem, -e
profession der Beruf, -e
professor der Professor, -en
program das Programm, -e; die Sendung, -en
proud stolz
pudding der Pudding, -s
to **pull** ziehen*
pullover der Pullover, -
purple lila

to **put (set down)** setzen; **(stand upright)** (hin·)stellen; **(lay down)** (hin·)legen; **(hang up)** (hin·)hängen; **to ~ on (clothing)** (sich) an·ziehen*

Q

quarter das Viertel; **a ~ to** Viertel vor; **a ~ past** Viertel nach; **in a ~ of an hour** in einer Viertelstunde
question die Frage, -n; **to ask a ~** eine Frage stellen
quick(ly) schnell
quite ziemlich

R

radio das Radio, -s
railway die Bahn, -en
to **rain** regnen ; **It's raining.** Es regnet.
rather lieber
to **read** lesen*
ready fertig
really wirklich
to **rebuild** wiederauf·bauen
to **receive** bekommen*
to **recognize** erkennen*
to **recommend** empfehlen*
record die (Schall)platte, -n; **~ player** der Plattenspieler, -
red rot (ö)
refrigerator der Kühlschrank, ̈e
region die Gegend, -en; das Gebiet, -e
regular normal
to **relax** sich aus·ruhen
to **remain** bleiben*
to **remember** sich erinnern (an + *acc.*)
to **remind (of)** erinnern (an + *acc.*)
to **renovate** renovieren
to **rent** mieten; **to ~ out** ver-mieten
to **repeat** wiederholen
reporter der Journalist, -en, -en
to **rescue** retten
to **reserve** reservieren
to **reside** wohnen
responsible verantwortungsvoll
restaurant das Restaurant, -s

to **restore** restaurieren
to **return** zurück·kommen*
return address der Absender, -
reunification die Wiedervereinigung
rice der Reis
rich reich
right rechts, recht-; **(correct)** richtig; **You're ~.** Du hast recht.; **Isn't it (right)?** nicht wahr?; **~ away** sofort
river der Fluß, ̈sse
roll das Brötchen, -
room das Zimmer, -; **bed~** das Schlafzimmer, -; **bath~** das Badezimmer, -; **dining ~** das Eßzimmer, -; **living ~** das Wohnzimmer, -; **guest ~** das Gästezimmer, -; **single ~** das Einzelzimmer, -; **double ~** das Doppelzimmer, -
roommate der Zimmerkollege, -n, -n, die Zimmerkollegin, -nen
to **run** laufen*; rennen*

S

sad traurig
safe sicher
salad der Salat, -e
salt das Salz
same gleich; **the ~ to you** gleichfalls
Saturday (der) Samstag; **on Saturdays** samstags
sausage die Wurst, ̈e
to **save (money)** sparen; **(rescue)** retten
to **say** sagen; **What did you ~?** Wie bitte?
scenery die Landschaft
schedule der Fahrplan, ̈e
scholarship das Stipendium, Stipendien
school die Schule, -n
science die Wissenschaft, -en
scientist der Wissenschaftler, -
second die Sekunde, -n
secretary die Sekretärin, -nen
secure sicher
to **see** sehen*
to **seek** suchen
to **seem** scheinen*
self-employed selbständig

to **sell** verkaufen
semester das Semester, -
seminar das Seminar, -e
to **send** schicken
sentence der Satz, ⸚e
September der September; **in ~** im September
several mehrer- *(pl.)*
to **shave** sich rasieren
shelf das Regal, -e
to **shine** scheinen*
shirt das Hemd, -en
shoe der Schuh, -e
shop das Geschäft, -e
to **shop** ein·kaufen; **to go ~ing** einkaufen gehen*
short kurz (ü)
to **show** zeigen
shower die Dusche, -n; **to take a ~** (sich) duschen
sick krank (ä)
to **sign up for** belegen
silly dumm (ü)
simple, simply einfach
since (time) seit (+ *dat.*)
to **sing** singen*
single (unmarried) unverheiratet, ledig
sister die Schwester, -n
to **sit (be sitting)** sitzen*; **to ~ down** sich (hin·)setzen
to **ski** Ski laufen*; **to go ~ing** Ski laufen gehen*
skinny dünn
skirt der Rock, ⸚e
slacks die Hose, -n
slender schlank
to **sleep** schlafen*
slim schlank
slow(ly) langsam
small klein
to **snow** schneien
soccer: to play ~ Fußball spielen
sofa das Sofa, -s
some etwas *(sg.)*; einig- *(pl.)*; **(many a)** manch-; **(a couple of)** ein paar
somebody jemand
something (to) etwas (zu)
sometimes manchmal
son der Sohn, ⸚e
song das Lied, -er
soon bald
sorry: I'm ~. Es tut mir leid.
so that *(conj.)* so daß
soup die Suppe, -n
south der Süden; **in the ~** im Süden; **~ of** südlich von
Spain (das) Spanien
Spanish *(adj.)* spanisch; **in ~** auf spanisch; **(language)**

Spanisch; **Do you speak ~?** Sprechen Sie Spanisch?; **(person)** der Spanier, -
to **speak** sprechen*; **~ up!** Sprechen Sie laut!
special : something ~ etwas Besonderes; **nothing ~** nichts Besonderes
spectator der Zuschauer, -
to **spend (money)** aus·geben*
spoon der Löffel, -
sport(s) der Sport
spring der Frühling, -e; **in (the) ~** im Frühling
square der Platz, ⸚e
stamp die Briefmarke, -n
to **stand, be standing** stehen*
start der Anfang, ⸚e
state der Staat, -en
to **stay** bleiben*
still noch
stomach der Bauch, ⸚e
stop (for buses etc.) die Haltestelle, -n
stopover der Aufenthalt, -e
to **stop (in a vehicle)** halten*; **(doing s.th.)** auf·hören (zu + *inf.*)
store das Geschäft, -e; **department ~** das Kaufhaus, ⸚er
story die Geschichte, -n; **detective ~** der Krimi, -s
straight gerade; **~ ahead** geradeaus
strange komisch
strawberry die Erdbeere, -n
street die Straße, -n; **main ~** die Hauptstraße, -n
streetcar die Straßenbahn, -en
strenuous anstrengend
to **stroll** bummeln (ist)
student der Student, -en, -en, die Studentin, -nen
study das Studium, Studien; **(room)** das Arbeitszimmer, -
to **study** lernen; **(a particular field, be a student at a university)** studieren (an + *dat.*)
stupid dumm (ü)
subject das Fach, ⸚er
subway die U-Bahn
such so ein *(sg.)*; solch *(pl.)*
sudden(ly) plötzlich
sugar der Zucker
suitcase der Koffer, -
summer der Sommer, -; **in (the) ~** im Sommer
sun die Sonne; **The ~ is shining.** Die Sonne scheint.
Sunday (der) Sonntag; **on Sundays** sonntags

supermarket der Supermarkt, ⸚e
supper das Abendessen; **for ~** zum Abendessen
to **support actively** sich ein·setzen für
sure sicher; doch; **for ~** bestimmt
surely bestimmt, sicher
surprise die Überraschung, -en
to **surprise** überraschen
surroundings die Umgebung; **(ecology)** die Umwelt
suspenseful spannend
sweater der Pullover, -
to **swim** schwimmen*; baden
Swiss (person) der Schweizer, -; *(adj.)* Schweizer
Switzerland die Schweiz

T

table der Tisch, -e
to **take** nehmen*; **to ~ along** mit·nehmen*; **to ~ off (clothing)** (sich) aus·ziehen*; **to ~ off (plane)** ab·fliegen*; **(last)** dauern; **to ~ a course** belegen; **to ~ an exam** eine Prüfung schreiben
talented talentiert; **un~** untalentiert
to **talk** reden, sprechen*; **to ~ to** reden mit, sprechen* mit; **to ~ about** reden über (+ *acc.*), sprechen* (von)
to **taste** schmecken; **That tastes good.** Das schmeckt gut.
taxi das Taxi, -s
tea der Tee, -s
to **teach** lehren
teacher der Lehrer, -
to **tear down** ab·reißen*
telephone das Telefon, -e
tell sagen; erzählen (von + *dat.*)
tennis Tennis
terrible, terribly furchtbar
terrific toll
test die Prüfung, -en; **to take a ~** eine Prüfung schreiben*
than *(after comp.)* als
to **thank** danken (+ *dat.*)
Thank you. Danke!; ~ very much. Danke schön! Vielen Dank!

that das; *(conj.)* daß; **so ~**
(conj.) so daß
the . . . the je (+ *comp.*) . . .
desto (+ *comp.*)
theater das Theater, -; **movie**
~ das Kino, -s
their ihr
then dann; **(in those days)**
damals
there da, dort; **over ~** da drüben; **~ is (are)** es gibt
therefore darum
thick dick
thin dünn
things: all sorts of ~ so
einiges
to **think (of)** denken* (an +
acc.); **(be of an opinion)**
meinen; **I ~ it's . . .** Ich
finde es . . .
thinker der Denker, -
thirst der Durst
thirsty: I'm ~. Ich habe
Durst.
this dies-
thought der Gedanke, -ns, -n
throat der Hals, ⸚e
through durch (+ *acc.*)
Thursday (der) Donnerstag;
on Thursdays donnerstags
ticket die Karte, -n; **(bus, etc.)**
die Fahrkarte, -n; **(return**
ticket) die Rückfahrkarte, -n
~ window der Schalter, -
time die Zeit, -en; **What ~ is**
it? Wie spät ist es? Wieviel
Uhr ist es?; **at what ~?**
wann?; **in the mean~** inzwischen; **one ~** einmal
tired müde
to zu (+ *dat.*); an (+ *acc.*); **(a**
country, etc.) nach
today heute
together gemeinsam, zusammen; **~ with** mit (+ *dat.*)
toilet die Toilette, -n
tomato die Tomate, -n
tomorrow morgen; **the day**
after ~ übermorgen
too (also) auch; **(too much)**
zu viel
tooth der Zahn, ⸚e
tourist der Tourist, -en, -en,
die Touristin, -nen
tower der Turm, ⸚e
town die Stadt, ⸚e
track das Gleis, -e
traffic der Verkehr
trail der Weg, -e
train der Zug, ⸚e, die
Bahn, -en; **~ station** der
Bahnhof, ⸚e

training die Ausbildung
to **travel** reisen (ist)
tree der Baum, ⸚e
trip die Reise, -n, die
Fahrt, -en; **to take a ~** eine
Reise machen
true richtig, wahr
to **try** versuchen
Tuesday (der) Dienstag; **on**
Tuesdays dienstags
to **turn: to ~ off (radio, etc.)**
aus·machen; **to ~ on (radio,**
etc.) an·machen
TV (medium) das Fernsehen;
(set) der Fernseher, -; **to**
watch ~ fern·sehen*
typical(ly) typisch

U

ugly häßlich
unathletic unsportlich
uncle der Onkel, -
under unter (+ *acc.* / *dat.*)
to **understand** verstehen*
understanding verständnisvoll
uneducated ungebildet
unfortunately leider
unfriendly unfreundlich
unification die Vereinigung
United States (U.S.)
die Vereinigten Staaten
(U.S.A.) *(pl.)*
university die Universität, -en
(die Uni, -s)
unlucky: to be ~ Pech haben*
unmarried unverheiratet
unmusical unmusikalisch
unique einmalig
untalented untalentiert
until bis; **not ~** erst
upset: to get ~ about sich
ärgern über (+ *acc.*)
upstairs oben
usual(ly) gewöhnlich
to **use** gebrauchen
to **utilize** gebrauchen

V

vacation die Ferien *(pl.)*
various verschieden-
vegetable(s) das Gemüse, -

very sehr; ganz
viewer der Zuschauer, -
village das Dorf, ⸚er
to **visit** besuchen; **(sightseeing)**
besichtigen

W

to **wait (for)** warten (auf + *acc.*)
waiter der Kellner, -, der
Ober, -; Herr Ober!
waitress die Kellnerin, -nen,
das Fräulein, -; Fräulein!
to **walk** zu Fuß gehen*, laufen*;
to go for a ~
spazieren·gehen*
wall die Wand, ⸚e; **(thick)** die
Mauer, -n
to **want to** wollen*, möchten*
war der Krieg, -e
warm warm (ä)
to **wash (o.s.)** (sich) waschen*
watch (clock) die Uhr, -en
to **watch: (TV)** fern·sehen*; **(pay**
attention) auf·passen; **~ out!**
Passen Sie auf!
water das Wasser
way der Weg, -e; **this ~** auf
diese Weise
to **wear** tragen*
weather das Wetter
wedding die Hochzeit, -en
Wednesday (der) Mittwoch;
on Wednesdays mittwochs
week die Woche, -n; **all ~**
long die ganze Woche; **this**
~ diese Woche
weekend das Wochenende;
on the ~ am Wochenende
weekly wöchentlich
welcome: You're ~. Bitte
schön! Nichts zu danken!
well *(adv.)* gut; *(gesture word)*
nun
west der Westen; **in the ~** im
Westen; **~ of** westlich von
what? was?; **~ did you say?**
Wie bitte?; **~'s new?** Was
gibt's (denn)?; **~'s on . . .?**
Was gibt's im . . .?; **So ~!** Na
und!; **~ kind of (a)?** was für
(ein)?
when (at what time) wann?;
(whenever) *(conj.)* wenn;
(conj., single action in past)
als; **just ~** *(conj.)* gerade als
where? wo?; **~ from?** woher?;
~ to? wohin?

whether *(conj.)* ob
which? welch-?
wide weit
while *(conj.)* während
white weiß
who? wer?
whole ganz
whom? wen?, wem?
whose wessen?
why? warum?, wieso?
wife die Frau, -en
wild wild
to **win** gewinnen*
window das Fenster, -;
  ticket ~ der Schalter, -
wine der Wein, -e
winter der Winter; **in (the) ~**
  im Winter
to **wish** (sich) wünschen

with mit (+ *dat.*); **(at the
home of)** bei (+ *dat.*); **~ me
(us . . .)** bei mir (uns . . .)
without ohne (+ *acc.*)
witty witzig
woman (Mrs., Ms.) die
  Frau, -en
wonderful(ly) wunderbar,
  prima
woods der Wald, -̈er
work die Arbeit
to **work** arbeiten
worker der Arbeiter, -
world die Welt, -en
to **write** schreiben*; **to ~ to**
  schreiben an (+ *acc.*); **to ~
about** schreiben über
  (+ *acc.*); **to ~ down**
  auf·schreiben*

wrong falsch; **You are ~.** Du
  hast unrecht.

Y

year das Jahr, -e; **all ~ long**
  das ganze Jahr; **next ~**
  nächstes Jahr
yellow gelb
yes ja; doch
yesterday gestern; **the day before ~** vorgestern
yet doch; **not ~** noch nicht
young jung (ü)
your dein, euer, Ihr
youth die Jugend
youth hostel die Jugendherberge, -n

Photo Credits *(Continued from page xii)*

INDEX

This index is limited to grammatical entries. Topical vocabulary (e.g., days of the week, food, hobbies, etc.) and material from the *Sprechsituationen* can be found in the table of contents. Entries appearing in the *Rückblicke* are indicated by parentheses.